Service Charges and Management: Law and Practice

AUSTRALIA
Law Book Co.
Sydney

CANADA and USA
Carswell
Toronto

HONG KONG
Sweet & Maxwell Asia

NEW ZEALAND
Brookers
Auckland

SINGAPORE and MALAYSIA
Sweet & Maxwell Asia
Singapore and Kuala Lumpur

Service Charges and Management: Law and Practice

Tanfield Chambers

Published in 2006 by
Sweet & Maxwell Ltd, 100 Avenue Road
Swiss Cottage, London NW3 3PF
http://www.sweetandmaxwell.co.uk

Typeset by Servis Filmsetting Ltd, Manchester
Printed in Great Britain by TJ International Ltd, Padstow, Cornwall

No natural forests were destroyed to make this product;
only farmed timber was used and replanted.

A CIP catalogue record for this book is available from the
British Library

ISBN 0 421 843 90X

Contributors

The authors are a team of barristers from Tanfield Chambers headed by

Philip Rainey

and including

Phillip Aliker
Robert Bowker
Michael Buckpitt
Andrew Butler
Tom Carpenter-Leitch
Adrian Carr
Christopher Coney
Taner Dedezade
Carl Fain
James Fieldsend
Ellodie Gibbons
Marc Glover
Tim Hammond
Christopher Heather
Geraint Jones QC
Charles Joseph
Mark Loveday
Timothy Polli
Lisa Sinclair
Paul Staddon
Mark Walsh

Contents

Preface

Scope of this book

This book sets out to encapsulate the law applicable to "service charges", which in general and non-technical terms may be said to mean sums payable for services in respect of land and buildings. Most commonly, service charges are a liability which tenants contract to pay to landlords or management companies under the terms of their leases, and the major part of this book is devoted to that subject. However, service charges also occur in respect of freehold land, either through covenants in freehold transfers, or under estate management schemes. Service charges will also arise in commonholds, and these are also dealt with.

This book also covers the law applicable to the management of real property. In the real world, it is the authors' experience that service disputes and disputes over management go hand-in-glove; indeed a dispute over the management fee is often a central part of a service charge dispute. Principally the law relating to management includes the statutory rights to appoint managers, and the statutory right to manage, which apply to residential leasehold property.

What this book does not include

This book sets out to provide a guide to the applicable law of service charges and management, in a practical and helpful format. It is not intended as a general handbook for the management of property, and does not attempt to summarise all the many areas of the general law with which a landlord or manager of property would be wise to be familiar.

It should go without saying that this book is not a substitute for legal and other professional advice for those who encounter specific problems in relation to the subjects it covers.

Structure of the book

The first section of the book considers the common law relating to service charges. There are two reasons for this: first, the common law and the contractual terms should always be the starting point for analysis of any service charge problem. Second, in the case of service charges arising under commercial leases, and freehold service charges, the common law is the end point as well as the starting point, as the complex statutory overlay applicable to residential leases does not apply.

The main body of the text considers the applicable law with a broadly topic-based approach. In practice, one needs to know what the law is in case of a dispute about insurance charges, or repairs, or legal costs, as the case may be, and the text attempts to bring together into one place the diverse cases and statutory provisions applicable to these topics. There are of course some provisions which are of wide application, for example the consultation requirements applicable in the case of long residential leases of flats, and these have a discrete section of their own.

Separate chapters deal with remedies and procedure in the courts and tribunals.

The statutory right to seek the appointment of a manager which applies to residential flats is dealt with separately, and the new right to manage, which is almost a book in itself, has its own set of chapters.

There are five appendices. Appendix A sets out the statutory material of most relevance to the topics covered. For reasons of space, this is not exhaustive, and in particular we have had to omit certain statutory instruments governing the law of service charges in Wales. Those readers who need to be aware of the law and practice in that principality should keep in mind that, while there is rarely any substantive difference from the law in England, commencement dates of statutory instruments are sometimes different and should be checked. They may conveniently be accessed through the LEASE website, along with most LVT decisions (www.lease-advice.org).

Thereafter, there are three appendices of precedents. Appendix B contains various miscellaneous notices which may be encountered in the context of service charge disputes; Appendix C contains materials relevant to leasehold valuation tribunals; Appendix D contains statements of case and forms encountered in county court proceedings. Again, constraints of space do not permit the inclusion of a comprehensive set of precedents in each case; the aim has been to provide examples sufficient to show what might be expected in terms of style and content.

Finally, Appendix E contains a list of web addresses which may be useful for those practising in this field.

Above all, our aim has been to provide a practical and straightforward guide to this increasingly complex area. We have endeavoured to state the law as at July 31, 2005, although thanks to the flexibility of our publishers it has also been possible to incorporate some more recent developments at the proof stage.

This book was the joint initiative of Philip Rainey and Paul Staddon of these chambers but, as the long list of contributing authors demonstrates, has been compiled through a genuine collective effort on the part of the property practitioners.

Table of Cases

Table of Statutes

Paragraph numbers in **bold** *indicate the locations where material is reproduced in full.*

Table of Statutory Instruments

Paragraph numbers in **bold** *indicate the locations where material is reproduced in full.*

Chapter 1

Construction of Service Charge Provisions

1–001 The purpose of this chapter is to deal with the construction of service charge provisions in leases, for (with the exception of cases falling within the provisions of s.11 of the Landlord and Tenant Act 1985, as to which see Chapter 3) whatever the statutory background, the landlord is only able to recover service charges if the lease, properly construed, so provides. Thus, the starting point is always the terms of the lease itself.

The usual approach to construction

1–002 The usual approach to construing contracts applies to service charge provisions in leases, for a lease is no more than a contract governing the terms on which land is let. When construing service charge provisions the Court will seek to determine the intentions of the parties to the lease by taking into account its words, read in the context of the underlying purpose of the parties in entering into a lease containing a service charge provision. That purpose was identified by the Court of Appeal in *Universities Superannuation Scheme Ltd v Marks & Spencer plc* [1999] 1 E.G.L.R. 13 where Munby L.J. held:

> "The purpose of the service charge provisions is relevant to their meaning and effect. So far as the scheme, context and language of those provisions allow, the service charge provisions should be given an effect that fulfils rather than defeats their evident purpose. The service charge provisions have a clear purpose: the landlord that reasonably incurs liability for expenditure in maintaining (the premises) for the benefit of all its tenants there should be entitled to recover the full cost of doing so from those

tenants and each tenant should reimburse the landlord a proper proportion of those service charges."

Unfortunately, the practitioner will gain only limited assistance from the interpretation given to the words of a lease in any given case. This was made clear by the Court of Appeal in *Berrycroft Management Co Ltd v Sinclair Gardens Investments (Kensington) Ltd* [1997] 1 E.G.L.R. 47 where it held:

"It is elementary that the specific covenants in each case have to be construed in the context of the lease in which they are contained. Construction of a clause in one lease in a particular way is no guide to the construction of a clause in another lease couched in different terms and set in a different context."

The factual matrix

1–003 In determining the meaning of those words, the Court may, in the case of any ambiguity, look at all of the relevant surrounding facts, sometimes called the factual matrix, to see if assistance can be found there. As Lord Hoffman said in *Mannai Investment Co Ltd v Eagle Star Life Assurance Co Ltd* [1997] A.C. 749 at 775, a case involving construction of a lease:

". . . commercial contracts are construed in the light of all the background which could reasonably have been expected to be available to the parties in order to ascertain what would objectively have been understood to be their intention . . ."

Exclusion of evidence as to prior negotiations

1–004 However, there is one exception to what the Court may look at as part of the factual matrix for the purposes of construing any contract, including a service charge provision. The Court will not look at anything that was said or written by the parties during the course of negotiations for the contract. As Lord Hoffman said in *Mannai*:

"There are certain special kinds of evidence, such as previous negotiations and express declarations of intent, which for practical reasons which it is unnecessary to analyse, are inadmissible in aid of construction. They can be used only in an action for rectification."

The application of "business common sense" and background

1–005 The Courts have moved away from a literal interpretation of commercial documents, including leases, where such an interpretation would result in commercial nonsense. As Lord Hoffman said in *Mannai*:

> "The fact that the words are capable of a literal application is no obstacle to evidence which demonstrates what a reasonable person with knowledge of the background would have understood the parties to mean, even if this compels one to say that they used the wrong words."

and in *Investors Compensation Scheme Ltd v West Bromwich Building Society* [1998] 1 W.L.R. 896 at 913:

> "The meaning which a document . . . would convey to a reasonable man is not the same thing as the meaning of its words. The meaning of words is a matter of dictionaries and grammars; the meaning of the document is what the parties using those words against the relevant background would reasonably have been understood to mean. The background may not merely enable the reasonable man to choose between possible meanings of words which are ambiguous but even (as occasionally happens in ordinary life) to conclude that the parties must, for whatever reason, have used the wrong words or syntax."

Lord Diplock made this point more vigorously when he said in *Antaios Compania Naviera SA v Salen Rederierna AB* [1985] A.C. 191, 201:

> "if detailed semantic and syntactical analysis of words in a commercial contract is going to lead to a conclusion that flouts business commonsense, it must be made to yield to business commonsense."

For an example of the application of this approach in the particular context of service charges, see *Billson v Tristrem* (2000) L. & T.R. 220 where the literal construction of a poorly drafted provision was made to yield to the parties' intention (which in the view of the Court was "abundantly plain" from the context).

Guidance on admissible background

1–006 In *BCCI v Ali* [2001] 1 All E.R., Lord Hoffman offered further guidance when he said:

"[admissible background] is not, for example, confined to the factual background but can include the state of the law (as in cases in which one takes into account that the parties are unlikely to have intended to agree to something unlawful or legally ineffective) or proved common assumptions which were in fact quite mistaken. But the primary source for understanding what the parties meant is their language interpreted in accordance with conventional usage: '. . . we do not easily accept that people have made linguistic mistakes, particularly in formal documents.' I was certainly not encouraging a trawl through 'background' which could not have made a reasonable person think that the parties must have departed from conventional usage."

Correction of obvious mistakes

1–007 Thus it is clear that as part of the process of the construction the Court has power to correct obvious mistakes in the written expression of the intention of the parties. In *Wilson v Wilson* (1854) 5 H.L. Cas. 40, Lord St Leonards said:

"If you find a clear mistake and it admits to no other construction, a Court of Law, as well as a Court of Equity, without impugning any doctrine about correcting things which can only be shown by parol evidence to be mistakes—without, I say, going into those cases at all, both Courts of Law and of Equity may correct an obvious mistake on the face of an instrument without the slightest difficulty."

Rectification not required

1–008 In *North Circular Properties Ltd v Internal Systems Organisations Ltd* (unreported, October 26, 1984, Mr Rattee Q.C.) the Court emphasised that the parties need not apply for rectification to correct an incorrectly drafted contract but could ask the Court to construe sensibly as it was, saying:

"Of course the court will not lightly, as part of the construction process, tamper with the actual words used, particularly in commercial documents such as a lease. On the other hand the law is not such an ass as to compel the court to hold the parties to the actual words used where it is, as in my judgment it is in this case, clear from the document itself, without looking at extrinsic evidence, that such words were used by virtue of a draftsman's blunder. Such a process of correction of obvious drafting errors in the process of construction is of course distinct from the equitable doctrine of rectification."

Cases of ambiguity

1–009 If after the application of the various principles set out above the service charge remains ambiguous, it will be construed contrary to the interests of the party who put the clause forward in the first place. In a service context this will almost invariably be the landlord. In *Gilje v Charlgrove Securities* [2001] E.W.C.A. Civ. 177 there was an issue as to whether the service charge clause required a contribution to the notional cost to the landlord of having one flat in the building occupied by a caretaker who paid no rent. Laws L.J. said:

> "The landlord seeks to recover money from the tenant. On ordinary principles there must be clear terms in the contractual provisions said to entitle him to do so. The lease, moreover, was drafted or proffered by the landlord. It falls to be construed *contra proferentem* . . . At the end of the day, I do not consider that a reasonable tenant or prospective tenant, reading the underlease which was proferred to him, would perceive that clause 4(2)(1) obliged him to contribute . . . Such a construction has to emerge clearly and plainly from the words that are used. It does not do so."

Implication of terms

1–010 As with all contracts, the Court will in the right circumstances be prepared to imply additional contractual terms into a service charge provision to meet the unexpressed contractual intention of the parties. For the Courts to imply a term into a contract the following conditions have to be fulfilled:

(a) the term must be necessary to give business efficacy to the service charge in issue; or

(b) it must be so obvious that it goes without saying (the officious bystander test); and

(c) the term to be implied must be reasonable, capable of clear expression and not be in conflict with any express provision.

Although in this context it has been held that:

> "Where parties have entered into written engagements with express stipulations, it is manifestly not desirable to extend them by any implication; the presumption is that having expressed some, they have expressed all the conditions by which they intend to be bound under the instrument"
>
> (*Aspdin v Austin* (1844) 5 Q.B. 671)

there are frequent examples where the Courts have implied terms into service charge provisions.

Thus in *Finchbourne Ltd v Rodrigues* [1976] 3 All E.R. 581 the Court of Appeal held that there was to be implied into a service charge provision a limitation that the costs claimed by the landlords were to be "fair and reasonable" and that it could not be supposed that the landlords were entitled to be as extravagant as they may choose in the standards of repair, the appointment of porters and other such matters, with Roskill L.J. holding:

> "In my opinion, the parties cannot have intended that the landlord should have an unfettered discretion to adopt the highest conceivable standard and to charge the tenant with it."

1–011 The case of *Embassy Court Residents' Association Ltd v Lipman* (1984) 271 E.G. 545 (CA) is an interesting example of the Court stretching the rules of construction to meet a problem that had arisen where the tenants of a block of flats held under leases, which contained service charge provisions enabling the landlord to recover a proportion of the costs of providing certain services but not expressly permitting him to recover any proportion of any costs necessarily incurred in providing administration of those services. Responsibility for providing those services was passed to a management company, the shares of which were held exclusively by the tenants of the various flats in the block, under the terms of an intermediate lease. The management company sued the defendant tenant for a proportion of the cost of providing administration. In these circumstances the Court of Appeal upheld the claim. Parker L.J. held:

> "This is a familiar scheme. It is a scheme which, whether the test of business efficacy as laid down in *The Moorcock* [1889] 14 PD 64, or the 'innocent bystander' test of *Reigate v Union Manufacturing (Ramsbottom) Co Ltd* [1918] 1KB 592 or any other test be applied, makes it abundantly apparent that an implied term must be incorporated in the lease providing for

> the tenants to pay any managing agent's fees if the company decides to employ managing agents. The contrary is simply unarguable. Having set up a company, that company is composed of a number of individuals none of whom may have the slightest ability to do accounts, to inspect properties, to manage properties, or anything else, but this scheme contemplated that the company would do all those things and it is simply out of touch with reality to suggest that, if they decide on employing managing agents, they are not entitled to recover from the tenants on the same basis as they recover in respect of the direct charges of fulfilling the landlord's obligations."

What is surprising in this case is that the Court of Appeal looked at events that had occurred after the granting of the lease, being the setting up of the management company, as an aid to construction of the lease. This common sense approach accords with the practical experience of the authors.

1–012 The *Lipman* case is difficult to reconcile with the decision in *Gilje* referred to in paragraph 1–009 above, where it was said that recovery was limited to sums the entitlement to which emerged "clearly and plainly" from the lease. The tension between the decisions perhaps demonstrates that courts and tribunals generally take a more benign attitude towards landlord companies or management companies that are beneficially owned by the tenants than they do to similar commercial enterprises. In a number of instances it has been held that terms may not be implied so as to widen the range of costs for which the landlord may charge. Thus it has been held that, in the absence of express provision, there is no entitlement to:

- the cost of collection of rent (*Woodtrek v Jezeck* (1982) 261 E.G. 571);
- the recovery of interest on money borrowed by the landlord (*Boldmark v Cohen* (1985) 277 E.G. 745 CA);
- the full cost of an insurance policy where the landlord enjoys a discount given by way of a "loyalty bonus" (*Williams v London Borough of Southwark* (2001) 33 H.L.R. 22—see further Chapter 5);
- the cost of replacement of windows, under a clause permitting recovery for "providing and maintaining additional services or amenities" (*Mullany v Maybourne Grange (Croydon) Management Co Ltd* (1986 277 E.G. 1350)).

No implication of a term just because it is reasonable

1–013 The Court will not imply a term in favour of either party simply because it would be reasonable to do so. In *Berrycroft Management Co Ltd v Sinclair Gardens Investments (Kensington) Ltd* [1997] 1 E.G.L.R. 47 the Court of Appeal declined to imply a term that the landlord should act reasonably in placing insurance, the cost of which he was entitled to recover from the tenant, holding:

> "It is axiomatic that a court will not imply a term which has not been expressed merely because, had the parties thought of the possibility of expressing that term, it would have been reasonable for them to have done so. Before a term which has not been expressed can be implied it has got to be shown not merely that it would have been reasonable to make that implication, but that it is necessary in order to make the contract work that such a term should be implied."

Further discussion of this topic can be found in Chapter 11.

Chapter 2

Particular Forms of Covenant Relevant to Service Charges

There are certain "standard" forms of covenant which are particular or relevant to service charge issues and are discussed below. **2–001**

Service charges payable/recoverable "as rent"

It is not unusual and appears to be modern practice for service charges to be expressly reserved in the lease as rent or an additional rent. In order for this to be achieved words to the effect that the service charge is payable and/or recoverable as rent/additional rent are required. The effect of such provision is that (in the case of commercial premises) arrears can be the subject of distraint. In addition a s.146 notice will not be required to forfeit and the service charges will likely be treated as "rent in arrear" which must be paid in order to obtain relief from forfeiture (see *Escalus Properties v Robinson and others* [1996] 2 Q.B. 321) including relief under s.138 of the County Courts Act 1984 (see *Maryland Estates v Barr-Joseph* [1999] 1 W.L.R. 83). **2–002**

"No set-off" clause

If the landlord wishes to prevent the lessee from setting off sums claimed against rent or service charge it is necessary for there to be an express provision to this effect. A covenant to pay the rent or service charge "without any deduction" has been held not to be sufficient to preclude a set-off being exercised (*Connaught Restaurants v Indoor Leisure* [1994] 1 W.L.R. 501). A clause containing the words "without any deduction or set-off whatsoever" was considered sufficient to preclude a set-off and such clause was not caught by the Unfair Contract Terms Act 1977 (*Electricity Supply Nominees Ltd v IAF Group Ltd* **2–003**

[1993] 2 All E.R. 95 and *Rider v Inntrepeneur Pub Co* [1998] 1 E.G.L.R. 53). The position is likely to be different in respect of residential premises insofar as the Unfair Terms in Consumer Contracts Regulations 1999 apply to the lease. A "no set-off" clause is subject of course to the statutory rights in respect of withholding service charges in force or likely to come into force (see Chapter 19).

Conditions precedent

2–004 Conditions precedent arise in a number of situations connected with service charges and their recovery. Landlords usually seek to include in a lease a provision that services need not be provided or works carried out unless payment of rent/service charge has been made. Historically the words usually preceding the landlord's obligation are "Subject to payment of rent/service charge the landlord covenants . . ." In *Yorkbrook Investments v Batten* [1985] 2 E.G.L.R. 100 the Court of Appeal was of the view that such clause did not make payment of rent/service charges a condition precedent to the landlord's obligation to provide the services in question. It was stated that the obligation to provide services was independent of the obligation to make payment and a clearer provision was required. The decision of *Yorkbrook* has been to some extent doubted by members of the Court of Appeal in *Bluestorm v Portvale Holdings* [2004] 2 E.G.L.R. 38. See Chapter 14 for a detailed analysis of these decisions.

Another example of where conditions precedent may arise is where the landlord is required to carry out certain tasks before works are carried out. In *CIN Properties v Barclays Bank plc* [1986] 1 E.G.L.R. 9 the clause required the landlord to obtain the tenant's approval to estimates/tenders prior to works commencing. The failure to do so precluded the landlord from recovering payment for such works through the service charge. The failure in *Northways Flats Management Company v Wimpey Pension Trustees* [1992] 2 E.G.L.R. 42 to comply with a clause requiring consultation with the tenants prevented recovery of the cost of major works from the tenants.

Similarly where the lease requires the landlord's surveyor or accountant to certify expenditure such certification is usually a condition precedent to the liability to pay. This is discussed in detail in Chapter 14.

"Sweeping up" clauses

2–005 Many leases contain at the end of the schedule listing the works/services covered by the service charge, a "sweeping up" clause allowing the landlord to add to or modify the services provided or works carried out. The effect of each clause obviously depends on the wording used. It appears from the cases that it will be difficult for a landlord to rely on a general sweeping up clause in order to carry out substantial works, i.e. works to external walls (*Jacob Isbiski & Co v Goulding & Bird* [1989] 1 E.G.L.R. 236) or replacement windows (*Mullaney v Maybourne Grange (Croydon) Management* [1986] 1 E.G.L.R. 70). If, however, the clause is clearly drafted and the proposed work on a proper construction is envisaged by it, effect will be given to it. (See *Sutton (Hastoe) Housing Association v Williams* [1988] 1 E.G.L.R. 56—replacing wooden windows with UVPC ones).

Surveyor's decision final

2–006 Leases frequently contain a clause to the effect that the decision of the landlord's surveyor shall be final and binding. There is conflicting case law as to whether such clauses stand up. Such clauses are discussed in detail in Chapter 14. The position appears to be that a clause drafted in the clearest terms may obtain such result.

Chapter 3

Repairs

Introduction

3–001 Obligations on the part of the landlord to repair and maintain the common parts of the building containing the demised premises and a concomitant obligation on the part of the tenant to contribute towards the costs incurred by the landlord in carrying out his obligations by way of the service charge provisions are commonly found in most modern leases where a building has been let in parts. Indeed, it is this aspect of service charges that has given rise to most reported cases regarding service charges and most disputes in practice.

The law relating to repairs is a complex area of law where a full consideration commands a specialist book to itself. An indication of the issues that may be involved is to be found in the judgment of Nicholls L.J. in *Holding & Management Ltd v Property Holdings & Investment Trust plc* [1990] 1 E.G.L.R. 65 where he considered the tests to be adopted when deciding whether particular works could fairly be regarded as constituting "repair", saying:

> "The exercise involves considering the context in which the word 'repair' appears in a particular lease and also the defect and remedial works proposed. Accordingly, the circumstances to be taken into account in a particular case under one or other of these heads will include some or all of the following: the nature of the building, the terms of the lease, the state of the building at the date of the lease, the nature and extent of the defect sought to be remedied, the nature, extent and cost of the proposed remedial works, at whose expense the proposed remedial works are to be done, the value of the building and its expected lifespan, the effect of the works on such a value and lifespan, current building practice, the likelihood of a recurrence if one remedy rather than another is adopted, the comparative cost of alternative remedial works and their impact on the use and enjoyment of the

building by the occupant. The weight to be attached to these circumstances will vary from case to case."

Although we cannot seek to deal with all aspects of repairs, the following considerations are those most likely to arise in service charge disputes.

The language of the lease

3–002 The first step is to consider the wording of the lease, to determine the extent of the landlord's repairing obligations. His obligations may be expressed in different ways—there is no common form of covenant—and the extent of his obligations will depend upon the actual wording of the lease under consideration. It is always to be borne in mind that an obligation to keep in repair includes an obligation to put in repair.

In modern and well-drafted leases of commercial properties the landlord will be responsible for all repairs to all parts of the fabric of the building, other than decorative repairs of the interior surfaces of the parts let, and all functional items serving it. In leases of residential properties, especially where there has been a conversion of a house into a number of flats, it is not unusual to find real difficulties in determining what parts of the building have been demised and consequently who is responsible for repairing those parts where the landlord has only covenanted to repair those parts retained by him.

An exception: s.11 of the Landlord and Tenant Act 1985—the landlord's obligation in short leases of dwellings

3–003 There is one notable exception to the general rule that the Court will look to the terms of lease to determine the parties' repairing obligations and responsibilities for paying for those repairs. The exception applies only to tenancies where the term of years is for less than seven years or where the landlord has an option to determine the tenancy before the expiration of seven years (s.13). Thus for the vast majority of leases containing service charge provisions, s.11 will have no effect at all.

The extent of the landlord's obligation under s.11

3–004 The extent of the landlord's repairing obligation is set out in subss.(1), (1A) and (1B) of s.11 of the Landlord and Tenant Act 1985 which provide:

"(1) In a lease to which this section applies (as to which see sections 13 and 14) there is an implied covenant by the lessor—

(a) to keep in repair the structure and exterior of the dwelling-house (including drains, gutters and external pipes),

(b) to keep in repair and proper working order the installations in the dwelling-house for the supply of water, gas and electricity and for sanitation (including basins, sinks, baths and sanitary conveniences, but not other fixtures, fittings and appliances for making use of the supply of water gas or electricity), and

(c) to keep in repair and proper working order the installations in the dwelling-house for space heating and heating water.

(1A) If a lease to which this section applies is a lease of a dwelling-house which forms part only of a building, then, subject to subs.(1B), the covenant implied by subs.(1) shall have effect as if—

(a) the reference in para.(a) of that subsection to the dwelling-house included a reference to any part of the building in which the lessor has an estate or interest; and

(b) any reference in paras (b) and (c) of that subsection to an installation in the dwelling-house included a reference to an installation which, directly or indirectly, serves the dwelling-house and which either—

(i) forms part of any part of a building in which the lessor has an estate or interest; or

(ii) is owned by the lessor or under his control.

(1B) Nothing in subsection (1A) shall be construed as requiring the lessor to carry out any works or repairs unless the disrepair (or failure to maintain in working order) is such as to affect the lessee's enjoyment of the dwelling-house or of any common parts, as defined in section 60(1) of the Landlord and Tenant Act 1987, which the lessee, as such, is entitled to use."

Subsection (5) of s.11 of the 1985 Act has the effect of preventing the landlord from recovering, by way of service charge or otherwise, the cost of carrying out repairs that he is obliged to carry out under the terms of subss.(1) or (1A). However, where the dwelling house consists of a flat in a block of flats, the structure and exterior is that of the particular flat and not of the whole building (*Campden Hill*

Towers v Gardner [1977] 1 Q.B. 823) but the roof over the top floor may be part of its "structure and exterior" although not part of premises demised (*Douglas-Scott v Scorgie* [1984] 1 All E.R. 1086). Thus a lessee can end up, where s.11 applies, in contributing to the cost of repairing the exterior of all the block of flats save for that part immediately enclosing his own flat and, perhaps, the roof of the block.

The standard of repair

3–005 The standard of repair is not affected by any qualifying words that might be used such as "good" or "tenantable" or "habitable" or "sufficient". In *Anstruther-Gough-Calthorpe v McOscar* [1924] 1 K.B. 716, Scrutton L.J. said:

> "In my view the matter can be dealt with as if the covenant was one to keep and yield up at the end of the term in repair. I do not think there is any substantial difference in construction between 'repair', which must mean 'repair reasonably and properly' and 'keep in good repair' or 'sufficient repair' or 'tenantable repair' or most of the various phrases cited to us."

Substantial repair rather than perfect repair

3–006 Not all damage or deterioration to the fabric of the building, or the functional items serving it, will oblige the landlord to act under his obligation to repair. A covenant to repair will generally be satisfied by keeping the building in substantial repair rather than in perfect repair. Whether a building is in disrepair, for the purposes of the repairing obligation, will be determined by having regard to the age, character and locality of the premises and what would make it reasonably fit for a reasonable minded tenant of the class who would be likely to take them. In the leading case of *Proudfoot v Hart* (1890) 25 Q.B.D. 42, Lord Esher M.R. put it thus:

> " 'Good tenantable repair' is such repair as, having regard to the age, character and locality of the house, would make it reasonably fit for the occupation of a reasonably minded tenant of the class who would be likely to take it. The age of the house must be taken into account, because nobody could reasonably expect that a house 200 years old should be in the same condition of repair as a house lately built; the character of the house must be taken into account, because the same class of repairs as would be necessary to a palace would be wholly unnecessary to a cottage; and

the locality of the house must be taken into account, because the state of repair necessary for a house in Grovesnor Square would be wholly different from the state of repair necessary for a house in Spitalfields. The house need not be put into the same condition as when the tenant took it; it need not be put into perfect repair; it need only be put into such a state of repair as renders it reasonably fit for the occupation of a reasonably minded tenant of the class who would be likely to take it".

Disputes as to whether the building is in disrepair

3–007 Before a landlord's obligation to repair arises (and thus, his ability to recover from the tenant), the fabric of the premises or the functional items serving it must be in disrepair. In other words the state of the part of the premises, or item in issue, must have deteriorated from some earlier state. In *Anstruther-Gough-Calthorpe v McOscar* [1924] 1 K.B. 716, Atkin L.J. stated that repair:

"... connotes the idea of making good damage so as to leave the subject so far as possible as though it had not been damaged".

It follows that if some lack of amenity or inefficiency results from the defective original design or construction of a building, rather than from some damage or deterioration in the fabric, the remedial works will not fall within the ambit of a repairing obligation. In *Quick v Taff-Ely Borough Council* [1986] Q.B. 809, Lawton L.J. held:

"... the landlord need not do anything until there exists a condition which calls for repair. As a matter of ordinary English that which requires repair is a condition worse than it was at some earlier time".

That passage was approved by the Court of Appeal in *Lee v Leeds City Council* [2002] 1 WLR 1488. In *Post Office v Aquarius Properties Limited* [1987] 1 All E.R. 1055, Slade L.J. held:

"a state of disrepair, in my judgment, connotes a deterioration from some previous physical condition".

However, there have been circumstances where the Courts have anticipated such deterioration rather than waiting for it to happen. In the right circumstances and on the right evidence, they will endeavour to apply a common sense approach and will allow a landlord to recover costs of replacing part of the fabric of a building even though that part of the fabric has not yet deteriorated or failed.

An example of this is to be found in *Postel Properties Ltd v Boots* [1996] 2 E.G.L.R. 60, where the landlord had decided to replace the roof, which was very extensive, under a phased programme that was expected to last four or more years. The tenants argued that replacement of the roof was premature because it had not failed. At the time of the action the roof was within five years of the end of its expected life. Dealing with this point, Kennedy J. held, finding for the landlord:

> "Clearly it is a matter for experience and judgment when the time has come to renew a roof. The cost of replacement must be balanced against the likely increasing cost of patch repairs. A consideration is that patch repairs are expensive in terms of preliminary elements in the overall cost. With an enormous building such as this centre, the work of replacement has to be phased over four or more years, to spread the cost and to minimise disturbance to the tenants' businesses".

Equally, it is not enough for it to fall within the ambit of a repairing liability that the item in question is obsolete or no longer meets modern standards, including modern building standards or health and safety standards. In *Secretary of State for the Environment v Euston Centre Investments Limited (No.2)* [1994] N.P.C. 130, Chadwick J. considered a rent review where the rent had been fixed on the assumption that the tenant was liable to remove dangerous asbestos from the property under his repairing obligation. In finding for the tenant he held that the tenant was not obliged to carry out this work under his repairing obligation and that there is no difference in principle between inherent defects resulting in hazards to health and safety and those resulting in a lack of efficiency or amenity.

Repairs v improvements

3–008 A distinction is frequently made between repairs and improvements. Usually, a tenant will be obliged to contribute towards the costs of repairs under a service charge provision but not towards the costs of improvements. Consequently, tenants will seek to argue that works are properly to be considered to be improvements, rather than repairs, so that they might avoid paying for them or landlords will make the same argument to avoid undertaking the works at all.

Although the distinction is frequently made between repairs and improvements, the distinction between them is occasionally far from obvious. In *Wates v Rowland* [1952] 2 Q.B. 12, Evershed L.J. referred to the distinction between repairs and improvements as follows:

> "In the course of the argument examples were given showing that what was undoubtedly repair might yet involve some degree of improvement, in the sense of the modern substitute being better than that which had gone before. At the other end of the scale, it was also clear that work done to satisfy modern standards, although it might involve restoration and might be said to be restoration . . . yet clearly would be an improvement. Between the two extremes, it seems to me to be largely a matter of degree, which in the ordinary case the county court judge could decide as a matter of fact, applying a common-sense man-of-the-world view".

Inherent defects

3–009 A factor that will concern the Court is an inherent defect in the building causing other parts of it to be out of repair and where the only practicable way of remedying the want of repair is to correct the inherent defect and thereby improve the building. Whether such works of improvement fall within the scope of the repairing obligation, although always a matter of fact and degree, will involve the Court in determining whether the works will result in the building being so different from that originally let that the works required to correct the inherent defect were outside the contemplation of the parties to the lease.

Thus in *Ravenseft Properties Ltd v Davestone (Holdings) Ltd* [1980] Q.B. 12 there was an inherent defect when the building, a relatively new one, was built in that no expansion joints had been included because it had not been realised that the different coefficients of expansion of the stone of the cladding and the concrete of the structure made it necessary to include such joints. There was, however, also physical damage to the subject matter of the covenant in that, because of the differing coefficients of expansion, the stones of the cladding had become bowed, detached from the structure, loose and in danger of falling. Forbes J. allowed in the damages under the repairing covenant the cost of putting in expansion joints, and in that respect improving the building, because:

> "In no realistic sense . . . could it be said that there was any other possible way of reinstating this cladding than by providing the expansion joints which were, in fact, provided."

Similarly, in *Elmcroft Investments Ltd v Tankersley-Sawyer* [1984] 1 E.G.L.R. 47 there was physical damage from rising damp in the walls of a flat that was due to an inherent defect in that when it had been built, the slate damp-proof course had been put in too low and was therefore ineffective. The remedial work necessary to eradicate the rising damp was, on the evidence, the installation of a horizontal damp-proof course by silicone injection and formation of vertical barriers by silicone injection. This was held to be within the landlord's repairing covenant. It was necessary in order to repair the walls and, although it involved improvement over the previous ineffective slate damp-proof course, it was held that, as a matter of degree, having regard to the nature and locality of the property, this did not involve giving the tenant a different thing from that which was demised.

Of course, once repairs are found to be necessary, it is proper for any remedial works to take modern building standards and methods into account. Just because the works of repair will provide an element of improvement does not prevent their being works of repair—please see below.

What works are to be carried out

The landlord's choice?

3–010 Because it is the landlord who has covenanted to carry out the repairs, the choice will be his where there is a proper choice between different appropriate methods of repair. In *Hi-Lift Elevator Services v Temple* [1995] 70 P. & C.R. 620, a landlord intended to repair a defective roof by entirely replacing it, whereas his tenant believed that it could be properly repaired with patch repairs at a far lower cost. The tenant obtained an interim injunction preventing the landlord going ahead with his proposed works. The injunction was discharged and the tenant ordered to pay damages under the undertaking he had given when obtaining his interim relief and the Court of Appeal apparently approved the following passage from Woodfall on Landlord and Tenant as correctly representing the law on this point:

> "As a matter of practice, it is often possible to remedy a disrepair in a variety of ways. In general it will be for the covenantor to decide upon the appropriate method of repair. Thus where a landlord covenants to keep the structure and exterior of a building in repair, and the tenant covenants to contribute towards the cost of so doing, it is for the landlord to decide how to repair, although his decisions must be reasonable."

When it is unreasonable to repair rather than replace

3–011 Nonetheless, the landlord will not have a proper choice and the duty to repair becomes a duty to replace when it is unreasonable to waste money on repairs—see *Greetings of Oxford Koala Hotel Pty Ltd v Oxford Square Investments* (1989) 18 N.S.W.L.R. 33 and *Minja Properties Ltd v Cussins Property Group plc* [1998] 2 E.G.L.R. 52.

Modern standards, etc.

3–012 Once repairs are found to be necessary, it is proper for any remedial works to take modern building standards and methods into account. In *Postel Properties Ltd v Boots* [1996] 2 E.G.L.R. 60, Kennedy J. had to consider the replacement of the roof of a shopping centre in Milton Keynes. The roof as it was constructed was to a significant extent liable to attack from condensation rising from the interior of the building. The tenants took the point that replacing the roof with a more expensive one complying with modern building standards constituted an improvement that took the works outside of the landlord's repairing obligation. Kennedy J. found for the landlord and took into account advances in technology, insulation standards imposed by modern building regulations (although not enforceable in cases of repair) as representing good building practice and the countervailing advantage to the tenants of lower heating bills.

Where the repair is also an improvement

3–013 Further, it is not only the immediate cost of the proposed works that need be considered. In *Wandsworth London Borough v Griffin* [2000] 2 E.G.L.R. 105, the Lands Tribunal had to consider a situation where the landlord council, which was the owner of an estate consisting of blocks of flats, had replaced flat roofs with pitched roofs and the windows with uPVC double-glazed units. The evidence showed that the works involved were best value if life-cycle costing were used as an analytical tool to evaluate an asset over its operating life. Mr Norman Rose, the Chairman, dealing with this point and finding for the landlord held:

> "It does not seem to me that a repair ceased to be a repair if it also effects an improvement. In my judgment, the works carried out by the (landlords) did constitute a repair, if they were indeed cheaper than the alternatives, taking into account both initial and future costs."

When is it reasonable to repair rather than replace

[illegible] landlord will [illegible] to repair becomes a duty to replace [illegible] *Gemmell v. Thrifty* [illegible] (VSM [illegible]) [illegible]

[illegible]

[illegible] relevant circumstances

[illegible] must be judged by [illegible] modern building [illegible] and [illegible]

[illegible] the replacement of the [illegible] The cost [illegible] from condensation [illegible] from the [illegible] the building. The [illegible] took the point that [illegible] constituted an [illegible] upon the obligation. [illegible] imposed by modern building regulations [illegible] [illegible]

Where the landlord is [illegible] cost

[illegible] the immediate cost of the proposed works [illegible] need be [illegible] (2003) [illegible] the landlord [illegible] blocks of flats and replaced [illegible] with uPVC double-glazed units. [illegible] the works [illegible] the windows with [illegible] [illegible]

[illegible] improvements to my judgment, the works carried out by the landlord [illegible] and future costs. [illegible]

Chapter 4

Statutory Control of Service Charges

A statutory overview

4–001

Statutes

- Landlord and Tenant Act 1985
- Landlord and Tenant Act 1987
- Commonhold and Leasehold Reform Act 2002
- Landlord and Tenant (Covenants) Act 1995
- Housing Act 1996
- Arbitration Act 1996
- Financial Service and Markets Act 2000
- Consumer Credit Act 1974

Statutory Instruments

- Service Charges (Consultation Requirements)(England) Regulations 2003 (SI 2003/1987)
- Unfair Terms in Consumer Contracts Regulations 1999 (SI 1999/2083)

Introduction

4–002 The purpose of this chapter is to give an overview of the statutory provisions as they apply to service charges. In the main, statutory control applies solely to dwellings.

Commercial premises

4–003 Service charges in leases of commercial premises, including those to which Pt II of the Landlord and Tenant Act 1954 applies, are not directly regulated by the Landlord and Tenant Acts 1985 and 1987. However, the Acts may have some relevance to commercial premises which include a dwelling. For example, s.25 of the Landlord and Tenant Act 1987 applies to buildings which include premises "occupied or intended to be occupied otherwise than for residential purposes and where the internal area of those parts (taken together) exceeds 50 per cent of the internal floor area of the premises (taken as a whole)". Section 35 of the Landlord and Tenant Act may also apply to premises which include non-residential commercial premises as part of the building containing the flat within the meaning of s.35(2)(ii). It is essential that the statutes are read closely and not generalised. It should be emphasised that the statutory provisions dealt with hereafter apply *mainly but not exclusively* to dwellings.

Importance of statute

4–004 Although the scope of service charge provisions in a lease of a dwelling is a matter of construction under that lease, there is very heavy statutory overlay. When considering the statutory landscape, it is essential to bear in mind that different *parts* of a statute—as much as different statutes—treat different types of dwelling differently. To avoid error, it is essential to refer to the particular description of "dwelling" and to the quality of the leasehold interest (e.g. whether a long lease, lease for less than seven years, etc.) under each section of any Act. For example, Pt IV s.35 of the Landlord and Tenant Act 1987 applies only to long leases of flats, whilst Pt II (s.21) has wider relevance applying to short and long leases.

That said:

- Service charges made in respect of dwellings are regulated primarily by ss.18–30 of the Landlord and Tenant Act 1985, and the Landlord and Tenant Act 1987 and the Commonhold and Leasehold Reform Act 2002 (which Acts supplement and amend the Landlord and Tenant Act 1985).
- Service charge consultation requirements are regulated by the Service Charges (Consultation Requirements)(England) Regulations 2003 (SI 2003/1987).

- The fairness of service charge terms in a lease are subject to the Unfair Terms in Consumer Contracts Regulations 1999 (SI 1999/2083) for natural person (i.e. non-company) lessees acting outside the course of their business.
- Landlords accepting credit card payments for service charges and those which refer arrears to mortgagees for payment are subject to challenge under the compulsory jurisdiction of the Financial Ombudsman Scheme pursuant to Pt XVI of the Financial Services and Markets Act 2000.
- A term in a lease providing for arbitration where the sum in dispute is less than £5,000.00 may be unfair under the Arbitration Act 1996 which extends the application of the Unfair Terms in Consumer Contracts Regulations 1994 (now superseded by the 1999 Regulations).

Section 18 of the Landlord and Tenant Act 1985

Service charge definition

4–005 Most statutory controls adopt the definition of "service charge" in s.18 of the Landlord and Tenant Act 1985:

"18(1) In the following provisions of this Act 'service charge' means an amount payable by a tenant of a dwelling as part of or in addition to the rent—

(a) which is payable, directly or indirectly, for services, repairs, maintenance, improvement or insurance or the landlord's costs of management, and
(b) the whole or part of which varies or may vary according to the relevant costs.

(2) The relevant costs are the costs or estimated costs incurred or to be incurred by or on behalf of the landlord, or a superior landlord, in connection with the matters for which the service charge is payable.

(3) For this purpose—

(a) costs includes overheads, and
(b) costs are relevant costs in relation to a service charge whether they are incurred, or to be incurred, in the period for which the service charge is payable or in an earlier or later period."

Tenant

4–006 The Courts, Leasehold Valuation Tribunals and the Lands Tribunal have considered the definition in s.18 on a number of occasions. "Tenant" includes a mesne landlord: *Heron Maple House v Central Estates* [2002] 1 E.G.L.R. 35.

Payable

4–007 "Payable" does not necessarily mean liability under a tenancy, but can include a contribution to water costs payable under an "informal" agreement: *re: Flat 25 Chalfont House* (August 27, 2004) LON/00AW/LSL/2004/024, LVT. A freeholder's own contribution to relevant costs is not "payable by a tenant": *re: 503 Nell Gwyn House* (August 20, 2004) LVT/00AW/LSL/2004/0070, LVT.

Dwelling

4–008 "Dwelling" means a building or part of a building occupied or intended to be occupied as a separate dwelling, together with any yard, garden, outhouses and appurtenances belonging to it or usually enjoyed with it: s.38 Landlord and Tenant Act 1985 and s.60(1) Landlord and Tenant Act 1987.

A dwelling does not include a site on a chalet park: *re: Saddlebrook Holiday Park* (October 25, 2004) CHI/29UM/LSC/2004/0046, LVT. It also does not include premises where over half the floor area is reserved for business use: *re: 63 Alphabet Square* (January 21, 2003) LVT/SC/CR/012/054/02, LVT. Costs payable "indirectly" for services was included in the Act to cover payments made to a superior landlord for services in the premises: *Minster Chalets Ltd v Irwin Park Residents Association* (April 27, 2000) LRX/28/2000, Lands Tribunal. In one case, it was held that "services" included the cost of notices under s.146 of the Law of Property Act 1925: *Forcelux Ltd* (January 20, 2004) LRX/33/2003, Lands Tribunal. However, they do not include application fees to the Tribunal itself: *re: Cascades and Quayside* (October 4, 2001) LVT/VOD/012/004/01 and *re: Flat 4 Kingsmead Lodge* (March 23, 1999) LVT/SC/0381098.

The word "dwelling" is commonly used in housing legislation: s.1 Rent Act 1977, s.1 Housing Act 1988, s.81 Housing Act 1996, s.38 Landlord and Tenant Act 1985, s.60 Landlord and Tenant Act 1987. Case law on these provisions will be of assistance: for example *Uratemp Ventures Limited v Collins* [2002] 1 All E.R. 46 HL, *Sutton (Hastoe) Housing Association v Williams* [1988] 1 E.G.L.R. 56

(CA) and *Re Bedfordshire Pilgrims Housing Association* (March 23, 2000, LT).

Improvements

4–009 The word "improvement" was added by s.150 of and Sch.9 para.7 to the Commonhold and Leasehold Reform Act 2002, and applies to costs incurred after September 30, 2003 in England and after March 31, 2004 in Wales.

Variable charges

4–010 The requirement that a service charge "varies . . . according to the relevant costs" means that charges that vary with a published index such as the Retail Price Index or an index of building costs do not fall within the definition of s.18: *Coventry City Council v Coles* [1994] 1 W.L.R. 398 (CA). It has been said in the Leasehold Valuation Tribunal that "the calculation of the amount is to be derived from the costs": *Minster Chalets* (above). It is plain that fixed service charges are not covered by the definition: *re:184 Stockwell Park Road* (August 1, 2000) P/SC/CR/008/027/00), LVT; *Room B, 42 Mornington Crescent* (June 5, 2003) LVT/SC/002/006/003, LVT; and *Flat 8 Springwell Court* (October 11, 2004) LON/00AU/LSL/2004/0075, LVT. However, a fixed management charge forming part of a variable service charge can still form part of a service charge within s.18: *Longmint Ltd v Marcus* (January 23, 2004) LRX/25/2003, Lands Tribunal.

"Relevant costs"

4–011 "*Relevant costs*" are defined as the costs or estimated costs incurred or to be incurred by or on behalf of the landlord, or a superior landlord, in connection with the matters for which the service charge is payable. For this purpose the word "costs" includes overheads and costs are "relevant costs" in relation to a service charge whether they are incurred or to be incurred in the period for which the service charge is payable or in an earlier or later period—see ss.18(2) and (3) of the Landlord and Tenant Act 1985. In *Cinnamon Ltd v Morgan* [2002] P. & C.R. 139, Chadwick L.J. observed that these definitions were somewhat circuitous because under s.30 of the Act "landlord" is defined as including any person who has a right to enforce payment of a service charge. That phrase is dependant on the meaning of "relevant costs", and "relevant costs" is itself defined by reference to the landlord. It was held however that a management company did, on the facts of the case, fall within the definition of "landlord", with the result that charges incurred by that company could not be passed on to the tenant other than in accordance with s.19.

Exceptions

4–012 By s.26 of the Landlord and Tenant Act 1985, the provisions of ss.18–25 do not apply to service charges payable by a tenant of a local authority, a National Park Authority, a new town corporation or the Development Board of Wales. However, if the tenancy is a "long tenancy" within the meaning of s.26(2), ss.18–24 but not s.25 apply.

"Long tenancies"

4–013 Under s.26(2) a long tenancy is defined as:

(a) a tenancy granted for a term certain exceeding 21 years, whether or not it is (or may become) terminable before the end of that term by notice given by the tenant or by re-entry or forfeiture;

(b) a tenancy for a term fixed by law under a grant with a covenant or obligation for perpetual renewal, other than a tenancy by sub-demise from one which is not a long tenancy; and

(c) any tenancy granted in pursuance of Pt V of HA 1985 (the right to buy), including any tenancy granted in pursuance of that Part as it has effect by virtue of s.17 of HA 1996 (the right to acquire).

A tenancy for life may also be a long tenancy if granted by a registered social landlord. By s.26(3) LTA 1985, a tenancy granted so as to become terminable by notice after a death is not a "long tenancy" for the purposes of s.26(1) unless all of the following circumstances are present:

(a) it is granted by a housing association which at the time of the grant is a registered social landlord;

(b) it is granted at a premium calculated by reference to a percentage of the value of the dwelling-house or the cost of providing it; and

(c) at the time it is granted it complies with the requirements of the regulations then in force under s.140(4)(b) of the Housing Act

1980 or s.4(2)(b) of Sch.4A to the Leasehold Reform Act 1967 (conditions for exclusion of shared ownership leases from Pt I of the Leasehold Reform Act 1967) or, in the case of a tenancy granted before any such regulations were brought into force, with the first such regulations to be in force.

Pursuant to s.27, ss.18–27 do not apply to a tenancy of a dwelling in respect of which the rent is registered under Pt IV of the Rent Act 1977 unless the amount registered is a variable amount under s.71(4) of the Rent Act 1977.

Look at the statute not the lease

4–014 There can be no substitute for reading the statutes. It should be apparent from a close reading of s.18 that the definition is a wide one. Contrary to the concession made before the Lands Tribunal in the case of *Forcelux Ltd v Sweetman and another* [2001] 2 E.G.L.R. 173, that litigation costs could not fall within the definition of service charge because the lease made a separate provision for the payment of the litigation costs and defined those costs as something else other than service charge, it is the statutory definition which is all important. The statutory definition of service charge is the determining factor and not the lease.

Were that not so, a landlord could drive a coach and horses through the protection afforded by the statute by defining service charge items as non-service charge items to circumvent the statutory control.

The rent/non-rent distinction relevant to the service of s.146 notices (i.e. by s.146(10) of the LPA 1925, a s.146 notice is not required in the case of a claim for forfeiture for non-payment of rent) is not relevant to the question as to what is or is not a service charge. Whilst a s.146 notice is not required in respect of a claim for a service charge item deemed rent and recoverable as rent, it nonetheless remains a service charge for the purposes of the statute: *Escalus Properties Limited v Robinson* [1996] Q.B. 231, [1995] 2 E.G.L.R. 23.

Service charges items and rent as defined in a lease are not mutually exclusive. The overlap is clearly recognised in the words "part of or in addition to the rent." It follows that costs of and incidental to the service of a notice pursuant to ss.146 and 147 of the LPA 1925 may be subject to an assessment of reasonableness under the statutory provision relevant to service charges as well as under the general provision of the CPR 1998 Pt 44.

It would be an abuse for a landlord to seek to forfeit a lease on the basis of the unpaid costs of service of a s.146 notice in respect of a disputed service charge. Since September 24, 1996, such a claim may well be premature unless the amount of the service charge has been agreed by the tenant, determined by the court or by an arbitral tribunal in accordance with ss.81 and 82 HA 1996 (amended by ss.170 and 180 and Sch.14 (repealing s.82 HA 1996) of the Commonhold and Leasehold Reform Act 2002).

Section 19 of the Landlord and Tenant Act 1985

Review by the LVT

4–015 For the purposes of determining what service charges are payable for a period:

- section 19(1)(a) provides that the costs must be *reasonably incurred*; and
- section 19(1)(b) provides that costs incurred on the provision of services or for the carrying out of works must be of a *reasonable standard*.

This is dealt with in Chapter 11. Both the Court and the Leasehold Valuation Tribunal have jurisdiction to determine the issue of reasonableness.

Anti-avoidance provisions

4–016 Under s.27A(6) of the Landlord and Tenant Act 1985 (as amended by the Commonhold and Leasehold Reform Act 2002) an agreement to contract out of the LVT jurisdiction conferred by statutory provisions is void.

- In the case of a consumer, such a term would also be void under the provision of reg.5 Sch.2 para.1(q) of the Unfair Terms in Consumer Contracts Regulations 1999.
- A post-dispute arbitration agreement is permissible under ss.27A(6) and 27A(4)(b) of the Landlord and Tenant Act 1985 despite s.91 of the Arbitration Act 1996, which provides that an arbitration agreement is unfair for the purpose of the 1994 Regulations (for which one should read the 1999 Regulations) so far as it relates to a pecuniary remedy which does not exceed the amount specified in the Unfair Arbitrations Agreement (Specified Amounts) Order 1999 (SI

1999/2167) (currently £5,000.00). The term would have to be optional.

Application to the LVT

Before September 30, 2003

4–017 Pursuant to s.19(2A), a landlord or a tenant could apply for a determination: (a) whether the service charge was reasonably incurred; (b) whether the services or works were to a reasonable standard; and (c) whether an amount payable would be reasonable. By s.19(2B), an application could be made in terms similar to s.19(2A) prospectively. By s.19(2C), no application may be made in respect of a matter which has been agreed or admitted by the tenant, is subject to an arbitration agreement to which the tenant is a party or is to be referred to arbitration or has been the subject of determination by a court or arbitral tribunal.

After September 30, 2003

4–018 Sections 19(2A)–(2C) (inserted by s.83(1) of the Housing Act 1996) have been repealed by s.180 of and Sch.14 to the Commonhold and Leasehold Reform Act 2002, having effect to an application to the LVT made after September 30, 2003 or proceedings transferred to the LVT from the County Court before that date in England, and in Wales after March 31, 2004.

Following the repeal of s.19(2A)–(3) of the Landlord and Tenant Act 1985, the LVT's jurisdiction in relation to service charge liability is set out at s.27A of the Landlord and Tenant Act 1985. The LVT now has a very wide jurisdiction and the right of the tenant to contest service charge arises whether or not the items in dispute have been paid (reversing *Daejan Properties*) (s.27A(2) Landlord and Tenant Act 1985)(see paragraphs 4–016–4–017 above).

LVT jurisdiction is fully discussed in Chapter 24.

Section 20 of the Landlord and Tenant Act 1985—consultation

4–019 The route to dispute avoidance as between landlord and tenant reposes in consultation. Consultation is required as a matter of statute. Consultation requirements are dealt with fully in Chapter 13.

Section 20B of the Landlord and Tenant Act 1985—limitation

4–020 Service charge demands must be made within 18 months of the service charge being incurred. A provision that the service charge is deemed rent and recoverable as rent cannot circumvent the truncated limitation period. This is dealt with in Chapter 23.

Section 20C of the Landlord and Tenant Act 1985—costs

4–021 Section 20C in its original form and as amended by the Commonhold and Leasehold Reform Act 2002 provides that a tenant may apply for litigation costs "not to be regarded as relevant costs to be taken into account in determining the amount of any service charge." The effect of the section is covered in Chapter 7.

Sections 21 and 22 of the Landlord and Tenant Act 1985—written summary

4–022 The landlord is obliged to supply tenants with a written summary of the service charge costs incurred over the previous 12 months. Within six months of the supply of the summary, the tenant or the secretary of a recognised tenant's association may request reasonable facilities for inspecting the accounts, receipts and other documents supporting the summary. This is dealt with in Chapter 10.

Section 23 of the Landlord and Tenant Act 1985—information

4–023 A landlord is required to make written requests of a superior landlord when required by a tenant. The superior landlord is required to respond within a reasonable time and the immediate landlord is then required to furnish the information sought by the tenant within the time allowed by s.21. Requests may also be made for inspection of documents held by a superior landlord. It is a summary offence for a person to fail, without reasonable excuse, to perform a duty imposed by ss.21–23. Statutory rights to information are dealt with in Chapter 10.

Schedule to the Landlord and Tenant Act 1985

Rights of tenant with respect to insurance

The tenant is entitled to a summary of insurance cover and inspection of the insurance policy and the landlord or tenant may make an application to the LVT for a determination as to the adequacy of that insurance and the amount of the premium payable. The provisions ensure that a landlord is not able to make a profit on the premiums, which should be competitive. This schedule was itself inserted by Sch.3 to the Landlord and Tenant Act 1987. **4–024**

Insurance is dealt with in Chapter 5.

Limitation of liability of former tenants—s.17 of the Landlord and Tenant (Covenants) Act 1995

If a claim is being made in respect of arrears of rent or service charge incurred following assignment of the lease against the original tenant, previous assignor of the lease or guarantor or against a previous tenant who has entered into an authorised guarantee agreement under the 1995 Act, the landlord must serve a notice under s.17 of the 1995 Act within six months of the sum falling due if the arrears are to be recoverable. It must not be overlooked that, notwithstanding that the section refers to the need for a notice where a "fixed charge" is being sought, a "fixed charge" includes service charges even though by their very nature they are not fixed in amount (s.17(6) LTCA 1995). Section 17 of the 1995 Act applies equally to service charges in respect of commercial premises as it does to residential premises. **4–025**

The Landlord and Tenant Act 1987 Part II—appointment of a Manager

The Landlord and Tenant Act 1987 complements the Landlord and Tenant Act 1985. By s.21 of the Landlord and Tenant Act 1987, a tenant alone, or with other tenants, may make an application to the Leasehold Valuation Tribunal for the appointment of a Manager (under s.24). The provisions of Pt II apply to premises consisting of the whole or part of a building if the building or part contains two or more flats. The provision excludes certain lettings by exempt landlords (s.58(1) Landlord and Tenant Act 1987). The Act does not apply to business tenants. The section allows tenants to have a Manager appointed to take over the management of a badly run building. **4–026**

Appointment of a Manager is dealt with in Chapter 23.

The Landlord and Tenant Act 1987 Part III—acquisition orders

4–027 Part III of the LTA 1987 (ss.25–34) has effect for the purpose of enabling qualifying tenants of flats contained in premises to which this Part applies to compulsorily acquire the landlord's interest. The orders are known as "acquisition orders". The Part applies if the premises consist of the whole or part of a building, and they contain two or more flats held by the tenants of the landlord who are qualifying tenants, and the total number of flats held by such tenants is not less than two-thirds of the total number of flats contained in the premises. Part III is excluded if any part or parts of the premises is or are occupied or intended to be occupied otherwise than for residential purposes and the internal floor area of that part or those parts (taken together) exceeds 50 per cent of the internal floor area of the premises (taken as a whole). Acquisition orders are dealt with in Chapter 28.

Landlord and Tenant Act 1987 Part IV—statutory variation of leases

4–028 The LVT has jurisdiction to vary the terms of leases. By s.35 Landlord and Tenant Act 1987, a party to a *long lease* of *a flat* may apply for the variation of a lease as to repair, maintenance generally and of installations, insurance, recovery of service charge, and computation of service charge. Consequential and necessary amendments to other leases may be made pursuant to s.36. Section 37 allows for applications to be made in respect of two or more leases. Variations are binding on third parties pursuant to s.39(2): *Selous Street Properties Limited v Oronel Fabrics Limited* (1984) 270 E.G. 643.

By s.40, any party to a long lease of a dwelling may make an application to the Leasehold Valuation Tribunal to vary insurance provisions in a dwelling *other than a flat* (s.40(5) Landlord and Tenant Act 1987). A dwelling to which the Landlord and Tenant Act 1954 Pt II applies is excluded from the insurance variation provisions (s.40(4)(b)). The application may be made by any party.

Variation of leases is dealt with in Chapter 21.

Landlord and Tenant Act 1987 Part V—trust accounts

4–029 Section 42 of the Landlord and Tenant Act 1987 requires a landlord to hold service charge contributions by tenants of two or more dwellings in a trust account (*23 Essex Mansions, Essex Road South, Leytonstone* LVT/SC/038/026 and 043/01 and LVT/SCC/038/017/01). The handling of service charge accounts is dealt with in Chapter 15.

Landlord and Tenant Act 1987 Part VI—landlord's name and address

4–030 Section 47 of the Landlord and Tenant Act 1987 requires a landlord to include his name and address in any demand for rent. The section provides that any demand for service charge "shall be treated for all purposes as not being due from the tenant to the landlord at any time before that information is furnished by the landlord by notice given to the tenant". This provision is dealt with in Chapter 14.

Section 48 of the Landlord and Tenant Act 1987 requires a landlord of premises to which this Part applies to furnish the tenant with an address in England and Wales at which notices may be served. Where the landlord fails to comply, any rent, service charge or administration charge shall be treated for all purposes as not being due from the tenant to the landlord at any time before the landlord does comply with that section. This provision is dealt with in Chapter 10.

Unfair Terms in Consumer Contracts Regulations 1999—fairness of term

4–031 The Unfair Terms in Consumer Contracts Regulations 1999 superseded the Unfair Terms in Consumer Contracts Regulations 1994. The Regulations apply a test of fairness to standard terms (terms which have not been individually negotiated). These provisions are dealt with in Chapter 11.

Financial Ombudsman Service—alternative statutory dispute resolution

4–032 Where a service charge dispute arises out of a relationship between the tenant and a financial institution, for example where the service charge is paid by credit card or the service charge arrear is met by a tenant's mortgagee, that complaint (dispute) may fall within the compulsory jurisdiction of the Financial Ombudsman Scheme pursuant to Pt XVI of the Financial Services and Markets Act 2000. The scheme allows individuals and certain companies to make complaints about financial institutions to the Financial Ombudsman Service. Credit card payments are of wide significance because of the provisions of s.75 of the Consumer Credit Act 1975 which would give the tenant a like claim against the issuer of a credit card where the landlord is in breach of contract. In a similar way, a mortgagee making an unauthorised payment on behalf of an objecting tenant in satisfaction of a service charge demand, may find itself paying compensation to the tenant on a determination by the Financial Ombudsman. The Ombudsman is empowered to determine complaints in accordance with what is fair and reasonable in all the circumstances of the case (s.228 Financial Services and Markets Act 2000 and DISP rule 3.8.1 of the FSA Handbook) and not necessarily under the principles of English law (*The Queen on the Application of IFG Financial Services Limited v Financial Ombudsman Services and Mr and Mrs Jenkins* [CO/5223/2004]).

The Consumer Credit Bill currently before parliament proposes provision for all credit disputes to be referred by the Office of Fair Trading to the Financial Ombudsman Scheme.

Chapter 5

Insurance

Introduction

5–001 In many modern leases, the lessor will seek to control how the demised property is insured. He will seek to do this generally for two reasons.

First, he will wish to be sure that the property is adequately insured. Thus he will wish to know that the property is insured against those risks that he considers to be important. This will almost always include the risk of fire, storm, and the other usual perils. It will also usually include the risk of being found guilty for third party liability, including environmental liabilities. He will also wish to be sure that the level of insurance is high enough to protect his interests and will fully cover the cost of rebuilding the building, replacing his plant and meeting his potential liabilities to third parties. Finally, he will wish to be sure that the insurance is placed with a reputable insurer.

Secondly, because of the very high levels of commission or discounts available to landlords placing bulk insurance, he will wish to take the income available from arranging the insurance. This is well illustrated by the figures in *Williams v Southwark B.C.* (2001) 33 H.L.R. 224 where the lessor first insured under a block policy where it was entitled to a discount or commission of 36.5 per cent of the gross premium and later insured under another block policy where it was entitled to a 25 per cent discount.

While these factors undoubtedly provide an incentive for landlords to retain control of insurance arrangements, there may also be a sound practical reason for this position, which is that in the case of blocks of flats, tenants will generally lack an insurable interest in the building outside of their flat. Furthermore, where leases are short, tenants may well have less "interest" in the colloquial sense in arranging adequate insurance as well.

Overview of the types of insurance provision commonly found in leases

5–002 Most commonly, particularly in the context of property in multiple occupation, the lessor will usually reserve to himself the right to insure and will seek to recover the cost either as a separate insurance rent or under the service charge provisions. The extent to which the lessor can recover all of his insuring costs will be a matter of construction of the particular lease. Authorities dealing with limitations on the recoverability of such costs are considered in Chapter 11.

Alternatively, in some instances the lessor will seek to control how the demised property is insured by reserving the right to nominate the insurer or by having a veto over the choice of insurer.

Occasionally a lease may restrict the amount that the lessor might seek to recover for insurance by, for example, expressly providing that the amount to be recovered is reasonable. However, such provisions are rarely encountered in practice.

Commissions or discounts

5–003 As stated above, frequently the lessor is able to negotiate a "commission" or "discount" on the gross premium. Whether the Court is prepared to require the lessor to pass on the benefit of the commission or discount will be a matter of construction or implication of a term into particular lease.

Thus in *Williams v Southwark B.C.* (2001) 33 H.L.R. 224, where the landlord covenanted to insure the building and the tenants covenanted to pay a service charge including an insurance element, it was conceded that the lessor was obliged to account for a discount or commission of 36.5 per cent of the gross premium to which it was entitled. However the lessor later insured under another block policy, where it was entitled to a 25 per cent discount, 5 per cent being attributable to a loyalty bonus and the remaining 20 per cent for rendering certain services. It was held that it need only account for 5 per cent (this point in fact being conceded). The remaining 20 per cent was not a rebate or reduction from the premium but was held on the facts to be remuneration for services.

Rights of tenants of dwellings under the Schedule to the Landlord and Tenant Act 1985

5–004 Section 30A of the Landlord and Tenant Act 1985 ("the 1985 Act") gives effect to a Schedule which lays down a set of rights for tenants of dwellings in respect of insuring obligations. The Schedule has been heavily amended by both the Housing Act 1996 and the Commonhold and Leasehold Reform Act 2002. The following paragraphs deal with the Schedule in its amended form.

The rights are exercisable by a "tenant of a dwelling". This includes a statutory tenant (para.1). There is no other qualification, so it presumably also includes assured tenants as well as long lessees. Both houses and flats qualify. However, secure tenants are in effect excluded by the landlord exception in para.9.

The rights are exercisable against "the landlord", which is defined widely to include any person who has a right to enforce payment of the service charge relating to insurance. They would therefore be exercisable against landlords, management companies, RTM companies and Managers.

The rights entitle a tenant to obtain a summary of cover (para.2), to inspect the policy (para.3), to notify insurers of a potential claim (para.7) and to challenge the lessor's choice of insurer (para.8).

Summary of cover

5–005 Paragraph 2 of the Schedule provides a right to the tenant to a summary of insurance cover from the landlord. This is exercisable by notice in writing from the tenant or the secretary of a registered tenants' association (RTA). Notice may be served on the landlord, any named agent or the person who receives the rent. It is considered that service on a LTA s.47 or s.48 address also suffices.

The right is exercisable by tenants who pay a service charge which includes an amount payable directly or indirectly for insurance. It does not matter whether the charge is a separate clause, a ring fenced payment or is one service charge item of many within a general clause.

The landlord has 21 days from service of the notice to supply the summary, which must include the name of the insurer, the insured risks, and the insured amount(s). Where the dwelling is a flat, the summary must identify the insured amount relating to the building containing the flat and (if the policy specifies it) the amount insured in relation to the flat itself. By virtue of sub-para.(6), a landlord sufficiently complies with this requirement if he supplies the policy itself.

Inspection of the policy

5–006 Paragraph 3 of the Schedule provides a further right to inspect and copy "any relevant policy or associated documents". The tenant has the choice of whether to do the inspection and copying himself or to require the landlord to do it for him.

The right is exercisable in the same instance as the right to demand a summary under para.2, and is exercised by notice in the same way. Again, the landlord has 21 days to comply.

No charge may be made for permitting the tenant to inspect, although any costs may be treated as a general management cost and included in the service charge as such (if the leases allow it). A reasonable charge may be made for anything else, such as copying. Such charges fall within the definition of "administration charges" and are subject to the controls under Sch.11 to the CLRA 2002 (see Chapter 12).

A relevant policy includes the previous policy as well as the current policy. Importantly, "associated documents" means accounts, receipts, etc. which evidence payment of the premiums for the current period of insurance and that immediately preceding it. This provides a means of checking just how much was paid, which may be highly relevant where the landlord is suspected of pocketing a discount.

As the Schedule was originally enacted, the right to inspect the policy could only be exercised if the right to inspect a summary had been exercised first. Since the amendments made by the CLRA 2002, the right to inspect the policy may be exercised without first exercising the right to a summary. It is difficult to see what benefit a tenant is likely to derive from asking for the summary instead of the policy itself, and it may therefore be that the right under para.2 becomes redundant.

Superior landlords

5–007 Paragraph 4(1) of the Schedule provides that where it is in fact a superior landlord who insures, the immediate landlord must pass on a tenant's para.2 request to his landlord, and so on up the chain until the responsible person is notified. That person is required to provide the information back down the chain until it reaches the tenant's direct landlord, who is then required to comply with his obligation within the 21 days specified or "such further time, if any, as is reasonable in the circumstances".

A slightly different mechanism exists in relation to requests for the policy under para.3. Here the immediate landlord is required to notify the tenant of the identity of the responsible landlord, and upon his doing so para.3 applies to the responsible landlord "as it applies to the immediate landlord" (para.4(2)). The tenant is therefore expected to deal directly with the responsible landlord instead of his immediate landlord. In a situation where there are a number of superior interests, this is likely to prove quicker than the route prescribed if requesting a summary, and provides a further incentive to a tenant to use para.3 in preference to para.2.

Effect of a change of landlord or tenant

5–008 Paragraph 4A makes provision for a change of landlord during the period when a notice under paras 2, 3 or 4 is pending.

If the outgoing landlord remains capable of performing the duty, he must do so.

The incoming landlord becomes liable to discharge the duty to the extent that he is capable of doing so (regardless of any continuing duty on the outgoing landlord). In this case the 21 day notice periods under paras 2(4) and 3(4) run instead from the date of disposal.

An assignment of the tenancy has no practical consequence; the landlord must discharge his duty regardless (para.5). The only restriction is that a person is not required to comply with more than a reasonable number of requirements imposed by any one person. Since *ex hypothesi* where an assignment has taken place the identity of the tenant will change, it is difficult to envisage this restriction having much application.

Enforcement

5–009 Where a person fails without reasonable excuse to comply with any of the duties prescribed by paras 2–4A of the Schedule, he commits an offence punishable by a fine not exceeding level four on the standard scale (para.6).

Other rights

5–010 There are two further rights exercisable by a tenant under the Act. The first is the right to notify insurers of a possible claim. The second is the right to challenge the landlord's choice of insurers.

Right to notify insurers of a possible claim

5–011 As with paras 2 and 3 of the Schedule, the right is exercisable by tenants who pay a service charge which includes an amount payable directly or indirectly for insurance. The phrase "directly or indirectly" presumably means that it does not matter whether the charge is a separate clause, a ring fenced payment, or is one service charge item of many within a general clause.

The right applies where it appears that there is such damage to the dwelling itself, or to the building which contains it, that an insurance claim could be made, but it is a term of the insurance (as is commonly the case) that notice of the claim be given within a specified period.

The tenant (defined in para.7(4) to include one of joint tenants) has the right to serve a notice on the insurer stating: (a) that damage has been caused to the dwelling (or, if the dwelling is a flat, to the dwelling or any other part of the building in which the flat is located); and (b) that a claim could be made in respect of the damage under the terms of the insurance policy.

The notice must be served within the specified period. It must be noted however that it is not the claim itself which must be made within that time, merely notice of the damage.

If a notice is given within that specified period, the effect of that notice is to extend time (if necessary) for the making of a claim until a date six months from the date of the notice.

Again, it is to be noted that the tenant is not given the right to make the claim itself. The purpose of this right is to permit the tenant if necessary to take proceedings to force the landlord to make a claim, if the landlord is obliged to do so under the terms of the lease. Provided the tenant serves the initial notice in time, it prevents landlords from relying on a defence that the time for making the claim has expired.

Sub-paragraphs (5) and (6) provide that the Secretary of State may prescribe the forms of notices under this section and the particulars which they must contain. At the time of writing, no regulations have been made under this section.

Right to challenge landlord's choice of insurer

5–012 The final right conferred on the tenant by the Schedule is to be found in para.8, which applies where a tenancy of a dwelling requires the tenant to insure the dwelling with an insurer nominated or approved by the landlord. It should be noted that this right has a significantly more limited scope than those which precede it; in particular, it does not apply where a tenant merely has to pay a contribution in respect of the landlord's choice of insurer.

Either the tenant or the landlord may make application to a County Court or LVT for a determination as to whether the insurance is unsatisfactory in any respect or the premiums payable are excessive (para.8(2)). It is thought that a landlord will rarely want to test whether an insurer he himself has nominated or approved is in fact satisfactory. Theoretically it could happen where, for example, he approves the tenant's choice of insurer without regard to the terms and subsequently forms the view that the terms are inadequate. Since however the remedies available on an application under sub-para.(2) are orders requiring the landlord to nominate or approve *either* a named insurer *or* an insurer satisfying such requirements in relation to the insurance as may be specified (para.8(4)), it is hard to see how conferring the right for a landlord to make an application is anything other than otiose.

No application may be made in respect of a matter which the tenant has agreed or admitted, which is to be referred to arbitration under an arbitration agreement or which has been the subject of a court or LVT determination (para.8(3)). Many of the other references to arbitration agreements in the landlord and tenant legislation have been amended by CLRA 2002 to refer only to post-dispute arbitration agreements, i.e. to avoid arbitration clauses written into the lease, but this provision appears to have been overlooked. If, as is often the case in a long lease, there is an arbitration clause, this will prevent a para.8 application to the court or LVT.

Finally, any agreement by the tenant which purports to provide for a determination, by a different means, of a question which could be the subject of an application under this paragraph, is void. This does not however extend to arbitration agreements.

Additional rights of tenants of houses under Commonhold and Leasehold Reform Act 2002

5–013 In addition to the rights arising under the Landlord and Tenant Act 1985, certain further rights are conferred on tenants under long leases of houses under s.164 of the 2002 Act.

What is a "long lease"?

5–014 The phrase "long lease" as used in the 2002 Act is defined in ss.76–77 of the Act. The definition is detailed but in essence there are, by virtue of s.76, six species of long lease:

- leases granted for terms certain exceeding 21 years;
- leases for a term fixed by law under a grant with a covenant or obligation for perpetual renewal;
- leases terminable after a death or marriage (s.149(6) of the Law of Property Act 1925);

- leases granted in pursuance of the right to buy or right to acquire on rent to mortgage terms under the Housing Act 1985;
- shared ownership leases (as defined in s.76(3) of the 2002 Act) where the tenant has a full 100 per cent share of the lease;
- leases granted in pursuance of the right to acquire under s.17 of the Housing Act 1996.

Certain refinements to these provisions are then contained in s.77, many of whose sub-sections are concerned with ensuring that leases which might otherwise fall through gaps in the provisions of s.76 should also come within the definition. So leases which have in fact exceeded (or will exceed) 21 years' duration (although granted for a shorter period originally), or which are continuations of long leases, are generally to be regarded as long leases for the purposes of s.76.

What is a "house"?

5–015 "House" is given the same meaning as under Pt 1 of the Leasehold Reform Act 1967. Section 2(1) of that Act defines "house" as including:

> ". . . any building designed or adapted for living in and reasonably so called, notwithstanding that the building is not structurally detached, or was not or is not solely designed or adapted for living in, or is divided horizontally into flats or maisonettes . . ."

The definition goes on to provide that where a building is divided horizontally or vertically into different units, the units themselves are not houses although the building as a whole might be.

There is a vast body of case law on the application of this definition, analysis of which is beyond the scope of this chapter. A comprehensive discussion can be found in *Hague on Leasehold Enfranchisement* (4th ed., 2003) at paras 2-02–2-09.

What are the rights conferred by s.164?

5–016 Essentially s.164 gives rise to a right to a tenant who comes within its terms not to effect insurance with the insurer nominated by the landlord.

In addition to the restriction of this section to tenants of houses under long leases, the following conditions are also required to be met:

- the house must be insured under a policy issued by an authorised insurer;
- the policy must cover the interests of both the landlord and the tenant;
- the policy must cover all the risks which the lease requires be covered by insurance provided by the landlord's insurer;
- the amount of the cover must be not less than that which the lease requires be provided by such insurance; and
- the tenant has satisfied certain requirements as to the giving of notice (s.164(2)).

An "authorised insurer" for these purposes means a person who is authorised to provide the kind of insurance required under the terms of the Financial Services and Markets Act 2000 (s.164(10)).

The notice requirements

5–017 Consideration of the notice requirements imposed on the tenant must begin by ascertainment of the "relevant date". That date is the inception of a policy or, if it has been renewed, its most recent renewal (s.164(4)(a)).

In order to satisfy the notice requirements, a tenant is required to give his landlord a notice containing certain information within 14 days of the relevant date (s.164(3)(a)). Alternatively, if after that date he is requested to do so by a new landlord, he must give the notice to that person within 14 days of their request (s.164(3)(b)). A "new landlord" is someone who has acquired the interest of the last landlord within the previous month (s.164(4)(b)).

The notice must specify the name of the insurer, the risks covered by the policy and the amount of the cover (s.164(5)(a)–(c)). There is further provision that it must contain such further information as may be prescribed (s.164(5)(d)), but there are no regulations under this provision at the present time.

Subsections 164(6)–(9) make provision for the service of the notice by post and the address for service, which is either the landlord's address for the service of notices given under s.48 of the Landlord and Tenant Act 1987 or, if no such address has been given, an address contained in a rent demand made under s.47 of that Act. Alternatively, if the landlord has notified the tenant that he wishes such a notice to be served on a different address, it must be served on that different address (s.164(9)).

Reasonableness

5–018 Contributions to insurance frequently give rise to questions of reasonableness under common law or under s.19 of the Landlord and Tenant Act 1987: see Chapter 11.

Over-insurance

5–019 If it is established that the landlord has over-insured, such over-insurance will generally be irrecoverable. Over-insurance can occur through the landlord insuring for higher value than necessary, more property than is necessary, or a greater variety of risks than is necessary. Examples in the Leasehold Valuation Tribunal are:

- *Scott & G&O Properties Ltd* LON/00AH/LSL/2004/0078, in which it was held unnecessary for the landlord to have obtained cover against terrorist attack for a property in Thornton Heath (but cf. *Takado v Dupenois* CHI/18/UG/NSP/2003/0015 (similar insurance recoverable in Totnes));
- *Mitchell v Jackson* (no reference number available—insurance against loss of rental income not necessary);
- *Serpes v Berger* LON/00BK/LSL/2004/0009 (business interruption premium not recoverable in residential context);
- *Gluck v Kashani* (no reference available—landlord insuring for entire block when, because of differing terms of leases, he was only obliged to insure one flat);
- *Hill v Martin Russell Jones* LVT/SC/021/063/00 (landlord insuring for shops and flats together—should have obtained quote relating to flats alone);
- *Morgan v Dewan* CAM/26UG/SC/2004/0028 (landlord only obliged to insure against damage by fire and aircraft—premium for general policy not recoverable in its entirety);
- *Loy v Marchwalk Ltd* LON/00AU/LSC/2004/0078 (lease required tenants to agree to landlord effecting insurance—tenants did not do so—premium not recoverable).

Under-insurance

5–020 The problem of under-insurance is rarely likely to arise in a service charges context, since few tenants are likely to complain about a problem that reduces their charge. However where a landlord did under-insure, and then had to meet the shortfall in the event of a claim, the shortfall was held irrecoverable from the tenants—*Cuthbert v Blackwell* LVT/SC/008/041.

Failure to insure adequately (or at all) will generally be regarded as a good reason to appoint a manager, at least if persistent—*Chechlowski v Cheung* (no reference available). See Chapter 27.

Excess

5–021 Conversely, where a landlord is obliged to make a claim and seeks to recover the excess from the tenants as part of a service charge, he will generally be entitled to do so (so long as it is not excessive)—*Sutcliffe v Bradford & Northern Housing Association Ltd* and *AEL Properties Ltd v Wallis* (no references available). The rationale is that the greater the excess, the lower the premium, and the tenant cannot take the benefit of that while at the same time rejecting the burden.

Chapter 6

Managing Agents

Recoverability of managing agents fees

The general rule

6–001 In ascertaining whether or not the cost of employing managing agents is recoverable, the starting point is, as with any other costs, the terms of the lease. As Cumming-Bruce L.J. said in *Embassy Court Residents' Association Ltd v Lipman* (1984) 271 E.G. 545 at 550:

> ". . .it is perfectly clear that if an individual landlord wants to [employ managing agents] and to recover the costs from the lessee, he must include explicit provision in his lease."

The exceptions

6–002 Embassy Court Residents' Association Limited was a residents' company established to take over the freeholder's obligations and to which the freeholder demised the whole of Embassy Court for a term of 99 years for that purpose. The company had no funds, yet somebody had to do the administrative work. In those circumstances it was held that there should be implied in the leases to the individual lessees a term that the residents' company could incur proper expenditure to carry out the functions imposed on it, including the cost of employing managing agents, and could recover contributions from the lessees.

In *Lloyds Bank PLC v Bowker Orford* [1992] 2 E.G.L.R. 44, the leases contained a clause allowing the lessor to recover "the total cost . . . of providing the services". It was held that this would include the cost of employing managing agents to organise and supervise the provision of such services (but not to carry out other tasks such as rent collection).

Appointment and employment of managing agents

Managing agents connected to the landlord

6–003 In *Skilleter v Charles* [1992] 1 E.G.L.R. 73, it was held that there was no reason why a landlord should not employ a company he owned, provided that it was not a complete sham. Mr Charles, the landlord, and his wife had formed a company after the creation of the leases to manage the property and other properties. There was no evidence that this was a sham and as the lease expressly permitted the employment of a manager and for that manager to be paid, the management fees of Mr Charles' company were recoverable.

In *Parkside Knightsbridge v Horwitz* (1983) 268 E.G. 49, the landlord company engaged its parent company to manage the block and by book entries paid the parent company a management fee. It was held that the parent company was a separate legal entity from its subsidiary, the landlord, and the book entries counted as payment. Consequently, the management fees could be included in the service charge.

The ability to employ a connected company is of particular importance where the lease provides for the recovery of expenses incurred by the landlord, but not its own overheads. In such circumstances, the landlord would not be able to recover the cost of in-house management, but could recover any fees paid to a managing agent. Where the landlord would prefer to manage its property in-house, a way of circumventing the problem is to establish a separate company, appoint it as the managing agent and pay it a reasonable fee for managing the property.

Consultation with tenants

6–004 There is no general requirement that tenants be consulted in relation to the appointment and employment of managing agents. It is possible for the terms of the lease to provide for such consultation and paragraphs 13–001 to 13–002 deal with express and implied covenants to consult.

Under s.30B of the Landlord and Tenant Act 1985, a tenants' association, which is a recognised tenants' association under s.29 of the Act, can require a landlord to consult the association in relation to the appointment or employment of managing agents. However, the association must first serve on the landlord a notice requesting him to consult them (s.30B(1)).

Prior to appointment

Section 30B(2) provides: **6–005**

> "(2) Where, at the time when any such notice is served by a recognised tenants' association, the landlord does not employ any managing agent for any relevant premises, the landlord shall, before appointing such a managing agent, serve on the association a notice specifying—
>
> (a) the name of the proposed managing agent;
> (b) the landlord's obligations to the tenants represented by the association which it is proposed that the managing agent should be required to discharge on his behalf; and
> (c) a period of not less than one month beginning with the date of service of the notice within which the association may make observations on the proposed appointment."

Post appointment

6–006 If at the time a notice is served by the association, the landlord already employs a managing agent, then within a month of service of the notice, the landlord must serve on the association a notice specifying the following:

(a) the landlord's obligations to the tenants represented by the association which the managing agent is required to discharge on his behalf; and

(b) a reasonable period within which the association may make observations on the manner in which the managing agent has been discharging those obligations, and on the desirability of his continuing to discharge them (s.30B(3)).

So long as the landlord employs a managing agent he must serve a notice on the association at least once every five years specifying any change in the managing agent's functions since the last notice and a reasonable period within which the association can make observations as in (b) above (s.30B(4)(a)). If the landlord proposes to appoint a new managing agent, then he must serve a notice specifying the matters mentioned in s.30B(2)(a)–(c) (s.30B(4)(b)). However, a landlord is not, by virtue of a notice served by an association under subs.(1), required to serve a notice under subs.(4)(a) or (b) if the association subsequently serves on the landlord a notice withdrawing its request under subs.(1) to be consulted by him (s.30B(5)).

Change of landlord

6–007 If the landlord changes, then the association's notice will be of no effect and a new notice needs to be served if the association still wishes to be consulted (s.30B(6)).

Generally

6–008 By virtue of s.30B(7), any notice served by a landlord must specify the name and the address in the United Kingdom of the person to whom any observations made in pursuance of the notice are to be sent; and the landlord must then have regard to any such observations that are received by that person within the period specified in the notice. However, the extent of the landlord's duty to have regard to observations is not set out in any greater detail in the statute.

In s.30B "landlord" means the immediate landlord of the tenants represented by the association or a person who has a right to enforce payment of service charges payable by any of those tenants. Consequently, a management company with whom the tenants covenant to pay service charges is a "landlord" for the purposes of s.30B (see *Cinnamon v Morgan* [2002] L.&T.R. 20). Where a RTM company has acquired the right to manage relevant premises (see Chapters 29 to 33), the RTM company is the "landlord" for the purposes of s.30B and subs.(6) is of no effect (Commonhold and Leasehold Reform Act 2002, s.102, Sch.7, para.6).

Further, "managing agent" means an agent of the landlord appointed to discharge any of the landlord's obligations to the tenants represented by the recognised tenants' association in question which relate to the management by him of those premises; and any premises (whether building or not) are "relevant premises" in relation to a recognised tenants' association if any of the tenants represented by the association may be required under the terms of their leases to contribute by payment of service charges to costs relating to those premises (s.30B(8)). Section 30B applies to crown land by virtue of s.172(1) of the Commonhold and Leasehold Reform Act 2002.

Level of fees

Terms of the lease

6–009 The lease itself may contain reference to the amount which can be recovered in respect of a managing agent's fees and therefore any such clause needs to be considered in the first instance. In *Thames Side Properties Ltd v Brixton Estate PLC* [1997] N.P.C. 5, the lease provided for payment by the tenant in respect of the landlord's managing agent's fees in accordance with a scale laid down by the R.I.C.S.

However, that scale had been abrogated by the R.I.C.S. and therefore it was held that the clause in the lease should be replaced by a provision that the tenant was to pay the percentage of the gross rental of the building representing the going rate for the job of managing the building.

Reasonableness

6–010 The reasonableness of service charges is dealt with in Chapter 11 and the common law principles and statutory controls set out therein apply equally to managing agents' fees as they do to other types of service charge.

As set out in Chapter 11, it seems unlikely that the Supply of Goods and Services Act 1982 applies to a lease, it being unrealistic to describe a lease as a "contract for the supply of a service". However, a contract between a landlord and a managing agent is a contract under which the managing agent ("the supplier") agrees to carry out a service. Consequently, it is implied into such a contract that the supplier will carry out the service with reasonable care and skill (s.13). Further, where the consideration for the service is not determined by the contract, left to be determined in a manner agreed by the contract or determined by a course of dealing between the parties, there is an implied term that the party contracting with the supplier will pay a reasonable charge (s.15(1)). What is a reasonable charge under s.15 is a question of fact (s.15(2)). It is important to note that it is the landlord who is the party contracting with the supplier and therefore the landlord and not the leaseholder/tenant who is entitled to the benefit of the implied terms. However, unlike the reasonableness control in s.19 of the Landlord and Tenant Act 1985, there is no reason why the Supply of Goods and Services Act cannot apply to a contract between a landlord of commercial property and a managing agent.

When are managing agents fees reasonable/"reasonably incurred"?
6–011 The general principles that apply are set out in Chapter 11.

Managing agents often charge on the basis of either a flat fee per property or as a percentage of expenditure. Where they seek to charge both, it is likely to be found that the fees have not been reasonably incurred (see for example *Park Court Residents Association v Flatfield Ltd* (unreported) 19/5/00 LVT).

A fee based upon a percentage of expenditure has the advantage over a flat fee in that it provides reasonable payment for years when exceptional items of work have to be done, for example major works. Consequently, where managing agents charge a fixed fee to cover standard management work of a recurring nature and additional sums in respect of non-standard items, such additional sums are likely to be found to have been reasonably incurred (see for example *Park Court Residents Association*). However, where a flat fee is charged and additional charges are made for standard items such as correspondence with tenants and others, it is likely to be found that these additional charges have not been reasonably incurred (see for example *McKay v G&O Investments Ltd* (unreported) undated LVT).

When any percentage charge is rendered on the VAT element of expenditure, it is unlikely to be found that the amount of the charge referable to the VAT element has been reasonably incurred (see, for example, *Swirlmanor Ltd v Murrell* (unreported) June 27, 2001 and *Jenkins v Nassibian* (unreported) June 4, 2001, LVT).

If costs have not actually been "incurred" i.e. the managing agents have not actually charged the landlord and/or are not entitled to charge the landlord under the terms of their contract, it is unlikely to be found that such costs have been reasonably incurred (see, for example, *McKay*).

When are the services of a reasonable standard?

6–012 The R.I.C.S. "Service Charge Residential Management Code" provides best practice advice for the management of residential property where leaseholders/tenants pay a separate and variable service charge. The code has been approved by the Secretaries of State for the Environment and for Wales under s.87 of the Leasehold Reform, Housing and Urban Development Act 1993 and became operative on March 17, 1997. If the managing agent's services are being provided in accordance with the code then they will invariably be found to be of a reasonable standard. Any breach of the code is a ground for appointing a Manager under s.24(2) of the Landlord and Tenant Act 1987, as to which see Chapter 27.

Chapter 7

Legal Costs

The recovery of legal costs through the service charge

7–001 It is common for landlords to try and recover through the service charge the legal costs incurred in proceedings brought against a defaulting tenant. Such provision will ordinarily only be relied upon where the landlord has been unsuccessful in recovering the costs from the defaulting tenant himself. Indeed leases will often incorporate a specific and separate covenant on the part of the tenant to pay the landlord's costs incurred in connection with the recovery or attempted recovery of arrears or in connection with remedying the breach of covenant by the tenant. Furthermore there may even be a duty on the landlord to endeavour to recover the expenses from the tenant before seeking to recover them through the service charge: see *Skilleter v Charles* [1992] 1 E.G.L.R. 73.

Whether a landlord is able to recover its costs or any outstanding balance of its costs through a service charge provision will depend upon the construction of the lease having regard to the nature of the proceeding in which the costs were incurred. In order to recover legal costs through the service charge clear and unambiguous terms are required (*St Mary's Mansions Ltd v Limegate Investments Co Ltd* [2003] 1 E.G.L.R. 41).

In *St Mary's Mansions*, the Court of Appeal held that the legal costs incurred in proceedings for the recovery of arrears of rent and service charge were not recoverable under service charge provisions entitling the landlord to recover: "The cost of all other services which the lessor may at its absolute discretion provide or install in the said Building for the comfort and convenience of the lessees" and "The reasonable and proper fees of the Lessor's Auditors and the reasonable and proper fees of the Lessor's managing agents for the collection of the flats in the said Building and for the general management thereof."

Similarly, in *Sella House Ltd v Mears* [1989] 1 E.G.L.R. 65, the Court of Appeal held that the legal costs incurred in recovering rent and service charge from defaulting tenants were not recoverable under a service charge provision encompassing the costs of employing "*. . . professional persons as may be necessary or desirable for the proper . . . administration of the Building*" and the costs of "*. . . collecting the rents and service charges. . . .*" See also *Morgan v Stainer* [1993] 2 E.G.L.R. 73 and *Reston Ltd v Hudson* [1995] 2 E.G.L.R. 51.

7–002 For an example of a case where the landlord's costs, incurred in an unsuccessful but properly brought claim for forfeiture, were held to be recoverable through a service charge provision allowing "The proper cost of management of [the Building]", see *Iperion Investments Corporation v Broadwalk House Residents* [1995] 2 E.G.L.R. 47.

However even where on the true construction of the lease the landlord is entitled to claim through the service charge costs incurred in legal proceedings, it does not necessarily follow that it may recover those costs. In *Holding & Management Ltd v Property Holding & Investment Trust plc* [1990] 1 All E.R. 938, the Court of Appeal held that the landlord in that case could on the proper construction of the lease only recover legal costs that had been "*reasonably or properly*" incurred in the enforcement of the tenant's covenants. In *Morgan v Stainer* it was held that it was to be implied into a clause permitting the recovery of "*legal and other costs*" through the service charge that the costs had to be reasonably and properly incurred before they could be claimed under the clause. Accordingly, where costs are not reasonably or properly incurred, they can not be recovered through a service charge provision, the reasonableness of the costs relates not only to their quantum but also their nature: see also *Finchbourne Ltd v Rodrigues* [1976] 3 All E.R. 581.

It is as Nicholls L.J. stated in *Holding Management Ltd v Property Holding & Investment plc*: the landlord cannot seek "to get through the back door what has been refused at the front." A landlord unsuccessful in litigation who has not acted reasonably or properly and who perhaps was not awarded his costs in that litigation (or even was ordered to pay the tenant's costs) cannot recover those costs through a service charge provision entitling the recovery of costs.

Iperion Investments Corporation v Broadwalk House is an example of where, despite an express provision in the relevant clause that the costs claimed had to be "properly incurred", the unsuccessful landlord in litigation was nevertheless entitled to recover through the service charge its legal costs, because it had not acted improperly or unreasonably.

Limiting the legal costs recoverable through the service charge

7–003 Section 20C of the 1985 Act enables a tenant to apply for an order that all or any of the costs incurred by a landlord in connection with any proceedings are not to be regarded as relevant costs to be taken into account in determining the amount of any service charge payable for the tenant or any other person or persons specified in the application; see s.20C(1) and (2) for the proceedings in which such an application may be made and for the court or tribunal to which the application must be made.

An order under s.20C may be made where it is just and equitable in the circumstances to do so (s.20C(3)), however the discretion is wide and unfettered: see *The Tenants of Langford Court v Doren Ltd* [2001] (LT) LRX/37/2000 (unreported) and *Veena SA v Cheong* [2003] 1 E.G.L.R. 175.

It does not necessarily follow that where, for example, a tenant makes an application in the LVT for a determination as to the reasonableness of an element of the service charge and he subsequently fails to achieve any reduction, the tribunal should not exercise its discretion to limit the amount of the landlord's costs recoverable through a service charge provision: see *Maryland Estates Ltd v Patsyanne Lynch and David Wilson* [2002] (LT) LRX/57/1999 (unreported). Indeed it may be unjust in the circumstances of the case, even where the landlord's costs have been reasonably and properly incurred, for the tenants or a particular tenant to pay the landlord's costs through the service charge. However it was noted by H.H.J. Rich Q.C. in *The Tenants of Langford Court v Doren Ltd* that there is "no automatic expectation of an Order under section 20C in favour of a successful tenant".

7–004 *Iperion Investments v Broadwalk House Residents Ltd* is an example of a case where, although the landlord had been unsuccessful in the litigation and notwithstanding the fact that it was entitled to recover through a service charge provision the costs of the litigation as it had not acted improperly or unreasonably, it was held that it was nevertheless appropriate to make an order under s.20C in respect of the service charge payable by the tenant. It was noted by the Court of Appeal that the tenant's conduct had been reflected in the order for costs made at trial.

As s.20C applies to the costs incurred in proceedings between landlords and tenants, there is an argument that proceedings brought under s.159 of the Commonhold and Leasehold Reform Act 2002 relating to charges under estate management schemes do not fall within s.20C and, in the absence of a corresponding provision within s.159 itself, there is no power for the LVT hearing a claim under that section to make a s.20C order. For s.159 and estate charges, see paragraph 12–010 *et seq.*

Notwithstanding the provisions of s.20C, it is always open for a tenant to argue at a later stage that the landlord's legal costs which it seeks to recover through the service charge are excessive, unreasonably incurred and therefore should be disallowed in accordance with s.19. The advantage however of making a s.20C application is, as noted by H.H.J. Rich Q.C. in *The Tenants of Langford Court v Doren Ltd*, that the tribunal who heard the original dispute is in a better position from which to assess whether the circumstances are such that an order under the section should be made. By adopting this approach the tribunal provides a short route by which the later arguments under s.19 can be avoided.

An additional argument has recently been raised that the Commonhold and Leasehold Reform Act 2002 in any event debars a landlord from adding the costs of proceedings before the Tribunal to the service charge. Paragraph 10(4) of Sch.12 to the 2002 Act provides that:

> "a person shall not be required to pay costs incurred in connection with proceedings before a leasehold valuation tribunal except by a determination under this paragraph or in connection with provision made by any enactment other than this paragraph".

There are conflicting first instance decisions on this at the date of publication, but both are subject to potential appeals. In *Shilling v Canary Riverside* (LON/00BG/LSL/2004/0064) May 3, 2005, the Leasehold Valuation Tribunal (by an unusual majority determination) upheld such an argument. It is understood that this determination is the subject of an appeal to the Lands Tribunal. However, in the recent County Court case of *Staghold Ltd v Takeda* (August 8, 2005), H.H.J. Levy Q.C. rejected such an argument. Permission was given to appeal to the Court of Appeal, although the tenant ultimately did not pursue the appeal.

Amount of costs recoverable

7–005 If a landlord is entitled to recover through the service charge its legal costs then the total amount of costs claimed may depend upon the basis upon which, in proceedings in the courts, the costs were assessed. For examples of where it was held there was a contractual provision entitling a claim for costs on an indemnity basis, see *Church Commissioners v Ibrahim* [1997] 1 E.G.L.R. 13 and *Bank of Baroda v Panessar* [1987] 2 W.L.R. 208. For an example of where a contractual provision for costs was construed as only entitling costs on a standard basis see *Primeridge Ltd v Jean Muir* [1992] 1 E.G.L.R. 273.

Chapter 8

Finance Costs and Interest

8–001 An issue that frequently arises is the matter of interest. Even under the terms of a well drawn service charge, where the lessor will be able to demand an interim sum or interim sums payable on account of the final sum payable for the service charge period, there is frequently a shortfall and a need to fund the expenditure before the final sum is paid. A lessor, who finds that he has had to finance service charge expenditure, will wish to recover the cost of financing the works. Typically this will be represented by the interest that he has had to pay on borrowed funds or, where he has financed the expenditure from his own resources, that he has forgone.

The position at common law and in equity

8–002 Unless there is a provision in the service charge provision permitting, in clear words, the lessor to recover the interest that he has had to pay or that he has forgone, he is not entitled to recover interest from the lessees. Likewise, unless there is a provision in the service charge provision requiring the lessor to account for any interest that he has received on sums paid on account, he is not obliged to account to the lessee for such interest.

In *Frobisher (Second Investments) v Kiloran Trust* [1980] 1 W.L.R. 425 (Walton J.), the landlord had covenanted to repair and keep in good order the reserved property, insure the block and pay for certain utilities used in the common parts and the tenants had in turn covenanted to pay a service charge including a proportion of "the reasonable and proper fees payable by the lessors to its managing agents". Walton J. held, following the coming into force of s.91A of the Housing Finance Act 1972, that the landlord could not recover interest payable by him on the monies borrowed to finance the cost of providing services and declined to imply a term to similar effect, holding:

> "... I do not think that in fact one can apply the doctrine of The Moorcock, [i.e. that a term will be implied into a contract if such implication is necessary to give the contract business efficacy as must have been intended by both parties] because I know of no case ... in which the doctrine of The Moorcock has been applied when there has been a disturbance to contractual arrangements because of statute."

Similarly in *Boldmark v Cohen* [1986] 1 E.G.L.R. 47 (CA), the lease contained provisions whereby the tenant covenanted to pay a yearly rent of £60, together with additional sums in respect of sums expended by the landlord in insuring the block and in respect of service charges. Disputes arose between a tenant and the landlord and in particular the landlord claimed the right to recover reasonable interest payments reasonably incurred as a result of reasonable borrowing to finance the provision of services under the lease. He argued principally that the words "such sums as the Lessors may from time to time expend in respect to the general administration and management of the Block" were wide enough to embrace interest that he had incurred in borrowing monies to discharge his obligations to the tenants; and in the alternative that the word "cost", found in the service charge provision relating to the expenditure incurred by the landlord in undertaking the matters he contracted to undertake, was wide enough to include reasonable interest on money borrowed to finance that expenditure. He did not seek to rely upon any implied term. The Court of Appeal held, allowing an appeal, that the onus lay on the lessor to show that under the terms of the lease the lessee had contracted to pay the interest claimed and that, on its true construction, the lease did not include payments by way of interest but left the door open for arguments in other cases, holding:

> "I do not doubt that in some contexts a reference to the 'cost' of doing a particular work will be perfectly apt to include interest on money borrowed to do it. ... I see no reason in principle why a lease should not provide for a landlord to be compensated for reasonable interest payments of this nature. ... It seems to me that in some contexts a provision of this nature might be a sensible one. I would even accept that in some other contexts a reference in general terms to expenditure in respect of the general administration of a block of flats might perhaps, on a liberal construction, be capable of including an interest element."

8–003 *Skilleter v Charles* [1992] 1 E.G.L.R. 73 is an example of a case where the Court of Appeal was prepared to imply a term into a service charge provision that the landlord could recover from the tenants the interest that he incurred on borrowing funds to finance other service charge expenditure. However, this was in the context of construing a lease where the parties had clearly intended that such interest should be recoverable under the service charge provision but where the word "incurred" had been mistakenly omitted from a provision that should have provided for the tenant to pay a proportion of "any interest charges payable by the Lessor on his Bank account or accounts in respect of any incurred for the purposes of the Maintenance Charge".

Interest on service charge monies held by the landlord is dealt with in Chapter 15.

Chapter 9

Miscellaneous Items

Employees, caretakers, porters and staff accommodation

9–001 Whether the costs associated with the employment of staff such as cleaners, caretakers or porters are recoverable by the landlord through the service charge ultimately is a question of construction of the lease. Where a landlord seeks to recover money from a tenant it has been said that there must be clear terms in the contractual provisions said to entitle him to do so; obligations on tenants for service charge are construed restrictively and are not likely to include ambiguous clauses: *Gilje v Charlgrove Securities Ltd* [2002] 1 E.G.L.R. 41. Mummery L.J. in that case approved the "obvious" proposition that "courts tend to construe service charge provision restrictively and are unlikely to allow recovery for items which are not clearly included." Where a lease has been drafted or proposed by a landlord then that lease will fall to be construed *contra proferentem*. See also paragraph 1–009.

Before deciding therefore whether to try and recover through a service charge the expenses incurred in employing staff, it is necessary to look closely at the terms of the lease to identify whether what is being sought can properly be recovered through the contractual provisions: was the landlord entitled to incur the expenditure under the terms of the lease and if so does the lease enable him to recover that particular expenditure from the tenants through the service charge?

Staff accommodation

9–002 One particular area of dispute relates to the provision of staff accommodation and the recovery through the service charge of the notional or alternatively actual cost of providing that accommodation.

Again it is a question of construction. First, what is the landlord required to provide? Is it for example the obligation to provide a resident caretaker (*Gilje v Charlgrove Securities Ltd* and *Lloyds Bank Plc v Bowker Orford* [1992] 2 E.G.L.R. 44) or is it alternatively to employ a caretaker whether resident or not (*Agavil Investments Co v Corner* unreported, October 1975). Secondly, having provided the service, what costs or expenses does the lease entitle the landlord to recover from the tenants? In *Lloyds Bank v Bowker Orford* and *Agavil Investments v Corner* the landlord was entitled to recover the notional rent for a caretaker's flat, whereas in *Gilje v Charlgrove Securities* the Court of Appeal refused the landlord's claim.

The factors to consider

9–003 Relevant factors in construing whether a landlord can charge through the service charge a notional rent for a caretaker's flat may include: whether the lease provided for how the notional rent would be calculated; any ambiguity in terms of the caretaker's residence; and whether a reasonable tenant or prospective tenant reading the lease would perceive that the provisions for service charge obliged the tenant to contribute towards the notional cost of providing the caretaker's flat.

In *Lloyds Bank v Bowker Orford*, Neuberger J. observed that where the lease enumerates a number of aspects of the costs of the provision of the caretaker's flat for which the tenant is liable, it is a fairly formidable argument for a tenant that the parties can not have intended any further aspects of the costs of the caretaker's flat to be included in the service charge. In *Gilje v Charlgrove Securities* [2000] 3 E.G.L.R. 89, H.H.J. Rich Q.C., sitting in the Lands Tribunal, found this argument to be determinative of the issue in question; the Court of Appeal in the same case was not so persuaded.

The requirement of reasonableness

9–004 In the case of residential service charges any costs associated with employing a caretaker that are recoverable through the service charge remain subject to the tests imposed by s.19. The questions are whether the costs have been reasonably incurred and where a service has been provided has that service been of a reasonable standard?

Simply because the cost of a caretaker is recoverable under a service charge provision does not mean that the cost claimed has been reasonably incurred. In *Veena SA v Cheong* [2003] 1 E.G.L.R. 175 it was held that, although the lease permitted in general terms the recovery through the service charge of the costs of maintenance of the services of a porter or porters, that was not an indication that the cost of a part-time or full-time or even two porters was a cost reasonably incurred. The test remains: first are the costs recoverable under the service charge provision in the lease? And secondly, are they reasonably incurred? The fact that the first question is answered in the affirmative does not mean that the same answer must be given to the second. In *Veena* it was held that a full-time porter and a part-time cleaner were unnecessary for a small block and that therefore the costs of their employment were not reasonably incurred. The recoverable costs were limited to those for a part-time porter.

Standard and extent of service

9–005 It is not uncommon for tenants to complain about the standard and extent of the service provided by a particular employee. What specific services or duties are to be undertaken by an employee may be recited in the lease or they may be found in the employee's contract of employment. Alternatively, reference might be made to what is considered trade standards in the particular line of employment.

The difficulty however often faced by tenants who challenge the standard of the service provided by an employee, is that the complaints made may relate only to a fraction of that employee's many duties. In such circumstances the tenant might find himself incurring considerable expense challenging the amount claimed by the landlord in respect of the cost of the employee and yet at best achieving only a very minor reduction in the overall service charge. Whilst a tenant might be justified in raising points of complaint in respect of many aspects of a porter's duties, a porter, particularly a resident porter, is valued for the security he provides by his very presence: see *Posner v Scott-Lewis* [1986] 1 E.G.L.R. 56.

Chapter 10

Rights to Information

Introduction

10–001 The service charge provisions in leases often provide the tenant with only limited rights to know how the service charge is calculated. Rights to investigate the landlord's management are usually non-existent. To redress the position, statute confers various rights on tenants to demand information from their landlords and those are discussed in this chapter. The statutory rights under the LTA 1985 and the LRHUDA 1993 are conferred on tenants of dwellings only.

Nevertheless, as always, one has to start with an examination of the lease to ensure that such information as the landlord is required to provide under the terms of the lease is being provided.

Statutory provisions

Consultation requirements and the supply of information

10–002 The new s.20ZA of the LTA 1985 introduces in subs.(5)(a) and (e) obligations on the landlord to provide details of proposed works or agreements to tenants or the recognised tenants' association representing them and to give reasons in prescribed circumstances for carrying out works or entering into agreements.

These matters are dealt with more fully in Chapter 13: Consultation Requirements.

Overview of summaries of relevant costs and statements of account

10–003 Under the current s.21, a tenant has the right to request the landlord to supply a summary of the relevant service charge costs which were incurred during the previous accounting year.

Section 152 of the CLRA 2002 introduces the new ss.21, 21A and 21B which entirely replace the old s.21. As at the date of going to press, the new ss.21, 21A and 21B are only in force in so far as they confer a power to make regulations (See Commonhold and Leasehold Reform Act 2002 (Commencement No. 1, Savings and Transitional Provisions) (England) Order 2001, SI 2002/1912, commencement date July 26, 2002; and Commonhold and Leasehold Reform Act 2002 (Commencement No. 1, Savings and Transitional Provisions) (Wales) Order 2002, SI 2002/3012, commencement date January 1, 2003).

Under the new s.21, landlords will be required to provide one yearly "statement of account" to every tenant, whether the tenant has requested one or not. The new s.21 confers a power on the Secretary of State to make regulations to prescribe the form of such statements of account.

If a landlord fails to provide a statement of account to a tenant or fails to provide it within the time allowed by the new s.21, under the new s.21A the tenant will have a statutory entitlement to withhold payment of service charges, although the entitlement to withhold is subject to the limitations set out within the new s.21A.

The old provisions and the new provisions will each be dealt with separately below.

Before the coming into force of s.152 of CLRA 2002: request for a summary of relevant costs

Who may make a request

10–004 Under the present s.21, a tenant may require a landlord to supply him with a written summary of the costs incurred:

(a) if the relevant accounts are made up for periods of 12 months, in the last such period ending not later than the date of the request; or

(b) if the accounts are not made up for periods of 12 months, in the period of 12 months ending with the date of the request,

and which are relevant costs in relation to the service charges payable or demanded as payable in that or any other period.

Note also that by s.102 of CLRA 2002, ss.18–30 of LTA 1985 have effect with the modifications provided by para.4 of Sch.7 to CLRA 2002, which came into force:

- in England, on September 30, 2003 (see the Commonhold and Leasehold Reform Act 2002 (Commencement No. 2 and Savings) (England) Order 2003, SI 2003/1986); and
- in Wales, on March 30, 2004 (see the Commonhold and Leasehold Reform Act 2002 (Commencement No. 2 and Savings) (Wales) Order 2004, SI 2004/669).

The expressions "service charge" and "relevant costs" are defined in s.18(1) of LTA 1985: see Chapter 4.

Request by the secretary of a recognised tenants' association

10–005 Under s.21(2), where a tenant is represented by a recognised tenants' association and he consents, the request may be made by the secretary of that tenants' association instead of by the tenant. The use of the words "instead of by the tenant" indicates that the tenant must make an election: he may either make the request himself or consent to the secretary of the recognised tenants' association making the request. It would seem that one tenant cannot make a request himself and consent to the secretary of the tenants' association making one as well.

Provisions not applicable to certain tenants under RA 1977

10–006 By s.27 of the LTA 1985, if the tenant has a tenancy with a registered rent under the Rent Act 1977, ss.18–25 of the LTA 1985 will not apply unless it is entered on the rent register as a variable rent.

Service of request on the landlord

10–007 The request may be served directly on the landlord himself.

In order to determine the landlord's proper address for service of such a request, a tenant should examine:

- the terms of his lease to establish whether there is an address for service for the landlord contained in the lease itself;
- any formal notices served under s.48 of the LTA 1987, to establish whether the landlord's address for service has changed (see paragraph 10–082 below);

- any demands for rent and service charges, which under ss.46 and 47 of the LTA 1987 are required to set out the name and address of the landlord; and if that address is not in England or Wales, an address in England or Wales at which notices (including notices in proceedings) may be served on the landlord by the tenant; and
- any other correspondence received from the landlord or on the landlord's behalf.

Note that by the modifications to LTA 1985 effected by s.102 of and para.4(2) of Sch.7 to CLRA 2002, references to the landlord are also to a RTM company.

Service of request on landlord's agent

10–008 By s.21(3) of the LTA 1985, a request is also deemed duly served on the landlord if it is served on:

(a) an agent of the landlord named as such in the rent book or similar document; or

(b) the person who receives rent on behalf of the landlord.

Such a person (other than the landlord) on whom a request is served by the tenant is obliged to forward it to the landlord as soon as may be.

Time limit for compliance

10–009 The landlord is obliged to comply with the request within one month of the request or within six months of the end of the relevant period set out in s.21(1)(a) or (b), whichever is the later.

Person to whom the summary should be supplied

10–010 Where the request is made by a tenant, the summary of relevant costs should be supplied to that tenant.

Where the request is made by the secretary of a recognised tenants' association with the consent of a tenant, by s.21(2) of the LTA 1985 the summary of relevant costs may be supplied to the secretary, although the wording of the statute appears to leave open the possibility of a request being made by the secretary with the consent of the tenant and the summary being supplied to the tenant.

Period

10–011 One crucial matter which the landlord must get right in the summary of relevant costs is the period over which he is obliged to supply such summary. The period over which the landlord is required to supply such summary should be determined as follows:

(a) where the service charge accounts are made up for periods of 12 months, the landlord must supply the summary of relevant costs incurred during the last accounting period which ended before the date of the request; or

(b) where the service charge accounts are made up over any other period, the landlord must supply the summary of relevant costs incurred during the period of 12 months ending with the date of the request.

10–012 In the latter case, the landlord will in effect have to draw up a new account, perhaps adapting an account made up over another period, to conform with the requirements of the section.

Costs to be summarised

10–013 Section 21 only refers to the costs "incurred" by the landlord during the relevant accounting period and does not cover the costs which were payable by the tenant or the body of tenants during that period.

Works paid or part-paid for by a grant or group repair scheme

10–014 The summary of relevant costs must state whether any of the costs relate to works:

(a) in respect of which a grant has been or is to be paid under s.523 of the HA 1985 or any provision of Pt I of the Housing Grants, Construction and Regeneration Act 1996 or any corresponding earlier statute and, where any of the costs relate to works in respect of which such a grant has been or is to be paid, the summary must set out the costs in a way showing how they have been or will be reflected in demands for service charges—see s.21(5) of the LTA 1985; or

(b) which are included in the external works specified in a group repair scheme within the meaning of Ch.II of Pt I of the Housing Grants, Construction and Regeneration Act 1996 or any corresponding earlier enactment, in which the landlord participated or is participating as an assisted participant—see s.21(5B) of the LTA 1985.

Matters to be summarised in summary of relevant costs

10–015 The summary of relevant costs must summarise each of the following items:

(a) under s.21(5)(a), any of the costs in respect of which no demand for payment was received by the landlord during the period referred to in s.21(1)(a) or (b);

(b) under s.21(5)(b), any of the costs in respect of which—

(i) a demand for payment was so received, but
(ii) no payment was made by the landlord within that period;

(c) under s.21(5)(c), any of the costs in respect of which—

(i) a demand for payment was so received, and
(ii) payment was made by the landlord within that period.

Information about sums received by landlord on account of service charges

10–016 The summary must also specify the aggregate of any amounts received by the landlord down to the end of that period on account of service charges in respect of relevant dwellings and still standing to the credit of the tenants of those dwellings at the end of that period, where s.21(5A) LTA 1985 defines "relevant dwelling" as meaning a dwelling whose tenant is either the person by or with the consent of whom the request was made, or a person whose obligations under the terms of his lease as regards contributing to relevant costs relate to the same costs as the corresponding obligations of the person by or with the consent of whom the request was made relate to.

Requirement for certification of summary of relevant costs by an accountant

10–017 If the service charges, in relation to which the costs are relevant costs as mentioned in s.21(1), are payable by the tenants of more than four dwellings, the summary of relevant costs must be certified by a qualified accountant as in his opinion a fair summary complying with the requirements of s.21(5) and being sufficiently supported by accounts, receipts and other documents which have been produced to him.

Meaning of qualified accountant

10–018 Section 28 of the LTA 1985 defines the meaning of the expression "qualified accountant" as a person who has the necessary qualification and is not disqualified from acting.

A person has the necessary qualification if he is eligible for appointment as a company auditor under s.25 of the Companies Act 1989.

A person is disqualified from acting if he is:

(a) an officer, employee or partner of the landlord or, where the landlord is a company, of an associated company (being a holding company of the landlord company, a subsidiary of the landlord company or another subsidiary of the landlord company's holding company, within the meaning of s.736 of the Companies Act 1985);

(b) a person who is a partner or employee of any such officer or employee;

(c) an agent of the landlord who is a managing agent for any premises to which any of the costs covered by the summary in question relate, being a person who has been appointed to discharge any of the landlord's obligations relating to the management by him of the premises and owed to the tenants who may be required under the terms of their leases to contribute to those costs by the payment of service charges; or

(d) an employee or partner of any such agent.

Request for summary of relevant costs relating to information held by superior landlord

10–019 Section 23 of the LTA 1985 contains provisions to take account of the problems which may occur where a tenant or the secretary of a recognised tenants' association has made a request to the tenant's landlord for a summary of relevant costs and the request relates in whole or in part to relevant costs which have been incurred by or on behalf of a superior landlord and the intermediate landlord to whom the request has been made is not in possession of the relevant information. In this situation, the following provisions will apply.

Intermediate landlord to make written request to superior landlord

10–020 By s.23(1)(a) the intermediate landlord is required to make a written request to the person who is his immediate landlord for the relevant information. Each intermediate landlord is in turn required to make the request of his immediate landlord until the superior landlord by or on behalf of whom the relevant costs have been incurred has been served with a request.

Compliance with request by superior landlord

10–021 Once the superior landlord by or on behalf of whom the relevant costs have been incurred has been served with a request, he is required by s.23(1)(b) to respond to it within a reasonable time. No further guidance is given on how the expression "reasonable time" is to be defined.

The tenant's immediate landlord is then required to comply with the tenant's or the secretary's request or that part of it which relates to the relevant costs incurred by or on behalf of the superior landlord within the time allowed by s.21 of the LTA 1985 (within one month of the request or within six months of the end of the relevant period set out in s.21(1)(a) or (b), whichever is the later) or within such further time, if any, as is reasonable in the circumstances.

After the coming into force of s.152 of CLRA 2002: statements of account

Supply of statements of account

10–022 The new s.21 is designed to ensure that landlords are obliged to supply statements of account in relation to service charge even where the tenant has not requested one.

Matters to be dealt with in statements of account

10–023 By the new s.21(1), the landlord will be obliged to supply each tenant by whom service charges are payable, in relation to each "accounting period" (as to the meaning of the expression "accounting period", see paragraph 10–026 below), a written statement of account dealing with:

(a) the service charges of the tenant and the tenants of the dwellings "associated with" his dwelling (as to the meaning of the expression "associated with", see paragraph 10–025 below);

(b) the relevant costs relating to those service charges;

(c) the aggregate amount standing to the credit of the tenant and the tenants of the associated dwellings:

  (i) at the beginning of the accounting period; and
  (ii) at the end of the accounting period; and
  (iii) related matters.

Time limit for landlord to supply statements of account

10–024 A landlord will be required to supply a statement of account in relation to an accounting period to each tenant by whom service charges are payable not later than six months after the end of the accounting period.

Meaning of "associated with"

10–025 For the purposes of the new s.21(1), the new s.21(8) provides that a dwelling is "associated with" another dwelling if the obligations of the tenants of the dwellings under the terms of their leases, as regards contributing to relevant costs, relate to the same costs.

Meaning of "accounting period"

10–026 For the purposes of the new s.21(1), the new s.21(9) provides that "accounting period" means such period beginning with the relevant date and ending with such date, not later than twelve months after the relevant date, as the landlord determines, where the "relevant date" is defined in the new s.21(10) as being:

(a) in the case of the first accounting period in relation to any dwelling, the later of the date on which service charges are first payable under a lease of any of them, and the date on which s.152 of the CLRA 2002 comes into force; and

(b) in the case of subsequent accounting periods, the date immediately following the end of the previous accounting period.

Other documents landlord obliged to supply with statement of account

10–027 Where the landlord supplies a statement of account to a tenant he will also be obliged to supply to him:

(a) a certificate of a qualified accountant that, in the accountant's opinion, the statement of account deals fairly with the matters with which it is required to deal and is sufficiently supported by accounts, receipts and other documents which have been produced to him (unless the requirement for an accountant's certificate is removed in circumstances by regulation); and

(b) a summary of the rights and obligations of tenants of dwellings in relation to service charges.

Tenant's address for the supply of statements of account

10–028 By the new s.21(6), if the landlord has been notified of an address in England and Wales at which he wishes to have the documents required to be supplied to him under the new s.21, the landlord is obliged to supply them to the tenant at that address.

Pursuant to the new s.21(7) the landlord is deemed to have been so notified if notification has been given to an agent of the landlord named as such in the rent book or other similar document or to the person who received the rent on behalf of the landlord and where notification has been given to such an agent or person he must forward it as soon as may be to the landlord.

Power to make regulations

10–029 The Secretary of State has the power under the new s.21 to make regulations, which are required to be made by statutory instrument which shall be subject to annulment in pursuance to a resolution of either House of Parliament. The Secretary of State has power to make regulations:

(a) under the new s.21(4) prescribing requirements for the form and content of:

  (i) statements of account;
  (ii) accountant's certificates; and
  (iii) summaries of rights and obligations,

  which are required to be supplied by landlords under the new s.21; and

(b) under the new s.21(5) to make exceptions from the requirement to supply an accountant's certificate.

By the new s.21(11), regulations made under the new s.21(4) may make different provision for different purposes. Even though the power of the Secretary of State to make regulations (but not the remainder of the section) came into force in England on July 26, 2002 under the Commonhold and Leasehold Reform Act 2002 (Commencement No. 1, Savings and Transitional Provisions) (England) Order 2001, SI 2002/1912 and in Wales on January 1, 2003 under the Commonhold and Leasehold Reform Act 2002 (Commencement No. 1, Savings and Transitional Provisions) (Wales) Order 2002, SI 2002/3012, as at the date of going to press, no regulations have been made under this part of this section.

After the coming into force of s.152 of CLRA 2002: tenant's right to withhold payment of service charges

10–030 In the event that the landlord fails to comply with the requirements to provide documentation in proper form, the new s.21A(1) provides that the tenant may withhold payment of service charges. This is dealt with in Chapter 19.

After the coming into force of s.152 of CLRA 2002: notice to accompany demands for service charges and tenant's right to withhold payment of rent for landlord's failure to comply

10–031 The new s.21B provides that a demand for the payment of service charges must be accompanied by a summary of rights and obligations of tenants of dwellings in relation to service charges. The Secretary of State has power to make regulations prescribing requirements as to the form and content of such summaries.

If a landlord fails to comply with his obligation to supply such a summary of rights and obligations with the demand, a tenant may withhold payment of a service charge which has been demanded from him in that demand.

Where a tenant withholds payment of service charges under the new s.21B, any provisions of his lease relating to non-payment or late payment of service charges do not have effect in relation to the period for which he withholds it.

Request to inspect supporting accounts, etc.

10–032 Where the tenant or the secretary of a recognised tenants' association has obtained a summary of relevant costs under s.21 of the LTA 1985, whether in pursuance of s.21 or otherwise, under s.22(1) and (2) the tenant or the secretary with the consent of the tenant may within six months of obtaining such summary of relevant costs require the landlord in writing to afford him reasonable facilities for—

(a) inspecting the accounts, receipts and other documents supporting the summary; and

(b) taking copies or extracts from them.

Tenant's exercise of the right to inspect

10–033 In order to exercise this right, the tenant must serve a written request to do so on the landlord. Under s.22(3) such written request will be deemed duly served if it is served on an agent of the landlord named as such in the rent book or similar document or on the person who receives rent on behalf of the landlord. Any such person who has a request served upon him by the tenant is obliged to forward it to the landlord as soon as may be.

Landlord to make available facilities for inspection

10–034 Where the tenant has made a request in writing to the landlord, under s.22(4) the landlord is required to make such facilities available to the tenant or secretary for a period of two months, which period must begin not later than one month after the request is made.

Costs of facilities for inspection

10–035 Under s.22(5)(a), where the landlord makes available facilities simply for the inspection of documents, he is obliged to make them so available free of charge.

Under s.22(5)(b), where the landlord makes available facilities for the taking of copies or extracts, the landlord is entitled to make them so available on the payment of such reasonable charge as he may determine.

Notwithstanding the requirement for the landlord to make facilities available for the inspection of any documents free of charge, by s.22(6) the landlord is not thereby precluded from treating as part of his costs of management any costs incurred by him in connection with making those facilities so available.

Request to inspect supporting accounts, etc. where documents are held by superior landlord

10–036 If a request under s.22 of the LTA 1985 to inspect supporting accounts and other documents relates to a summary of relevant costs where such relevant costs or part of them have been incurred by or on behalf of a superior landlord, the tenant's immediate landlord, on whom the request to inspect supporting documents has been served is required forthwith to inform the tenant or secretary of the recognised tenant's association of that fact and of the name and address of the superior landlord.

Once the tenant's immediate landlord has done so, by s.23(2) the provisions of s.22 apply to the superior landlord as they apply to the tenant's immediate landlord.

In particular the superior landlord should pay attention to the time limits imposed by s.22: the superior landlord will be required to make facilities available to the tenant or secretary for a period of two months, which period must begin not later than one month after the request is made.

Effect of assignment on request for summary of relevant costs and request to inspect

10–037 By s.24 of the LTA 1985, the assignment of a tenancy does not affect the validity of a request:

(a) for a summary of relevant costs;

(b) to make facilities available to the tenant or the secretary of a recognised tenants' association to inspect accounts and documents supporting a summary of relevant costs; or

(c) made to a superior landlord for either the supply of relevant information or to make available facilities to inspect.

However, a person is not obliged to provide a summary or to make facilities available more than once for the same dwelling and for the same period.

Failure to comply with ss.21, 22 and 23 of the LTA 1985 an offence

10–038 By s.25 of the LTA 1985, it is a summary offence for a person to fail, without reasonable excuse, to perform any duty imposed on him by ss.21, 22 and 23 of the LTA 1985. By s.26(1), the summary penalties do not apply to local authority landlords.

A person convicted of committing such an offence is liable to a fine not exceeding level four on the standard scale.

In *Taber v MacDonald and Another* (1998), the Divisional Court held that the landlord's obligation was to make available to the tenant all documents which had been seen by the qualified accountant for the purpose of providing the certificate that the summary of relevant costs was in accordance with s.21 of LTA 1985. Although the tenant had not seen the supporting documentation, the landlord had a reasonable excuse for his failure to produce the documents because the supporting documentation was in relation to composite service charges of which a part only was applied to the service charge payable by the appellant.

Management audit

10–039 Chapter V of the LRHUDA 1993 establishes the right to a "management audit". Its purpose is to ascertain both the extent to which the landlord's obligations, which are owed to qualifying tenants and involve the discharge of management functions in relation to the relevant premises and any appurtenant property, are being discharged in an efficient and effective manner and the extent to which sums payable by those tenants by way of service charges are being applied in an efficient and effective manner.

Whilst in itself toothless, an adverse management audit report may provide a springboard for an application to appoint a Manager (see Chapter 27). It may also be useful for tenants to require an audit before making a RTM claim.

Premises to which the right applies

10–040 The right to a management audit may be exercised where the relevant premises consist of or include two or more dwellings let to qualifying tenants of the same landlord. In the case of the right to a management audit exercisable by two or more qualifying tenants, "relevant premises" means so much of the building or buildings containing the dwellings let to those tenants and any other building or buildings as constitutes premises in relation to which management functions are discharged, in respect of the costs of which common service charge contributions are payable under the leases of the qualifying tenants. Common service charge contributions are payable if the tenants may be required under the terms of their leases to contribute to the same costs by the payment of service charges.

The right to a management audit may also be exercised by a single qualifying tenant of a dwelling where the relevant premises contain no other dwelling let to a qualifying tenant apart from that let to him. In the case of the right to a management audit exercisable by a single qualifying tenant, "relevant premises" means so much of the building containing the dwelling let to him and any other building or buildings as constitutes premises in relation to which management functions are discharged in respect of the costs of which a service charge is payable under his lease, whether as a common service charge contribution or otherwise.

Who may require a management audit

Qualifying tenants

10–041 The right may be exercised by the "qualifying tenants". For a person to be a qualifying tenant he must satisfy a number of conditions:

(a) his tenancy must be of a "dwelling";

(b) his tenancy must be a long lease falling within any of paras (a)–(c) of s.7(1), other than a business lease; and

(c) any service charge must be payable under that lease.

Sub-tenants and joint tenants

10–042 No single dwelling may have more than one qualifying tenant at a time. Accordingly the LRHUDA 1993 contains provisions to determine who is the qualifying tenant.

Where a dwelling is for the time being let under two or more long leases which fall within s.77(1), any tenant under any of those leases which is superior to that held by any other such tenant is not a qualifying tenant for the purposes of the right to have a management audit.

Where a dwelling is let to joint tenants under a lease falling within s.77(1), the joint tenants shall be regarded as jointly constituting the qualifying tenant of the dwelling and any one or more of such joint tenants may sign a notice calling for a management audit on behalf of both or all of them.

However, the fact that no single dwelling may have more than one qualifying tenant at a time does not prevent a person from being a qualifying tenant of each of two or more dwellings at the same time, whether he is the tenant of those dwellings under one lease or two or more leases.

Number of tenants joining in exercising the right

10–043 The following minimum numbers of qualifying tenants must participate in exercising the right:

(a) One dwelling let to a qualifying tenant where the relevant premises contain no other dwelling let to a qualifying tenant apart from him—that tenant alone may exercise the right.

(b) Two dwellings only let to qualifying tenants of the same landlord—either or both of those tenants may participate.

(c) Three or more dwellings let to qualifying tenants of the same landlord—at least two thirds of those tenants must participate.

Appointment of auditor

10–044 Qualifying tenants have the right to appoint their own auditor and are free to appoint an auditor of their own choice. All that is required is that the person is appointed by the qualifying tenants (or the requisite majority of them) and is qualified to be appointed to act as an auditor according to the restrictions set out below.

Who may be appointed auditor

10–045 The following rules apply to the appointment of an auditor:

(a) A "qualified accountant" as that expression is defined in s.28(1) of the LTA 1985 (see paragraph 10–018 above); or a "qualified surveyor", meaning that he must hold the qualifications FRICS or FISVA; or a professional associate of the RICS or ISVA may be appointed to act as auditor.

(b) A person may not be appointed to act as an auditor if he has been "disqualified" from acting within the meaning of s.28 of the LTA 1985 or is a tenant of any premises contained within the relevant premises.

(c) Regulations may be made by the Secretary of State extending the categories of persons who may be appointed to act as auditor (s.78(5)). To date, no such regulations have been made.

(d) The LRHUDA 1993 is silent on the question of remuneration of the auditor and certainly there is no provision requiring the landlord to pay for the audit. It therefore seems that the tenants will have to pay for the audit themselves and this is a matter which will have to be agreed between the tenants and the auditor prior to his appointment.

Rights exercisable by the auditor

10–046 Section 79 of the LRHUDA 1993 confers a number of statutory rights on the auditor in connection with management audits and these are discussed below.

To information

10–047 The auditor has limited powers to obtain information both from the landlord and from "relevant persons".

Meaning of "relevant persons"

10–048 Section 79(7) defines "relevant persons" as a person other than the landlord who:

(a) is charged with responsibility for either:

(i) the discharge of any obligations of the landlord which are owed to the qualifying tenants of the constituent dwellings and involve the discharge of management functions in relation to the relevant premises or any appurtenant property; or

(ii) the application of service charges which are payable by the qualifying tenants of the constituent dwellings; or

(b) has a right to enforce payment of any such service charges.

Information which may be obtained from the landlord only

10–049 By s.79(2)(a), the auditor has the right to require the landlord only:

(a) to supply him with a summary of relevant costs within the meaning of s.21(1) of the LTA 1985 (in relation to which, see paragraph 10–004) in connection with any service charges payable by the qualifying tenants of the constituent dwellings; and

(b) to afford him reasonable facilities for inspecting or taking copies or extracts from the accounts, receipts and other documents supporting such a summary of relevant costs.

Landlord and relevant persons to afford auditor reasonable facilities

10–050 By s.79(2)(b) and (c), the auditor has the right to require the landlord or any relevant person to afford him reasonable facilities for:

(a) inspecting any other documents, sight of which is reasonably required by the auditor for the purpose of carrying out the audit; and

(b) taking copies of or extracts from any such documents.

The rights to information conferred by s.79 are exercisable by the auditor:

(a) in relation to the landlord, by the service on the landlord of a notice under s.80; and

(b) in relation to any relevant person, by the giving of a notice to that person by the auditor at (so far as reasonably practicable) the same time as a notice under s.80 is served on the landlord. Note that the auditor is also required to give a copy of any notice given to a relevant person to the landlord.

Auditor's entitlement to inspect

10–051 The auditor is entitled to carry out an inspection of any common parts comprised in the relevant premises or any appurtenant property.

Auditor's power to delegate

10–052 By s.78(6), the auditor has a power to appoint such persons to assist in carrying out the management audit as he thinks fit. This discretion afforded to the auditor is unfettered and appears to be extremely broad.

Note also that by s.79(8), references to the auditor in the context of being afforded reasonable facilities:

(a) for inspecting or taking copies or extracts from the accounts, receipts and other documents supporting a summary of relevant costs;

(b) for inspecting any other documents, sight of which is reasonably required for the purpose of carrying out the audit;

(c) for taking copies of or extracts from any other such documents; and

(d) to carry out an inspection of any common parts comprised in the relevant premises or any appurtenant property,

shall be read as including a person appointed by the auditor under s.78(6).

Costs of landlord or relevant person

10–053 Where the auditor (or any person appointed by him) has a right to require the landlord or a relevant person to afford him reasonable facilities to inspect documents, those facilities are required to be made available free of charge, although that does not preclude the landlord (and the landlord only) from treating as part of his costs of management any costs incurred by him in connection with making those facilities available.

Where the auditor has a right to require the landlord or any relevant person to supply him with documents or facilities for taking copies of or extracts from documents, the landlord or the relevant person shall be entitled to make such facilities available on payment of such reasonable charge as he may determine.

Exercise of the right to a management audit

10–054 The right of qualifying tenants to have a management audit carried out on their behalf is exercised by the giving of a notice under s.80.

There is no prescribed form for a notice under s.80. However, by s.99(1) the notice must be in writing. There are certain formalities prescribed by s.80 with which the notice must comply, and these are discussed below.

Notice to landlord

10–055 The notice must:

(a) be given by the auditor, rather than the qualifying tenants, and must state the name and address of the auditor;

(b) be given to the landlord. By s.80(5), a notice will be deemed to have been duly given to the landlord of any qualifying tenants if it is given to a person who receives the rent payable by such qualifying tenants on behalf of the landlord;

(c) state the full name and address of each of those tenants on behalf of whom it is given and the address of the dwelling of which he is the qualifying tenant;

(d) be signed by each of the tenants on whose behalf it is given;

(e) specify any documents or description of documents which the landlord is required to supply to the auditor under s.79(2)(a)(i) (a summary of relevant costs) and those in respect of which the landlord is required to afford the auditor facilities for inspection and for taking copies or extracts; and

(f) state the date on which the auditor intends to carry out an inspection pursuant to s.79(4) of any common parts comprised in the relevant premises or any appurtenant property, which date must be a date falling not less than one month nor more than two months after the date of the giving the notice under s.80.

Notice to relevant persons

10–056 If the auditor wants to exercise his right to require a relevant person to afford him reasonable facilities for either inspecting any document, sight of which is reasonably required by him for the purpose of carrying out the audit, or his right to require or take copies of or extracts from any such documents, the auditor must serve notice on the relevant person at (so far as reasonably practicable) the same time as a notice under s.80 is given to the landlord.

Although the LRHUDA 1993 does not set out any further details of the form of notice to be given to a relevant person, it is suggested that the form of a notice given under s.79 should be similar to any notice given under s.80, and should, as far as possible, contain the same information as a notice given under s.80, since it is envisaged by s.81(3) that the notice will at least specify the documents the auditor requires to inspect and copy. Further, by s.99(1) the notice must be in writing.

Procedure following giving of notice under s.80 to landlord where landlord has documents

10–057 Within the period of one month of the giving of the notice under s.80, the landlord must:

(a) supply the auditor with the summary of relevant costs and afford the auditor facilities for the inspection of and the taking of copies of or extracts from the accounts, receipts and other documents supporting the summary of relevant costs;

(b) in the case of other any other documents, sight of which is reasonably required by the auditor for the purpose of carrying out the management audit, afford the auditor facilities for the inspection of and the taking of copies of or extracts from such documents within one month of the giving of the notice under s.80, or alternatively the landlord must give the auditor a notice stating that he objects to doing so for such reasons as are specified in the notice; and

(c) if the auditor has suggested a date in the s.80 notice on which he intends to carry out an inspection of any common parts comprised in the relevant premises or appurtenant property, either approve that date or propose an alternative date for the carrying out of such inspection, although such date to be suggested by the landlord must be a date falling not later than the period of two months beginning with the date of the giving of the notice under s.80.

Supply of summary where superior landlord has documents

10–058 Where the landlord is required by a notice given to him under s.80 to supply a summary of relevant costs and any information necessary for complying with the requirement to supply such summary is held by a superior landlord, the landlord must make a written request for the relevant information to his immediate landlord. If the landlord's immediate landlord is not himself the superior landlord, he must make the same request of his immediate landlord and so on up the chain until the superior landlord is reached.

The superior landlord must comply with the request within one month beginning with the date of the making of the request to him.

The landlord who originally received the notice under s.80 shall then comply with it so far as it relates to the supply of such summary within the one month allowed by s.81(1) or such further time, if any, as is reasonable.

Affording facilities for inspection and copying where superior landlord has documents

10–059 Where the landlord is required by a notice given under s.80 to afford the auditor facilities for the inspection or the taking of copies of or extracts from any documents specified in the notice and any of the documents in question are in the custody or control of a superior landlord, the landlord must, upon receipt of the notice, inform the auditor as soon as possible of that fact and the name and address of the superior landlord.

The auditor may then give the superior landlord a notice requiring him to afford the auditor the facilities for the inspection of and making copies of or taking extracts from the relevant documents. No form of notice has been prescribed, but by s.99(1) it must be in writing.

When a superior landlord is given notice under s.82(2) by the auditor, the superior landlord must comply with it in the same way as a relevant person is required to comply with a notice given under s.79, with such modifications as are necessary.

Procedure following giving of notice under s.79 to relevant person

10–060 Where a relevant person has been given notice by the auditor under s.79, requiring him to afford the auditor facilities for the inspection or the taking of copies of or extracts from documents, he must within the period of one month from the giving of the notice in the case of every document or description of documents either afford the auditor the facilities required by him or give him a notice stating that he objects to doing so for the reasons specified on that notice.

Enforcement

10–061 Any application for the enforcement of the auditor's rights required in a notice under ss.79 or 80 must be made before the end of the period beginning with:

(a) in the case of an application in connection with a notice to the landlord given under s.80, the giving of that notice; or

(b) in the case of an application in connection with a notice to a relevant person given under s.79, the date of the giving of that notice.

Inspection and copying of documents

10–062 If by the end of the period of two months beginning with the giving of a notice under either ss.79 or 80 the landlord or the relevant person has failed to comply with any requirement of such notice, the auditor may apply to the court for an order requiring the person in default to comply with that requirement within such period as may be specified within the order.

Upon an application to the court for such an order, the auditor must adduce sufficient evidence to satisfy the court that any document or documents, sight of which is required by the auditor, falls or fall within para.(a) or (b) of s.79(2). The court shall not make an order under s.81(4) unless it is so satisfied and even if the court is so satisfied, it retains an overriding discretion not to make the order.

Inspection of common parts

10–063 If by the end of the period of two months beginning with the date of the giving of the notice under s.80 no inspection of the common parts of the relevant premises or appurtenant has been carried out, the auditor may apply to the court for an order providing for the inspection to be carried out on such date as may be specified in the order.

Supplementary provisions

Landlord disposing of his interest after giving of s.80 notice

10–064 Where a landlord has been given a notice under s.80 and at a time when any obligations arising out of the notice remain to be discharged by him and he disposes of the whole or part of his interest as landlord of the qualifying tenants of the constituent dwellings and the person who has acquired any such interest of the landlord is in a position to discharge any of the obligations arising out of the notice to any extent, that person is responsible for discharging those obligations to the extent which he is able, as if he had been given the notice under s.80.

If the landlord remains, despite such a disposal, in a position to discharge any obligations arising out of the notice, he shall remain liable for so discharging them, but otherwise the person who has acquired the interest shall be responsible for discharging those obligations to the exclusion of the landlord.

Relevant person ceasing to be a relevant person after giving of s.79 notice

10–065 Where a notice has been given to a relevant person under s.79 and, at a time when any obligations arising out of the notice remain to be discharged by him, he ceases to be a relevant person but he remains, despite so ceasing, in a position to discharge those obligations to any extent, he shall remain responsible for discharging those obligations to that extent and s.81 continues to apply to him as if he remained a relevant person.

Restriction on giving of further notices under ss.79 and 80

10–066 Where a notice or notices have been given under either or both of ss.79 and 80 then during the period of 12 months beginning with the date (not the giving) of such notice, no subsequent such notice may be given to the landlord or that relevant person on behalf of any persons who, in relation to the earlier notice, were qualifying tenants of constituent dwellings.

The right to appoint a surveyor to advise on matters relating to service charges

10–066.1 By s.84(1) of the HA 1996, a recognised tenants' association may appoint a surveyor to advise on any matters relating to, or which may give rise to, service charges payable to a landlord by one or more members of the association.

The provisions of Sch.4 to HA 1996 have effect to confer on a surveyor appointed under s.84(1) rights of access to documents and premises.

By the operation of s.102 of and para.15 of Sch.7 to the CLRA 2002, s.84 has effect as if references to the landlord were to the RTM company.

Persons who may be appointed as surveyor

10–067 A person may not be appointed under s.84 unless he is a "qualified surveyor" and for this purpose "qualified surveyor" has the same meaning as in s.78(4)(a) of the LRHUDA 1993 (persons qualified for appointment to carry out a management audit)—see further paragraph 10–045 above.

Duration of appointment of surveyor and notice to landlord

10–068 The appointment of the surveyor takes effect only upon notice being given to the landlord by the recognised tenants' association stating:

- the name and address of the surveyor;
- the duration of his appointment; and
- the matters in respect of which he is appointed.

An appointment of the surveyor shall cease to have effect if:

- the recognised tenants' association gives notice in writing to the landlord to that effect; or
- that recognised tenants' association ceases to exist.

By s.84(5), a notice under s.84 is duly given to the landlord of any tenants if it is given to a person who receives on behalf of the landlord the rent payable by those tenants.

Note that by the modifications effected by s.102 of and para.15 of Sch.7 to CLRA 2002, s.84(5) of the HA 1996 applies as if the reference to a person who receives the rent were to a person who receives service charges.

Rights exercisable by the surveyor

10–069 The rights exercisable by the surveyor are set out in detail in Sch.4 to HA 1996.

Appointment of assistants

10–070 By para.2 of Sch.4, the surveyor is entitled to appoint such persons as he thinks fit to assist him in carrying out his "functions". The surveyor's functions are defined in para.1 of Sch.4 as being his functions in connection with the matters in respect of which he was appointed.

References in Sch.4 to the surveyor, in the context of being afforded facilities and carrying out an inspection, include a person appointed by the surveyor to assist him.

The right to inspect documents

10–071 The surveyor has the right to require the landlord or any "other relevant person" (as to the definition of which, see below) to afford him:

- reasonable facilities for inspecting any documents, sight of which is reasonably required by him for the purposes of his functions; and
- reasonable facilities for the taking of copies of or extracts from any such documents.

In subpara.1 of para.3, "other relevant person" means a person other than the landlord who is or, in relation to a future service charge, will be:

- responsible for applying the proceeds of the service charge; or
- under an obligation to a tenant who pays the service charge in respect of any matter to which the service charge relates.

Exercise of the right to inspect

10–072 The rights conferred on the surveyor by para.3 of Sch.4 are exercisable by him by notice in writing given by him to the landlord or the other relevant person concerned.

Note that where the surveyor gives a notice to any other relevant person, the surveyor is also obliged to give a copy of such notice to the landlord.

Compliance by landlord or other relevant person

10–073 Where a landlord or other relevant person has been given a notice by a surveyor, he is obliged within one week of the date of the giving of the notice or as soon as is reasonably practicable thereafter, either:

(a) to afford the surveyor the facilities required by him for inspecting and taking copies or extracts of the documents to which the notice relates; or

(b) to give the surveyor a notice stating that he objects to doing so for the reasons specified in the notice.

Cost of providing reasonable facilities for inspection

10–074 The landlord is obliged by para.3(5) to make the facilities available for the inspection of any documents free of charge, although this does not prevent the landlord from treating any costs incurred by him in connection with making the facilities for inspection available as part of his costs of management.

However, by para.3(6), a landlord is entitled to make a reasonable charge for facilities for the taking of copies of or extracts from documents.

The right to inspect premises

10–075 By para.4 of Sch.4, the landlord has the right to inspect any "common parts" comprised in "relevant premises" or any "appurtenant property", where the following definitions apply:

- "common parts" in relation to a building or part of a building, includes the structure and exterior of the building or part and any common facilities within it;
- "relevant premises" means so much of the building or buildings containing the dwellings let to members of the relevant tenants' association and any other building or buildings as constitute premises in relation to which management functions are discharged in respect of which service charges are payable by members of the recognised tenants' association; and
- "appurtenant property" means so much of any property not contained in relevant premises as constitutes property in relation to which any such management functions are discharged.

The expression "management functions" in the context of para.4 includes functions with respect to the provision of services or the repair, maintenance, improvement or insurance of the property.

Request to inspect

10–076 Upon being requested to do so, the landlord is obliged to afford the surveyor reasonable access for the purposes of carrying out of an inspection.

By para.4(5), such a request is duly made to the landlord if it is made to a person appointed by the landlord to deal with such requests or, if no such person has been appointed, to a person who receives on behalf of the landlord the rent payable by the tenant.

By s.102 of and para.15(2) of Sch.7 to CLRA 2002, para.4(5) of Sch.4 to HA 1996 should be read as if the reference to a person who receives rent on behalf of the landlord were also to a person who receives service charges.

Any such person who receives such a surveyor's request is obliged to inform the landlord of it as soon as may be.

Cost of reasonable access

10–077 By para.4(4), the landlord is obliged to afford the surveyor such reasonable access for inspection free of charge, although this does not mean that the landlord cannot treat the cost incurred by him in connection with affording such reasonable access to the surveyor as part of his costs of management.

Enforcement of rights by the court

Failure to afford facilities for inspection

10–078 If the landlord or any other relevant person, to whom a notice has been given under para.3 of Sch.4 to afford a surveyor reasonable facilities for the inspection and copying of or the taking of extracts from documents, has not complied with the notice by the end of the period of one month beginning with the date on which the notice was given to him, the court may, on the application of the surveyor, make an order requiring him to do so within such time as is specified in the order.

Failure to afford reasonable access for an inspection

10–079 If the landlord does not, within a reasonable period after a surveyor has made a request to be afforded reasonable access for an inspection, so afford the surveyor such reasonable access, the court may, on the application of the surveyor, make an order requiring the landlord to do so on such date as is specified in the order.

Time limit for applications to the court under para.5

10–080 An application for an order under para.5 of Sch.4 to HA 1996 must be made before the end of the period of four months beginning with the date on which the notice was given under para.3 or the request was made under para.4.

Documents held by superior landlord

10–081 Where a surveyor has served a notice on the landlord under para.3 of Sch.4, requiring the landlord to afford the surveyor reasonable facilities for the inspection of and taking copies of or extracts from any documents which are in the custody of a superior landlord, the landlord is obliged to inform the surveyor of the name and address of the superior landlord as soon as may be and the surveyor may serve a notice in writing to the superior landlord requiring the superior landlord to afford him reasonable facilities for the inspection and taking of copies of such documents.

By para.6(2), the superior landlord is obliged to give such inspection in the same way as the landlord and is subject to the same court enforcement procedures.

Feedom of Information Act 2000

10–081.1 Practitioners should also be aware that the Freedom of Information Act 2000 is now fully in force. By s.1 of the FIA 2000, a person is entitled to request a "public authority" to communicate information held by that public authority, provided that the information is sufficiently identified and is not either the subject of legal professional privilege or one of the categories of exempt information as set out in Pt II of the FIA 2000.

The expression "public authority" is defined in s.3 of the FIA 2000 as any body which is listed in Sch.1 to the FIA 2000. By para.7 of Sch.1 to the FIA 2000, any local authority within the meaning of the Local Government Act 1972 is a public authority for the purposes of the FIA 2000. The effect of local authorities being obliged to communicate information appears to be twofold:

- A tenant of a local authority may well be able to request the local authority to communicate information held by it in relation to the calculation of service charges and the tendering for works to premises occupied by the tenant; and
- A landlord may apply for a grant under s.523 of the HA 1985 or any provision of Pt I of the Housing Grants, Construction and Regeneration Act 1996 and such grant is awarded by a "local housing authority", which is defined by s.101 of the HGCRA 1996 as having the same meaning as in the HA 1985. In s.1 of the HA 1985 a "local housing authority" is defined as a district council, a London borough council, the Common Council of the City of London, a Welsh county council or county borough council or the Council of the Isles of Scilly. If such a grant has been granted, a tenant may make a request for information in relation to the award of the grant, which may in turn provide the tenant with a useful avenue to obtain further information in relation to service charges.

Section 42A of the Landlord and Tenant Act 1987

10–081.2 Where s.42 of the LTA 1987 applies, a payee in receipt of service charges payable by contributing tenants or by a sole contributing tenant under the terms of their/his lease(s) is obliged to hold such sums, or any investments representing such sums, on trust.

Section 156 of the CLRA 2002 introduces the new s.42A into the LTA 1987. By s.42A(1), the payee must hold sums standing to the credit of any trust fund in a designated account or accounts at a relevant financial institution. Section 42A(3) creates a right for a contributing tenant to require the payee by notice in writing:

- to afford reasonable facilities to inspect documents evidencing that s.42A(1) has been complied with and for taking copies of or extracts from them; or
- to supply copies of or extracts from any such documents or to afford reasonable facilities for their collection.

As at the date of going to press, s.42A of the LTA 1987 is only in force in so far as it empowers the Secretary of State to make regulations.

Section 42A of the LTA 1987 is dealt with in more detail in Chapter 15 below.

Landlord's identity and address for service

10–082 By s.48 of the LTA 1987, no rent or service charge is due from the tenant of premises which are or include a dwelling unless the landlord has served on the tenant a notice in writing giving the tenant an address for service in England or Wales at which notices may be served on the landlord by the tenant.

There is no prescribed form for the s.48 notice, but a suggested form of s.48 notice may be found in Appendix B.

In the context of disputes relating to service charges, practitioners acting on behalf of landlords should take great care to ensure at an early stage that a s.48 notice has been served on each and every tenant who may become involved in the dispute.

The Court of Appeal held in *Dallhold Estates (UK) Property Limited v Lindsay Trading Properties* [1994] 1 E.G.L.R. 99 that rent is not due until a s.48 notice has been served, but once it has been served the rents which would otherwise have been in arrears immediately fell due. In order for the sums to become due under s.48, the information must be provided in writing: see *Rogan v Woodfield Building Services* (1995) 27 H.L.R. 484.

If there is a change of landlord, it is incumbent on the incoming landlord to inform the tenant of the change of landlord: see s.3 of the Landlord and Tenant Act 1985. Generally under s.151 of the Law of Property Act 1925, where the reversion has been assigned the tenant is entitled to continue to pay rent, etc. to the previous landlord until notice of the change has been given.

The Civil Procedure Rules 1998

10–083 The Civil Procedure Rules 1998 (as amended) ("the CPR") contain provisions relating to the disclosure of documents in Pt 31.

Lawyers will be very familiar with the onerous duty of disclosure imposed by the CPR in the course of litigation, which of course applies to all parties alike, be they landlord or tenant.

However, it should not be forgotten that the CPR contains provisions which allow a person to apply to the court before any proceedings have been issued for an order requiring the respondent to the application to disclose documents to the applicant. It is anticipated that this provision may be of some assistance to tenants in service charge disputes, particularly in circumstances where a landlord has failed to comply with his statutory duties to provide information.

In appropriate circumstances a person may apply to the court under s.33 of the Supreme Court Act 1981 or s.52 of the County

Courts Act 1984 for an order that another person discloses documents to him before proceedings have started.

Such an application should be made under rule 31.16 of the CPR and should be supported by evidence.

The court may grant such an application only where all of the following circumstances apply:

(a) the respondent to the application is likely to be a party to subsequent proceedings;

(b) the person who makes the application is also likely to be a party to those proceedings;

(c) if proceedings had already started, the respondent to the application would have a duty under the ordinary rules for standard disclosure to disclose the documents or those classes of documents disclosure of which the applicant requires; and

(d) pre-action disclosure is desirable to:

  (i) dispose fairly of the anticipated proceedings;
  (ii) assist the dispute to be resolved without the issue of proceedings; or
  (iii) save costs.

The Leasehold Valuation Tribunal also has power to require documents from a party to an application before the Tribunal: see Chapter 22.

Chapter 11

The Reasonableness of Service Charges

Although service charge provisions quite frequently contain express limitations as to the level of professional fees which may be recovered, it is rare to find any similar restriction on charges of other kinds. This chapter explores the limitations imposed by common law and statute on what a landlord may reasonably charge when no express limitation is to be found in the lease. **11–001**

In this chapter reference is made to reasonableness of expenditure on works and insurance. In the context of residential service charges, there are a huge range of LVT decisions on how questions of reasonableness are applied in relation to specific kinds of work as well as the various types of professional fees and other expenses which habitually make up a service charge. It is suggested that the reader who is in search of such specific guidance should visit www.lease-advice.org.uk and view the table of decisions on the Landlord and Tenant Acts of 1985 and 1987. That table currently runs to in excess of 1,400 entries and can easily be searched by the use of appropriate keywords.

The position at common law

Given the limited application of the statutory regimes controlling the recovery of service charges, the position at common law continues to be a matter of importance. **11–002**

Implied limitation to charges which are "fair and reasonable"

The courts have generally been willing to imply at common law a term that service charges recoverable under a lease are limited to those which are fair and reasonable. **11–003**

Cases on repairs

11–004 In *Finchbourne v Rodriguez* [1976] 3 A.E.R. 581, the lease provided that the landlord was entitled to recover from the tenant a percentage of "the outgoing costs expenses and liabilities" of meeting his service charge obligations. The court at first instance was confronted with a preliminary issue as to whether the landlord could recover "costs and outgoings other than fair and reasonable costs and outgoings". It was held that he could not, and the Court of Appeal upheld this finding.

The basis for the Court of Appeal's decision was that it was necessary to imply a term to that effect in order to give business efficacy to the lease, in accordance with ordinary principles as set out in *Liverpool City Council v Irwin* [1997] A.C. 239. As Cairns L.J. said at 587b "the parties cannot have intended that the landlords should have an unfettered discretion to adopt the highest conceivable standard". Agreeing, Orr L.J. made the further point that the lessee's contribution was to be checked by the managing agents in an expert capacity. He said that it would require expertise to determine what works were reasonably required, and what a reasonable cost for those works would be, but not simply to add up figures provided by the landlord.

Finchbourne was followed in *Morgan v Stainer* [1993] 2 E.G.L.R. 73. In *Morgan*, the standard form lease required the individual tenants to pay to the landlord "all legal and other costs that may be incurred by the landlord in obtaining the payment of maintenance contributions from any tenant in the building". Proceedings were brought by 30 of 55 tenants against the landlord, those proceedings eventually being compromised by an order under the terms of which the landlord agreed to bear the claimants' costs in the sum of £88,585.91. The landlord then sought to recover those costs, as well as his own costs, from the tenants as a whole.

David Neuberger Q.C. (as he then was) rejected the landlord's claim on three separate grounds, including by reference to the *Finchbourne* requirement that costs must be fair and reasonable not only with regard to their *quantum* but also with regard to their nature. He found that the mere fact of an adverse order for costs did not mean that those costs had been unreasonable, but would give rise to a presumption that they were. Where the landlord had consented to such an order, a heavy onus would fall on him to establish that the position was otherwise and that the costs incurred were reasonable.

11–005 In *Pole Properties v Feinberg* (1981) 43 P.&C.R. 121 the court went even further. There, the lease required the tenant to contribute to heating costs in a particular proportion. During the tenancy, the landlord purchased adjoining premises and changed the heating system in such a way as to improve the heating to other flats in the newly enlarged building, but not to the tenant's. The Court of Appeal held that there had been such a radical change of circumstances as to mean that the lease as originally understood by the parties was no longer of any application in this regard. It held that it had power to impose a charge which was fair and reasonable in all the circumstances. On the basis of expert evidence put before the court at first instance, it significantly reduced the tenant's liability.

The basis on which the court regarded itself as having jurisdiction to impose a fair and reasonable charge without reference to the terms of the lease is not made clear in the decision. The existence of this jurisdiction does not appear from the report to have been contentious. There would appear to be a number of possible ways in which it might arise. One analysis might be that the court was doing no more than enforcing the agreement the parties had in substance made, albeit that that agreement was no longer (by virtue of the change in circumstances) accurately expressed by the words in the lease. An alternative is that the landlord's entitlement to remuneration for the services arose not under the express terms of the lease but solely on a *quantum valebant* basis. A further approach, were the same problem to arise now, would be to invoke s.15 of the Supply of Goods and Services Act 1982. The application of this Act to leases was considered in *Havenridge v Boston Dyers Ltd* [1994] 2 E.G.L.R. 73 (see below) but no concluded view was expressed.

A further aspect of the common law approach to reasonableness is that the standard of what is reasonable must be judged by reference to the duration of the tenant's interest. It has been successfully argued in a number of cases that works undertaken by the landlord, although reasonable in themselves, could nevertheless not reasonably be charged to the tenant in view of the fact that the remaining period of the tenant's occupation was limited and it would therefore derive limited benefit from the works. Examples are:

- *Holding & Management Ltd v Property Holding & Investment Trust plc* [1989] 1 W.L.R. 1313 (owners of 75 year leases not liable to pay for major scheme of rebuilding of external walls despite the fact that such rebuilding could justifiably be undertaken by a "prudent building owner");
- *Scottish Mutual Insurance Co v Jardine* (1999) E.G.C.S. 43 (short term tenant not liable for the cost of expensive roof repairs);
- *Fluor Daniel Properties Ltd v Shortlands Investment Ltd* [2001] E.G.C.S. 8 (landlord not entitled to effect complete overhaul to air-conditioning *inter alia* on grounds of tenant's limited interest).

An interesting consequence of this is that, in a block occupied by tenants under identical leases, works might be chargeable to a tenant whose term has a long period still to run, but not to another whose term is close to expiry.

As with any implied term, the implication of a requirement of reasonableness will not be made if it would be inconsistent with the express wording of the lease—*Wigglesworth v Property Holdings & Investment Trust Ltd* (1984) 270 E.G. 555.

Cases on insurance

11–006 It is often thought that a different approach has been taken in cases involving the recovery of insurance premiums. In this context the courts have traditionally been unwilling to hold that the landlord is limited to the recovery of what might be regarded as a reasonable sum. In *Bandar Property Holdings v J.S. Darwen (Successors)* [1968] 2 All E.R. 305, the lessor had covenanted to keep the premises insured at "some insurance office or offices of repute, or at Lloyds", and the lessee had covenanted to repay to him "such sum as the landlord shall from time to time pay or be called on to pay by way of premium or premiums for insuring the demised premises in accordance with the provisions of clause 3(1) hereof".

Roskill J. summarised the law saying:

> "It is axiomatic that a court will not imply a term which has not been expressed merely because, had the parties thought of the possibility of expressing that term, it would have been reasonable for them to have done so. Before a term which has not been expressed can be implied it has got to be shown not only that it would be reasonable to make that implication, but that it is necessary in order to make the contract that such a term should be implied."

and went on to hold:

> "I can see no justification for making the implication sought [that there was an implied term that the landlord would act reasonably in placing the insurance so as not to impose an unnecessary heavy burden on the tenant] since no implication is necessary and the bargain made between the parties works perfectly sensibly without making any implication."

Reference should also be made to *Havenridge* (see paragraph 11–005 above) and *Berrycroft Management Co Ltd v Sinclair Gardens Investments (Kensington) Ltd* [1997] 1 E.G.L.R. 47. It is notable however that in *Havenridge*, Evans J., far from departing from the approach adopted in *Finchbourne*, expressly followed it, acknowledging that there must be a limitation on the recoverable premium so as to avoid an "outlandish" result. The test adopted in *Havenridge* was whether the landlord had procured insurance in the normal course of business. If he had, it did not matter that a lower premium could have been obtained elsewhere. It was not incumbent on the landlord to "shop around". A similar approach was taken in *Berrycroft*.

11–007 What the cases may disclose is a difference in approach as to what constitutes excessive expenditure in the context of insurance placement, and what in the context of service charges of other kinds. Some conceptual justification for this distinction may lie in the nature of insurance placement. Different insurers may justifiably take different approaches to risk or alternatively may legitimately price policies in accordance with different pricing structures. On the other hand, the question of what repairs might be reasonable in any particular case, or what legal costs or other professional fees were justifiably incurred, is one which tends to admit of only one right answer.

It is also notable that in both *Havenridge* and *Berrycroft*, some weight was attached to the existence of a measure of protection for the tenants in the wording of the respective leases. In *Havenridge*, the landlord was limited to the recovery of sums paid or expended "properly". In *Berrycroft*, the protection for the tenant was that the landlord was obliged to insure with an insurer "of repute". The position under a lease in which such words of protection were absent might therefore be regarded as uncertain. But it would be odd if a tenant holding under such a lease was better off as a result of the implication of some restraint than one whose lease expressly contains restraining words. Furthermore, in *Havenridge*, Evans J. stated that in his view it did not matter whether one approached the question by reference to the proper construction of the word "properly", or by implying a limitation on what was recoverable (75M).

The best advice that can be given in the light of these cases to a tenant who believes that he is being over-charged for the insurance element in his service charge is that he should: (1) obtain alternative quotes to see if what his landlord is being charged appears to be unduly high; and (2) if it does so appear, write a formal letter to his landlord, exhibiting the quotes he has obtained, and inviting the landlord to show what steps he has taken to obtain insurance or to prove that there was no special feature to take his placing of the insurance outside the normal course of business.

Statutory intervention

Section 19(1) of the Landlord and Tenant Act 1985

11–008 In the residential context, the principal legislative intervention on the common law framework is s.19(1) of the Landlord and Tenant Act 1985. This provides:

"(1) Relevant costs shall be taken into account in determining the amount of a service charge payable for a period—

(a) only to the extent to which they are reasonably incurred, and
(b) where they are incurred on the provision of services or the carrying out of works, only if the services or works are of a reasonable standard

and the amount payable shall be limited accordingly."

Definitions of the expressions "service charge" and "relevant costs" are set out in s.18: see Chapter 4.

Section 19(1) is commonly referred to as a "test of reasonableness", but it is noteworthy that what s.19(1)(a) actually requires to be scrutinised is whether or not costs were "reasonably incurred". The distinction has been commented on in at least two cases. In *Forcelux v Sweetman* [2001] 2 E.G.L.R. 173, the issue was whether a landlord was justified in insuring the building under a "block" policy, which resulted in higher premiums than might have been obtained if the property had been insured individually. Mr P.R. Francis FRICS, sitting in the Lands Tribunal, accepted the landlord's submission that what the subsection required was consideration of the decision-making process. He went on to say however that this could not be a "licence to charge a figure that is out of line with the market norm", and identified a further stage, being consideration of whether the amount charged was reasonable in the light of evidence about that process.

This approach was developed by Mr Peter Clarke FRICS in *Veena SA v Cheong* [2003] 1 E.G.L.R. 175, another Lands Tribunal case. Mr Clarke again identified the two-stage test involved, being consideration not only of whether the action taken by the landlord was reasonable, but also whether the costs incurred in taking that action were too. He held that the landlord needed to demonstrate both in order to succeed, and found on the facts (which concerned the employment of a full-time porter at premises in Mayfair) that the landlord could not establish the first requirement.

It would seem to follow that the phrase "reasonably incurred" imposes a somewhat more stringent test than that which would be required if the test were simply that the costs be "reasonable".

11–009 Some tribunals have gone further. In *O'Sullivan v Regisport* LVT/INS/027/003/00 the tribunal held that a mechanistic application of *Havenridge* to cases under s.19(1) "would largely emasculate the protection afforded to leaseholders" by that section. And in *Maryland Estates v Ayton* LVT/SC/CR/123/166/01, it was said that *Berrycroft* "was not intended to defeat the clear and literal meaning as well as the obvious intention of s.19 and the tribunal does not think that the Court of Appeal could have intended this result to occur."

On the other hand, perhaps unsurprisingly, where the landlord has satisfied the *Berrycroft* test, he is also likely to satisfy s.19. See:

- *Gerolaki v Chappell* LVT/SC/002/235/99
- *Jenkins v Nassibian* LVT/SC/024/218/99
- *Curtis v Glass* LVT/SC/035/075
- *Kyte v Rolvendale Ltd* LVT/SC/014/07/03
- *Mayor v Westleigh Properties Ltd* LON/00BK/LSL/2004/0040.

Section 19(1)(b) provides that, in relation to works, recovery is only permissible "if the services or works are of a reasonable standard". It would seem to follow from the wording of this sub-paragraph that if the works are not of a reasonable standard, there can be no recovery. However in *Yorkbrook Investments Ltd v Batten* [1985] 2 E.G.L.R. 100, the Court of Appeal shortly rejected a submission to this effect in relation to very similar provisions of s.91A(1) of the Housing Finance Act 1972. It may be that the correct approach is to take a composite view of any particular item of work. This will allow a court to make a deduction from that item to reflect any shortcoming in the manner of its performance.

It is often argued that a particular charge has not been reasonably incurred because, for example, the landlord's delay in dealing with the problem in question has exacerbated it and rendered its repair more expensive than would have been the case if it had been addressed promptly. It is thought that such an argument places more strain on the words "reasonably incurred" than they can bear. What is under scrutiny is whether the actual incurring of the cost was reasonable. That must depend on whether the landlord's response, at the point in time when the decision was made to act, was a reasonable one. It does not depend on whether the action (or inaction) on the part of the landlord which gave rise to the need to incur the cost was reasonable. The tenant may undoubtedly have other remedies in respect of such a failure, for example by way of set-off, but it is submitted that on a true analysis no such remedy is available on the basis of s.19(1) alone.

The Supply of Goods and Services Act 1982 ("SoGSA")

11–010 A contract for the supply of services is defined in s.12 of the SoGSA simply as "a contract under which a person ('the supplier') agrees to carry out a service". Section 15 provides that where under such a contract "the consideration for the service is not determined by the contract, or is left to be determined in a manner agreed by the contract . . . there is an implied term that the party contracting with the supplier will pay a reasonable charge."

As mentioned above, the question of whether or not this Act is applicable to leases was considered in *Havenridge*. Evans L.J. declined to express a concluded view as to whether the Act could ever apply to a lease. But he commented that where parties reach agreement as to the allocation of risk and responsibilities between them, it would be unrealistic to describe the arrangement as "the supply of services". On the slender basis of this dictum, it seems unlikely that, in the ordinary course, SoGSA will apply to a lease. If SoGSA did apply, its effect would be that the vast majority of service charge provisions in leases both residential and commercial would be subject to a test of reasonableness. It is not easy to see how this would sit with s.19(1) of the 1985 Act which, as suggested above, gives rise to a stricter test as to what costs can be recovered.

Evans J. also expressly left open the scenario where for example the tenant covenants to insure but it is provided that the landlord will obtain quotes and put in place the insurance on the tenant's behalf. Clearly it is possible to envisage covenants such as this which genuinely do give rise to the provision of services, as distinct from the basket of corresponding rights and obligations which ordinarily characterise a contract such as a lease.

Unfair Terms in Consumer Contract Regulations 1999 ("UTCCR")

11–011 It is outside the scope of this chapter to provide exhaustive guidance to the UTCCR, but in summary its purpose is to release consumers from any term which is "unfair" (reg.8(1)), and to ensure that terms which are not expressed in plain, intelligible language are interpreted in a manner most favourable to the consumer (reg.7). "Unfair" in this context means that the term "contrary to the requirement of good faith . . . causes a significant imbalance in the parties' rights and obligations arising under the contract, to the detriment of the consumer" (reg.5(1)). The reference to "the requirement of good faith" is somewhat opaque to the eyes of an English lawyer, but is described by the editors of Chitty on Contracts as little more than "a bow in the direction of" the German statute on which the Directive was based (see para.15–045, 29th ed., Vol.1).

A recent decision of the Court of Appeal (*R (Khatum) v Newham LBC* [2004] 1 W.L.R. 417) has confirmed that the UTCCR apply to contracts relating to land, including contracts of tenancy.

An early demonstration of the potentially far-reaching consequences of this decision is provided by the case of *Schilling v Canary Riverside Development PTE* LON/00BG/LSL 2004/0064. In this case the landlord had successfully resisted an application by tenants to appoint a manager. It tried to recover the significant costs incurred in doing so by way of a provision which, it argued, gave rise to an entitlement to levy such costs from its tenants by way of service charge. The LVT held that it could not do so. Among other grounds for this refusal, it held that the clause in question fell foul of the UTCCR. The tribunal said:

> "Any term which entitles the landlord on one side to recover from tenants its costs of proceedings against tenants, without conferring any reciprocal rights, must cause a significant imbalance in the parties' rights and obligation arising under the lease/contract within regulation 5(2) of the 1999 regulations".

11–012 Certain limitations on the application of UTCCR should however be noted. First, under reg.3(1) a "consumer" means a "natural person who, in contracts covered by these Regulations, is acting for the purposes which are outside his trade, business or profession." Accordingly, while the UTCCR may well impact on residential service charges, it will have no bearing on commercial tenancies. Second, the test of fairness in the UTCCR applies only to contractual terms which have not been individually negotiated (reg.5(1)). However, since by reg.5(2) this will include terms which have been drafted in advance and whose substance the tenant has not been able to influence, it would seem likely that the majority of service charge provisions will satisfy this test.

Schedule 2 to UTCCR contains what is described in reg.5(5) as "an indicative and non-exhaustive list" of terms which might be regarded as unfair. Those that might be expected to be of particular significance to service charge provisions include (b) (the inappropriate exclusion of rights of set-off), (c) (performance by supplier at supplier's own discretion) and (k) (supplier entitled to alter unilaterally the service provided).

The latter kind of clause clearly has a resonance in the context of service charges where it is common to find "sweeping-up" clauses enabling the landlord to provide services of a kind not specified in the lease. The courts have grappled with such clauses on many occasions and have frequently gone to considerable lengths to limit a landlord's right to recover. Examples include *Jacob Isbicki & Co Ltd v Goulding & Bird Ltd* [1989] 1 E.G.L.R. 236 and *Mullaney v Maybourne Grange (Croydon) Management Ltd* [1986] 1 E.G.L.R. 70. The UTCCR may provide an alternative means of reaching a similar result.

Chapter 12

Related Charges

This chapter is concerned with two matters: control of "administration charges" and control of "estate charges" under estate management schemes.

The statutory provisions: commencement

12–001 The controls were introduced by s.158 (and Sch.11) and s.159 of the Commonhold and Leasehold Reform Act 2002, which were brought into force on September 30, 2003 in England and March 30, 2004 in Wales: see the Commonhold and Leasehold Reform Act 2002 (Commencement No.2 and Savings) (England) Order 2003 (SI 2003/1986) (C.82) and the Commonhold and Leasehold Reform Act 2002 (Commencement No.2 and Savings) (Wales) Order 2004. The respective Commencement Orders provided that the provisions did not apply to charges payable before the relevant commencement dates.

Section 158 and Sch.11: control of "administration charges"

12–002 Many leases impose charges payable in certain circumstances, which are not "service charges", for example, a fee for registering notice of assignment. Leases may also contain "default" charges of one sort or another, such as a "late payment fee" or interest on late payments or a fee for preparation of a s.146 notice.

Such charges were uncontrolled and there was evidence of abuse by unscrupulous landlords. Section 158 of and Sch.11 to the Commonhold and Leasehold Reform Act 2002 aim to remedy this by introducing a concept new to statute of "Administration Charges", with an associated control mechanism. The scheme is similar to that under s.19 of the Landlord and Tenant Act 1985 in that it imports a requirement of reasonableness, but there are differences, principally the remedy of variation of the lease itself.

To whom does Sch.11 apply?

12–003 Schedule 11 applies to amounts payable by "a tenant of a dwelling". This is the same formulation as used in s.18 of the LTA 1985, and reference should be made to the detailed consideration of this formulation at paragraphs 4–006 to 4–008.

Definition of administration charge

12–004 An Administration Charge is defined in para.1(1) of Sch.11 as:

> " . . . an amount payable by a tenant of a dwelling as part of or in addition to the rent which is payable, directly or indirectly—
>
> (a) for or in connection with the grant of approvals under his lease, or applications for such approvals,
> (b) for or in connection with the provision of information or documents by or on behalf of the landlord or a person who is party to his lease otherwise than as landlord or tenant,
> (c) in respect of a failure by the tenant to make a payment by the due date to the landlord or a person who is party to his lease otherwise than as landlord or tenant, or
> (d) in connection with a breach (or alleged breach) of a covenant or condition in his lease".

- The definition provides for amounts which are payable "directly or indirectly". The intent is plainly to cast the net as widely as possible. Amounts payable "indirectly" could include amounts which are claimed in respect of a third party's charges, such as the landlord's solicitors.
- It should be noted that a charge need not be a fixed fee in order to fall within the basic definition of an administration charge.
- It should also be noted that the definition does not restrict itself to sums payable under an express term of the lease itself. Sums which have to be paid because there is a lease may be caught. For example, leases rarely provide expressly that a landlord is entitled to costs of considering applications for permission or licence under the lease, but as a matter of general law the landlord may be entitled to require the payment of a reasonable sum in respect

of any legal or other expense incurred in relation to such licence or consent (see the proviso to s.144 of the Law of Property Act 1925). Such costs will fall within the scope of "administration charges" under Sch.11.

- It also does not appear to matter to whom the administration charge is payable. Payments, for example, to management companies will be covered.

12–005 *Sub-paragraph (a)* covers landlords' costs of considering and/or granting licence to assign, licence to sub-let, licence to alter and so on. However, the drafting of sub-para.(a) may be defective. It plainly covers landlord's costs of considering applications for consent to assign, where the lease provides that the landlord's consent to any assignment is required, but in the authors' experience it is more common in long residential leases to find no restriction on assignment but a covenant requiring the fact of any assignment to be registered with the landlord, coupled with a fee. It is arguable that sub-para.(a) does not cover such a fee, which has nothing to do with "approval" of the assignment.

Sub-paragraph (b) is fairly self explanatory, covering the costs of provision of information. Examples of such information which might be sought, and for the provision of which a landlord might seek to charge a fee, include the provision of a letter to a potential purchaser to confirm that the service charge is paid up to date, and for plans of the building to enable repairs to be made to a flat. Payment to "a person who is party to his lease otherwise than as landlord or tenant" would include, for instance, payment to a management company/managing agent.

Sub-paragraph (c) is very widely drafted and would appear to catch any and all "default" charges for non-payment of money due under the lease, such as "administration fees" for chasing letters (again, whether payment is to the landlord or someone who is party to the lease otherwise than as landlord or tenant). Although not expressly mentioned, it is submitted that interest on late payments is within sub-para.(c) of the definition of administration charge.

Sub-paragraph (d) dovetails with sub-para.(c). Again it is widely drafted and covers charges arising out of any breach or alleged breach of the lease. A common example is a clause providing that the landlord is entitled to its costs of the preparation and service of a s.146 notice, whether or not forfeiture takes place or relief is granted. The cost of preparing a detailed schedule of dilapidations in the case of forfeiture for disrepair may, of course, be considerable.

Exceptions from and extensions of the definition

12–006

- Power to *amend* the definition in sub-para.(1)(a) by delegated legislation is provided by sub-para.(4). This will permit any loopholes which appear in practice to be plugged quickly and easily by regulation.
- Paragraph 1(2) *excepts* from the definition an amount payable by the tenant of a dwelling the rent of which is registered under Pt 4 of the Rent Act 1977 unless the amount registered is entered as a variable amount in pursuance of s.71(4) of that Act. This is not commonly encountered these days.

Variable administration charges

12–007 Sub-paragraph 1(2) of Sch.11 goes on to divide administration charges into those which are "variable" and those which are not. A "variable administration charge" is defined in a negative manner as:

> ". . . an administration charge payable by a tenant which is neither
>
> (a) specified in his lease, nor
> (b) calculated in accordance with a formula specified in his lease."

Whilst it appears that the meaning of "formula" in sub-para.1(3)(b) of Sch.11 is restricted to a clause which lays down method of calculation of a charge which necessarily produces a certain result, nevertheless the concept of a "variable" administration charge is rather narrower than one would expect.

Examples:

(1) A contractual interest provision applicable to arrears of service charge, which provides for interest at 10 per cent over base rate. The payment due will vary as the base rate varies from time to time and depending on the level of arrears, but this would not be a "variable administration charge" because it is calculated in accordance with a formula under the lease.

(2) By contrast, a clause which provides for all costs, fees and expenses of service of a s.146 notice is not a "formula", no matter how detailed the provisions of the clause, as the charge is in the end variable on the same facts (the costs would be higher if the landlord used a more expensive firm of solicitors to prepare exactly the same notice).

The significance of the distinction between "variable" and other administration charges lies in the method of control under paras 2 (variable) or 3 (other) administration charges. As discussed in detail below, the method of control is quite different under each paragraph:

- variable administration charges are subject to a reasonableness requirement;
- where the administration charge is not variable, the fixed fee or formula may be challenged under para.3 of Sch.11 and the remedy to be granted on a successful challenge is variation of the lease itself.

In the result, it will not be possible for a tenant to ask the LVT to vary a clause which provides that the landlord may recover costs on an indemnity basis. The tenant will be restricted to challenging particular bills as unreasonable.

Restrictions on administration charges

Variable administration charges

12–008 Paragraph 2 of Sch.11 provides that:

> "A variable administration charge is payable only to the extent that the amount of the charge is 'reasonable' ".

Whilst calling this a "reasonableness" test is no doubt a useful shorthand, this "reasonableness test" is different from the s.19(1)(a) of the Landlord and Tenant Act 1985 "reasonableness test". As discussed in paragraph 11–008, the s.19(1)(a) test is that costs must be "reasonably incurred".

Paragraph 5 of Sch.11 gives the LVT jurisdiction to decide whether the charge is contractually payable, but assuming that the LVT so finds, it is not clear whether a para.2 challenge to an administration charge is limited to challenging quantum, or whether it is open to the tenant to argue that although strictly claimable under the lease, it was unreasonable for the landlord to make a charge at all in the particular circumstances.

Schedule 11 also does not say on whom the burden of proof falls to establish whether or not an administration charge is reasonable. Section 19 of the 1985 Act did not make explicit upon whom the burden lay either, although in *Yorkbrook Investments v Batten* [1985] 2 E.G.L.R. 100, the Court of Appeal said at 102L that having examined the statutory provisions "we can find no reason for suggesting that there is any presumption for or against a finding of reasonableness of standard or of costs. The court will reach its conclusion on the whole of the evidence . . ..”

This raises an interesting question in relation to clauses which provide for the payment of the landlord’s legal fees on an indemnity basis. The basis for assessment of litigation costs is set out in CPR 44.4(1). On both the indemnity and standard bases of assessment, the court will not allow any cost unreasonably incurred or unreasonable in amount. CPR 44.4(3) provides that the effect of the indemnity basis of assessment is that any doubt as to reasonableness is resolved in favour of the receiving party. The interrelationship of CPR 44.4(1) and (3) with para.2 of Sch.11 to the CLRA 2002 is unclear—does para.2 require that the burden of proof is on the landlord and thus override the indemnity costs provision, or does it add nothing to CPR 44 thus leaving the effect of an indemnity costs clause unchanged?

Under para.5 of Sch.11 to the Commonhold and Leasehold Reform Act 2002 the Leasehold Valuation Tribunal has the power to determine liability to pay an administration charge. This is similar to its jurisdiction under s.27A of the Landlord and Tenant Act 1985 to determine liability to pay a service charge.

It has always been open to a tenant who is bound to pay his landlord’s solicitor’s costs to have those costs assessed pursuant to s.71 of the Solicitors Act 1974. Such assessment is on the same basis as between a solicitor and his own client. It is unclear how the LVT’s new powers and the reasonableness test under Sch.11 dovetail with the existing costs jurisdictions.

Non-variable administration charges

12–009 Where the administration charge is not “variable”, i.e. where it is specified by the lease or calculated in accordance with a formula under the lease, any party to the lease may apply to a LVT under para.3 of Sch.11 for an order varying the lease on the grounds that the charge or formula specified in the lease is unreasonable. This is dealt with in Chapter 21.

Section 159: control of estate charges under estate management schemes

What is an estate management scheme?

12–010 In moving the amendment to the Commonhold and Leasehold Reform Bill during the Committee Stage of the Bill, Lord Richard said that estate management schemes are there "to maintain the character of an area—for example, the Grosvenor Estate or the Dulwich Estate—and to protect it from any possible damage by enfranchising freeholders; for example, the hideous crime of pebble-dashing a house in Grosvenor Square". (See Hansard, March 22, 2001, C.W.H. 254).

Many houses which qualified for enfranchisement under the Leasehold Reform Act 1967 were part of developments where the common landlord had imposed covenants on the leaseholders for the purpose of maintaining the character and standards of the area (or estate) as a whole. It was recognised when the 1967 Act was passed that enforcement of such schemes was of general benefit, and that it would be unfortunate if the exercise of the right to enfranchise by one or more tenants had the side-effect of making them inoperable.

Consequently, s.19 of the 1967 Act made provisions for continuing the management powers of the landlord by establishing a legally binding scheme to preserve the quality and appearance of the area. The scheme had to be certified by the minister and approved by the court. The provisions were both complex and limited. Consequently, when the Leasehold Reform Housing and Urban Development Act 1993 extended enfranchisement to long leases of flats and provided for collective enfranchisement, Ch.IV of Pt 1 of the Act made new provision for such schemes, to be approved by the LVT. The provisions of the 1993 Act cover property which can be enfranchised under the provisions of the 1967 and 1993 Acts.

What sorts of matters are covered by such schemes?

12–011 Section 69 of the 1993 Act (which follows s.19(6) of the 1967 Act) provides that a scheme may provide for all or any of the following matters:

(a) for regulating the redevelopment, use or appearance of property in which tenants have acquired the landlord's interest (i.e. under the 1967 or 1993 Act);

(b) for empowering the landlord for the time being to carry out works of maintenance, repair, renewal, or replacement in relation to any such property to comply with the scheme, or for making the operation of any provisions of the scheme conditional on his doing so or on the provision or maintenance by him of services, facilities or amenities of any description;

(c) for imposing on persons from time to time occupying or interested in any such property obligations in respect of the carrying out of works of maintenance, repair, renewal or replacement in relation to the property or property used or enjoyed by them in common with others, or in respect of costs incurred by the landlord for the time being on any matter referred to in this paragraph or in paragraph (b) above;

(d) for the inspection from time to time of any such property on behalf of the landlord for the time being, and for the recovery by him of sums due to him under the scheme in respect of any such property by means of a charge on the property.

The purpose of s.159

12–012 When the Commonhold and Leasehold Reform Bill was debated in Committee in the House of Lords in November 2001 it was pointed out that, whereas leaseholders who paid service charges already had statutory protection against unreasonable charges (which were to be extended), and that the Bill provided for control of administration charges, there was *no* control proposed in respect of estate management charges. Lady Gardner of Parkes said that "people are being asked to pay much more now as so-called freeholders than they ever were when they were leaseholders" (Hansard, November 13, 2001 col.552). Accordingly, when the Bill reached the House of Commons the Government inserted what is now s.159 of the Act to deal with the anomaly. Without such a provision, anyone who enfranchised and was subject to an estate management scheme would "move from having protection against unreasonable charges under their lease to having no protection against unreasonable charges under the estate management scheme" (Hansard, March 11, 2002 col.690). The purpose of s.159 is accordingly to provide the same protection in respect of estate management charges as for service charges. Charges under estate management schemes ("estate charges") are payable only to the extent that they are reasonable, and there is recourse to the LVT in respect of them.

When does s.159 apply?

12–013 The section applies where an estate management scheme set up under the 1967 Act or the 1993 Act "includes provision imposing on persons occupying or interested in property an obligation to make payments ('estate charges')".

Restrictions on estate charges

12–014 The protection afforded in respect of estate charges follows the protection afforded in respect of administration charges (see the first part of this chapter).

Variable estate charges

12–015 Subsection (2) follows para.2 of Sch.11 and provides that a "variable estate charge" is "payable only to the extent that the amount of the charge is reasonable". The definition of a "variable" estate charge under s.159(2) follows the definition of a "variable" administration charge in para.1(3) of Sch.11; see above.

Application to the LVT to vary the scheme

12–016 The provisions of subss.(3)–(5) in respect of estate charges are, *mutatis mutandis*, the same as paras 3(1)–(3) of Sch.11 in respect of administration charges: application may be made to the LVT on the ground that any estate charge or formula specified in the scheme is unreasonable, and the LVT has the same powers in respect of variation.

Liability to pay estate charges

12–017 The provisions of subs.(6) in respect of an application to the LVT for a determination are, *mutatis mutandis*, the same as para.5 of Sch.11 in respect of administration charges. It should be noted:

- as with service charges and administration charges, application may be made whether or not payment has been made;
- by subs.10, and again as with service charges and administration charges, simply making payment is not to be taken as an agreement or admission that the charge is accepted;
- the jurisdiction of the LVT is in addition to the jurisdiction of the court;
- there are similar bars to making an application to the LVT (where the matter has been agreed or admitted; where there is a post-dispute arbitration agreement; where there has been determination by a court or arbitrator)

- an agreement is void in so far as it purports to provide for a determination in a particular manner or on particular evidence of any question which may be the subject matter of an application under subs.(6).

Chapter 13

Consultation Requirements

Contractual requirements

Express clauses

13–001 Occasionally, the lease itself provides for consultation. This is most likely to be the case in a lease of non-residential premises, where the statutory consultation requirements under the Landlord and Tenant Act 1985 ("LTA 1985") do not apply. If the lease does provide for consultation, the court is likely to hold that these contractual requirements must be followed if the cost is to be recovered under the service charge covenant.

In *CIN Properties Ltd v Barclays Bank plc* [1986] 1 E.G.L.R. 59, the lease provided that the landlord had to obtain estimates or tenders for proposed work, and further that the landlord should not proceed without first submitting the estimate or tender to the tenant for approval (not to be unreasonably withheld or delayed). The landlord failed to comply and the tenant refused to pay the relevant part of the service charge. The court held that compliance was a condition precedent to the landlord's rights to recover the cost of the work under the service charge covenant, and the claim was dismissed.

The same outcome occurred in *Northways Flats Management Co (Camden) Ltd v Wimpey Pension Trustees Ltd* [1992] 2 E.G.L.R. 42. There the lease provided that in the case of major repairs, before carrying out such works the landlord must submit to the tenant the specification of the works and the contractor's estimate for consideration. If the tenant failed to object within 21 days, the lease provided that the tenant be deemed to have accepted the specification and estimate as reasonable. The landlord failed to comply, and the court dismissed the claim to recover the cost of the works under the service charge, again on the basis that compliance with the consultation requirement was a condition precedent to recovery of the costs.

While it is considered that these cases are indicative of the courts' general approach to contractual consultation requirements, each was a decision on the construction of a particular lease. If a lease is drafted so as to provide for consultation as a condition precedent to recovery of service charge, failure to comply with contractual consultation requirements will render the service charge irrecoverable. It is conceivable, however, that a lease might be drafted in such a way that, on its true construction, compliance with the consultation requirement is not a condition precedent to recovery of the corresponding costs through the service charge. In such circumstances a failure to comply will not provide the tenant with a defence to a claim for the costs as part of the service charge.

Implied terms as to consultation

13–002 Applying the conventional tests for the implication of terms into a contract (see paragraph 1–010), it would seem unlikely that any term as to prior consultation would be implied into a lease. Such prior consultation would not be necessary for a lease to work satisfactorily, and indeed there are tens of different ways in which a consultation requirement could be drafted.

Interrelationship with LTA 1985

13–003 The statutory consultation requirements under ss.20 and 20ZA of the LTA 1985 do not override any contractual requirement. Therefore, if a lease of a dwelling included contractual consultation requirements, the landlord would have to comply with both those and the statutory requirements (subject to any application to dispense with the statutory requirements).

The statutory power (now under s.20ZA(1) of the LTA 1985) to dispense with statutory consultation requirements does not empower the court to dispense with any contractual requirements.

Statutory consultation requirements

Checklist

13–004 The following statutory consultation requirements may apply:

- Sections 20 and 20ZA of the LTA 1985 as amended by s.151 of the Commonhold and Leasehold Reform Act 2002. Section

151 of the Commonhold and Leasehold Reform Act 2002 came into force on October 31, 2003.

- The Service Charges (Consultation Requirements) (England) Regulations 2003 as amended by the Service Charges (Consultation Requirements) (Amendment) (No.2) (England) Regulations 2004. The Service Charges (Consultation Requirements) (England) Regulations 2003 came into force on October 31, 2003 whilst the Service Charges (Consultation Requirements) (Amendment) (No.2) (England) Regulations 2004 came into force on November 12, 2004.
- Section 30B of the LTA 1985 (specific to managing agents)—see paragraph 6–004.

Sections 20 and 20ZA of the LTA 1985 requirements

13–005 In a case to which it applies, the LTA 1985 requires consultation as a pre-condition to the recoverability of service charge contributions from tenants over a certain financial level.

The applicability of the LTA 1985 is dealt with in detail in Chapter 4 but, broadly, it applies to tenancies of dwellings.

Old consultation requirements—prior to October 31, 2003

13–006 By s.20 of the Landlord and Tenant Act 1985, costs incurred on carrying out qualifying works (discussed later) over and above a prescribed limit shall not be taken into account in determining the amount of service charge unless the relevant requirements as to consultation have been complied with or, dispensed with by the court. The statutory maximum limit is the greater of £50 multiplied by the number of units or £1,000 or such other sum as may be prescribed under the Service Charge (Estimates and Consultation) Order 1988 (SI 1988/1285).

The original s.20 of the LTA 1985 applies to works begun before October 31, 2003 (in England) and March 30, 2004 (in Wales), in relation to which the landlord has given or displayed a notice under s.20 before the commencement date or are carried out within two months of the commencement date pursuant to an agreement with the landlord made before the commencement date. The transitional provisions are set out in the Service Charges (Estimates and Consultation) Order 1988 (SI 1988/1285).

The power of the *court* (old s.20(9) of the LTA 1985) (but not the LVT) to dispense with the consultation is subject to reasonableness;

it is not generally available. There must be a reasonable explanation for non-compliance. Where the statutory maximum is exceeded, it is reasonable for the landlord to consult thereafter: *Martin v Maryland Estates Limited* [1999] 2 E.G.L.R. 53, CA.

The court (and not the LVT) remains, even after the introduction of s.151 of the Commonhold and Leasehold Reform Act 2002, the only venue in which to bring applications to dispense with service of a s.20 notice in respect of qualifying works covered by the old s.20 of the LTA 1985.

New consultation requirements—after October 31, 2003

13–007 The former consultation provisions, contained in s.20 of the LTA 1985, are repealed and replaced by an entirely new s.20 and s.20ZA of the Landlord and Tenant Act 1985 (inserted by s.151 of the Commonhold and Leasehold Reform Act 2002) and by the further detailed requirements laid down in The Service Charges (Consultation Requirements) (England) Regulations 2003 ("the Consultation Regulations").

The new requirements apply in England from October 31, 2003 and in Wales from March 30, 2004. They apply to qualifying works and qualifying long-term agreements over a prescribed amount which amount is set by regulations made by the Secretary of State pursuant to s.20(5) of the LTA.

Sections 20 and 20ZA of the LTA 1985 and the Consultation Regulations lay down a statutory procedure for prior consultation before service charges may be recovered. These provisions are additional to any consultation procedures that may be laid down in the lease itself.

The procedure laid down in the Consultation Regulations is very much more extensive and rigorous than was provided for under the old s.20 of the LTA 1985 and cases on the old s.20 of the LTA 1985 (and its predecessors) must be treated with caution.

It is now the "relevant contribution" of the tenants that is limited where there is non-compliance by the landlord with any consultation procedures.

In an effort to deal with the problem of recurring items of expenditure, specific provision is now made for consultation on what are now defined as qualifying long term agreements (discussed later).

Basic mechanism of the consultation regime

Section 20(1) and 20(2) of the LTA 1985 provide that: **13–008**

"(1) Where this section applies to any qualifying works or qualifying long term agreement, the relevant contributions of tenants are limited in accordance with subsection (6) or (7) (or both) unless the consultation requirements have been either—

(a) complied with in relation to the works or agreement, or
(b) dispensed with in relation to the works or agreement by (or on appeal from) a leasehold valuation tribunal.

(2) In this section "relevant contribution", in relation to a tenant and any works or agreement, is the amount which he may be required under the terms of his lease to contribute (by the payment of service charges) to relevant costs incurred on carrying out the works or under the agreement."

The meaning of "qualifying works" is discussed in paragraph 13–009 below. The meaning of "qualifying long term agreement" (usually abbreviated to "QLTA") is discussed in paragraph 13–015 below.

The underlying mechanism of the consultation requirements contained within sections 20(1) and 20(2) of the LTA 1985 is straightforward:

- unless the consultation requirements are complied with, the amount that a tenant can be required to contribute to the relevant costs is capped;
- if the consultation requirements are not complied with, the landlord's only escape is to persuade the LVT to dispense with the requirements.

It should be noted that it is only liability to contribute to the relevant costs that is capped, so that if, for example, the consultation requirements only applied to one item out of five in a service charge account, the tenant's liability to pay the costs relating to the other four items would remain unaffected.

Definition of "qualifying works"

Section 20ZA(2) of the LTA 1985 provides that "qualifying works" means works on a building or any other premises. **13–009**

"Works" are not defined in either s.20 or s.20ZA of the LTA 1985 or in the Consultation Regulations. Reference to s.18 of the LTA 1985, however, demonstrates that the term "works" does not include "services".

It is plain whether or not some common service charge items are "works". Agents' fees are plainly "services" not "works", whereas repairs are plainly "works" not "services". Difficult questions can however arise in practice. To take the example of retaining a caretaker, taking on an employee and making payments for his wages is a service, but retaining a contractor to maintain the garden would probably be "works".

One set of "works" or several sets of "works"?

13–010 A question frequently arises as to what represents one set of works. Landlords may be tempted to split works contracts up so that the value of each contract is below the consultation level.

This point arose in *Martin v Maryland Estates* (1999) 2 E.G.L.R. 53. It was held that a landlord was not entitled artificially to split up works into separate contracts. It was further held that where additional work was found necessary during the course of carrying out works in respect of which consultation had taken place, further consultation was necessary, as the additional work formed part of the same works and ought to have been consulted upon. On the other hand, depending on the circumstances, it may be appropriate to split a contract in two parts to permit further consultation once, say, opening up work has been carried out.

Where the line is to be drawn, whether a scheme of repairs is one set of works or more than one, can raise difficult questions and is a question of fact in each case. As Robert Walker L.J. stated in *Martin v Maryland Estates* (1999) 2 E.G.L.R. 53 at 57, since Parliament has not attempted to spell out any precise test, a common-sense approach is necessary.

Supervision costs

13–011 On larger contracts, it may well be necessary and prudent for the employer landlord to retain a clerk of works, supervising architects, quantity surveyors and so forth.

In cases where damages are awarded for disrepair, the cost of repair includes the costs deriving from the supervision of those repairs. It is submitted that the better view is that such costs form part of the costs of works and are not a separate cost. Therefore by analogy the cost of supervision should form part of the calculation of the cost of works for the purposes of the qualifying cost threshold for consultation.

Application of consultation requirements to qualifying works

13–012 Section 20(3) of the LTA 1985 provides that the consultation requirements apply to qualifying works if the relevant costs incurred on carrying out the works exceed an appropriate amount.

The "appropriate amount" is a threshold level for the relevant costs set by regulations made by the Secretary of State. The purpose of there being a threshold level is to exclude works of limited value from the consultation requirements where the cost of the landlord's compliance with the requirements would exceed the potential benefit to the tenants in reducing an already small bill by a few pounds.

Section 20(5) of the LTA 1985 provides that:

> "(5) An appropriate amount is an amount set by regulations made by the Secretary of State; and the regulations may make provision for either or both of the following to be an appropriate amount—
> (a) an amount prescribed by, or determined in accordance with, the regulations, and
> (b) an amount which results in the relevant contribution of any one or more tenants being an amount prescribed by, or determined in accordance with, the regulations."

The LTA 1985 therefore permits the appropriate amount to be fixed on two distinct bases.

The s.20(5)(a) basis is a single fixed sum or a sum calculable under regulations made by the Secretary of State. This basis reflects the thresholds under the old s.20 of the LTA 1985 where the consultation requirements were triggered if the cost of works exceeded £50 per lessee or £1,000 (whichever was greater).

The s.20(5)(b) basis is new and is a sum referable to the service charge contribution of any one or more tenants. In effect, this means that, in those blocks where service charge contributions vary from flat to flat, one looks at the contribution to the cost of the works in question payable by the tenant liable for the highest proportion of service charge under his lease. At the date of publication the threshold is more than £250.

13–013 In respect of qualifying works, the Secretary of State opted for the s.20(5)(b) basis.

Regulation 6 of the Consultation Regulations provides that for the purposes of s.20(3) of the LTA 1985 and qualifying works the appropriate amount is an amount which results in the relevant contribution of any tenant being more than £250.

Since the appropriate amount is fixed by reference to the contribution of individual tenants, the cost of the works needed to trigger the consultation requirements will differ from block to block depending upon how many tenants there are among whom the service charge is divided. It will also depend upon how the service charge is split between the tenants. One tenant's contribution for a penthouse flat, for which he pays twice as much service charge as any other tenant in the block, may cross the £250 threshold when the other tenants' contributions are still well below that level.

In such a circumstance, a landlord might conclude that it would be more advantageous for him to accept that any service charge claim against that one lessee be limited by the provisions of the LTA 1985 to £250 in order to avoid the costs and aggravation of consultation. It will be recalled (see paragraph 13–008 above) that s.20(1) of the LTA 1985 provides that where there is a failure to consult, the tenant's contribution is limited to the figure set out in s.20(7) of the LTA 1985.

Section 20(7) provides that:

> "(7) Where an appropriate amount is set by virtue of [s.20(5)(b)], the amount of the relevant contribution of the tenant, or each of the tenants, whose relevant contribution would otherwise exceed the amount prescribed by, or determined in accordance with, the regulations is limited to the amount so prescribed or determined."

Therefore, if only one tenant's contribution is over the appropriate amount, a failure to consult will limit that tenant's contribution to £250 but will not effect the service charge contributions of the other tenants.

Qualifying long term agreements

13–014 Sections 20 and 20ZA of the LTA 1985 introduce the new concept of the qualifying long term agreement ("QLTA"). This is intended to meet the difficulty that arose in practice when applying the old s.20 of the LTA 1985 to situations where a landlord had entered into agreements for periods which extended into more than one service charge year and/or gave rise to recurring expenditure.

It is crucial to appreciate that the purpose of introducing the QLTA regime was not necessarily to enhance tenants' rights in respect of long term agreements. On the contrary, the new regime was introduced to permit landlords to enter into long term agreements with a "once only" consultation process and then to disapply the usual consultation requirements from works carried out pursuant to a long term agreement.

In short, the QLTA concept was largely driven by a desire to facilitate PFI deals by local authority landlords and to make it easier for such local authority landlords to enter into long-term contracts for the management or maintenance of their housing stock without having to consider alternative contractors or quotes for each set of works. Once a QLTA is in place it is of great benefit to the landlord not to have to comply with consultation requirements.

Definition of qualifying long term agreements

13–015 Section 20ZA(2) of the LTA 1985 defines a QLTA in broad and simple terms as, subject to s.20ZA(3) of the LTA 1985, an agreement entered into, by or on behalf of the landlord or a superior landlord, for a term of more than 12 months.

As a result of this broad definition, the subject matter of QLTAs extends beyond "works". Therefore any agreement relating to a matter falling within the basic definition of "service charge" in s.18(1) of the LTA 1985 is potentially a QLTA.

Exceptions to s.20ZA(2) of the LTA 1985

13–016 Section 20ZA(3) of the LTA 1985 permits the Secretary of State to make regulations excluding classes of agreement from being QLTAs. This power has been exercised and a list of exceptions is found in reg.3 of the Consultation Regulations (see Appendix A). The principal exceptions are contracts of employment and the costs of management by a local housing authority.

There will hence be no service charge recoupment cap imposed on a landlord who, without consulting his tenants, enters into a long term agreement that is not a QLTA as defined by reg.3 of the Consultation Regulations.

Application of consultation requirements to QLTAs

13–017 Section 20(4) of the LTA 1985 provides that:

"(4) The Secretary of State may by regulations provide that this section applies to a qualifying long term agreement—

(a) if relevant costs incurred under the agreement exceed an appropriate amount, or

(b) if relevant costs incurred under the agreement during a period prescribed by the regulations exceed an appropriate amount."

As explained in paragraph 13–012, s.20(5) of the LTA 1985 provides that an appropriate amount is an amount set by regulations and is determined on one of two bases.

The appropriate amount

13–018 The Secretary of State followed his approach in respect of qualifying works and opted to apply the s.20(5)(b) basis when calculating the appropriate amount in respect of QLTAs. As will be remembered from paragraph 13–012, the s.20(5)(b) basis is a sum referable to the service charge contribution of any one or more tenants and therefore one looks at the contribution payable by the tenant liable for the highest proportion of service charge under his lease.

The set amount for the appropriate amount in respect of QLTAs is laid down in reg.4 of the Consultation Regulations (see Appendix A) as being more than £100. This is intended to catch more agreements and ensure that initial consultation takes place under the regime applicable to QLTAs since, once the QLTA is in place, further consultation in respect of works under the QLTA is not required.

Regulation 4 of the Consultation Regulations is less straightforward than the equivalent reg.6 provision for qualifying works. This is inevitable however because of the long term nature of QLTAs.

The relevant date

13–019

- Regulation 4 of the Consultation Regulations is based upon the premise that conventional service charge provisions levy the service charge by reference to accounting periods, usually of one year. The accounting period begins with the relevant date and ends on the date that falls 12 months after the relevant date.

- Where the service charge accounting period under the lease is annual, for the first accounting period the relevant date would be the date upon which the 12 month service charge period that includes October 31, 2003 (the date that the Consultation Regulations came into force) ends. In the unusual case where the service charge accounting period is not annual, the relevant date for the first accounting period is October 31, 2003.

- Under reg.4(3A) of the Consultation Regulations, where a landlord intends to enter into a QLTA on or after November 12, 2004 (the date that the Service Charges (Consultation Requirements) (Amendment) (No.2) (England) Regulations 2004 came into force) and that same landlord has not at any time between October 31, 2003 and November 12, 2004 prepared service charge accounts referable to a QLTA and payable in respect of the dwellings to which the intended agreement is to relate, the relevant date is the date upon which the first 12 month service charge period begins (for which service charges are payable) under the terms of the leases of the dwellings.
- In the case of all subsequent accounting periods, the relevant date will be the date immediately after the last date of the previous accounting period. The effect of reg.4(4) of the Consultation Regulations is that each subsequent accounting period will be a period of 12 months.

As provided by s.20(7) of the LTA 1985, a failure to consult in respect of a QLTA will limit each qualifying tenant's contribution to costs payable in respect of the QLTA to £100 per service charge year. Section 20(7) of the LTA 1985 is set out in paragraph 13–013 above. Given that the costs payable under a QLTA may fluctuate, a failure to comply with consultation requirements under a QLTA may have very serious consequences. The option of deliberate non-consultation that may sometimes be attractive to landlords in respect of qualifying works where only one tenant qualifies is unlikely to recommend itself in respect of QLTAs. Since the appropriate amount is only £100 and it may prove difficult to forecast if any (and how many) of the tenants' contributions will be higher than this amount, it is always advisable for a landlord to consult on a QLTA in advance.

Consultation Regulations

13–020 Regulation 1(3) of the Consultation Regulations states that the Consultation Regulations will apply where a landlord:

(a) intends to enter into a "qualifying long term agreement" to which s.20 of the Landlord and Tenant Act 1985 applies on or after the date on which these Regulations come into force [October 31, 2003]; or

(b) intends to carry out qualifying works to which that section applies on or after that date.

Introduction

13–021 The draftsman of the Commonhold and Leasehold Reform Act 2002 adopted the modern approach of laying down a fairly general power in subss.(5)–(7) of s.20ZA of the LTA 1985 to make regulations laying down consultation requirements. The Consultation Regulations contain requirements very much more stringent than those found in the old s.20 of the LTA 1985.

Consultation requirements

13–022 The consultation requirements in respect of QLTAs and qualifying works are set out in the Schedules to the Consumer Regulations, as identified by regs 5 and 7 of the Consultation Regulations respectively (see Appendix A).

Right to buy leases

13–023 As can be seen from reg.5(3) and reg.7(5) of the Consultation Regulations, exceptions exist that provide that in respect of a right to buy lease a landlord does not have to comply with any QLTA consultation requirements before the 31st day of the tenancy.

Transitional provisions in respect of qualifying works

13–024 Regulations 7(2) and 7(3) of the Consultation Regulations contain in effect a limited transitional provision by which the Sch.3 consultation requirements (usually applicable only where a QLTA is in place) apply to certain qualifying works as set out in reg.7(3) of the Consultation Regulations. Regulation 7(3) of the Consultation Regulations applies where:

(a) qualifying works are carried out at any time on or after December 31, 2003 under an agreement entered into by or on behalf of the landlord or a superior landlord before October 31, 2003; or

(b) qualifying works for which public notice has been given before October 31, 2003 are carried out at any time on or after October 31, 2003 under an agreement for a term of more than 12 months entered into by or on behalf of the landlord or a superior landlord.

The consultation requirements of the new s.20 of the LTA 1985 do not apply however to certain qualifying works which are contained in s.3 of the Commonhold and Leasehold Reform Act 2002 (Commencement No.2 and Savings) (England) Order 2003 (SI 2003/1986):

(a) where work is begun before October 31, 2003;

(b) where a s.20 notice has been served before October 31, 2003;

(c) where, in respect of a contract for 12 or less months entered into on or after October 31, 2003, a public notice was served before October 31, 2003;

(d) work carried out and completed at any time between October 31, 2003 and December 31, 2003.

Schedules

13–025 The application of the Schedules to the Consultation Regulations setting out the various consultation requirements is as follows:

(a) Part 2 of Sch.4 to the Consultation Regulations contains the basic scheme applicable to qualifying works where there is no QLTA in place;

(b) Part 1 of Sch.4 to the Consultation Regulations contains a slightly different scheme for qualifying works where no QLTA is in place which is applicable where the European Union derived procurement regimes apply (only applicable to public bodies);

(c) Schedule 3 of the Consultation Regulations contains the (fairly limited) basic scheme in respect of qualifying works where a QLTA is in place;

(d) Schedule 1 of the Consultation Regulations contains the basic scheme applicable to QLTAs; and

(e) Schedule 2 of the Consultation Regulations contains a slightly different scheme for QLTAs that is applicable where the European Union derived procurement regimes apply (only applicable to public bodies).

Terminology used in the Schedules

"Notice of Intention"

13–026 This was what used to be known as a "section 20 notice" but it is now more appropriate to adopt the nomenclature of the Consultation

Regulations. The landlord must give notice in writing of his intentions to each tenant and, where applicable, to a recognised tenants' association ("RTA"). The notice should set out the proposed work or relevant matters, or instead specify a place and time at which a description of the proposed work or relevant matters can be inspected. It should also state the landlord's reasons for considering it necessary to carry out the proposed work or enter into the agreement. It should invite the submission of written observations in respect of the proposed work or the proposed agreement, stating the address to which the observations should be sent, that observations must be submitted within the relevant time and the date upon which the relevant period ends. Under Sch.1, Sch.2 and Sch.4 Pt 2, the notice should also invite each tenant or RTA to propose the name of an individual from whom the landlord should try to obtain an estimate. Under Sch.3 and Sch.4 Pt 1, it is instead necessary for the landlord to include a statement of the total estimated expenditure.

"Relevant period"

13–027 Regulation 2(1) of the Consultation Regulations sets out the relevant period in respect of a notice as meaning the period of 30 days beginning with the date of the notice.

"Relevant matters"

13–028 Regulation 2(1) of the Consultation Regulations provides that the relevant matters, in relation to a proposed agreement, mean the goods or services to be provided or the works to be carried out (as the case may be) under the agreement.

Inspection

13–029 Where a notice specifies a place and time for inspection, the place and time specified must be reasonable and the landlord must make available at that place and time a description of the proposed works or relevant matters for inspection, free of charge. If copies of the description cannot be taken at the time, the landlord must provide a copy of the description to any tenant upon request, free of charge.

Observations

13–030 Where any tenant or RTA makes observations within the relevant period, the landlord shall have regard to those observations. The duty of the landlord in such circumstances appears to be limited, although under certain Schedules he will be required to respond in writing to any observations submitted.

Estimates

13–031 Under Sch.1 and Sch.4 Pt 2 the notice of intention invites any tenant or RTA to submit the name of an individual from whom the landlord should try to obtain an estimate for the proposed works or relevant matters. The process for obtaining estimates is as follows:

(a) if a single nomination is made by an RTA, the landlord should try to obtain an estimate from that nominated person;

(b) if a single nomination is made by only one of the tenants, the landlord should try to obtain an estimate from that nominated person;

(c) if a single nomination is made by more than one tenant, the landlord should try to obtain an estimate from the person who received the most nominations, or, if there is no such person but two (or more) persons received the same number of nominations (being a number of nominations in excess of the nominations received by any other person), the landlord should try to obtain an estimate from one of those two (or more) persons. In any other case the landlord should try to obtain an estimate from any nominated person; and

(d) if more than one nomination is made by any tenant and more than one nomination is made by a RTA, the landlord should try to obtain an estimate from at least one person nominated by a tenant and at least one person nominated by a RTA (other than a person nominated by a tenant from whom an estimate is already being sought).

Provisional figures

13–032 It sometimes arises in practice that a contractor provides only a provisional or estimated sum for elements of the proposed works. An example would be a provision for the cost of dry rot works within a wider contract for structural repair.

Various issues arise. To what extent is a notice including a provisional or estimated sum valid? Can a landlord recover a higher sum if the provisional sum turns out to be insufficient? In answer to the former question there will be certain dangers in respect of validity. In response to the latter question, the answer is no (see *Martin v Maryland Estates* (1999) 2 E.G.L.R. 53).

Connection

13–033 In certain circumstances the Consultation Regulations require that the landlord obtain an estimate from an individual that is wholly unconnected with him. It shall be assumed that there exists a connection between a landlord and another party in the following circumstances:

(a) where the landlord is a company, if the party is, or is to be, a director or manager of the company or is a close relative of any such director or manager;

(b) where the landlord is a company, and the party is a partner in the partnership, if any partner in that partnership is, or is to be, a director or manager of the company or is a close relative of any such director or manager;

(c) where both the landlord and the party are companies, if any director or manager of one company is, or is to be, a director or manager of the other company;

(d) where the party is a company, if the landlord is a director or manager of the company or is a close relative of any such director or manager; or

(e) where the party is a company and the landlord is partner in a partnership, if any partner in that partnership is a director or manager of the company or is a close relative of any such director or manager.

Consultation in respect of qualifying works, no QLTA applying

13–034 This is probably the most common situation in practice, so it seems appropriate to deal with it first. The consultation requirements are set out in Pt 2 of Sch.4 to the Consultation Regulations (see Appendix A).

Overview

13–035

(1) The landlord serves a "notice of intention" on all tenants and any RTA describing the proposed works;

(2) The tenants or RTA then have 30 days to:

  (a) make observations as to the works proposed;
  (b) nominate a person or persons from whom the landlord should try to obtain an estimate for the carrying out of the proposed works;

(3) The landlord then obtains a minimum of two estimates:

  (a) he must try to obtain an estimate from one and in some cases two of the tenants' nominees;

(b) at least one estimate must be from a contractor wholly unconnected with the landlord;

(4) The landlord serves on all tenants and any RTA a "paragraph (b) statement" free of charge summarising at least two of the estimates, setting out any observations received and his response to observations. All estimates should be made available for inspection;

(5) At the same time, the landlord should make the estimates available to all tenants and any RTA, inviting observations on the estimates. The tenants or RTA have 30 days to respond;

(6) The landlord is obliged to consider the observations but is otherwise free to enter into a contract for the carrying out of the works if he contracts either with a person nominated by the tenants or RTA or with the person who supplied the lowest estimate;

(7) Otherwise, the landlord must within 21 days of entering into the contract serve notice on the tenants or RTA stating his reasons for awarding the contract, setting out observations received, and his response to those observations.

Consultation in respect of qualifying works, QLTA applying

13–036 By way of contrast with the extensive consultation scheme applicable where there is no QLTA, the consultation requirements in respect of qualifying works under a QLTA are very limited. This is inevitable, as once a QLTA is in place the contractor will usually have the exclusive right to carry out the proposed works, and very often it will be the contractor that has decided that the works need to be done.

The relevant consultation requirements are set out in Sch.3 to the Consultation Regulations (see Appendix A).

Overview

13–037

(1) The landlord serves a "notice of intention" on all tenants and any RTA describing the proposed works and inviting observations;

(2) The tenants or RTA then have 30 days to make any observations as to the works proposed and as to the landlord's estimated expenditure;

(3) The landlord is obliged to consider the observations and must within 21 days of receipt of observations state his response by notice to the person who made the observations;

(4) Otherwise the landlord is free to carry out the works.

Consultation in respect of QLTAs

13–038 As a quid pro quo for the advantages of a QLTA, the consultation scheme applicable where the landlord proposes to enter into a QLTA is the most extensive of all the schemes laid out in the Consultation Regulations.

The relevant consultation requirements, in respect of QLTAs to which the public procurement regime does not apply, are set out in Sch.1 to the Consultation Regulations. The differences between this scheme and that which applies to public bodies where the public procurement regime is applicable, are dealt with in paragraph 13–042 below, but the principal difference is that where the public procurement regime applies, the tenants do not have the right to nominate a contractor from whom an estimate must be sought.

Overview

13–039 (1) The landlord serves a "notice of intention" to enter into the QLTA on all tenants and any RTA describing the goods or services to be supplied or works to be carried out under the QLTA and his reasons for wishing to enter into the QLTA;

(2) The tenants or RTA then have 30 days to:

- (a) make observations as to the proposed QLTA;
- (b) nominate a person or persons from whom the landlord should try to obtain an estimate for the carrying out of the goods or services to be supplied or works to be carried out under the QLTA;

(3) The landlord then obtains a minimum of two estimates:

- (a) He must try to obtain an estimate from one and in some cases two of the tenants' nominees;
- (b) At least one estimate must be from a contractor unconnected with the landlord;

(4) The landlord prepares at least two "proposals" for the carrying out of the goods or services to be supplied or works to be carried out, at least one of which must be by a person unconnected with

the landlord and one of which must be based on an estimate from a nominated person;

(5) The landlord serves the proposals on all tenants and any RTA inviting observations on the proposals. All proposals should be made available for inspection;

(6) The proposals should include:

   (a) where it is reasonably practicable for the landlord to estimate the relevant contribution of each tenant, a statement of that estimated contribution;
   (b) alternatively where it is reasonably practicable for the landlord to estimate the total amount of his expenditure, a statement of that estimated expenditure;
   (c) alternatively where it is reasonably practicable for the landlord to ascertain the current unit cost or hourly or daily rate applicable to the relevant matters, a statement of that cost or rate;
   (d) if the landlord proposes to appoint an agent in his place, a statement containing details of the membership of that proposed agent to any professional body or trade association and the agent's subscription to any code of practice or voluntary accreditation scheme;
   (e) a statement as to the provisions (if any) for variation of any amount specified or determined under the proposed agreement;
   (f) a statement of the intended duration of the proposed agreement;
   (g) the landlord's response to any observations received.

(7) Tenants/RTA have 30 days to respond with observations;

(8) The landlord is obliged to consider the observations but is otherwise free to enter into a QLTA if he contracts either with a person nominated by the tenants/RTA or with the person who supplied the lowest estimate;

(9) Otherwise, the landlord must within 21 days of entering into the agreement serve notice on the tenants/RTA stating his reasons for entering into the agreement, setting out observations received, and his response to observations.

Consultation in respect of qualifying works, no QLTA applying, EU derived procurement regime applying

13–040 The Consultation Regulations make reference to works for which public notice is required. These are works where the sum of money involved will be of a level where European Union public procurement rules apply. In such cases the proposed works must be advertised by public notice in the Official Journal of the European Union. While the tenants are invited to submit their observations, they do not have a right to nominate a contractor for these works. The relevant consultation provisions are set out in Sch.4 Pt 1 to the Consultation Regulations.

Overview

13–041 (1) The landlord serves a "notice of intention" to carry out qualifying works on all tenants and any RTA describing the goods or services to be supplied or works to be carried out and his reasons for considering it necessary to carry out the proposed work. The notice should also state that the reason why the landlord is not inviting nominations for contractors is because public notice of the relevant matters is to be given;

(2) The tenants or RTA then have 30 days to make observations as to the proposed works;

(3) The landlord then prepares a statement in respect of the proposed contract. The proposal should contain a statement of the name and address of every party to the proposed agreement and any connection between a party and the landlord;

(4) The proposal should include:

(a) where it is reasonably practicable for the landlord to estimate the relevant contribution of each tenant, a statement of that estimated contribution;
(b) alternatively, where it is reasonably practicable for the landlord to estimate the total amount of his expenditure, a statement of that estimated expenditure;
(c) alternatively, where it is reasonably practicable for the landlord to ascertain the current unit cost or hourly or daily rate applicable to the relevant matters, a statement of that cost or rate;
(d) alternatively, a statement of the reasons why the landlord cannot provide a statement of cost or rate and the date by which he expects to be able to provide an estimate;
(e) the landlord's response to any observations received.

(5) The proposal should be served on the tenants/RTA who then have 30 days to respond with observations;

(6) The landlord is obliged to consider the observations and must within 21 days of receipt of observations state his response by notice to the person who made the observations.

Consultation in respect of QLTAs, EU derived procurement regime applying

13–042 The Consultation Regulations also make reference to QLTAs for which public notice is required. These are agreements where the sum of money involved will be of a level where European Union public procurement rules apply, with the proposed agreement needing to be advertised by public notice in the Official Journal of the European Union. While the tenants are invited to submit any observations that they wish to make, they do not have a right to nominate a contractor for these agreements. The relevant consultation provisions are set out in Sch.5 Pt 2 to the Consultation Regulations.

Overview

13–043

(1) The landlord serves a "notice of intention" to enter into the QLTA on all tenants and any RTA describing the goods or services to be supplied or works to be carried out under the QLTA and his reasons for wishing to enter into the QLTA. The notice should also state that the reason why the landlord is not inviting nominations for contractors is because public notice of the relevant matters is to be given.

(2) The tenants or RTA then have 30 days to make observations as to the proposed QLTA;

(3) The landlord then prepares a "proposal" in respect of the proposed agreement. The proposal should contain a statement of the name and address of every party to the proposed agreement and any connection between a party and the landlord;

(4) The proposal should include:

   (a) where it is reasonably practicable for the landlord to estimate the relevant contribution of each tenant, a statement of that estimated contribution;
   (b) alternatively, where it is reasonably practicable for the landlord to estimate the total amount of his expenditure, a statement of that estimated expenditure;
   (c) alternatively, where it is reasonably practicable for the landlord to ascertain the current unit cost or hourly or daily rate applicable to the relevant matters, a statement of that cost or rate;

(d) alternatively, a statement of the reasons why the landlord cannot provide a statement of cost or rate and the date by which he expects to be able to provide an estimate;
(e) if the landlord proposes to appoint an agent in his place, a statement containing details of the membership of that proposed agent to any professional body or trade association and the agent's subscription to any code of practice or voluntary accreditation scheme;
(f) a statement of the intended duration of the proposed agreement;
(g) the landlord's response to any observations received.

(5) The proposal should be served on the tenants/RTA who then have 30 days to respond with observations;

(6) The landlord is obliged to consider the observations and must within 21 days of receipt of observations state his response by notice to the person who made the observations.

Dispensation with the requirements of consultation

13–044 The LVT is given power under s.20(1)(b) of the LTA 1985 to dispense with the consultation requirements. Section 20ZA(1) of the LTA 1985 states that where an application is made to the LVT for a determination to dispense with all or any of the consultation requirements in relation to any qualifying works or qualifying long term agreement, the tribunal may make the determination if satisfied that it is reasonable to dispense with the requirements.

"Reasonable"

13–045 Section 20ZA of the LTA 1985 does not elaborate on when it might be reasonable to dispense with the consultation requirements. It is submitted, however, that when a question arises as to whether it is reasonable to make an order, it is necessary to give consideration to all relevant factors.

It should be noted that under s.20ZA of the LTA 1985, the LVT only has to be satisfied that it is reasonable to dispense with consultation requirements. The section does not require the tribunal to be satisfied that the landlord has acted reasonably. This is in marked contrast with the old s.20(9) provision that the court could dispense with consultation requirements if it was satisfied that the landlord had acted reasonably.

Indeed under the old s.20 provisions, it was the court, and not the LVT, that had the power to dispense with consultation requirements. It seems unfortunate that the new s.20 has wholly removed from the court the power to dispense with the consultation requirements, while the court retains in parallel to the LVT its jurisdiction under s.19 of the LTA 1985 in respect of reasonableness of service charge and its general contractual jurisdiction to deal with service charge disputes.

If the landlord is aware before the event that it is likely that the consultation requirements cannot be complied with, a pre-emptive application must be made before commencing the work. The section confers a discretion as to whether to dispense with consultation, and the LVT is unlikely to be sympathetic to applications after the event in circumstances where the application could and should have been made earlier. To permit such applications, even where the works were otherwise not subject to challenge, would be to render the consultation requirements optional.

The consultation paper gave, as an example of a situation where a pre-emptive application would be appropriate, the case where only one contractor could possibly carry out certain works. The example given was repairs to an alarm system where only the installer could carry out maintenance.

The plain intent in permitting after the event applications is to provide for situations where it is not possible to comply with the consultation requirements and not possible to make an application to dispense with the requirements prior to carrying out the works. This will generally require some sort of emergency or urgency. It is submitted that the bare fact that the relevant costs were reasonably incurred and/or works were of a reasonable standard is unlikely to be sufficient ground to obtain a dispensation from the consultation requirements

13–046 In *Wilson v Stone* (1998) 28 E.G. 153 (LVT), a building in which flats were situated was found to be in danger of collapse and the landlord immediately contracted with a builder for urgent work to alleviate the immediate danger. The LVT granted the landlord's retrospective application to dispense with the consultation requirement. It is noteworthy that although the LVT acted in this way, it did not in fact have jurisdiction to dispense with the consultation requirements. This is because the LVT hearing of *Wilson v Stone* pre-dated the introduction on October 31, 2003 of the LVT's new power to dispense with the consultation requirements under s.20(1)(b) of the LTA 1985. As set out in paragraph 13–006 above, under the old s.20(9) of the LTA 1985 and prior to October 31, 2003 it was only "the court" that had the relevant jurisdiction to deal with applications to dispense with consultation requirements.

This principle must not however be stretched too far. Sections 20/20ZA of the LTA 1985 are there for the protection of the tenants and are there to be complied with. Retrospective dispensation for emergency work should be limited to such work as is necessary to deal with the emergency itself; further work should await compliance with the consultation requirements.

Consequently, it is difficult to envisage circumstances in which a retrospective application to dispense with the requirements to consult before entering a QLTA could succeed.

It should be noted that the dispensation power under s.20 of the LTA 1985 applies only to the statutory consultation requirements. It confers no power to dispense with any consultation requirement which may be present in the lease itself: *Northways Flats Management Co (Camden) Ltd v Wimpey Pension Trustees Ltd* [1992] 2 E.G.L.R. 42 (CA) (see paragraph 13–001).

Failure to comply with s.20

13–047 The consequence of failure either to comply with ss.20 and 20ZA of the LTA 1985 and the Consultation Regulations, or to obtain a dispensation, is set out in s.20(1), (6) and (7) of the LTA 1985: the relevant contributions of the tenants are limited to the "appropriate amount" fixed by regulations under s.20(5) of the LTA 1985.

Failure to comply with ss.20 and 20ZA of the LTA 1985 is not a criminal offence.

Consultation requirements relating to commercial properties

13–048 Such leases occasionally include express contractual consultation requirements (see paragraph 13–001). There is no statutory equivalent to ss.20 and 20ZA LTA 1985 applicable to commercial leases.

What there is, however, is "*Service Charges in Commercial Property—a Guide to Good Practice*", first published by the RICS in 1996 and now in a new edition. Paragraph 38 of the Guide recommends, in respect of "substantial works", prior communication to occupiers of "full information on the programme of works, costs and the process to be adopted for keeping occupiers informed."

The Guide professes itself to reflect good practice in the industry. A good landlord will no doubt comply with it. If a landlord does not comply, it has (subject to the caveat below) no teeth and does not affect liability for service charge. It should be noted that the Guide is not a Code of Practice with statutory recognition.

The caveat lies in the courts' powers as to costs. Under CPR 44.3(4), when deciding what order (if any) to make about costs, the court must have regard to (among other circumstances) the conduct of a party to litigation. CPR 44.3(5)(a) makes clear that "conduct" includes conduct prior to the issue of proceedings. It is considered that failure to comply with the RICS Code of Practice is something which the court might take into account when deciding whether to make a costs order in favour of (or against) a landlord, particularly if the judge takes the view that the landlord's uncooperative attitude is one reason why the dispute ended up being the subject of litigation.

Chapter 14

The Machinery of Service Charges—Demands, Certification and Accounts

Service charge contribution

14–001 Older leases occasionally provided for payment by the tenant of fixed service charges, rising year on year by a fixed percentage, or by reference to an inflation index. All modern service charge covenants, however, provide for the tenant to contribute towards the landlord's costs of providing amenities and services. Such clauses frequently provide for an accounting period, often a calendar year, by reference to which the service charge is to be calculated. As has already been discussed in Chapter 1, it is a matter of construction of the lease in question whether the cost of any particular amenity or service provided by the landlord is recoverable through the service charge covenant.

Recovery of future costs?

14–002 Most service charge covenants provide for the tenant to pay a contribution towards the costs or expenses that the landlord has "expended" or "incurred" or which "become payable" by the landlord during an accounting period. In each case, it is a matter of construction of the lease whether the landlord can recover in advance through the service charge such costs or expenses for which he knows he will become liable pursuant to a contract into which he has entered. Such issues might become particularly important should the tenant's term expire after the contract has been entered into, but before the landlord's obligation to pay for the works has arisen.

In general, in the absence of clear words to the contrary, a landlord will only be able to charge to the service charge account costs and expenses which he has paid, or which he has become liable to pay during the accounting period. For example, in *Capital & Counties Freehold Equity Trust Ltd v B L plc* [1987] 2 E.G.L.R. 49, the court was concerned with a tenant's covenant to contribute a proportion of the costs and expenses "which may from time to time during the said term be expended or incurred or become payable". It was argued on behalf of the landlord that "expended" referred to monies actually paid by the landlord, "incurred" referred to monies for which the landlord had become liable but which had not yet been paid, and "become payable" referred to monies for which the landlord had not yet become liable but for which he would do so in due course. The court noted the "surprising results" that would follow should such a construction prevail, and found that, in that lease, the words "incurred" and "become payable" had the same meaning, referring to costs for which the landlord had become liable during the accounting period but which he had not yet actually paid.

In this context, it must be remembered that some leases provide for a sinking fund or reserve fund into which tenants are to pay on a regular basis and from which major capital works are to be paid. Sinking funds are considered in detail in Chapter 16.

Apportioning service charge contributions

14–003 Typically, the landlord's costs of providing amenities or services to a building or to an estate are split between all the various tenants occupying the building or the estate. Most modern, residential leases specify a fixed percentage that is to be paid by the tenant holding under the lease. Older leases, or commercial leases, might instead provide that the tenant's proportion of the service charge is to be calculated by reference to the rateable value of the tenant's demise as compared with the rateable values of the other lettable parts of the building or estate, or by reference to the floorspace demised to the tenant as compared with the floorspace of the other lettable parts of the building or estate. Any provision that the proportion is to be calculated by reference to the ratios of rateable values "from time to time", or by reference to the ratios of floorspace "from time to time", requires the proportion to be recalculated each time the rateable values and/or layouts of any part of the building or estate are changed. Accordingly, if a service charge covenant provides that the tenant's contribution is to be calculated by reference to the ratios of rateable values "from time to time", then, the ratios to be applied are to be based upon the rateable values applying at the time that the landlord paid or incurred each item of cost or expense that he seeks to recover *via* the service charge (*Moorcroft Estates v Doxford* (1980) 254 E.G. 871).

"Fair" or "proper" or "due" or "reasonable" proportion

14–004 Rather than specify any formula by reference to which the tenant's contribution is to be calculated, the lease might simply provide that the tenant is to pay a "fair", or "proper", or "due", or "reasonable" proportion of the costs incurred by the landlord. Such clauses usually provide that it is for the landlord's surveyor to determine what might be such a "fair", "proper", "due" or "reasonable" proportion. In doing so, the landlord's surveyor is acting as an expert, and must act fairly and reasonably to reach a decision that is justifiable. He is likely to take into account the number of lettable parts of the building or estate, the relative rateable values of those lettable parts, the relative floorspaces of those lettable parts, and the relative use which those various lettable parts make of the common amenities and services. It may be, for example, that some parts of a building might consume more heat than other parts of a building. Some tenants may not require the use of lifts. The landlord's surveyor must take all these various factors into account.

In *Scottish Mutual Assurance plc v Jardine Public Relations Ltd* (1999) E.G.C.S. 43, the court was concerned with a lease providing that the tenant pay a "fair proportion" of the costs "reasonably and properly" incurred by the landlord in, amongst other things, repairing and maintaining the structure and exterior of the building. The roof to the building was in significant disrepair, although some patch repairs had recently been carried out. Notwithstanding that the tenant's lease had only a few months left to run, the landlord carried out expensive and long-term repairs, rather than further short-term, patch repairs. Mr Recorder David Blunt Q.C. held that the cost of such long-term repairs was not a cost "reasonably and properly" incurred by the landlord because it was not reasonable *vis-à-vis* the tenant for the landlord to carry out such substantive repair works when short-term patch repairs had only recently been carried out, and the tenant was only going to occupy the building for a few more months. He therefore found that the tenant was liable for 39.88 per cent of the cost of only the short-term repairs. However, he commented, *obiter*, that, if he was wrong and the long-term repairs were "reasonably and properly" incurred by the landlord *vis-à-vis* the tenant, then he would have held that the "fair proportion" of the cost of those long-term repairs to be paid by the tenant should be determined by reference to the fact that the tenant enjoyed the benefit of those long-term repairs for only a few months of their 25–30 year life-span. Such an approach would have produced a very small contribution on the part of the tenant.

It may well be, therefore, that when determining the "fair", or "proper", or "due", or "reasonable" proportion to be paid by a tenant, the landlord's surveyor must also take into account the extent of the tenant's remaining unexpired term, and the extent to which the tenant will benefit from the works.

Interim service charges

14–005 Unless, on the true construction of the lease, payment by the tenant of service charges is a condition precedent to the landlord's repairing obligations, the non-payment of service charges will rarely provide a defence to a tenant's claim for damages for breach of a repairing covenant: see for example *Marenco v Javamel Co Ltd* (1964) 191 E.G. 433; *Francis v Cowcliffe* (1977) 33 P.&C.R. 368).

14–006 Leases frequently provide for the landlord's repairing obligations to be "subject to" or to arise "upon" payment by the tenant of the service charges. In *Yorkbrook Investments v Batten* (1985) 52 P.&C.R. 51, the landlord's repairing obligations were said to be "subject to" the tenant paying the service charge. The Court of Appeal held that, as a matter of construction, it was not a condition precedent to the landlord's repairing obligations that the tenant paid the service charges. Over the years since, *Yorkbrook Investments* had come to be regarded as authority for the proposition that *any* such clause purporting to make a landlord's repairing obligations subject to a condition precedent that the tenant pay the service charges would be of no effect. In *Bluestorm v Portvale Holdings* [2004] 22 E.G. 142, however, Buxton L.J. stated, *obiter*, that he did not regard *Yorkbrook Investments* as binding authority for the proposition that any such clause can *never* be of effect, particularly where (as in *Bluestorm*) the words used in the lease were different from those used in *Yorkbrook Investments*. Sir Martin Nourse also appeared to doubt that *Yorkbrook Investments* was binding authority that such clauses in leases can never be of any effect, although he did not appear to be willing to construe such clauses as literally as Buxton L.J. appeared to be. It was only Maurice Kay L.J. who took the view that *Yorkbrook Investments* was binding on the Court of Appeal and appeared to achieve an acceptable balance. It is presently unclear which of three judicial opinions expressed in *Bluestorm v Portvale Holdings* will prevail.

Further and in any event, a tenant's failure to pay service charges can never be a defence to a claim brought in reliance upon any statutory provisions imposing an obligation upon the landlord to repair (such as s.11 of the Landlord and Tenant Act 1985 or s.4 of the Defective Premises Act 1972).

Therefore, whilst it is of fundamental importance to ensure that the cost of providing services and undertaking works can be recovered from the tenant, it is of great practical importance to ensure that the landlord is in a position, financially, to comply with his obligations as and when they arise. The provision of a reserve or sinking fund may ameliorate the position of the landlord in respect of items which can be paid for from that fund and wholly from that fund, but in respect of the more mundane and regular annual expenses the solution for the landlord is a properly drafted provision in the lease allowing him to make interim or on-account demands in respect of service charges.

Older leases usually required either payment towards actual expenditure when demanded, or an advance payment of a fixed sum (sometimes with reference to the previous accounting year). Modern leases tend to be more sophisticated with explicit provision for regular payments on account spread across the accounting period. Those provisions often specify procedures for the ascertainment of those anticipated costs by a chartered surveyor. There are usually procedures provided for balancing out or even carrying over at the end of the financial year.

The right to make an interim demand

14–007 The right to demand an interim payment should be expressly provided for in the terms of the lease itself. It appears that, in the absence of any express right to an interim payment, no such right will be implied (see the comments of Harman J. in *Daitches v Blue Lake Investments* [1985] 2 E.G.L.R. 67).

The lease may specify conditions precedent to the right to make an interim demand. For example, on a proper construction of the lease, it may be that the landlord is only entitled to make an interim demand following a formal computation of the estimated costs of repair and maintenance for the coming year. A failure by a landlord to comply with such a condition precedent will render invalid any interim service charge demand. For example, in *Gordon v Selico Co Ltd* [1986] 1 E.G.L.R 71, the lease provided that the maintenance trustee was to make a computation of the estimated costs of maintenance for the year, on which the interim service charges were to be based. In fact, the maintenance trustee sought interim service charges which were not supported by any proper computation. The Court of Appeal held that no proper demand for interim service charges had been made.

The absence of an interim service charge covenant

14–008 In the absence of such a clause, difficulties often arise, especially in the case of cash-poor landlords—most notably management companies owned by the tenants themselves. The landlord may be forced to borrow (if it can) in order to comply with its obligations. Even if the landlord does not have to borrow, without an appropriate provision permitting an interim or on-account demand, it loses the use of its money until the costs are recovered from the tenants. The circumstances in which interest on borrowing, or upon money expended pending recoupment under the service charge provisions, can be recovered from the tenants within the service charge is discussed at Chapter 8 in this book.

The amount of the interim service charge demand

14–009 Ordinary principles discussed elsewhere in this book apply to the amount of interim service charges. The amount that may be demanded by the landlord by way of interim service charges is to be determined by reference to the lease. Most leases purport to give the landlord or his surveyor absolute freedom to set the level of interim service charges. The interim charge is subject to any common law requirement of reasonableness, and in the case of residential leases the interim charge is subject to s.19 of the Landlord and Tenant Act 1985.

Balancing payments/credits at the end of the accounting period

14–010 A lease that provides for the payment of interim service charges ought properly also to provide for the payment of a balancing charge to reflect the difference between the sums paid by the tenant on account of the service charge, and the actual service charge payable by the tenant for that accounting period. Occasionally a lease provides for such balancing payments to be payable on demand. Typically, however, leases provide for such balancing payments to fall due following preparation by the landlord of accounts, and the submission to the tenant of a demand based upon those accounts. When that is the case, the preparation of such accounts is usually a condition precedent to the payment by the tenant of any balancing payment.

On rare occasions, the payments of interim service charges made by the tenant might exceed the service charge for which the tenant is liable in any given accounting year. In principle, the landlord then falls under a common law duty to return the excess payment to the tenant. Many leases provide, however, for any such excess payment to be carried over as a credit towards the following year's service charge or into the reserve fund.

Certification and demands

14–011 It is common for a lease to provide for the service costs to be recovered by the landlord for any given accounting period to be certified by a landlord's surveyor or accountant. In such circumstances, the issue of a valid certificate will usually be a condition precedent to the tenant's obligation to pay. It is, therefore, essential that the accounts should be prepared and certified strictly in accordance with the provisions of the lease. Further, it will usually be implicit that the landlord and the certifier (whether a surveyor or accountant) be legally distinct persons. For example, in *Finchbourne v Rodrigues* [1976] 3 All E.R. 581, the managing agents engaged by the landlord were a firm of which he was the sole proprietor. The Court of Appeal upheld the judge's decision that, as a consequence, the landlord and the managing agent were, in effect, the same person, and that the tenant's contribution had not been "ascertained and certified by the [landlord's] managing agents acting as experts and not as arbitrators". On the other hand, in *New Pinehurst Residents' Association (Cambridge) v Silow* [1988] 1 E.G.L.R. 227, the landlord residents' association appointed a management committee of six tenants who were shareholders of the association to act as managing agents pursuant to the provisions of the lease. The court held that the committee was validly formed because its members were separate legal persons from the landlord residents' association and would exercise an independent judgment in relation to management of the blocks. Further, no particular expertise being specified in the lease, they were competent to act as experts.

"Conclusive" certification

Common law

14–012 It is common for leases to provide that the certificate of the landlord's surveyor or accountant is "conclusive" or "binding and conclusive". It is, in principle, unobjectionable for the parties to a lease to agree that the certificate of the landlord's surveyor or accountant is to be conclusive and binding as to matters of fact. It is unclear whether a certificate can also be binding as to matters of law.

Re Davstone Estates Ltd's Leases [1969] 2 Ch. 378

14–013 *Re Davstone Estates Ltd's Leases* [1969] 2 Ch. 378 concerned a provision that the certificate of the lessor's surveyor "shall be final and not subject to any challenge whatsoever". The landlord was pursuing a claim for service charges in respect of various items of repair works that he carried out. The tenants objected, alleging, amongst other things, that the works for which the landlord was charging did not fall within the landlord's repairing obligations. The landlord argued that his surveyor's certificate was final and above challenge. The court held that, on a true construction of the lease, whether the works carried out by the landlord fell within the landlord's repairing obligations was not a matter that fell within the ambit of the surveyor's certificate. Accordingly, the tenants could challenge the landlord's service charges. Ungoed-Thomas J. nevertheless also held that a clause that sought to oust the court's jurisdiction from matters of law was contrary to public policy. If, contrary to his conclusion, the ambit of the surveyor's certificate did extend to determination as to whether, as a matter of law, the repair works carried out by the landlord fell within the landlord's repairing obligations, then that would be contrary to public policy. There was nothing objectionable to the surveyor's certificate being conclusive and binding as to matters of fact, but as there was no way to sever that part of the clause that purported to make the surveyor's certificate binding as to matters of law from the rest of the clause, the whole clause would be void.

Jones v Sherwood Computer Services plc [1992] 1 W.L.R. 277

14–014 It has been doubted whether *Re Davstone Estates Ltd's Leases* was correctly decided. In *Jones v Sherwood Computer Services plc* [1992] 1 W.L.R. 277, the parties agreed to refer their dispute as to the valuation of shares in a company to accountants who were to act as experts and not as arbitrators. The parties agreed that the accountants' determination was to be "conclusive and final and binding for all purposes." The claimants sought a declaration that the accountant's report was of no effect on the grounds that the accountants had made a mistake by failing to take into account relevant sales. The Court of Appeal held that, if the parties had agreed, as a matter of contract, to remit matters (including matters of law) to the expert, they were entitled to do so. Further, if the expert answered the questions put to him, and did not depart from his instructions in a material respect, then the parties could not subsequently deny that the expert's certificate was binding on them. In *Nikko Hotels Ltd v MEPC Ltd* (1991) 28 E.G. 85, a case concerning the determination of a rent review by an expert, Knox J. disapproved *Re Davstone Estates Ltd's Leases* and instead applied *Jones v Sherwood Computer Services plc.*

Mercury Communications Ltd v Director General of Telecommunications [1996] 1 W.L.R. 48

14–015 The case of *Mercury Communications Ltd v Director General of Telecommunications* [1996] 1 W.L.R. 48 concerned a dispute between two telecommunications companies as to the terms of an agreement. They agreed to refer their dispute to the Director General of Telecommunications for determination. Mercury was unhappy with the Director General's determination and sought declaratory relief. Lord Slynn, giving the unanimous judgment of the House of Lords, accepted that the dispute to be resolved by the Director General involved the interpretation of various phrases in an agreement and therefore included questions of law. He commented, however, that if the Director General misinterpreted those phrases and made a determination on the basis of that misinterpretation then he would not be doing what he had been asked to do. Accordingly, his interpretation could be reviewed by the court. Thus far, Lord Slynn appears both to support *Jones v Sherwood Computer Services plc*, but also to undermine the effect of that decision. His Lordship continued as follows ([1996] 1 W.L.R. 48, 59A):

> "There is no provision expressly or impliedly that these matters were remitted exclusively to the Director, even though in order to carry out his task he must be obliged to interpret them in the first place for himself. Nor is there any provision excluding altogether the intervention of the court. On the contrary clause 29.5 contemplates that the determination shall be implemented 'not being the subject of any appeal or proceedings.' In my opinion, subject to the other points raised, the issues of construction are ones which are not removed from the court's jurisdiction by the agreement of the parties."

It therefore seems to be arguable that the parties to a lease may, by a properly drafted clause, provide that issues concerning the service charge payable (including issues of construction or other issues of law) may be conclusively determined by an expert: see also, *British Shipbuilders v VSEL Consortium plc* [1997] 1 Lloyd's Rep. 106. In practice, however, and in the absence of clear words to the contrary, a provision in a lease providing that the certificate of a surveyor or accountant is conclusive is likely to be construed narrowly such that it is conclusive only to those matters within the expertise of the certifier in question.

Statutory regulation

14–016 In a lease to which s.19 of the Landlord and Tenant Act 1985 applies, any such provision purporting to make a certificate of the service charge account "conclusive" is void (formerly s.19(3) of the Landlord and Tenant Act 1985 and now s.27A of that Act).

Time-limits for preparation and certification of accounts

Common law

14–017 At common law, and unless a lease provides otherwise, time is not of the essence in the preparation by a landlord of service charge accounts for any particular accounting period. Accordingly, in *West Central Investments v Borovik* (1977) 241 E.G. 609, the lease required the landlord to have accounts prepared and served within two months of the end of each accounting year. In fact, the accounts for the years 1970 to 1973 were not prepared until 1974. The court held that the two month stipulation did not make time of the essence and the landlord was nevertheless entitled to recover the service charges shown on those accounts as owing.

Statutory regulation

14–018 As far as residential leases are concerned, however, s.20B of the Landlord and Tenant Act 1985 provides that the costs are not recoverable if they were incurred more than 18 months before being demanded.

> **"20B Limitation of service charges: time limits on making demands**
>
> (1) If any of the relevant costs taken into account in determining the amount of any service charge were incurred more than 18 months before a demand for payment of the service charge is served on the tenant, then (subject to subsection (2)), the tenant shall not be liable to pay so much of the service charge as reflects the costs so incurred.

(2) Subsection (1) shall not apply if, within the period of 18 months beginning with the date when the relevant costs in question were incurred, the tenant was notified in writing that those costs had been incurred and that he would subsequently be required under the terms of his lease to contribute to them by the payment of a service charge."

The bar to recovery does not apply in the event that the tenant was informed within 18 months in writing that those costs had been incurred and that the same would be recoverable from the tenant. It is not entirely clear whether the tenant must be informed of the precise sum that has been incurred, or whether notice in more general terms, e.g. indicating the nature of the works rather than their precise costs, suffices. It has been held in the county court that the tenant must be informed of the precise sum: *Westminster City Council v Hammond*, December 1995, L.A.G. Bulletin p.19. It is questionable whether this decision is correct as it is often difficult, particularly with major works where there are extras and variations, to determine the exact cost until all matters have been agreed with the contractor. If such a notice is necessary, the safest approach is to keep lessees informed at regular intervals of the precise costs incurred and any variations that arise.

For the purposes of s.20B, a relevant cost is incurred by a landlord when he pays the said cost, or when he becomes legally liable to do so.

When s.20B applies, the landlord must ensure that his final accounts are prepared and certified as necessary in order that any balancing payment can be demanded within 18 months of the date on which the earliest of the relevant costs were incurred. If the accounting period is 12 months, say, then the landlord must have his service accounts prepared and any balancing payment demanded within six months of the end of the accounting period or else run the risk that any costs or expenses incurred towards the start of the accounting period may have become irrecoverable.

Section 20B has no effect where payments on account have been made in respect of service charges and the actual expenditure by the lessor does not exceed the payments on account, such that there is no need for any further demand to be made of the tenant and no such demand is made: *Gilje v Charlgrove Securities Limited* (2003) 36 E.G. 110.

Sections 152 to 154 of the Commonhold and Leasehold Reform Act 2002

14–019 Sections 152–154 of the Commonhold and Leasehold Reform Act 2002 will substitute new ss.21, 21A, 21B and 22 into the Landlord and Tenant Act 1985. Those provisions, which have not been brought into force at the time of writing, are considered in detail in Chapter 10. In summary, however, the proposed new s.21 (1)–(3) of the 1985 Act will require landlords to serve on each tenant not later than six months after the end of the accounting period a written statement of account certified by a qualified accountant. Should the landlord fail to comply with the requirement, then the tenant will be entitled to withhold payment of the service charge until the documents are served (the proposed s.21A of the 1985 Act).

"Re-opening" service charge accounts and the correction of errors

14–020 Where the lease does not provide that the certification of the service charge account for a particularly accounting period is conclusive, the courts will be most reluctant to imply such a provision. Where a certificate is not conclusive (either because it is not said to be conclusive or because the provision purporting to do so is void), then either the landlord or the tenant can seek to have the account reopened if a mistake was made in the calculation. On the other hand, where a lease provides for a certificate to be conclusive and that provision is effective, then neither party will normally be permitted to re-open the account.

It is also important to distinguish between the service charge account for any given accounting period and the statements setting out the liability of individual tenants. Certificates as to the service charge account for any given accounting period, setting out the total service costs spent by the landlord in that period, are often said to be conclusive; statements setting out the liability of individual tenants are rarely said to be conclusive.

In *Universities Superannuation Scheme v Marks & Spencer* (1999) 04 E.G. 158, the lease provided for the tenant's liability in respect of service charges to be in proportion to the relative rateable values of its demise. The lease also provided for the total service costs incurred by the landlord to be certified. The certificate was not said to be conclusive, but the lease provided that the tenant could only challenge the certificate within 42 days of receipt of the same. Certificates for the years ending March 31, 1992 and March 31, 1993 were issued but an error was made in calculating the tenants' contributions. The result of that error was that the landlord did not demand (and therefore did not recover) the full service costs that he had incurred. The landlord subsequently sought to recover the shortfall, issuing proceedings in 1996. The Court of Appeal found that it was entitled to do so. The tenant's obligation was to pay its due proportion of the proper service costs incurred by the landlord. The tenant had not paid its due proportion of the service costs incurred by the landlord and there was nothing in the lease to preclude the landlord from seeking the balance. The certificate was not said to be final and conclusive. In any event, the certificate did not specify the service charges payable by the tenant; simply the total service costs incurred by the landlord.

The form of demands

14–021 When preparing a service charge demand, it is important to have in mind the possibility that it might one day be closely scrutinised by a court or LVT in order to determine its validity. It is, therefore, important to ensure that it is in valid form.

At common law there are no particular requirements for the form of a service charge demand; the demand need only comply with the provisions of the lease.

Statutory regulation in relation to residential leases

14–022 As far as leases of dwellings are concerned, however:

- section 47 of the Landlord and Tenant Act 1987 provides that any written demand given by a landlord to a tenant must contain the name and address of the landlord and, if that address is not in England and Wales, an address in England and Wales at which notices (including notices in proceedings) may be served on the landlord by the tenant; and
- sections 21 and 22 of the Landlord and Tenant Act 1985 provide a statutory code for the provision by landlords of information as to the service charge costs, the form of statements of account, the certification of the accounts by a qualified accountant, and the inspection of documentation by the tenant. These provisions will be substantially amended by ss.152–154 of the Commonhold and Leasehold Reform Act 2002, although those latter provisions have not been brought into force at the time of writing. These issues are considered in detail in Chapter 10. In particular, the new s.21B will require a notice containing specified information to accompany service charge demands.

Breakdown in the service charge machinery

14–023 On occasions, landlords and tenants may be faced with leases that do not make proper or adequate provision for the maintenance of the block or estate or for the provision of services to the block or estate or for the payment of service charges in respect of maintenance or services. It may be that the leases of the block or estate never provided for any proper service charge machinery. Alternatively, the landlord may have carried out alterations to the block or estate thereby creating extra dwellings or he may now be providing more extensive services than those specified in the leases.

In such circumstances, Pt IV of the Landlord and Tenant Act 1987 provides the court and the LVT with a limited jurisdiction to vary the terms of the leases and only then with the consent of a sizeable majority of the relevant parties. These issues are considered in greater detail in Chapter 21.

Chapter 15

Handling Service Charge Funds

Introduction

15–001 This chapter deals with:

- The ownership of service charge funds generally;
- The statutory trust (s.42 of the 1987 Act) and:
  - provisions supplementing the statutory trust;
  - modifications to the statutory trust where a RTM company has acquired the right to manage;
  - the jurisdiction of the county court in respect of the statutory trust;
- Ownership of service charge funds where a lease falls outside of the 1987 Act;
- The consequences where service charge funds are held on trust including:
  - general consequences;
  - the obligation to invest;
  - insolvency;
  - where a receiver or manager is appointed;
- The investment of service charge funds;
- Interest on service charges.

Ownership of service charge funds generally

15–002 Whilst in practice funds generated by service charge provisions (referred to in this chapter as "service charge funds") will be controlled and administered by the landlord or a management company or agent, the beneficial entitlement to the funds will generally depend upon the terms of the lease, and in the case of properties let as dwellings, with some limited exceptions, will be regulated by statute.

The general principles dealt with in this chapter apply equally to all service charge funds whether generated by final or interim payments, or contributions towards reserve or sinking funds (as to which see Chapter 16).

Property let as a dwelling—the statutory trust

Overview

15–003 In broad terms, s.42 of the Landlord and Tenant Act 1987 ("the 1987 Act") imposes a statutory trust upon monies paid in respect of service charge liability by tenants of dwellings. The advantages of this to the tenant are considerable—see paragraph 15–034 *et seq.*

"Tenant(s)" and "exempt landlords"

15–004 For the purposes of s.42, "tenant" is defined as *not* including a tenant of an "exempt landlord". Accordingly, the statutory trust does not apply in respect of payments made by tenants of "exempt landlords" as defined by s.58(1) of the 1987 Act; specific reference should be made to that section as required but, for the most part (but note not exclusively), the landlords specified there are what might be described as social landlords. Section 58(1) includes:

- most local authorities (s.58(1)(a));
- a housing action trust (s.58(1)(ca)), the Housing Corporation (s.58(1)(e)) or a charitable housing trust (s.58(1)(f));
- a registered social landlord or a fully mutual housing corporation which is not a registered social landlord (s.58(1)(g));
- the Commission for New Towns or a development corporation established under the New Towns Act 1981; or an urban development corporation (s.58(1)(b) and (c));
- the London Fire and Emergency Planning Authority and police authorities (s.58(1)(a));
- waste disposal authorities (s.58(1)(h)).

Other exceptions and variations

15–005 Specific provisions regulate the application of s.42 to the Isles of Scilly (see s.55 1987 Act) and to Crown Land (see s.56 1987 Act).

Where a RTM has acquired the right to manage the property, there are some minor amendments in the application of s.42–42B. These are dealt with below at paragraph 15–029.

Note also that in respect of the amendments to s.42 (which are made by CLRA 2002) separate commencement orders bring them into force in England and Wales on different dates (see paragraph 15–008 *et seq.*).

"Dwelling"

15–006 The statutory trust applies only in respect of service charges paid by tenants of dwellings. "Dwelling" is defined (see s.60 1987 Act) as a building or part of a building occupied or intended to be occupied as a separate dwelling, together with any yard, garden, outhouses and appurtenances belonging to it or usually enjoyed with it.

Scope of the statutory trust

15–007 The statutory trust will apply to any sums paid in respect of service charges whether they are paid in respect of expenditure already incurred by the landlord or on account of such expenditure (for example interim service charges or contributions towards a reserve or sinking fund), but it does not apply to sums claimed by a landlord, or court appointed manager, but as yet unpaid (see *Maunder Taylor v Blaquiere* [2003] 1 W.L.R. 379).

For the purposes of s.42, "service charge" has the meaning given by s.18(1) of the Landlord and Tenant Act 1985, save that it does not include a service charge payable by the tenant of a dwelling the rent of which is registered under Pt IV of the Rent Act 1977, unless the amount registered is, in pursuance of s.71(4) of the Rent Act 1977, entered as a variable amount.

One or more tenants—extension of s.42 by CLRA 2002

15–008 As originally enacted, the statutory trust applied where the tenants of two or more dwellings (referred to as "the contributing tenants" in the section) could be required under the terms of their leases to contribute to the same costs by the payment of service charges.

The Commonhold and Leasehold Reform Act 2002 (s.157, Sch.10) has introduced an obvious and sensible extension to the statutory trust, which now applies to situations where a tenant of a dwelling may be required, under the terms of his lease, to contribute to costs to which no other tenant of the dwelling may be required to contribute (such a tenant is referred to as "the sole contributing tenant" in the section).

The relevant amendments were brought into force on February 28, 2005 in England (SI 2004/3056) and May 31, 2005 in Wales (SI 2005/1353).

"The payee"

15–009 The person to whom the service charges are payable under the terms of the contributing tenants' leases (or sole contributing tenant's lease) is referred to in the section as "the payee". In practice the payee will generally be the landlord, but might of course be a management company or agent of the landlord.

Interest, and investments representing the monies paid

15–010 It is specifically provided (s.42(2)) that any investments representing the monies paid in respect of service charges, and any income accruing thereon (which would include interest), will also be held upon trust.

The reference in s.42(2) to investments representing the sums paid will be repealed from a day to be appointed (s.180, Sch.14, CLRA 2002)—presumably the same day upon which s.42A will be brought into force compelling the payee to place sums paid into a designated account (see further below at paragraph 15–017 *et seq.*).

The reference in s.42(2) to income accruing on the sums will not be repealed, leaving no room for doubt (should there have been any) that interest on the sums in the designated account will also be subject to the statutory trust.

Section 42(5) (power of the Secretary of State to authorise investment of funds held pursuant to the statutory trust in a particular manner—for more detail see paragraph 15–039 below) remains in force at the time of writing but, like s.42(2), is due to be repealed from a day to be appointed, again, presumably, the same day upon which s.42A is brought into force.

Holding the trust monies as single or multiple funds

15–011 The payee is obliged to hold the trust monies either as a single fund or, if in his discretion he thinks fit, as two or more separate funds (s.42(2)).

Purpose of the trust

15–012 The purpose of the trust upon which the funds are held is: first, to defray costs incurred in connection with matters for which relevant service charges were payable (whether those charges were incurred by the payee or were incurred by another person) (s.42(3)(a)); secondly, subject to that, for the persons who are the contributing tenants *for the time being* (or the person who is the sole contributing tenant *for the time being*) (s.42(3)(b)). (But note the special provisions applicable on termination of tenancies—see below, paragraph 15–014).

Proportions in which funds are held

15–013 To the extent that there is any residue upon which s.42(3)(b) bites (see above, paragraph 15–012), and subject in appropriate cases to express provision in the lease to the contrary (see below, paragraph 15–015), the funds are held in such shares as are proportionate to the respective liabilities of the contributing tenants to pay relevant service charges (s.42(4)) or, in the case of a sole contributing tenant, the entire residue is held for the benefit of that person. (But note the special provisions applicable on termination of tenancies—see below, paragraph 15–014).

Entitlement of tenants to funds on termination of their leases

15–014 Subject to what follows (see below and also paragraph 15–015), upon termination of a tenant's lease, he loses any beneficial entitlement he may previously have had under the trust as a contributing tenant (s.42(6)), as the funds are held (after defraying of costs) for the contributing tenants *for the time being* (s.42(3)(b)). In other words, his "interest" is lost to him but the funds representing that interest remain part of the funds held upon the statutory trust with the purpose described above at paragraph 15–012.

Unless otherwise provided (see below, paragraph 15–015), where a tenant's lease comes to an end and there are no remaining contributing tenants, the trust fund is dissolved as at the date of termination of the tenant's lease and the landlord is entitled to any assets comprised in the fund immediately before its dissolution (s.42(7)).

Contracting out and application

15–015 The provisions outlined above relating to:

- the shares in which the contributing tenants for the time being are beneficially entitled to the trust funds (s.42(4), see paragraph 15–013 above);
- a tenant's entitlement upon termination of a lease where contributing tenants continue to exist (s.42(6), see paragraph 15–014 above);
- a tenant's entitlement upon termination where no contributing tenants remain (s.42(7), see paragraph 15–014 above);

are subject to any express provisions in the lease relating to the distribution (either before or at its termination) of amounts attributable to relevant service charges paid under the terms of the lease; this is so whether the lease was granted before or after the commencement of s.42 (s.42(8)).

Other than as outlined above, and in the following paragraph, the provisions of s.42 prevail over the terms of any express or implied trust created by a lease to the extent that the provisions are inconsistent with s.42 (s.42(9)), and so it is not possible to contract out of the essential features of the statutory trust.

Note that the provisions of s.42 will not, however, prevail over those of:

- an express trust created by a lease, in the case of contributing tenants, before the commencement of s.42 of the 1987 Act (being April 1, 1989 in England and Wales, SI 1988/1283);
- an express trust created by a lease, in the case of a sole contributing tenant before the commencement of para.15 of Sch.10 to CLRA (being February 28, 2005 in England SI 2004/3056, and May 31, 2005 in Wales SI 2005/1353).

(See s.42(9) 1987 Act).

Property let as a dwelling—supplementary provisions (ss.42A and 42B)

Overview and commencement

15–016 The protection afforded to a tenant by s.42 has been given teeth, on paper at any rate, by the insertion of two new sections, ss.42A and 42B, by the Commonhold and Leasehold Reform Act 2002 (inserted by s.156(1)).

At the time of writing, neither s.42A nor s.42B have been brought into force other than to the extent that they confer power to make regulations (SI 2002/1912 England, SI 2002/3012 Wales). Note that in relation to situations where a right to manage company (an "RTM company") has acquired the right to manage the property modifications to ss.42–42B are made by para.11 Sch.7 to CLRA 2002 (see paragraph 15–029 for more details). Despite the fact that Sch.7 has been brought into effect, and despite the terms in which para.11 is expressed, it is considered that on its proper construction para.11 presupposes that ss.42A–42B are already in effect. The RTM and the RTM company are given full treatment in Chapter 29.

Section 42A provides for funds held upon the statutory trust to be held in a separate and identified bank/building society account and grants to contributing tenants the right to inspect and obtain copies of documents evidencing that this has been done.

Of considerable note is that s.42A also provides that service charges may be withheld, and certain ancillary covenants, such as the accrual of interest on unpaid service charges, may be suspended by a contributing tenant who has reasonable grounds for believing that the payee has failed to place the relevant funds in an appropriate account (see paragraph 15–024 below).

Furthermore, failure to comply with the obligations imposed by s.42A is made the subject of criminal sanctions by s.42B.

Specific provision is made in respect of the application of ss.42A and 42B to the Crown (see s.172 CLRA 2002).

Section 42A

15–017 The Secretary of State is given power to make regulations specifying situations in which s.42A will not apply (s.42A(10)); at the time of writing no such regulations have been made.

In all other situations, s.42A(1) provides that any sums standing to the credit of any trust fund must be held by the payee in a "designated account" at a "relevant financial institution", although, as noted above (paragraph 15–011), the payee has a discretion to hold the monies in more than one account (s.42(2)) which facilitates, amongst other things, the creation and physical separation of reserve and sinking accounts (these are dealt with in greater detail in Chapter 16).

"Relevant financial institution"

15–018 A "relevant financial institution" has the meaning given by regulations made by the Secretary of State (s.42A(11)); at the time of writing no such regulations have been made.

"Designated account"

15–019 An account is a "designated account" if the relevant financial institution has been notified in writing that sums standing to the credit of the trust fund are to be (or are) held in it, there are no other funds held in the account, and the account is an account of a description specified in regulations made by the Secretary of State (s.42A(2)). As at the time of writing, no such regulations have been made.

The separation of the funds in this manner, and the fact that the relevant financial institution is on notice that the monies are held on trust (and thereby potentially exposed to a claim for knowing assistance in a breach of trust), should, in theory, give significant protection to tenants where the payee becomes insolvent.

Section 42A notice—inspection and copying of documents

15–020 Any of the contributing tenants (or the sole contributing tenant) may, by notice in writing, require the payee either to afford him reasonable facilities for inspecting documents evidencing that s.42A(1) is being complied with, and for taking copies of or extracts from those documents, or, alternatively, requiring the payee to take copies of or extracts from such documents and either send them to him or afford him reasonable facilities for collecting them. The choice as to whether the payee shall send such copies to the tenant or afford facilities for collecting them is that of the tenant. (See generally s.42A(3)).

If a tenant is represented by a recognised tenants' association (as to which s.42A(11) provides that "recognised tenants' association" is to have the same meaning as in the Landlord and Tenant Act 1985 (which is defined in s.29 of that Act)), and if he consents, the notice referred to above can be served by the secretary of the association instead of the tenant, in which case any requirement imposed by the notice is to afford reasonable facilities or send copies or extracts to the secretary (s.42A(4)).

Service of a s.42A notice

15–021 The notice will be properly served on the payee if it is served on his agent, named as such in the rent book or similar document, or if served upon the person who receives the rent on behalf of the payee; in either case, such a person is under an obligation to forward the notice to the payee "as soon as may be" [sic] (s.42A(5)).

Time for compliance

15–022 The payee must comply with a requirement imposed by the notice within 21 days beginning with the day upon which he receives the notice (s.42A(6)).

Costs of compliance with a s.42A notice

15–023 The payee cannot charge for providing facilities for inspecting documents but may treat any costs incurred by him in doing so as part of his costs of management (s.42A(7)). He may, however, make a reasonable charge for doing anything else in compliance with a requirement imposed by the notice (s.42A(8)).

Effect of payee's non-compliance upon the tenants' obligations

15–024 Any of the contributing tenants, or the sole contributing tenant, may withhold payment of service charges if he has reasonable grounds for believing that the payee has failed to comply with the duty imposed upon him by s.42A(1). Additionally, in such circumstances, any provisions of the tenant's lease relating to non-payment or late payment of service charges (for example the accrual of interest) will not have effect in relation to the period for which the tenant withholds the service charges (see generally s.42A(9)).

Section 42B

15–025 Section 42B creates a summary offence of failing, without reasonable excuse, to comply with a duty imposed by or by virtue of s.42A (s.42B(1)). The drafting of the section would seem to mean that the offence may be committed not merely by the payee, but, for example, his agent or even a person who is not his agent but has been held out as such: see, for example, the obligation imposed by s.42A(5) in relation to the prompt passing to the payee of a notice served pursuant to s.42A(3), above, paragraph 15–021.

Persons liable

15–026 It is clear that a body corporate can be guilty of an offence under this section (s.42B(3)) but the section also makes specific provision for the personal liability of directors, managers, secretaries and other similar officers, or persons purporting to act as such, of a body corporate (s.42B(3)).

Where the affairs of a body corporate are managed by its members, provision is made for the liability of those members in connection with their functions of management as if they were directors of the body corporate (s.42B(4)).

The personal liabilities discussed in the preceding two paragraphs will arise where it is proved that the body corporate committed the offence with the consent or connivance, or due to the neglect, of the relevant individual (s.42B(3)and(4)).

Prosecutions

15–027 Proceedings for an offence under the section may be brought by a local housing authority within the meaning of s.1 of the Housing Act 1985 (s.42B(5)).

Sanction on conviction

15–028 A person guilty of an offence under s.42B is liable on summary conviction to a fine not exceeding level four on the standard scale. At the time of writing, level four on the standard scale is £2,500.

Property let as a dwelling—modifications where a RTM company has acquired the right to manage

15–029 At the time of writing, neither s.42A nor s.42B have been brought into force other than to the extent that they confer power to make regulations (SI 2002/1912 England, SI 2002/3012 Wales) (but see comment at paragraph 15–016). In relation to situations where a Right to Manage company (a "RTM company") has acquired the right to manage the property, modifications to ss.42–42B are made by para.11 Sch.7 to CLRA 2002:

- references to the "payee" are references to the RTM company;
- the definition of "tenant" in s.42(1) (i.e. as not including tenants of "exempt landlords") does not apply;
- references to a tenant of a dwelling include a person who is landlord under a lease of the whole or any part of the premises;
- the reference in s.42(2) to sums paid to the payee by the contributing tenants by way of relevant service charges includes payments made to the RTM company under s.94 (transfer of uncommitted service charges to the RTM company) or s.103 (landlord's contribution to service charges) of CLRA 2002;
- section 42A(5) (service of a s.42A notice) applies so as to provide that service of a s.42A notice is effective if it is served on a person who receives service charges on behalf of the RTM company, and that person must forward the notice "as soon as may be" [sic] to the RTM company.

Note that where a RTM company has acquired the right to manage the property, specific provisions apply to the right to collect service charges and the transfer of uncommitted service charge funds to the RTM company.

Property let as a dwelling—jurisdiction of the county court

15–030 By s.52(2) of the 1987 Act, the county court is given jurisdiction to hear and determine any question arising under any provision of s.42.

Note also the effect of s.52(3) of the 1987 Act, so that where any proceedings are being taken in the county court under s.42, the county court has jurisdiction to hear and determine any other proceedings joined with those proceedings, notwithstanding that those other proceedings would otherwise be outside its jurisdiction.

Leases falling outside s.42 of the 1987 Act

Generally

15–031 Where the funds generated by the service charge provisions in a lease do not fall within s.42 of the 1987 Act, the lease may expressly provide that service charge funds are held on trust, for what purposes they may be used, and with whom any residual beneficial entitlement to the funds lays.

Where the service charge provisions are neither caught by s.42 nor provide expressly that service charge funds are to be held upon trust, those funds will generally be the property of the landlord absolutely unless:

- the construction of the lease and/or the circumstances give rise to a trust. (Such questions are most likely to arise in the context of reserve or sinking funds).
- the terms of the lease constitute a third party, for example a managing agent, as stakeholder to hold the monies pending some future event, see *Frobisher (Second Investments) Ltd v Kiloran Trust Co Ltd* [1979] 1 W.L.R. 425.

Where the funds are the property of the landlord, he may do with them as he pleases: whilst he will have obligations to fulfil under the lease he will not be obliged to use *these specific funds* to discharge those obligations.

Examples of cases in which a trust argument has been advanced

15–032 A claim by a tenant that monies paid under the terms of a lease with a view to future expenditure on fixtures and fittings gave rise to a trust failed as a matter of construction in the case of *Secretary of State for the Environment v Possfund (North West) Ltd* [1997] 39 E.G. 179. The fund, including interest, of some £1 million, which had been accumulated by the landlord through payments made by the tenant, was earmarked by the landlord and set aside to cover the cost of replacement of the air conditioning system. In the event, this was not done during the term of the lease and after the lease had expired the tenant claimed repayment of the fund on a number of bases, including the argument that the fund was held upon trust.

The clause of the lease pursuant to which the fund had been accumulated provided for contribution by the tenant to "the cost of periodically maintaining overhauling and where necessary replacing any and every part of the building . . . including where necessary the provision for future expenditure on fixtures and fittings by means of depreciation allowance". The last words of the clause were not, Rimer J. considered, mere surplusage, rather they showed that the landlord had in mind depreciation as a specific head of annual cost, and the purpose of the payments in respect of "depreciation allowance" was nothing more than the indemnification of the landlord by the tenant in respect of this specific cost. The terms of the lease did not result in the fund thus accumulated being held upon trust and the landlord was entitled to retain the fund. The absence of any machinery in the lease for returning an unspent balance, whilst not decisive, provided support for this interpretation.

In *Frobisher (Second Investments) Ltd v Kiloran Trust Co Ltd* [1979] 1 W.L.R. 425, in the context of a long lease of a residential property at a low rent, the court had to consider whether monies which, under the terms of the lease, could be demanded on account of service charges were themselves "service charges" within the meaning of s.91A of the Housing Finance Act 1972 and therefore (under that Act) only recoverable after the expenditure had been incurred.

The scheme of the lease was that service charges were assessed on a percentage basis. Payment of any given tenant's contribution was to be made on March 25 in every year in respect of the landlord's expenditure over the previous 12 months. The terms of the lease provided expressly that during the course of that previous 12 months the landlord could require the tenant to pay interim sums half-yearly in advance on March 25 and September 29.

On behalf of the landlord, in an attempt to take the interim sums outside the ambit of s.91A (and therefore, in effect, uphold its *prima facie* contractual entitlement to make on-account demands), it was argued that these interim sums were not service charges within the meaning of the section but were funds held on trust for the discharge of the tenant's "contribution" liability when ultimately ascertained at the end of each year.

15–033 In the course of rejecting this argument as ignoring the reality of the matter, Walton J. observed that there was nothing in the lease to prevent the lessor's managing agents from applying the monies as they received them to whatever purpose they thought fit and that, as a matter of practice, that was what had happened.

Had the sums been trust monies, to be applied in the way contended for by the landlord (only at the end of the year in meeting the contribution) it would, considered Walton J., be the duty of the managing agents to keep all those monies together during the year until payment of the contribution became due.

In *Re: Chelsea Cloisters Ltd (In liquidation)* [1980] P.&C.R. 98, the landlords of a block of flats had entered into an underlease with a company which thereafter managed the block and granted tenancies to various tenants. Pursuant to the terms of their leases, tenants had provided the company with a sum equal to one or two weeks rent as a deposit against sums due at the end of their tenancy for breakages and so forth, any positive balance after deductions for such matters being returned to the tenant at the end of the tenancy. The company ran into financial difficulty and a chartered accountant, a Mr Iredale, was appointed to supervise the running of the company. After his appointment he opened a separate bank account designated "tenants' deposit account". Into this account he transferred all deposits received since his appointment a couple of months earlier and all new deposits were also paid into this account. Shortly thereafter the underlease expired and the company went into voluntary liquidation. The liquidator issued a summons to determine how it should deal with the funds in the account. At first instance, Slade J. held that the sums in the account formed part of the company's general assets available for the creditors. The landlord appealed on the basis that, first, the terms of the lease relating to the deposit gave rise to a trust, alternatively that Mr Iredale's actions in setting up and running a separate account of the deposit monies created a trust of those monies. The relevant term provided that "the Tenant shall on the signing of this agreement pay to the landlord the sum of [blank] pounds as and by way of a deposit against any such sum which may be due from or payable by the tenant at the end of the tenancy for damage breakages compensation etc . . . any balance to be credited to the tenancy at the termination of the tenancy". There was no requirement for the money to be held in a separate account. The Court of Appeal declined to express an opinion as to whether this form of words gave rise to a trust but allowed the landlord's appeal on the basis of the alternative argument that Mr Iredale's actions had given rise to a trust. Lord Denning M.R. drew attention to earlier case law establishing that there is no need for an express declaration of trust or for the use of the words "trust" or "confidence" or the like, and to the importance of looking at the nature of the transaction. The court, and particularly Bridge L.J., emphasised the evidence of Mr Iredale's intention that the fund be kept separate from the company's general cashflow to be available solely for the purpose of repaying tenants.

The background against which this was done, namely the parlous state of the company, was also a factor in determining the view taken by the court of the consequences of Mr Iredale's actions. In other circumstances in which the lease does not expressly require the service charges funds to be kept separately but, as a matter of practice, they are kept separately, it is not possible to say more than that whether or not a trust is thereby constituted will be a matter of evidence and/or inference of intention as to the reasons for so doing in the circumstances of the case. On the other hand, where a lease provides expressly for service charge funds to be kept in a separate account, in the absence of any particular reason for doing so other than discharge of service charge liabilities, it may well be that the service charge funds are impressed with a trust. The precise purpose of that trust, and therefore the expenditure towards which it can be put, and any residual beneficial interest will be a matter of construction.

Consequences of service charge funds being held on trust

Generally

15–034 Important reasons for identifying situations in which the service charge funds are held upon trust include the following:

- the purposes for which the fund can be expended will be limited by the terms of the trust;
- there will be obligations and limitations as to what may be done with the funds pending expenditure;
- it is necessary to understand the terms of the trust upon which the service charge funds are held when considering matters of ownership, specifically in the context of assignment of the lease, termination of the lease, 1954 Act renewal and, not infrequently, insolvency of the landlord or management company holding the funds.

If the service charge funds are held upon trust, the normal substantive rules applicable to trusts will provide the tenant with considerable protection against loose accounting and/or misuse of funds and the insolvency of the person holding the fund. The reader should consult specialist textbooks on the duties of trustees and remedies for breach of trust but for the purposes of this book it suffices to note that incautious dealing with service charge funds held on trust or sloppy accounting procedures may mean that the landlord or other person holding the funds subject to the trust finds that:

- he has left himself open to a claim for breach trust;
- if he has mixed the fund with his own property, the burden will be upon him to identify what part of the mixed fund or derivative property is his own;
- in addition to recovering monies dissipated in breach of trust, the tenant may in certain circumstances be entitled to an account of any profit made on the back of that dissipation; and
- furthermore, the tenant may be entitled to equitable interest upon, as well as return of, dissipated funds.

Whether residential or commercial property, the tenant may be well advised to insist on an express clause providing for any excess in service charge funds to be held on trust for the tenants according to their contributions/liability to contribute during and at termination of the lease. It has already been noted that, in the absence of express provisions in the lease to the contrary, the landlord will ultimately be entitled to the residue of any service charge funds held pursuant to the statutory trust (see paragraph 15–014).

Obligation to invest

15–035 Where monies are held upon trust, there is a general obligation on the trustees to invest the monies within a reasonable time and if they omit to do so they will be charged interest (see *Gilroy v Stephens* (1882) 30 W.R. 745, *Stafford v Fiddon* (1857) 23 Beav. 386, *Re: Jones* (1883) 49 L.T. 91, and *Cann v Cann* (1884) 51 L.T. 770 in which Kay J. considered that six months was the maximum period of time) and if the fund is lost they will be liable to make it good (see *Moyle v Moyle* (1831) 2 Russ. & M. 710).

The precise duties of the trustees and their powers of investments will be determined by the terms of the trust and relevant enactments (see generally the Trustees Investment Act 1961 and the Trustees Act 2000). A detailed consideration of these matters is outside the scope of this work. In the context of service charge funds held upon trust, in most cases, the need to preserve the service charge funds accumulated and the need for liquidity will dictate that they be placed in an interest bearing account with a credit worthy institution. See below, "Investment of service charge funds", paragraph 15–038 *et seq*.

Insolvency

15–036 If the service charge funds are held upon trust for the benefit of the tenant(s) they will not form part of the assets of the insolvent landlord or managing agent available for distribution to creditors. In practice, it is important that the funds are held in a separate bank account identified as being a fund related to a particular building. In the case of residential property, s.42A of the 1987 Act makes retention of the fund in a separate account mandatory (see above, paragraph 15–017 *et seq*., for further details and provisions).

Where a Manager or receiver is appointed

15–037 For a detailed discussion of the appointment of a Manager see Chapter 27. In the case of *Hart v Emelkirk* [1983] 1 W.L.R. 1292, which predated the 1987 Act, the court granted an application (pursuant to s.37(1) Supreme Court Act 1981) for the appointment of a receiver to receive the rents and profits and any other monies payable under a number of long leases of residential flats. It is normal practice when granting applications under that jurisdiction to require security from the receiver. Although it was not part of the tenants' application that the receiver should provide security, Goulding J. directed that the receiver be appointed upon giving security and that, subject to such security, he be entitled to give good receipt for sums representing what remained of a reserve fund. However, as regards appointment of receivers (or managers) pursuant to the provisions contained in the 1987 Act, the experience is that it has not been the practice to require the proposed receiver to give such security, although he is generally expected to set out what he proposes to do with any existing funds. Normally the proposal is to place the funds in an interest bearing deposit account with a credit worthy institution.

As to the extent to which jurisdiction to appoint a receiver pursuant to s.37(1) of the Supreme Court Act 1981 in the case of leases remains, see the commentary at paragraph 27–003.

Investment of service charge funds

Generally

15–038 There will usually be periods of time during which the landlord or managing agent is holding service charge funds pending payment out to third parties for the provision of services or the execution of works. Where there is a reserve or a sinking fund then the monies so held, and the period over which they are held, may be significant. The landlord or managing agent may be under an obligation to invest the funds. The entitlement to interest or other proceeds of investment of service charge funds will, as a general rule, follow the entitlement to the fund itself.

Property let as a dwelling

15–039 Where s.42 of the 1987 Act applies (see above), the service charge funds will be held pursuant to statutory trust. Although s.42 does not (pending implementation of s.42A) provide expressly that such sums must be invested, as a matter of the general law of trusts a trustee ought to invest the sums (see above, paragraph 15–035). Furthermore, s.42(5) provides for such sums to be invested in any manner prescribed by regulations made by order by the Secretary of State. The only regulations made pursuant to that sub-section are the Service Charge Contributions (Authorised Investments) Order 1988 (SI 1988/1284), which provide that such sums may be:

(a) deposited at interest with the Bank of England; or

(b) deposited in the United Kingdom at interest with a person carrying on in the United Kingdom a deposit-taking business within the meaning of the Banking Act 1987; or

(c) deposited at interest with, or invested in shares in, a building society within the meaning of the Building Societies Act 1986.

As noted earlier (paragraph 15–010), in due course s.42(5) will be repealed and ss.42A and 42B will be brought into force imposing an obligation to hold funds in a designated account (see above, paragraph 15–017 *et seq.*).

Leases falling outside the 1987 Act

15–040 Where service charge funds are subject to a trust (other than s.42 of the 1987 Act), the lease may specifically provide for the investment of the funds, in which case the landlord, or managing agent as the case may be, will be obliged to invest the funds as per the terms of the lease. (Indeed, it may be that the inclusion in a lease of an express requirement that service charge funds be invested is a good indication that the funds are in fact held upon trust, as to which see generally paragraph 15–031 *et seq.*).

Where the funds are subject to a trust but there is no express provision, because of the general obligations of a trustee to invest trust funds (subject to limitations—see above, paragraph 15–035 *et seq.*), the landlord or person with control of the funds would be well advised to place the funds in an interest bearing account with a credit-worthy institution.

Where service charge funds are not subject to a trust, they will either be the absolute property of the landlord or be held by a stakeholder (perhaps a managing agent) upon the terms set out in the lease. If the funds are the absolute property of the landlord then he may deal with them as he pleases and there is no obligation to invest them. If they are held by a stakeholder then the terms of the lease should be consulted; in the absence of any express or implied obligation upon the stakeholder to invest the funds there will be no such obligation.

Interest on service charges

Accounting for interest earned on service charge funds

15–041 Where service charge funds are held upon trust the landlord will be obliged to invest the funds pending use. In practice, this usually means placing them in an interest bearing account—see above, paragraphs 15–038 to 15–040. Where the funds are held on trust pursuant to the statutory trust, it is expressly provided (see above, paragraph 15–010) that the interest earned will accrue to the trust fund. Where the funds are held on trust otherwise than pursuant to the statutory trust, normal trust principles apply, which in practice will normally mean that the trustee will have to account to the beneficiaries of the trust for any interest received on the service charge funds, unless the lease specifically provides otherwise.

Where the service charge funds are not held on trust, the landlord will not have to account for interest accrued on money held by him, subject to any provision in the lease to the contrary.

Interest on arrears of service charge

15–042 Where, under the terms of a lease, a tenant is obliged to pay interest on any arrears of service charge or interim charges, the landlord is entitled to retain such interest for his own benefit and not to credit it to the service charge fund, unless the lease provides otherwise.

Thus in *St Mary's Mansions v Limegate Investment Co* [2003] 1 E.G.L.R. 41, where the landlord had covenanted to carry out certain services and the tenants had covenanted to pay interest on late paid service charges, the Court of Appeal held that on the terms of the lease interest was the property of the landlord and that he need not account for it to the trust that arose by virtue of s.42 of the Landlord and Tenant Act 1987 (there is no reason in principle why the answer would have been any different if the trust had arisen under the lease, in the absence of any express clause requiring the interest on arrears to be credited to the trust). It is of note that interest in the lease in this case was reserved as rent and the Court of Appeal decided that it must be treated as rent and therefore payable to the lessor.

Chapter 16

Reserve Funds, Sinking Funds and Depreciation Allowances

Introduction

16–001 This chapter deals with:

- The rationale for the use of reserve funds and sinking funds;
- Terminology;
- The establishment of reserve funds and sinking funds and the contrast with depreciation allowances;
- The operation of reserve funds and sinking funds, including:
  - income to the fund;
  - expenditure from the fund;
  - a comment on some practical considerations;
- Tax considerations.

Rationale

16–002 The obvious problems of cash-flow for a landlord obliged to carry out works under the terms of the lease can be ameliorated by the use of a suitably drafted clause providing for the levying of interim or on-account service charges; this is discussed elsewhere in this book (see paragraph 14–005 *et seq.*). Equally, however, fluctuation in service charge demands from year to year and, more especially, the imposition upon the tenant of large demands at infrequent, irregular and sometimes unforeseeable points in the term in order to cover items of extraordinary capital expenditure (common examples include lifts, boilers, air conditioning units, roofs, etc.) can be a cause of considerable friction between landlord and tenant and are a frequent source of litigation and reference to the LVT. The solution is for the parties to adopt a means of spreading recurring but irregular expenditure, and also extraordinary expenditure, evenly over the accounting periods of the lease. This is commonly done by the use of "reserve" and/or "sinking" funds.

Terminology

"Reserve fund"

16–003 Although more and more the terms are used interchangeably, traditionally the term "reserve fund" is used in relation to a fund created for the purposes of equalising across accounting periods demands made on the tenant in respect of items of expenditure which, whilst recurring on a regular basis, tend to vary in amount from period to period (for example, internal cleaning and decorating).

"Sinking fund"

16–004 A "sinking fund", on the other hand, is a fund accumulated for the purpose of repairing or renewing major items of plant and equipment (for example, lifts, air conditioning plant, etc.). Such items may only require renewal or repair once or twice, or possibly not at all, during the term of a lease.

"Depreciation allowance or charge"

16–005 A "depreciation allowance" or "depreciation charge" is a charge to the tenant made to reflect the cost to the landlord of the depreciation in plant and machinery, etc. (see below at paragraph 16–006.)

Establishment of reserve and sinking funds, contrasted with depreciation allowances

16–006 Whilst leases frequently make express provision for the establishment of a reserve and/or sinking fund (and often, but not always, actually refer to the fund(s) as a "sinking fund" or "reserve fund") this is not invariably the case. Where such express authorisation is given by the lease then, naturally, establishment of such a fund is permitted in accordance with the terms of the lease subject to any applicable overriding statutory provisions (for example, s.19 of the Landlord and

Tenant Act 1985). As regards beneficial entitlement to the fund, see generally Chapter 15. As regards what monies can be brought into the fund, see below at paragraph 16–007.

Even in the absence of a provision in the lease expressly providing for the establishment of a reserve or sinking fund (whether or not referred to as such), on a proper construction of the lease, the landlord may be entitled to establish such a fund. In *St. Marys' Mansions Limited v Limegate Investment Company Limited* [2002] EWCA Civ 1491, the terms of the lease provided that the amount of service charge due from a given lessee was to be ascertained and certified by a certificate signed by the lessor's auditor. A further sub-clause provided that the certificate should contain a summary of the expenses and outgoings incurred by the lessor. A further sub-clause defined "the expenses and outgoings incurred by the lessor" as including not only those expenses *actually* disbursed or incurred in the year in question but also "such a reasonable part of all such expenses, outgoings and other expenditure hereinbefore described which are of a periodically recurring nature . . . including a sum or sums of money by way of reasonable provision for anticipated expenditure . . . as the lessor or its accountants or managing agents may in their discretion allocate to the year in question as being fair and reasonable . . .". The landlord set-up a reserve fund and a substantial sum was accumulated. In those circumstances, the court appears to have thought it clear that the lessor was entitled to establish and maintain a reserve fund, subject to complying with the procedural requirements imposed by the lease relating to certification. (Perhaps a more interesting argument, which did not arise on the facts of the case as s.42 of the 1987 Act applied, would have been whether the lessor, if it made provision for future expenditure pursuant to the terms of the lease, would have held the monies upon trust.)

In other cases, even where there is express reference in the service charge provisions of the lease to payment of sums towards the cost of provision for future expenditure, it may not be clear whether such provisions give rise to a reserve or sinking fund. In *Secretary of State for the Environment v Possfund (North West) Ltd* [1997] 39 E.G. 179, it was held that, on proper construction of the relevant term in the lease, the monies paid by the tenant were merely an indemnity against the cost actually and irreversibly incurred by the landlord during each year by virtue of the depreciation of its plant, i.e. a "depreciation allowance".

Note, however, Rimer J.'s view that where payments made in respect of the cost of making provision against future expenditure by way of a "depreciation allowance" proved to exceed that which was necessary, the landlord would ordinarily be expected at least to give credit to the tenant for the excess against future depreciation payments.

Depreciation charges must be properly assessed and demanded in accordance with the terms of the lease as tenants may, subject to the precise terms of the lease and any limitation arguments, have a claim in restitution for return of any excess charges (see *"The extent of mistake"* J. Brock E.G. 6/3/99 173, *Nurdin & Peacock plc v D.B. Ramsden & Co Ltd (No.2)* [1999] 1 W.L.R. 1249, *Kleinwort Benson Ltd v Lincoln City Council* [1998] 3 W.L.R. 1095).

Operation of reserve and sinking funds

Income

16–007 In the absence of a clause permitting, directly or indirectly, the establishment of such a fund, there is probably no entitlement to demand contributions in order to establish one—by analogy with the position where the lease makes no provision for making interim service charge demands (see paragraph 14–007 and *Daitches v Blue Lake Investments* [1985] 275 E.G. 462).

Note also *Parker & Beckett v Parham* (L.T. ref. LRX/35/2002), in which the boot was on the other foot. The tenants of residential property applied for an order spreading the cost of payment for anticipated major works. The application, apparently based on the invocation of the s.19(2B)(c) jurisdiction, was rejected on the basis that there was no power to make an order of that sort.

Where the establishment of such a fund is permitted by the lease, the provisions relating to precisely what may be brought into the fund should be complied with strictly. The case of *St Marys' Mansions Limited v Limegate Investment Company Limited* [2002] EWCA Civ 1491 highlights the need for any reserve or sinking fund account to be run according to the terms which provide (whether directly or, in this case, indirectly) for the establishment of the fund, and the nightmarish accounting scenario that may follow if this is not done. Having held that the lessor was entitled to establish a reserve account, Ward L.J. went on to consider precisely what, by reason of the terms of the lease, could stand in the reserve account. The broad scheme of the service charge provisions was that at the end of the financial year there was to be an account taken between amounts paid during the year pursuant to the interim service charge demand provisions and the amount actually payable by the tenant in respect of that year. If there was a shortfall, the tenant was obliged to make it up; if there was an excess, that excess was to be "allowed by the lessor to the lessee".

The auditor's certificate, prepared at the end of the year, was determinative of what was properly due from the tenant in respect of that year and, therefore, of whether there was a shortfall or an excess. The auditors certificate had to contain details of: (1) the relevant expenses or outgoings actually paid in the previous year; and (2) if provision for future expenditure was being made (pursuant to the clause referred to above), details of that future anticipated expenditure.

The question posed by the parties for the court was whether the lessor was "entitled to apply *any* [emphasis added] year end service charge surplus to the reserve fund". This question was, considered Ward L.J., framed too widely because a surplus could arise in different circumstances. Any overpayment made in respect of expenses *actually incurred* in the previous year could not be taken to the reserve fund but had to be "allowed" to the lessee. The only sums which the lessor was entitled to take into the reserve account were those sums in category (2) above, and even then only subject to compliance with the procedural requirements contained in the lease relating to allocation by the lessor, its accountant or managing agents, and certification by its auditors.

Incidentally, although the court was not concerned with whether "allowed by the lessor to the lessee" meant repaid to the lessee or merely placed to his credit in the account to be set-off against demand in the following year, Ward L.J. indicated that he was "inclined to think that either may be appropriate".

It must also be borne in mind that, in the case of property let as a dwelling, demands for monies destined for the reserve or sinking fund will, in addition to complying with the terms of the lease itself, have to satisfy the test set out in s.19(2) of the Landlord and Tenant Act 1985 (see Chapters 4 and 11), and the monies received will be held upon statutory trust (s.42 of the 1987 Act, see paragraph 15–003 *et seq*.).

In the case of leases falling outside of s.19 of the L&T Act 1985, it may be that there is an implied term that any demands for contribution to the reserve or sinking fund will be reasonable, however, it is often the case that such demands are expressly subject to some form of limitation referable to reasonableness, for example, where the tenant covenants to "pay such sum of money by way of reasonable provision for anticipated expenditure as the Lessor shall reasonably require".

Ownership of accumulated funds is discussed at Chapter 15.

Expenditure

16–008 Where the lease makes specific provision for the establishment of a reserve or sinking fund it may do so in general or specific terms. Not infrequently the service charge clause in a lease will simply provide for service charges to include an amount towards "future anticipated expenditure", or some such very general form of words, but sometimes it will be more specific than this, identifying the subject matter of the future anticipated expenditure, for example "plant and machinery". In such cases the fund can be used only for the specified purposes. Where the terms of the lease are more general, it will be a matter of construction in each case.

Of course, where the fund is held upon statutory trust (s.42 of the 1987 Act) the use to which the fund can be put is governed by s.42(3) (see paragraph 15–012).

Practical considerations

16–009 Where there is a limitation on the amount that may be demanded by the landlord in respect of contribution to a reserve or sinking fund (for example, by reason of s.19(2) L&T 1985 where applicable, or expressly or impliedly on proper construction of the lease) the landlord will usually need to be able to point to some rationale basis for the amount demanded. Indeed, good landlord and tenant relations demand that this should be normal practice in any event.

Demands are usually based upon an analysis involving consideration of the life expectancy of the relevant item (or frequency of expenditure in the case of matters such as redecoration) and the projected cost of replacement/repair (or service).

Interest and inflation will also play a greater or lesser role according to the time intervals and the amounts involved.

In practice, the calculation of contributions required for a reserve fund (i.e. a fund for regularly recurring items such as redecoration) is likely to be relatively straightforward because:

- the contribution will usually be calculated across a short period of time, perhaps five or seven years, with the result that interest on monies and inflation held will play less of a part in the calculation;
- there is more likely to be recent (and therefore accurate) historical evidence of the likely costs involved.

Sinking funds for the replacement or repair of major items present more difficulty. Generally speaking the present day capital cost of any given item will be known but, because of the time scales involved (10, 20, 30, etc. years), interest on the monies held in the account, the effects of inflation, and even changes in technology and the standards of the construction industry become more important considerations.

By using a rolling analysis (i.e. recalculating the analysis each year in the light of accumulated funds, interest, inflationary changes and changes in technology) the possibility of large variations can be reduced.

Reserve and sinking funds at termination of the lease

16–010 It is sometimes the case that at the termination of a lease, for whatever reason, a substantial amount of money is held by the landlord or managing agent in a reserve or sinking fund. Entitlement to those funds may become an issue between parties. The question of ownership of service charge funds (including reserve and sinking funds) is dealt with in Chapter 15.

Tax

16–011 Reserve and sinking funds give rise to specific questions of taxation (see generally Chapter 25). There may, in any given case, be particular tax advantages and disadvantages to making provision for future expenditure by means of such funds, as opposed to the use of a depreciation allowance or some other system. Those involved in drafting leases are advised to obtain specialist advice on such issues.

Chapter 17

Service Charges and Right to Buy Leases

Introduction

17–001 This chapter concerns leases of dwellings which have come into existence as a result of the exercise by a tenant of a local authority of the "right to buy" first given by the Housing Act 1980 and now contained in the Housing Act 1985.

The chapter will discuss the geography of the lease which is likely to be encountered, the relevant legislation, "the cost floor" (a feature of the method of calculation of the discount under the right to buy scheme) and the issue of waiver as it relates to local authorities.

The lease

Generally

17–002 Whether acting for the local authority or for the lessee, it is imperative that the geography of the lease is understood. This might appear trite but in the experience of the authors many local authorities demand service charges according to internal policy documents rather than according to the terms of the lease in question. Those policy documents can be outdated or simply wrong (and disclosure of which can be useful for those acting for lessees).

Demands for a contribution towards major works can often ignore the timetable set by the lease, a local authority often believing that the cost of major works is recoverable as of right without the need to conform to the strict terms of the lease.

Variations

17–003 The lease will (usually) have been drafted by the local authority's legal department, following one of its standard forms; there might be three or four variations which have been executed in the 20 or so years that the right to buy regime has been in existence.

For example, many leases executed in the early days of the scheme made provision for a sinking fund or "Capital Expenditure Reserve Fund". Generally, such funds are no longer implemented and newer leases contain no such provision. However, rarely will this defunct provision have been varied.

It is quite possible that individual lessees (most local authorities do not use "tenant" and "lessee" interchangeably, "tenant" being used to describe only secure tenants) in a block of flats will hold their property under standard-form leases with widely differing covenants.

Covenants implied by statute

17–004 Statute requires certain covenants to be incorporated into the lease (see Housing Act 1985 s.139 and Pts I and III to Sch.6). This is common sense because a lessee might be the *only* occupier in a building to have exercised the right to buy and cannot be out of kilter with other occupiers who enjoy the benefits of extensive express and implied repairing obligations. Service charges are dealt with more particularly under paras 16A–16E of Pt III to Sch.6.

The "reasonableness" of covenants can be challenged prior to the lease being executed. After the lease has been entered into, challenge must be by claim for judicial review or direction of the Secretary of State under the Housing Act 1985 ss.167 and 168 (see *Sheffield City Council v Jackson* [1998] 3 All E.R. 260, *per* Nourse L.J. at 261j–262a, 262j–263b, 268a–b, g and j, 270b; *Guinan v Enfield London Borough Council* (1997) 29 H.L.R. 456, *per* Staughton L.J. at 461–3; and *Coventry City Council v Cole* (1993) 25 H.L.R. 555, *per* Neill L.J. at 564–5. Although on a different point, some guidance can also be gained from *Hackney London Borough Council v Thompson* [2001] L.&T.R. 7, *per* Aldous L.J. at 71 para.5 and 74 paras 15–17).

The typical lease

17–005 The geography of a typical lease executed under the right to buy scheme will often be as follows.

Definitions

17–006 The lease will define "the building", "the estate", "the flat" and "the services". There will also be definitions of the amount of discount the purchase attracted, the premium paid and the term (always 125 years). Many service charge disputes will turn on these definitions.

"The services" will generally be defined as including the provision of central heating, hot water, lifts, caretaking, lighting, entry-phones, maintenance of common television aerials or landline, maintenance of estate roads and paths, estate lighting, gardening and landscaping in respect of the flat and other flats in the building and estate as defined. Many lessees are aggrieved by the notion that they are required to pay a contribution toward the provision of services not only to their home but to the homes of others.

Payment of service charge

17–007 The lessee will generally covenant to pay the service charges at the times and in the manner defined in one of the schedules to the lease. It is the timing and manner of payment which the local authority sometimes overlooks when demanding payment for major works. A department dealing with service, charge recovery might have its policy guides and software firmly established for making regular demands for the provision of services, but become lost when attempting to integrate into this system demands for much larger amounts.

Generally, the lease will require the local authority to estimate the service charge for the coming year and notify the lessee of that estimate. Payment in advance on account is often not on the usual quarter days but on the first day of April, July, October and January in each year (which runs April to March). At the end of the year, the local authority will calculate any balance due to the lessee or shortfall due to the local authority and notify the lessee accordingly. If this process appears all too familiar to those who advise on landlord and tenant matters, it must be borne in mind that, as already stated, the procedure is not infrequently overlooked when the local authority seeks to recover the cost of major works.

The lease will generally require the lessee to pay a fair proportion of the costs and expenses which the lease defines as being a service charge. The lease will often include a covenant which entitles the local authority to adopt any reasonable method of ascertaining this proportion and entitling it to adopt different methods of apportioning the different items and costs which comprise the service charge. As to the definition of service charge, this is generally as follows.

Repairs

17–008 The lessee will have to pay for the repairs which the local authority covenants to carry out. These are imposed by statute (see para.14 of

Pt III of Sch.6 to the Housing Act 1985) and mirror, in part, the covenant implied by s.11 of the Landlord and Tenant Act 1985 and, probably, the express covenants contained in the leases of secure tenants.

It is not uncommon for a major works project to involve the repair of the structure and exterior of buildings which have, for many years, not benefited from regular repair and maintenance. Notwithstanding the lessee's covenant to pay for such work, this cost may be legitimately challenged if, for example, those costs have been exacerbated by the local authority's breach of covenant.

Maintenance, etc.

17–009 As well as the cost of repairs, service charges will often include the provision of the services defined by the lease, insurance, maintenance and management of the building and estate as defined and the employment of managing agents appointed by the local authority. There might well be an express exclusion of the right to recover the cost of the maintenance of any other building comprised in the estate. In the event that managing agents are not employed by the local authority, the lease might provide for the addition of a percentage figure for administration.

Improvement contributions

17–010 Improvement contributions by way of service charge will often be limited by the lease to items such as the cost of installing double-glazed windows and an entry-phone system, with the decision to introduce the improvement being in the local authority's absolute discretion. It is not unusual for disputes over service charges to centre on the reluctance of lessees to pay for perceived "improvements", whereas the anticipated work is merely a *repair* which inevitably includes an element of improvement owing to technological advancement (see *The Sutton (Hastoe) Housing Association v Williams* (1988) 20 H.L.R. 321, *per* Glidewell L.J. at 328–9).

Other disputes regularly concentrate on the refusal of a lessee to pay for the costs of new windows which conform to a block-specification. It will often be the case that the lessee will not want the style chosen by the local authority, or will have found a cheaper quote. However, the failure to introduce new windows to all but the three or four flats in a building will be unacceptable to most local authorities and it will be entirely proper to charge under the lease. To continue the example, the economy of scale derived by the local authority paying its contractor to install uniform windows across an estate might persuade the LVT that such costs are reasonable in amount, despite the fact that the lessee complainant's preferred style is cheaper. The desirability of uniformity when maintaining those same windows and negotiating future contracts will often convince the LVT that it would be unreasonable for a lessee, or even a group of lessees, to break rank. The problem is often that the local authority fails to explain this to an irate lessee until a final hearing in the LVT takes place.

The grace period

17–011 It makes sense that a tenant who exercises the right to buy should be afforded something of a grace period. Often the transition from security under the 1985 Act to home-ownership will place a seemingly intolerable financial burden on the new lessee. It will have been extremely difficult to budget for the years following the purchase of a lease, particularly where a major works project could confront the lessee out of the blue.

With this in mind, para.16B of Pt III of Sch.6 to the Housing Act 1985 provides a grace period which curtails the ability of the local authority to demand service charge for the first five years of the lease.

The notice which the local authority serves pursuant to s.125 of the Housing Act 1985 must estimate the lessee's contribution for a particular item, the purpose of the scheme being the ability of the potential lessee to budget and borrow accordingly.

This means that the lessee or his advisor will not only have to look carefully to see whether any service charge levied within this first five year period is recoverable, but also whether the local authority has waited until the five year period has elapsed before making a demand for payment. If a local authority knew that the roof of a building was in disrepair, but waited until after the five period had ended simply in order to recover at least part of the cost of the works, the lessee might well have an argument that those costs have not been reasonably incurred or are not reasonable in amount (see *Payne v Barnet London Borough Council* (1998) 30 H.L.R. 295, *per* Brooke L.J. at 312).

Summary

17–012 To recap, those representing local authorities, and lessees and those advising them, should ask themselves the following questions:

- Is the local authority adhering to the strict terms of the lease, or is it simply following its policy?
- Does the demand accord with the definitions of flat, estate, building and services in the lease?

- Has the cost of repairs been exacerbated by the local authority's failure to act more quickly?
- Did the local authority fail to carry out repairs during the five year grace period?
- Can the local authority justify its demand by economies of scale or uniformity across the building or estate?

Procedure

The consultation requirements

17–013 The Service Charges (Consultation Requirements) (England) Regulations 2003 ("the consultation requirements") govern service charge demands made by local authorities just as they do private landlords. Regulation 2 contains definitions of right to buy tenancies and right to buy tenants. This includes those lessees whose right to buy has been preserved by s.171A of the Housing Act 1985, that is, where a person ceases to be a secure tenant because the local authority landlord disposes of the property (generally by stock-transfer to a registered social landlord). Note, however, the provisions of the Anti-Social Behaviour Act 2003, s.14 and Sch.1 para.2, by which this preserved right to buy ceases where the tenancy has been demoted to an assured shorthold tenancy so as to jeopordise the tenant's security of tenure as a method of regulating anti-social behaviour.

Regulations 5(3) (qualifying long-term agreements) and 7(5) (qualifying works) of the consultation requirements provide that those requirements do not apply to the first 30 days of a right to buy tenancy. This provision is, of course, unlikely to be of great practical effect.

Management agreements

17–014 By reg.3(1) of the consultation requirements, an agreement is not a qualifying long term agreement if it is a management agreement made by a local housing authority and either a tenant management organisation or a body established under s.2 of the Local Government Act 2000.

A "management agreement" is defined by reg.3(4) of the consultation requirements as having the meaning given by s.27(2) of the Housing Act 1985, that is, an agreement which devolves the local housing authority's management functions to another as specified in that agreement.

TMOs

17–015 A "tenant management organisation" has the meaning given by s.27AB(8) of the Housing Act 1985. Section 27AB(8) merely defines a TMO as being a body which satisfies such conditions as may be determined by or under the regulations. The regulations to which s.27AB(8) refers are the Housing (Right to Manage) Regulations 1994 (SI 1994/627) which set out the procedure for establishing a TMO.

LGA 2002 empowerment

17–016 Section 2 of the Local Government Act 2000 forms part of the rather curiously sweeping provisions of Pt I of that Act, which empowers local authorities to do anything which they consider likely to promote or improve the economic, social and environmental well-being of their area. Sections 3 and 4 contain limits on that power and impose the need for each local authority to develop a community strategy (including consultation requirements) in order to implement the objective of Pt I.

Practical effect

17–017 The consultation requirements distinguish between those works in respect of which a "public notice" is required and those for which it is not. "Public notice" is defined in reg.2. The majority of service charge disputes will not involve works by a local authority carrying with them the need to give public notice.

Furthermore, most cases will not concern a management agreement made by a local authority which is a TMO, or set up under the Local Government Act 2000.

In a case involving a right to buy lease, it is, accordingly, more likely that the dispute will be governed by the consultation requirements which are found in Pt 2 of Sch.4. It is through these hoops that the local authority will have to jump, unless it can persuade the LVT to exercise its jurisdiction to dispense with the consultation requirements.

Summary

17–018 To recap, the following questions should be asked:

- Has the right to buy ceased owing to demotion of the tenancy pursuant to the Anti-Social Behaviour Act 2003?
- Is it within the first 30 days of the lease?
- Does the case concern a management agreement which is either a TMO (possible) or set up under the powers to promote well-being of an area (unlikely)?

- Has a public notice been served?
- Is there a qualifying long term agreement?
- Are these qualifying works to which Pt 2 of Sch.4 apply (most likely)?
- Has the local authority complied or is there any basis for dispensing with the consultation requirements?

Cost floor

HA 1985, s.131

17–019 By s.131 of the Housing Act 1985, the discount to be given to a tenant exercising the right to buy cannot be reduced below a price which is to be taken as representing so much of the costs incurred in respect of the property during a 10 year period prior to the date on which the tenant exercised the right to buy.

1999 Determination

17–020 This notional cost is set by the local authority in accordance with The Housing (Right to Buy) (Cost Floor) (England) Determination 1999. Paragraph 3 of the Determination provides that the local authority shall perform its calculation by aggregating the costs which are "relevant costs" as defined by para.5. "Relevant costs" include not only the direct cost of construction of the property but, in the case of land which was purchased, the cost of that land and, in the case of existing land which was developed, the cost of site development works including, it is submitted, demolition and statutory home loss payments.

Service charges

17–021 Excluded from "relevant costs" are a series of items set out in para.6 of the Determination. Any costs which are recoverable by the landlord as a service charge or improvement contribution cannot be included as relevant costs. Accordingly, the discount cannot be reduced by this amount.

In practice, this provision means that when calculating the discount which a newly-built property attracts, the local authority or the lessee's representative must be clear about what the lease does and does not permit the local authority to recover as a service charge. The starting point will be not only the lease itself, but also the estimate which the local authority makes as part of its s.125 notice.

Generally speaking, the only way a would-be lessee is able to satisfy himself that the discount is accurate is to go back to the local authority, refer to paras 5 and 6 of the Determination, and ask for a breakdown of precisely what has been excluded from and included in the calculation. Doubtless, this provision will become increasingly important as more public sector housing is constructed and the right to buy is exercised in respect of new-builds. This is all the more likely given that s.131(1) can have the effect of eliminating the discount in its entirety. It must be borne in mind, however, that what the lessee gains by the discount might well be lost by the service charge.

Summary

17–022 Therefore, the following questions should be asked:

- Has the property been built or purchased within the last 10 years?
- Does the s.125 notice refer to a limit on the discount by reason of s.131 of the Housing Act 1985?
- For what service charges does the lease permit recovery?
- Is there any duplication between the cost floor calculation and service charge estimate contained in the s.125 notice?

Waiver

17–023 The basic principle is that once the right to forfeit has arisen by, for example, a breach of a covenant against sub-letting without consent, the landlord may elect to treat the lease as having come to an end or as continuing. If the landlord elects to treat the lease as continuing by, for example, demanding ground rent or service charge, the right to forfeit is lost. A claim for possession would fail.

Local authorities are, by their nature, large and complicated organisations. The department responsible for the recovery of service charge arrears is often distinct from the department responsible for issuing demands for ground rent and service charge. Indeed, such demands may well be generated and despatched automatically.

Will an automatic demand for rent or service charge by a local authority, or a demand despatched by a department which is wholly ignorant of a breach giving rise to the right to forfeit, amount to a waiver of that right? This is a question which all too frequently confronts those advising local authorities and lessees. The answer, it is submitted, is "yes". The local authority cannot hide behind the suggestion that its right hand did not know what its left hand was doing (see *David Blackstone Ltd v Burnetts (West End) Ltd* [1973] 1 W.L.R. 1487, *per* Swanick J. at 1501E–H).

Therefore:

- check precisely when the local authority knew that the right to forfeit arose, i.e. its knowledge of the breach of covenant;
- check whether rent or service charge was demanded after the date of knowledge;
- if acting for the local authority, make sure that as soon as a breach giving rise to the right to forfeit is known of, the relevant department is told to put a "stop" on demands for rent and service charge;
- if a lessee or acting for a lessee and if forfeiture is threatened, obtain disclosure of all demands for rent or service charge (bearing in mind that where automatically created and posted, copies of demands are often not retained; in such circumstances the document retained by the lessee might be the only evidence that a demand was made).

Chapter 18

Landlords' Remedies

Introduction

18–001 The purpose of this chapter is to consider the range of legal remedies available to a landlord, and to offer practical advice on the merits and the tactical considerations which apply to each.

The choice of remedies

18–002 The principal remedies available are:

- Money claim for the unpaid amount;
- Distress;
- Forfeiture of the lease;
- Application to the court for a declaration;
- Application to a leasehold valuation tribunal under s.27A of the Landlord and Tenant 1985 and under s.158 and Sch.11 to the Commonhold and Leasehold Reform Act 2002 (residential premises only);
- Application to a leasehold valuation tribunal under s.159(6) of the Commonhold and Leasehold Reform Act 2002;
- Application to a leasehold valuation tribunal to vary one or more leases (residential premises only).

Money claim

18–003 A money claim is a claim for a liquidated sum, or a debt, which is due under the terms of the lease. The advantages of a money claim are:

- Simplicity—in the county court the claim can be prepared and issued online under CPR 7.12 and Practice Direction 7E.
- Speed—if the tenant does not file a defence, judgment in default may be entered by the landlord under CPR 12. If a defence is filed and the claim is strong, an application for summary judgment under CPR 24 can be made.
- The lease is preserved, unlike forfeiture. In a non-residential dispute where the rental market is depressed, it may be more attractive to a landlord to keep a solvent tenant locked into the lease and to claim the arrears of service charge, rather than to forfeit the lease and have to re-let at a lower rent.
- A money judgment is a gateway to forfeiture in residential cases.

However, it is open to a residential tenant to ask the court to transfer the claim to the leasehold valuation tribunal for determination under s.27A of the Landlord and Tenant 1985 if the liability is disputed.

Interim or final account?

18–004 Where the lease provides for payments on an interim or on-account basis, with a balancing charge at the conclusion of the service charge year, the decision will need to be taken as to whether to issue proceedings based upon an unpaid interim bill or to wait until the conclusion of the service charge year and claim on the basis of the final account.

Waiting until the final account has the advantage of certainty but involves waiting for possibly several months until the year is complete and any certification process has occurred. If a claim for an interim bill is defended, by the time that the trial takes place the final account may have been prepared, and it would seem that the claim could therefore be amended to the final account.

For a discussion of interim and final accounts generally, see paragraphs 14–007 to 14–009.

Claiming interest

18–005 If the lease provides for interest to be paid on unpaid service charges, or service charges reserved as rent, the claim should include a claim for interest in accordance with the lease. Otherwise, s.69 of the County Courts Act 1984 or s.35A of the Supreme Court Act 1981 should be utilised.

Choice of venue

18–006 If the amount claimed is less than £15,000, the claim must be brought in the county court; otherwise it may be brought in either the county court or the High Court: County Courts Act 1984, s.15; High Court and County Courts Jurisdiction Order 1991 (SI 1991/724) arts 2, 4A.

Restrictions in residential cases

18–007 Section 166(1) of the Commonhold and Leasehold Reform Act 2002 (in force from February 28, 2005: SI 2004/3056) provides that a tenant under a long lease of a dwelling is not liable to make a payment of rent under the lease unless the landlord has given him a notice relating to the payment and the date on which he is liable to make the payment is that specified in the notice. That date must not be less than 30 days or more than 60 days after the day on which the notice is given, or before that on which the tenant would have been liable to make it in accordance with the lease: s.166(3). However, "rent" does not include a service charge within the meaning of s.18(1) of the Landlord and Tenant 1985: s.166(7)(a).

Care must therefore be taken if a residential lease reserves service charges as rent. If a money claim is to be brought for recovery of both ground rent and service charge, notice must be given under s.166 in relation to the ground rent element, but not the service charge, and the date specified in the notice must have passed before the claim is issued.

Distress

18–008 Distress is the seizure and impounding of chattels without legal process to compel the satisfaction of a demand for rent. The chattels may be sold if, after seizure, the tenant does not pay.

It has been held that where service charges are recoverable as rent and have been ascertained they may be distrained for: *Concorde Graphics v Andromeda Investments* (1983) 265 E.G. 386. Discussion of the remedy of distress is beyond the scope of this book.

Forfeiture

18–009 Forfeiture, or re-entry, is the premature bringing to an end of the lease by a landlord pursuant to a right contained in the lease by either the issue and service of possession proceedings, or by peaceable re-entry. The right to forfeit is security for the rent and therefore also for service charges if they are reserved as rent: *Howard v Fanshaw* [1895] 2 Ch. 581; *Escalus Properties Ltd v Robinson* [1996] Q.B. 231. It enables a landlord to recover possession of his property, often where the arrears of rent or service charge are a small proportion of the value of the property recovered. It is said that the courts lean against forfeiture: *Goodright d. Walter v Davids* (1778) Cowp. 803.

The advantages of forfeiture are:

- It is often an effective method of securing payment of unpaid rent and service charges;
- The landlord's costs are often paid in full;
- If possession is obtained, the onus is passed to the tenant to apply for relief from forfeiture.

The disadvantages are:

- It is open to abuse by landlords, and therefore treated circumspectly by the courts;
- In residential cases, statute has made significant reductions to the scope, procedure and preconditions of forfeiture for unpaid rent and service charge.

The fundamentals of forfeiture for unpaid service charges

18–010

- The lease must have a forfeiture clause. Absent one, there is no right to forfeit for unpaid service charges at all: *Doe d. Dixon v Roe* [1849] 7 C.B. 134.
- The forfeiture clause must cover unpaid service charges, which will usually be reserved as rent.
- If the service charge is reserved as rent there is no need for a notice under s.146 of the Law of Property Act 1925: s.146(11).
- Forfeiture may be effected by the issue and service of a claim for possession: *Billson v Residential Apartments* [1992] 1 A.C. 494.
- Alternatively, forfeiture may be effected by peaceable re-entry, but not in residential cases: see below. The courts frown upon peaceable re-entry in all cases: *Billson*.

Relief from forfeiture

18–011 In many cases, it is an application by the tenant for relief from forfeiture which results in payment of outstanding service charges.

Relief where service charges are reserved as rent—county court

18–012 In the county court, application for relief from forfeiture for non-payment of rent may be made by the tenant under s.138 of the County Courts Act 1984 if the forfeiture resulted in proceedings for possession being issued, or in the making of an order for possession. To obtain relief, the tenant must either pay into court or to the lessor not less than five clear days before the return day all the rent in arrear and the costs of the action, or pay into court or to the lessor all the rent in arrear and the costs of the claim within such period specified by the court, which may not be less than four weeks from the date of the order for possession: s.138(2) and 138(3). The period for payment specified by the court may be extended at any time before possession of the land is recovered: s.138(5).

It has been held that "all the rent in arrear" means the rent in arrears at the time when the court makes its order (i.e. not only the arrears at the date of the issue of the proceedings) because the court assumes that payment of that rent will result in the lease continuing: *Maryland Estates Ltd v Bar Joseph* [1998] 2 E.G.L.R. 47. That decision was made in the context of arrears of service charges which would now fall within s.81 of the Housing Act 1996 (see below). However, once a right to forfeit has arisen, it raises the question whether in order to obtain relief the tenant must pay amounts of service charge which have not been the subject of a determination or agreement satisfying s.81 of the Housing Act 1988. This point was considered in *Mohammadi v Anston Investments Ltd* [2004] L.&T.R. 6, but was not determined because the lease did not reserve service charges as rent. The jurisdiction of the leasehold valuation tribunal under s.27A(2) of the Landlord and Tenant Act 1985 to determine an application after payment has been made suggests that it is open to the court to order payment of the disputed sums as a term of relief and it will then be open to the tenant to apply to the leasehold valuation tribunal for a determination. The alternative courses will be either for the court to try the issue of the disputed service charge or to transfer the matter to the leasehold valuation tribunal.

Where the landlord recovers possession of the land at any time after the making of the order, the lessee may, at any time within six months from the date on which the lessor recovers possession, apply to the court for relief and the court may, if it thinks fit, grant to the lessee such relief, subject to such terms and conditions as it thinks fit: s.138(9). After the expiry of six months, all relief is barred: *United Dominions Trust Ltd v Shellpoint Trustees Ltd* [1993] 4 All E.R. 310.

If the landlord has obtained possession by peaceable re-entry, the lessee may, at any time within six months from the date on which the lessor re-entered, apply to the county court for relief, and on any such application the court may, if it thinks fit, grant to the lessee such relief the High Court could have granted: County Courts Act 1984, s.139(2). Reference should be made to the following paragraphs which deal with the terms on which the High Court will grant relief.

Service charges reserved as rent—High Court

18–013 The High Court's jurisdiction to grant relief from forfeiture by proceedings is s.38(1) of the Supreme Court Act 1981. Relief will usually be granted on payment of the arrears and the landlord's costs: *Standard Pattern Co v Ivey* [1962] Ch. 432

By s.210 of the Common Law Procedure Act 1852, any application for relief following execution of a judgment for possession based upon a half year's rent arrears must be made within six months of execution. The six month period will be treated as a guide in cases of less than a half year's rent: *Di Palma v Victoria Square Property Co* [1986] Ch. 150.

Where the landlord has peaceably re-entered without obtaining a court order, the High Court retains a jurisdiction in equity to grant relief. The six month limit does not apply but will be treated as a guide: *Thatcher v CH Pearce & Son (Contractors) Ltd* [1968] 1 W.L.R. 748.

Statutory limits on forfeiture of residential premises

18–014 Parliament has enacted a number of measures to restrict the scope of forfeiture of residential premises over the preceding three decades.

Protection from Eviction Act 1977

18–015 Peaceable re-entry of premises let as a dwelling is unlawful. Section 2 of the Protection from Eviction Act 1977 states that where any premises are let as a dwelling on a lease which is subject to a right of re-entry or forfeiture, it shall not be lawful to enforce that right otherwise than by proceedings in the court while any person is lawfully residing in the premises or part of them. It is also a criminal offence by s.1 of the Protection from Eviction Act 1977.

Housing Act 1996, s.81—forfeiture for unpaid service charges

18–016 Section 81(1) of the Housing Act 1996 (as amended by the Commonhold and Leasehold Reform Act 2002, s.170 and in force from February 28, 2005: SI 2004/3056) provides, that a landlord may not, in relation to premises let as a dwelling, exercise a right of re-entry or forfeiture for failure by a tenant to pay a service charge or administration charge unless:

(a) it is finally determined by (or on appeal from) a leasehold valuation tribunal or by a court, or by an arbitral tribunal in proceedings pursuant to a post-dispute arbitration agreement, that the amount of the service charge or administration charge is payable by him; or

(b) the tenant has admitted that it is so payable.

The landlord may not exercise a right of re-entry or forfeiture by virtue of subs.(1)(a) until after the end of the period of 14 days beginning with the day after that on which the final determination is made: s.81(2). It is finally determined that the amount of a service charge or administration charge is payable:

(a) if a decision that it is payable is not appealed against or otherwise challenged, at the end of the time for bringing an appeal or other challenge; or

(b) if such a decision is appealed against or otherwise challenged and not set aside in consequence of the appeal or other challenge, at the time specified in subs.(3A): s.81(3).

"The time" is the time when the appeal or other challenge is disposed of:

(a) by the determination of the appeal or other challenge and the expiry of the time for bringing a subsequent appeal (if any); or

(b) by its being abandoned or otherwise ceasing to have effect: s.81(3A).

In *Southwark London Borough Council v Tornaritis* [1999] C.L.Y. 3744 it was held that a prior judgment in default of a defence obtained under the predecessor to Pt 12 of the CPR amounted to a determination for the purposes of s.81. It is submitted that the amendments to s.81 made by s.170 of the Commonhold and Leasehold Reform Act 2002 do not affect this decision and that it will often be prudent to commence a money claim for unpaid service charges first.

Section 81 may apparently be raised at any stage in the proceedings: *Mohammadi v Anston Investments Ltd* [2004] L.&T.R. 6.

Failure to pay a small amount for a short period

18–017 Section 167(1) of the Commonhold and Leasehold Reform Act 2002 (in force in England from February 28, 2005: SI 2004/3056; but not yet in force in Wales) provides that a landlord under a long lease of a dwelling may not exercise a right of re-entry or forfeiture for failure by a tenant to pay an amount consisting of rent, service charges or administration charges (or a combination of them) unless the unpaid amount exceeds the prescribed sum or consists of or includes an amount which has been payable for more than a prescribed period.

By s.167(2) the prescribed sum may not exceed £500. It is currently set at £350 and the prescribed period is three years: The Rights of Re-entry and Forfeiture (Prescribed Sum and Period) (England) Regulations 2004 (SI 2004/3086). The effect of these provisions is that a landlord may not forfeit a lease for amounts of ground rent, service charges or administration charges less than £350 unless a proportion of the sum outstanding is more than three years old.

Any default charges, meaning administration charges payable in respect of the tenant's failure to pay any part of the unpaid amount, are excluded from the unpaid amount which is counted: s.167(3).

No requirement for a determination of breach before a forfeiture notice

18–018 In the (comparatively unusual) case of service charges not having been reserved as rent by the terms of the lease, the restrictions in s.167(1) of the Commonhold and Leasehold Reform Act 2002 do not prevent a landlord from serving notice under s.146 of the Law of Property Act 1925. That is because s.169(7) expressly disapplies s.168 in respect of a failure to pay a service charge or an administration charge.

Conclusions

18–019 The hurdles to forfeiting a lease for unpaid service charges must be carefully negotiated. In particular, s.81 of the Housing Act 1996 and s.167 of the Commonhold and Leasehold Reform Act 2002 would appear to have a cumulative effect. Therefore, it is submitted that a landlord may only exercise a right of forfeiture for failure to pay a service charge if the amount has been agreed/admitted/determined and exceeds £350 or consists of or includes an amount which has been payable for more than three years.

Declaration

18–020 The High Court has an inherent jurisdiction, and by s.38(1) of the County Courts Act 1984 the county court has a statutory jurisdiction, to make a declaration. In a service charge dispute this may include a declaration as to the (un)reasonableness of a charge, whether a sum is due under the terms of a lease, or who is liable to pay.

These powers are unaffected by the jurisdiction given to the leasehold valuation tribunal under s.27A of the Landlord and Tenant 1985: s.27A(7). Nor are they affected by the jurisdiction given to the leasehold valuation tribunal with regard to estate management charges under s.159 the Commonhold and Leasehold Reform Act 2002: s.159(8).

It should be noted that a declaration in favour of a landlord does not of itself give a right to payment. However, it may give a basis for forfeiture proceedings of premises let as a dwelling: Housing Act 1996 s.81(1)(b).

Application to the Leasehold Valuation Tribunal

Service charges

18–021 Under s.27A(1) of the Landlord and Tenant Act 1985 a landlord may apply to the leasehold valuation tribunal for a determination of any of the matters set out in s.27A(1) or (3). Reference should be made to Chapter 22 which contains a detailed analysis of the leasehold valuation tribunal's powers.

An application under s.27A can be used as a precursor to forfeiture in a situation where a dispute as to liability is anticipated.

Estate management charges

18–022 There is a parallel jurisdiction with regard to estate management charges in s.159(6) of the Commonhold and Leasehold Reform Act 2002, enabling a freeholder to apply to the leasehold valuation tribunal for a determination and for which reference should be made to Chapter 12.

Administration charges

18–023 Section 158 of and Sch.11 to the Commonhold and Leasehold Reform Act 2002 provide for the determination of administration charges by the leasehold valuation tribunal and reference should be made to Chapter 12.

Variation of leases

18–024 Leases of flats occasionally fail to provide for full recovery of expenditure incurred by a landlord *via* the service charge, either as a result of inadequate drafting or of changes to the property. Section 35(1) of the Landlord and Tenant Act 1987 gives any party to a long lease of a flat the right to apply to the leasehold valuation tribunal for an order varying the lease. The grounds on which an application may be made include that the lease fails to make satisfactory provision with respect to the computation of a service charge payable under the lease: s.35(2)(f). Reference should be made to Chapter 21 for a full treatment of this topic.

Chapter 19

Tenants' Remedies

Introduction

19–001 The purpose of this chapter is to identify the range of remedies available to a tenant and to give guidance as to the uses of each.

The following remedies are potentially available:

- Set-off;
- Right to withhold payment of service charge;
- Injunction;
- Claim for breach of trust;
- Application to the court for a declaration;
- Claim for repayment of overpaid service charges;
- Application to leasehold valuation tribunal under s.27A of the Landlord and Tenant Act 1985 in respect of service charges (residential premises only);
- Application to the leasehold valuation tribunal under s.159(6) of the Commonhold and Leasehold Reform Act 2002 in respect of estate management charges;
- Application to the leasehold valuation tribunal under s.157 of and Sch.11 to the Commonhold and Leasehold Reform Act 2002 in respect of administration charges (residential premises only);
- Inspection of documents pursuant to s.154 the Commonhold and Leasehold Reform Act 2002 (residential premises only);
- Management Audit under Pt V of the Leasehold Reform, Housing and Urban Development Act 1993 (residential premises only);

- Appointment of a Manager under Pt II of the Landlord and Tenant Act 1987 (residential premises only);
- Appointment of a surveyor under s.84 of the Housing Act 1996 (residential premises only);
- Exercising the right to manage given by Pt 2 Ch.1 of the Commonhold and Leasehold Reform Act 2002 (residential premises only);
- Collective enfranchisement under Pt 1 of Ch.1 of the Leasehold Reform, Housing and Urban Development Act 1993 (residential premises only).

Set-off

19–002 Where a landlord is in breach of his obligations under the lease, for example the repairing obligations, the tenant may set off against the service charge a claim for damages for breach of obligation under the lease: *Filross Securities v Midgeley* [1998] 3 E.G.L.R. 43. However, where it is the non-payment of service charges that has rendered the landlord unable to perform its obligations under the lease, a further set-off operates in favour of the landlord which cancels out the tenant's claim for damages: *Bluestorm Ltd v Portvale Holdings Ltd* [2004] 2 E.G.L.R. 38.

A tenant may set off a claim for damages for breach of repairing obligation by his former landlord against a claim by the assignee of the reversion for rent due before the assignment that has been assigned under s.141 of the Law of Property Act 1925: *Muscat v Smith* [2003] 1 W.L.R. 2853. The question whether the set-off can be raised against rent due after the assignment has not been determined.

The right to withhold service charges

19–003 Section 152 of the Commonhold and Leasehold Reform Act 2002 (which amends s.21 of the Landlord and Tenant Act 1985) introduces a new statutory right for a tenant to withhold payment of service charges in certain circumstances. At present, s.152 is only in force for the purposes of making regulations: Commonhold and Leasehold Reform Act 2002 (Commencement No.1, Savings and Transitional Provisions) (England) Order (SI 2002/1912).

When it comes into force, s.21(1) will provide that the landlord must supply to each tenant by whom service charges are payable, in relation to each accounting period, a written statement of account. This is dealt with in Chapter 10. Section 21A(1) of the Landlord and

Tenant Act 1985 will enable a tenant to withhold payment of a service charge if—

(a) the landlord has not supplied a document to him by the time by which he is required to supply it under s.21; or

(b) the form or content of a document which the landlord has supplied to him under that section (at any time) does not conform exactly or substantially with the requirements prescribed by regulations under subs.(4) of that section.

The maximum amount which the tenant may withhold is an amount equal to the aggregate of—

(a) the service charges paid by him in the accounting period to which the document concerned would or does relate; and

(b) so much of the aggregate amount required to be dealt with in the statement of account for that accounting period by s.21(1)(c)(i) as stood to his credit: s.21A(2).

An amount may not be withheld under s.21A—

(a) in a case within para.(a) of subs.(1), after the document concerned has been supplied to the tenant by the landlord; or

(b) in a case within para.(b) of that subsection, after a document conforming exactly or substantially with the requirements prescribed by regulations under s.21(4) has been supplied to the tenant by the landlord by way of replacement of the one previously supplied: s.21A(3).

Section 21A(4) provides that if, on an application made by the landlord to a leasehold valuation tribunal, the tribunal determines that the landlord has a reasonable excuse for a failure giving rise to the right of a tenant to withhold an amount under this section, the tenant may not withhold the amount after the determination is made.

It should be noted that it is a summary offence, punishable by a fine not exceeding level four on the standard scale for a person to fail, without reasonable excuse, to perform a duty imposed on him by s.21: Landlord and Tenant Act 1985, s.25.

Injunction

19–004 It is possible in an appropriate case to restrain a landlord by injunction from carrying out works, the cost of which would be recovered *via* the service charge, pending an application to the leasehold valuation tribunal for a determination of the reasonableness under s.19 of the Landlord and Tenant Act 1985: *Bounds v Camden LBC* [1999] C.L.Y. 3728. However, see also *Hi-Lift Elevator Services v Temple* (1995) 70 P.&C.R. 620 which might now be decided differently.

Breach of trust

19–005 Service charges are held on a statutory trust by reason of s.42 of the Landlord and Tenant 1987, which is discussed in Chapter 15 of this book. The landlord will therefore have the duty of a trustee to use such due diligence and care in the management of the trust as businessmen of ordinary prudence and vigilance would use in the management of their own affairs: *Bartlett v Barclays Bank Trust Co Ltd* [1980] Ch. 515. If the landlord is remunerated by way of an administration charge, he will be subject to the more stringent duties of a paid trustee: *Bartlett*.

This may provide a remedy against a former landlord who has dissipated the service charges, or a sinking fund, on works which are not of a reasonable standard or cost, or not within the terms of the lease. The former landlord would be required to compensate the trust fund. In such a situation, although the lessees could apply to the leasehold valuation tribunal under s.27A of the Landlord and Tenant Act 1985, any determination in their favour would be of little practical use because they were no longer in a landlord and tenant relationship, and it is suggested that the breach of trust route may provide a remedy.

Application to the court for a declaration

19–006 The High Court has an inherent jurisdiction, and by s.38(1) of the County Courts Act 1984 the county court has a statutory jurisdiction, to make a declaration. In a service charge dispute this may include a declaration as to the (un)reasonableness of a charge, whether a sum is due under the terms of a lease, or who is liable to pay.

The remedy is available to tenants as well as landlords. This is dealt with at paragraph 18–020.

Claim for repayment of overpaid service charges

19–007 Where the tenant has paid service charges which are not due, for example, in a residential case where it has subsequently been determined by either a leasehold valuation tribunal or a court that the service charge is unreasonable, the tenant may recover the overpaid sums by a claim for money paid under a mistake of fact or of law. In the light of the decision of the House of Lords in *Kleinwort Benson v Lincoln City Council* [1999] 2 A.C. 349 the distinction between mistake of fact and of law will not be relevant to this kind of claim.

In many cases, there will not be any need for a restitutionary claim of this kind as the remedy of set-off will suffice. However, there may be situations where it is appropriate, for example, when the tenant is assigning his interest, or where the amount of the overpayment is so substantial that the tenant will be out of pocket for a prolonged period even if he sets off against future payments. In such cases, a claim for unjust enrichment will lie. For an example of a case involving recovery of overpaid rent see *Nurdin & Peacock plc v DB Ramsden & Co (No.2)* [1999] 1 W.L.R. 1249.

Application to the Leasehold Valuation Tribunal

19–008 Application to the Leasehold Valuation Tribunal with regard to service charges under s.27A of the Landlord and Tenant Act 1985 is considered in Chapters 11 and 22.

Application to the Leasehold Valuation Tribunal in relation to estate management charges under s.159(6) of the Commonhold and Leasehold Reform Act 2002 is considered in Chapter 12.

Application to the Leasehold Valuation Tribunal in relation to administration charges under s.158 of and Sch.11 to the Commonhold and Leasehold Reform Act 2002 is considered in Chapter 12.

Inspection of documents

19–009 The right to inspect documents found in s.22 of Landlord and Tenant Act 1987 (as amended by s.154 of the Commonhold and Leasehold Reform Act 2002) is considered in Chapter 10.

The right to a management audit

19–010 The right to a management audit under Ch.V of the Leasehold Reform, Housing and Urban Development Act 1993 is considered in Chapter 10.

Appointment of a Manager

19–011 Appointment of a Manager under Pt II of the Landlord and Tenant Act 1987 is considered in Chapter 27.

Appointment of a surveyor

19–012 Appointment of a surveyor under s.84 of and Sch.4 to the Housing Act 1996 is considered in Chapter 10.

Exercise of the right to manage

19–013 The exercise of the right to manage under Pt 2 Ch.1 of the Commonhold and Leasehold Reform Act 2002 is considered in Chapter 29.

Collective enfranchisement

19–014 Collective enfranchisement of flats under the Leasehold Reform, Housing and Urban Development Act 1993 Pt 1 Ch.1 is the ultimate remedy for dissatisfied lessees in that it allows them to acquire, at a price determined by the Act, the freehold of the building. It is beyond the scope of this book.

Chapter 20

Commonhold Finances

Commonhold

Introduction to commonhold

20–001 Commonhold is an alternative to the conventional method of owning flats and other interdependent properties under a lease. It is not a new estate in land but a new form of freehold ownership.

The major advantage of commonhold for property owners is that possession is not restricted to a set period of time, as it is under the leasehold system.

The relevant primary legislation is the Commonhold and Leasehold Reform Act 2002 ("CLRA 2002"), which received Royal Assent on May 1, 2002. Part 1 of the CLRA 2002, which deals with commonhold, was implemented on September 27, 2004.

The CLRA 2002, in conjunction with the Commonhold Regulations 2004 (SI 2004/1829) ("the Regulations"), Commonhold (Land Registration) Rules 2004 (SI 2004/1830) and the Land Registry Practice Guide 60, govern the procedures for setting up, running and registering commonhold land.

Commonhold is intended to eventually replace long leasehold in residential property ownership. As of June 7, 2005, no commonholds have been registered.

Commonhold features

20–002 All commonholds will have a commonhold association (which must be a private company limited by guarantee, see CLRA 2002, s.34), a commonhold community statement ("CCS"), and two or more commonhold units. The unit holders are freehold proprietors of their respective units and also the only members of the commonhold association.

The CCS makes provision for the rights and duties of the commonhold association and unit holders (CLRA 2002, s.1(c)), and acts as a contract between the unit holders and the commonhold association. The CCS is in a predominantly prescribed form (CLRA 2002, s.31 of and Sch.3 to the Regulations)(the "Model CCS"). The commonhold association, comprised of directors and members, manages the commonhold within the parameters of the CCS.

Charges for services

20–003 The unit-holders meet the costs of running a commonhold and maintaining a commonhold association. The costs have the same function as service charge in leasehold developments, but the term "service charge" is conspicuously absent from the legislation governing commonhold. However, the legislation does not offer a new definition to describe the contribution paid by unit-holders.

Statutes that do not apply to commonhold define the term "service charge", and since commonhold is presented as a new and distinct concept from the legislation and jurisprudence governing leaseholds, there is a move away from adopting leasehold terminology. Accordingly, the term "commonhold contribution" is currently favoured as an alternative to "service charge".

The statutory framework

20–004 Section 38 of the Act states:

"38 Commonhold Assessment

(1) A commonhold community statement must make provision—

(a) requiring the directors of the commonhold association to make an annual estimate of the income required to be raised from unit-holders to meet the expenses of the association,

(b) enabling the directors of the commonhold association to make estimates from time to time of income required to be raised from unit-holders in addition to the annual estimate,

(c) specifying the percentage of any estimate made under paragraph (a) or (b) which is to be allocated to each unit,

(d) requiring each unit-holder to make payments in respect of the percentage of any estimate which is allocated to his unit, and

(e) requiring the directors of the commonhold association to serve notices on unit-holders specifying payments required to be made by them and the date on which each payment is due.

(2) For the purpose of sub-section (1)(c)—

(a) the percentages allocated by a commonhold community statement to the commonhold units must amount in aggregate to 100;

(b) a commonhold community statement may specify 0 per cent in relation to a unit."

Commonhold contributions

Annual commonhold estimate and additional occasional estimate

20–005 The commonhold association must prepare an annual estimate of expenditure in advance. Paragraph 4.2.1 of the Model CCS provides that "the directors of the commonhold association must make an annual estimate of the income required to be raised from unit-holders to meet the expenses of the commonhold association".

If the annual estimate proves incorrect or additional expenses arise (which do not qualify under the emergency procedure, see below), the commonhold can raise an additional estimate. Paragraph 4.2.1 of the Model CCS goes on to provide that the directors of the commonhold:

> ". . . may from time to time make estimates of income required to be raised from unit-holders in addition to the annual estimate".

The annual estimate and additional estimates must follow the standard notice procedures, which includes a consultation requirement.

Commonhold assessment consultation

20–006 The consultation procedure, which must be followed when raising an assessment, is as follows:

(a) The directors of the commonhold association must provide notice to all unit-holders of a proposed assessment (Model CCS, para.4.2.2) using Form 1 "*Notice of Proposed Commonhold Assessment*".

(b) A unit-holder may make a representation in writing to the commonhold association within one month (Model CCS, para.4.2.3).

(c) The directors must consider any representation duly made by a unit-holder (Model CCS, para.4.2.4).

(d) The directors must serve a second notice on each unit holder detailing the amount to be paid and the date(s) for payment using Form 2 "*Demand for Payment of Commonhold Assessment*".

(e) The date for payment (or first instalment) must not be less than 14 days after the notice is given.

Emergency commonhold assessment

20–007 An emergency commonhold assessment can be raised where the directors consider that "the commonhold association requires income to meet its expenses in an emergency" (Model CCS, para.4.2.5). An emergency may be determined by reference to a situation whereby income is required and there is insufficient time to permit an assessment by normal means (which would take approximately two months). There are no specific remedies provided to a unit-holder by the legislation if directors abuse the emergency assessment procedure. An approach could be to address concerns through association meetings.

An emergency commonhold assessment does not require the consultation procedure to be followed but the commonhold association must give unit-holders notice of an Emergency Commonhold Assessment using Form 3 "*Demand for payment of emergency commonhold assessment*", which requires a reason to be provided for the emergency assessment.

Unlike demands under standard assessments, payment can be demanded by a date earlier than 14 days after the notice is given.

Reserve funds

20–008 Section 39 of the CLRA 2002 provides for reserve funds and raising a levy in respect of the same.

A reserve fund is restricted to the "repair and maintenance of the common parts . . . [and] . . . of commonhold units" (CLRA 2002, s.39(1)(a) and (b)).

Section 39 of the Act, the Regulations and the Model CCS do not contain an obligation to establish or maintain a reserve fund, which is in contrast to s.38 which makes it mandatory for a commonhold to raise an annual assessment.

Creating a reserve fund

20–009 When first registering a commonhold, the directors may choose to establish a reserve fund in the CCS. However, the Model CCS imposes the following requirements:

(a) The directors must "consider" whether to commission a reserve study by an appropriately qualified person within the first year in which the commonhold is registered (Model CCS, para.4.2.6);

(b) The directors must commission a reserve study a minimum of once every 10 years (Model CCS, para.4.2.7);

(c) The directors must, in light of the mandatory study, decide whether to establish a reserve fund or to maintain any existing reserve fund (Model CCS, para.4.2.8);

(d) Additionally, the directors must at appropriate intervals consider whether to establish or maintain a reserve fund (independently of a mandatory study) (Model CCS, para.4.2.9).

If the directors determine a need for a reserve fund, they must establish one (Model CCS, para.4.2.9).

The unit-holders may by ordinary resolution require the directors to establish a reserve fund (Model CCS, para.4.2.10). There is no like provision to enable unit-holders to require the directors not to maintain a reserve fund, albeit that unit-holders could bring a special resolution or remove directors to force such a change.

A unit-holders liability to a reserve fund will be set out in para.3 of Annex 3 to the CCS. The percentage of a reserve fund levy allocated to a unit may differ from the commonhold assessment allocation and a single unit can contribute a different percentage to different reserve funds.

If a reserve fund is established, or subdivided after the inception of the original CCS, the CCS will need to be amended. This can only be achieved by a special resolution (Model CCS, para.4.8.9), save when a unit-holder proposes a fund is established by ordinary resolution.

Reserve fund contributions

20–010 The directors must set a levy from time to time for a reserve fund that is established (Model CCS, para.4.2.11), but they must also seek to ensure that unnecessary reserves are not accumulated. However, there is no obligation to ensure that sufficient funds are accumulated. The following procedure must be followed in setting and collecting fund contributions:

(a) The directors must notify each unit-holder of the total levy, the percentage allocation to each unit, the date(s) and amount(s) of payments required, and the right to make representations. Form 4 "*Notice of Proposed Reserve Fund Levy*" must be used.

(b) Representations in response to Form 4 must be made within one month (Model CCS, para.4.2.13).

(c) The directors must consider any representations.

(d) The demand for payment of the levy is made using Form 5 "*Demand for Payment of Reserve Fund Levy*".

(e) The earliest date for payment under the levy must not be less than 14 days after the notice (Model CCS, para.4.2.14).

Protecting reserve funds

20–011 A reserve fund is protected against judgment creditors, and cannot be used for the purpose of the enforcement of any debt whilst the commonhold endures, save for a judgment debt referable to a reserve fund activity (CLRA 2002, s.39(4) and s.56(a)–(b)). A reserve fund activity is an activity that can be financed from the fund in compliance with the Act (CLRA 2002, s.39(5)(a)).

The Act does not expressly prohibit directors from using a reserve fund for a commonhold purpose other than that for which the fund was conceived, and occasions may arise that would justify monies from a reserve fund being redirected to pressing expenses of the commonhold for which the fund was not established.

Payment

20–012 A unit-holder must meet a demand for payment within the time frame prescribed on Form 2 (the commonhold assessment), Form 3 (an emergency assessment) or Form 4 (reserve fund levy) (Model CCS, para.4.2.15). Interest is payable at the prescribed rate on late payments (Model CCS, para.4.2.16).

However, the commonhold association is restricted to standard recovery remedies between creditor and debtor, save as follows.

Third party rental payments

Identifying tenants

20–013 The commonhold association can secure the diversion of rent from the tenant of a defaulting unit-holder to the association to settle that unit-holder's arrears. To that end a commonhold association must be notified within 14 days of the date of a tenancy being granted by a unit-holder or tenant granting a sub-tenancy (Model CCS, para.4.7.15).

A copy of the written tenancy agreement or details of any oral tenancy must be supplied, using Form 14 "*Notice of a Grant of a Tenancy in a Commonhold Unit*". In default of notice of a tenancy, the commonhold association can request the details of a tenancy by Form 8 "*Notice requesting further details about a tenancy*". The recipient (the occupier and/or unit holder) must reply within 14 days, giving the requested information (Model CCS, para.4.2.42).

Procedure

20–014 Following a default by a unit-holder to pay sums owing to the commonhold, the commonhold association can serve Form 6 "*Notice to Tenant of Diversion of Rent*" on the unit-holder's tenant, specifying the payments the tenant is required to make. The notice cannot "require the tenant to pay more rent than is due under the tenancy agreement, to pay rent earlier than is due under the tenancy agreement or to pay rent earlier than the diversion date" (Model CCS, para.4.2.19).

Form 6 can be served immediately following the date for payment by the unit-holder (Model CCS, para.4.2.18), but the "diversion date" must be at least 14 days after the notice is given (Model CCS, para.4.2.18).

Following service of Form 6, the tenant becomes personally liable to the commonhold association for the rent (Model CCS, para.4.2.20), and would therefore be foolish to continue to pay rent to his landlord.

The tenant is liable to pay interest at the prescribed rate for late payments to the commonhold association (Model CCS, para.4.2.26), and further "may not rely on any non-statutory right of deduction, set-off or counterclaim that he has against the unit-holder to reduce the amount to be paid to the commonhold association" (Model CCS, para.4.2.23).

The effect of payment of rent to the commonhold association is to discharge the liability of the unit-holder to the association and the tenant's rental obligation to the unit-holder. (Model CCS, paras 4.2.24 and 4.2.25).

The commonhold association must notify the tenant and the unit-holder that the diversion of rent has ended within 14 days of the arrears being cleared (Model CCS, para.4.2.22) and a tenant is entitled to be reimbursed for any overpayment to the commonhold association by the unit-holder (Model CCS, paras 4.2.39 and 4.2.40). The unit-holder must reimburse the tenant within 14 days of being given notice of an overpayment (Model CCS, para.4.2.40).

Sub-tenants

20–015 Following default on payment by a unit-holder, the commonhold association must first look to the tenant of the unit but may thereafter seek to enforce payment against a sub-tenant. The procedure is similar to that for enforcement against a tenant and is detailed in paras 4.2.28–4.2.38 of the Model CCS.

New unit-holders

20–016 Unit-holders are not liable for sums owing to the commonhold association once they have transferred their interest in the unit (CLRA 2002, s.16(2) and (3)(b)). Rather, the commonhold association is able to give notice requiring a new unit-holder to pay debts owed to the commonhold association by the former unit-holder (Model CCS, paras 4.2.15 and 4.2.16).

A new unit-holder can be liable for the debts of "any former unit-holder" (Model CCS, para.4.7.3) of the unit being purchased, meaning that the liability can be accumulated from more than one predecessor in title.

A prospective new unit-holder can request a commonhold unit information certificate (Form 9) from the commonhold association, which should detail any debt associated with the relevant unit. The new unit-holder can only be required to pay the amount specified on the certificate as at the date of the certificate (Model CCS, para.4.7.4), but will remain liable for any indebtedness arising after the date of the certificate (Model CCS, para.4.7.3). It is therefore important for commonhold associations to ensure that certificates do not understate sums owed by a unit, and for conveyancers to address liability for post-certificate debts that may arise before completion.

A failure to provide the certificate does not exempt the purchaser from liability for any sums owing. A purchaser should not complete without the certificate and could make an urgent application to court requiring specific performance of the commonhold association's obligations to provide the certificate.

A new unit-holder must settle any debt within 14 days of the notice (Model CCS, para.4.7.5), after which interest becomes payable at the prescribed rate (Model CCS, para.4.7.6). The new unit-holder is entitled to an indemnity from his predecessor in title for any such sums paid (Model CCS, para.4.7.7).

It remains for conveyancing solicitors, as with leasehold transfers, to ensure that the vendor of a unit meets any indebtedness to the commonhold association to avoid liability passing to the purchaser.

Commonhold finances v leasehold finances

20–017 There is both overt and subtle legal and practical disparity between the financing of a commonhold and a leasehold development. By way of illustration, the following list provides a number of such differences:

(a) The commonhold assessment is only restricted to meeting "the expenses of the association". The commonhold directors are thereby able to require commonhold contributions to meet any genuine expense of the association. This is in contrast to a service charge, which is restricted in scope by the terms of a given lease and, for example, argument over whether an expense is a repair or an improvement.

(b) The commonhold can only provide a single undivided commonhold assessment, whereas a service charge can be levied in separate "Parts". For example, under a lease it is possible in a mixed development of flats and houses that all properties may be required to contribute towards a "Part A" of the service charge for items such as communal gardens and roadways, whilst only the flats would contribute to "Part B", being costs associated with maintaining the block of flats. It is further possible that the percentage payable by a leaseholder would differ under Part A and Part B.

(c) The aggregate of the percentages allocated to unit-holders must total 100 per cent. There cannot therefore be a profit element by raising from the unit holders more than the amount required under the commonhold assessment.

(d) The CCS details the percentage of the commonhold assessment and reserve fund allocated to each unit, and therefore each unit-holder will be able to determine the commonhold contribution of other unit-holders, a degree of transparency often lacking in leasehold.

(e) A lease may only allow for landlord's expenditure to be recovered after it has been incurred, and may not provide for advance payments. This situation is not possible under commonhold, where an advance budget must be set.

(f) Failure to consider representations made in regard to service charge may prejudice a landlord seeking to establish that charges were reasonably incurred if challenged under s.19 of the Landlord and Tenant Act 1985. There is no similar risk to a commonhold association that fails to consider representations on the commonhold assessment. The only recourse for a dissatisfied unit-holder is to raise concerns at an annual general meeting or extraordinary general meeting.

(g) A contribution to a reserve fund is invariably collected as part of the service charge in a lease, in the same proportions as the service charge. The CLRA 2002 keeps the commonhold assessment and reserve fund entirely separate.

Chapter 21

The Variation of Terms in Residential Leases

Introduction

21–001 The Nugee Committee Report 1985 (The Committee of Inquiry into the Management of Privately Owned Blocks of Flats) recommended that the court should have the power to vary leases after identifying the difficulties in amending defective or badly drafted long leases. That recommendation evolved into Pt IV of the Landlord and Tenant Act 1987 which sets out a statutory code for the variation of long leases by the court in specified circumstances. It has given rise to few reported decisions, perhaps because the broad concepts of "reasonableness" that underpin its application to varying factual situations will seldom attract the attention of the higher courts. Before considering the statutory provisions in their application to certain types of clause, the following should be observed in respect of any variation application under Pt IV:

(i) Any party to a long lease of a flat (or any dwelling if it relates to insurance—s.40 of the Landlord and Tenant Act 1987) can bring the application;

(ii) If the lease fails "to make satisfactory provision" in respect of;

(iii) Any of the matters set out in s.35(2) of the Act.

The Act gives scant guidance on what amounts to "satisfactory provision" but does include some non-exhaustive and rather vague factors to be taken into account when deciding whether a flat provides a reasonable standard of accommodation.

The main areas where Pt IV is likely to be invoked are:

(i) Service charges;

(ii) Insurance provisions; and

(iii) Miscellaneous other clauses.

All applications under Pt IV from September 30, 2003 lie to the Leasehold Valuation Tribunal (by reason of s.163 of the CLRA 2002).

Service charges

21–002 The provisions dealing with service charges are ss.35(2)(e) and (f), (3A), (4) and 36.

In reality s.35(2)(f) should give rise to no difficulty. It expressly provides for that which seems to be obvious. It applies when a lease does not make satisfactory provision in respect of the computation of service charges (but not the amount of those service charges). Then, s.35(4) provides that satisfactory provision is not made if the lease computes each tenant's liability to pay the service charge as a percentage or proportion of the entire service related expenditure and the aggregate of those percentages or proportions adds up to more than 100 per cent of the expenditure incurred (or to be incurred). Many will find this so obvious that its inclusion may seem surprising. However, s.35(4) does not purport to set out the only circumstances in which service charge provisions in a lease might fail to make satisfactory provision. There may be one other instance where the ability to rely upon s.35(2)(f) will be important. If a landlord increases the number of flats within a given development the computation of the service charge payable under the then existing leases may need revision, but the several leases may make no provision for any such revision. Perhaps the existing tenants would be unlikely to object given that they might expect their share of the overall service charge liability to reduce. However, in a situation where the existing tenants' objection is, in reality, an objection to the proposed increase in the number of flats, a landlord may need to rely upon s.35(2)(f) to seek a variation of the leases so as to provide for a new mechanism for computing the service charge. In *Devonshire Reid Properties Ltd v Treneman* (1997) 20 E.G. 148, the landlord proposed to add one more flat to a building that comprised four flats. The existing tenants objected to the principle of another flat being added and did so partly on the basis that the intention of the parties, as objectively ascertained from the several leases (which were held to amount to a letting scheme), did not contemplate the addition of a further flat. In that case it seems that no reference was made to s.35(2)(f) with a view to arguing that the terms of the several leases dealing with service charges should not be taken into account as part of the objective consideration because there existed a statutory mechanism for varying the several service charge clauses in the event that the additional flat was created.

Section 35(2)(e) allows the Leasehold Valuation Tribunal to vary a lease that fails to make satisfactory provision with respect to the recovery by one party to the lease from another party to it of expenditure incurred or to be incurred by him or on his behalf for the benefit of that other party or of a number of persons who include that party. The only specific guidance given as to what is included is in s.35(3A) where the factors to be considered specifically include whether the lease makes satisfactory provision for interest on unpaid service charges.

21–003 The issue common to both subsections is whether a lease "fails to make satisfactory provision" only if the provision is unsatisfactory to all parties to the lease or to one only. The complete answer cannot be that an objective test is applied. For example, in the *Treneman* case, the tenants could properly argue that the service charge clause, from their viewpoint, was entirely satisfactory in that the service charge was shared equally. Thus, in that case, it was properly arguable that the fact of the equal sharing of the service charge was not a factor to be taken into account in determining whether the landlord could create another flat, but that if he could do so, then even though the tenants were not dissatisfied with the existing service charge provisions in their leases, they were nonetheless objectively unsatisfactory because they failed to provide a mechanism for the variation of the proportion to be paid by each lessee in the event of the number of flats being increased. This approach may be justified by reference to the High Court decision in *Paul Hanson v 169 Queen's Gate Ltd* (2000) 1 E.G.L.R. 40 where Mr Bernard Livesey Q.C. (sitting as a judge of the Chancery Division), on facts similar to those in *Treneman* held that the envelope of a flat letting scheme was to be found in the horizontal plane only and not in a vertical plane, so that the landlord should not be restrained by interlocutory injunction from creating two additional flats, one within the existing roof space and the other above an existing flat roof. Whilst s.35(2)(f) was not specifically referred to in that case, the addition of the two extra flats would have resulted in a situation where a variation under that provision was necessary. Equally, in *Stapel v Bellshore Property Investments Ltd* (2001) 3 E.G.L.R. 7 it was argued by the landlord that the draftsman of the service charges provisions in certain residential leases deliberately provided for the lessees to pay for repairs to parts of a "building" that they did not occupy. On that argument, the lease would make satisfactory provision for the landlord but not the lessee.

Section 35(e) of the Act provides for an application to be made if the lease does not make "satisfactory provision" dealing with "the recovery" of "expenditure incurred or to be incurred . . . for the benefit of" another party to the lease. That provision is open to two possible constructions. The narrow construction is that it applies only to the mechanics of recovery. The wider construction is that it applies to the amount sought to be recovered and the bases upon which recovery is said to be justified. It seems likely that the courts would find that the narrower construction is the proper construction because the Leasehold Valuation Tribunal already has jurisdiction (see below) to adjudicate upon the reasonableness or recoverability of service charges and insurance premiums. In *Berrycroft Management Company Ltd v Sinclair Gardens* (1997) 1 E.G.L.R. 47 the Court of Appeal ruled upon the recoverability of insurance premiums paid by the landlord in a situation where lower premiums were readily available in the market. The litigation partly turned upon ss.19 and 30(A) Landlord and Tenant Act 1985, and it is notable that Pt IV of the 1987 Act was not argued as applicable nor raised by the Court of Appeal, as well it might have been if the wider interpretation mentioned above is to be preferred.

21–004 Despite these issues, in practice the Leasehold Valuation Tribunal had no difficulty in applying the statutory criteria in the limited number of reported cases determined by it under s.35(e) and (f):

(a) In *McKay v G&O Investments*, CAM/22UG/NAM/2003/0002, a Tribunal varied a provision in a lease that fixed interest at 20 per cent per annum to an interest rate of 4 per cent above Barclays Bank base rate. The Tribunal found that both s.35(2)(e) and (3A) applied.

(b) In *re: Sollershott Hall, Letchworth* CAM/22UF/LVT/2004, a successor to the original freeholder had granted leases without proper reflection on their relation to the earlier leases. None of the parties argued against a change in apportionment, the tenants contending for a different percentage to that argued for by the landlord. The Tribunal found that s.35(2)(f) was applicable and varied the apportionment of service charges in all the leases to reflect the current user.

(c) In *Tickmean v Iterasia* LON/00BK/LVL/2004/0002/01, a number of leases had a blank space by the percentage liability for service charges and the total recoverable charges amounted to under 90 per cent of the landlord's expenditure. The Tribunal found that both s.35(2)(f) and (4) were applicable and varied the proportions to amount to 100 per cent.

(d) In *Sussex Property Development v Amin* CHI/00ML/LSC/2004/0003, a small extension had been built on another part of the building after the original lease was granted. The Tribunal declined to adjust the percentage apportionment downwards to reflect the new development.

Insurance provisions

21–005 If a lease fails to make "satisfactory provision" relating to insurance of the flat or dwelling, the court can vary the relevant clause in the lease. No statutory criteria are set out for determining when an insurance provision might not be satisfactory. Perhaps one of the most common complaints from tenants is that their leases provide for the insurance to be effected by the landlord or on his behalf, with a nominated insurer and, often, through the landlord's agency with that insurer. However, that is not usually the real complaint. The real complaint is that the premium payable as a result of those provisions is not the cheapest reasonably obtainable for any given cover. Section 38(7) expressly provides that a variation cannot be effected which would deprive the landlord of his right to nominate an insurer or to provide a list of insurers from which the tenants can choose or which requires the insurance to be placed with a specified insurer who is not the insurer specified by the landlord. This indicates that Pt IV is limited to situations where unsatisfactory provision has been made for insurance cover to be obtained or maintained or where the scope of the cover is unsatisfactory, rather than being directly applicable to disputes between a lessor and lessees concerning the reasonableness of the cost of such cover. In some instances, directly relevant to cost, Pt IV may nonetheless be applicable. This will arise, for example, where the lease provides for the lessor to insure against the "usual insured perils" which may exclude terrorism cover. If a lessor declines to arrange or include terrorism cover then the lessees would plainly have a sufficient interest to seek a variation of the terms of their leases to extend the lessor's insuring obligation to cover such a peril.

Other provisions

21–006 Sections 35(2)(a) of the Act relates to the repair of the building and to any land or building "in respect of which rights are conferred on him under it". Thus where the lease also grants a legal easement of way over land not contained within the demise, for example, the lessor's next door premises as an emergency fire escape route, Pt IV might come into play. If the grant of the easement does not provide for the emergency escape route to be properly maintained so as to be properly useable, a conflict will arise. An easement of way does not carry with it an obligation upon the owner of the servient tenement to maintain the way. Thus the only mechanism open to the lessee, if the way is not maintained so that it is safely useable, will be to seek a variation of the lease so that it imposes an obligation upon the lessor to maintain the way so that it is safely useable as an escape route. On the basis that satisfactory provision will not have been made for the escape route to be used throughout the term of the demise, unless it is maintained so as to be safely useable, it is to be expected that in such a situation s.35(2)(a) would result in the lease being varied notwithstanding that any such variation will impose on the servient owner an obligation that he would not usually bear.

Section 35(2)(d) relates to the provision or maintenance of services which are reasonably necessary to ensure that the occupiers of flats enjoy a reasonable standard of accommodation. Although in very wide terms and governed by the uncertainty of what might be reasonable, this provision must be applied using both an objective and subjective standard. What may amount to a reasonable standard of accommodation may vary depending upon the type of flats and the general condition of the common parts, as expressly provided by s.35(3)(b). Thus a failure to make provision for a concierge may allow lessees of upmarket Mayfair flats to show that a lease fails to provide for services necessary to provide them with a reasonable standard of accommodation, whilst lessees in Grimethorpe might struggle to make good the same argument. In short, s.35(3) envisages both an objective and subjective element to the test of what is reasonable in any factual situation.

Who can apply

21–007 Section 35(1) is clear in providing that any party to the long lease of a flat can make an application to vary its terms. It is likely that most variation applications will be multi-party and s.37 sets out the requirements to be observed when it is proposed that more than one lease should be varied. What at first sight appears to be a drafting oddity in s.37, is explained by appreciating that under s.37(6) each tenant and the landlord are to be counted in reckoning the number of "parties" involved.

In a situation where there are less than nine leases, all or all but one of the parties must consent to the application. Thus if there are two lessees, one of them can make the application notwithstanding that the other lessee does not consent to it, provided that the landlord consents to it (s.37(6)) as it is important to note that the landlord is counted as one party for the purpose of s.37(5) and when determining whether the necessary number of parties consent as required by s.37(5). Indeed, the practical effect of s.37(6) is to make these variation applications conditional upon them being backed by a sizeable majority of the parties concerned. If, notwithstanding opposition to a variation, the variation order is made, any party to the application can be ordered to pay compensation to another in respect of any loss or disadvantage that he is likely to suffer as a result of the variation.

Assessing compensation

21–008 The statute gives no indication of how such compensation is to be assessed but the general principles for assessing compensation are set out in s.38(10). Given that a variation order cannot be made if one party would be substantially prejudiced (s.37(6)), unless that substantial prejudice can be adequately compensated, it seems that compensation may fall to be awarded in two distinct types of situation:

(a) where a party will suffer substantial prejudice that is considered to be capable of monetary compensation; and

(b) where a party will suffer prejudice that does not reach the threshold of substantial prejudice.

The quantification of compensation will need to be fact sensitive, as the following illustrations show. In a case where a lessee opposes the variation of several leases to provide for a 24 hour concierge service, only one lessee may object on the basis that he would be substantially prejudiced by having to bear a fair share of the cost involved in the provision of concierge services but, having fallen on hard times, will be unable to afford the extra cost. If compensation is calculated by reference to any reduction in the capital value of his residuary term, it seems likely that expert evidence may show there to be no capital loss. Thus, if that is the correct basis of assessment, no compensation would be payable. Any assessment of compensation based upon applying a (discounted) multiplier to the extra annual cost (the multiplicand) would be unfair to both the landlord and the tenants. The landlord would probably agree to the variation application on the basis that if the tenants want a 24 hour concierge and they pay for it, then he suffers no prejudice. That would be scant justification for ordering the landlord to pay the compensation. If the other tenants were ordered to pay any such compensation, the one objecting tenant would, in effect, obtain the benefit of the additional service free of cost. Additionally he might benefit from an increase in the capital value of his leasehold interest if the provision of the extra service had the effect of raising the market profile of the flats which fed into increasing the capital values of the several leasehold interests. Perhaps the only fair basis of assessment, in a case involving a variation to provide additional services, is to ascertain by what sum, if any, the capital values of the residual leasehold interests increase as a result of having the additional service. A notional rate of interest (say 3.5 per cent at current interest rates) should be applied to that capital sum. The product should then be deducted from the additional annual cost of the service to the tenant. In that way the tenant would be compensated for his actual loss given that he will, despite his objections, benefit from the new service.

The problem about who is to pay the compensation is even more difficult. The landlord may reasonably be expected to become an objecting party if he believes that he may be required to pay compensation. Indeed, a prudent landlord may well make his consent conditional upon his being indemnified in respect of any compensation that he may be ordered to pay. It would offend basic principles of fairness for a landlord to be ordered to pay the compensation where he was gaining no benefit from the variation, but consenting to it so as not to frustrate what he considers to be a reasonable request from the vast majority of his tenants. The tenants who want to enjoy the additional service would seem to be the obvious party to pay any appropriate compensation as the price of their desire to impose on a fellow tenant an extra service that he does not want and has hitherto not had to fund. They will be able to know in advance the sum for any likely compensation and thus they will be able to factor that consideration into their decision on whether to pursue the variation application.

In the converse case, where the proposed variation is to delete a service, the objecting tenant may argue that its deletion will cause a reduction in the desirability of the flats and thus in the value of his estate. The amount of any diminution in value will be ascertainable, if necessary, with the assistance of expert evidence. A compensable loss will only then arise if the difference between the before and after service charge does not represent a fair return on the reduction in capital value. If it does not, the same problems arise concerning who should pay the compensation and again, as a matter of principle, it seems that this should be the majority tenants who have imposed their will upon a fellow tenant.

In *re: Sollershott Hall, Letchworth* CAM/22UF/LVT/2004, the Tribunal awarded lessees compensation of £4,222 and £3,000 to reflect the loss of an advantageous apportionment of service charges. The former was awarded for an increase in the service charge proportion from 1.40 per cent to 2.38 per cent and the latter was awarded for an increase in the service charge proportion from 2 per cent to 5.5 per cent.

Variation of administration charges

21–009 Chapter 12 deals with the remedies available in respect of fixed administration charges. Paragraph 3 of Sch.11 to the Commonhold and Leasehold Reform Act 2002 provides:

"(1) Any party to a lease of a dwelling may apply to a leasehold valuation tribunal for an order varying the lease in such manner as is specified in the application on the grounds that—

(a) any administration charge specified in the lease is unreasonable, or
(b) any formula specified in the lease in accordance with which any administration charge is calculated is unreasonable.

(2) If the grounds on which the application was made are established to the satisfaction of the tribunal, it may make an order varying the lease in such manner as is specified in the order.

(3) The variation specified in the order may be—

(a) the variation specified in the application, or
(b) such other variation as the tribunal thinks fit.

(4) The tribunal may, instead of making an order varying the lease in such manner as is specified in the order, make an order directing the parties to the lease to vary it in such manner as is so specified.

(5) The tribunal may by order direct that a memorandum of any variation of a lease effected by virtue of this paragraph be endorsed on such documents as are specified in the order.

(6) Any such variation of a lease shall be binding not only on the parties to the lease for the time being but also on other persons (including any predecessors in title), whether or not they were parties to the proceedings in which the order was made."

Either party may apply for such a variation. Although it is likely that the bulk of applications will come from tenants seeking to reduce excessive fixed charges, landlords could equally use this provision to increase charges set at anachronistically low levels: see for example *Flat 1 Malcolm Court* LON/NL/02090/03.

Chapter 22

The Leasehold Valuation Tribunal

The majority of disputes about residential service charges are now dealt with by the leasehold valuation tribunal rather than the courts. The general ethos of the leasehold valuation tribunal is that it is a low cost and relatively informal method of resolving service charge issues. **22–001**

Jurisdiction of the leasehold valuation tribunal

The rent assessment committee and enfranchisement jurisdictions

The leasehold valuation tribunal is the rent assessment committee by another name: Commonhold and Leasehold Reform Act 2002, s.173(2). The rent assessment committee was established by s.67 of the Rent Act 1977 to consider appeals against fair rents. By Sch.10 to the Rent Act 1977 members of each rent assessment committee are drawn from regional rent assessment panels consisting of persons nominated by the Lord Chancellor and the Secretary of State. **22–002**

The Housing Act 1980 transferred to the rent assessment committee the jurisdiction to determine certain matters relating to the enfranchisement of leasehold houses. By s.142(2) a committee sitting in this capacity was for the first time known as "a leasehold valuation tribunal". The enfranchisement jurisdictions were extended to leasehold flats by the Leasehold Reform Housing and Urban Development Act 1993.

The administration of the leasehold valuation tribunal (including the convening of hearings and clerking) is carried out by the Residential Property Tribunal Service.

For many years the original leasehold powers of the tribunal were known as the "old LVT" jurisdiction, but the label "enfranchisement" jurisdiction is now more commonly used.

"Leasehold management" jurisdictions

22–003 The tribunal's power to deal with service charges arises under the Landlord and Tenant Act 1985. Section 19 of the 1985 Act originally gave the court the power to determine that residential service charges were reasonably incurred and/or that services provided were of a reasonable standard. Under s.24 of the Landlord and Tenant Act 1987 the court was also originally given the power to appoint managers and receivers "for cause". Both provisions were amended by the Housing Act 1996 which granted these powers to the leasehold valuation tribunal. Before 2003, the tribunal's remit in relation to residential service charges was therefore limited to determining reasonableness under s.19(2A) and (2B) of the 1987 Act. The tribunal had no power to construe the terms of a tenancy or to consider whether there were statutory bars on the right to recover the service charges, such as under s.20 of the 1987 Act: see for example *Aylesbond Estates v MacMillan* [1999] L.&T.R. 127 and *Gilje v Charlegrove Securities* [2002] 16 E.G. 182.

The Commonhold and Leasehold Reform Act 2002 clarified the powers of the tribunal in respect of service charges and greatly extended the leasehold valuation tribunal's jurisdiction.

The tribunal's powers in relation to service charges and management have for many years been known as the "new LVT" jurisdiction, but the label "leasehold management jurisdictions" is now more commonly used.

Service charge jurisdiction

22–004 Since September 30, 2003 the leasehold valuation tribunal's principal leasehold management jurisdiction has been to determine whether a service charge is payable under ss.27A and 27B of the Landlord and Tenant Act 1985. The jurisdiction extends to service charges payable under short terms, periodic tenancies and leases of houses, but in practice most disputes arise from charges in long leases of flats. "Service charge" is defined in s.18 of the 1985 Act: see Chapter 4.

Liability to pay service charges

22–005 "27A Liability to pay service charges: jurisdiction

(1) An application may be made to a leasehold valuation tribunal for a determination whether a service charge is payable and, if it is, as to—

(a) the person by whom it is payable,
(b) the person to whom it is payable,
(c) the amount which is payable,
(d) the date at or by which it is payable, and
(e) the manner in which it is payable.

(2) Subsection (1) applies whether or not any payment has been made.
(3) An application may also be made to a leasehold valuation tribunal for a determination whether, if costs were incurred for services, repairs, maintenance, improvements, insurance or management of any specified description, a service charge would be payable for the costs and, if it would, as to—

(a) the person by whom it would be payable,
(b) the person to whom it would be payable,
(c) the amount which would be payable,
(d) the date at or by which it would be payable, and
(e) the manner in which it would be payable.

(4) No application under subsection (1) or (3) may be made in respect of a matter which—

(a) has been agreed or admitted by the tenant,
(b) has been, or is to be, referred to arbitration pursuant to a post-dispute arbitration agreement to which the tenant is a party,
(c) has been the subject of determination by a court, or
(d) has been the subject of determination by an arbitral tribunal pursuant to a post-dispute arbitration agreement.

(5) But the tenant is not to be taken to have agreed or admitted any matter by reason only of having made any payment.
(6) An agreement by the tenant of a dwelling (other than a post-dispute arbitration agreement) is void in so far as it purports to provide for a determination—

(a) in a particular manner, or
(b) on particular evidence, of any question which may be the subject of an application under subsection (1) or (3).

(7) The jurisdiction conferred on a leasehold valuation tribunal in respect of any matter by virtue of this section is in addition to any jurisdiction of a court in respect of the matter."

Section 27A(1) enables the LVT to determine any issue arising as to liability to pay service charges. Section 27A(3) contains similar powers in relation to future service charges. By s.27A(2) it is no longer relevant that the tenant has paid the sums allegedly due: reversing *Daejan Properties v London LVT* [2001] 3 E.G.L.R. 28, CA.

By contrast with the exclusive jurisdiction to appoint managers, the leasehold valuation tribunal shares with the court the power to determine liability to pay service charges: s.27A(7).

Limitation on applications to determine liability

22–006 The Act is retrospective in that the tribunal can consider service charges that were allegedly payable before the amendment of the 1985 Act. However, a more significant restriction is the question of limitation. In *Daejan Properties v London LVT* (above) the Court of Appeal effectively upheld a decision of Sulivan J. that the Limitation Act 1980 was not relevant to leasehold valuation tribunal proceedings. This part of the judgment in *Daejan* also appears to have been reversed by s.27A.

In *re: 3,12,23 and 29 St Andrew's Square* (February 26, 2004) LON/00AW/NSI/200/0054, LVT, the leasehold valuation tribunal determined that the Limitation Act 1980 did apply to the tribunal. The tribunal adopted various different limitation periods:

(a) An application by a tenant in relation to service charges contained in a tenancy not under seal (typically a periodic tenancy) is an action on a simple contract. It is subject to the six-year limitation period under s.5 of the Limitation Act 1980.

(b) An application brought by a landlord in relation to service charges contained in a tenancy under seal (typically a long lease) where the service charge is *not* reserved as rent is an action on a specialty. It is subject to the 12-year limitation period under s.8 of the Limitation Act 1980.

(c) An application brought by a landlord in relation to service charges contained in a tenancy under seal (typically a long lease) where the service charge is reserved as rent is an action to recover rent. It is subject to the six-year limitation period under s.19 of the Limitation Act 1980.

(d) An application brought by a tenant in relation to service charges contained in a tenancy under seal where the service charge is reserved as rent is not covered by the Limitation Act 1980. Such applications (which form the bulk of new applications to the tribunal) are not subject to any limitation period.

Although this test is complex, it is considered it represents the applicable limitation periods under s.27A. It should also be noted that a written acknowledgement of liability by the tenant may mean that the limitation periods start afresh: s.30(1) of the Limitation Act 1980.

Liability to pay service charges—the three stage test

22–007 Once it is satisfied that it has jurisdiction to determine an application, the leasehold valuation tribunal will apply a three stage test to applications under s.27A:

(a) Are the service charges recoverable under the terms of the lease? This depends on common principles of construction: see Chapter 1.

(b) Are the service charges reasonably incurred and/or services of a reasonable standard under s.19 of the 1985 Act? Even though s.19(2A) and (2B) of the Act have been repealed, s.19(1) and (2) have not.

(c) Are there any other statutory limitations on recoverability? These will include s.20 of the Landlord and Tenant Act 1985 (notices of works and qualifying long term agreements), s.20B of the Landlord and Tenant Act 1985 (18 month limitation), ss.47 and 48 of the Landlord and Tenant Act 1987 (provision of information), s.21 of the Landlord and Tenant Act 1985 (withholding of service charges) and the Limitation Act 1980.

Appointment of Managers "for cause"

22–008 The leasehold valuation tribunal has the exclusive jurisdiction to appoint a manager of premises "for cause": s.24(1) of the Landlord and Tenant Act 1987. It also has the power to dispense with service of a preliminary notice to the landlord under s.22(3). These powers are dealt with in Chapter 27.

In practice, a tribunal will invariably require a proposed manager to attend a hearing and be questioned about his/her experience and knowledge of general management and the particular requirements of a tribunal-appointed manager under the Act.

During the continuance of an order, the manager may apply to the tribunal for further directions under s.24(4). "Any interested person" may apply to the tribunal under s.24(9) to vary or discharge the order. This is also dealt with in Chapter 27. "Any interested person" includes the manager himself, but the manager may not resign without a variation or discharge of the order: *Flat 5 The Keir* (February 5, 2005) LON/00BE/LIS/2004/0038, LVT.

The right to manage

22–009 The leasehold valuation tribunal has the power to determine that a RTM company is entitled to acquire the freehold of flats under ss.84(3) and 85(2) of the Commonhold and Leasehold Reform Act 2002. It has the power to determine the amount of costs payable by a RTM company under s.88(4), the amount of any accrued uncommitted service charges under s.94(3), to grant approvals under long leases notwithstanding an objection under s.99(1) and to allow an application for the right to manage to be made earlier than four years after a previous application has lapsed under para.5(3) of Sch.6 to the Act. These are dealt with in Chapters 32–33. The tribunal has no general power to make directions to facilitate the exercise of the right to manage: *re: Waterloo Warehouse* (August 10, 2004) LVT/RTM/106MAN/00.

Dispensing with consultation requirements—s.20ZA

22–010 Under s.20ZA of the Landlord and Tenant Act 1985, the tribunal has the power to dispense with the consultation requirements of the Service Charges (Consultation Requirements) (England) Regulations 2003. This is dealt with in Chapter 13.

However, the power under s.20ZA is not retrospective and this leads to an anomalous situation. If a s.20 notice was required before October 31, 2003, only the court can dispense with service of the notice: s.20(9). Under s.27A, the leasehold valuation tribunal may determine that a s.20 notice was required for relevant costs incurred prior to October 31, 2003—but it cannot dispense with the notice. The matter must be remitted back to the county court. In such a situation, some tribunals may be prepared to give an indicative determination on dispensation to assist the parties with settlement. However, such determinations cannot bind the county court in the event of an application under s.20(9).

Variation of leases

22–011 Part IV of the Landlord and Tenant Act 1987 sets out the power to vary defective leases of flats. By s.162 of the Commonhold and Leasehold Reform Act 2002, that power was transferred from the county court to the leasehold valuation tribunal. These powers are dealt with in Chapter 21.

Specifically, under s.38(4) the tribunal can vary a lease or direct the parties to make such a variation. It may also order compensation to be paid to any other person under s.38(10). The tribunal can also order that the variation becomes binding on the parties and others. A person who should have been served with a preliminary notice may also apply to the tribunal to cancel or modify the order under s.39(3) and seek compensation.

Other jurisdictions

22–012 The leasehold valuation tribunal has a number of other statutory powers in relation to service charges and management:

(a) Variation of insurance provisions in the case of dwellings other than flats: s.40 of the Landlord and Tenant Act 1987. These powers are subject to important limitations in s.38(7) of the Act and s.164 of the Commonhold and Leasehold Reform Act 2002.

(b) Landlord's insurance of dwellings: para.8 of Sch.1 to the Landlord and Tenant Act 1985. The tribunal may require the landlord to nominate a new insurer.

(c) Orders that the costs of proceedings before the tribunal shall not be added to the service charge: s.20C of the Landlord and Tenant Act 1985.

(d) Charges under Estate Management Schemes: s.159(3) and (6) of the Commonhold and Leasehold Reform Act 2002.

(e) Administration charges: paras 3 and 5 of Sch.11 to the Commonhold and Leasehold Reform Act 2002. These powers are similar to the tribunal's jurisdiction to vary a lease or to determine liability for service charges under s.27A of the 1985 Act.

(f) The jurisdiction (on the application of a landlord), to determine whether a tenant is in breach of any covenant other than failure to pay service charges or administration charges before a lease is forfeit: s.168(4) of the 2002 Act.

(g) The power to grant a certificate of recognition of a tenant's association and the power to cancel it: s.29(1)(b) and (3) of the Landlord and Tenant Act 1985. This is an anomalous jurisdiction since strictly speaking it is an administrative act of a single member of the rent assessment panel rather than a judicial determination by the leasehold valuation tribunal.

(h) The determination of the terms of acquisition under s.31(1) of the Landlord and Tenant Act 1987. This power is exercised very rarely (but see *139 Finborough Road Management v Mansoor* [1990] 2 E.G.L.R. 225).

(i) Section 152 of the Commonhold and Leasehold Reform Act 2002 introduces a statutory right to withhold service charges in the form of a new s.21A of the Landlord and Tenant Act 1985. The Leasehold Valuation is to have the power under s.21A(4) to override the tenant's right to withhold payment. At the date of this publication, these provisions are not yet in force.

Practice and procedure in the leasehold valuation tribunal

Procedure regulations

22–013 The current procedure regulations in England are the Leasehold Valuation Tribunals (Procedure) (England) Regulations 2003. The Welsh equivalent is the Leasehold Valuation Tribunals (Procedure) (Wales) Regulations. The procedure regulations cover all jurisdictions referred to above except s.29(1)(b) of the Landlord and Tenant Act 1985. The English regulations were amended by the Leasehold Valuation Tribunals (Procedure) (Amendment) (England) Regulations 2004 and the Welsh regulations were amended by the Leasehold Valuation Tribunals (Procedure) (Amendment) (Wales) Regulations 2005. Since the English and Welsh regulations are to all intents and purposes identical, references in this chapter to the procedure regulations are to the English regulations as amended: see Appendix A.

Applications

22–014 Most matters are brought before the tribunal by application. These are dealt with by reg.3 of the procedure regulations. Schedule 2 to the procedure regulations sets out additional requirements for particulars and documentation in relation to specific types of application. The tribunal has the power to dispense with any of these formal requirements if the application is sufficient to enable the application to be determined and no prejudice is caused to any party: reg.3(8) of the procedure regulations.

The Residential Property Tribunal Service produces five forms for common types of application. These are:

(a) An application for determination of liability to pay service charges under s.27A of the Landlord and Tenant Act 1985;

(b) An application to vary a lease or leases under Pt IV of the Landlord and Tenant Act 1987;

(c) An application for a reduction or waiver of fees;

(d) An application for the dispensation of all or any of the consultation requirements contained in s.20 of the Landlord and Tenant Act 1985;

(e) An application for the determination of the liability to pay for or for the variation of an administration charge.

Any other application may be made by letter provided that the letter complies with reg.3 and Sch.2.

In practice, many applications to the tribunal, particularly those made by unrepresented parties, lack proper particulars. Failure to give proper particulars runs the risk of the tribunal striking out the application as an abuse of process under reg.11(1) of the procedure regulations. In *Yorkbrook Investments v Batten* [1985] 2 E.G.L.R. 100, the Court of Appeal stated that a claim to the court in respect of service charges, a tenant needed to "specify the item, complained of and the general nature—not the evidence—of his case". Similar principles probably apply to applications to the leasehold valuation tribunal.

A precedent for sections 7 and 10 of an application to determine the liability to pay service charges under s.27A of the Landlord and Tenant Act 1985 is given in Appendix C. Apart from the documents required by the above provisions, an applicant should avoid sending a large volume of supporting documentation with the application.

The application is to be submitted together with any fee to the appropriate office of the Residential Property Tribunal Service. These offices are listed on the application forms in Appendix C.

Withdrawal of applications

22–015 There is no specific procedure for withdrawing an application, and strictly speaking a withdrawal need not be in writing. However a second application may be struck out as an abuse of process if it covers the same ground as one that has been withdrawn: see the employment case of *E Okoturo v Tesco Stores plc* (September 18, 2001), Employment Appeal Tribunal.

Fees

22–016 Fees are not necessary for many applications such as an application relating to an estate management scheme, an application under s.20C of the Landlord and Tenant Act 1985 that costs should not be added to a service charge or an application in respect of the right to manage.

The rates of fee payable in other matters are set out in the Leasehold Valuation Tribunal (Fees) Regulations 2003 and the Leasehold Valuation Tribunals (Fees) (Wales) Regulations 2004. Once again, the regulations are in similar form and references to the fees regulations in this chapter are to the English regulations. Separate fees are payable for making an application and for a hearing.

Under reg.3 of the fees regulations the current rate of application fee is as follows:

Service charges insurance and administration charges	
Amount in dispute not more than £500	£50
Amount more than £500 but less than £1,000	£70
Amount more than £1,000 but less than £5,000	£100
Amount more than £5,000 but less than £15,000	£200
Amount more than £15,000	£350
Section 20ZA, suitability of insurer, appointment of managers and variation of leases	
5 or fewer dwellings	£150
6 to 10 dwellings	£250
More than 10 dwellings	£350

The fee payable on a transfer is more advantageous to an applicant because it may set off the costs of any application to the court against fees due to the tribunal: fees regulation para.4. A person who makes multiple applications only pays one set of fees (the highest): reg.3(5) of the fees regulations. If there are several applicants, the fees are shared between them equally: reg.7(4) of the fees regulations.

The hearing fee is £150. However, no specific fee is prescribed for preliminary hearings or determinations on paper without a hearing.

If a fee has not been paid "the Tribunal shall not proceed further with the application to which the fee relates until the fee is paid". The tribunal therefore has no discretion to continue if a fee is not paid. After one month, the application is then treated as withdrawn: para.7 of the fees regulations.

It is not uncommon during the course of a hearing in relation to service charges for a landlord to apply to dispense with consultation requirements under s.20ZA of the 1995 Act. This cannot be done until the relevant application has been made and a fee has been paid.

Under reg.8 of the fees regulations, the tribunal may waive or reduce fees payable by certain applicants. There is a specific form available for such an application. Under reg.9 of the fees regulations it may also order a party to reimburse the fees to the other.

Service of the application

22–017 The tribunal serves a copy of the application (whether a regular application or an application transferred from the court) on the persons named by the applicant under reg.5 of the procedure regulations. For service charges, administration and estate charges, the tribunal also "gives notice" of the application to the secretary of any residents' association and any person the tribunal thinks is likely to be significantly affected by the application. Such a notice can be given by advertisement: reg.5(5) of the procedure regulations.

If the application is for a variation of a lease under Pt 4 of the 1987 Act, reg.4 of the procedure regulations requires the *applicant* to serve. In practice the tribunal will also serve on any named respondents. Such an application must be given to the respondent and to any person the applicant knows or has reason to believe is likely to be affected by the variation. The respondent must then notify anyone who it knows or has reason to believe is likely to be affected by the variation.

All notices (including notices of applications) are properly served by delivering or sending them to the recipient's usual or last known address, sent by fax or "other means of electronic communication" (presumably by email) or sent to an agent: reg.23 of the procedure regulations.

Transferred applications from the court

22–018 The alternative means of bringing a matter before the tribunal is by a "transferred application" from the court. Paragraph 3 of Sch.12 to the Commonhold and Leasehold Reform Act 2002 gives all courts a general power to transfer proceedings whenever there falls for determination a question falling within the jurisdiction of the leasehold valuation tribunal. This replaced the more limited power to transfer under s.31C of the Landlord and Tenant Act 1985.

The courts will apply para.15 of the Practice Direction to CPR 56. This states:

> "56PD.29 **Transfer to leasehold valuation tribunal under the Commonhold and Leasehold Reform Act 2002**
> 15.1 If a question is ordered to be transferred to a leasehold valuation tribunal for determination under paragraph 3 of Schedule 12 to the Commonhold and Leasehold Reform Act 2002 the court will—
>
> (1) send notice of the transfer to all parties to the claim; and
> (2) send to the leasehold valuation tribunal—
>
> (a) the order of transfer; and
> (b) all documents filed in the claim relating to the question."

Thereafter, a transferred application is treated by the tribunal in the same way as a direct application. A fee is payable upon transfer from the court: reg.4 of the fees regulations.

Whether or not the matter should be transferred will depend on a number of factors including the complexity of the issues, the likely saving in costs, the benefit of an expert tribunal and whether there are other issues which will remain in court: see *Aylesbond Estates Ltd v (1) Fiona Macmillan (2) Dr R N Garg (3) Abbey National Plc* (1998) CA (2000) 32 H.L.R. 1. If the service charge matter is one aspect of the claim it is possible for the court proceedings to be stayed pending resolution of the service charge issues and then restored for final determination

Case management

22–019 On receipt of an application, it is allocated to a clerk who will generally arrange for the papers to be considered by a procedural chairman—a tribunal chairman with particular experience of this type of work. The procedural chairman will consider any preliminary procedural points that arise. The application will be allocated to one of three tracks either at this stage or at the pre-trial review:

(a) The paper track: essentially this involves an application being dealt with by a procedural chairman sitting alone on the basis of written representations. The procedure is set out in reg.13 of the procedure regulations.

(b) The fast track: this is a matter that can be dealt with in less than 10 weeks. This will typically involve a hearing of less than half a day and but it will be considered by a full tribunal.

(c) The standard track: this is the most usual track in service charge disputes.

Any person may request to be joined as a party under reg.6 of the procedure regulations. Once joined, such a party becomes liable to pay all or part of the fees: reg.7(7). The tribunal can also propose to determine one of numerous matters as a "representative application" under regs 8–10 of the procedure regulations.

Striking out

22–020 Under para.7 of Sch.12 to the Commonhold and Leasehold Reform Act 2002 and reg.11 of the procedure regulations the tribunal has the power to strike out any application that is frivolous or vexatious or otherwise an abuse of process. This provision is similar to the old Ord.18 r.19 of the Rules of the Supreme Court. Thus, a party would not be permitted to bring forward in a second action a matter that properly belonged to or could have been raised in earlier proceedings between the same parties: *Henderson v Henderson* (1843) 3 Hare 100. Before striking out an application, the tribunal must give notice that it is minded to dismiss the application and allow the applicant at least 21 days to reply and request a hearing: reg.11(3) of the procedure regulations. These matters are often dealt with during the course of the pre-trial review.

Pre-trial review

22–021 Most applications to the leasehold valuation tribunal are set down for a pre-trial review. In London, they are often listed for a one hour oral hearing before a procedural chairman. Under reg.12(2) of the procedure regulations at least 14 days notice must be given to the parties. It should be noted that at this stage, it is unlikely the tribunal will have had a formal documentary response from the respondents, so the issues may not be clear.

Regulations 12(b) and (c) of the procedure regulations provide that the tribunal *shall* "endeavour to secure that the parties make all such admissions and agreements as ought reasonably to be made by admission or agreement" and record any admission, agreement or refusal to make an admission or agreement. The procedural chairman is therefore under an express obligation to encourage the parties to reach agreement and make concessions at the pre-trial review. For this reason, it is advisable that both parties attend. Because the procedural chairman takes an active role in attempting to secure concessions at this stage, the general practice is that he will not chair the substantive hearing of the application.

Directions

22–022 The procedure regulations provide that at the pre-trial review, the tribunal shall give any necessary or desirable directions. The directions given at the pre-trial review will usually provide for exchange of witness evidence at the same time as disclosure of each party's evidence. The final hearing date is fixed at this stage. An example of directions used by the leasehold valuation tribunal appears at Appendix C.

A common order is that the parties serve further details of their arguments. This will almost always be necessary for the respondent who has not yet formally set out its response to the application, and it may also be necessary if the applicant has failed to give proper particulars in the application form. Although such documents are sometimes referred to as "statements of case", this label is not appropriate in most cases before the tribunal (and it is not used in most directions issued). The form varies from case to case. In a simple issue a letter with perhaps one or two bullet points would suffice. In a complex issue, a formally pleaded statement of case as used in court proceedings would be more appropriate. A precedent for details of a response appears in Appendix C.

Documentation frequently causes problems. Typically, a tenant challenging the reasonableness of a service charge will need to provide evidence of alternative estimates. A landlord justifying service charge costs would need to provide copies of service charge demands, accounts, final certificates, underlying vouchers for items in dispute, management contracts, insurance estimates, policies and so on.

The tribunal has limited powers to enforce compliance with directions. Under para.4 of Sch.12 to the Commonhold and Leasehold Reform Act 2002, the tribunal can serve a notice on a party requiring it to give any information that is reasonably required. If this information has not been given after 14 days a person commits an offence: para.4(4) of Sch.12. The notice must contain the warning in para.22 of the procedural regulation. In practice, such notices are very rare. In addition, breach of a direction may give rise to liability under the limited costs jurisdiction in para.10 of Sch.12 to the Commonhold and Leasehold Reform Act 2002.

The tribunal can extend time for complying with any direction, provided that the application to extend time is made before the time limit expires: reg.24 of the procedure regulations.

Hearing

22–023 Membership of the leasehold valuation tribunal is prescribed by Sch.10 to the Rent Act 1977. Each tribunal comprises two or three members. The chairman must be a panel President, Vice President or a member of the panel appointed by the Lord Chancellor. The former requirement (under Sch.22 to the Housing Act 1980) that a member of the tribunal should also have experience of valuation was abolished by the Commonhold and Leasehold Reform Act 2002. In practice, the tribunal will usually comprise a lawyer chairman sitting with a professional member (generally a valuer) and a lay member of the Rent Assessment Panel. However, it is not uncommon for the third member also to be another professional member, particularly where some special expertise is an advantage.

Hearings in London are generally held at the London Residential Property Tribunal Service at 10 Alfred Place, London, WC1E 7LR. Outside London, hearings are held in rooms hired for the purpose of the hearing close to the subject premises.

The hearing requires at least 21 days notice. Hearings are in public but there is the power to hold all or part of a hearing in private. This might be appropriate if a "domiciliary" hearing was held at the home of a disabled party.

There is power to postpone or adjourn a hearing, but reg.16 of the procedure regulations contains a presumption against postponement. The party causing the adjournment may be made liable to pay the costs of adjournment under para.10 of Sch.12 to the Commonhold and Leasehold Reform Act 2002.

Procedure at the hearing

22–024 A member of a tribunal holds judicial office and must therefore recuse (or withdraw) himself if there is a conflict of interest: *Locabail (UK) Ltd v Bayfield Properties Ltd* [2000] 2 W.L.R. 870, *R v Gough* [1993] 2 W.L.R. 883.

If a person turns up with a document on which they rely, there is a presumption the hearing shall be adjourned to enable the other party to deal with it: reg.16(2).

Otherwise, the tribunal has a wide discretion as to the conduct of the hearing and the order of evidence: reg.14 of the procedure regulations. Although complex cases will be conducted like court proceedings (especially if there are expert witnesses), there is no sworn evidence. Smaller disputes typically involve litigants in person who are permitted to give evidence and make submissions together. In the majority of matters, there is no representation on at least one side.

The leasehold valuation tribunal is an expert tribunal. It frequently adopts an inquisitorial style to disputes. It has the power to make its own independent investigations under reg.16(1)(b) of the procedure regulations.

It is common practice to carry out an inspection of the premises particularly where the standard of works or cleaning is in dispute. The procedure regulations set out detailed requirements at reg.17. It may take place before, after or during the course of the hearing. It should be noted that the parties cannot give evidence during then course of the inspection—other than to indicate where particular areas of dampness and so on are present. If the tribunal identifies matters on the inspection which are unfavourable to either party, it must draw their attention to those matters at the hearing or a later hearing: *R v Paddington Rent Tribunal Ex p. Bell London Properties* [1949] 1 K.B. 666.

Special considerations apply to the appointment of managers under s.87 of the 1987 Act. The tribunal will expect the proposed manager to attend and give evidence of qualifications, familiarity with the RICS code and his appreciation of the difference between a managing agent and leasehold valuation tribunal appointed manager/receiver: see Chapter 27.

Decisions

22–025 Although a decision can be given orally at the conclusion of a hearing, this is comparatively rare. The tribunal may not meet to reach an agreed decision until a reconvened meeting at a later date. The decision of the tribunal needs to be recorded in a written document and written reasons must also be produced: reg.18(5) of the procedure regulations. Under reg.18(7) the chairman may correct a clerical error under the slip rule in analogous situations to those under r.40.12 of the Civil Procedure Rules.

Appeals

22–026 An appeal from the leasehold valuation tribunal lies to the Lands Tribunal under Sch.22 to the HA 1980. The appeal is by way of rehearing: *Wellcome Trust v Romines* [1999] 3 E.G.L.R. 229.

Permission to appeal is now required—Lands Tribunal Rules 1996 as amended by Lands Tribunal (Amendment) Rules 2003—and the tribunal will adopt similar criteria to those that apply to courts under r.52.3 of the Civil Procedure Rules. Such applications are generally made on paper. The time limit for an appeal is 21 days from the date the reasons are sent out by the tribunal: reg.20 of the procedure regulations. It should be noted that application for permission to appeal *must* be made to the LVT as the Lands Tribunal has no jurisdiction to grant permission unless application is first made to the LVT. It should also be noted that application to the LVT for permission to appeal *must* be made within the 21 days as there is no jurisdiction to extend time.

The Lands Tribunal has limited powers to award any costs of the appeal in the event that a party has behaved frivolously, vexatiously, disruptively or otherwise unreasonably: Commonhold and Leasehold Reform Act 2002 s.175(6). In such a case the amount it may order to be paid shall not exceed the maximum amount that the tribunal can order in similar circumstances.

Costs

22–027 The tribunal has no general power to award costs. The tribunal can order that up to £500 in costs is paid by a party who has made an application that is dismissed as frivolous, vexatious or an abuse of process. It may make a similar order if any party has acted frivolously, vexatiously, abusively, disruptively or otherwise unreasonably in connection with the proceedings: para.10(2) of Sch.12 to the Commonhold and Leasehold Reform Act 2002.

In the majority of service charge and management applications to the tribunal, the tenants make applications under s.20C of the Landlord and Tenant Act 1985 for the costs of proceedings not to be added to the service charge. Section 20C applications and the related arguments under para.10(4) of Sch.12 to the Commonhold and Leasehold Reform Act 2002 are dealt with in Chapter 7.

Under para.9(4) of Sch.12 to the Commonhold and Leasehold Reform Act 2002, the tribunal has the power to waive or reduce fees. The circumstances are set out in the fees regulations, and cover parties receiving income support, housing benefit, jobseeker's allowance, certain forms of tax credits or a guarantee credit, parties with a funding certificate in related county court proceedings, and some parties in receipt of working tax credits. The tribunal may also order that a party reimburse all or part of the fees incurred by another party under para.9(2) of Sch.12 to the Commonhold and Leasehold Reform Act 2002. The tribunal will not require a party to make such reimbursement if, at the time the tribunal is considering whether or not to do so, the tribunal is satisfied that the party is in receipt of similar benefits, allowances or the above certificates.

Alternative dispute resolution

22–028 The ethos of the legislation and the tribunal is very much to encourage alternative means of determining service charge and management disputes. Several situations are set out in s.27A(4) of the 1985 Act where an application may not be made. Under s.27A(4)(1) any matter which has been agreed or admitted by the tenant cannot be the subject of an application. There is no requirement for such an agreement or admission to be in writing. Under s.27A(4)(b) and (d) an agreement after the dispute has arisen that the matter should be referred to arbitration (or an actual award by an arbitrator) will also oust the leasehold valuation tribunal's jurisdiction. Therefore the mere existence of an arbitration clause in a tenancy will not be sufficient. Furthermore, it is probable that a post-dispute arbitration agreement must be in writing: Arbitration Act 1999, s.6. Finally, the tribunal will not have jurisdiction if the court has already determined liability: s.27A(c).

In addition, the London Residential Property Tribunal Service is presently piloting a mediation scheme for parties to service charge disputes.

Enforcement

22–029 Before the Commonhold and Leasehold Reform Act 2002, there was no direct means of enforcing an order of the tribunal. However, an order of the tribunal may now be enforced in the same way as a court order with the permission of the county court: reg.19 of the procedure regulations made under para.11 of Sch.12 to the 2002 Act. The procedure for making such an application is governed by CPR 70.5 and CPR PD 70.

An award of money may be enforced by an application to the court without notice, and such an application must be made to the court for the district where the defendant resides or carries on business (unless the court orders otherwise): CPR 70.5(4). The application must be made on an application notice in Form N322A: CPR 70 PD 4. It must be accompanied by a copy of the award: CPR 70.5(6).

The order may be made by a court officer without a hearing: CPR 70.5(7). It is made in form N322. Once permission is obtained, the following remedies are available:

(a) A writ of *fieri facias* or warrant of execution;

(b) A third party debt order;

(c) A charging order, stop order or stop notice;

(d) An attachment of earnings order;

(e) Appointment of a receiver.

The Civil Procedure Rules make no specific provision for enforcement of non-monetary awards in court—even though both reg.19 of the procedure regulations and CPR 70.5(1) envisage that the courts permission is needed to enforce such a decision. It is considered that any application to enforce non-monetary decisions of the tribunal should be made on Form N322A with appropriate adaptations.

Chapter 23

Court Proceedings in Respect of Service Charges

23–001 Before making the decision to issue court proceedings reference should be made to what is said about alternatives to bringing proceedings in Chapter 24. Of course attempts should be made to settle if possible before getting too embroiled in proceedings.

In arriving at a settlement either during or under threat of court proceedings, care must be taken to ensure that the sums agreed are binding. It is often prudent to recite in any written compromise agreement that the sums agreed are reasonable in the context of s.19 of the LTA 1985 and are agreed in the context of the HA 1996.

If the matter is negotiated in the throes of a hearing it may be prudent to attempt to get the court to sanction the settlement either formally by recording the same in an order or at least by noting the same.

Preparing for litigation—a checklist

23–002 If a settlement has not been achieved then litigation is the only real option. In a standard type of dispute where the lease adopts conventional service charge machinery and where the issue is whether or not sums are due, the following matters should be considered:

- Has ADR been exhausted?
- Is there an arbitration clause prohibiting proceedings?
- Is it due/recoverable at common law?
- Is there some statutory bar to recovery?
- In the case of commercial premises: is there some more effective remedy?

- Are there any pre-action protocols to be complied with or followed in spirit?
- Has some protection in respect of costs been obtained by offers to settle re costs/s.20c?
- Has the client been informed of likely costs?

Is it due/recoverable at common law?

23–003 This usually includes some or all of the following issues:

- Is the item of work or service provided within the landlord's obligation?
- Is there any condition precedent to be fulfilled?
- Is the sum caught by the payment provisions?
- Is the mathematics correct—has the correct percentage/apportionment been applied?
- Is it due as "rent"?

Is it within the landlord's obligation?

23–004 This is covered in detail in earlier chapters. The short question which must be asked is whether the item of work or service provided is within the landlord's obligations in the lease. Sometimes landlords undertake work beyond that which the lease requires. If this is so (and unless, for example, the lease expressly permits improvements at the tenant's cost) the sum sought will not be recoverable from the tenant.

Is the sum caught by the payment provisions?

23–005 Assuming the item of work or service provided is within the landlord's rights/obligations, the question then is whether the lease makes provision for payment towards it. This is ultimately a question of construing the lease and the service charge machinery, and checking that the tenant is obliged to make payment for the item in question.

Condition precedent

23–006 Advisors should ensure that all conditions precedent have been performed. It is possible for there to be conditions precedent to the works being carried out as well as for the costs being recovered. The more usual conditions concern final accounts and accountant's certificates, prior demand for payment, and such like.

Mathematics/correct percentage

23–007 It should also be confirmed that the figures add up. One area of dispute is often as to whether the percentage charged is correct. Complications may arise where the building has been extended, for example by adding flats to the roof.

Is it due as rent?

23–008 It should be determined whether the sum due or owing is payable or recoverable as if rent: see *Escalus Properties Ltd v Robinson* [1995] 3 W.L.R. 524 for a discussion as to when a service charge is properly recoverable as rent. Section 146 of the LPA 1925 (which prohibits forfeiture without prior service of a notice under that section) does not apply in respect of forfeiture for non-payment of rent. In the case of commercial premises only, it is open to the landlord to distrain. Again in the case of commercial premises only, the remedy of forfeiture by peaceable re-entry is available (without the need for service of a s.146 notice). Any forfeiture and the issue of relief from forfeiture are governed by s.138 of the County Courts Act 1984.

Is there some statutory bar to recovery of the sum?

23–009 The main statutes which may preclude recovery of sums on account of service charges are:

- Limitation Act 1980;
- Section 20B of the LTA 1985;
- Section 17 of the LT(C) Act 1995;
- Section 3 of the LTA 1985 and ss.47 and 48 of the LTA 1987;
- Sections 166–167 of the CLRA 2002 and s.81 of the 1996 Act;
- Section 19 of the LTA 1985;
- Unfair Terms in Consumer Contracts Regulations 1999.

These topics are dealt with in greater detail in other parts of this book.

Limitation

23–010 The sum claimed may be outside the limitation period fixed under the Limitation Act 1980.

- For service charges recoverable as rent, the period is 6 years from when the same fell due for payment (s.19 of the Limitation Act 1980).
- Where the service charge is not recoverable as rent, in the event that the tenancy/lease is created by a *deed* the period in question is 12 years from the date that the payment fell due (s.8 of the Limitation Act 1980).
- Where the tenancy is not created by deed the limitation period will be 6 years whether or not the service charges are recoverable as rent (ss.5 and 19 of the Limitation Act 1980).

Section 20B of the Landlord and Tenant Act 1985

23–011 Section 20B of the Landlord and Tenant Act 1985 in effect imposes its own limitation period in respect of service charges for residential premises caught by the 1985 Act. Costs are not recoverable insofar as they were incurred more than 18 months before being demanded unless the tenant was informed within 18 months in writing that those costs had been incurred and that the same would be recoverable from the tenant.

Section 17 of the Landlord and Tenant (Covenants) Act 1995

Claims against the original tenant, etc.

23–012 If a claim is being made in respect of arrears of rent or service charge incurred following assignment of the lease against the original tenant, previous assignor of the lease or guarantor, or against a previous tenant who has entered into an authorised guarantee agreement under the 1995 Act, the landlord must serve a notice under s.17 of the 1995 Act within six months of the sum falling due. A "fixed charge" includes service charges (even though by their very nature they are not fixed in amount) (s.17(6) of the LTCA 1995).

Section 3 of the Landlord and Tenant Act 1985 and ss.47 and 48 of the Landlord and Tenant Act 1987

23–013 These sections apply to residential premises only and require the landlord's name and address to be included on the written demands. Also the tenant has to be furnished with an address in England and Wales at which notices including notices in proceedings can be served (ss.47 and 48 of the LTA 1987). Rent, service charges and administration charges are not due until such information has been provided in writing (see *Rogan v Woodfield Building Services* [1995] 27 H.L.R. 484).

In addition, if there is a change of landlord it is incumbent on the incoming landlord to inform the tenant of the change of landlord (s.3 LTA 1985).

Generally, under s.151 of the LPA 1925, where the reversion has been assigned the tenant is entitled to continue to pay rent, etc. to the previous landlord until notice of the change has been given.

Sections 166–167 of the CLRA 2002 and s.81 of the HA 1996

23–014 A demand notice containing the prescribed information must be served before ground rent payable under a lease of a dwelling falls due. "Rent" in this context does not include service charges payable as rent (s.166(7)).

Even if a money judgment has been obtained for arrears of service charge (and/or administration charges) and assuming there has been no waiver of the right to forfeit, forfeiture cannot be obtained in respect of a dwelling if the arrears are less than the prescribed amount—at present £350—or, if less than this sum, the amount has been owing for more than three years.

Forfeiture in respect of residential premises for non-payment of service charges is precluded until the service charges have been subject to such determination or agreement (s.81 HA 1996).

Section 19 of the Landlord and Tenant Act 1985

23–015 Section 19 of the 1985 Act in respect of residential premises only permits recovery of costs incurred where the costs have been reasonably incurred and/or the works, etc. are of a reasonable standard. (This is discussed in detail in Chapter 12).

Unfair Terms in Consumer Contract Regulations 1999

23–016 In the event that the regulations apply, it should be ascertained whether the clause relied upon falls foul of the regulation.

In the case of commercial premises is there some more effective remedy?

23–017 By reason of the statutory protection in place in respect of residential premises, a landlord's hands are somewhat tied as to the remedies available, which require proceedings to be brought in court or before the LVT followed, perhaps, by the ultimate sanction: forfeiture.

In respect of commercial premises it is often the case that the landlord does not want to forfeit, as the premises without the lease may be of limited value, and/or the rent payable under the lease is a favourable rent.

In such circumstances the advisor should consider whether it may be better to seek a money judgment for arrears of service charge or, perhaps (and again stressing only in respect of commercial premises), distrain. In the event that there is a subtenant able to pay its rent, it is open to the landlord to serve a "by-pass" notice under s.6 of the Law of Distress Amendment Act 1908.

Another option may be to pursue the original tenant or a previous tenant (under the terms of a licence to assign) or a surety. This is more likely to be of use in respect of commercial premises where as the term is shorter the previous/original tenant is more likely to be easily located and may have the resources to satisfy any judgment. Before such claim can be made a notice must be served as set out above. In respect of new tenancies caught by the Landlord and Tenant Covenants Act 1995, an original or previous tenant and an original guarantor will not be liable for arrears after assignment of the lease unless caught by an authorised guarantee agreement (ss.5, 16 and 24(1) of the 1995 Act).

Is there an arbitration clause prohibiting proceedings?

23–018 Most leases contain arbitration clauses, yet historically it was very rare for them to be utilised in a service charge dispute. With the creation of the LVT—and now with its extended jurisdiction—it is unlikely that parties would choose to go down the arbitration route. It may be that if the party has a strong case arbitration is the wiser course as costs can be awarded in an arbitration, whereas the jurisdiction to award costs in the LVT is limited.

If it is decided to rely upon an arbitration clause care should be taken not to "take part" in court proceedings (save to apply for a stay in order for the arbitration clause to be set in motion).

The existence of an arbitration clause will not oust the LVT's jurisdiction unless there has been a post-dispute arbitration agreement (s.27A(6) of the LTA 1985).

Are there any pre-action protocols to be complied with or followed in spirit?

23–019 There are no specific pre-action protocols designed for service charge disputes. The CPR Practice Direction (Protocols) para.4 states that, in cases not covered by any approved pre-action protocol, the court will expect the parties, in accordance with the overriding objective, to act reasonably in exchanging information and documents relevant to the claim and generally in trying to avoid the necessity for the start of proceedings.

Where the issues concern (at least in part) the appropriateness of works carried out, it is suggested that the pre-action protocol for construction and engineering disputes may be adapted and followed.

Where the challenge to payment of a service charge arises out of a set-off for failure to repair, it is suggested that the pre-action protocol for housing disrepair be followed.

Has some protection in respect of costs been obtained by offers to settle re costs/s.20C

23–020 Tactical advantage can be gained in making admissible and sensible offers to settle at an early stage. Such offers should be on a "without prejudice save as to costs basis" (purely "without prejudice" offers being of no use when the matter progresses to proceedings).

There would appear to be no reason why such offers cannot be "without prejudice save as to costs including the issue of whether or not a section 20C order should be made".

Genuine and reasonable attempts to avoid the costs of proceedings may well have an impact on the court or the LVT's decision whether or not to make a s.20C order.

The purpose of an offer is twofold. First, it is made with a view to compromising the dispute. The other purpose is to provide protection on costs. There is often some merit in making a generous "without prejudice save as to costs offer" at the outset of a dispute when feelings are running high. The other side may well turn down an offer which in retrospect it should have accepted. If so, it may face an adverse costs order. The risk with such strategy, of course, is that the offer might be accepted and the client must be prepared to live with such consequence.

Where the matter is before the LVT, and where the landlord is entitled under the lease terms to add the cost of proceedings to the service charges and/or seek them in the event of default, similar considerations apply. The LVT are likely to take into account admissible offers to compromise in determining whether to make a s.20C order and/or whether costs as administration charges were reasonably incurred.

As stated there appears to be no reason why such offer cannot be "without prejudice save as to costs including orders under section 20C and/or paragraph 10 of Schedule 12 to the 2002 Act."

Informing clients of the likely costs

23–021 Apart from advisors' usual professional obligations to inform clients of their terms of business charging rates, etc. it is suggested that in a service charge dispute it is incumbent on the advisor to inform the client at an early stage how very expensive the dispute may turn out to be and to try to give some estimate of the costs involved.

This is all the more important if the matter is to be litigated in the LVT, for (not surprisingly as the same work is involved) the rates of solicitors, counsel and experts are the same as in proceedings in court, yet these will not be recovered. There is nothing more depressing for a client than the hollow victory of winning the case having spent more on the case than was in issue in the first place.

Procedure

The appropriate venue/jurisdiction

Commercial premises

23–022 If the dispute concerns purely commercial premises the LVT has no jurisdiction to determine it.

Where the premises are mixed premises but the dispute is between the landlord and commercial tenant, again the LVT has no jurisdiction.

In short, the LVT's jurisdiction only covers a dispute where the service charge in question arises out of the provisions of a lease of residential premises. It is often the case, however, that the LVT has to decide issues affecting premises with commercial units. As the commercial tenant will not be a party to such dispute the decision will not be binding on it. It would likely be very persuasive in any proceedings in court as the LVT are an expert tribunal.

In the case of a service charge dispute between landlord and commercial tenant, the appropriate venue is the court. Whether that is the county court or the High Court will depend on the value of the claim and the issues. If the arguments concern difficult issues of construction, the High Court Chancery Division may be the appropriate place to issue. Some county courts (e.g. Central London County Court) have a Chancery or business list, which may again be an appropriate venue. If the case is particularly complex factually and/or concerns issues over building works, the Technology and Construction Court may be an appropriate venue. In a case which appears suitable for one or other of the above mentioned courts it may be worthwhile to ascertain how long the wait will be for a trial before the forum is selected.

Residential premises

23–023 ***The LVT*** With its extended jurisdiction the LVT is able to deal with all aspects of service charge disputes concerning residential premises. What it cannot do however is give judgment in respect of sums it has found due. The decision of the LVT is enforceable in the county court (para.11 of Sch.12 to the 2002 Act and the regulations made thereunder) (see Chapter 22). The LVT cannot give judgment in favour of a landlord for sums due, and likewise cannot give judgment for a lessee in respect of sums overpaid.

It is arguable that as part of the process of determining whether a service charge "is payable" under s.27A of the Landlord and Tenant Act 1985 the LVT can determine whether the tenant has a counterclaim for damages that can be set off against a claim for service charges. There is no logical reason why a right to set-off damages should be different to any other defence available to a tenant. There may well be advantages to this in a simple case where the LVT is likely to be well placed to decide such a matter. Where the "counter-claim" giving rise to the set-off is complex and concerns difficult issues of fact and law, the LVT is less obviously an appropriate venue to determine such matters—particularly with the absence of formal pleadings, detailed witness statements, etc. In practice, tribunals generally decline to try counter-claims by tenants. The position remains, however, that in determining whether a sum "is payable" by a tenant it is at least arguable that the LVT is able to take into account set-off arguments.

The court

23–024 The court has jurisdiction to deal with all areas of service charge disputes save that it no longer has jurisdiction to appoint managers or to dispense with the consultation requirements under s.20 of the 1985 Act, such matters now falling within the LVT's jurisdiction. It retains jurisdiction to determine issues of reasonableness under s.19 of the 1985 Act. As set out above there are a number of factors to take into account in determining in which court or division to commence proceedings.

There are certain statutory provisions which provide that the county court has exclusive jurisdiction. Issues arising under ss.81 and 82 of the Housing Act 1996 (restrictions on forfeiture and s.146 notices) are within the exclusive jurisdiction of the county court unless coupled with other issues which are properly before the High Court (s.95 Housing Act 1996).

Ordinarily proceedings should be issued in the local county court. When initially enacted, s.19 of the 1985 Act provided (s.19(5)) that if proceedings were issued in the High Court when they could have been issued in the county court, no costs would be recoverable. This subsection has been repealed but advisors should be aware that the High Court should only be utilised where the case merits it. A case which is unsuitable for the High Court will be transferred with possible adverse costs orders attached.

Possession claims

23–025 A possession claim based on forfeiture for non-payment of service charges only (i.e. not including a claim based on non-payment of rent or service charges payable as rent) will have been preceded by a s.146 notice.

In the case of residential premises, s.81 of the 1996 Act must also have been complied with.

It is arguable that if a possession claim is based upon non-payment of ground rent (provided the ground rent is above the prescribed limit and has been subject to a written demand in the prescribed form (ss.166–167 of the 2002 Act)) and there is included a money claim for service charges *recoverable as rent* which are found by the court to be due, the sum required to obtain relief from forfeiture under s.138 of the County Courts Act 1984 should include the service charges payable as rent (see *Maryland Estates v Barr-Joseph* [1999] 1 W.L.R. 83).

- Claims for possession based upon forfeiture (and generally) are governed by CPR Pt 55.
- The claim must be started in the county court for the district in which the land is situated. If in error it is commenced in the wrong court it can be transferred.
- The claim may be started in the High Court if the claimant files with his claim form a certificate stating the reasons for bringing the claim in that court, verified by a statement of truth in accordance with CPR r.22.1(1). The practice direction (PD 55.1) refers to circumstances which may justify starting the claim in the High Court which include where there are complicated disputes of fact or there are points of law of general importance.
- Where the claim concerns residential premises, a prescribed form of Particulars of Claim (Form N119) must be used. If there are matters which cannot sensibly be included within the form, a bespoke Particulars of Claim can be attached and reference made to the same in the form N119.

The Practice Direction states that the Particulars of Claim for possession (whether the premises are residential or commercial) should:

- identify the land to which the claim relates;
- state whether the claim relates to residential property;
- state the ground on which possession is claimed;
- give full details about any mortgage or tenancy agreement; and
- give details of every person who, to the best of the claimant's knowledge, is in possession of the property.
- if the claimant knows of any person (including a mortgagee) entitled to claim relief against forfeiture as underlessee under s.146(4) of the Law of Property Act 1925 (or in accordance with s.38 of the Supreme Court Act 1981 or s.138(9C) of the County Courts Act 1984), state the name and address of that person and the claimant must file a copy of the particulars of claim for service on him.

Residential property

23–026 55PD.3 provides that if the claim relates to residential property let on a tenancy and if the claim includes a claim for non-payment of rent (which arguably includes services charges payable as rent) the Particulars of Claim must set out:

- the amount of due at the start of the proceedings;
- in schedule form, the dates when the arrears of rent arose, all amounts of rent due, the dates and amounts of all payments made and a running total of the arrears;
- the daily rate of any rent and interest;
- any previous steps taken to recover the arrears of rent with full details of any court proceedings; and
- any relevant information about the defendant's circumstances, in particular:
  - whether the defendant is in receipt of social security benefits; and
  - whether any payments are made on his behalf directly to the claimant under the Social Security Contributions and Benefits Act 1992.

The procedure for the progress of a possession claim is governed by Pt 55. There will be a first hearing where the case will be given a five-minute slot in a possession list usually before a district judge and, if uncontested, the court will dispose of the matter. Otherwise the court will give directions for trial and the matter will progress like most other forms of proceedings.

Debt claims

23–027 Perhaps the most frequent use of court proceedings, particularly in a residential context, is where landlords issue debt claims (under Pt 7 of the Civil Procedure Rules) seeking a money judgment in respect of service charges. In the event that the proceedings are not acknowledged or no defence is filed a default judgment can be obtained under CPR Pt 12. The advantage of proceeding in this way (apart from being able to enforce the money judgment in the usual way) is that such default judgment has been held (in the county court) to constitute a "determination" within the meaning of s.81 of the Housing Act 1996 entitling forfeiture proceedings to be commenced. It was held that the phrase "determination by a court" does not require a judicial determination: see *Southwark LBC v Tornaritis* [1999] 7 C.L.D. 330, Lambeth County Court, H.H.J. Cox.

Summary judgment

23–028 In a case where an acknowledgement of service has been filed but:

- the claimant has no real prospect of succeeding on the claim or issue; or
- the defendant has no real prospect of successfully defending the claim or issue; *and*
- there is no other compelling reason why the case or issue should be disposed of at a trial;

it is possible to apply under CPR Pt 24 for summary judgment. On such application the court will determine the matter on reading the statements of case and witness statements filed in respect of the application for summary judgment. Ordinarily summary judgment applications concern money claims.

It is, however, possible to seek judgment for forfeiture and possession by way of summary judgment in respect of both residential and commercial premises, provided in the case of residential premises that the tenant's occupation is not protected under the Rent Act 1977 or Housing Act 1988 (CPR Pt 24.3).

By reason of the procedure under Pt 55, which provides for a short hearing date being listed between four and eight weeks after issue, this often acts as a filter where cases without merit are weeded out. This to some extent removes the need for summary judgment applications in possession claims. As the hearing on such "return date" is very short and there is often insufficient time to consider the matter in detail it is suggested that in a clear case there is still some advantage in making an application for summary judgment.

Declarations

23–029 There are certain situations where it may be advantageous to apply to the court for a Declaration in a service charge dispute.

- In the case of *residential* premises this is less likely to be advantageous, as an application can be made to the LVT before works are carried out under s.27A(3) of the 1985 Act for a determination. Examples of when an application to the court might be made are:
  - where the issue is one of construction of the terms of the lease;
  - where there are conflicting LVT decisions and the matter is of some general importance.
- In the case of *commercial* premises, where there is some doubt as to whether if works are carried out the cost will be recoverable, it is possible to apply to the court for a Declaration resolving the issue.

An application for a Declaration where there is no substantial dispute of fact is best made utilising the CPR Pt 8 procedure. This provides for evidence in support of the application to be served with the Claim Form and for evidence in response prior to the first hearing.

At the hearing the court can dispose of the matter on the evidence before it, or give directions for the further conduct of the claim (for instance, if there is any dispute of fact) as if Pt 8 had not been utilised (CPR Pt 8.1(3) and 8PD.1 para.1.6). Default judgment is not available in a Pt 8 claim (8PD.3 para.3.5).

Transfer to the LVT

23–030 If a claim issued in the court based upon arrears of service charge is properly contested there is a likelihood that it will be transferred to the LVT for determination. This is discussed in detail in Chapter 22.

Interim payments

23–031 In the event that a case is disputed and is proceeding to a full trial, the claimant should consider an application for an interim payment under CPR 25.6.

Where the claim includes a claim for possession and the matter is adjourned at the first hearing the court has specific power to order an interim payment if it is satisfied that whatever the outcome of the proceedings further sums will have fallen due in respect of the tenant's occupation of the premises pending trial: CPR 25.7(1)(d). There is no reason why this could not included service charges, or alternatively a portion of the service charge which cannot be disputed.

The court also has power under its general case management powers when making an order to order a sum to be paid into court: CPR 3.1(3). On an adjournment of a possession claim out of the undefended list, such order could be made as a term of the adjournment in respect of service charges due, or about to fall due, pending trial.

Matters to be included in the claim form and statements of case under the CPR

23–032 The Civil Procedure Rules Pt 16 set out certain matters which must be included in the claim form and statements of case. Reference should be made to the Rules of Court and the standard texts for details of all matters required. By way of summary set out below are the key matters which are likely to arise and/or should be covered in a service charge dispute in court.

Claim form

23–033 The claim form should (CPR 16.2):

- include a concise statement of the nature of the claim;
- specify the remedy which the claimant seeks;
- where the claimant is making a claim for money, contain a statement of value in accordance with r.16.3; and
- contain such other matters as may be set out in a Practice Direction.

Particulars of claim

The particulars of claim in a service charge dispute must include: **23–034**

- a concise statement of the facts on which the claimant relies;
- if the claimant is seeking interest, a statement to that effect including:

  whether he is doing so—

  (i) under the terms of a contract (e.g. pursuant to the terms of the lease);
  (ii) under an enactment and, if so, which (s.69 of the County Courts Act 1984, s.35A of the Supreme Court Act 1981); or
  (iii) on some other basis and, if so, what that basis is; if the claim is for a specified amount of money—

    – the percentage rate at which interest is claimed;
    – the date from which it is claimed;
    – the date to which it is calculated, which must not be later than the date on which the claim form is issued;
    – the total amount of interest claimed to the date of calculation; and
    – the daily rate at which interest accrues after that date.

Practice Direction 16PD.7 specifies other matters to be included in the particulars of claim:

- Where a claim is made for an injunction or Declaration in respect of or relating to any land or the possession, occupation, use or enjoyment of any land, the particulars of claim must:
  - state whether or not the injunction or Declaration relates to residential premises; and
  - identify the land (by reference to a plan where necessary).
- Where a claim is based upon a written agreement:
  - a copy of the contract or documents constituting the agreement should be attached to or served with the particulars of claim and the original(s) should be available at the hearing.

Defence

23–035 The matters to be included in a defence are set out at CPR 16.5. These include:

- which of the allegations in the particulars of claim are denied;
- which allegations the defendant is unable to admit or deny, but which he requires the claimant to prove; and
- which allegations the defendant admits.
- Where the defendant denies an allegation—
  (a) he must state his reasons for doing so; and
  (b) if he intends to put forward a different version of events from that given by the claimant, he must state his own version.
- A defendant who—
  (a) fails to deal with an allegation; but
  (b) has set out in his defence the nature of his case in relation to the issue to which that allegation is relevant;

  shall be taken to require that allegation to be proved.

Limitation

23–036 Under the Practice Direction to CPR Pt 16 it is provided that the defendant must give details of the expiry of any relevant limitation period relied on: CPR 16PD.13. This clearly covers defences under the Limitation Act 1980 and, it is suggested, any challenge under s.20B of the 1985 Act.

Defence of tender

23–037 If a landlord has refused to accept rent or service charge sums notwithstanding that the same has been tendered, it is open to the tenant to rely on the defence of "tender before action", which impacts not only against liability to make payment and the right to forfeit, but also as to any interest claimed.

If the defence of tender is to be entertained by the court it must not be overlooked that the sum tendered must be paid into court. CPR 37.3 provides:

"(1) Where a Defendant wishes to rely on a defence of tender before claim he must make a payment into court of the amount he says was tendered.

(2) If the Defendant does not make a payment in accordance with paragraph (1) the defence of tender before claim will not be available to him until he does so.

(3) Where the Defendant makes such payment into court—

(a) he may choose to treat the whole or any part of the money paid into court as a Part 36 payment;
(b) if he does so, he must file a Part 36 payment notice."

Statement of truth

23–038 All statements of case should be verified by a statement of truth: CPR Pt 22.

Statements of case generally

23–039 Whether claimant or defendant, applicant or respondent, it is worth spending some time getting the statement of case right from the outset. It will have a significant impact not only on the issues to be determined but also the way in which the parties and judge or tribunal deal with the manner. If the statement of case is clear and focused, it is more likely that the other party and those determining the matter will be clear and focused. If it is jumbled and consists of irrelevant matters, the response in dealing with it will likely be equally as cumbersome. This spirals on into the experts' reports and the hearing.

In a simple case in the LVT it is possible to use the application form as the statement of case. In anything other than a simple case it is suggested that it is worthwhile to have a separate statement of case.

A well-drafted statement of case (whether in court or the LVT) should be as clear and as concise as possible. Ideally it should set out the issues in a succinct way and be the template for the resolution of the dispute. It is suggested that the use of headings within the statement of case is helpful and should be adopted whether in court or the LVT. The items of expenditure which are challenged should be given an item number in a way that they can be identified throughout the proceedings.

Claimant/applicant's statement of case

23–040 It is suggested (for there is no right or wrong way to do it) that in a service charge dispute the following matters should be covered in the following order (there are sample precedents in the appendices).

The parties

23–041 Introduce the parties and the address of the property (i.e. *The Applicants are lessees of flats 1–10 and the Respondent is the freehold owner and company wholly owned by residents*).

The building

23–042 Give a brief description of the building (i.e. *The Building is a 1920s block of 20 flats with two commercial shop units on the ground floor*).

The leases

23–043 Give details of leases (i.e. *The Applicants are lessees under leases granted between 1989 and 1994 by XY Limited for terms of 99 years from 24.06.89 at a rent of £50 per annum together with a service charge payable as rent*).

The terms of the leases

23–044 Give details in summary form by reference to clauses of lease terms and service charge clauses (i.e. *The leases are in identical terms and contain the following covenants/terms . . .* [set out landlord's obligations first and then the mechanism for collection of charges including proportions]).

Summary of service charge machinery

23–045 In a complex case, give a simple summary of how it is contended the service charge machinery works.

Details of items in dispute

23–046 Where the claim is a claim by lessees challenging service charges and the case concerns several years of service charge, it may be best to set out the items in issue on a year by year basis. If there are recurring items and the arguments are the same this can be dealt with by stating "*see above*". The basis of challenge should be made clear, e.g. "*The works constitute improvements not within the repairing obligations for which service charges are payable and/or the costs were incurred unreasonably*". If a proportion of the sum is admitted it is usually better to say so. If possible, figures should be included in the right hand column.

Section 20C/costs generally

23–047 If a s.20C application is to be made, any grounds in support should be set out. Likewise if the matter is before the court, it is often a good idea to include a statement in respect of costs indicating/warning why costs will be sought and if there is good reason why they should be paid on an indemnity basis this should be stated. In court proceedings where a landlord has a contractual right to seek indemnity costs arising out of breach of covenant/non-payment such clause should be pleaded and indemnity costs claimed pursuant to it.

Summary of relief

23–048 In a statement of case in court proceedings there is a formal way to set out the relief sought in the prayer. It is suggested that in a more complex case in the LVT it is prudent to give a summary of the relief sought at the end of the document.

Defendant/respondent's statement of case

23–049 The statement of case in response should if possible follow the claimant/applicant's statement of case. If it is poorly drafted it is often better for the defendant/respondent to deal with the matters above (parties, lease terms, etc.) so that the court/tribunal will be aware of the relevant matters. If there is to be a counter-claim or set-off (which arguably can be made in the LVT) it should be set out clearly and, if possible, quantified. The defence should deal with all items and if matters are to be admitted there is often real merit in making admissions at the outset.

Burden of proof

23–050 It is beyond the scope of this book to enter into academic debate over the burden and standard of proof in a service charge claim.

- Generally: the landlord must prove that the sums claimed are due and owing.
- Calling evidence from, say, a managing agent that works/services were provided, paid for and properly billed to the lessees should suffice.
- As regards issues of reasonableness, there is no presumption that an item is or is not reasonable.

In *Yorkbrook Investments Ltd v Batten* [1985] 2 E.G.L.R. 100, Wood J. (at 102 L) stated that there is no such presumption for or against a finding of reasonableness of standard of costs and that the court will reach its conclusion on the whole of the evidence. He went on to say that if the normal rules of pleading are followed there should be no difficulty: the position was analogous to a *quantum meruit* claim and the courts over the years have not been hampered by considerations as to the burden of proof. Thus:

- In the *defence* the tenant will need to specify the item complained of and the general nature—but not the evidence—of his case.
- If the tenant gives evidence establishing a *prima facie* case, then it will be for the landlord to meet the allegations and ultimately the court will reach its decision.

From this case it appears that the position is that the landlord must get over the hurdle that work has been done and properly billed. If there is to be a challenge, in the first instance the tenant must raise it with sufficient supporting material for such argument to get off the ground. It then falls upon the landlord to counter such challenge. As suggested by Wood J., in the courts and tribunals on a day to day basis such matters are determined in the round.

Group litigation

23–051 It is not unusual in a residential service charge dispute that a number of lessees dispute the sums in issue more or less on the same grounds. In such circumstances there is real merit in such lessees acting together and instructing the same solicitors, and having the claims heard at the same time.

In the LVT this poses no real problem as it is relatively simple for parties to be joined and, in the absence of any costs orders (save for the ability of the landlord to reclaim them *via* the service charge), several individuals being a party does not present any real difficulties.

In court proceedings where there are connected claims it is often sensible from all sides' perspectives for an application to be made for the claims to be heard together.

Participation agreement

If lessees are to act together and to instruct the same lawyers and experts, it is prudent at an early stage for the lessees to enter into a participation agreement governing how instructions will be given and costs, etc. paid. There is no ideal form of agreement and similar agreements are used for enfranchisement claims which may be adapted to cover the matters in issue.

Representative proceedings and group litigation orders ("GLOs") in court proceedings

Representative orders

23–052 Historically, where multiple parties were interested in the same or related claims, a representative order could be made entitling all the parties to be represented by one or more parties. This right has been preserved in the CPR in Pt 19 and in particular CPR Pt 19.6.

Put broadly, r.19.6 provides for legal persons to be represented in civil proceedings by other legal persons provided they have the same interest in the claim. The phrase "the same interest" in a claim must be interpreted to give effect to the overriding objective. Specifically, it should be interpreted in a way that makes the representative proceedings machinery available in cases where its use would save expense and enable a matter to be dealt with expeditiously.

Group litigation orders

23–053 Perhaps more suited to service charge disputes with multiple lessees is a group litigation order. GLOs were introduced to deal with problems encountered in the handling of representative proceedings under the former rules.

- An order may be made where there are multiple claimants or multiple defendants, or both.
- There must be common or related claims of issues of fact or law raised by the proceedings that make it desirable for the court to make a GLO in order to provide for the better management and progress of the claim.
- The procedure is governed by CPR 19 rr.10–15.

CPR 19.10 provides that a GLO means an order made under r.19.11 to provide for the case management of claims which give rise to common or related issues of fact or law (the "GLO issues").

- The GLO issues need not be the same issues but common or related.
- The court may make a GLO where there are or are likely to be a number of claims giving rise to the GLO issues. The practice direction provides the procedure for applying for a GLO.

The rules and procedure are somewhat complex and outside the scope of this work and reference should be made to the actual rules and practice direction.

Costs in respect of GLOs

Apart from the obvious advantage in having the claims "case managed" as one claim, there are real costs advantages. CPR 48.6A deals with the position as to costs where the court has made a GLO and in particular provides that unless the court orders otherwise:

- any order for costs against group litigants imposes several (rather than joint) liability for an equal proportion of the common costs: CPR 48.6(A)(3).
- Where a group litigant is the paying party he will be liable for:

  a) any costs he is ordered to pay to the receiving party;
  b) the individual costs of his claim;
  c) an equal proportion, together with other group litigants, of the common costs (r.48.6(A)(4)); and

  individual litigants can be ordered to pay their share of any common costs incurred before he joined the group action, but not after he has left the action (this could be as a result of filing an admission or settlement or withdrawal of claim) (CPR 48.6(A)(6) and (7)).

The costs provisions under GLOs are beneficial for lessees in a multiple dispute as they are not ordinarily exposed to paying the whole of the costs of the litigation. The court does retain a discretion to depart from the orders covered by CPR 48.6 but it is difficult to envisage a situation where an individual party would be required to pay more than his due proportion.

Whilst it is provided in the rule that a group litigant should pay an equal proportion of the common costs, this may work injustice where some lessees have only a limited interest (and others a significant interest) in the claim. One way around this in a service charge dispute may be that such proportion should reflect the percentages payable under the lease. A well-drafted participation agreement should cover this issue.

Appeals

23–054 Appeals from decisions of the court are dealt with comprehensively in CPR Pt 52 and the Practice Direction thereto and are beyond the scope of this book.

Chapter 24

Alternative Dispute Resolution: Negotiation, Mediation, Arbitration, Expert Determination and Adjudication

Introduction

24–001 This chapter considers aspects of alternative dispute resolution. Proceedings before the leasehold valuation tribunal are considered in Chapter 22 and proceedings before the courts are considered in Chapter 23. In this chapter, negotiation, mediation, arbitration, expert determination and adjudication are considered.

The issue of proceedings (whether before the LVT or a court) should be considered a last resort.

The costs of proceedings are expensive, involving as they usually do two sets of professional fees per side: those of the lawyers and those of surveyors.

It is the experience of the authors that the professional costs of dealing with a particular item in dispute may well exceed its value.

It must be borne in mind that in court proceedings the winning party rarely recovers 100 per cent of his costs on detailed assessment and, in particular, may well lose out when the test of "proportionality" is applied.

In respect of proceedings before the LVT, costs are not usually awarded to the winning party. The jurisdiction to award costs is limited to a maximum award (at present £500) and to instances where the party has acted frivolously, vexatiously, etc. Those familiar with proceedings before the employment tribunals will be aware that a similar rule applies there and, also, that the jurisdiction to award costs is very rarely exercised. Costs before the LVT are dealt with in paragraph 22–027.

The courts now actively encourage the use of ADR: Civil Procedure Rules 1998 Pt 1.4 reads "(1) The court must further the overriding objective by actively managing cases. (2) Active case management includes . . . (e) encouraging the parties to use an alternative dispute resolution procedure if the court considers that appropriate and facilitating the use of such procedure." Part 1.3 CPR states in terms that the parties have a duty to further the overriding objective.

Failure to negotiate, refusal of offers of settlement or refusal to submit to mediation will be taken into account in court proceedings in costs awards. Indeed, even a party who wins at trial may lose all or part of his costs: see *Dunnett v Railtrack* [2002] 1 W.L.R. 2434, discussed later.

Essentially there are two forms of alternative dispute resolution:

- Forms that encourage the parties to resolve disputes: e.g. negotiation, mediation.
- Forms that impose a determination: e.g. arbitration, expert determination, adjudication (binding but temporary).

Negotiation

24–002 Accordingly, parties should be encouraged to seek to resolve (or at least narrow) issues without recourse to proceedings. In the first instance, this may be dealt with in correspondence. Parties should ensure that the letters sent are constructive and helpful: it must always be remembered that in due course and some way down the line if the matter comes to trial the letters will be read by the judge. A judge who takes the view that a party has been difficult or obstructive will have little sympathy for the party at trial and may well take such matters into account in deciding what to do about costs.

As a matter of tactics in order to afford some protection on the issue of costs, particularly if court proceedings are anticipated, there is some logic in making genuine offers to mediate/negotiate on a "without prejudice save as to costs basis". Failure to agree to mediate may be the basis of an adverse costs order in court proceedings. Even if not entirely successful on the main claim, on the question of costs the court will take into account the stance adopted and steps taken by the respective parties in order to achieve a settlement: see *Halsey v Milton Keynes General NHS Trust* [2004] 4 All E.R.

The decision whether or not to compromise is likely to depend on many factors including the strength of the case, whether others are likely to be affected and/or change their position as a result of the compromise, and the costs of litigating the matter.

In a block situation a landlord however must be aware that any compromise may have a knock on effect and lead other lessees to challenge the service charges (whether already paid or not). A negotiated settlement in global terms, which may be non-specific as to the precise basis of settlement, is often preferable for a landlord than an adverse and public finding in the leasehold valuation tribunal, which is then seized and relied upon by the other tenants. Similarly, a negotiated agreement in respect of charges payable by a commercial tenant may have less impact on capital values and rent reviews within a portfolio.

If the parties do reach an agreement that agreement should be formally recorded. By s.27A of the Landlord and Tenant Act 1985 (as added by the Commonhold and Leasehold Reform Act 2002), the LVT has no jurisdiction where the matter "has been agreed or admitted by the tenant" (subs.(4)).

Mediation

24–003 If the parties are unable to reach a settlement by negotiation the next step to consider is mediation.

The Centre for Effective Dispute Resolution (CEDR) defines mediation as:

> "A flexible process conducted confidentially in which a neutral person actively assists parties in working towards a negotiated agreement of a dispute or difference, with the parties in ultimate control of the decision to settle and the terms of resolution. It is possible to distinguish between facilitative mediation, where the mediator aids or assists the parties' own efforts to formulate a settlement; and evaluative mediation where the mediator additionally helps the parties by introducing a third-party view over the merits of the case or of particular issues between the parties."

Lord Justice Brooke (with whom Lord Justice Sedley and Lord Justice Robert Walker agreed) in *Dunnett v Railtrack* [2002] EWCA Civ. 303, observed that:

> "Skilled mediators are now able to achieve results satisfactory to both parties in any cases which are quite beyond the power of lawyers and courts to achieve. This court has knowledge of cases where intense feelings have arisen, for instance in relation to clinical negligence claims. But when the parties are brought together on neutral soil with a skilled mediator to help them resolve their

> differences, it may very well be that the mediator is able to achieve a result by which the parties shake hands at the end and feel that they have gone away having settled the dispute on terms with which they are happy to live. A mediator may be able to provide solutions which are beyond the powers of the court to provide."

Various bodies and individuals provide mediation services. As the reference to mediation is voluntary, the procedure is in the hands of the parties, but in the authors' experience most mediations generally follow the same pattern.

The costs of the mediator are usually shared equally between the parties, although the authors have had experience of cases where one party pays all the fees by reason of the impecuniosity of the other party (to avoid the necessity of trial).

The mediator usually asks for a "statement of case" from each party plus copies of documents deemed relevant by each party.

On the day of the mediation the parties usually meet for a joint session at which each party puts its position to the other. The parties then retire to separate rooms where they are visited in turn by the mediator. Anything said to the mediator is confidential and will not be revealed to the other side without express consent. The mediator having heard the respective parties can then put forward suggested solutions to either party (on the instructions of the respective parties). Some mediators are more proactive than others and may put forward their own solutions (again restrained by confidentiality). The hope is that as the issues have been thrashed out, the parties may see that there is a workable solution between the parties and embrace/find a solution to the dispute(s).

The parties should be prepared for the session to last long into the evening.

The advantages of mediation are:

- It is relatively cheap;
- The method of proceeding can be controlled by the parties;
- It can take place at a time and place to suit the parties and their professional advisors;
- If successful there is an obvious saving of costs of trial/LVT proceedings;
- There is a very high success rate;
- If an offer to go to mediation is refused this will very likely sound in costs.

The potential disadvantages of mediation are:

- Parties may disclose documentation/arguments that tactically they would have potentially kept "closer to their chest" if they were proposing to litigate. The current ethos of the Civil Procedure Rules, however, encourages early identification of issues.
- There are uncertain standards at mediation. Often it is not possible to predict what approach a mediator will take and there is a vast difference between a highly skilled mediator and a novice mediator. Usually, however, recognised organisations such as CEDR provide the requisite training to ensure the high standards required from a qualified mediator.
- The parties have to be on reasonably good terms to agree to enter into mediation. Often parties do not consider mediation as they feel that their entrenched position is so far away from the other party's position and relations between the parties have deteriorated to such an extent that it is difficult to consider that mediation will achieve anything. The authors reiterate that it is surprising how some mediators can resolve situations and instil confidence back to the relationship between the parties.

Effect on costs at trial if mediation is refused

24–004 In the *Dunnett* case, the Court of Appeal held that it was bound under CPR Pt 44 to take into account all the circumstances of the case in considering what order to make in respect of costs, and the refusal of the defendants to contemplate alternative dispute resolution led to their not being awarded their costs even though they won.

In *Halsey v Milton Keynes NHS Trust* [2004] EWCA Civ. 576, the Court of Appeal held that a party will only be penalised for refusing to take part in a mediation if the refusal was unreasonable. The burden was on the unsuccessful party to show why there should be a departure from the general rule on costs in the form of an order to deprive a successful party of some or all of his costs on the grounds that he had refused to agree to alternative dispute resolution (ADR). The fundamental principle was that such a departure was not justified unless it had been shown that the successful party had acted unreasonably in refusing to agree to ADR. In deciding whether a party had acted unreasonably, the court should bear in mind the advantages of ADR over the court process and have regard to all the circumstances of the particular case. Factors that could be relevant included:

(i) the nature of the dispute;

(ii) the merits of the case;

(iii) the extent to which other settlement methods had been attempted;

(iv) whether the costs of ADR would be disproportionately high;

(v) whether any delay in setting up and attending the ADR would have been prejudicial;

(vi) whether the ADR had a reasonable prospect of success.

Where a successful party had refused to agree to ADR despite the court's encouragement, that was a factor that the court would take into account when deciding whether his refusal was unreasonable.

There has been much commentary on the effect of these two cases and the importance of ADR in relation to costs.

As to the comment above that mediation is relatively cheap, although the parties will bear the costs of the mediation (i.e. the mediator's fees, costs of accommodation, etc.), such costs generally pale into insignificance compared with the costs of going to trial or appearing before the LVT. Mediations are usually over within a day.

The courts themselves offer mediation, and the London Residential Property Tribunal Service is also piloting a mediation scheme. However, the disadvantage of court mediation is that usually only half a day is given to each matter, and this may be an insufficient time-frame.

Arbitration

24–005 Section 1 of the Arbitration Act 1996 sets out the clear principles that are expected from arbitration:

"(a) the object of arbitration is to obtain the fair resolution of disputes by an impartial tribunal without unnecessary delay or expense.

(b) the parties should be free to agree how their disputes are resolved, subject only to such safeguards as are necessary in the public interest".

Advantages of arbitration:

- Arbitration can be quicker and more cost-effective than the courts or the LVT.

- In arbitration the parties have an input as to what procedures to adopt in determining the dispute. These may be provided for in the lease or in the alternative tailored for the dispute in a post-dispute arbitration agreement.
- Parties have the ability to choose their arbitrator for their expertise. In service charge disputes the arbitrator should invariably have some experience in property/construction. It is not uncommon for reference to be made to the President of RICS.
- Arbitration awards have the advantage of being final and binding subject to very limited exceptions (See s.58 of the Arbitration Act 1996).
- Arbitration awards by agreement between the parties can remain confidential. This can be an overwhelming factor in going to arbitration.

Section 9 of the Arbitration Act 1996 provides that a party to an arbitration agreement against whom legal proceedings are brought (whether by way of a claim or counter-claim), in respect of a matter which under the agreement is to be referred to arbitration, may (upon notice to the other parties to the proceedings) apply to the court in which the proceedings have been brought to stay the proceedings so far as they concern the matter. Section 66 of the Arbitration Act 1996 provides that an arbitration award may be enforced in the same way as a judgment of a court. An in-depth analysis of arbitration is obviously outside the scope of this book. For a detailed commentary on the Arbitration Act 1996, see the third edition of "The Arbitration Act 1996, a commentary" by Bruce Harris, Rowan Planterose and Jonathan Tecks, published in association with the Chartered Institute of Arbitrators by Blackwell Publishing.

Disadvantages of arbitration include:

- The costs savings are not necessarily achieved, particularly as the costs of the arbitration are borne by the parties (in addition to the costs of the parties' representatives and experts);
- The arbitration is only as good as the appointed arbitrator.

Arbitration proceedings involving service charges may be initiated as follows.

Express provision in the lease

24–006 The lease may provide expressly that disputes relating to service charges be resolved by arbitration. Express terms may be caught by the Unfair Terms in Consumer Contracts Regulations 1999 (SI 1999/2083) (which implement Council Directive 93/13).

Regulations 5.1 and 8.1 of Sch.2 to the regulations contain an indicative and non-exhaustive list of terms which may be regarded as unfair. It includes at para.1q:

> "terms which have the object or effect of excluding or hindering the consumer's right to take legal action or exercise any other legal remedy, particularly by requiring the consumer to take disputes exclusively to arbitration not covered by legal provisions, unduly restricting the evidence available to him or imposing on him a burden of proof which, according to the applicable law, should lie with another party to the contract".

Section 91 of the Arbitration Act 1996 renders consumer arbitration agreements automatically non-binding where the claims are small (currently under £5000)—in all other cases it is for the consumer to show that the arbitration clause is unfair. Lord Justice Laws, at para.83 of his judgment in *The London Borough of Newham v Khatun, Zeb and Iqbal* [2004] EWCA Civ. 55, held that the Directive and Regulations apply to contracts relating to land. For guidance on the meaning of good faith see *Director General of Fair Trading v First National Bank* [2001] 1 All E.R. 97, *Bryen & Langley Limited v Boston* [2004] EWHC 2450 (TCC), *Lovell Projects Limited v Legg & Carver* [2003] 1 B.L.R. 452 and *Westminster Building Company Limited v Beckingham* [2004] 1 B.L.R. 265. *Zealander v Laing Homes Ltd* [1996] C.I.L.L. 1510 is an example of a case where an arbitration clause was struck down under the 1994 Regulations (the Regulations that preceded the current 1999 Regulations).

See also Chapter 11.

Arbitration clauses in leases of dwellings

24–007 Section 27A(6) of the LTA 1985 provides that:

> "an agreement by the tenant of a dwelling (other than a post-dispute arbitration agreement) is void in so far as it purports to provide for a determination—
>
> (a) in a particular manner, or
> (b) on particular evidence,

of any question which may be the subject of an application under subsection (1) or (3)".

See paragraph 24–010 as to commencement.

This provision renders an arbitration clause void if it is contained in the lease of a dwelling. Of course, the parties would be free to enter into a post-dispute arbitration agreement.

Post-dispute arbitration agreements

24–008 Once a dispute has arisen the parties may voluntarily enter into a post-dispute arbitration agreement. Section 27A(4) of the Landlord and Tenant Act 1985 states that no application to the LVT may be made under subs.(1) or (3) in respect of a matter which:

(a) has been agreed or admitted by the tenant;

(b) has been, or is to be, referred to arbitration pursuant to a post-dispute arbitration agreement to which the tenant is a party;

(c) has been the subject of determination by a court; or

(d) has been the subject of determination by an arbitral tribunal pursuant to a post-dispute Landlord and Tenant Act 1985 arbitration agreement.

Note of caution

24–009 Inconsistent decisions of differently constituted arbitral tribunals may result if each lease relating to different tenants have separate arbitration clauses making no reference to disputes of a similar nature between landlord and multiple tenants. This arises due to the contractual nature of an arbitration clause between the parties (and not any third parties, in this case other tenants). Unless otherwise agreed between all the parties, there would be no means of joining similar disputes. Arguably, a way round this problem would be for the parties to include a clause in the lease that would provide a right to consolidate the arbitration with others concerning the same/similar issues but relating to other tenants, perhaps, at the same building. Such a clause may be difficult to draft as decisions would need to be made on which tenants should be party to such a clause. Problems may also arise in interpreting such a clause as it may be that the parties have different ideas as to what might constitute "similar issues".

Expert determination

Leases of dwellings

24–010 Section 27A(6) of the Landlord and Tenant Act 1985 was inserted by the Commonhold and Leasehold Reform Act 2002, s.155(1). It came into force (in relation to England) on September 30, 2003 (except in relation to any application made to a LVT under s.19(2A) or (2B) or any proceedings relating to a service charge transferred to a LVT by a county court before that date): see SI 2003/1986, arts 1(2) and 2(c)(i) and Sch.2, para.6. It came into force (in relation to Wales) on March 30, 2004 (except in relation to any application made to a LVT under s.19(2A) or (2B) or any proceedings relating to a service charge transferred to a LVT by a county court before March 31, 2004): see SI 2004/669, art. 2(c)(i) and Sch.2, para.6.

Section 27A(6) of the LTA 1985 provides that:

> "an agreement by the tenant of a dwelling (other than a post-dispute arbitration agreement) is void in so far as it purports to provide for a determination—
>
> (a) in a particular manner, or
> (b) on particular evidence,
>
> of any question which may be the subject of an application under subsection (1) or (3)".

The mischief aimed at was the practice of landlords of including a clause providing for determination by (for instance) the landlord's surveyor.

Apart from statute

24–011 Prior to this clause coming into force, the case of *Concorde Graphics Ltd v Andromeda Investments SA* (1983) 265 E.G. 386, Ch.D. was relevant in relation to expert determinations. The lease examined by the court contained a provision that in case of a "difference" as to the contribution of service charges the matter was to be settled "by the landlord's surveyor", whose decision was to be "final and binding" on the parties. The demands for contributions were made by a firm who were both the landlord's managing agents and the landlord's surveyors. The court held that as the function of deciding a "difference" as to the amount of tenant's contribution was "essentially arbitral", involving an impartial holding of the balance between landlord and tenant, the landlord's managing agents who had made the disputed claim could not, in their capacity as the landlord's surveyors, make a "final and binding" decision on such a "difference". The landlord would have to appoint other surveyors for that purpose.

This authority will govern the position in respect of non-residential leases.

Adjudication

24–012 Adjudication is in the main relevant to disputes between a landlord and its builder. Such disputes may have some impact as to works for which service charges are payable. There is some suggestion that adjudication is also applicable to a dispute between landlord and tenant.

What is adjudication?

24–013 Adjudication is similar to arbitration in that a decision is made by a third party which is binding upon the parties. It differs from arbitration in that the decision only has temporary effect: i.e. until finally resolved either by the court or an arbitral award. The adjudicator is someone with specialist knowledge of the subject matter of the dispute, e.g. a surveyor or architect.

Adjudication, created by the Housing Grants, Construction and Regeneration Act 1996 (the "1996 Act"), provides a scheme for ADR in written construction contracts entered into since May 1, 1998.

The contract between landlord and contractor

24–014 The 1996 Act applies to all "construction contracts" made after May 1, 1998. The definition of that term appears in s.104 of the 1996 Act. Clearly, a contract entered into by a landlord (or one in a similar position such as a RTM company) with a building contractor, whereby the latter would carry out repairs, decoration, maintenance (standard service charge undertakings), would come within the ambit of the adjudication provisions of the 1996 Act.

Application to a dispute between landlord and tenant over service charges

24–015 It has been suggested that a contract entered into between landlord and tenant, could also be covered by the adjudication provisions:

see "Cut to the Quick", Hastie & Armitage, Estates Gazette No.0105 p.164. Consideration of ss.104 and 105 led to the view that by the inclusion of the words "provisions of any kind", an agreement is a "construction contract" for the purposes of the Act even if only one of its facets is construction operations. There is a Scottish authority that if a contract is mostly concerned with operations which do not fall within the ambit of the Act, nevertheless the Act may still be invoked: *Homer Burgess v Chirex (Annan) Ltd* (2000) S.L.T. 277. This case was cited with approval in *ABB Power Construction Limited v Norwest Holst Engineering Ltd* (2000) 77 Con.L.R. 20.

In any case where there is a complaint about the standard of works (etc.) being carried out by the contractor, the landlord should consider referring the matter to adjudication. Further, in such circumstances the tenant should consider urging such a course upon the landlord. Reference to adjudication—or failure to refer to adjudication and the stance adopted in respect thereof—may well be relevant when the question of reasonableness of a service charge comes to be considered.

Basics of adjudication

24–016 The legislative framework is contained in ss.104–108 of the 1996 Act. What has to be in writing is the contract, not just evidence of the contract or evidence of the terms: *RJT Consulting Engineers Ltd v DM Engineering (Northern Ireland) Limited* [2002] B.L.R. 79.

The 1996 Act states that either the contract itself must provide for an adjudication process in terms no less favourable than those prescribed, or the 1996 Act will step in with its own scheme. That scheme is contained in the Scheme for Construction Contracts (England and Wales) Regulations 1998 (SI 1998/649) (the "Scheme").

Disputes may be referred to adjudication at the option of either party to the building contract. The non-referring party is then bound to adjudicate.

Challenges to the process can only be resolved at the enforcement stage: *Pegram Shopfitters Ltd v Tally Wiejl UK Ltd* [2003] EWHC 984; [2003] B.L.R. 296. In practice this means that the responding party to the adjudication should submit his response without prejudice to the challenge which itself should be clearly identified.

The courts will enforce an adjudicator's decision unless the question actually referred to adjudication can be said not to have been answered, because the adjudicator was referred to—or referred himself to—the wrong documentation/principles: *Joinery Plus Limited (In Administration) v Laing Limited* (February 15, 2003) unreported H.H.J. Thornton Q.C.

Advantages

Advantages are: **24–017**

Speed—

- Once notice of referral of any dispute between the parties is made, the adjudicator is appointed either by agreement between the parties or, in default of agreement, by the referring party. The adjudicator then sets the timetable for the parties to adduce submissions and evidence to him and specifies in what manner. A decision must be made within 28 days of the date of the Notice of Referral or such longer period as the parties agree.
- The timetable may only be challenged if the rules of natural justice have been clearly breached. Attempts to challenge the limit under the auspices of the Human Rights Act 1998 have failed.
- Disputes may be referred to adjudication at the option of either party to the building contract. The non-referring party is then bound to adjudicate.

The disadvantages are:

- There is no time limit on referring a matter to adjudication so parties can be caught out long after the dispute has arisen.
- The adjudicator has no power to award costs. The parties can agree between themselves that the adjudicator has power to make a costs order. A party may not unilaterally give the adjudicator the power to do so.
- An adjudicator has no power to decide on matters of jurisdiction unless the parties agree that he shall do so. Such technical matters should always be referred to the Technology and Construction Court for a determination as a preliminary issue.
- The adjudicator does not have power to stay the process pending the outcome unless the parties agree or he considers that to do so is required by natural justice. As agreement is unlikely to be obtained, it is all the more necessary to raise this issue at the outset if it is to be "live" for the purposes of any enforcement proceedings.

Chapter 25

VAT and Tax

VAT

VAT basics

VAT is a charge on the supply of goods and services. Unless the supply is in a category "exempt" from the VAT charge, VAT must generally be charged on any supply of goods or services made: **25–001**

- In the UK or Isle Of Man made for consideration;
- By a person registered (or who ought to be registered) for VAT;
- In the course of furtherance of a business of a person registered (or who ought to be registered) for VAT.

Any supply of goods and services which is not within the above categories, for example services supplied other than in furtherance of a business or supplied outside the UK and Isle Of Man, is outside the scope of VAT and no VAT accounting need be carried out.

Exempt categories include the provision of most insurance, financial, health, postal, education and training services.

VAT rates

There are three rates of the charge, applied to the consideration payable or deemed payable: **25–002**

- The "standard rate" of 17.5 per cent which applies to the vast majority of supplies unless some other rate applies;

- The "reduced rate" of 5 per cent applies to supplies of domestic fuel, some energy-saving installations and certain renovations of dwellings;
- The "zero rate" of 0 per cent applies to some foods, books and children's clothes and also to certain works to listed buildings.

Zero rated and exempt supplies must be carefully distinguished for, whilst they have the superficial similarity of not giving rise to liability to pay VAT, zero rated suppliers must account for VAT in the usual way and are entitled to claim deduction of input tax even though suffering no output tax.

Partial exemption

25–003 A business that makes wholly exempt supplies cannot register for VAT. Where the business makes supplies some of which are exempt and some of which are not, then it is "partially exempt" and only a part of its input tax in proportion to its non-exempt business, may be reclaimed.

VAT accounting

25–004 A person registered for VAT must keep records and file regular returns with HM Customs & Excise of his business sales and purchases and the VAT thereon. The VAT suffered when purchasing goods or services for use in the business is termed "input tax" and that charged on the sales of the business goods and services is termed "output tax". The difference between the output tax charged on sales by the trader and the input tax suffered by him on purchases in any set period must be accounted for to HM Customs & Excise.

Example

25–005 A manufacturer buys raw materials for £1,000 plus standard rate VAT at 17.5 per cent, being £175. Those materials are made into a product that the manufacturer sells for £2,000 plus standard rate VAT at 17.5 per cent, being £350. The manufacturer also incurs charges for subcontracted services of £200 plus standard rate VAT at 17.5 per cent, being £35.

At the end of its VAT period the business must pay £140 to HM Customs & Excise, being:

	Output tax		£350
Less:	Input tax—materials	£175	
	Input tax—services	£35	
			(£210)
			£140

General

25–006 The overall effect of VAT is to tax the end consumer of goods and services in proportion to the amount spent. Businesses supplying other businesses are generally able to pass on the VAT charged on their purchases to their customers—VAT on the difference between the amount paid for purchases and charged to customers on sale (the "value added") being remitted to HM Customs & Excise. Thus in general only the end consumer or unregistered business will be unable to pass on the VAT charge and will end up shouldering the tax burden.

Persons registered for VAT must keep their relevant records for six years and must issue VAT invoices containing prescribed information and displaying their VAT registration number.

VAT legislation and practice is extremely complex and reference should be made to specialist texts for detailed guidance.

VAT bad debt relief

25–007 Other than for businesses permitted to account on a cash basis, VAT must be accounted for on the difference between sales and purchases made in a defined period, usually quarterly, rather than on receipts and payments.

Where a sale that includes VAT remains unpaid and a debt is outstanding at the end of a VAT period then the business must usually account for the VAT on that debt regardless of whether or not payment has been received. Similarly input VAT should be reclaimed on unpaid purchases.

Where the debt from a sale arising after January 2003 has not been paid within six months, the seller is permitted to write off the debt and reclaim the output VAT by deduction from other output VAT in the period in which the six-month limit is passed. Likewise the purchaser, if VAT registered, must repay the input VAT on invoices not paid within the six-month period.

VAT and leases

25–008 The letting of property, whether residential or commercial, is exempt from VAT (Sch.9 VAT Act 1994) and thus no VAT ordinarily need be or can be charged by a landlord to its tenants on rent. Whilst this means that rent payments would not carry VAT, the corresponding effect is that the landlord cannot recover input VAT on its purchases (such as VAT charged by maintenance contractors or solicitors).

Waiver of exemption

25–009 From April 1, 1989 however, a landlord may elect to waive this exemption in respect of commercial property only. The effect of such a waiver is that the letting is to be treated as subject to VAT at the standard rate; and correspondingly to allow the landlord to reclaim input VAT on its purchases.

No waiver is permitted in respect of domestic property or of property used for charitable purposes—where a single property has mixed use, the waiver can only apply to the commercial part. If there are separate lettings of the commercial and domestic parts then only the rent for the commercial parts can be subject to VAT—otherwise an apportionment between the parts will have to be agreed with HM Customs & Excise.

The effect on a commercial tenant will depend upon the tenant's own VAT status:

- Tenants who are not VAT registered or who make exempt supplies will be unable to reclaim the VAT on their rent as input VAT and will therefore suffer the VAT inclusive cost.
- Tenants who are VAT registered and make standard or zero rated supplies will be able to reclaim the VAT on rent as input VAT in their own VAT returns. Their rent cost will be treated as any other taxable purchase and the true cost to the business will be the net rent paid.
- Tenants whose supplies are partially exempt will fall between the two categories above and will incur increased costs in proportion to the percentage of exempt supplies they make.

The election

25–010 The landlord's election to waive the exemption must be notified to HM Customs & Excise in writing within 30 days of the election having been made.

The election must relate to the whole of a building and land within its curtilage although, as noted above, mixed commercial and domestic property has a special treatment.

The election is binding upon the property to which it applies for a period of 20 years unless:

- it is revoked by the landlord within the first three months (and then only with permission from HM Customs & Excise, such permission usually being granted if the election has not been put into practical effect); or
- the property becomes used for domestic or charitable purposes (during which time the effect of the election is suspended).

It follows that great care must be taken by landlords in deciding whether to elect to waive exemption. If the election is made then any supply relating to the property, including lettings or a sale, will become taxable for the period of at least 20 years. It is particularly important to consider the nature of potential tenants or purchasers, for their own VAT status will determine the impact of VAT upon them and thus the effective cost of the lease or purchase. For example a bank or similar financial institution is likely to be wholly or partially exempt and thus will be unable to reclaim all of the input VAT charged on a sale or letting of a property to which an election applies.

VAT on service charges—the nature of services provided

25–011 We have seen that rent may be subject to VAT for commercial properties where the landlord has elected to waive the VAT exemption, but for all domestic properties and also for commercial properties where there has been no election, VAT is not chargeable on rent.

Whether VAT is chargeable on service charges depends upon whether the service charge is in the nature of rent, i.e. it is a charge directly related to the tenant's right of occupation of the property or not. If it is in the nature of rent, then VAT will only be chargeable on the service charge in the same circumstances as it is on rent; if not, then VAT will be chargeable by the landlord to the tenant on the supply of those services at the appropriate rate for those services.

Charges in the nature of rent

25–012 Charges in the nature of rent are those which are direct incidents of the tenant's right of occupation under the lease and include:

- maintenance of the structure of the building;
- cleaning, lighting and repairing the common parts;
- lift maintenance;
- porterage and security.

Where a property is in multiple occupation, these communal charges will be apportioned between the various occupiers in accordance with the provisions of their leases.

Charges otherwise than in the nature of rent

25–013 Charges which are not in the nature of rent are those which are personal to the tenant and include:

- cleaning or repairing the tenant's demise;
- reception, telephone or office services.

Disbursements

25–014 Where a landlord pays for services on behalf of a tenant, as opposed to recharging their cost, the service of the landlord is outside the scope of VAT as he is simply making a disbursement and not providing a taxable service. For example if a telephone account is in the name of the tenant but the landlord pays it and reclaims the sum paid this would be a disbursement; conversely if the account were in the name of the landlord and the landlord recharged the sum paid this would be a service subject to VAT.

Tax

The landlord's tax treatment

25–015 A landlord's income arising from the ownership of land will be assessable to income or corporation tax on the basis allowed by Schedule A. The general application of the Schedule A rules is that:

- Expenses incurred wholly and exclusively for business purposes are allowable as deductions from income in calculating taxable profit.

- Profits and losses from all properties are pooled so that losses from one property are relieved first against profits in the same period from others.
- If there is an overall loss for the pool then it is carried forward against Schedule A profits in future years (although losses relating to capital allowances can be set off against other income sources in the year incurred or subsequently).
- Capital expenditure is not deducted from profit and neither is depreciation. Instead capital allowances at approved rates (usually 25 per cent per year on a reducing balance basis) are deducted to write off capital expenditure over time. It is essential that capital and revenue expenditure is clearly distinguished.

Service charge income is treated as rent and simply as an additional part of the landlord's income from the ownership of the land. Revenue expenditure is likely to be entirely allowable as a deduction from income.

Capital expenditure, even if reimbursed by tenants during the accounting period, remains treated as the landlord's capital expenditure and only the proportion represented by the capital allowance set against income in any year. Landlords will frequently therefore face timing differences in that receipts in respect of the bulk of capital expenditure will be taxable in the year of receipt and the benefit of the writing down allowances will take several years to be effectively recouped.

The tenant's tax treatment

25–016 Commercial tenants will account for rent payments, suitably apportioned between periods, as an allowable deduction from taxable income as with any other allowable expenditure.

Commercial tenants should probably only deduct from taxable income the proportion of payments from the service charge payments in any one period that represents revenue expenditure in that period. Any service charge payment that represents a payment of capital is arguably not deductible against income. The application of these provisions depends to a great extent upon the precise drafting of the lease and the nature of the payments made or fund created.

Sinking fund capital expenditure

25–017 Particular difficulties arise where a sinking fund is held. The treatment of the fund and its investment income for tax purposes will depend upon the nature of the fund:

- Where the fund is a trust fund then the Inland Revenue treats receipts as capital. Investment income is chargeable in the hands of the trustee at the special rates applicable to trusts.
- Where the "fund" is part of the general funds of the landlord it is taxed as the landlord's income.

Accordingly, where a sinking fund (other than a trust fund) is accumulated for future capital expenditure the landlord will be obliged to treat the receipts of the fund as part of his Schedule A income chargeable to tax.

From the tenant's position, if the service charge or a defined part of it is levied in order that the landlord might incur specified capital expenditure, then that payment or part is to be treated as capital expenditure by the tenant and not allowed as a deduction against income. Capital allowances on the expenditure, when it occurs, are to be claimed by the landlord and not the tenant as the common areas concerned will be retained by the landlord. Where the service charge levied is not identified as being in respect of specific capital expenditure and the tenant ceases to have any control over or interest in the monies paid then they can usually be treated as revenue expenditure by the tenant.

Trust funds

25–018 Where the sinking fund is held on trust for tenants then the landlord (or other trustee) will be treated as having received payments of capital into the trust fund. Investment income will be taxable in the hands of the trustee under the normal rules applicable to trustees.

Payments into the trust fund that are treated as capital receipts in the hands of the trustee are also treated as capital payments by the tenants. Commercial tenants cannot therefore deduct any part of the payments from taxable income and, for the same reasons as given in paragraph 25–017, cannot claim capital allowances.

General

25–019 It follows that the drafting of the particular terms of the lease dealing with the nature of the fund and the allocation of service charge payments demanded is critical to any understanding of the likely tax treatment. Specialist advice should be sought as to the likely alternatives.

Chapter 26

Company Law

Introduction

26–001 The purpose of this chapter is to demonstrate how problems which involve aspects of company law may arise in the context of service charges and the management of properties held on long leases, and to suggest certain solutions which might be found to be useful. This chapter deals with companies other than RTM companies, for which reference should be made to Chapters 29–33. It is sufficient to note that, while most aspects of company law apply to RTM companies, there are some exceptions provided by the Commonhold and Leasehold Reform Act 2002, including restrictions on the ability to alter the memorandum and articles of association (s.74(7) of CLRA 2002).

Frequently found arrangements

26–002 It is commonplace, particularly in urban areas, for a house to be converted into two, three or four flats. The freehold will typically be owned by a company. The flats will be let on 99, 125 or even 999 year leases. Often the owners of the company, i.e. the shareholders, will be the individuals who own the long leases of the flats.

It is frequently a stipulation of such an arrangement that the proprietor of each of the long leasehold interests must be a shareholder of the company which owns the freehold and that his share is (broadly) not transferable except to a successor in title to the long leasehold interest in question.

Generally there will be one share per flat. The leases will normally contain some provision for a service charge to be levied so that, in general terms, the fabric of the building and the common parts can be maintained. The rent payable by the long leaseholder will often be a peppercorn and even if it is not it is invariably a very small sum.

Possible difficulties

26–003 How can this arrangement be faulted? It appears on the face of it to provide the owners of the flats with just what they want, namely the security of knowing that the fate of the building in which they live is safely in their own hands, and it enables them to grant new or extended leases should it be necessary, at will.

The fundamental difficulty with the scheme is economic. The company which owns the freehold is under-capitalised and has no or no significant income stream.

It is under-capitalised because, on the above analysis, its only capital asset is the freehold reversion of the building. This is probably worth very little, and in any event it cannot readily be turned into cash since the entire raison d'etre of the company is, and is only, to own the freehold of the building. The articles of association may make this explicit.

The company has no significant income because, of course, its only source of income is the ground rents payable by the long leaseholders, and those rents will be very low or non-existent, together with whatever service charges can be agreed or imposed. One of the reasons that the sort of arrangement described above is entered into is precisely so that the long leaseholders can minimise the ground rents payable to the freeholder.

Accordingly difficulties will arise when the company needs to spend money. This may occur in a variety of circumstances, including, of course, collection of disputed service charges. Two examples may be given.

First example—house divided into four flats

26–004 In a house which has been divided into four flats it becomes apparent that external works are required after some years of neglect. Each of the four flats is owned by a long leaseholder, and the four leaseholders own the only four shares in a company which owns the freehold reversion. The works required include complete redecoration of the exterior, some work to the roof and the replacement of gutters and downpipes. Estimates are obtained but no agreement can be reached about who is to do the works or at what price. Of the four long leaseholders, two (A and B) want to go ahead with an expensive quotation from a reputable builder. One (C) wants to go ahead with the cheapest quotation, which has been provided by an individual with a strong foreign accent who can only be contacted by a mobile phone number. The whereabouts of the fourth long leaseholder (D) are unknown. D's flat has been let on an assured shorthold tenancy and the subtenant pays rent monthly to an offshore bank account. All four of the long leaseholders are directors and (as indicated above) shareholders of the company.

The lease

26–005 The provisions in the leases concerning the levying of a service charge are likely to be of little use at this stage because in order to levy a charge the landlord (i.e. here the company) must first have decided what works are intended to be done and at what cost.

This assumes that the service charge provisions allow the landlord to levy a charge for work which has not yet been done (i.e. payment in advance), which is not always the case. It may be necessary for the works to be done before the service charge can be claimed, thereby introducing further potential difficulties in relation to interim funding.

Nevertheless, however the matter is looked at, it is necessary for the reversioner (here the company owning the freehold) to decide the extent and cost of the works.

The company

26–006 The articles of association of the company will govern the holding of meetings both by the directors and by the shareholders. Typically the company will be what is known as a "Table A" company, that is to say one where its articles of association are the model articles set out in Table A of the Companies Act 1985, or, for older companies, Table A of the Companies Act 1948, together with whatever variations were thought appropriate when the company was formed.

In this example, the individual long leaseholders, as directors of the company, cannot agree the way forward. They vote, *as directors*, in favour of the expensive option by two (A and B) to one (C). They have not voted as shareholders because no notice of a general meeting has been given. C says that he will not pay the cost of the expensive option under any circumstances and relationships break down completely. C calls a general meeting of the company and threatens proceedings which might involve its winding up (see below) if he doesn't get his way. He serves the relevant notice on D through his bank. Much to everyone's surprise the notice is effective and D becomes involved. He votes with C. The result is deadlock.

Deadlock

26–007 By art.42 of Table A 1985 the chairman of the board of directors shall chair the meeting. If there is none, the chairman shall be a director voted by the board of directors. If there is no chairman of the board already in place (as will often be the case with this sort of inactive company) then it will be impossible to elect a chairman in the case of deadlock. The relevance of this is that the chairman of the meeting has a casting vote (art.50 of Table A 1985). If there is no chairman then there can be no casting vote. The deadlock will continue and no decision can be made.

Leaving aside any form of alternative dispute resolution, the solution from the point of view of company law is an application to the court for its assistance. The application will be by one or more of the shareholders in their capacity as such, and will be made pursuant to s.459 of the Companies Act 1985 ("the Act"). The nature of the application and the powers of the court are explained in more detail in the next two sections below.

Let it be supposed, however, that there is a chairman, perhaps appointed at the court's direction, and even assuming that the more expensive option mentioned above is forced through on his casting vote, what then might be the situation? Two (C and D) of the four long leaseholders may say that they will not pay because they have not voted for the works, whatever the court may direct. Unless A and B are willing to risk putting up the whole of the cost of the works themselves, and risk the costs of the litigation which may be required to recover the relevant proportion of the cost of the works from C and D, still nothing will happen.

Remedy of disgruntled shareholders

26–008 Moreover there remains the question of what the outvoted shareholders will do. Any member of a company can seek relief from the court under s.459(1) of the Act 1985 on the ground that:

> "the company's affairs are being or have been conducted in a manner which is unfairly prejudicial to the interests of its members generally or some part of its members (including at least himself) or that any actual or proposed act or omission of the company (including an act or omission on its behalf) is or would be so prejudicial".

It can be seen that it is not necessary for the company to be deadlocked for an application to be made. The application is made by petition (s.459(1) of the Act) to the Companies Court. See below for the wide range of orders which can be made. It can also be seen that the prejudicial conduct must be prejudicial to at least one person in his capacity as a *member*, not, e.g. as a director.

Rule in *Foss v Harbottle*

26–009 Apart from the rights given by statute, however, the right of access to the court by a shareholder is somewhat restricted. This is the result of rule in *Foss v Harbottle* (1843) 2 Hare 461. The rule can broadly be stated as two propositions, namely:

(i) that the court will not interfere with the internal affairs of a company; and

(ii) that where a company has suffered a loss or other wrong the proper claimant is the company itself.

There are a few exceptions, however, e.g. in cases of fraud where the fraudsters are in control of the company, and so no vote can be passed which would enable it to sue them.

Unfair prejudice

26–010 In the brief facts of the example given above there is nothing to indicate whether the affairs of the company are or are not being conducted in a manner which is unfairly prejudicial to C or D (s.459(1) of the Act). An infinite variety of circumstances may arise in such a company ranging from, at one end of the scale, *mala fides* where there is some underlying personal animosity and the service charge issue is simply being used as a vehicle to get rid of an unpopular neighbour, to at the other end of the scale, a situation where genuinely necessary works are bona fide required for the preservation of the property. The question whether the conduct complained of is unfairly prejudicial is one of fact depending on all the circumstances. Of course, A or B could themselves apply for relief, e.g. in the form of an order that the company carries out the proposed works. They might argue that their interests as shareholders are being prejudiced because the value of the property is being reduced while the works are not done.

Possible court orders

26–011 The court can make such order as it thinks fit, pursuant to s.461(1) of the Act. This can include an order requiring the company to make such alteration in its memorandum or articles of association as it may specify (which takes effect without a resolution of the company in general meeting (s.461(4)). Other examples of orders which the court can make are given at s.461(2).

These are:

(i) an order regulating the future conduct of the company's affairs;

(ii) an order that the company does or does not do some specified thing or things;

(iii) an order authorising one or more persons to bring proceedings in the name of and on behalf of the company; and

(iv) an order for the purchase, by other shareholders or by the company itself, of the shares of any member of the company.

Buy back

26–012 In the case of the sort of company under discussion, however, it is hard to see how this latter provision, an order that the member's share be purchased, could work satisfactorily if the only person who is permitted to own the share in question is the proprietor of the long leasehold interest which he owns. It is also possible that the articles may stipulate that only one share may be held by any one individual.

Authorisation

26–013 An order authorising one or more persons (e.g. A and/or B in the example above) to bring proceedings on behalf of the company may well be suitable if the question is only the collection of service charge which is due and unpaid, although it might be said that in such a case the company should be funded by A and/or B so that it can itself bring the proceedings. Of course, if the company was deadlocked that might be a good reason for authorising individuals to act for it.

It almost goes without saying that the sort of procedures contemplated here will result in extreme bad feeling and great hostility amongst the owners of the flats in the house. They may still see each other on a daily basis and legal advisers should not lose sight of the stress and tension which this sort of litigation can engender.

Winding up

26–014 The court can also wind up the company on the just and equitable ground provided for by s.122(1)(g) of the Insolvency Act 1986 if an application is made under that section. Again, the application is by petition (s.124(1)). The application is unlikely to succeed, however, if there is another remedy available (i.e. other than winding up the company) since if there is another remedy and the petitioner is acting unreasonably in seeking a winding up then the court will not make the order (s.125(2) of that Act). The possible undesirable consequences of a winding up are mentioned later.

Receiver/Manager

26–015 By s.37 of the Supreme Court Act 1981, the High Court may appoint a receiver whenever it appears to the court to be just and convenient to do so. There may be a conflict here with Pt II of the Landlord and Tenant Act 1987 (appointment of a Manager). For a discussion of this aspect, reference should be made to Chapter 27.

Summary

26–016 The difficulties which may arise in the sort of example mentioned above are an inability to agree amongst the directors/shareholders or a complete breakdown in relationships, and/or a deadlocked company. The remedy may frequently lie with an application to the court, usually to invoke the assistance of the court to allow the company to carry on its proper functions rather than to wind it up.

Second example—blocks of flats

26–017 A second example may illustrate further difficulties. The freehold of a development of 18 flats on a site comprising three small blocks each of six flats, is owned by a company. The company is limited to 18 shares, and each share must be owned by the long leaseholder of a flat. Works need to be done to the exterior and communal parts of the blocks. Seventeen of the 18 long leaseholders vote in favour of the works which are then carried out. A service charge is levied under the relevant service charge provisions.

The dissenting long leaseholder and one other decline to pay on the ground, *inter alia*, that a substantial proportion of the costs are referable to improvements rather than repair or maintenance. The terms of the relevant leases provide that service charges may be levied for the costs of repair or maintenance but not for improvements. The view of the remaining long leaseholders is that the works are not improvements. Proceedings are commenced.

In due course the dissenters' view is upheld, but only after the company has expended further substantial sums on its own litigation costs such as legal fees, experts, etc. Moreover it has, almost inevitably, been ordered to pay the costs of the victorious dissenters.

The company's problem

26–018 This leaves the company theoretically out of pocket not only as to the cost of the works which amount to improvements, but also as to the costs incurred in the resolution of the dispute. Realistically, of course, some or all of the individuals who wanted the works done and who voted for them will already have paid for them by funding the company, since the builder will have required payment as the works were being carried out. The point here is that the company is unable to recover any share of the cost of the disputed works, or of the costs of the dispute, from the dissenting long leaseholders. This is because so far as concerns the cost of the works, not only are they not recoverable as service charge but there is no other mechanism available which can oblige an unwilling tenant to pay (see below as to a general meeting).

So far as concerns the costs of the dispute, it is not likely that such costs will be recoverable by the company from the tenants who were the winners, since:

(i) they may not be contractually recoverable as service charges in any event;

(ii) even if they are contractually recoverable, they might very well not be recoverable as being unreasonable (Landlord and Tenant Act 1985, s.19); and

(iii) even if not unreasonable, the winning tenants can apply under s.20C of the Landlord and Tenant Act 1985 for an order that such costs are not to be taken into account in calculating the service charge.

Otherwise, of course, the winning tenants would end up funding the costs of the losing party and, in effect, paying for their own costs despite the court order which entitles them to recover their costs from the company itself.

Consequence

26–019 The result of this is that the dissenters will have all the benefits of the works of improvement without having to pay for them.

Restitution and unjust enrichment

26–020 In the example given above it will have been noted that one of the two successful long leaseholders in the service charge dispute had earlier voted in favour of carrying out the works. If the meeting had been a properly convened general meeting of the company, i.e. a shareholders' meeting and not simply a meeting of the long leaseholders, the consequences might be rather different. As a result of his vote (amongst others, of course) the company had entered into the commitment to have the works done and had in fact paid for them. Assuming for the moment that he had not voiced any reluctance to pay his proportionate share until after he had been presented with the service charge bill (rendered after the works had been completed), and assuming also that he knew that the cost of the works would be funded by contributions from the tenants, it might reasonably be said that he had impliedly promised to pay his share. The company for its part had relied, to its detriment, on his implicit promise to pay his proper share of the costs. He might also be said to be estopped from reneging on his implied promise. Of course, promissory estoppel as a shield not a sword is said to operate, so this will not necessarily found a cause of action.

If the company had been funded for the costs of the works by the remaining tenants it is arguable that the loss is suffered not by the company, but rather by those remaining tenants, since they will have had to pay a greater proportion of the overall costs than they might reasonably have expected. Nevertheless the implied promise might found an action in contract by the company, particularly if it was known to the promisor that the company could not pay from its own existing funds but would have to raise the money proportionately from the long leaseholders. Depending on the circumstances, it might also be argued that there was a similar implied promise to the other shareholders, thus giving them a cause of action.

The more satisfactory argument in terms of legal analysis may be that the tenant who voted for the works has taken the benefit of them and will continue to enjoy the benefit of them permanently, without payment. He is enriched by virtue of that benefit, and it is unjust that he should enjoy it without payment because he was instrumental in causing the costs of providing it to be incurred. He should, as a matter of conscience or equity, pay his proper share of the costs. This may be arguable even if the meeting at which the vote was taken was not formally a meeting of the company. Since the matter is one of equity, the court is not likely to be dissuaded simply by reliance on a technical point from providing a remedy where one exists, if it has formed the view that the remedy is a proper one.

The case of *Villatte v 38 Cleveland Square Management Limited* [2002] EWCA Civ. 1549 may conveniently be noted here. There had been no annual general meetings of the company (which owned the freehold and which was itself owned by the long leaseholders) for over seven years. As a result all the directors had ceased to be in office. Notwithstanding this, various purported appointments and resignations had taken place in the meantime. In the proceedings a number of points were taken about company procedure and the jurisdiction of the company to engage in the proceedings, all of which were ultimately rejected. Parker L.J. suggested, *obiter*, at para.67 of his judgment, that the nature of the real dispute could properly be reflected by the majority of the tenants (who had voted for the works) bringing an application as individuals against the dissenting tenant (who refused to pay) under s.19(2A) of the Landlord and Tenant Act 1985 in the Lands Valuation Tribunal as to the reasonableness of the service charge proposed, saying:

> "to allow the proceedings to founder on a technical ground related to the workings of the management company would, in the circumstances, be to countenance a triumph of form over substance."

He suggested that the company could be an additional and nominal respondent to the application. It will be recalled that s.19(2A) of the Act applied to "any tenant", and accordingly the proceedings suggested would not be by or on behalf of the company, and so the rule in *Foss v Harbottle* (see above) would not be offended.

General meeting

26–021 The holding of a general meeting of the company after the event would be unlikely to assist since it is doubtful whether any conventionally drafted articles of association would give the company the power to require some of its members to pay additional sums sought by the company, over and above the costs of the shares already paid up. See below, however, for shares with a deferred call.

Winding up

26–022 In general terms, one option is (as mentioned above) the winding up of the company, whether by the court (a compulsory winding up) or by the members of the company themselves where disputed matters cannot be resolved (a voluntary winding up). Winding up is a remedy of last resort. In the type of case under consideration here, however, such a solution is likely to be profoundly unsatisfactory.

On the liquidation of a company it is the task of the liquidator to administer the company's assets for the benefit of the company's creditors and then its contributories, i.e. the shareholders. Since *ex hypothesi* the only asset is the freehold reversion (which may well be of quite limited value), it is entirely possible that a sale, even if desirable, will not be sufficient to pay for the cost of the works. In any event a sale is very unlikely to be considered desirable since the whole point of the company is that the ownership and control of the freehold reversion is vested in the tenants of the flats.

On the other hand a sale will at least provide a solution as between the warring long leaseholders, who will no longer be members of a company with conflicting interests as between themselves. They will, of course, still have their differences but it will be for the new owner of the freehold reversion to make the relevant decisions. The new owner could, of course, be a RTM company in suitable circumstances. Reference should be made to Chapters 29–33 of this work for a discussion of RTM companies.

Summary

26–023 The problems which may arise and which are identified in the second example are that the company might find itself out of pocket, either as to legal costs or as to an inability to recover the cost of works for which the shareholders have voted—or both. A general meeting is unlikely to help. Winding up is not likely to be considered to be satisfactory by the shareholders (unless, perhaps, a RTM company has been formed). One possibility, at least as to the cost of the works, might in appropriate circumstances be an action based on the principles of unjust enrichment.

Possible solutions

26–024 Ideally one would wish to prevent the sort of situations described above from happening at all.

Sinking fund

26–025 The provision of a substantial sinking fund under the terms of the lease might make disputes about the cost of works to the property less bitter, since the funds would already be available to pay for them. Even if not in the leases, the long leaseholders could agree an ad hoc arrangement to contribute annually to a sinking fund, but that might not bind successors in title, so a more formal arrangement set out in the long leases is clearly desirable. Consideration should be given, however, to possible taxation issues here, and reference should be made to Chapter 25 of this work.

Shares—deferred call on shares

26–026 The company's articles of association might be drafted or, if not so drafted, might be altered to provide for the company to raise money from its members for specified purposes and calculated in a specified manner. This could be achieved by providing for a substantial share price, perhaps a very substantial price, with a deferred call for part or even all of the price. There is no reason in principle why a company should not have long term uncalled capital, although this would imply a par value very much greater than the usual £1. The articles of association will usually deal with the directors' powers to make calls and the means by which such calls are to be made (e.g. Table A 1985 arts 12–18). If the call is not paid the share can be forfeited by the company, with the effect that the defaulting shareholder ceases to be a member of the company (assuming that the shareholder is in default in respect of all the shares he owns). He would, of course, remain the proprietor of the long leasehold interest in the property.

Shares—issue of further shares

26–027 The company might, like any other company, raise money by the issue of further shares at an appropriate price, subject always to the provisions in the articles of association concerning the issuing of shares. By art.32 of Table A 1985, a company may increase its share capital by ordinary resolution, but of course many companies such as those under discussion here will have a strict limitation both on share capital and on who may own the shares, so the existing articles would require alteration by the relevant majority, depending on what, if anything, the articles said about alterations. By s.9 of the Companies Act 1985, a company can alter its articles by special resolution. Naturally the power to alter the articles must be exercised bona fide for the benefit of the company as a whole (e.g. *Allen v Gold Reefs of West Africa Ltd* [1900] 1 Ch. 656).

The issue of new shares would ordinarily provide an opportunity for existing shareholders to buy into the new issue if they wanted to do so. It is to be observed that by s.16 of the Companies Act 1985 the consent of *each individual member* is needed if he is to be *required* to subscribe for further shares, or to increase his liability to contribute to the company's share capital or pay money to the company.

It should also be noted that the document containing provisions about shares, or e.g. classes of shares, might instead be the memorandum of association. This too can be altered by special resolution so far as concerns the objects of the company (s.4 of the Act), and any provision in the memorandum which could lawfully have been in the articles can again be altered by special resolution, in this case pursuant to s.17 of the Act.

In order for a special resolution to be passed, three-quarters of the persons voting (personally or by proxy) must be in favour (s.378(2) of the Act).

Effect of increase in share capital

26–028 The possible effects of an increase in share capital are interesting to contemplate. For example, if the company was deadlocked and the court made orders which had the effect of authorising the issue of new shares, e.g. of equal status with the existing shares, then if the existing but dissenting shareholders did not take up their allocation, their existing shareholding would be diluted, perhaps significantly. It would be easier for other shareholders to outvote them in future. Conversely, if the dissenting shareholders did take up their allocation in order to avoid a dilution of their voting rights, then they would thereby have made the very contribution to the cost of the works which they sought to avoid. The proposed increase in share capital would, as above, have to be proposed and implemented bona fide for the benefit of the company (*Allen v Gold Reefs of West Africa Ltd, op. cit.*) otherwise it might trigger a s.459 petition by the dissenting shareholders who would say that the purpose of the proposed increase in capital was indeed to dilute their shareholding.

Winding up—sale of asset

26–029 As mentioned above, it is possible, e.g. in cases of deadlock, although on the face of it undesirable, that a winding up order might be made or that the shareholders decide voluntarily to wind up the company. This might be done with a view to the purchase of the only asset, namely the freehold reversion, by one or more of the shareholders. While permissible by a shareholder simpliciter, there might be difficulties if the purchaser was also a director. By s.310 of the Companies Act 1985 implicitly and by s.317 of the Act explicitly, a director must disclose his interest in any proposed dealing (but see here Table A 1985 art.86). By s.320 of the Act, shareholder approval in general meeting is required for a transaction between a director (or a connected person) and the company if it is a substantial property transaction, as defined. Absent such approval, the transaction is in general terms unlawful and is liable to be set aside.

By way of limited exception to the rule, under s.321(3) of the Act, a person who is a director and a member of a company can acquire an asset from the company if he does so only in his capacity as a member. It is not always easy in connection with a small private company to discern the difference between the actions of a person as director and the actions of the same person as a member of the company.

Directors' duties

26–030 Hitherto this chapter has looked at matters largely as possible disputes between individuals or groups of individuals because that is in practical terms how these issues arise. However it cannot be overlooked that a company has its own independent existence. The directors owe their duties, as directors, *to the company*, and they must exercise those duties in good faith for the benefit of the company. There are also statutory obligations placed on directors in connection with the running of the company. Although this is not the place for an exposition on the obligations of company directors generally, the following points should be noted.

Directors' duties at common law

26–031 The general duties of directors are usefully set out in the Law Commission report entitled *Company Directors: Regulating Conflicts of Interests and Formulating a Statement of Duties* (Report No.261 (1999)) and quoted by Arden J. in *Re Benfield Greig Group plc* [2001] B.C.C. 92 at 105. Importantly, those duties include duties of loyalty and good faith based on the fiduciary relationship between the directors and the company, and duties of skill and care and diligence rather like the duties of professional persons as known to the law of negligence.

Statutory obligations

26–032 So far as statutory obligations are concerned, there are a wide range of administrative responsibilities for directors (and also company secretaries). Examples are the obligations to file notices of appointments and resignations at Companies House, to hold an annual meeting, to submit returns (including a list of shareholders) and to produce and file accounts. This latter obligation is less onerous for small companies, which all the companies contemplated by this chapter are likely to be, since by s.246 of and Sch.8 to the Companies Act 1985 there is special provision for less detailed reports and accounts to be filed.

Elective resolutions

26–033 The directors of private companies (i.e. all companies which are not public limited companies—s.1(3) Companies Act 1985) can make life considerably easier for themselves by the passing of elective resolutions under the provisions of s.379A of the Act. If passed and delivered to the Registrar of Companies according to the statutory requirements, such resolutions can, *inter alia*:

(i) permit the company to dispense with holding an annual general meeting;

(ii) permit it to dispense with the requirement to lay reports and accounts before a general meeting; and

(iii) permit it to dispense with the annual appointment of auditors.

Written resolutions

26–034 By ss.381A–C of the Companies Act 1985 (and Sch.15A), provision is made for written resolutions to be effective, thereby dispensing with the need for a meeting of the company at all. It is to be observed, however, that the resolution (which need not be on a single document) must be approved and signed by all the members entitled to vote at a meeting in order to be effective. Article 53 of Table A 1985 also authorises the use of written resolutions.

Generally

26–035 In general terms, the directors must be aware that the company is not their private fiefdom to do with what they will, but rather they should be alert to the fact that they have important statutory and common law duties and responsibilities which must be complied with. Breaches can lead to both civil and criminal liability. Taking office as a director is far from being a mere formality.

[illegible] and resignations at Companies House (Forms [illegible]) annual [illegible] resultant return (including [illegible]) and the balance and the accounts. In latter [illegible] small companies which [illegible] the companies [illegible] Chapter are likely to be [illegible] ss.249A and [illegible] their respect [illegible] only [illegible] [illegible]

Elective resolutions

The directors of private companies [illegible] which are not public limited companies [illegible] Companies Act 1985 [illegible] considerably easier for [illegible] by [illegible] provisions [illegible] of the Act [illegible] Registrar of Companies [illegible] supplement [illegible] [illegible]

(i) [illegible] to [illegible] positions [illegible] annual [illegible]

(ii) [illegible] to [illegible] [illegible]

(iii) [illegible]

Written resolutions

By s.381A [illegible] of the Companies Act 1985 and Sch. [illegible] provisions [illegible] made for [illegible] required to be [illegible] the [illegible] meeting [illegible] that the resolution [illegible] must be [illegible] signed by all the members [illegible] [illegible] Table A 1985 [illegible] necessary [illegible] written resolutions [illegible] [illegible]

Generally

In [illegible] the directors [illegible] that the company [illegible] a private [illegible] should be [illegible] important [illegible] duties, and responsibilities which [illegible] breaches [illegible] and criminal liability [illegible] not of [illegible] being [illegible]

Chapter 27

The Appointment of a Manager

Introduction

27–001 This chapter deals with the appointment of a Manager under Pt II of the Landlord and Tenant Act 1987 (as amended). This is a fault-based right exercisable "for cause" where statutory fault-based grounds are made out and it is "just and convenient" to appoint a Manager. Chapter 28 considers acquisition orders under Pt III of the 1987 Act, one ground for the making of such an order being the previous appointment of a Manager.

Interrelationship with the right to manage

27–002 It is a common misconception that the right to manage (RTM) under the CLRA 2002 supersedes or even repeals the existing right to seek the appointment of a Manager. This is incorrect. The two regimes are intended to co-exist. Indeed, it is conceivable that a RTM company will mismanage a property, and discontented tenants may seek the appointment of a Manager against the RTM company.

RTM is dealt with in Chapters 29–33.

Interrelationship with the jurisdiction to appoint a receiver

27–003 The High Court and county court have a general jurisdiction (see CPR 69) to appoint a receiver. There were instances before the LTA 1987 came into force of this jurisdiction being exercised in service charge or similar disputes, for example *Hart v Emelkirk Ltd* [1983] 1 W.L.R. 1289.

However, in *Styli v Hamberton Properties Inc* [2002] E.G.C.S., it was held that the statutory jurisdiction to appoint a Manager under

Pt II of the LTA 1987 ousts the general jurisdiction to appoint a receiver. See also s.21(6) of the LTA 1987 which prohibits application by a tenant to the court for the appointment of a receiver or Manager in any circumstances in which an application could be made by him for an order under s.24 of the LTA 1987 appointing a Manager.

More seriously, it was also held that the High Court had no power to appoint a receiver on an *interim* basis pending a hearing before the LVT. Although the LVT has power to make an interim Manager appointment, the LVT's procedures are not well suited to urgent applications for interim relief. This may potentially present a serious difficulty, for instance if the property is uninsured.

Manager's status

27–004 The status of the Manager was clarified in *Maunder Taylor v Blacquiere* [2003] 1 W.L.R. 379 (CA). It was held that a Manager carries out his functions in his own right as a LVT appointed official and does so in a capacity independent of the landlord. His powers and authority derive from the order which appoints him, underpinned by the LTA 1987, and not from the leases. Indeed, he may be given powers or duties which are not present in the leases. This represents a significant difference from RTM, as the RTM company's powers of management are derived from the leases. The order appointing a Manager may empower the Manager to collect service charge, or recover fees, for which defective leases make no provision.

Who may apply

27–005 Section 21(1) of the LTA 1987 provides that the application may be made by the tenant of a flat contained in any premises to which Pt II of the Act applies. There is no requirement that the tenancy be a long lease. "Tenancy" includes statutory tenancies (s.60(1)). However, business tenancies protected by Pt II of the LTA 1954 are excluded by s.21(7), which has the effect of excluding mixed-use properties such as artisans' studios or live/work units, so long as business use is taking place. It is relatively easy to circumvent this exception by ceasing business use or by sub-letting parts used for business.

Where a flat is held on a joint tenancy, any one of the joint tenants may apply alone—s.21(5).

A qualifying tenant may make an application for the appointment of a Manager to act in relation to those premises, i.e. the premises in which the flat is contained.

Although in principle an application by a lone tenant may succeed, s.21(4)(a) expressly provides for applications to be made jointly by a number of tenants. An application made jointly by a significant proportion of the tenants in the premises is more likely to find favour with the LVT.

Premises to which Pt II of the Act applies

27–006 Part II of the Act applies to the whole or part of a building which contains two or more flats—s.21(2). Note that this is a physical requirement only, there is no need for the flats to be let.

Where a building contains flats and other premises, there is no requirement to limit the application to the part containing the flats, although the LVT would still need to be satisfied that it was just and convenient to appoint the Manager over the whole building.

Certain premises are excluded by s.21(3):

- premises included in the functional land of a charity (defined in s.60(1));
- premises where the landlord is exempt, as defined in s.58(1) of the Act;
- premises where there is a resident landlord, as defined in s.58(2) of the Act.

Flat

27–007 "Flat" is defined in s.60(1) as meaning a separate set of premises (whether or not on the same floor, so including most maisonettes) which forms part of a building, which is constructed or adapted for use for the purposes of a dwelling and which is divided horizontally from some other part of that building. (Note this last requirement is not worded in quite the same way as the equivalent part of the definition of flat in s.112 of the CLRA 2002 in relation to RTM, but the difference does not appear material).

This definition is fairly comprehensive and will include almost all premises which one might expect to refer to as a flat. What may be excluded include:

- demised parts which are physically divorced from the flat, such as a store-room on a different floor (*Cadogan v McGirk* [1996] 4 All E.R. 643);

- parts of a flat, which could arise if, say, what was originally two flats has been knocked into one, but only one of those flats was on a qualifying lease;
- conceivably, in some circumstances, a maisonette, for example where there is a large house with a back addition, converted into a number of "flats", but where the back addition is entirely filled with a single maisonette.

Exempt landlords

27–008 Section 58(1) contains a list of exempt landlords, including:

- most local authorities, the LFEPA, and police authorities (s.58(1)(a)) and waste disposal authorities (s.58(1)(h));
- the Commission for New Towns or a development corporation established under the New Towns Act 1981, or an urban development corporation (s.58(1)(b) and (c));
- a housing action trust (s.58(1)(ca)), the Housing Corporation (s.58(1)(e)) or a charitable housing trust (s.58(1)(f));
- a registered social landlord, or a fully mutual housing corporation which is not a registered social landlord (s.58(1)(g)).

Resident landlords

27–009 There is a resident landlord exception in s.58(2) and (3):

- The exemption is limited in scope, applying only where the premises were not purpose built as flats (s.58(2)(a)). The intention is to limit the exception to converted houses and similar properties.
- Section 21(3A) of the LTA 1987 provides that the resident landlord exception does not apply where at least half the flats in the premises are held on long leases which are not business tenancies subject to Pt II of the LTA 1954. "Long lease" is defined in s.59(3) and means a lease for a term in excess of 21 years, a perpetually renewable lease, or a right-to-buy/right-to-acquire lease.
- The resident landlord or family member must have been resident for a continuous period of the last 12 months (s.58(2)(c)).

Application to the Crown

27–010 Section 172(1)(b) of CLRA 2002 provides that Pt 2 of the LTA 1987 applies to Crown Land as it applies in relation to other land.

Applications relating to more than one premises

27–011 Section 21(4)(b) expressly provides that an application to appoint a Manager may be made in respect of two or more premises to which Pt II of the Act applies. Such an application would of course need to be made jointly by at least one tenant in each of the premises.

The purpose of permitting applications covering more than one set of premises appears to be to provide for situations where various separate premises are set in a single estate, such as a multi-building development set in common grounds and where the lessees of more than one building may contribute to a common service charge fund for the management of the grounds, service roads and so on. On its face s.21(4)(b) is not restricted to such circumstances and on the face of it entirely unconnected premises could be the subject of a joint application. However, the LVT would be unlikely to consider it just and convenient to make a single order covering unconnected premises.

Circumstances in which a Manager may be appointed by the LVT

27–012 The jurisdiction under Part II of the LTA 1987 to appoint a Manager was transferred from the court to the LVT by the Housing Act 1996. An order may only be made by the LVT appointing a Manager where one or more of the circumstances set out in s.24(2) of the LTA 1987 are established. Those circumstances are, in summary:

- Breach by any "relevant person" of obligation relating to management (s.24(2)(a)); or
- Unreasonable service charges (s.24(2)(ab)); or
- Unreasonable variable administration charges (s.24(2)(aba)); or
- Failure by any "relevant person" to comply with a Code of Management Practice (s.24(2)(ac));

  AND

- in all cases, that it is further "just and convenient" to appoint a Manager (s.24(2)(a)(iii), (ab)(ii) and (ac)(ii)).

There is also a "sweeping up" provision in s.24(2)(b) permitting the LVT to appoint a Manager in "other circumstances" where it is just and convenient to do so.

"Relevant person"

27–013 Part II of the LTA 1987 was extended to any "relevant person" by CLRA 2002. The extension to any "relevant person" permits the LVT to appoint a Manager in respect of the management obligations owed by persons or entities which are not technically "the landlord", most obviously, management companies which are parties to the leases and owe obligations separate from those of the landlord, and RTM companies (see s.22(1)(ii)).

Breach of obligation relating to management—s.24(2)(a)

27–014 This applies only to obligations owed to the tenant. However, it extends also to cases where, technically, there is no breach because the obligation is dependent on notice and it has not been reasonably practicable for the tenant to give him the appropriate notice. An example might be a repairing covenant under which the landlord's obligation arises only on notice but the landlord has disappeared.

The majority of obligations owed to tenants by landlords under their leases will fall within the wide ambit of an obligation "relating to the management of the premises". Obligations in respect of repairs, cleaning, and insurance are obvious examples, as are the various statutory obligations such as to consult in respect of major works, provide service charge accounts and to keep service charge funds in trust accounts. Those last obligations, although relating to service charge, are not themselves the raising of unreasonable service charges and so fall within s.24(2)(a) rather than (2)(ab).

In *Petrou v Metropolitan Properties Company Ltd* (10/5/00, LVT, unreported), the LVT held that to satisfy s.24(2)(a) it had to be established that a breach was in existence as at the date of the application to the LVT, not at the date of the hearing where the order was sought.

Unreasonable service charges—s.24(2)(ab)

27–015 This largely mirrors the statutory limitation on service charge costs under ss.18 and 19 of the LTA 1985. "Service charge" bears the same meaning as under s.18 of that Act. However, the two sets of provisions are not precisely the same because s.19 of the LTA 1985 limits service charge costs, not the service charge itself, whereas s.24 refers to "unreasonable service charges". Section 24 therefore appears to be wider in scope.

"Reasonableness" is further defined in s.24(2ZA) as including unreasonable amounts claimed having regard to the items for which it is payable, amounts claimed for items of an insufficient standard and also for items of an unnecessarily high standard. That last provision is intended to give tenants relief against landlords who decide to increase the overall standard of blocks (and thus increase the value of the reversion, or drive the tenants to ruin so that they may forfeit the leases).

Unreasonable variable administration charges—s.24(2)(aba)

27–016 "Variable administration charge" is defined by s.24(2B) as bearing the same meaning as under para.1 of Sch.11 to CLRA 2002 (see paragraphs 12–004 and 12–007). There is no amplification of what is to be considered "unreasonable".

Breach of RICS Code—s.24(2)(ac)

27–017 The importance of the fourth ground, breach of a code of management practice, can not be understated. The RICS Service Charge—Residential Management Code is approved under s.87 of the LRHUDA 1993. The Code is very extensive and prescriptive and it is almost inevitable that a landlord can be established to be in breach of one or more of its provisions.

There are also at present two other approved codes which may be of relevance in some cases: the RICS Rent Only Management Code and the Code of Practice for the Management of Leasehold Sheltered Housing (promulgated by the Association of Retirement Housing Managers).

Materiality of breach

27–018 There is no requirement that a breach of obligation under s.24(2)(a)(i), unreasonable service charge or administration charge under s.24(2)(ab) or (aba), or breach of the Code under s.24(2)(ac) needs to be material. The structure of s.24(2) is such that the need to establish a breach is in effect a threshold criterion, which once crossed brings the question on whether it is "just and convenient" to make the order—see, for example, the LVT's decision in *Petrou v Metropolitan Properties Company Ltd* (10/5/00, LVT, unreported), where only one allegation was actually proven before the LVT but on the basis of which the LVT went on to consider what was just and convenient.

Exercise of the right—preliminary notice

27–019 Before an application to the LVT for an order appointing a Manager can be made, a preliminary notice under s.22 must be served on the landlord and any person other than the landlord by whom obligations relating to the management of the premises or any part of them are owed (s.22(1)), unless the LVT makes an order under s.22(3) dispensing with service of the notice. The dispensation power is strictly limited, see paragraph 27–025 below.

Form and content of a preliminary notice

27–020 There is no prescribed form of s.22 notice. The required content of a notice is set out in s.22(2) of the LTA 1987, which provides that a notice under s.22 must:

- specify the tenant's name, the address of his flat and his address for service;
- state that the tenant intends to make an application to the LVT to appoint a Manager of the premises;
- state (if applicable) that he will not do so if the requirement for remedy specified in the notice is complied with;
- specify the grounds on which the tribunal would be asked to make such an order and the matters that would be relied on by the tenant for the purpose of establishing those grounds;
- where those matters are capable of being remedied by any person on whom the notice is served, require him, within such reasonable period as is specified in the notice, to take such steps for the purpose of remedying them as are so specified.

There is power to add to this list by regulation, but no such regulations have been made.

Errors and omissions on the preliminary notice

27–021 There is no specific "saving" provision in respect of inaccuracies, errors or omissions in the notice. The usual tests for the validity of statutory notices will apply. In *M25 Group v Tudor* [2004] 1 WLR 2319 (a case on the equivalent preliminary notice under Part III of the LTA 1987, see Chapter 28) it was held that the requirement to specify addresses was "directory" rather than "mandatory", so that failure to comply did not invalidate the notice. This approach to statutory notice requirements has been applied more generally in *7 Strathray Gardens v Pointstar Shipping & Finance* [2005] 07 EG 144, in which the *M25 Group* case was analysed.

Nor is there any power to amend or add to the notice. What there is, is a power in the LVT under s.24(7)(b) to make an order appointing a Manager notwithstanding that the s.22 preliminary notice failed to comply with any of the requirements of s.22.

Power to make order despite defects in the preliminary notice

27–022 On the face of it, s.24(7)(b) is an untrammelled power and would permit the lessees to raise matters not set out in the notice. However, the purpose of the notice is to give the landlord an opportunity to remedy the breaches of which complaint is made. Consequently, it would seem that in arguing the application before the LVT, the tenants would be limited more or less to the grounds set out in the s.22 notice. It would no doubt be just in many cases to allow variations or amplifications of grounds specified, but surely not just to permit something wholly new to be argued.

Section 24(7)(b) also is only capable of operation where some sort of s.22 notice was served on the landlord. Even if something was sent to the landlord, wholesale failure to comply with s.22(2), such that a reasonable recipient would not appreciate that a notice was indeed a s.22 notice, would lead to the conclusion that no s.22 notice had been served at all and that s.24(7)(b) would be of no application. Section 24(3) provides for dispensation with the service of any preliminary notice in limited circumstances: see paragraph 27–025 below.

Reasonable period for remedy

27–023 The requirement that a reasonable period be specified for the landlord to remedy the matters of which complaint is made is very similar to the requirement set out in s.146 of the Law of Property Act 1925 for notices preliminary to forfeiture of a long lease.

It will be impossible for a landlord to remedy a past breach, so by analogy with the case law under s.146, only say 14 days needs to be given (to allow time for the landlord to take legal advice).

Where the breach complained of is continuing, such as disrepair to the premises, then a realistic period must be given to take the remedial steps specified in the notice. This could in some cases be a period of many months, conceivably even years in respect of major repairs to a large block. However, what must be given is a reasonable period for taking the "steps" for the purpose of remedying the breaches as are specified in the notice. For a large project such as major repair there would be a number of steps to be taken, including commissioning a scheme, tendering and so on. Service of notices to consult under s.20/20ZA of the LTA 1985 may well be required at various stages. The s.22 notice may specify reasonable periods for taking each step in the process, failure to comply with which would permit application to the LVT.

If the periods specified are not reasonable, all is not lost. Section 24(7)(a) permits the LVT, if it thinks fit, to make an order notwithstanding that any period specified in the notice was not a reasonable period. The LVT tends to think fit in most cases where the landlord has still not taken appropriate steps by the date of the LVT hearing (by which time of course a considerable further period of time will have passed).

In practice, if the landlord takes the point that the s.22 notice is not valid, the LVT will order that this be decided at a preliminary hearing. The LVT also takes the view that it can exercise the discretion under s.24(7) at that preliminary hearing—see, for example, *Petrou v Metropolitan Properties Company Ltd* (10/5/00, LVT, unreported).

Service of the notice

27–024 Section 54(1) of the LTA 1987 provides that any notice under s.22 shall be in writing and "may be sent by post".

Dispensation with notice altogether

27–025 Section 24(3) permits an LVT to dispense with the need for a s.22 notice (only) "where it is satisfied that it would not be reasonably practicable to serve such a notice on the landlord". There is no general power to dispense on "just and equitable" grounds.

The dispensing power under s.24(3) would appear to cover two main situations: where the landlord is missing, and where the application is made urgently and an interim order is sought.

Where notices are dispensed with, the LVT has power to direct that such other notices are served, or steps taken, as it thinks fit. In a missing landlord situation, the LVT might order that steps are taken to trace the landlord, or advertisement of the s.24 application be made. Where no notice was served because of urgency, the LVT might order that a notice in s.22 form be served retrospectively.

The power to dispense with notice may be exercised either at the final hearing of the Manager application or otherwise. If a notice point is seriously being relied upon by the landlord, it will often be appropriate (given the potential waste of costs if the matter is determined against the tenants at the final hearing) to have this matter dealt with at a preliminary hearing.

Service on mortgagee

27–026 Section 22(4) requires a landlord in receipt of a s.22 notice to serve a copy on his mortgagee. The reason for this is that the appointment of a Manager may seriously impinge on the rights of a mortgagee.

Application to the LVT

27–027 No application may be made unless:

- a s.22 notice has been served and the reasonable period for remedy of a breach has expired, or the breach was not capable of remedy; or
- service of the s.22 notice has been dispensed with and any directions made by the LVT as to further steps or notices have been complied with.

The content of an application is prescribed by procedure regulations, currently the Leasehold Valuation Tribunal (Procedure) (England) Regulations 2003 and the Leasehold Valuation Tribunal (Procedure) (Wales) Regulations 2004, but there is no prescribed form.

LVT procedure is dealt with in Chapter 22.

Focus of the argument before the LVT

27–028 It follows from the structure of s.24(2) (discussed at paragraph 27–018 above) that the hearing before the LVT will focus on whether it is "just and convenient" to make an order. Although the circumstances which establish the jurisdiction to make an order appointing a Manager are by their nature historic, the Manager's appointment deals with the future only. Therefore, in considering whether it is just and convenient to make an order, the LVT will be most concerned with:

- the landlord's likely future management;
- the Manager himself and his plans for management.

It is also critical to appreciate that when considering whether it is just and convenient to make an order, the LVT will be considering the particular order for which the tenants contend. Circumstances might arise where in principle the LVT would be prepared to make an order but not the particular order sought, for example because the proposed Manager is unsatisfactory. Considerations as to the form of order are dealt with in paragraph 27–032 below.

Anticipated future conduct of the landlord

27–029 Even landlords who have been poor landlords for many years may change their ways, perhaps having dismissed the incumbent managing agents. Some consideration of the history may be relevant to consideration of the landlord's likely future conduct, but it is usually a mistake for tenants to become bogged down in attempting to establish each and every allegation as to past misconduct. Certain factors may be of continuing relevance:

- Persistent poor management which casts doubt on whether the landlord really has improved or may suggest that a relapse will occur once the proceedings are over;
- Conduct which was flagrant or deliberate, which again may colour the tribunal's view of the landlord's present intentions.

The landlord's response to being served with the s.22 notice is therefore of central importance.

The case law on "just and convenient" is discussed at paragraph 27–031 below.

Identity of the Manager

27–030 The LVT will be intensely interested in the identity, experience and so on of the proposed Manager. It is almost invariable practice for the LVT to direct that the Manager attend personally before the tribunal, and the tribunal will usually question the Manager as to his experience, suitability, familiarity with the RICS Residential Management

Code and understanding of the particular role and function of a Manager appointed under Pt II of the LTA 1987. In one LVT hearing (*The Keir, 24 Westside, Wimbledon Common*, (2002 LEASE No.720)), during questioning the proposed Manager changed his mind about accepting an appointment and left! The case was adjourned for an alternative Manager to be nominated.

There is a substantial body of LVT decisions dealing with this issue, some of the more instructive of which are as follows:

Petrou v Metropolitan Properties Company Ltd (10/5/00, LVT, unreported) raised many of the factors which the tribunal will take into account. Appointment of a Manager was refused on the grounds that:

- the proposed Manager lacked experience of London mansion blocks of the type and age of the premises in question;
- the proposed Manager lacked experience of repair works of the value of the works required (£2 million);
- the proposed Manager was based too far from the property;
- the majority of residents had expressed hostility towards the proposed Manager;
- the Manager's fees would be higher than the existing managing agents' fees.

Betts v 180 Devonport Road Management Company limited (2002 LEASE No.835). The tenants proposed an unqualified but experienced professional agent. The landlord counter-proposed a person formerly employed by the existing unsatisfactory managing agents. The tribunal rejected both candidates and adjourned for the parties to propose alternatives.

Where the proposed Manager is closely connected with the premises, this has rarely found favour with the tribunal:

- *Edwards v Brighton & Hove Securities* (2001 LEASE No.675). Decision: not appropriate to appoint the secretary of the residents' association because the leases expressly provided for professional management and the lessees purchased their leases on that basis.
- *58 Claremont Road, Seaford* (2001 LEASE No.671 and 2002 LEASE No.847). In the earlier 2001 decision, although unhappy, the LVT was persuaded to appoint an applicant tenant as Manager, but on conditions including obtaining professional indemnity insurance and appointing managing agents. In the later 2002 decision, the Manager was forced to obtain his own discharge as he could not comply with the conditions.

The LTA 1987 does not state that a Manager must be an individual, as opposed to a firm or company. However, it seems implicit in the status of a Manager as an officer of the tribunal (or in the case of older appointments, the court) that he or she must be an individual. LVT decisions where a firm or company has been appointed are probably wrong.

Case law on "just and convenient"

27–031 LVTs have repeatedly stated that the appointment of a Manager is a remedy of "last resort". Whether this restrictive approach is consistent with the statutory requirement that it be "just and convenient" is open to question.

In any event, examination of those decisions of the LVT which are available suggests that the LVT is prepared to find that the "last resort" has been reached rather more frequently than the principle might suggest.

The LVT has repeatedly found that it was not just and convenient to make an order appointing a Manager with whose identity it was not satisfied. The relevant case law is set out in paragraph 27–030 above.

Factors suggesting that appointment of a Manager may be just and convenient:

- Very serious breaches of covenant;
- Breaches of covenant over a lengthy period;
- Failure to respond meaningfully to the s.22 notice;
- There had been three professional Managers in as many years and the block was being managed de facto by the secretary to the residents' association (*The Keir, 24 Westside, Wimbledon Common* (2002 LEASE No.720));
- Failure to comply with the s.20 consultation requirements during the pendency of a Manager application, despite express warnings to do so (*The Keir, 24 Westside, Wimbledon Common* (2002 LEASE No.720)).

Factors suggesting that appointment of a Manager may not be just and convenient:

- Isolated breaches which could be dealt with appropriately and completely under other jurisdictions, such as disallowing service charge costs;
- Inadvertent breaches;

- Changes in ownership of landlords which are companies;
- The Manager's management proposals were open to criticism (*Petrou v Metropolitan Properties Company Ltd* (10/5/00, LVT, unreported));
- A group of lessees were in the process of collectively enfranchising at the same time as the Manager application was made (*Edwards v Brighton & Hove Securities* (2001, LEASE No.675));
- The freeholder had responded positively and agreed to appoint independent managing agents (*Petrou v Metropolitan Properties Company Ltd* (10/5/00, LVT, unreported) and *58 Claremont Road, Seaford* (2002 LEASE No.847));
- The freeholder appointed well known independent managing agents, for a five-year term, on a contract jointly with the landlord and the residents' association, and which included a clause providing that the residents' association's consent was required to termination (*Petrou v Metropolitan Properties Company Ltd* (10/5/00, LVT, unreported));
- The majority of lessees had considered the landlord's proposals and backed them (*Petrou v Metropolitan Properties Company Ltd* (10/5/00, LVT, unreported)).

Form and content of order

27–032 The extent of the order which may be made, and the matters which may be included in it, are laid down by s.24(1) and (3)–(6).

Section 24(1) empowers the LVT to make an order (whether interim or final) to appoint a Manager to carry out such functions in connection with the management of the premises, or such functions of a receiver, or both, as the tribunal thinks fit. Section 24(4) permits the order to provide for matters relating to the exercise of those functions, including incidental or ancillary matters, while s.24(6) permits the tribunal to impose conditions or to suspend the order.

"Management" is defined in s.24(11) as including the repair, maintenance, improvement or insurance of premises. This is plainly not an exhaustive definition.

Section 24(5) provides a list of specific matters for which the order may make provision:

- for rights and liabilities arising under contracts to which the Manager is not a party to become rights and liabilities of the Manager;

- for the Manager to be entitled to prosecute claims in respect of causes of action (whether contractual or tortious) accruing before or after the date of his appointment;
- for remuneration to be paid to the Manager by any relevant person, or by the tenants of the premises in respect of which the order is made or by all or any of those persons.

A suggested form of order is included in Appendix C. This form of order is appropriate where the terms of the leases are satisfactory. In the case of unsatisfactory terms, for example as to service charge, provisions should be added creating an appropriate service charge regime under which the Manager may operate.

Manager or receiver?

27–033 There is a significant difference between appointment to carry out management functions under s.24(1)(a) and the functions of a receiver under s.24(1)(b). A receiver stands in the landlord's shoes, whereas a Manager under the 1987 Act does not. The difference between the two halves of subs.(1) was one of the grounds on which the Court of Appeal in *Maunder Taylor v Balquiere* [2003] 1 W.L.R. 379 held that a Manager acted in his own capacity and not in the landlord's shoes. This distinction can be extremely important. In the *Maunder Taylor* decision itself, one of the tenants attempted to set off against service charges claimed by the Manager damages which he claimed he was entitled to from the landlord. The attempted set off failed because the Manager claimed in a capacity impendent of the landlord. However, it appears that a receiver would have been subject to set off.

In most cases the order should therefore make clear that the functions to be carried out by the Manager arise under s.24(1)(a). The basic function of a receiver is to gather assets of the party over whom he has been appointed receiver. A possible circumstance in which the Manager should *additionally* be appointed receiver to a limited extent would be where the landlord is holding service charge funds. The effect of a receivership order of those funds would be to restrain the landlord from dealing with those funds and require him to pass them to the Manager (compare s.94 of the CLRA 2002—uncommitted service charge funds are expressly to be made over to a RTM company under the RTM regime). Receivership operates as an injunction—*Sartoris v Sartoris* [1892] 1 Ch. 11 (CA)—so any failure by the landlord to make over the funds would amount to a contempt of court. As the LVT is not a court and has no contempt jurisdiction, presumably contempt proceedings could be brought in court, but this is by no means clear.

Manager as officer of the tribunal

27–034 It is made clear by *Maunder Taylor v Blacquiere* that the Manager is an officer of the tribunal which appointed him. This concept underpins certain other provisions, such as the capacity of the Manager to apply to the tribunal for directions, and the necessity to serve the appointing tribunal if a claim to RTM is made (see paragraph 30–031).

The concept of an "officer of the court" is well established, whereas the concept of an officer of a tribunal is, so far as the authors are aware, unprecedented. It is to be expected that the approach to the Manager's duties as officer will be analogous to that applied to officers of courts.

In particular, the Manager is not the agent of the tenants who appointed him—he must be autonomous and independent.

Order as the basis of functions and powers

27–035 Following *Maunder Taylor v Blaquiere*, it is also clear that it is the order itself (*not* the leases of the flats) which forms the entire basis of the Manager's functions and powers. If the Manager is supposed to repair, the order must say so. If he is to collect service charge, the order must say so.

To date, orders have often been made in a form which makes provision along the lines that the Manager is to manage the premises in accordance with the rights and obligations of the landlord under the leases in the premises. The difficulty with this form of order is that it imposes direct, personal liability on the Manager for breach of each and every landlord covenant. Further, leases generally include provisions which may not be appropriate to a Manager, such as giving consent to make structural alterations. This could affect the reversion, which remains vested in the landlord. In this context, it is to be noted that the RTM provisions give landlords the right to challenge before the LVT approvals given by RTM companies (ss.98 and 99 of CLRA 2002) and landlords may wish to argue that it would be inappropriate to give Managers an unrestricted right to give approvals under the lease.

Orders improving on or varying the lease terms

27–036 The form of order discussed at paragraph 27–035 above also misses an opportunity in effect to improve upon the terms of the leases. It was made clear in *Maunder Taylor v Blacquiere* that an order appointing a Manager may confer rights or obligations not present in the leases. In some cases, defects or omissions in the leases may be one factor contributing to the poor management of which the tenants have made complaint. The order appointing the Manager may remedy such defects. To take a mundane example: the lease may contain no provision for payment of an interim or on account service charge. The order may empower the Manager to levy an interim service charge (indeed, if it does not, the Manager would either have to fund works himself or borrow, but with no security, neither of which is satisfactory).

To take an example from the *Maunder Taylor* case, the lease provided estimates for repairs to be obtained through the landlord's surveyor. Such requirements are inappropriate for a Manager and the provision was not applied to the Manager.

The Manager's duties will ordinarily cover managing the premises, repair and insurance. The leases may provide a guide as to the sort of obligations to be dealt with but not necessarily the ambit of those obligations. In framing the Manager's duties, it is important to qualify or limit them to "best endeavours" and to make the duty to carry out functions subject to the Manager being able to obtain sufficient prior funding.

Existing contracts

27–037 The order may also provide for the rights and liabilities under contracts to become rights and liabilities of the Manager. Section 24(5)(a) in effect permits the LVT to impose the Manager as a contracting party into any existing contract. This is useful as it prevents the other party refusing to deal with the Manager or attempting to alter the terms on which it is prepared to continue providing services in respect of the building.

The sorts of contracts which the Act contemplates are contracts which the landlord has with third parties for the management of the premises. Whether it is appropriate to make such provision will depend on the contract in question. It seems unlikely to be appropriate for the Manager to take over a contract with managing agents—it is more or less implicit in the application for a Manager that the existing managing agents if any should cease to fulfil that role. On the other hand, the Manager may consider it appropriate to retain the existing garden maintenance contractor. In some circumstances, for example where prices have risen and a contractor would welcome the opportunity to be released from a contract, it may be beneficial for the order to provide for the Manager to become the party to the contract, in order to keep the contractor on the hook.

Levy of service charge

27–038 Specific provision should always be made for the levying of a service charge. If correctly framed, this should entitle the Manager to levy his own service charge to pay for the actions he proposes to take, regardless of the state of any tenant's existing service charge account. This may obviate the need for provision for the Manager to take over claims to service charge under the leases, which might be provided for under s.24(5)(b).

Remuneration of the Manager

27–039 Specific provision also needs to be made in all cases for the remuneration of the Manager, as contemplated by s.24(5)(c). This may be a bone of contention—the tenants may consider that the landlord ought to pay, whereas the Manager will simply be concerned that he is paid and may not be prepared to depend on a successful recovery against a (necessarily bad) landlord. The order might provide for the landlord to be ultimately responsible for the Manager's remuneration but for the tenants to pay in the first instance. The level of remuneration also needs to be fixed.

Period for which the order is effective

27–040 Section 24(5)(d) provides that an order appointing a Manager may be open ended or for a fixed term. Although an open-ended order may sound attractive, eventually the Manager will no longer be capable of fulfilling his functions. Given that the power to vary the order includes a power to extend, without reconsidering the s.24(2) criteria (see paragraph 27–045 below) it is suggested that in most cases the order should be made for such fixed period as appears just and convenient on the facts of the case.

Exercise of his functions by the Manager

27–041 The Manager should act in his own name, not that of the lessor. Service charge demands are issued in his name and cheques in payment of service charge are made payable to the Manager personally.

The Manager makes contracts, for example to carry out repairs, personally.

Any proceedings brought by the Manager in respect of the exercise of his functions, such as to enforce payment of service charge, are brought in the Manager's own name, as in *Maunder Taylor v Blacquiere*.

Directions from the LVT

27–042 Section 24(4) permits the Manager to make application to the LVT for directions to be given with respect to the exercise of his functions.

Registration of the order

27–043 A Manager order should be registered against the landlord's title (s.24(8)).

Variation or discharge of the order

27–044 Section 24(9) of the LTA 1987 provides that a LVT may vary or discharge an order appointing a Manager. Such application may be made "by any person interested", which includes the Manager himself, the tenants of the premises (including those who were not party to the application for an order), the landlord, and any mortgagees.

However, "any person interested" is a deliberately wide formulation and there may be others who are so interested. A possible example would be the personal representatives of a Manager who had died in office. However, a tenants' association is probably not sufficiently interested (*Petrou v Metropolitan Properties Company Ltd* (10/5/00, LVT, unreported)).

Only in the case of the landlord are there restrictions on the making of an order for discharge or variation. In the case of a landlord's (or other managing party's) application, s.24(9A) provides that such an order shall not be made unless the LVT is satisfied that variation or discharge will not lead to a recurrence of the circumstances which led to the making of the order and that it is just and convenient to vary or discharge the order.

The plain intent is to stop attempts by landlords to re-open the issues decided against it at the appointment hearing, and to prevent continuous re-litigation by the landlord which might hamper the Manager's carrying out of his functions.

In the case of an application by any person interested other than a landlord, presumably the LVT would consider whether it was just and convenient to make the order sought. Circumstances in which variation might be sought are many and varied, examples being where the terms of the original order have proven to be unsatisfactory in some respect, or where the Manager wishes to be released from his obligations perhaps because of illness. The LVT has decided that a Manager may not resign without a variation or discharge of the order which appointed him—*Re Flat 5, The Keir* (5/2/05, LVT, unreported).

Section 24(10) provides that the fact that premises cease to be premises to which Pt II of the LTA 1987 applies is not of itself a ground for discharge (although there is nothing to stop that circumstance being taken into account if some other reason for discharge is also present).

Extending the period of a Manager order

27–045 The power to vary the order plainly includes a power to extend an order beyond the fixed period for which it was made. The exercise of this power was considered by the Court of Appeal in *Orchard Court Residents Association v St Anthony's Homes Ltd* [2003] 2 E.G.L.R. 28, where it was held that on such application under s.24(9) it was not necessary for the LVT to consider again whether the threshold criteria for making an order in s.24(2) were met. The jurisdiction to extend an order exists whenever it is just and convenient to do so, taking into account all relevant circumstances at the date the variation is considered.

Appeals

27–046 An appeal lies from any "final" order of the LVT to the Lands Tribunal. The precise ambit of the right of appeal is not settled, but in the context of applications under Pt II of the LTA 1987, this will include any order appointing a Manager (whether "interim" or final) and any order varying or discharging a Manager order.

The appeal procedures are discussed at paragraph 22–026.

Chapter 28

Acquisition Orders

Introduction

The right to an acquisition order is conferred by Pt III of the Landlord and Tenant Act 1987. An acquisition order is a form of compulsory acquisition of the landlord's interest in cases of prolonged default in management obligations owed to the long lessees of flats. It has been described as a "last resort" but this is not a phrase found in the Act and may have discouraged its use. The authors would suggest that the position is that if the relevant grounds are made out, the order may be made in appropriate cases. **28–001**

The previous appointment of a Manager is one of the grounds for the making of an acquisition order, but it is not the only ground. In cases of persistent breaches of management obligations by the landlords with no prospect of remedy, the tenants are entitled to seek an acquisition order without first seeking the appointment of a Manager.

Premises which may be subject to an acquisition order

The basic qualifying provision is found in s.25(2), which provides that the right to an acquisition order applies to premises: **28–002**

- which are the whole or part of a building; and
- which contain two or more flats held by qualifying tenants; and
- in which the total number of flats held by such tenants is not less than two-thirds of the total number of flats contained in the premises.

It should be noted that this basic qualifying provision does not represent the limit of the property which may be acquired: s.29(4)(a) permits the acquisition order to include any yard, garden outhouse or appurtenance belonging to or usually enjoyed with the specified premises, and s.29(4)(b) permits the court to exclude parts of the specified premises from the order.

Exceptions

28–003 Premises with substantial non-residential parts are excepted from Pt III of the 1987 Act by s.25(4) despite otherwise meeting the basic qualifying criteria. These are premises to which Pt III of the Act does not apply.

Premises with certain types of landlord are premises in respect of which no application for an acquisition order may be made (although they are still premises to which Pt III of the Act applies):

- premises with exempt landlords (s.25(4)(a) and see s.58(1));
- premises with resident landlords (s.25(4)(a) and see s.58(2), (3));
- premises within the functional land of a charity (s.25(4)(b) and see s.60(1)).

The exempt landlord and resident landlord exemptions are the same as those in respect of the right to appoint a Manager under Pt II of the Act and are discussed in detail at paragraphs 27–008 to 27–009 above. The exception from Pt III for premises with substantial non-residential parts does not apply under Pt II of the Act, and is discussed below.

Buildings with substantial non-residential parts

28–004 Section 25(4) excludes a building with more than 50 per cent "non-residential" parts, measured by reference to internal floor area. This 50 per cent threshold is higher than the 25 per cent which applies to RTM and the right to collective enfranchisement under the Leasehold Reform Housing and Urban Development Act 1993. The 50 per cent threshold may be amended by delegated legislation (s.25(6)).

A part of premises is a non-residential part if it is neither occupied, nor intended to be occupied, for residential purposes. Any common part of the premises is disregarded.

See *Indiana Investments v Taylor* [2004] 3 EGLR 63 as to calculating floor areas.

Relevant date for considering the qualifying criteria

28–005 In general the premises must continue to meet the qualifying criteria right up to the time the court considers making an acquisition order (s.29(1)(a)). However, the relevant time for considering the exceptions for exempt landlords, resident landlords and charities is the date the application for the acquisition order is made and it does not matter if there is such a landlord by the date of the hearing (s.29(7)).

"Flat"

28–006 The definition of a "flat" (see s.60(1)) is the same as applies under Pt II of the Act, discussed in paragraph 27–007 above.

Applications relating to more than one premises

28–007 Section 28(3) expressly provides that an application for an acquisition order may be made in respect of two or more premises to which Pt III of the Act applies. Such an application would of course need to be made jointly by the requisite majority of qualifying tenants in each of the premises (see paragraph 28–017).

The purpose of permitting applications covering more than one set of premises appears to be to provide for situations where various separate premises are set in a single estate, such as a multi-building development set in common grounds. On its face s.28(3) is not restricted to such circumstances and on the face of it entirely unconnected premises could be the subject of a joint application. However, the court would be unlikely to consider it appropriate to make a single order covering unconnected premises.

In this regard, s.29(5) may also be relevant. This obliges the court to refuse to make an acquisition order where the application relates to premises which consist of part only of more extensive premises in which the landlord has an interest and that the interest can not reasonably be severed.

Who may apply

28–008 Section 25(1) of the LTA 1987 provides that the application may be made by the qualifying tenants of flats contained in any premises to which Pt III of the Act applies. In fact, as set out in paragraph 28–017 below, the right to seek an acquisition order can only be exercised by the requisite majority of such tenants.

Qualifying tenants are dealt with in s.26. Unlike the position in respect of the appointment of a Manager, "qualifying tenant" means a tenant under a long lease (defined in s.59(1)), unless that lease is in one of the excepted categories in s.26.

"Long lease"

28–009 "Long lease" is defined in s.59(1) and as one would expect means a lease granted for a term in excess of 21 years. For this purpose, the term can not be back dated, so the term must expire more than 21 years after the date of grant of the lease (*Roberts v Church Commissioners* [1972] 1 Q.B. 278).

In addition, leases with a clause for perpetual renewal, where the term is fixed by law (except by way of a sub-tenancy from a lease which is not a long lease), are deemed to be long leases, as are all right-to-buy leases.

Sub-leases

28–010 There can only be one qualifying tenant of a flat. A lessee is excluded by s.26(3) if his landlord is a qualifying tenant—i.e. it is the long lease highest up a chain of sub-tenancies which qualifies, the opposite of the position under RTM and the right to enfranchise under the Leasehold Reform Housing and Urban Development Act 1993.

Exceptions—business tenancy

28–011 Business tenancies to which Pt II of the Landlord and Tenant Act 1954 applies which would otherwise qualify are expressly excluded by s.26(1). This has the effect of excluding mixed-use properties such as artisans' studios or live/work units, so long as business use is taking place. However, this exclusion is poorly drafted, because tenancies are only 1954 Act business tenancies if business use is being carried on at the relevant time. Therefore the exclusion can be evaded fairly easily by ceasing business use or granting a (short) sub-tenancy of the commercial part of the unit. (See *Bishopsgate Foundation v Curtis* [2004] 3 EGLR 57.)

Exceptions—multiple tenancies

28–012 A qualifying tenant who is a long lessee of two or more other flats is also excluded by s.26(2). This exception operates in such a way that there is no qualifying lessee of any of the three or more flats concerned. As an anti-avoidance measure, where the tenant is a corporate body, it is treated by s.26(4) as being the tenant of any flat let to an associated company. This measure is easily evaded by vesting legal title in a nominee such as a company director personally.

No application to the Crown

28–013 Section 56(1) of the LTA 1987 provides that Part III of the Act applies to a tenancy of the Crown (only) if there has ceased to be a Crown interest in it. In other words (and unlike the right to appoint a Manager under Part II of the Act) the right to an acquisition order does not apply to Crown land.

Circumstances in which an acquisition order may be made

28–014 There is a common misconception that an acquisition order is only available as a second stage to a previous successful application to appoint a Manager under Pt II of the 1987 Act. This is not so. An acquisition order may only be made where one or either of the conditions laid down by s.29(2) and (3) of the LTA 1987 are established.

Those circumstances are, in summary:

- Breach by the landlord of an obligation relating to management (s.29(2)); or
- Where there has been a Manager appointment in force on the date of the application and throughout the period of two years prior to the application being made (s.29(3));

  AND
- in either case that it is "appropriate" to make an acquisition order in the circumstances of the case (s.29(1)(c)).

Under s.29(2), cases where there has been no previous appointment of a Manager, it used to be a further condition of making an order that the court be satisfied that the appointment of a Manager would not be an adequate remedy. This condition was repealed by the Leasehold Reform Housing and Urban Development Act 1993. It may be inferred from this that the intention of Parliament was to make acquisition orders easier to obtain. The case of *Gray v Standard Home & Counties Properties Ltd* [1994] 1 E.G.L.R. 119, the only reported case on s.29(2), was decided under the old law and should be treated with caution.

Breach of obligation relating to management

28–015 This applies only to obligations owed to the tenant. However, it extends also to cases where, technically, there is no breach because the obligation is dependent on notice, and it has not been reasonably practicable for the tenant to give him the appropriate notice. An example might be a repairing covenant under which the landlord's obligation arises only on notice, but the landlord has disappeared.

Unlike the equivalent ground for appointment of a Manager under Pt II of the Act, the obligation must be owed by the landlord. Obligations owed by others such as management companies do not suffice. This is presumably because the effect of an acquisition order is to deprive the landlord of his property interest. Note that the ground is directed to contractual liability: landlords remain responsible for breaches by their appointed managing agents.

The majority of obligations owed to tenants by landlords under their leases will fall within the wide ambit of an obligation "relating to the management of the premises". Obligations in respect of repairs, maintenance, improvement and insurance are specifically included by s.29(2A). This list is probably not intended to be exhaustive, so for example the various statutory obligations such as to consult in respect of major works, provide service charge accounts and to keep service charge funds in trust accounts may all be considered "management" obligations.

There is no requirement that a breach of management obligation needs to be material. The structure of s.29(1) is such that the need to establish a breach is in effect a threshold criterion, which once crossed raises the question as to whether it is "appropriate" to make the order in the circumstances of the case. However, unless the breach is substantial and continuing, it will probably be inappropriate to make an acquisition order.

Preliminary notice

28–016 Before an application (to the court) for an acquisition order appointing a Manager can be made, a preliminary notice under s.27 must be served on the landlord by the requisite majority of qualifying tenants, unless the LVT makes an order under s.27(3) dispensing with service of the notice. The dispensation power is strictly limited, see paragraph 28–022 below.

Requisite majority

28–017 Although expressed in terms of "votes", there is one vote per flat let to a qualifying tenant and the requisite majority is not less than two-thirds of the qualifying tenants (s.27(4)). The persons who constitute the requisite majority in one context need not be the same as constitute it in another context (s.27(5)). The composition of the majority of qualifying tenants may therefore alter so, for example, the majority who serve the notice need not be composed of the same persons who subsequently apply to the court.

Form and content of a preliminary notice

28–018 There is no prescribed form of s.27 notice. The content of a notice is set out in s.27(2) of the LTA 1987 and it is expressly provided by s.54(1) that the notice must be in writing. This is similar to the content prescribed by s.22(2) in respect of preliminary notices under Pt II of the Act. A notice under s.27 must:

- specify the names of the qualifying tenants by whom it is served, the addresses of their flats and the name and address (in England and Wales) of a person on whom the landlord may serve notices in connection with Pt III of the Act. In principle this list must be accurate and up to date—see *El Naschie v The Pitt Place (Epsom) Ltd* (1999) 78 P.&C.R. 44 dealing with an equivalent provision in s.19 of the Act—but this must now be read subject to *M25 Group v Tudor* [2004] 1 W.L.R. 2319 (discussed below). The list must also expressly identify the tenants on whose behalf the notice is served: *El Naschie*, probably unaffected by the *M25 Group* case on this point.
- state that the tenants intend to make an application to the court for an acquisition order in respect of the specified premises.
- state (if applicable) that they will not do so if the requirement for remedy specified in the notice is complied with.
- specify the grounds on which the court would be asked to make such an order and the matters that would be relied on by the tenants for the purpose of establishing those grounds.
- where those matters are capable of being remedied by the landlord, require him within such reasonable period as is specified in the notice to take such steps for the purpose of remedying them as are so specified.

There is power under s.27(2)(e) to add to this list by regulation, but no such regulations have been made.

In *Gray v Standard Home & Counties Properties Ltd* (above), the notice slightly misnamed the landlord to whom it was addressed (the word "Properties" was omitted from the name). This was held not to be sufficiently substantial an error to invalidate the notice.

It should go without saying, but a s.27 notice will only be valid if it is served with the authority of all those on whose behalf it purports to be given: *El Naschie v The Pitt Place* (above), a case about a notice under Pt I of the Act but the same principle will apply.

Errors and omissions on the preliminary notice

28–019 There is no specific "saving" provision in respect of inaccuracies, errors or omissions in the notice. Nor is there any power to amend or add to the notice. However the usual tests for the validity of statutory notices will apply. In *M25 Group v Tudor* [2004] 1 W.L.R. 2319 it was held that the requirement under s.27(2)(a) to specify addresses was merely "directory" not mandatory or substantive, with the consequence that failure to comply properly with this requirement did not invalidate the notice. This approach to statutory notice requirements has been applied more generally in *7 Strathray Gardens v Pointstar Shipping & Finance* [2005] 07 E.G. 144, in which the *M25 Group* case was analysed.

Additionally, there is a power in the court under s.29(6)(b) to make an acquisition order notwithstanding that the s.27 preliminary notice failed to comply with any of the requirements of s.27(2).

On the face of it, s.27(6)(b) is an untrammelled power and would permit the lessees to raise matters not set out in the notice. However, the purpose of the notice is to give the landlord an opportunity to remedy the breaches of which complaint is made. Consequently it would seem that in arguing the application before the court, the tenants would be limited more or less to the grounds set out in the s.27 notice. It would no doubt be just in many cases to allow variations or amplifications of grounds specified, but surely not just to permit something wholly new to be argued.

Section 27(6)(b) also is only capable of operation where some sort of s.27 notice was served on the landlord. Even if something was sent to the landlord, wholesale failure to comply with s.27(2), such that a reasonable recipient would not appreciate that a notice was indeed a s.27 notice, would lead to the conclusion that no s.27 notice had been served at all, and that s.27(6)(b) would be of no application. Section 27(3) provides for dispensation with the service of any preliminary notice in limited circumstances: see paragraph 28–022 below.

Reasonable period for remedy

28–020 As to what is a reasonable period, the same issues arise as arise in respect of notices preliminary to applications to appoint a Manager, discussed in paragraph 27–023. The LVT had like powers to make an acquisition order notwithstanding that any period specified in the notice was not a reasonable period (s.29(6)(a)) and presumably will take the view that this power can be exercised at a preliminary hearing deciding on the validity of the notice.

Service of the notice

28–021 Section 54(1) of the LTA 1987 provides that any notice under s.27 shall be in writing and "may be sent by post".

Dispensation with notice altogether

28–022 Section 24(3) permits a court to dispense with the need for a s.27 notice (only) "where it is satisfied that it would not be reasonably practicable to serve such a notice on the landlord". There is no general power to dispense on "just and equitable" grounds. The dispensing power under s.27(3) would appear to cover only a missing landlord situation. The power to dispense with notice may be exercised at any stage of proceedings.

Where notices are dispensed with, the court has power to direct that such other notices are served, or steps taken, as it thinks fit. The court might order that steps are taken to trace the missing landlord, or that advertisement of the application be made.

Application to the court

28–023 Although many of the 1987 Act jurisdictions have been transferred to the LVT in their entirely, an application for an acquisition order is made in the first instance to the county court.

Application must be made by the requisite majority of qualifying tenants (s.28(1)) although as noted earlier these need not be the same qualifying majority who served the s.27 notice (s.27(5)). All those tenants must be claimants in the action. This is different from claims for RTM, or collective enfranchisement, where the tenants' nominee is the claimant. Where an application is made in respect of two or more separate premises, as permitted by s.28(3), it follows that the requisite majority of qualifying tenants in each of those premises must join in the claim.

No application may be made unless:

- a s.27 notice has been served and the reasonable period for remedy of a breach has expired, or the breach was not capable of remedy; or
- service of the s.27 notice has been dispensed with and any directions made by the LVT as to further steps or notices have been complied with.

The application is made by a CPR Pt 8 Claim Form. Paragraphs 8.2 to 8.4 of the Practice Direction supplementing CPR 56 provide for the form and content of the Claim Form, which must:

- identify the property and provide details as to why s.25 of the Act applies to it;
- give details of the claimants to demonstrate that they are a requisite majority of qualifying tenants;
- state the names and addresses of the claimants;
- state the name and address of the landlord or, if he cannot be found or his identity can not be ascertained, the steps taken to ascertain his identity;
- state the name and address of the nominee purchaser (the requirement to specify a nominee purchaser in the application is statutory, see s.30(3));
- state the name and address of every other person known to be likely to be affected by the application, including but not limited to non-participating tenants (including non qualifying tenants), mortgagees, superior landlords, and any recognised tenants' association;
- state the grounds of the claim;
- be accompanied by the s.27 notice (if any);
- name the landlord (and the nominee purchaser, if he is not a claimant) as defendants. (The nominee purchaser will only be a claimant if he is a qualifying tenant forming part of the requisite majority, and the obligation to join him into the claim is statutory, s.30(4)).

Oddly, there is no obligation to serve any Manager or the court of tribunal which appointed him.

Paragraph 8.5 of PD 56 requires the Claim Form to be served on all those identified as being likely to be affected, together with a notice informing the recipient that they may apply to be joined as a party.

Paragraph 10.1 of PD 56 provides that the parties must serve all documents, i.e. the usual option of service by the court is not available.

Paragraph 10.2 of PD 56 purports to lay down requirements for service of documents before a claim is made. With respect, there is no power for the Practice Direction to do so. In respect of documents to be served during proceedings, para.10.2(1) requires service in accordance with s.54(1) of the Act, which is either of no meaning since s.54(1) is permissive only, or positively requires postal service under s.54 and so prohibits any other mode of service. Paragraph 10.2(2) obliges the parties to serve a landlord at his address given under s.48(1) of the Act.

Focus of the argument before the court

28–024 It follows from the structure of s.29(1) (discussed at paragraph 28–015 above), that once the tenants have satisfied the court that the premises qualify under Pt III of the Act and that they are the requisite majority, the hearing before the court will focus on whether (where applicable) there is a continuing breach and whether it is "appropriate" to make an order.

The court is likely to pay most regard to the likely future (mis)management of the property. Some assistance may be gained from consideration of the LVT's approach when considering whether it is just and convenient to appoint a Manager under Pt II of the Act (see paragraph 27–031 above), always bearing in mind that an acquisition order is a more draconian order than the appointment of a Manager, and is an irreversible deprivation of property rights, so presumably any application should be subjected to anxious scrutiny.

Presumably, where there is an existing Manager appointment, the success or otherwise of that appointment will be highly relevant: *Gray v Standard Home & Counties Properties* [1994] 1 E.G.L.R. 119. In cases where there has not been the previous appointment of a Manager, the position is less clear following the repeal of the pre-condition in the former s.29(2)(c) that the court consider whether the appointment of a Manager would be an adequate remedy. *Gray* was decided before the repeal and is of doubtful authority now. Probably the court will still consider whether the appointment of a Manager is a more proportionate and suitable remedy but without giving the consideration any overriding weight.

It is difficult to see why an acquisition order ought not to be appropriate in a missing landlord case where the landlord has been missing for some time. There can hardly be any prospect of the landlord complying with any of his obligations. The appointment of a Manager—at the tenants' expense and for an indefinite period given the absence of the landlord—would not seem sufficient or appropriate in such a case.

Extent and terms of acquisition orders

28–025 As noted earlier, the basic order of the court is that the tenants acquire the specified premises.

The court has power to include any yard, garden outhouse or appurtenance belonging to or usually enjoyed with the specified premises (s.29(4)(a)), and conversely s.29(4)(b) permits the court to exclude parts of the specified premises from the order. Section 29(5) obliges the court to refuse to make an acquisition order where the application relates to premises which consist of part only of more extensive premises in which the landlord has an interest and that the interest can not reasonably be severed.

The court has power to impose conditions on the acquisition order, and in particular to make acquisition orders suspended on conditions (s.30(2)).

The order made by the court will otherwise be fairly bland and will not set out the precise terms of acquisition. Two quite different forms of order (and procedures) apply depending on whether or not the landlord is missing:

- In the ordinary case where the landlord is not missing, the order must provide for acquisition by the nominee purchaser on such terms as may be agreed between the claimant qualifying tenants and the landlord or in default determined by the LVT (s.30(1)).
- Where the landlord can not be found or his identity can not be ascertained, s.33(1) provides for the property to be vested in the nominee purchaser on terms determined by the court on payment into court of the open market value of the property and any sums due to the landlord under the leases of any tenants of the premises.

It should be noted that once an acquisition order is made, the nominee purchaser can not be changed save with the approval of the court under s.30(4).

Costs

28–026 An acquisition order is a fault-based remedy. There appears to be no reason why when making an order the court should not exercise its general powers to order costs against the landlord, whether or not the acquisition order is resisted. In *Gray v Standard Home & Counties Properties Ltd* (above) a costs order was made against the landlord even though it had not contested either the s.27 notice or the court proceedings. Similarly, if the landlord is entirely missing, and so in complete breach of obligation as lessor, that might also justify a costs order.

Once made, a costs order can be enforced against the consideration due to the landlord, after redemption of any charges: *Gray v Standard Home & Counties Properties Ltd* (above).

Registration of the order

28–027 An acquisition order may be (for which read "should be") registered against the landlord's title (s.30(6)).

Reference to LVT to determine the terms of the order

28–028 The content of an application is prescribed by procedure regulations, currently the Leasehold Valuation Tribunal (Procedure) (England) Regulations 2003 and the Leasehold Valuation Tribunal (Procedure) (Wales) Regulations 2004. The application may only be made by the nominee purchaser (s.31(4)). Neither the qualifying tenants in favour of whom the order was made, nor the landlord, may apply.

LVT procedure is dealt with in Chapter 22.

The consideration payable is the amount which the LVT determines that the landlord's interest might be expected to realise if sold on the open market on the "appropriate terms" by a willing seller and assuming that none of the tenants seek to buy (s.31(2)). The "appropriate terms" are the other terms determined by the LVT (s.31(3)). Those are to be determined on the basis of what appears to the LVT to be "fair and reasonable".

In *139 Finborough Road Management v Mansour* [1990] 2 E.G.L.R. 225, the LVT took the valuation date as the date of the hearing, while acknowledging that the valuation date might arguably be the date of the court order. This authority is of little weight as the landlord did not appear, there was no argument on the point, and no reasons were given for adopting that valuation date. There is no higher authority as to the valuation date.

On the face of it, this valuation basis is favourable to the tenants, as it does not appear to include any marriage value realised through the tenants' nominee gaining control of the reversion to the long leases, and the capacity to grant new long leases to which this may give rise.

Excluded from the LVT jurisdiction is any jurisdiction over the discharge of mortgages. Complex provision is made for their discharge by s.32 and Pt II of Sch.1 to the Act (see paragraph 28–030 below).

Where the landlord can not be found

28–029 Where the landlord can not be found or his identity can not be ascertained, the LVT has no part to play. The court makes in effect a true vesting order (s.33(3)). The terms of acquisition, other than the price, are fixed by the court (s.33(1)(b)), and are to correspond so far as possible to the terms which would be included in a transfer if the property were being transferred by the missing landlord.

The consideration for the acquisition of the property must be ordered to be paid into court. The consideration payable is the same as under s.31(2) (see paragraph 28–028 above) but it is determined by a surveyor selected by the President of the Lands Tribunal (s.33(1)(a)). There is no provision for appealing the surveyor's certificate. There is no authority as to the valuation date—for consistency with the valuation date in cases where the landlord is not missing, the date of the reference to the surveyor might be taken, but equally it could be the date the court decides all the terms of the vesting order.

In addition, any amounts or estimated amounts due from *any* tenants to the landlord, as determined by the court, must be paid into court (s.33(2)(b)). This includes sums due from qualifying tenants who are not participating in the claim to an acquisition order, and in principle from non-qualifying tenants such as assured tenants (in practice, the landlord entitled to a rack rent will usually be identifiable and the missing landlord procedure will not apply).

Mortgages and charges

28–030 In general, an acquisition order discharges charges secured against the premises (s.32(1)). The same applies to mortgages and liens, but not rent charges (s.32(3)). The exceptions are:

- Where the landlord and either the nominated person or the qualifying tenants in whose favour the order was made have agreed that the property be acquired subject to the charge (s.32(2)(a)).

- Where the court is satisfied that in the exceptional circumstances of the case it is fair and reasonable that the landlord's interest be acquired subject to the charge (s.32(2)(b)). The court can consider this either when making the order, or on the application of the mortgagee.

Where there is a charge, the nominated person must apply the consideration to redemption of the charge or charges (Sch.1, para.7(1)). As long as all the consideration is applied to the redemption, the charge is redeemed even though the consideration may fall short of the redemption figure (para.7(2)). A chargee's right to consolidate securities is excluded by para.8(1), and para.8(2) obliges chargees to accept three months' notice of redemption regardless of the terms of the charge documentation.

In case of dispute over the redemption figures, or other difficulty such as where the chargee is missing or will not provide a discharge, para.9 of Sch.1 provides for the payment of the disputed sums into court.

Discharge of acquisition orders and withdrawal by the tenants

28–031 Once a landlord's interest has been acquired, there is no power under the Act to discharge the order (s.34(8)). Up to that point, there are a number of situations where the claim may fail.

Section 34(1) of the Act provides for a number of situations where the acquisition order may be discharged on the application of the landlord:

- Where the nominated person has had a reasonable period to effect the acquisition but has not done so;
- Where the number of qualifying tenants who wish to proceed has dropped below a qualifying majority;
- Where Pt III of the Act has ceased to apply to the premises.

Section 34(2) provides for service of a notice of withdrawal by the tenants, in which case the landlord is entitled to his costs in connection with the disposal (this does not include court or LVT costs, which are dealt with under s.34(4)). Such notice of withdrawal may be served at any time between service of the preliminary notice under s.27 and the completion of the acquisition.

Section 34(3) obliges the nominated person to serve notice of withdrawal if he becomes aware:

- that the number of qualifying tenants who wish to proceed has dropped below a qualifying majority;
- that Pt III of the Act has ceased to apply to the premises.

Although not explicitly set out in s.34, it is implicit in s.34(4)(b) that if the person nominated indicates that he is no longer willing to act, and no replacement is nominated, the claim will cease to be effective.

Section 34(4) provides for the landlord to recover his costs of court or Lands Tribunal (but not the LVT—see s.34(5)) where:

- an acquisition order is discharged under s.34(1); or
- notice of withdrawal is served under s.34(2) or (3); or
- the person nominated indicates that he is no longer willing to act and no replacement is nominated; or
- the number of qualifying tenants who wish to proceed has dropped below a qualifying majority; or
- Part III of the Act has ceased to apply to the premises.

Where the costs liability arises before application is made for an acquisition order, the liability is jointly and severally that of the tenants who served the s.27 notice. Where the liability arises after the making of the application, the liability is jointly and severally that of the tenants who made the application (s.34(6)). The nominated person is also liable in either case. Tenants who have assigned their interest escape liability, the present tenant is liable (s.34(7)).

Somewhat bizarrely, if the landlord against whom an acquisition order is made requires the consent of another person to transfer his interest, the acquisition order is defeated and ceases to have effect if that other person refuses consent (s.30(5) and (6)). The landlord's obligation is limited to seeking the necessary consent and, if it appears to him that consent has been unreasonably withheld, to seek a declaration to that effect.

Presumably, if there is a dispute as to whether the landlord should have issued such proceedings, the court will be able to rule upon it when considering whether the acquisition order has ceased to have effect.

On the face of it, if assignment of the landlord's interest is absolutely prohibited, then the above does not apply and there is nothing in the Act to deprive the acquisition order of effect in those circumstances. Whether the court would accept this interpretation is perhaps open to question.

Where the order ceases to have effect under s.30(5) and (6), this does not appear to give rise to a costs liability.

Appeals

28–032 Appeals from the court and the LVT may be made in the usual way. The relevant appellate procedures are considered at paragraph 23–054 (court) and paragraph 22–026 (LVT).

Chapter 29

The Right to Manage—Introduction, Qualifying Criteria and RTM Companies

Structure of this part of the book

29–001 Acquisition of the right to manage is a complex subject and has been split into several chapters for ease of use:

- This chapter introduces RTM generally, and deals first with the question as to whether RTM applies to a particular property. It goes on to consider RTM companies, what they are and how they are run.
- Chapter 30 deals with the two essential steps to be taken towards acquiring RTM—the notice of intention to participate and the claim notice.
- Chapter 31 deals with the procedure after service of the claim notice, up to any reference to the LVT. This includes service of contractor notices and counter notices.
- Chapter 32 considers references to the LVT, costs and withdrawal of the claim.
- Chapter 33 deals with the exercise of RTM once acquired, and also the circumstances in which RTM may cease.

To avoid confusion, the acronym "RTM" and the epithet "RTM company" is used in respect of the right to manage, with "Manager" used in respect of a manager appointed under Pt II of the LTA 1987. Appointment of a Manager is dealt with in Chapter 27.

Introduction

29–002 The right to manage (or "RTM") is an entirely new right arising under Pt 2 of the Commonhold and Leasehold Reform Act 2002. It confers on qualifying leaseholders of flats (broadly speaking those with leases granted for terms in excess of 21 years) the right to take over the management of their block of flats through the vehicle of a dedicated, tenant-owned company known as a "RTM company" (s.71(1) of CLRA 2002). Unlike the jurisdiction to appoint a Manager under Pt II of the Landlord and Tenant Act 1987, RTM is a no-fault right, exercisable without proving any complaint against the landlord or his managing agents.

Upon the lessees exercising RTM, the RTM company takes over not simply management, but all the obligations and duties arising under the leases of the flats in the block, except the right to forfeit the leases. For most practical purposes, the RTM company will in effect act as "the landlord".

A RTM company is simply the vehicle for the exercise of RTM. The RTM company may well wish to employ a professional managing agent to actually manage the block day to day.

The qualifying conditions for RTM are the same as those for collective enfranchisement under Pt 1 of the Leasehold Reform etc. Act 1993 amended by CLRA 2002. The RTM may prove an attractive alternative to collective enfranchisement (or perhaps a first step towards it), because the lessees will thereby almost entirely replace their landlord with their own RTM company but need not find the capital to purchase the freehold itself. In a falling property market, with a long time left to run on the leases, RTM may be a sounder option than enfranchisement, with the RTM company then a ready vehicle for enfranchisement once property prices bottom out.

Interrelationship with the right to appoint a Manager

29–003 RTM does not replace the fault-based right to appoint a Manager under Pt II of the LTA 1987. The two regimes co-exist. A failing RTM company could be on the receiving end of an application to appoint a Manager, and an unpopular Manager could be replaced by a RTM company. The right to appoint a Manager is dealt with in Chapter 27.

The right to appoint a Manager is fundamentally different from RTM in that a Manager's powers derive from the order which appoints him, whereas a RTM company's powers are derived from the leases. If the leases are seriously defective in terms of the right to recover service charge, the lessees may be well advised to apply together for the appointment of a Manager rather than invoke RTM.

In force dates

29–004 The in force dates are as follows:

- All the RTM provisions were brought into force in England on September 30, 2003 by the Commonhold and Leasehold Reform Act 2002 (Commencement No.2 and Savings) (England) Order 2003;
- All the RTM provisions were brought into force in Wales on March 30, 2004 by the Commonhold and Leasehold Reform Act 2002 (Commencement No.2 and Savings) (Wales) Order 2004;
- Section 104 (registration of RTM) was repealed in both England and Wales on November 17, 2004 by the Commonhold and Leasehold Reform Act 2002 (Commencement No.5 and Saving and Transitional Provision) Order 2004 (Note: replacement provision for s.104 of the CLRA 2002 is made under the Land Registration Act 2002).

Qualifying for the RTM—introduction

29–005 The qualifying rules are set out in ss.72 and 75–77 of the CLRA 2002. As noted earlier, the qualifying rules for RTM are the same as for collective enfranchisement under the LRHUDA 1993 following amendments to that Act by the CLRA 2002. Reference may therefore be made to a standard text on leasehold enfranchisement, such as *Hague on Leasehold Enfranchisement,* 4th ed., by Radevsky and Greenish, for a more detailed treatment of the qualifying rules, and what follows is a summary.

Premises to which RTM applies

29–006 The basic qualifying provision is found in s.72(1), which provides that the right to acquire RTM applies to premises:

- which are a self-contained building or part of a building, with or without appurtenant property;

- which contain two or more flats held by qualifying tenants; and
- in which the total number of flats held by such tenants is not less than two-thirds of the total number of flats contained in the premises.

A building is "self-contained" if it is structurally detached (s.72(2)), and a part of a building is "self-contained" if it is a vertical division which could be developed independently of the rest of the building (s.72(3)) and either has independent services or such services could be provided without a significant interruption in services to the rest of the building (s.72(4) and (5)). For the meaning of "structurally detached", see *Parsons v Henry Smith's Charity* [1974] 1 W.L.R. 435.

Thus a row of mansion blocks is a series of self-contained parts of a building, and each block can acquire RTM, but where there is significant overlap between parts of a building, RTM can not be acquired for any of those parts. RTM might also be sought globally for a series of non-detached buildings, again taking the example of a row of mansion blocks, so long as the whole may reasonably be called one "building" and so long as they are in the same freehold ownership (para.2 of Sch.6).

A consequence of adopting the same qualifying rules as under Pt 1 of the LRHUDA 1993 is that the RTM can probably only be claimed in relation to single buildings and their appurtenant property (see in relation to the 1993 Act the county court decision in *Garden Court NW8 Property Co Ltd v Becker Properties* (7/9/1995, unreported, Mr Recorder Knott)). This contrasts with the right to seek the appointment of a Manager under Pt 2 of the LTA 1987 where an application may be made in respect of two or more blocks together (as expressly provided by s.21(4)(b) of the LTA 1987). However, it may be possible to treat a series of structurally attached and overlapping premises as one large building and acquire RTM for the whole.

The meaning of "flat" and "qualifying tenant" is dealt with in paragraphs 29–015 to 29–020 below.

Multiple premises covered by a single RTM company

29–007 It is arguable that the restriction of RTM to single buildings can be circumvented by using a single RTM company to acquire RTM over more than one set of premises. This argument was upheld by the LVT in *Dawlin RTM Ltd v Oakhill Park Estates* (LVT, 21/9/05, unreported) where a single RTM company was held to be entitled to acquire RTM in respect of five separate blocks on a single estate (together with the estate grounds). At the time of writing that decision is subject to appeal, and in the view of the authors there are strong arguments to the contrary:

- The multiple premises would have to be specified in the company's objects clause.
- The company would only be a RTM company to the extent that its objects satisfy s.73(2)(b). "Premises" as used in that subsection must mean the same as in the primary definition in s.72.
- Therefore, the objects of the company would be to acquire RTM to premises to which the Act does not apply. The company would appear not to be a RTM company at all and to have no power to invoke any right under the Act.
- Analysis of the complex voting rights for members of the company (paragraphs 29–028 to 29–030) demonstrates that the scheme is unworkable if multiple premises are covered—for example, RTM might be acquired for one building but not another, thus permitting tenants from blocks where RTM had not been acquired to vote at a general meeting of the company in respect of matters concerning a block where RTM had been acquired, and where there might be landlord members.
- If the position were otherwise, a single large landlord could set up a single RTM company for all its properties. If the landlord had sufficient flats held by associated entities, all could join the company, and vote against RTM being acquired for any of the properties.

Exceptions

29–008 Section 72(6) and Sch.6 import a long list of exceptions where premises are excepted from the RTM despite otherwise meeting the basic qualifying criteria:

- premises with substantial non-residential parts;
- premises with resident landlords;
- premises with an immediate landlord which is a local housing authority;
- premises where there is already a RTM company;
- premises where RTM has been acquired but ceased within the past four years.

Buildings with substantial non-residential parts

29–009 The most important of these exceptions is contained in Sch.6 para.1, which excludes a building with more than 25 per cent "non-residential" parts, measured by reference to internal floor area (para.1(1)). The method of calculating the floor areas is helpfully explained in *Indiana Investments v Taylor* [2004] 3 E.G.L.R. 63.

A part of premises is a non-residential part if it is neither occupied, or intended to be occupied, for residential purposes, nor comprised in any common part of the premises (para.1(2)). A part of premises can be occupied for residential purposes even if held on a commercial lease: *WHRA RTM Co Ltd v Gaingold* (7/12/04, LVT unreported, LEASE No.9) (staff accommodation and staff kitchen attached to a restaurant). Any part of the premises used or intended for use in conjunction with a particular dwelling (for example, a garage, parking space or storage area) is taken to be occupied, or intended to be occupied, for residential purposes (para.1(3)).

Resident landlords

29–010 There is a resident landlord exception in para.3 of Sch.6. This is limited in scope, applying only where the premises contain not more than four units (para.3(1)(b)) and were not purpose built as flats (para.3(2)(a)). The intention is to limit the exception to converted houses and similar properties. The residence requirement does however extend to adult members of the landlord's immediate family (para.3(4) and 3(8)). The resident landlord or family member must have been resident for a continuous period of the last 12 months (para.3(4)). Provision is made for purchase by one resident landlord from another (para.3(5)).

Local housing authorities

29–011 There is no right to RTM if the immediate landlord of any qualifying tenant is a local housing authority.

Duplicate RTM/ lapsed RTM

29–012 It is a fundamental part of the overall scheme of RTM that there should not be duplication of RTM. Consequently, the RTM can not be exercised if there is already a RTM company exercising RTM (See paragraph 29–021).

RTM is also unavailable where the RTM was exercisable by a RTM company during the past four years but has ceased to be so (other than under s.73(5)). The LVT has power to disapply this restriction if it would be "unreasonable" for the restriction to apply (para.5(3) of Sch.6).

Crown land

29–013 RTM does apply to premises despite the existence of a Crown interest (s.108).

No contracting out

29–014 Agreements which seek to exclude lessees rights to join RTM companies, or which seek to impose any penalty (for example termination of their leases) on lessees who join RTM companies or act through RTM companies, are void by virtue of s.106.

"Flat"

29–015 "Flat" is defined in s.112(1) as meaning a separate set of premises (whether or not on the same floor, so including most maisonettes) which forms part of a building, which is constructed or adapted for use for the purposes of a dwelling, and either the whole or a material part of which lies above or below some other part of the building.

This definition is fairly comprehensive and will include almost all premises which one might expect to refer to as a flat. What may be excluded include:

- demised parts which are physically divorced from the flat, such as a store-room on a different floor (*Cadogan v McGirk* [1996] 4 All E.R. 643);
- parts of a flat, which could arise if, say, what was originally two flats has been knocked into one but only one of those flats was on a qualifying lease;
- conceivably in some circumstances, a maisonette, for example where there is a large house, with a back addition converted into a number of "flats", but where the back addition is entirely filled with a single maisonette.

Qualifying tenants

29–016 Qualifying tenants are dealt with in s.75. A qualifying tenant is a tenant of a flat under a "long lease" (s.75(2), see paragraphs 22–017 to 22–019 below) unless that lease is in one of the excepted categories (paragraph 29–020 below).

"Long lease"

29–017 The basic definition of a long lease is a lease granted for a term in excess of 21 years (s.76(2)(a)). For this purpose, the term can not be back dated, so the term must expire more than 21 years after the date of grant of the lease (*Roberts v Church Commissioners* [1972] 1 Q.B. 278).

A number of further types of leases are deemed to be long leases by ss.76(2)(b)–(f) and 77(2)–(4):

- Any tenancy (however short) granted subsequent to a long lease if granted to the tenant who was tenant under the previous long lease (s.77(2));
- Leases with perpetual covenants for renewal (s.76(2)(b)) and leases with non-perpetual covenants for renewal for no premium which have been renewed so that the total period of grant exceeds 21 years (s.77(3));
- Right-to-buy leases and rent-to-mortgage leases (s.76(2)(d), but note the premises will not qualify for RTM if the immediate landlord remains a local housing authority—see paragraph 29–011), shared ownership leases where the tenant has a 100 per cent share (s.76(2)(e)), and right to acquire leases (s.76(2)(f));
- Tenancies continuing under Pt I of the Landlord and Tenant Act 1954 or Sch.10 to the Local Government and Housing Act 1989 (s.77(4));
- Lease taking effect under s.149(6) of the Law of Property Act 1925 (leases terminable after a death or marriage, s.76(2)(c)) and which are not within the exception at s.77(1).

Provision is also made in s.77(5) for cases where a flat and/or appurtenant property is held on two or more leases and the broad scheme is to treat such leases as if there were a single long lease.

Sub-leases

29–018 There can only be one qualifying tenant, so a tenant under any lease which is superior to that of a qualifying tenant does not qualify.

Joint tenants and trustees

29–019 Joint tenants qualify jointly (s.75(7)). Therefore, all joint tenants must act together to validly participate in RTM.

Where the lessees are trustees, s.109 extends the trust powers to permit participation in RTM, unless there is express provision in the Trust Deed to the contrary.

Exceptions—leases which do not qualify

29–020 A number of leases which would otherwise qualify are expressly excluded:

- Business tenancies (s.75(3));
- Unlawful sub-tenancies (s.75(4));
- Inalienable tenancies terminable on death or marriage (s.77(1)).

Probably the most important of those exclusions is that of business tenancies to which Pt II of the Landlord and Tenant Act 1954 applies. However, this exclusion is poorly drafted because tenancies are only 1954 Act business tenancies if business use is being carried on at the relevant time. Therefore the exclusion can be evaded fairly easily by ceasing business use (see *Bishopsgate Foundation v Curtis* [2004] 3 EGLR 57) or granting a (short) sub-tenancy of the commercial pert of the unit.

The exception for unlawful sub-tenancies applies unless the breach has been waived (s.75(4)).

Section 77(1) excepts tenancies which are not assignable nor capable of being sub-let as a whole and are terminable by not more than three months notice after the death or marriage or civil partnership of the tenant. *Skinns v Greenwood* [2002] 2 E.G.L.R.137 explains the meaning of the notice provisions under this exception.

The RTM company

29–021 The first step towards exercise of the RTM is that the participating lessees must set up a RTM company. This is a critical step because, in order to avoid competing bids for the RTM being mounted, a company can not be a RTM company in relation to premises if a RTM company already exists in respect of the premises or any premises contained in, or containing, the premises (s.73(4)).

A company is a RTM company in relation to premises if it is a company limited by guarantee (i.e. there are no shareholders), and the objects of which include the acquisition and exercise of the right to manage the premises in question (s.73(2)). The form of objects clause is prescribed by RTM Companies (Memorandum and Articles of Association) (England) (Regulations) 2003, or their Welsh equivalent, which also requires that the company name end with the style "RTM Company Limited".

It is of critical importance to appreciate that it is the very formation of the relevant company which leads to it being the one and only RTM company for a given set of premises.

Reference may be made to Chapter 26 which deals with some basic aspects of company law and which will be applicable to RTM companies.

Membership of the RTM company

29–022 Any qualifying leaseholder is entitled to be (but is not required to be) a member of the RTM company at any time. In order to exercise the RTM and serve a valid "claim notice" under s.79, a minimum of half the qualifying tenants must be members of the RTM company at that time, but the RTM company can be incorporated without waiting for the necessary numbers of lessees to become members. Once the RTM is exercised, the number of qualifying lessees who are members can fall below the 50 per cent needed to exercise the RTM without any adverse consequence in law.

Once the RTM has been acquired by the RTM company, any landlord is also entitled to become a member of the RTM company. The reason why the landlord can not become a member any earlier is to avoid any spoiling action by the landlord in the running of the company.

How valuable a right the right of membership really is to the landlord remains to be seen. Certainly it gives the landlord a voice in the RTM company's affairs, and it gives the landlord the rights of any member to attend the AGM, receive accounts and so on. On the other hand, the landlord will often (save in the case of a very small block) be a tiny minority liable to be outvoted by the tenant members.

A matter of concern is as to the ability of a disgruntled landlord to wage some sort of "guerrilla war" using its membership of the RTM company. There are many, many technicalities to company law and the proceedings in general meetings and meetings of directors. Difficult landlords might threaten the weight of action in the Companies Court on the basis of trivial alleged breaches of company law or the articles of the RTM company. The officers of a RTM company will almost always have less funds to fight a Companies Court application, so the threat of action by the landlord may well be enough to cow the tenants into toeing the landlord's line.

No person other than a qualifying tenant (or, after RTM has been acquired, a landlord) may be a member of the RTM company. To the extent this is not made clear by the Act, it is prescribed by art.5 of the prescribed articles of association. However, this does not appear to apply to the initial subscribers (see arts 4 and 10 of the articles of association, and s.81(2) CLRA) but—assuming that the company is a valid RTM company—they will automatically cease to be members as soon as the formation process is complete (art.10).

This means that third parties to leases, such as management companies which do not have any demised property and so are not a "landlord", are not entitled to join the RTM company. The thinking presumably was that such companies would wither away once RTM was acquired, but this may not be so in all cases.

Directors of the RTM company

29–023 There is no restriction on who may be a director of a RTM company. Article 49 of the prescribed articles of association expressly provides that a director need not be a member, i.e. need not be a qualifying tenant or a landlord. This is deliberate. It usefully allows the employment of an outsider—most obviously a professional managing agent, or an accountant—to run the RTM company on a day-to-day basis.

The constitution

29–024 The RTM Companies (Memorandum and Articles of Association) (England) (Regulations) 2003 provide a complete memorandum of association and articles of association. Section 74(5) and reg.2(3) each provide that the prescribed forms have effect whether or not they are adopted by the RTM company, so there can be no contracting out. In principle, the memorandum and articles could be added to, so long as there were no conflict with the prescribed articles, but in practice the articles are comprehensive and there is little scope for addition.

In any case, art.95 of the prescribed articles of association empowers the directors to make rules or by-laws which may regulate among other things the conduct of members of the RTM company towards each other and towards the RTM company's servants, and which may regulate procedure at meetings.

A comprehensive treatment of the company law applicable to companies limited by guarantee would be a book in itself and is beyond the scope of this work. Reference should be made to Chapter 26 for a summary of some of the more important points which may arise in practice.

The running of a RTM company—quorum and voting rights of members

29–025 The quorum for a general meeting of members is 20 per cent, or two members, whichever is the greater number (art.23). There is no requirement that any one of those forming the quorum need be tenant members, so it is possible that a quorum could be formed of landlord members, or that landlord members form the majority of members present.

Voting rights—no landlords

29–026 As long as there are no landlord members of a RTM company, it is a simple "one flat, one vote" system—art.38. There is no weighting for size of flat, proportion of service charge paid or otherwise.

Voting rights—joint parties

29–027 The position of joint tenants is that as each of several joint tenants is individually admitted to membership (see art.5) but to be regarded as jointly being a member with the other joint tenants (art.6). Any one of the joint members may cast the vote for the flat but where more than one is present, the "senior" member casts the vote (art.40). "Seniority" is denoted by the order in which the joint tenants' names are entered in the register of members, something which must be stated in the initial application for membership (see art.8).

Precisely the same provisions apply in the case of joint landlords.

Voting rights—where there are landlord members

Introduction

29–028 By contrast with the simplicity of the situation where there are no landlord members, the provisions in art.39 for determining voting rights where there are landlord members of the RTM company are Byzantine in their complexity, and may change from time to time. Article 39 plainly contemplates that the voting rights need to be determined every time a vote is taken.

Determination of voting rights under art.39 is a two stage process:

- First, determine the votes available to be cast;
- Secondly, determine who may cast those votes.

A real difficulty with the provisions is that it will be uncertain until a vote actually comes to be taken at a meeting how many votes are available to be cast and by whom. For example, a freeholder with an empty residential unit (not entitled to any votes for that unit, see paragraph 29–030 below) could let the unit on the day of a general meeting and without any warning seek to cast the allocated votes at the general meeting. There appears to be a significant potential for argument as to the validity of any motion voted on in such circumstances.

Votes available

29–029 Every "residential unit" is allocated a number of votes equal to the number of landlord members of the RTM company (art.39(a)). The following points arise:

- "residential unit" is defined in art.1 and is not limited to flats held by qualifying tenants, so the number of votes attributed to the qualifying lessees' flats depends how many residential units there are physically in the premises;
- the number of landlord members will be variable from time to time, given that any sub-letting will create a landlord who may wish to be a member.

Votes that are also attributable to non-residential parts of the premises are calculated by application of the formula set out in art.39(b). This is calculated as:

(Total votes of residential units) x A/B

In the A/B factor:
A = total internal area of non-residential parts
B = total internal area of residential parts

The A/B factor can never exceed ¼, otherwise the premises would not qualify for RTM in the first place.

Detailed provision is made for calculating the internal areas and the rounding up of fractions of those areas, but no provision is made for any fractions of a vote which emerge from the application of the formula (unlike under art.39(d), discussed below). It is unclear whether or not those fractions are lost—in principle that fraction of a vote might carry a close vote.

It is possible that in a building with a large commercial element, and a number of flats let by the freeholder on short leases, the landlord(s) may have a majority of the available votes, or at any rate enough votes to carry the day unless almost all the qualifying lessees are present and vote together.

Casting the available votes

29–030 As might be expected, where a residential unit has a qualifying tenant, the attributable votes are cast by the member who is the qualifying tenant (art.39(c)).

Where the residential unit has no qualifying tenant, but is let on some sort of lease or leases, art.39(c) provides that the attributable votes are cast by the "immediate landlord", defined in art.1 as the landlord or, in the case of multiple leases, the landlord under the most inferior lease (but other landlords may be entitled to one vote, see below).

Where a residential unit is not subject to any lease, the votes attributable to it may not be cast at all (art.39(e)). It seems odd that a freeholder with an empty flat may not cast any vote in respect of that flat but if the flat is let on an assured shorthold then the votes may be cast. Equally, it is a simple restriction to evade by granting a lease to an associated person or company.

The votes allocated to any non-residential part which is subject to a lease are cast by the "immediate landlord" (art.39(d)).

Where a non-residential part has no lease, the votes are cast by the freeholder (art.39(d)).

For the purposes of voting, there can be only one "non-residential part". If that part is in fact a number of separate non-residential parts, art.39(d) provides for the votes allocated to be split in proportion to the respective internal floor areas. Any resulting fraction of a vote is ignored.

Finally, any landlord member who, after the complex provisions of art.39 are applied, is not entitled to any votes, is given one vote by art.39(e). This is likely to apply to intermediate landlords and landlords of open areas (external "floor" area attracts no votes).

Dispute resolution

29–031 Article 42 provides that objections as to qualifications to vote or computation of votes shall be referred to the chairman of the meeting whose decision is "for all purposes relating to that meeting . . . final and conclusive". Consequently a decision by a chairman properly holding office under the articles is conclusive absent bad faith—see *Wall v London and Northern Assets* [1899] 1 Ch. 550 and *Wall v Exchange Investment Corp* [1926] Ch. 143. The position is different where the chairman is not properly appointed as such: *Re Bradford Investments* [1991] B.C.L.C. 224. There may be arguments that the complexity of the voting provisions is such that it would be bad faith for the chairman to refuse an adjournment to clarify genuinely disputed points.

The position is rendered less clear still because art.42 goes on to provide that, subject to the conclusivity of the chairman's decision, any dispute which arises out of the measurement of floor areas shall be referred to a chartered surveyor for expert determination which is final and conclusive. It is not clear how such determination interacts with the chairman's decision.

No other provision is made for the resolution of disputes arising out of the internal running of the RTM company. Any such dispute, for example as to whether a general meeting had been validly called, would have to be referred to the Companies Court if incapable of resolution by agreement.

Proceedings of directors

29–032 Subject to ordinary resolution of the members to the contrary, the minimum number of directors is two, and there is no maximum (art.50). If there are few members, and no landlord members, it may be appropriate for all members also to be directors. With larger RTM companies, this is unlikely to be appropriate.

The default quorum of a meeting of directors is 50 per cent, or two, whichever is the greater (art.75), but the quorum may be fixed by the directors at a greater number.

Each director has one vote, decisions are by simple majority (art.74). The chairman has a casting vote.

Chapter 30

The Right to Manage—Notice of Intention to Participate and Claim Notice

Exercise of the RTM—participation

30–001 Before any notice may be served on the landlord, the RTM company must first have served a "notice of invitation to participate" under s.78 (hereafter referred to as a "NITP") on all qualifying lessees who are not already members of the RTM company. The non-participating lessees have the right to become members of the RTM company.

In the case of joint lessees, each must be served. If one only has joined the company, the non-member must be served.

The intention behind this and the similar provision relating to right to enfranchise companies under the LRHUDA 1993 ("RTE companies") is to prevent the exclusion of minority groups of lessees by a majority clique, which is something that has occurred under the collective enfranchisement provisions in the LRHUDA 1993 and which could have become common under RTM with the minimum number of participating lessees set at a bare 50 per cent.

Form and content of notice of invitation to participate

30–002 A valid NITP must be in the form of Sch.1 to the Right to Manage (Prescribed Particulars and Forms) (England) Regulations 2003, including all the notes (regs 3(2)(j) and 8(1)).

The prescribed form pre-supposes that the identity of the tenant is known, as it requires the tenant's name and address to be specified. It is unclear whether an NITP addressed to "the tenant" of a particular flat would be valid.

Section 78(2) provides that an NITP must:

(a) state that the RTM company intends to acquire the right to manage the premises;

(b) state the names of the members of the RTM company; and

(c) invite the recipients of the notice to become members of the company.

Regulation 3(2) prescribes a further long list of particulars which must be included in an NITP, designed to provide sufficient information to the recipient lessees in order for them to make an informed choice as to whether to join the RTM company.

The most important of these additional particulars is set out in reg.3(2)(g), which obliges the RTM company to state whether or not it intends to appoint a managing agent, and:

- if it does intend to appoint a managing agent, to give the name and address of the proposed managing agent (if known) and to state (if it be the case) that the person is the landlord's managing agent; or
- if it does not intend to appoint a managing agent, to state the qualifications or experience (if any) of the existing members of the RTM company in relation to the management of residential property.

This is a highly significant requirement, as it focuses on the core issue of the likely competence of future management of the premises should RTM be acquired.

The balance of reg.3 requires the inclusion of a summary of the more significant aspects of RTM, and a suggestion that the recipient may wish to seek professional advice as to the implications of the NITP.

Section 78(4) provides that an NITP must either be accompanied by a copy of the memorandum of association and articles of association of the RTM company or include a statement (see s.78(5)) about inspection and copying of the memorandum of association and articles of association of the RTM company. Since the form of the memorandum and articles is also prescribed, this latter provision appears superfluous, except to save photocopying in the case of large blocks.

It is of critical importance that the notice of invitation to participate is in the correct form, accompanied by the necessary documentation and served on all lessees. Failure by the RTM company to comply in a material way with s.78 of the CLRA 2002 (and which is not saved by s.78(7)) would appear to render a nullity any subsequent purported claim notice for the RTM itself. Failure to comply with s.78 is a ground on which the landlord can serve a counter-notice and resist a RTM claim.

Errors and omissions in the notice of invitation to participate

30–003 Section 78(7) provides that a notice of invitation to participate is not invalidated by "any *inaccuracy* in any of the *particulars* required" by s.78 or the Regulations. This is not as generous a saving provision as may at first seem to be the case. It also gives rise to the question as to what are "particulars" and what is an "inaccuracy".

"Particulars"

30–004 In the similar saving provisions found in the Leasehold Reform Act 1967 and the LRHUDA 1993, the courts have taken a restrictive approach to the meaning of "particulars". In *Earl Cadogan v Morris* [1999] 1 E.G.L.R. 99 (a case on s.42(3) of the LRHUDA 1993), it was held that as a matter of ordinary construction "particulars" meant those matters expressly referred to as "particulars" by the relevant section or regulation (for a case where a wider view of the word "particulars" was taken, see *Marath v Macgillivray* (1996) 28 H.L.R. 484).

Other than in subs.(7) itself, in s.78 of the CLRA 2002 the word "particulars" only appears in subs.(2)(d), providing that Regulations may provide that the notice "contain such other particulars (if any)" as the national authority thinks fit to require. Subsection (d) appears to assume that it is part of a sub-section dealing with "particulars".

In those circumstances, the matters laid down in reg.3 are therefore particulars, but it may be debatable whether the matters laid down by s.78(2)(a)–(c) are particulars. The basic requirement in subs.(2)(a) that the notice state that the RTM company intends to acquire the right to manage the premises is probably not a particular, and the requirement under subs.(4) to include a copy of the memorandum and articles (or a statement as to place of inspection and provision of copies) is not a particular and failure to comply with these requirements will invalidate the notice. This interpretation is reinforced by subs.(6), providing that the notice is treated as not having been given if the recipient lessee is, following service of the notice, not actually allowed to inspect or is not given a copy of the memorandum and articles when requested.

"Inaccuracy"

30–005 The wording "any inaccuracy in any of the particulars" is lifted from the LRHUDA 1993 and may be contrasted with the superficially similar saving in the Leasehold Reform Act 1967 applicable to "any inaccuracy in the particulars". The difference appears to indicate that under s.78(7) of the CLRA 2002 some attempt must be made to provide each of the required particulars, otherwise that particular will not be "inaccurate", it will be omitted entirely. A notice which wholly omits a mandatory particular will not be saved by s.78(7). The case law under the 1967 and 1993 Acts will apply to s.78 of the CLRA 2002.

- In *Cresswell v Duke of Westminster* [1985] 2 E.G.L.R. 151 (CA), in respect of the similar saving under the Leasehold Reform Act 1967, the test for an inaccuracy was suggested to be:

  > " 'Looking at the facts as they were and what was stated in the notice, can this fairly be said to be an inaccuracy, or is it simply a notice which does not on a fair view relate to the facts?' Where we draw the line I do not know, and doubt that it is in anybody's interests that I should attempt to draw that line. Many cases will answer the question themselves on their own facts."

- In the subsequent case of *Dymond v Arundel-Timms* [1991] 1 E.G.L.R. 109 (CA) (also a 1967 Act case) it was held (at 113E) that an omission from particulars which was deliberate and intended to mislead did not qualify as an "inaccuracy"and so was not within the saving provision.
- In the more recent case of *Speedwell Estates v Dalziel* [2002] 1 E.G.L.R. 55 (CA), the approach of the court was to consider whether the information supplied in a notice was sufficient (and sufficiently accurate) to provide the critical particulars required by the statutory provisions under which the notice was given. The wholesale omission of one important particular was held to invalidate the notice.

Other errors

30–006 The Regulations contain no saving for "notices substantially to the same effect" as the prescribed form of NITP and, as noted earlier, all the information set out in the notes is a mandatory part of the "particulars" to be provided. From this it appears clear that failure to include some or all of the notes will invalidate an NITP, as has been held to be the case in respect of a claim notice served without the notes (*23 Albert Road RTM Company Ltd v Oasis Properties Ltd* (LVT 15/10/04, LEASE No.10)).

Minor deviations from the form may be overlooked by application of the principle in *Sinclair Gardens Investments (Kensington) Ltd v Oak Investments RTM Company Ltd* (Lands Tribunal, 1/3/05 George Bartlett Q.C., P. discussed at paragraph 30–013 below) but the only sound advice to a RTM company is that any NITP must be carefully checked for strict compliance with the prescribed form.

Service of the notice of invitation to participate

30–007 Although the aim of the notice of invitation to participate is laudable, the drafting of the provisions may pose a significant problem. Failure to serve even one lessee who is not a member of the RTM company *may* invalidate any subsequent RTM claim notice (but see paragraph 30–013 below).

Method of service

30–008 Section 111(5) provides that any notice may be served by post, but does not require that it be served by post. For the reasons explained below, to avoid any arguments over either the fact of service or the date of service, RTM companies would be well advised to arrange delivery *by hand* of the NITP through the lessee's letterbox at the flat.

As a first step, the RTM company must obtain from HM Land Registry *up-to-date* Official Copies for the leases of all non-member lessees. It must be remembered that "the lessee" is the legal owner of the residue of the term of the lease, regardless of who may be the beneficial owner or the occupier. Where, as is usually the case, the leasehold interests are registered land, the legal owner is (with one or two minor exceptions) the registered proprietor.

Postal service

30–009 The Interpretation Act 1978, s.7 will apply to postal service of any notice under the RTM provisions. This provides that service is deemed to be effected by properly addressing, pre-paying and posting a letter containing the document and, unless the contrary is proved, to have been effected at the time at which the letter would be delivered in the ordinary course of post.

It should be noted that the provisions of CPR 6.7 dealing with deemed dates of service by various methods of documents served under the CPR have no application whatever to notices under the CLRA.

Service by hand

30–010 If a notice is put through the letterbox of a property by hand, it will be served on the date of delivery—even if that takes place in the evening after business hours. This method of service (particularly if effected in the presence of a witness) is the surest method.

Address for service

30–011 Section 111(5) of the CLRA 2002 provides that notice may be given by the RTM company to a tenant at the flat in the premises, unless the tenant has notified the RTM company of an alternative address for service. This makes service by hand relatively simple as one would expect some of the members of the RTM company to live in the premises concerned.

Significance of the date of service

30–012 Section 79(2) of the CLRA 2002 provides that a minimum of 14 days must have elapsed since the date of service of the notice of invitation to participate before a RTM claim notice may be validly served. RTM companies are strongly urged to allow an extra few days at least, to allow a margin of error for service of all non-member lessees—particularly if one of the lessees has given an address for service other than the flat.

Where there is more than one non-member lessee who must be served, the date of service from which the 14 day minimum period under s.79(2) runs (see below) is calculated from the date when service has been effected on all non-member lessees—i.e. the date when the last of those lessees is served.

Consequences of failure to serve all non-participating qualifying tenants

30–013 There is no saving provision in respect of other failures to comply with s.78, such as failure validly to serve one of the lessees. This has been suggested to be a serious potential pitfall.

However, in the first RTM case to reach the Lands Tribunal, *Sinclair Gardens Investments (Kensington) Ltd v Oak Investments*

RTM Company Ltd (1/3/05 George Bartlett Q.C., P.) it was held that the requirement to serve all lessees was a "directory" requirement, and that the consequences of non-compliance depended on whether there was any real prejudice. This decision was arrived at by applying the authority of *R v Immigration Appeal Tribunal Ex p. Jeyeanthan* [1999] 3 All E.R. 231. The failure in *Sinclair Gardens* was to serve one of two joint lessees, who were a couple living together in the flat. On the evidence the failure of one of them to join the RTM company was an oversight and he knew all about the claim. Consequently, it was held that the failure to serve him was not fatal to the validity of the subsequent claim notice.

Claim notice

30–014 RTM is exercised by serving a claim notice in accordance with s.79 of the CLRA 2002. As noted earlier, s.79(2) provides that a valid claim notice can not be served until at least 14 days have elapsed from service of the notice of invitation to participate. There is however no maximum period beyond which a claim notice may not be served. It therefore appears possible to delay service of the claim notice indefinitely after service of the notice of invitation to participate.

"Relevant date"

30–015 The date the claim notice is given is "the relevant date" for the purposes of the CLRA 2002 (s.79(1)).

Minimum number of qualifying tenants who are members

30–016 If on the relevant date there are only two qualifying tenants of flats contained in the premises, both must be members of the RTM company (s.79(4)). In any other case, the membership of the RTM company must on the relevant date include a number of qualifying tenants of flats contained in the premises which is not less than one half of the total number of flats so contained (s.79(5)).

It is plain from the reference to "relevant date" in subs.(5) that the RTM company only needs to satisfy these conditions on the date the notice of claim is given. The number of qualifying lessees who are members can decline after that date (perhaps because a lease is assigned and the assignee is uninterested in the RTM) without adverse effect on the claim notice.

Right to obtain information

30–017 Before serving a claim notice, the RTM company has the right under s.82 of the CLRA 2002 to give notice to third parties seeking information with a view to including the necessary particulars in the claim notice.

Section 82(1) provides the RTM company with the right to serve on any person a notice requiring him to provide any information which the RTM company reasonably requires to be included in a claim notice. Section 82(2) provides a corresponding right for agents of the RTM company to inspect documents containing such information and be supplied with copies.

The information to which there is a right under s.82 is narrowly defined: it only relates to information needed to include in a claim notice the required particulars. It does not permit a more general interrogation of the landlord to obtain information which might be used for a wider purpose, such as to decide whether or not to claim the RTM. However, the lessees have other rights to information which may be used for this purpose (see Chapter 10).

Notice may be given to "any person". This is a formulation which is, on the face of it, without limit, and certainly the draftsman deliberately opted not to restrict the class of persons on whom notice may be given. However, it is submitted that caution should be exercised before service of a notice on anyone other than obvious candidates such as the landlord or his managing agent. A notice may only be given under subs.(1) where the RTM company "reasonably requires" the information. It may be open to a recipient to argue that the information is not reasonably required from him as it could more reasonably be obtained from, say, the landlord.

This is especially so because there is no provision for costs under s.82. On the face of it, a third party may be put to cost by service of the notice without any recourse.

A similar point arises in respect of timing of a s.82 notice. There is no express restriction on how early a s.82 notice may be served—in theory it could be served as soon as the RTM company is incorporated—but again, it might be argued that until enough lessees have become members of the RTM company to enable a claim notice to be served, the RTM company can not reasonably require the information under s.82.

Compliance with a notice to provide information

30–018 Recipients have 28 days from when the notice was given to them to provide the information sought (s.82(3)). If the recipient refuses to comply with the notice, the RTM company's remedy is to apply under s.107 to the county court, having first served a 14 day default notice. The s.107 procedure is considered in detail in paragraph 33–026 below.

Form and content of a claim notice

30–019 A valid claim notice must be in the form of Sch.2 to the Right to Manage (Prescribed Particulars and Forms) (England) Regulations 2003, or the Welsh equivalent, including all the notes (regs 4(e) and 8(2)).

Section 80(2) provides that a claim notice must specify the premises and contain a statement of the grounds on which it is claimed that they are premises to which the RTM applies.

Section 80(3) and (4) require that the claim notice must state the full name of each person who is both the qualifying tenant of a flat contained in the premises, and a member of the RTM company, it must give the address of his flat and it must contain, in relation to each such person, such particulars of his lease as are sufficient to identify it, including:

(a) the date on which it was entered into;

(b) the term for which it was granted; and

(c) the date of the commencement of the term.

The claim notice must also state the name and registered office of the RTM company (s.80(5)).

Regulation 4 of the Right to Manage (Prescribed Particulars and Forms) (England) Regulations 2003, or the Welsh equivalent, prescribes a further list of "particulars" which must be included in a claim notice, which are in fact a series of "statements" given to the recipient explaining the more important elements of the claim notice procedure.

The claim notice must also specify a date for service of a counter-notice (s.80(6), see paragraph 30–021 below) and a date upon which the RTM company intends to acquire the right to manage the premises (s.80(7), see paragraph 30–022 below). By analogy with the case law under the LRHUDA 1993, failure to specify one or either of those dates, or specifying an invalid date, will render the claim notice invalid.

Failure by the RTM company to comply in a material respect with ss.79 or 80 of the CLRA 2002 (and which is not saved by s.81(1)) would appear to render the claim notice a nullity. Failure to comply with ss.79–80 or the Regulations is a ground on which the landlord can serve a counter-notice and resist a RTM claim.

Errors and omissions in the claim notice

30–020 There is no substitute for getting the notice right in the first place and little excuse for errors of substance given the right to request information under s.82 prior to service of the claim notice (see paragraph 30–017).

If an error is made, then, like s.78(7) in respect of notices of invitation to participate, s.81(1) provides that a claim notice is not invalidated by any *inaccuracy* in any of the *particulars* required by s.80 or the Regulations. This again gives rise to the question as to what are "particulars" and what is an "inaccuracy" (see paragraphs 30–003 to 30–005 above).

In s.80, the word "particulars" appears twice—once in subs.(4) referring to particulars of the leases of qualifying tenants who are members of the RTM company, and once in subs.(8), providing that Regulations may provide that the notice "contain such other particulars (if any)" as the National Authority thinks fit to require. However, reg.4(c) of the Regulations is based on the construction that all matters in subss.(2)–(7) of s.80 are "particulars", as well as all requirements of the Regulations themselves.

In *23 Albert Road RTM Company Ltd v Oasis Properties Ltd* (LVT 15/10/04, LEASE No.10) a claim notice was served without any of the supporting notes. This was held to be an invalid notice. By analogy with the case law on notices in similar contexts, for example the Landlord and Tenant Act 1954, this decision was surely right, although the LVT does not appear to have had such case law cited to it.

Section 81(2) provides that wrongly including in the claim notice a lessee who was not on the relevant date a qualifying lessee does not invalidate the notice so long as the RTM company would otherwise have been entitled to serve a claim notice.

Date for counter-notice

30–021 Section 80(6) requires that the claim notice specify a date, not earlier than one month after the notice is given, by which each person who was given the notice under s.79(6) may respond to it by giving a counter-notice under s.84. This does not include the non-member lessees or a Manager—these persons do not have the right to serve a counter-notice.

The date of service from which the one month period runs is calculated from the date when service has been effected on all those required to be served (which includes those who are not entitled to give a counter-notice)—i.e. the date when the last of the persons to be served is actually served.

RTM companies are strongly urged to allow an extra few days at least, to allow a margin of error for service to be effected on all necessary persons.

Date for commencement of management

30–022 Section 80(7) provides that the claim notice must further specify a date, at least three months after the expiry of the one month period for service of a counter-notice specified under s.80(6), on which date the RTM company intends to acquire the right to manage the premises. If no counter-notice is served disputing the entitlement to RTM, s.90(2) provides that this date will be the date that RTM is acquired and the RTM company takes over management. In other words, the RTM can not be acquired for a minimum of four months after the date the claim notice is given.

This extra three month period is actually a practical necessity—there is a great deal for both landlord and RTM company to do in this period if the transition to RTM is to be anything other than a shambles. It is also a minimum period—in a complex case the RTM company should consider whether it would be wise to specify a longer period.

Unless there is some desperate need to acquire RTM earlier, it will almost certainly be good sense to specify a convenient date for the acquisition of the RTM. In many cases, the preferred date would be the first day of the next service charge accounting year. Another possibility is the day before an interim service charge instalment is payable by the lessees. Acquiring the right to manage in the middle of a service charge accounting period or, worse, in the middle of a programme of works could cause very difficult and costly wrangles over contracts and/or accounting. There are real fears among LVT members that specification of inappropriate dates will have disastrous consequences.

It is therefore most unfortunate that if the claim notice is challenged, and the matter is referred to the LVT, the acquisition date is postponed until three months after the determination becomes final (as to which, see paragraph 32–003 below) and that the LVT is not given power to fix the acquisition date itself. The almost inevitable consequence of an unsuccessful challenge to a claim notice is that the date the RTM is acquired will be an unhelpful date that the RTM company would not have chosen if it had any way to influence the matter. It is to be hoped that having failed in a challenge to the RTM, landlords will reach a sensible agreement with the RTM company as to the acquisition date.

Service of the claim notice and copies of the claim notice

30–023 Section 79(6) provides that the claim notice must be given to each person who is, on the date the claim notice is given:

- a landlord under a lease of the whole or any part of the premises;
- a party to such a lease otherwise than as landlord or tenant; or
- a Manager appointed under Pt 2 of the LTA 1987 to act in relation to the premises, or any premises containing or contained in the premises.

There are also requirements to serve copies of the claim notice, see paragraph 30–031 below.

Landlords

30–024 The landlord requirement applies not just to the freeholder because "lease" includes sub-leases (see s.112(2)). If there is an intermediate lease, the lessee under that lease will be the landlord in respect of occupational leases.

In *Charton RTM Co v Longmint Ltd* (LVT, 9/6/04, LEASE No.1) an LVT held that a claim notice addressed to and served on the managing agents, and addressed to and served on a director of the landlord, was not validly given to the landlord company by either route. The LVT also held that such notice was a complete nullity and so s.81 did not preclude the service of a fresh notice on the landlord company.

Address for service on landlords

30–025 Section 111(3) provides that, unless a landlord has notified the RTM company that it wishes to be served at a different address (s.111(4)), a landlord shall be served at an address given to a member of the RTM company under s.47 or s.48 of the LTA 1987, both of which require landlords to provide to their tenants addresses for the service of notices.

This actually precludes service at the landlord's registered office or principal place of business, unless that happens to be the s.47/s.48

address. The s.47/s.48 address will often be the address of the managing agent, and in such cases it is important not to fall into the trap (see *Charton RTM Co v Longmint Ltd* (above)) of addressing the notice to the agent. It must be addressed to the landlord, but care of the address of the managing agent.

No provision is made for cases where the only tenant of the landlord is not a member of the RTM company, or no s.47 or s.48 address has been provided. In such cases, service should be effected at the landlord's address (if it can be ascertained—if not, see paragraph 30–029 below).

Parties to leases

30–026 The requirement to serve a party to a lease who is neither landlord nor tenant requires service on, for example, management companies who are parties to leases, or sureties. An odd result of the drafting is that a surety of a lease of commercial parts is required to be served but the tenant of those parts is not.

A further possible reading of the drafting is that the original landlord and original tenant under any lease must be served, because he will not be "the landlord" or "the tenant" at the relevant date but will nevertheless be "a party to the lease". Whether this is intended must be open to doubt. A similar question arises under s.42 of the LRHUDA 1993, which requires that a notice of claim to an extended lease must be given to any "third party" under the tenant's lease. In *Wellcome Trust v Bellhurst Ltd* [2002] 2 E.G.L.R. 57, the Court of Appeal ruled that it was only necessary to serve third parties who had some continuing involvement with the lease at the time the notice was given. A similar result would probably be reached under s.79(6)(b) of the CLRA 2002.

Address for service on other parties

30–027 There is no express provision for an address for service on other parties, and service should be effected at their address (if it can be ascertained—if not, see paragraph 30–029 below).

Service on a Manager

30–028 The purpose of serving any Manager is to facilitate as smoothly as possible a transition to RTM.

Missing parties

30–029 By virtue of s.79(7) the claim notice need not be given to a person who cannot be found or whose identity cannot be ascertained; but if as a result the claim notice is not required to be given to anyone at all, s.85 applies (discussed in paragraphs 30–032 below).

Method of service

30–030 As with the NITP, a claim notice may be given by post (s.111(1)).

Copies of the claim notice

30–031 A copy of the claim notice must be given to:

- each person who on the date the claim notice is served is the qualifying tenant of a flat contained in the premises (s.79(8));
- the leasehold valuation tribunal or court by which any Manager was appointed (s.79(9)).

At first sight it is odd that all the qualifying tenants must be served with the claim notice (i.e. including those who are members of the RTM company). The purpose is to make sure all members are aware that the RTM company is proceeding with the claim and to give non-members a further opportunity to become members. As noted earlier, there may also be a substantial delay between service of the NITP and the claim notice and some leases may have been assigned in the intervening period.

As noted above, the purpose of serving any Manager is to facilitate as smoothly as possible a transition to RTM. The appointing court or LVT is also served because a Manager is an officer of the court (or tribunal) and upon acquisition of RTM an order will be required bringing an end to his appointment.

Special case—no party to be served

30–032 Provision is made in s.85 for the special case where there is no party *at all* who can be found or identified to be served under subs.(6). Even if there is only one out of a number of the parties who should be served who can be found or identified (perhaps a Manager), the normal procedure is followed and that person is served.

Where s.85 applies:

- Instead of serving a claim notice, the RTM company applies to the LVT for an order that it is to acquire RTM (s.85(2)).
- Notice of the application must be given to all qualifying tenants (s.85(3)).
- The LVT may order that further steps be taken to trace the missing parties, therefore the RTM company should take reasonable steps to trace missing parties before making the application. If it does not, and the missing parties are easily found, the costs will have been wasted, because if any of the missing parties are traced during the pendency of the application, s.85(5) provides that no further proceedings may be taken on the application and the matter proceeds as if a claim notice had been given on the date of the LVT application (s.85(6)(a)).
- The LVT will then give directions under s.85(6)(b).

It should be noted that the application can not be withdrawn without the consent of the LVT once any missing party has been traced.

This procedure was invoked in *Re 59 Astbury Road RTM Company Ltd* (LVT 7/9/04, LEASE No.6). A number of interesting points arise out of the decision:

- A copy claim notice was served on the qualifying tenants, even though it could not be served on landlord/third parties/ Manager.
- The LVT identified a number of defects in the form of notice to the qualifying tenants and in the documents filed in support of the claim. The LVT was content to make directions at a series of preliminary hearings directing what the RTM company had to do to cure the defects, which included re-service of an amended claim notice on the qualifying tenants, and did not require a fresh application to be made.
- When the LVT was satisfied that the RTM company had fully complied with s.85, an order was made providing for the right to manage to be acquired only 28 days after (re-)service of the claim notice on the qualifying tenants (the property was in a seriously dilapidated condition and overrun with vermin).

Chapter 31

The Right to Manage—Procedure After Service of the Claim Notice

Consequences of service of a valid claim notice

31–001 Service of a valid claim notice has a number of important consequences:

- no further RTM claim notice in respect of the premises or any part of the premises may be served while the claim notice continues in force (s.81(3));
- the right to access under s.83 arises;
- the obligation on the landlord/third party/Manager to serve "contractor notices" and "contract notices" under ss.91 and 92 is triggered;
- a duty to provide information arises (s.93);
- the recipients of the claim notice must consider whether to serve a counter-notice;
- the RTM company and the members of it become potentially liable for costs under ss.88 and 89.

The first of those consequences is self-explanatory. The other consequences will be considered in turn.

Right of access

31–002 After service of a claim notice, s.83(1) provides for a right of access to any part of the premises if that is reasonable in connection with any matter arising out of the claim to acquire the right to manage.

This is a very wide formulation. The only restriction on the exercise of the right is that it must be reasonable. Presumably this means that it must be reasonable for the person exercising the right to require access to the particular part of the premises to which they seek access.

This right is exercisable by those identified in s.82(2):

- the RTM company;
- a landlord under a lease of the whole or any part of the premises;
- any person who is party to such a lease otherwise than as landlord or tenant;
- any Manager appointed under Pt 2 of the 1987 Act to act in relation to the premises, or any premises containing or contained in the premises.

Those persons are entitled to authorise others to act on their behalf in exercising the right of access.

"Reasonable"

31–003 As stated above, the right of access only exists if it is reasonable. Therefore, it may be necessary to justify exercise of the right. Circumstances in which it may be necessary could include where the landlord serves a counter-notice denying the RTM on the ground that the premises have more than 25 per cent of the floor space used for a non-residential use—the RTM company may wish to check the measurements.

What is reasonable may also depend on the area to be accessed. Access into flats may be difficult to justify without very good reason and/or no viable alternative.

Where the part of the premises to be accessed is occupied, the right is exercisable by giving not less than 10 days' notice to the *occupier* of the relevant part of the premises or, if empty, the person entitled to occupy (s.83(3)). This may give rise to problems in practice, as the occupier may not have been a person who needed to be served with the claim notice—for example an assured shorthold sub-tenant of a qualifying tenant—and who may be completely unaware of the RTM claim or indeed of what RTM is in the first place. In such circumstances it would no doubt be wise to inform the long lessee or his agent of the service of the notice.

Contractor notices and contract notices

31–004 The obligation to serve "contractor notices" and "contract notices" arises under ss.91 and 92. The structure of these sections is that s.91 contains the relevant definitions and s.92 the substantive obligations. In respect of all "management contracts" (see paragraph 31–006 below), the landlord, third party management company or Manager (given the nomenclature of "the manager party" by s.91(4)) gives a notice to both the relevant contractors under those contracts ("contractor parties"—s.91(2)(b)) and to the RTM company.

The intention is to ensure that:

- contractor parties have notice that RTM has been claimed;
- the RTM company is aware of all management contracts before RTM is acquired.

The underlying aim is to enable both contractor parties and the RTM company to make informed decisions as to how to proceed. Contractors may or may not wish to have their contracts adopted by the RTM company, or they may wish to terminate their contract with the manager party and make arrangements for orderly cessation of business. The RTM company may wish to adopt some contracts but not others. The contractors and the RTM company need to consider the position before the acquisition date.

Although not spelt out as such, the obligation to serve contractor notices and contract notices can only arise after a claim notice is served because the obligation arises after "the determination date", as defined in s.91(5).

"Determination date"

31–005 The determination date is defined in s.91(5) as:

- in a case where the right to acquire RTM is not disputed, the date specified in the claim notice pursuant to s.80(6) for service of a counter-notice;
- in a case where the right to acquire RTM is disputed, either the date when the LVT determination in favour of RTM becomes final or the date when the objecting party or parties agree in writing under s.84(5)(b) that RTM may be acquired.

"Management contract"

31–006 "Management contract" is defined very widely by s.91(2) and includes not just "management agreements" in the conventional sense but extends to any contract for services or to do "any other thing" in connection with any matter relating to a function which will be a function of the RTM company once it acquires RTM.

Although not expressly limited to "management functions" transferred to the RTM company under s.96(5), it is to those functions that the definition is directed (see paragraph 33–003).

Section 91(3) separately defines "existing management contract" as a management contract which is subsisting at the determination date or entered into between that date and the acquisition date. This dual definition of "management contract" and "existing management contract" appears somewhat tortuous given that the obligations to service contractor notices and contract notices under s.92 apply only to "existing management contracts".

"Contractor notice", "contract notice"

31–007 Section 92(1) obliges service by "the manager party" in relation to each "existing management contract" of a "contractor notice" and a "contract notice".

The "contractor notice" is served on the contractor and the "contract notice" on the RTM company.

Provision is made in s.92(4)–(6) for the service of further contractor notices and contract notices down any chain of sub-contracts, discussed in paragraph 31–008 below.

Where there are sub-contracts

31–008 Where there is an "existing management sub-contract", the contractor party must, by virtue of s.92(4):

- send a copy of the contractor notice to the sub-contractor ("the sub-contractor party");
- serve on the RTM company a contract notice in respect of the sub-contract.

"Existing management sub-contract" is defined by s.92(5) in similar terms to "existing management contract" in s.91(5).

There may be a chain of sub-contracts. If so, the obligations under s.92(4) are repeated down the chain of sub-contracts.

Time for service of contractor notices and contract notices

31–009 The contractor notice and contract notice must be served by the manager party either on the determination date or as soon as reasonably practicable thereafter (s.92(2)(a)) or, in the case of contracts entered into after the determination date, on the date the contract was entered into or as soon as reasonably practicable thereafter (s.92(2)(b)).

In the case of sub-contracts, the contractor party must serve the copy contractor notice and the contract notice in respect of the sub-contract, either on the date the contractor notice is received or as soon as reasonably practicable thereafter (s.92(6)(a)) or, in the case of sub-contracts entered into after the determination date, on the date the sub-contract was entered into or as soon as reasonably practicable thereafter (s.92(6)(b)).

Form and content of contractor notices

31–010 There is no prescribed form of contractor notice. A valid contractor notice must:

- give details sufficient to identify the contract in relation to which it is given;
- state that the right to manage the premises is to be acquired by a RTM company;
- state the name and registered office of the RTM company;
- specify the acquisition date (these requirements derived from s.92(3)); and
- contain a statement advising the contractor party that if it wishes to continue providing services to the RTM company, it should contact the RTM company (see reg.6 of the Right to Manage (Prescribed Particulars and Forms) (England) Regulations 2003).

Form and content of contract notices

31–011 There is no prescribed form of contract notice. A contract notice must:

- give particulars of the contract (s.92(7));
- give particulars of the contractor party, or sub-contractor party (s.92(7));

- give the address of the contractor party, or sub-contractor party (reg.7 of the Right to Manage (Prescribed Particulars and Forms) (England) Regulations 2003);
- contain a statement that if the RTM company wishes to avail itself of the services of the contractor party or sub contractor party, it should contact that party (reg.7).

Duty to provide information

31–012 Section 93 of the Act requires landlords, management companies under leases and 1987 Act Managers to provide information (s.93(1)) and/or provide copy documents (s.93(2)) which are reasonably required "in connection with" the exercise of RTM.

The procedure is a straightforward notice, which must be answered within 28 days.

In principle, this is an important right, as the RTM company will probably need quite a considerable volume of information relating to the existing management arrangements for the property, the state of the service charge accounts of the tenants, and so on. Without this information ahead of the acquisition date, the transition to RTM may be shambolic.

RTM companies would be well advised to have a comprehensive s.93 notice drafted ready for service soon after the claim notice.

Unfortunately, the notice may not require the recipient to do anything before the acquisition date. This is unfortunate as it permits recalcitrant or inefficient landlords (i.e. those likely to be responding to a RTM claim) to withhold information until RTM is actually acquired, which is far later in the process than is desirable.

Section 93 does not specify any date beyond which a notice may not be served. It would appear that a s.93 notice or notices may be served whenever necessary once the RTM is acquired. To hold otherwise would greatly reduce the utility of this notice procedure.

If the notice is not obeyed, compliance may be enforced through the county court by the s.107 default procedure.

Counter-notice

31–013 Section 84(1) provides that any recipient of a claim notice under s.79(6) may give a counter-notice—that is to say, the right is not confined to the landlord. Third parties to leases and Managers are also entitled to serve a counter-notice. A landlord usually has the most to lose and is the most likely candidate but a tenant's management company which is a party to the leases may wish to resist RTM—especially if the membership of the RTM company does not include all the tenants. It is at first sight odd that a Manager has the right to serve a counter-notice resisting RTM but a Manager is an independent officer and it is conceivable that a Manager might properly consider that it was not in the interests of all "stakeholders" in the building that RTM be resisted.

On the other hand, the qualifying tenants, even those who are not members of the RTM company and who may be deeply opposed to the exercise of the RTM, are only served with a copy of the claim notice under s.79(8) and therefore have no right to serve a counter-notice.

Counter-notice not mandatory

31–014 Section 84(1) provides that recipients of the claim notice "may" give a counter-notice. This is to be contrasted with the position in respect of the scheme under the collective enfranchisement provisions of the LRHUDA 1993 where it is provided that the landlord "shall" serve a counter-notice. Under the scheme of the RTM provisions of the CLRA 2002, there is no real point in serving a counter-notice admitting the RTM and there is no need to do so if the RTM is not disputed. A landlord who wishes to deny the RTM must, however, serve a counter-notice.

Challenging the validity of the claim notice

31–015 If the experience of leasehold enfranchisement is any guide, many claim notices will be served in circumstances where there is in substance a good claim to the RTM but where the claim notice itself is defective and can not be saved either by s.81(1) or (2) or by application of general principles.

It is arguable that references to a claim notice must be construed as meaning a valid claim notice: an invalid notice is not a claim notice at all, and no requirement to serve a counter-notice arises. This is the position under the enfranchisement/lease extension provisions of the LRHUDA 1993, the machinery of which is evidently the model for the RTM machinery.

It is also arguable that disputes over the formal validity of a claim notice should be referred to the court:

- The notice and counter-notice provisions are modelled on those found in the enfranchisement/lease extension provisions in the LRHUDA 1993. Like that Act, the provisions relating to counter-notices under s.84 of the CLRA are designed to deal with the situation where the underlying right (in this case, the RTM itself) is disputed, not where the objection is to the form of the notice.

- Section 84(3) of the CLRA 2002 is modelled on ss.22(1) and 46(1) of the LRHUDA 1993, giving (in this case) the LVT jurisdiction to make a determination that the RTM company was on the relevant date entitled to acquire the right to manage the premises. The similar wording of ss.22(1) and 46(1) of the LRHUDA 1993 is not usually considered apt to cover disputes as to the formal validity of the initial notice.
- Under the LRHUDA 1993, a procedure has grown up by which disputes as to the validity of an initial notice are decided by the county court by way of proceedings seeking a declaration as to the validity or otherwise of the notice.
- Although the scheme of the RTM is to refer disputes to the LVT, the LVT only has the jurisdiction given to it by statute. If the claim notice is invalid, the LVT's jurisdiction under s.84 does not arise.

There are counter arguments:

- That the "automatic" nature of the acquisition of RTM is such that the scheme does not work if the claim notice can simply be ignored.
- That the only purpose of a counter-notice is to deal with whether there is a right to RTM, unlike the equivalent LRHUDA provisions where landlords are also concerned with matters such as adequacy of the price proposed.
- That aside from enforcement by the court under s.107, the scheme of the RTM provisions disputes as to entitlement to acquire RTM are all referred to the LVT. This is not the case under the LRHUDA 1993 where the court has significant jurisdiction.
- The RTM provisions in CLRA 2002 contain no equivalent of s.90(2) of the LRHUDA 1993 which gives the county court jurisdiction to determine any matter arising under that Act which is not expressly within the jurisdiction of the LVT.

In *Dawlin RTM Ltd v Oakhill Park Estates* (LVT, 21/9/05, unreported) the tribunal ruled on the validity of the claim notice.

On a practical note, a landlord or other recipient who seeks to argue that a claim notice is invalid should always serve a counter-notice disputing RTM (if that course is open to him) and disputing the validity of the claim notice, served without prejudice to the contention that because the claim notice is invalid, no requirement to serve a counter-notice arises.

Time limit for giving a counter-notice

31–016 Any counter-notice must be given by the date specified in the claim notice under s.80(6) (see paragraph 30–021 above), which must be not less than one month from the date the claim notice is given.

This does not leave the recipients of the claim notice with very much time. Under the LRHUDA 1993, landlords have two months to serve a counter-notice to an initial notice in respect of collective enfranchisement. The time period under s.84 of the CLRA 2002 appears to have been set at a shorter period because the recipient of the notice has less to consider: all he is concerned with is whether or not the RTM company is entitled to the RTM.

Late counter-notice

31–017 It seems plain from the overall scheme of the 2002 Act that the time limit is strict and that late counter-notices will be invalid and of no effect. In this regard it is similar to the scheme for collective enfranchisement under the LRHUDA 1993. In particular, this follows from the provisions of s.90(2), which provides that the RTM is acquired on the date specified in the claim notice where there is no dispute as to entitlement to RTM.

There is no power under the 2002 Act for an extension of time to be granted by the court or LVT.

Content of a valid counter-notice

31–018 The fundamental requirement of a valid counter-notice is that it either admit or deny that the RTM company is entitled to acquire the RTM (s.84(2)(a) or (b)). By analogy with the equivalent provisions of the LRHUDA 1993, a counter-notice which is ambiguous about this fundamental requirement will be held invalid: *Burman v Mount Cook Land Ltd* [2002] Ch. 256 (CA).

A counter-notice may be served admitting the RTM although, as noted earlier, there is no need to serve such a notice.

A counter-notice denying the RTM must "by reason of a specified provision of this Chapter" deny the RTM (s.84(2)(b)). In order to be valid, the counter-notice must therefore refer to a particular section or sub-section of the Act which the giver of the counter-notice relies upon. In *Dawlin RTM Ltd v Oakhill Park Estates* (LVT, 21/9/05, unreported), the LVT held a counter-notice to be invalid because it merely identified a section of the Act with which it was said there had been non compliance and failed to indicate why it was contended that the claim notice was not valid or why it was contended that the Act had not been complied with.

A valid counter-notice must be in the form set out in Sch.3 to the Right to Manage (Prescribed Particulars and Forms) (England) Regulations 2003, or the Welsh equivalent, including all the notes (regs 5(c) and 8(2)).

A counter-notice denying the RTM must also inform the RTM company of its right to apply to the LVT (reg.5(a)) and that RTM is not acquired unless the RTM so determines or the person giving the counter-notice agrees in writing (reg.5(b)).

Errors and omissions in the counter-notice

31–019 There is no equivalent of s.81(1) providing for the notice to be valid despite inaccuracies in particulars. Any failure to comply with the regulations will invalidate the counter-notice.

Anyone proposing to give a counter-notice would be well advised to use one of the pre-printed forms available from law stationers as this will minimise the risk of omitting anything.

Chapter 32

The Right to Manage—Reference to the LVT, Withdrawal and Costs

Application to the LVT—where counter-notice challenging the RTM is given

32–001 A RTM company which has been given a counter-notice challenging the RTM must apply to a leasehold valuation tribunal for a determination that it was on the relevant date entitled to acquire the right to manage the premises (s.84(3)).

The application must be made within two months of the date the counter-notice was given (s.84(4)). If more than one counter-notice is given, the two month period runs from the date the last notice was given. However, the RTM company will not know how many counter-notices it may receive until the one month period for giving counter-notice has expired, so in practice the RTM company will have to work on the assumption that it has two months from the date the first counter-notice was received.

There is no power to extend the time limit for making an application to the LVT. Pursuant to s.87(1) and (2) of the CLRA 2002, failure to apply in time to the LVT results in the deemed withdrawal of the claim notice at the end of the two month period.

It is not clear whether at any hearing before the LVT under s.84, the landlord (or other giver of the counter-notice) is limited to arguing the point raised in the counter-notice. In *Dawlin RTM Ltd v Oakhill Park Estates* (LVT, 21/9/05, unreported) the LVT held that the landlord was limited to those points.

Suspension of the date of acquisition of the RTM

32–002 The most significant consequence of service of a counter-notice denying RTM is that the RTM company does not acquire the RTM on the date specified in the claim notices. Section 84(5) provides that the RTM company does not acquire the RTM until either:

(a) final disposal of the LVT application; or

(b) all persons who gave a counter-notice agree that the RTM company is entitled to the RTM.

The effect of s.84(5)(b) is evidently intended to be that if the parties reach agreement, there is no need to appear before the LVT to obtain a formal order disposing of the LVT application before the RTM company may acquire the RTM. However, the drafting is imperfect in that it is not clear on what date the RTM is acquired in such circumstances—and it is entirely possible that the concession or agreement will be made after the date given in the claim notice has passed. For that reason, the RTM company (and indeed the landlord) may wish to proceed to an unopposed final hearing or determination on paper in order for the LVT decision to set the date the RTM will be acquired. This procedure was adopted in *BCL (RTM) Company Ltd v Barrington Developments Ltd* (LVT 23/6/04, LEASE No.4).

If on an application under s.84(3) it is finally determined that the RTM company was not entitled to acquire the right to manage the premises, the claim notice ceases to have effect.

"Final determination"

32–003 A determination becomes final:

- if not appealed against, at the end of the period for bringing an appeal; or
- if appealed against, at the time when the appeal (or any further appeal) is disposed of (s.84(7)).

An appeal is disposed of:

- if it is determined and the period for bringing any further appeal has ended; or
- if it is abandoned or otherwise ceases to have effect.

Appeal lies to the Lands Tribunal, but only with permission of the LVT or the Lands Tribunal, consequently:

- An application for permission must be made within 21 days of the date the LVT decision was sent out (para.20(a) of the Procedure Regulations).

- If permission to appeal is not sought, the LVT determination will become final 21 days after it is sent out.
- If permission is sought and refused, application for permission may be made to the Lands Tribunal itself within 28 days of the refusal by the LVT (r.5C(2) of the Lands Tribunal Rules 1996).
- Where permission to appeal is sought from the LVT and refused, there will be no final disposal until the further 28 day period for applying to the Lands Tribunal has elapsed.
- If permission is sought from the Lands Tribunal and permission is refused, final disposal occurs when the Lands Tribunal so decides.
- If permission to appeal is granted by the LVT, notice of appeal must be filed at the Lands Tribunal within 28 days (r.6(1)(a) of the Lands Tribunal Rules 1996). Failure to comply will result in final disposal on the expiration of that 28 day period.
- If permission is sought from the Lands Tribunal and permission is granted, then (unless notice is given under r.5F(2)), final disposal occurs when the Lands Tribunal disposes of the appeal *and* a further 28 days has elapsed, being the period during which an appeal to the Court of Appeal on a point of law might be made (see the Practice Direction to CPR 52, para.21.9).

Form and content of application to the LVT

32–004 There is presently no form produced by the LVT for applications under s.84 of the CLRA 2002.

Paragraph 4 of Sch.2 to the Leasehold Valuation Tribunals (Procedure) (England) Regulations 2003, and their Welsh equivalent, requires various particulars to be given: see generally as to LVT procedure, Chapter 22.

Withdrawal of the claim notice

32–005 A claim notice may be withdrawn by the RTM company at any time before it actually acquires the RTM. The procedure is to give a "notice of withdrawal" to the persons specified in s.86(2)—essentially those persons on whom the claim notice had to be served, with the exception of the court or LVT which appointed a Manager. This may be a drafting oversight but will be of no importance in practice.

There is no saving provision where there is a failure to serve one of the parties to be served. Because the section provides that the claim is withdrawn by giving the notice of withdrawal (as opposed to providing that the RTM company may unilaterally withdraw the claim, and give notice of its decision to the relevant parties), it follows that failure to serve the notice of withdrawal on one of the parties to be served means that the notice of withdrawal is ineffective. In theory at least, the situation could arise where some interested parties (perhaps some of the lessees who wanted the RTM company to proceed) claim that the RTM company has acquired the RTM by reason of failure validly to serve notice of withdrawal.

Deemed withdrawal

32–006 There are a number of situations where the claim notice is deemed withdrawn:

- where a counter-notice is served denying the RTM but the RTM company fails to apply to the LVT in time;
- where the LVT application is withdrawn;
- where the LVT finds that the RTM company was not entitled to acquire the RTM.

A further list of situations is given in s.87(4), namely:

- where the RTM company is wound up or placed into administration;
- where administrative receivers or managers of property of the RTM company are appointed;
- if a corporate voluntary arrangement is approved;
- if the RTM company is struck off the register of companies under s.652 (failure to make statutory returns to Companies House) or s.652A (voluntary striking off) of the Companies Act.

Given that RTM companies will generally be incorporated not long before giving the claim notice, deemed withdrawal under s.87(4) will be a rare event.

Costs of the claim to acquire RTM

32–007 The provisions about costs are split between ss.88 and 89:

- Section 88(1) deals with the issue in general terms and provides that a RTM company is liable for "reasonable costs" incurred by various other parties, who are those persons on whom the claim notice must be served under s.79(6), i.e. landlords, third parties to leases and Managers;

- Section 89 provides for costs on withdrawal of the claim notice or where it otherwise ceases to have effect.

Costs of proceedings in the LVT

32–008 The RTM company is only liable for costs which such person incurs in respect of proceedings in the LVT if an application to acquire RTM is dismissed (s.88(3)). However, there is no express power given to the LVT to refuse to award costs against the RTM company in such circumstances.

It is unclear how s.88(3) interacts with the LVT's general power to order reimbursement of fees by one party to another (up to £500) under para.9(2) of Sch.12 to CLRA 2002 and to award limited costs (up to £500) under para.10 of Sch.12. Presumably the LVT can make an award of costs under its general powers in favour of the RTM company where the validity of the claim notice is unsuccessfully disputed. Nevertheless, there is an imbalance in that if the landlord successfully disputes the validity of the notice, he receives all his reasonable costs at the LVT, but if he is unsuccessful, he does not have to pay the RTM company all its reasonable costs of the LVT application, the LVT's general powers being limited.

"Reasonable costs"

32–009 Section 88(2) attempts to limit "reasonable costs". Any costs incurred in respect of professional services are to be regarded as reasonable only if and to the extent that costs in respect of such services might reasonably be expected to have been incurred by such person if the circumstances had been such that he was personally liable for all such costs.

The LVT has jurisdiction to determine any dispute as to costs in default of agreement.

- It is considered that the LVT will probably take the view that the successful respondent to a RTM application ought not usually be left out of pocket;
- The "reasonableness" requirement does not for example lead to the conclusion that the party should use the cheapest possible solicitors;

- "Reasonableness" is neither an indemnity basis, nor the less generous "standard basis" for assessment in court—it is a free standing test;
- See on the equivalent provisions under the LRHUDA 1993, *Daejan Investments Ltd v Parkside 78 Ltd* (5/5/04, LVT unreported, LEASE No.652) and *Jacobs v City & Country Properties (Midlands) Ltd* (30/9/04, LVT unreported, LEASE No.713).

Section 89 contains supplemental provisions applicable where the claim notice is withdrawn or deemed withdrawn.

Chapter 33

The Right to Manage—Acquisition, Exercise and Cessation of RTM

Acquisition and exercise of the RTM—overview

33–001 Sections 95–103 of the CLRA 2002 are intended to provide a comprehensive code for the exercise of the RTM by the RTM company, although as noted below, there is the extraordinary omission of any provision dealing with the effect on existing contracts for the management of the building.

Once the RTM is acquired:

- all management functions over the qualifying flats pass to the RTM company;
- existing management contracts are probably frustrated or perhaps discharged by breach;
- uncommitted service charges must be passed to the RTM company (s.94);
- flats held directly as part of the freehold become liable for service charge;
- the RTM company takes over part of the responsibility for the grant or withholding of approvals (consents) under the leases;
- the RTM company gains parallel rights to enforce untransferred tenant covenants;
- various statutory provisions are applied to the RTM company in modified form;
- the RTM company owes duties to the landlord.

What the RTM company does not acquire, and are retained by the landlord, are as follows:

- rights to enforce in respect of breaches of covenant arising before the acquisition date;
- management of non-qualifying flats and commercial parts;
- right to grant approvals (consents) in respect of non-qualifying units;
- the right to collect ground rent;
- the power to forfeit leases (s.96(6)).

Transfer of management responsibility

33–002 Once the RTM is acquired, "management functions" which a person who is landlord or another party under a lease of the whole or any part of the premises has under the lease are instead functions of the RTM company—s.96 (2) and (3). Section 96(4) provides that the landlord or other party may not exercise any such functions. Section 96(6) excludes management functions relating solely to units which are not qualifying flats—these remain the responsibility of the existing management party.

For example, if a building has commercial tenants, the landlord retains responsibility for management of those parts. Also excluded from the RTM company's functions is the right to forfeit leases.

By these simple provisions, the RTM company supplants the landlord (or management company) as the party entitled to, and responsible for, management of the qualifying flats.

Transfer of "management functions"

33–003 "Management functions" are defined in s.96(5) as functions with respect to:

- services;
- repairs;
- maintenance;
- improvements;
- insurance; and
- management.

It should be noted that this list by no means covers all covenants commonly found in a long lease, and s.100 makes other provisions for the enforcement of all other tenant covenants ("untransferred covenants") (see paragraph 33–021 below).

The definition of "management functions" is problematic in that it is partly circular, as "management functions" includes a function relating to "management", which is not further defined. "Management" is a concept which may mean different things to different people, and disputes may arise as to the limits of a RTM's company's rights and liabilities in this regard.

Delegation back of management responsibility

33–004 Although at first blush it is a strange provision, it appears that the RTM company may effectively delegate back to the landlord (or third party management company or Manager) the management functions transferred to it under s.96. This is because s.97(2) provides that the landlord/third party/Manager may not exercise any transferred function except by agreement with the RTM company. Unilateral delegation back by the RTM company would not appear to be possible.

Wholesale delegation back would defeat the object of acquiring RTM, so presumably specific delegation back is what the draftsman had in mind. A possible example is insurance, where a large landlord may be able to obtain better terms than a RTM company and it may be in everyone's interests to retain the current arrangement.

Presumably the agreement to delegate back can include other terms, such as that any discount which the landlord obtains is passed on to the lessees (or more likely that it is split, otherwise the landlord will have no incentive to accept the delegation back). It is less clear to what extent an agreement to delegate back can provide for a fixed term or otherwise fetter the capacity of the RTM company to terminate it.

It is also unclear whether an agreement to delegate back under s.97(3) absolves the RTM company of liability for the exercise of the relevant management function. Any RTM company contemplating entering such an agreement would be wise to extract an express indemnity from the landlord.

Nature of the RTM company's rights and liabilities

33–005 It is not absolutely clear whether the RTM company becomes liable on the covenants under the lease, or whether it is subject to an equivalent liability by statute. The reference in s.100 to all other covenants as being "untransferred" might suggest that the RTM company is liable on the other (presumably "transferred") covenants. However, the authors suggest that the liability of the RTM company is statutory rather than contractual, similar in this respect to the position of Managers appointed under Pt II of the LTA 1987 (*Maunder Taylor v Blacquiere* [2003] 1 W.L.R. 379). A number of factors point towards this conclusion:

- in particular, s.96(4) which provides that the landlord-tenant provisions of the lease cease to have effect;
- section 97(1) which refers to the RTM's obligations owed by virtue of s.96;
- the drafting of Sch.7 is of a list of statutory responsibilities;
- it would follow that the RTM company is liable only to the landlord and the tenants, not to any other party under the lease;
- it would follow that the RTM company's claims to service charge would not be subject to set off of accrued claims against the landlord for damages under the leases: see, *Maunder Taylor v Blacquiere* [2003] 1 W.L.R. 379.

Acquisition of the RTM—effect on existing contracts

33–006 It is, frankly, extraordinary that nowhere in the Act is it spelt out what happens to existing contracts relating to the management of the property once the RTM is acquired by the RTM company. The omission is very difficult to understand because this is one of the more important issues to arise under RTM and because of the great detail devoted to other less important issues, such as the provisions for "contractor notices" and "contract notices" under ss.91 and 92.

It was assumed by the Government that such a contract would not be capable of being performed because the employer loses the right to manage. Logically, this must be right. However, Lord Falconer, then the responsible Minister in the House of Lords, went on to state that it was the view of the Government that such contracts would be frustrated (Hansard, HL, 22/10/01, col.844).

Frustration?

33–007 Whether the acquisition of RTM will frustrate management contracts in all cases is seriously open to doubt. In the wartime case of *Re Shipton Anderson & Co* [1915] 3 K.B. 676, exercise of a statutory power by the Government which rendered performance of a contract illegal was held to frustrate the contract. It is clear that exercise of a statutory power by a private company will have the same result: *Baily v de Crespigny* (1869) 4 L.R. Q.B. 180, and see also *Metropolitan Water Board v Dick, Kerr & Co* [1918] A.C. 119. However, in *Walton Harvey Ltd v Walker and Homfrays Ltd* [1931] 1 Ch. 274, the result was different. There, a private Act conferred compulsory purchase powers over specific, identified properties. With knowledge of this, the defendants, who owned one of those properties, contracted with the claimant to permit an advertising hoarding. When the property was compulsorily purchased, and the hoarding removed, it was held that because the compulsory purchase was foreseen, the contract was not frustrated and the defendants were liable in damages for breach.

A definitive exposition of the position will have to await a decision of a court, but in the light of existing authority the law is probably this:

- Contracts entered into before the CLRA was passed will probably be held to have been frustrated by the acquisition of RTM;
- Contracts entered into since the CLRA was passed but when there appeared to be no real possibility that the right to acquire RTM would be exercised will probably be held to have been frustrated by the acquisition of RTM; however
- Contracts entered into where there was known to the managing party to be a real possibility that RTM might be exercised will probably be held not to have been frustrated—in the extreme case of a contract entered into after a claim notice has been served, it seems most unlikely that the contract would be frustrated. Unless the parties have provided in the contract for it to terminate when RTM is acquired, the managing party will probably be held to be in breach.

Consequences of frustration

33–008 In summary, the consequences of frustration are these:

- The contract is terminated automatically;

- Advance payments made for services not yet performed or for goods not yet supplied may be recovered (s.1(2) of the Law Reform (Frustrated Contracts) Act 1943);
- Liability for payments which have fallen due but remain unpaid is discharged save to the extent that the payee is entitled to recover so much of his expenses as is just, not exceeding the payment due (s.1(2) of the Law Reform (Frustrated Contracts) Act 1943);
- The cost of services rendered/goods delivered which exceeds any payments due can *not* be recovered;
- The parties remain liable for breaches of contract (other than to pay money) which occurred before the contract was discharged.

Consequences of a finding that a contract is breached on acquisition of RTM

If a court finds that the acquisition of RTM did not frustrate a management contract, then the impossibility of performance following the acquisition of RTM would amount to a breach of contract by the managing party unless the contract provides this eventuality. If the contract does provide for the eventuality, then it is a matter of working through the contractual provision. If not, the consequences are likely to be as follows:

- The contract will be discharged by breach;
- The contractor party will be discharged from his obligations under the contract;
- The managing party will be liable in damages for loss arising from the non-performance of the contract.

Effect on employees

33–009 It is also entirely unclear how the Transfer of Undertakings (Protection of Employment) Regulations 1981 (TUPE) regime will apply to employees of landlords or management companies stripped of their management function. The difficulties may be acute where there are staff, such as resident caretakers, employed to work solely at the premises of which RTM is being acquired. Landlords and RTM companies should take specialist advice in such circumstances.

Effect on contracts relating to transferred management functions

33–010 Notwithstanding the difficulties noted above, it seems clear that contracts made with the landlord or other former managing party relating to transferred management functions become incapable of performance unless expressly adopted by the RTM company.

Such adoption would probably be construed as a novation and would discharge the landlord or other managing party from any further obligations under it.

Effect on a 1987 Act Manager

33–011 The Manager's appointment is not terminated by the exercise of the RTM but s.97(2)(c) provides that the Manager may no longer exercise any functions which have become functions of the RTM company. In many cases, there will be nothing left for the Manager to do and he may seek to terminate his appointment. However, there will be cases where the Manager will still retain some functions. For example where the Manager order covered more than one building and only one of the buildings has become subject to RTM. In all cases, the order appointing the Manager, from which his functions are derived, will require amendment.

Service charges for costs incurred prior to acquisition of RTM

33–012 The landlord remains entitled to collect service charges in respect of costs incurred prior to the acquisition date (s.97(5)).

Payment over to the RTM company of uncommitted service charges

33–013 Section 94(1) provides that any landlord, third party to leases or Manager must pay to the RTM company a sum equal to the amount of any "accrued uncommitted service charges" held by him on the acquisition date. The inclusion of third parties to leases is to cover management companies under leases who may be responsible for the collection and disposition of service change funds. As the obligation to pay over service charge only arises at the acquisition date, the RTM company must therefore "live with" expenditure incurred between the date of the claim notice and the acquisition date.

"Accrued uncommitted service charges" are defined by s.94(2). This is a two part definition. First, it in effect defines "accrued service charges" as the aggregate of:

(a) service charge payments made; and

(b) investments representing those sums including any income which has accrued on them (most obviously interest but potentially other returns on investment).

Section 94(2) then provides for the deductions to be made to arrive at the "accrued uncommitted service charge". The permitted deductions are such sums as are required to meet the "costs incurred" before the acquisition date in connection with the matters for which the service charges were payable.

The accrued service charges therefore include reserve funds, sinking funds and other contributions otherwise carried over from previous years.

"Costs incurred" is not defined but reference should be made to s.97(5). Presumably, "costs incurred" must have a limited meaning because any pending contract will probably be frustrated or discharged by breach, so the service charge will not be needed to pay for it.

Payment must be made on the acquisition date or as soon as reasonably practicable after that (s.94(4)). In case of dispute as to the amount of payment to be made, either the payee or the RTM company can make application to the LVT to determine the amount of the payment which must be made (s.94(3)). It is implicit that the tribunal will be able to adjudicate on any matter which gives rise to the dispute, not limited to matters of accounting. For example, the tribunal might have to decide whether or not a cost allegedly incurred was properly included within the service charge.

Future service charge contributions

33–014 The RTM company is entitled to collect service charge contributions amounting to 100 per cent of the applicable service charge expenditure.

Qualifying tenants

33–015 The lessees of the qualifying flats remain obliged to pay the share of service charge due under their leases, but they pay them to the RTM company. Variation of those lease terms can not be effected by RTM—an application to the LVT under Pt IV of the LTA 1987 would need to be made if the service charge clauses in the qualifying leases are unsatisfactory.

Consequently, if the landlord has set up the service charge contributions so that the long lessees of flats in a block pay 100 per cent of the service charge but the commercial units pay nothing, no service charge will be due from those units as "excluded units".

Other units—"excluded units"

33–016 Where there are other units within the premises (defined as "excluded units" in s.103), such as non-qualifying flats, or commercial units, and the amount due from the qualifying tenants is less than 100 per cent of the total service charge, provision is made for payment of a share of the service charge relating to those excluded units. These provisions are effective whether or not the leases (if any) of those units make any service charge provision and regardless of the terms of any service charge clauses in such leases.

The person liable to pay in respect of each excluded unit is "the appropriate person" under s.103(5):

- If there is no lease of the excluded unit, the freeholder is liable;
- If there is a lease (of any length or character), the landlord under a lease of the unit is liable;
- Where there is more than one lease of an excluded unit, the appropriate landlord is the landlord under the most inferior lease (usually the occupational lease).

Where there is more than one excluded unit, the service charge payable by the excluded units is apportioned under s.103(4) in proportion to their respective net internal areas. This applies regardless of lease terms. It also applies regardless of the differences between residential flats and commercial units, and ignores external area. There appears to be considerable potential for unfairness in practice.

Approvals under the lease

33–017 As noted earlier, the scheme of the Act relating to the grant or withholding of approvals under the leases is complex and in effect shares the function between the landlord(s) and the RTM company.

Although subject to considerable fetters, ss.98 and 99 do provide that the consideration and grant of approvals under the leases of qualifying tenants become functions of the RTM company. This includes any "approval" which may be required, most obviously consent to assign, to sub-let or to alter the premises but also such approvals as may be required by virtue of a restriction registered against title at HM Land Registry.

Consequently:

- application for the approval must be made to the RTM company;
- the RTM company makes the initial decision whether or not to grant the approval;
- statutory requirements in relation to approvals apply to the RTM company, for example the duties under the Landlord and Tenant Act 1988 not unreasonably to withhold consent to assign (para.13 of Sch.7).

Notice to landlords

33–018 However, the RTM company must not grant an approval without having under s.98(4) given to each landlord under the relevant lease notice of the application for consent. The length of notice is either 14 days or 30 days:

- in the case of an approval relating to assignment, underletting, charging, parting with possession, the making of structural alterations or improvements or alterations of use, 30 days' notice; or
- in any other case, 14 days' notice.

There is no requirement to refer refusals of consent, so the RTM company is entitled to refuse consent even though the landlord may wish to grant it (a situation which could arise where the relevant lessee and the relevant landlord are associated companies). In practice, for the reason set out in the next paragraph, the RTM company may have to give notice of all applications, but the giving of such notice will not prevent the RTM company deciding to refuse.

The statutory time limits in s.98(4) may require some reconsideration of the case law as to the length of time which is reasonable to consider an application for an approval—for example, in *Footwear v Amplight Properties* (1999) 77 P.&C.R. 418 it was held that one month was long enough to consider consent to assign. It is to be anticipated that the courts will take the view that the RTM company should give the s.98(4) notice to the landlord immediately upon receipt of the tenant's application (i.e. before the RTM company has decided what to do). Even a short delay in doing so may be held unreasonable, and consequently the RTM company's withholding of consent during the 30 day period may be held unreasonable.

Landlord's objection to approval

33–019 The landlord is entitled to object to the grant of an approval only if it would be entitled to do so if there were no RTM (s.99(2)). An objection also includes seeking to impose conditions beyond those imposed by the RTM company, and again any such conditions may only be imposed if it would be entitled to do so if there were no RTM (s.99(3)).

The landlord must give notice of the objection both to the RTM company and the applicant tenant (s.99(4)). Where the application is from a sub-tenant and the landlord is a superior landlord, the landlord must also give notice to the applicant sub-tenant. There is no requirement to give notice to a prospective assignee or sub-tenant.

If the landlord objects, the RTM company can not grant the approval without the landlord's written consent or a favourable LVT determination (s.99(1)).

Determination by the LVT

33–020 Application for such determination can be made by the RTM company, the landlord, or the applicant tenant or sub-tenant, but not a prospective assignee or sub-tenant.

Conferring this jurisdiction on the LVT may create something of a problem. The LVT is presently very slow, certainly by comparison with the potential for obtaining a quick summary judgment from the court under the 1988 Act. The LVT also can not award damages, so if a tenant is seriously prejudiced by a landlord's refusal to assign, he first has to obtain an LVT determination, then sue for any damages by fresh proceedings before a court.

Enforcement of "untransferred" tenant covenants

33–021 Enforcement of "untransferred tenant covenants" is provided for by s.100(1):

- "untransferred" means a covenant which is not enforceable by a RTM company under any section of the Act other than s.100;

- "tenant covenant" means a covenant falling to be complied with by a tenant under the lease (s.100(4)).

Such untransferred tenant covenants remain enforceable by the person(s) otherwise entitled to enforce, but in addition are enforceable by the RTM company (s.100(2)). The RTM company is entitled to use any method of enforcement open to the person otherwise entitled to enforce, except forfeiture (s.100(3)). This does not mean that the result will be the same—for example, the RTM company may not have suffered any loss from a breach, and may have no substantial damages claim, but the landlord may have suffered loss.

Section 100(5) additionally confers on the RTM company any "power under a lease" to enter any part of the premises to determine whether a tenant is complying with any untransferred tenant covenant. Although not entirely clear, "power under the lease" probably extends to implied rights and to any rights at common law which arise by reason of the landlord/tenant relationship under the lease.

By analogy with the decision in *Maunder Taylor v Blacquiere*, and indeed the limits on set off generally, it is suggested that tenants will not be able to set off damages claims against the landlord against sums claimed by the RTM company.

Statutory obligations of the RTM company

33–022 By s.102 of and Sch.7 to the Act, the RTM company is written into a long list of statutory provisions. The effect is in some case to impose on the RTM company potential duties and liabilities under statutory provisions, in other cases to extend to the RTM company duties owned to tenants, and in yet further cases to disapply provisions. The paragraph numbers below relate to Sch.7:

1. Section 19 of the Landlord and Tenant Act 1927 (c.36) (provisions as to consents to assign extended to RTM companies).
2. Section 4 of the Defective Premises Act 1972 (c.35) (duties to occupiers extended to RTM companies).
3. Section 11 of the Landlord and Tenant Act 1985 (c.70) (repairing obligations in short leases extended to RTM companies).
4. Sections 18–30 of the Landlord and Tenant Act 1985 (c.70) (save s.26) (control over service charges extended to RTM companies).
5. Section 30A and Schedule to the Landlord and Tenant Act 1985 (c.70) (provision of information about insurance applies to RTM companies, duty owed to landlord as well as tenants).

6. Section 30B of the Landlord and Tenant Act 1985 (c.70) (consultation with recognised tenants' associations extended to RTM companies).
7. Section 5 of the Landlord and Tenant Act 1987 (any notice informing the tenants of their right of pre-emption on sale of the reversion must also be served on the RTM company);
8. Part 2 of the Landlord and Tenant Act 1987 (the grounds for appointment of a Manager are extended to defaults by the RTM company, and in such a case the landlord as well as the tenants may apply).
9. Part 3 of the Landlord and Tenant Act 1987 (compulsory acquisition of landlord's interest—disapplied where there is RTM).
10. Sections 35, 36, 38 and 39 of the Landlord and Tenant Act 1987 (the RTM company is deemed to be a party to a lease for the purposes of applications to vary lease terms under those sections of the LTA 1987).
11. Sections 42–42B of the Landlord and Tenant Act 1987 (requirement to hold service on trust extended to RTM companies).
12. Sections 46–48 of the Landlord and Tenant Act 1987 (addresses for service to be provided by RTM company).
13. Landlord and Tenant Act 1988 (duties to consider applications for licence to assign or sub-let extended to RTM companies).
14. Chapter 5 of the LRHUDA 1993 (management audits available to landlords and tenants of premises where RTM acquired).
15. Section 84 of the Housing Act 1996 (c.52) (right of recognised tenants association to appoint a surveyor extended to premises where RTM acquired).
16. Schedule 11 to the CLRA 2002 (control over administration charges extended to RTM companies).

Schedule 7 is set out in full at Appendix A and reference must be made to the detailed provisions of the Schedule for their full terms and effect.

Monitoring and reporting performance of tenant covenants

33–023 Section 101(2) obliges the RTM company to keep under review whether tenant covenants of leases of the whole or any part of the premises are being complied with, and report to any person who is landlord under such a lease any failure to comply with any tenant covenant of the lease.

It seems clear from the wording of s.101(1) that this obligation applies to any lease of any part of the premises, that is to say it is not limited to the qualifying leases or to the residential parts, nor is the obligation limited to tenant covenants relating to the transferred management functions under s.96. However, the RTM company may agree with the landlord that it need not report particular types of failure (s.101(4)(c)) and it may be appropriate to agree that the RTM company need not be concerned with those parts of the premises over which the landlord retains management.

There is no amplification of what the RTM company is expected to do by way of "review". It is suggested that the RTM company will be expected to be pro-active in monitoring compliance by the lessees, and to act as one would expect a professional managing agent to act. However, less may be expected in respect of untransferred tenant covenants.

A report must be made within three months of any breach of covenant coming to the attention of the RTM company (s.101(3)). "Report" is not defined—it is suggested that no particular formality is required.

In addition to providing for the possibility of excluding by agreement certain failures from the reporting requirement, s.101(4) excludes from the reporting requirement cases where the failure has been remedied or reasonable compensation has been paid for the failure. It is unclear who is to decide whether a breach has been remedied or whether compensation is reasonable. Because of this lack of clarity, and because making a report is not onerous, RTM companies may be well advised simply to report all failures whether or not they appear to have been remedied or compensation paid.

Section 101 does not provide for the consequences of any failure to review or report. Failures to comply could be used by a landlord as grounds for applying to appoint a Manager under Pt 2 of the LTA 1987 to replace the RTM company. If the failure to review or report was causative of loss, presumably the landlord could mount a damages claim for breach of statutory duty.

Cessation of RTM

33–024 Once RTM is acquired, it can in principle continue indefinitely. Nevertheless, there are a number of situations in which, after a RTM company has acquired the right to manage, RTM will cease to be exercisable by it:

- By agreement with every landlord under a lease within the premises (s.105(2));
- On the insolvency of the RTM company (including winding up whether compulsory or voluntary, administration, receivership, debenture holder takes possession, or the RTM company proposes a corporate voluntary arrangement) (s.105(3)(a)–(c));
- If the RTM company is struck off the register of companies (s.105(3)(d));
- If a Manager is appointed under Pt 2 of the LTA 1987 (s.105(4));
- If the RTM company ceases to be a RTM company in respect of the premises (s.105(5)).

Insolvency may be a particular threat to RTM companies as, by their nature, they will tend to be undercapitalised, will have no property which is suitable for security against loans and will often be taking over properties which require significant expenditure. It is obvious that a RTM company in liquidation should lose RTM. However, it may be thought unfortunate that RTM is also lost automatically if the RTM company goes into administration, or proposes a corporate voluntary arrangement, the purpose of which would be the rescue of the RTM company as a going concern. The loss of RTM in such circumstances renders any attempt at rescue pointless.

Turning to s.105(5), it should be noted that the RTM company does not cease to be a RTM company simply because lessees cease to be members so that the number of qualifying lessee members falls below the initial qualifying threshold for RTM. It is unclear whether a RTM company would cease to be so if an attempt were made to alter the memorandum or articles of association away from the form prescribed by the RTM Companies (Memorandum and Articles of Association) (England) Regulations 2003, as it is unclear whether such attempt would be effective given the mandatory wording of reg.2(2). One example of a situation where the RTM company ceases to be such a company is that provided for in s.73(5), where the RTM company acquires the freehold.

Effect of cessation of RTM

33–025 There is nothing in the Act providing for the effect of the RTM ceasing to be exercisable under s.105. If the cessation follows the appointment of a Manager, the LVT will no doubt provide for the handover of management functions by express terms of the order appointing the Manager.

In the other situations provided for, it appears that the management obligations will simply revert to the party or parties responsible under the leasehold structure, save in the unlikely event that all parties to all leases agreed otherwise. If the structure is no longer complete—for example, if a third party management company has ceased to exist since RTM was acquired—there will be real difficulties. If no solution can be found by agreement, it will probably be appropriate to apply to the LVT to appoint a Manager under Pt 2 of the LTA 1987 because, as discussed in Chapter 27, the order appointing a Manager can cure any deficiencies in the leasehold structure. Alternatively, a new RTM company could be formed and application made to the LVT to disapply para.5 of Sch.6, which otherwise excludes any claim to RTM within four years after cessation of RTM.

This leaves the question of the status of contracts relating to the management of the premises which have been entered into by the RTM company. Presumably such contracts are in the same position as contracts with the landlord when RTM is acquired (see paragraphs 33–006 to 33–008 above). They may well be frustrated. Alternatively, they may be discharged by breach (particularly if a manager is appointed, as this will involve fault by the RTM company and frustration can not be "self-induced"). If the contracts were held to have been breached by the RTM company, claims to damages may be mounted. Insolvency will follow if the RTM company has not already been liquidated. Such damages claims could cause real difficulties, despite the limited liability of members of RTM companies, because the directors might be vulnerable to claims for wrongful trading.

One further effect of the cessation of RTM is that no fresh claim to RTM can be made for a period of four years (para.5 of Sch.6). The LVT has power to disapply this restriction if it is unreasonable for the restriction to apply. It will probably only be unreasonable for the restriction to apply if either the loss of RTM was not the fault of the RTM company, or perhaps where the new RTM company is to be run by a different set of lessees. This restriction also does not apply if RTM ceases on acquisition of the freehold by the RTM company.

Enforcement of obligations

33–026 Enforcement of obligations imposed under the RTM provisions of the CLRA 2002 (and the various Regulations made under those provisions) is a matter for the county court under s.107, which empowers the county court to make an order requiring the default to be made good within a specified period. This provision is identical to s.92 of the LRHUDA 1993.

Before application for an order under s.107 can be made, a default notice must have been given to the defaulting party under s.107(2) requiring him to remedy the default. A minimum of 14 days must have elapsed since the default notice was given before application to the court can be made.

There is no prescribed form of default notice, but it must be in writing, should be addressed to the defaulting party, should identify the premises, must identify the default, and must expressly demand remedy. It is good practice to recite the fact that the notice is a default notice under s.107(2). It is not necessary to specify any particular period by which remedy must be made, although it may be helpful to recite the fact that failure to comply within 14 days will cause application to the court to be made.

There is no power to waive the need for a default notice nor to waive any defect in such a notice.

Application for an order may be made by "any person interested". Plainly this will include, where applicable, the RTM company, landlords, third parties to leases and Managers. It probably also includes qualifying tenants who are not participating in RTM. It is not clear whether it includes qualifying lessees who are members of the RTM company—it may be argued that the RTM company should represent their interests. It is also not clear whether a recognised tenants association would be entitled to apply in its own right.

If a person failed to comply with such an order of the court, then a penal notice could be endorsed on the order and continued failure to comply would constitute a contempt of court.

The county court also retains its power to award costs, potentially on an indemnity basis, against a defaulting party.

Appendices

Contents

Appendix A

Statutes and Statutory Instruments

COMMON LAW PROCEDURE ACT 1852 CHAPTER 76

Ejectment

s 210 Proceedings in ejectment by landlord for nonpayment of rent.

A1–001 In all cases between landlord and tenant, as often as it shall happen that one half year's rent shall be in arrear, and the landlord or lessor, to whom the same is due, hath right by law to re-enter for the nonpayment thereof, such landlord or lessor shall and may, without any formal demand or re-entry, serve a writ in ejectment for the recovery of the demised premises, [. . .][1], which service [. . .][2] shall stand in the place and stead of a demand and re-entry; and in case of judgment against the defendant for nonappearance, if it shall be made appear to the court where the said action is depending, by affidavit, or be proved upon the trial in case the defendant appears, that half a year's rent was due before the said writ was served, and that no sufficient distress was to be found on the demised premises, countervailing the arrears then due, and that the lessor had power to re-enter, then and in every such case the lessor shall recover judgment and execution, in the same manner as if the rent in arrear had been legally demanded, and a re-entry made; and in case the lessee or his assignee, or other person claiming or deriving under the said lease, shall permit and suffer judgment to be had and recovered on such trial in ejectment, and execution to be executed thereon, without paying the rent and arrears, together with full costs, and without proceeding for relief in equity within six months after such execution executed, then and in such case the said lessee, his assignee, and all other persons claiming and deriving under the said lease, shall be barred and foreclosed from all relief or remedy in law or equity, other than by bringing error for reversal of such judgment, in case the same shall be erroneous; and the said landlord or lessor shall from thenceforth hold the said demised premises discharged from such lease; [. . .][3], provided that nothing herein contained shall extend to bar the right of any mortgagee of such lease, or any part thereof, who shall not be in possession, so as such mortgagee shall and do, within six months after such judgment obtained and execution executed pay all rent in arrear, and all costs and damages sustained by such lessor or person entitled to the remainder or reversion as aforesaid, and perform all the covenants and agreements which, on the part and behalf of the first lessee, are and ought to be performed.

[1] Words repealed by Statute Law Revision Act 1892 (c.19)
[2] Words repealed by Statute Law Revision Act 1892 (c.19)
[3] Words repealed by Statute Law Revision Act 1892 (c.19)

LAW OF PROPERTY ACT 1925 CHAPTER 20

PART V LEASES AND TENANCIES

s 141 Rent and benefit of lessee's covenants to run with the reversion.

(1) Rent reserved by a lease, and the benefit of every covenant or provision therein contained, having reference to the subject-matter thereof, and on the lessee's part to be observed or performed, and every condition of re-entry and other condition therein contained, shall be annexed and incident to and shall go with the reversionary estate in the land, or in any part thereof, immediately expectant on the term granted by the lease, notwithstanding severance of that reversionary estate, and without prejudice to any liability affecting a covenantor or his estate. **A2–001**

(2) Any such rent, covenant or provision shall be capable of being recovered, received, enforced, and taken advantage of, by the person from time to time entitled, subject to the term, to the income of the whole or any part, as the case may require, of the land leased.

(3) Where that person becomes entitled by conveyance or otherwise, such rent, covenant or provision may be recovered, received, enforced or taken advantage of by him notwithstanding that he becomes so entitled after the condition of re-entry or forfeiture has become enforceable, but this subsection does not render enforceable any condition of re-entry or other condition waived or released before such person becomes entitled as aforesaid.

(4) This section applies to leases made before or after the commencement of this Act, but does not affect the operation of—

(a) any severance of the reversionary estate; or

(b) any acquisition by conveyance or otherwise of the right to receive or enforce any rent covenant or provision;

effected before the commencement of this Act.

s 146 Restrictions on and relief against forfeiture of leases and underleases.

(1) A right of re-entry of forfeiture under any proviso or stipulation in a lease for a breach of any covenant or condition in the lease shall not be enforceable, by action or otherwise, unless and until the lessor serves on the lessee a notice— **A2–002**

(a) specifying the particular breach complained of; and

(b) if the breach is capable of remedy, requiring the lessee to remedy the breach; and

(c) in any case, requiring the lessee to make compensation in money for the breach;

and the lessee fails, within a reasonable time thereafter, to remedy the breach, if it is capable of remedy, and to make reasonable compensation in money, to the satisfaction of the lessor, for the breach.

(2) Where a lessor is proceeding, by action or otherwise, to enforce such a right of re-entry or forfeiture, the lessee may, in this lessor's action, if any, or in any action brought by himself, apply to the court for relief; and the court may grant or refuse relief, as the court, having regard to the proceedings and conduct of the parties under the foregoing provisions of this section, and to all the other circumstances, thinks fit; and in case of relief may grant it on such terms, if any, as to costs, expenses, damages, compensation, penalty, or otherwise, including the granting of an injunction to restrain any like breach in the future, as the court, in the circumstances of each case, thinks fit.

(3) A lessor shall be entitled to recover as a debt due to him from a lessee, and in addition to damages (if any), all reasonable costs and expenses properly incurred by the lessor in the employment of a solicitor and surveyor or valuer, or otherwise, in reference to any breach giving rise to a right of re-entry or forfeiture which, at the request of the lessee, is waived by the lessor, or from which the lessee is relieved, under the provisions of this Act.

(4) Where a lessor is proceeding by action or otherwise to enforce a right of re-entry or forfeiture under any covenant, proviso, or stipulation in a lease, or for non-payment of rent, the court may, on application by any person claiming as under-lessee any estate or interest in the property comprised in the lease or any part thereof, either in the lessor's action (if any) or in any action brought by such person for that purpose, make an order vesting, for the whole term of the lease or any less term, the property comprised in the lease or any part thereof in any person entitled as under-lessee to any estate or interest in such property upon such conditions as to execution of any deed or other document, payment of rent, costs, expenses, damages, compensation, giving security, or otherwise, as the court in the circumstances of each case may think fit, but in no case shall any such under-lessee be entitled to require a lease to be granted to him for any longer term than he had under his original sub-lease.

(5) For the purposes of this section—

(a) "Lease" includes an original or derivative under-lease; also an agreement for a lease where the lessee has become entitled to have his lease granted; also a grant at a fee farm rent, or securing a rent by condition;

(b) "Lessee" includes an original or derivative under-lessee, and the persons deriving title under a lessee; also a grantee under any such grant as aforesaid and the persons deriving title under him;

(c) "Lessor" includes an original or derivative under-lessor, and the persons deriving title under a lessor; also a person making such grant as aforesaid and the persons deriving title under him;

(d) "Under-lease" includes an agreement for an under-lease where the under-lessee has become entitled to have his under-lease granted;

(e) "Under-lessee" includes any person deriving title under an under-lessee.

(6) This section applies although the proviso or stipulation under which the right of re-entry or forfeiture accrues is inserted in the lease in pursuance of the directions of any Act of Parliament.

(7) For the purposes of this section a lease limited to continue as long only as the lessee abstains from committing a breach of covenant shall be and take effect as a lease to continue for any longer term for which it could subsist, but determinable by a proviso for re-entry on such a breach.

(8) This section does not extend—

(i) To a covenant or condition against assigning, underletting, parting with the possession, or disposing of the land leased where the breach occurred before the commencement of this Act; or

(ii) In the case of a mining lease, to a covenant or condition for allowing the lessor to have access to or inspect books, accounts, records, weighing machines or other things, or to enter or inspect the mine or the workings thereof.

(9) This section does not apply to a condition for forfeiture on the bankruptcy of the lessee or on taking in execution of the lessee's interest if contained in a lease of—

(a) Agricultural or pastoral land;

(b) Mines or minerals;

(c) A house used or intended to be used as a public-house or beershop;

(d) A house let as a dwelling-house, with the use of any furniture, books, works of art, or other chattels not being in the nature of fixtures;

(e) Any property with respect to which the personal qualifications of the tenant are of importance for the preservation of the value or character of the property, or on the ground of neighbourhood to the lessor, or to any person holding under him.

(10) Where a condition of forfeiture on the bankruptcy of the lessee or on taking in execution of the lessee's interest is contained in any lease, other than a lease of any of the classes mentioned in the last sub-section, then—

(a) If the lessee's interest is sold within one year from the bankruptcy or taking in execution, this section applies to the forfeiture condition aforesaid;

(b) If the lessee's interest is not sold before the expiration of that year, this section only applies to the forfeiture condition aforesaid during the first year from the date of the bankruptcy or taking in execution.

(11) This section does not, save as otherwise mentioned, affect the law relating to re-entry or forfeiture or relief in case of non-payment of rent.

(12) This section has effect notwithstanding any stipulation to the contrary.

(13) The county court has jurisdiction under this section—

[. . .][1]

[1] subject to savings specified in art12 by SI 1991/724 (High Court and County Courts Jurisdiction Order). Sch.1 (1) Para.1

PROTECTION FROM EVICTION ACT 1977 CHAPTER 43

PART I UNLAWFUL EVICTION AND HARASSMENT

s 1 Unlawful eviction and harassment of occupier.

A3–001

(1) In this section "residential occupier", in relation to any premises, means a person occupying the premises as a residence, whether under a contract or by virtue of any enactment or rule of law giving him the right to remain in occupation or restricting the right of any other person to recover possession of the premises.

(2) If any person unlawfully deprives the residential occupier of any premises of his occupation of the premises or any part thereof, or attempts to do so, he shall be guilty of an offence unless he proves that he believed, and had reasonable cause to believe, that the residential occupier had ceased to reside in the premises.

(3) If any person with intent to cause the residential occupier of any premises—

(a) to give up the occupation of the premises or any part thereof; or

(b) to refrain from exercising any right or pursuing any remedy in respect of the premises or part thereof;

does acts [likely][1] to interfere with the peace or comfort of the residential occupier or members of his household, or persistently withdraws or withholds services reasonably required for the occupation of the premises as a residence, he shall be guilty of an offence.

[(3A) Subject to subsection (3B) below, the landlord of a residential occupier or an agent of the landlord shall be guilty of an offence if—

(a) he does acts likely to interfere with the peace or comfort of the residential occupier or members of his household, or

(b) he persistently withdraws or withholds services reasonably required for the occupation of the premises in question as a residence,

and (in either case) he knows, or has reasonable cause to believe, that that conduct is likely to cause the residential occupier to give up the occupation of the whole or part of the premises or to refrain from exercising any right or pursuing any remedy in respect of the whole or part of the premises.

(3B) A person shall not be guilty of an offence under subsection (3A) above if he proves that he had reasonable grounds for doing the acts or withdrawing or withholding the services in question.

(3C) In subsection (3A) above "landlord", in relation to a residential occupier of any premises, means the person, who, but for—

(a) the residential occupier's right to remain in occupation of the premises, or

(b) a restriction on the person's right to recover possession of the premises,

would be entitled to occupation of the premises and any superior landlord under whom that person derives title].[2]

(4) A person guilty of an offence under this section shall be liable—

(a) on summary conviction, to a fine not exceeding £400 or to imprisonment for a term not exceeding 6 months or to both;

(b) on conviction on indictment, to a fine or to imprisonment for a term not exceeding 2 years or to both.

(5) Nothing in this section shall be taken to prejudice any liability or remedy to which person guilty of an offence thereunder may be subject in civil proceedings.

(6) Where an offence under this section committed by a body corporate is proved to have been committed with the consent or connivance of, or to be attributable to any neglect on the part of, any director, manager or secretary or other similar officer of the body corporate or any person who was purporting to act in any such capacity, he as well as the body corporate shall be guilty of that offence and shall be liable to be proceeded against and punished accordingly.

[1] Word substituted by Housing Act 1988 (c.50), s.29(1) (read with s.44(2)(b))
[2] s.1(3A)–(3C) inserted by Housing Act 1988 (c.50), ss.29(2), 44(2)(b)

s 2 Restriction on re-entry without due process of law.

A3–002 Where any premises are let as a dwelling on a lease which is subject to a right of re-entry or forfeiture it shall not be lawful to enforce that right otherwise than by proceedings in the court while any person is lawfully residing in the premises or part of them.

SUPREME COURT ACT 1981 CHAPTER 54

PART II JURISDICTION

CHAPTER 002 THE HIGH COURT

Powers

s 38 Relief against forfeiture for non-payment of rent.

A4–001

(1) In any action in the High Court for the forfeiture of a lease for non-payment of rent, the court shall have power to grant relief against forfeiture in a summary manner, and may do so subject to the same terms and conditions as to the payment of rent, costs or otherwise as could have been imposed by it in such an action immediately before the commencement of this Act.

(2) Where the lessee or a person deriving title under him is granted relief under this section, he shall hold the demised premises in accordance with the terms of the lease without the necessity for a new lease.

COUNTY COURTS ACT 1984 CHAPTER 28

PART IX MISCELLANEOUS AND GENERAL

Forfeiture for non-payment of rent

s 138 Provisions as to forfeiture for non-payment of rent.

A5–001 (1) This section has effect where a lessor is proceeding by action in a county court (being an action in which the county court has jurisdiction) to enforce against a lessee a right of re-entry or forfeiture in respect of any land for non-payment of rent.

(2) If the lessee pays into court [or to the lessor][1] not less than 5 clear days before the return day all the rent in arrear and the costs of the action, the action shall cease, and the lessee shall hold the land according to the lease without any new lease.

(3) If—

(a) the action does not cease under subsection (2); and

(b) the court at the trial is satisfied that the lessor is entitled to enforce the right of re-entry or forfeiture,

the court shall order possession of the land to be given to the lessor at the expiration of such period, not being less than 4 weeks from the date of the order, as the court thinks fit, unless within that period the lessee pays into court [or to the lessor][2] all the rent in arrear and the costs of the action.

(4) The court may extend the period specified under subsection (3) at any time before possession of the land is recovered in pursuance of the order under that subsection.

(5) [. . .][3], if—

(a) within the period specified in the order; or

(b) within that period as extended under subsection (4),

the lessee pays into court [or to the lessor][4]—

(i) all the rent in arrear; and

(ii) the costs of the action,

he shall hold the land according to the lease without any new lease.

(6) Subsection (2) shall not apply where the lessor is proceeding in the same action to enforce a right of re-entry or forfeiture on any other ground as well as for non-payment of rent, or to enforce any other claim as well as the right of re-entry or forfeiture and the claim for arrears of rent.

(7) If the lessee does not—

(a) within the period specified in the order; or

(b) within that period as extended under subsection (4),

pay into court [or to the lessor][5]—

(i) all the rent in arrear; and

(ii) the costs of the action,

the order shall be [enforceable][6] in the prescribed manner and so long as the order remains unreversed the lessee shall[, subject to subsections (8) and (9A),][7] be barred from all relief.

(8) The extension under subsection (4) of a period fixed by a court shall not be treated as relief from which the lessee is barred by subsection (7) if he fails to pay into court [or to the lessor][8] all the rent in arrear and the costs of the action within that period.

(9) Where the court extends a period under subsection (4) at a time when—

(a) that period has expired; and

(b) a warrant has been issued for the possession of the land, the court shall suspend the warrant for the extended period; and, if, before the expiration of the extended period, the lessee pays into court [or to the lessor][9] all the rent in arrear and all the costs of the action, the court shall cancel the warrant.

[(9A) Where the lessor recovers possession of the land at any time after the making of the order under subsection (3)(whether as a result of the enforcement of the order or otherwise) the lessee may, at any time within six months from the date on which the lessor recovers possession, apply to the court for relief; and on any such application the court may, if it thinks fit, grant to the lessee such relief, subject to such terms and conditions, as it thinks fit.

(9B) Where the lessee is granted relief on an application under subsection (9A) he shall hold the land according to the lease without any new lease.

(9C) An application under subsection (9A) may be made by a person with an interest under a lease of the land derived (whether immediately or otherwise) from the lessee's interest therein in like manner as if he were the lessee; and on any such application the court may make an order which (subject to such terms and conditions as the court thinks fit) vests the land in such a person, as lessee of the lessor, for the remainder of the term of the lease under which he has any such interest as aforesaid, or for any lesser term.

In this subsection any reference to the land includes a reference to a part of the land.][10]

(10) Nothing in this section or section 139 shall be taken to affect—

(a) the power of the court to make any order which it would otherwise have power to make as respects a right of re-entry or forfeiture on any ground other than non-payment of rent; or

(b) section 146(4) of the Law of Property Act 1925 (relief against forfeiture).

[1] Words inserted by Courts and Legal Services Act 1990 (c.41), s.125(2), Sch.17 para.17
[2] Words inserted by Courts and Legal Services Act 1990 (c.41), s.125(2), Sch.17 para.17
[3] Words repealed by Administration of Justice Act 1985 (c.61), ss.55(2), 67(2), Sch.8 Pt III
[4] Words inserted by Courts and Legal Services Act 1990 (c.41), s.125(2), Sch.17 para.17
[5] Words inserted by Courts and Legal Services Act 1990 (c.41), s.125(2), Sch.17 para.17
[6] Words substituted by Administration of Justice Act 1985 (c.61), s.55(3)(a)
[7] Words inserted by Administration of Justice Act 1985 (c.61), ss.55(3)(b)
[8] Words inserted by Courts and Legal Services Act 1990 (c.41), s.125(2), Sch.17 para.17
[9] Words inserted by Courts and Legal Services Act 1990 (c.41), s.125(2), Sch.17 para.17
[10] ss.138(9A), (9B), (9C) inserted by Administration of Justice Act 1985 (c.61), ss.55(4), 69(5), Sch.9 para.13

s 139 Service of summons and re-entry.

A5–002 (1) In a case where section 138 has effect, if—

(a) one-half-year's rent is in arrear at the time of the commencement of the action; and

(b) the lessor has a right to re-enter for non-payment of that rent; and

(c) no sufficient distress is to be found on the premises countervailing the arrears then due,

the service of the summons in the action in the prescribed manner shall stand in lieu of a demand and re-entry.

(2) Where a lessor has enforced against a lessee, by re-entry without action, a right of re-entry or forfeiture as respects any land for non-payment of rent, the lessee may [. . .][1] at any time within six months from the date on which the lessor re-entered apply to the county court for relief, and on any such application the court may, if it thinks fit, grant to the lessee such relief as the High Court could have granted.

(3) Subsections (9B) and (9C) of section 138 shall have effect in relation to an application under subsection (2) of this section as they have effect in relation to an application under subsection (9A) of that section.

[1] Words repealed this effect shall not apply to: (a) family proceedings within the meaning of Part V of the Matrimonial and Family Proceedings Act 1984; (b) proceedings to which 27(1) of the County Court by SI 1991/724 (High Court and County Courts Jurisdiction Order), Sch.1 (I) para.1

s 140 Interpretation of sections 138 and 139.

A5–003 For the purposes of sections 138 and 139—

"lease" includes—

(a) an original or derivative under-lease;
(b) an agreement for a lease where the lessee has become entitled to have his lease granted; and

(c) a grant at a fee farm rent, or under a grant securing a rent by condition;

"lessee" includes—

(a) an original or derivative under-lessee;
(b) the persons deriving title under a lessee;
(c) a grantee under a grant at a fee farm rent, or under a grant securing a rent by condition; and
(d) the persons deriving title under such a grantee;

"lessor" includes—

(a) an original or derivative under-lessor;
(b) the persons deriving title under a lessor;
(c) a person making a grant at a fee farm rent, or a grant securing a rent by condition; and
(d) the persons deriving title under such a grantor;

"under-lease" includes an agreement for an under-lease where the under-lessee has become entitled to have his under-lease granted; and

"under-lessee" includes any person deriving title under an under-lessee.

LANDLORD AND TENANT ACT 1985 CHAPTER 70

Repairing obligations

s 11 Repairing obligations in short leases.

A6–001 (1) In a lease to which this section applies (as to which, see sections 13 and 14) there is implied a covenant by the lessor–

(a) to keep in repair the structure and exterior of the dwelling-house (including drains, gutters and external pipes),

(b) to keep in repair and proper working order the installations in the dwelling-house for the supply of water, gas and electricity and for sanitation (including basins, sinks, baths and sanitary conveniences, but not other fixtures, fittings and appliances for making use of the supply of water, gas or electricity), and

(c) to keep in repair and proper working order the installations in the dwelling-house for space heating and heating water.

[(1A) If a lease to which this section applies is a lease of a dwelling-house which forms part only of a building, then, subject to subsection (1B), the covenant implied by subsection (1) shall have effect as if—

(a) the reference in paragraph (a) of that subsection to the dwelling-house included a reference to any part of the building in which the lessor has an estate or interest; and

(b) any reference in paragraphs (b) and (c) of that subsection to an installation in the dwelling-house included a reference to an installation which, directly or indirectly, serves the dwelling-house and which either—

(i) forms part of any part of a building in which the lesser has an estate or interest; or
(ii) is owned by the lessor or under his control.

(1B) Nothing in subsection (1A) shall be construed as requiring the lessor to carry out any works or repairs unless the disrepair (or failure to maintain in working order) is such as to affect the lessee's enjoyment of the dwelling-house or of any common parts, as defined in section 60(1) of the Landlord and Tenant Act 1987, which the lessee, as such, is entitled to use.][1]

(2) The covenant implied by subsection (1) ("the lessor's repairing covenant") shall not be construed as requiring the lessor–

(a) to carry out works or repairs for which the lessee is liable by virtue of his duty to use the premises in a tenant-like manner, or would be so liable but for an express covenant on his part,

(b) to rebuild or reinstate the premises in the case of destruction or damage by fire, or by tempest, flood or other inevitable accident, or

(c) to keep in repair or maintain anything which the lessee is entitled to remove from the dwelling-house.

(3) In determining the standard of repair required by the lessor's repairing covenant, regard shall be had to the age, character and prospective life of the dwelling-house and the locality in which it is situated.

[(3A) In any case where—

(a) the lessor's repairing covenant has effect as mentioned in sub-section (1A), and

(b) in order to comply with the covenant the lessor needs to carry out works or repairs otherwise than in, or to an installation in, the dwelling-house, and

(c) the lessor does not have a sufficient right in the part of the building or the installation concerned to enable him to carry out the required works or repairs,

then, in any proceedings relating to a failure to comply with the lessor's repairing covenant, so far as it requires the lessor to carry out the works or repairs in question, it shall be a defence for the lessor to prove that he used all reasonable endeavours to obtain, but was unable to obtain, such rights as would be adequate to enable him to carry out the works or repairs.][2]

(4) A covenant by the lessee for the repair of the premises is of no effect so far as it relates to the matters mentioned in subsection (1)(a) to (c), except so far as it imposes on the lessee any of the requirements mentioned is subsection (2)(a) or (c).

(5) The reference in subsection (4) to a covenant by the lessee for the repair of the premises includes a covenant—

(a) to put in repair or deliver up in repair,

(b) to paint, point or render,

(c) to pay money in lieu of repairs by the lessee, or

(d) to pay money on account of repairs by the lessor.

(6) In a lease in which the s repairing covenant is implied there is also implied a covenant by the lessee that the lessor, or any person authorised by him in writing, may at reasonable times of the day and on giving 24 hours' notice in writing to the occupier, enter the premises comprised in the lease for the purpose of viewing their condition and state of repair.

[1] Ss. 11(1A), 11(1B) inserted by Housing Act 1988 (c.50), s. 116(1)(4)

[2] S. 11(3A) inserted by Housing Act 1988 (c.50), s. 116(2)(4)

Service charges

s 18 Meaning of "service charge" and "relevant costs".

A6–002 (1) In the following provisions of this Act "service charge" means an amount payable by a tenant of a dwelling as part of or in addition to the rent—

(a) which is payable, directly or indirectly, for services, repairs, maintenance[, improvements][1] or insurance or the landlord's costs of management, and

(b) the whole or part of which varies or may vary according to the relevant costs.

(2) The relevant costs are the costs or estimated costs incurred or to be incurred by or on behalf of the landlord, or a superior landlord, in connection with the matters for which the service charge is payable.

(3) For this purposes—

(a) "costs" includes overheads, and

(b) costs are relevant costs in relation to a service charge whether they are incurred, or to be incurred, in the period for which the service charge is payable or in an earlier or later period.[. . .][2]

[1] word inserted by Commonhold and Leasehold Reform Act (2002 c.15), Sch 9 Para 7
[2] word inserted by Commonhold and Leasehold Reform Act (2002 c.15), Sch 9 Para 7

s 19 Limitation of service charges: reasonableness.

A6–003 (1) Relevant costs shall be taken into account in determining the amount of a service charge payable for a period–

(a) only to the extent that they are reasonably incurred, and

(b) where they are incurred on the provisions of services or the carrying out of works, only if the services or works are of a reasonable standard;

and the amount payable shall be limited accordingly.

(2) Where a service charge is payable before the relevant costs are incurred, no greater amount than is reasonable is so payable, and after the relevant costs have been incurred any necessary adjustment shall be made by repayment, reduction or subsequent charges or otherwise.

[. . .][1]

(5) If a person takes any proceedings in the High Court in pursuance of any of the provisions of this Act relating to service charges and he could have taken those proceedings in the county court, he shall not be entitled to recover any costs.[. . .][2]

[1] repealed subject to savings specified in SI 2004/669 Sch.2 para.6 by Commonhold and Leasehold Reform Act (2002 c.15), Sch 14 Para 1
[2] repealed subject to savings specified in SI 2004/669 Sch.2 para.6 by Commonhold and Leasehold Reform Act (2002 c.15), Sch 14 Para 1

s 20 Limitation of service charges: consultation requirements

[20 Limitation of service charges: consultation requirements **A6–004**

(1) Where this section applies to any qualifying works or qualifying long term agreement, the relevant contributions of tenants are limited in accordance with subsection (6) or (7) (or both) unless the consultation requirements have been either—

(a) complied with in relation to the works or agreement, or

(b) dispensed with in relation to the works or agreement by (or on appeal from) a leasehold valuation tribunal.

(2) In this section "relevant contribution", in relation to a tenant and any works or agreement, is the amount which he may be required under the terms of his lease to contribute (by the payment of service charges) to relevant costs incurred on carrying out the works or under the agreement.

(3) This section applies to qualifying works if relevant costs incurred on carrying out the works exceed an appropriate amount.

(4) The Secretary of State may by regulations provide that this section applies to a qualifying long term agreement—

(a) if relevant costs incurred under the agreement exceed an appropriate amount, or

(b) if relevant costs incurred under the agreement during a period prescribed by the regulations exceed an appropriate amount.

(5) An appropriate amount is an amount set by regulations made by the Secretary of State; and the regulations may make provision for either or both of the following to be an appropriate amount—

(a) an amount prescribed by, or determined in accordance with, the regulations, and

(b) an amount which results in the relevant contribution of any one or more tenants being an amount prescribed by, or determined in accordance with, the regulations.

(6) Where an appropriate amount is set by virtue of paragraph (a) of subsection (5), the amount of the relevant costs incurred on carrying out the works or under the agreement which may be taken into account in determining the relevant contributions of tenants is limited to the appropriate amount.

(7) Where an appropriate amount is set by virtue of paragraph (b) of that subsection, the amount of the relevant contribution of the tenant, or each of

the tenants, whose relevant contribution would otherwise exceed the amount prescribed by, or determined in accordance with, the regulations is limited to the amount so prescribed or determined.][1]

[1] ss.20–20ZA substituted for s.20 subject to savings specified in SI 2004/669 art.2(d)(i)–(vi) by Commonhold and Leasehold Reform Act (2002 c.15), Pt 2 c 5 s 151

s 20ZA Consultation requirements: supplementary

A6–005 (1) Where an application is made to a leasehold valuation tribunal for a determination to dispense with all or any of the consultation requirements in relation to any qualifying works or qualifying long term agreement, the tribunal may make the determination if satisfied that it is reasonable to dispense with the requirements.

(2) In section 20 and this section—

"qualifying works" means works on a building or any other premises, and

"qualifying long term agreement" means (subject to subsection (3)) an agreement entered into, by or on behalf of the landlord or a superior landlord, for a term of more than twelve months.

(3) The Secretary of State may by regulations provide that an agreement is not a qualifying long term agreement—

(a) if it is an agreement of a description prescribed by the regulations, or

(b) in any circumstances so prescribed.

(4) In section 20 and this section "the consultation requirements" means requirements prescribed by regulations made by the Secretary of State.

(5) Regulations under subsection (4) may in particular include provision requiring the landlord—

(a) to provide details of proposed works or agreements to tenants or the recognised tenants' association representing them,

(b) to obtain estimates for proposed works or agreements,

(c) to invite tenants or the recognised tenants' association to propose the names of persons from whom the landlord should try to obtain other estimates,

(d) to have regard to observations made by tenants or the recognised tenants' association in relation to proposed works or agreements and estimates, and

(e) to give reasons in prescribed circumstances for carrying out works or entering into agreements.

(6) Regulations under section 20 or this section—

(a) may make provision generally or only in relation to specific cases, and

(b) may make different provision for different purposes.

(7) Regulations under section 20 or this section shall be made by statutory instrument which shall be subject to annulment in pursuance of a resolution of either House of Parliament. [. . .][1]

[1] ss.20–20ZA substituted for s.20 subject to savings specified in SI 2004/669 art.2(d)(i)–(vi) by Commonhold and Leasehold Reform Act (2002 c.15), Pt 2 c 5 s 151

s 20A Limitation of service charges; grant-aided works.

A6–006 Where relevant costs are incurred or to be incurred on the carrying out of works in respect of which a grant has been or is to be paid under section 523 of the Housing Act 1985 (assistance for provision of separate service pipe for water supply) or any provision of Part I of the Housing Grants, Construction and Regeneration Act 1996 (grants, &c. for renewal of private sector housing) or any corresponding earlier enactment[or article 3 of the Regulatory Reform (Housing Assistance) (England and Wales) Order 2002 (power of local housing authorities to provide assistance)][1], the amount of the grant shall be deducted from the costs and the amount of the service charge payable shall be reduced accordingly.

(2) In any case where–

(a) relevant costs are incurred or to be incurred on the carrying out of works which are included in the external works specified in a group repair scheme, within the meaning of Part I of the Housing Grants, Construction and Regeneration Act 1996, and

(b) the landlord participated or is participating in that scheme as an assisted participant,

the amount which, in relation to the landlord, is the balance of the cost determined in accordance with section 69(3) of the Housing Grants, Construction and Regeneration Act 1996 shall be deducted from the costs, and the amount of the service charge payable shall be reduced accordingly.

[1] words inserted by SI 2002/1860 (Regulatory Reform (Housing Assistance) (England and Wales) Order), Sch 1 Para 2

s 20B Limitation of service charges: time limit on making demands.

A6–007 [20B.— Limitation of service charges: time limit on making demands.

(1) If any of the relevant costs taken into account in determining the amount of any service charge were incurred more than 18 months before a demand for payment of the service charge is served on the tenant, then (subject to subsection (2)), the tenant shall not be liable to pay so much of the service charge as reflects the costs so incurred.

(2) Subsection (1) shall not apply if, within the period of 18 months beginning with the date when the relevant costs in question were incurred, the

tenant was notified in writing that those costs had been incurred and that he would subsequently be required under the terms of his lease to contribute to them by the payment of a service charge.][1]

[1] Ss. 20B, 20C inserted by Landlord and Tenant Act 1987 (c.31), s. 41, Sch. 2 para.4

s 20C Limitation of service charges: costs of proceedings.

A6–008 [20C.— "Limitation of service charges: costs of proceedings.

(1) A tenant may make an application for an order that all or any of the costs incurred, or to be incurred, by the landlord in connection with proceedings before a court or leasehold valuation tribunal, or the Lands Tribunal, or in connection with arbitration proceedings, are not to be regarded as relevant costs to be taken into account in determining the amount of any service charge payable by the tenant or any other person or persons specified in the application.

(2) The application shall be made—

(a) in the case of court proceedings, to the court before which the proceedings are taking place or, if the application is made after the proceedings are concluded, to a county court;

(b) in the case of proceedings before a leasehold valuation tribunal, to the tribunal before which the proceedings are taking place or, if the application is made after the proceedings are concluded, to any leasehold valuation tribunal;

(c) in the case of proceedings before the Lands Tribunal, to the tribunal;

(d) in the case of arbitration proceedings, to the arbitral tribunal or, if the application is made after the proceedings are concluded, to a county court.

(3) The court or tribunal to which the application is made may make such order on the application as it considers just and equitable in the circumstances."][1]

[1] substituted subject to savings specified in SI 1997/1851 Sch.1 para.1 by Housing Act (1996 c.52), Pt III c I s 83 (4)

s 21 Regular statements of account

A6–009 [21 Regular statements of account

(1) The landlord must supply to each tenant by whom service charges are payable, in relation to each accounting period, a written statement of account dealing with—

(a) service charges of the tenant and the tenants of dwellings associated with his dwelling,

(b) relevant costs relating to those service charges,

(c) the aggregate amount standing to the credit of the tenant and the tenants of those dwellings—

(i) at the beginning of the accounting period, and
(ii) at the end of the accounting period, and

(d) related matters.

(2) The statement of account in relation to an accounting period must be supplied to each such tenant not later than six months after the end of the accounting period.

(3) Where the landlord supplies a statement of account to a tenant he must also supply to him—

(a) a certificate of a qualified accountant that, in the accountant's opinion, the statement of account deals fairly with the matters with which it is required to deal and is sufficiently supported by accounts, receipts and other documents which have been produced to him, and

(b) a summary of the rights and obligations of tenants of dwellings in relation to service charges.

(4) The Secretary of State may make regulations prescribing requirements as to the form and content of—

(a) statements of account,

(b) accountants' certificates, and

(c) summaries of rights and obligations,

required to be supplied under this section.

(5) The Secretary of State may make regulations prescribing exceptions from the requirement to supply an accountant's certificate.

(6) If the landlord has been notified by a tenant of an address in England and Wales at which he wishes to have supplied to him documents required to be so supplied under this section, the landlord must supply them to him at that address.

(7) And the landlord is to be taken to have been so notified if notification has been given to—

(a) an agent of the landlord named as such in the rent book or similar document, or

(b) the person who receives the rent on behalf of the landlord;

And where notification is given to such an agent or person he must forward it as soon as may be to the landlord.

(8) For the purposes of this section a dwelling is associated with another dwelling if the obligations of the tenants of the dwellings under the terms of their leases as regards contributing to relevant costs relate to the same costs.

(9) In this section "accounting period" means such period—

(a) beginning with the relevant date, and

(b) ending with such date, not later than twelve months after the relevant date, as the landlord determines.

(10) In the case of the first accounting period in relation to any dwellings, the relevant date is the later of—

(a) the date on which service charges are first payable under a lease of any of them, and

(b) the date on which section 152 of the Commonhold and Leasehold Reform Act 2002 comes into force,

and, in the case of subsequent accounting periods, it is the date immediately following the end of the previous accounting period.

(11) Regulations under subsection (4) may make different provision for different purposes.

(12) Regulations under this section shall be made by statutory instrument which shall be subject to annulment in pursuance of a resolution of either House of Parliament.][1]

[1] ss.21–21A substituted for s.21 by Commonhold and Leasehold Reform Act (2002 c.15), Pt 2 c 5 s 152

s 21A Withholding of service charges

A6–010 (1) A tenant may withhold payment of a service charge if—

(a) the landlord has not supplied a document to him by the time by which he is required to supply it under section 21, or

(b) the form or content of a document which the landlord has supplied to him under that section (at any time) does not conform exactly or substantially with the requirements prescribed by regulations under subsection (4) of that section.

(2) The maximum amount which the tenant may withhold is an amount equal to the aggregate of—

(a) the service charges paid by him in the accounting period to which the document concerned would or does relate, and

(b) so much of the aggregate amount required to be dealt with in the statement of account for that accounting period by section 21(1)(c)(i) as stood to his credit.

(3) An amount may not be withheld under this section—

(a) in a case within paragraph (a) of subsection (1), after the document concerned has been supplied to the tenant by the landlord, or

(b) in a case within paragraph (b) of that subsection, after a document conforming exactly or substantially with the requirements prescribed by regulations under section 21(4) has been supplied to the tenant by the landlord by way of replacement of the one previously supplied.

(4) If, on an application made by the landlord to a leasehold valuation tribunal, the tribunal determines that the landlord has a reasonable excuse for a failure giving rise to the right of a tenant to withhold an amount under this section, the tenant may not withhold the amount after the determination is made.

(5) Where a tenant withholds a service charge under this section, any provisions of the tenancy relating to non-payment or late payment of service charges do not have effect in relation to the period for which he so withholds it. [. . .][1]

[1] ss.21–21A substituted for s.21 by Commonhold and Leasehold Reform Act (2002 c.15), Pt 2 c 5 s 152

s 21B Notice to accompany demands for service charges

A6–011 (1) A demand for the payment of a service charge must be accompanied by a summary of the rights and obligations of tenants of dwellings in relation to service charges.

(2) The Secretary of State may make regulations prescribing requirements as to the form and content of such summaries of rights and obligations.

(3) A tenant may withhold payment of a service charge which has been demanded from him if subsection (1) is not complied with in relation to the demand.

(4) Where a tenant withholds a service charge under this section, any provisions of the lease relating to non-payment or late payment of service charges do not have effect in relation to the period for which he so withholds it.

(5) Regulations under subsection (2) may make different provision for different purposes.

(6) Regulations under subsection (2) shall be made by statutory instrument which shall be subject to annulment in pursuance of a resolution of either House of Parliament.[. . .][1]

[1] added by Commonhold and Leasehold Reform Act (2002 c.15), Pt 2 c 5 s 153)

s 22 Request to inspect supporting account &c.

A6–012 (1) This section applies where a tenant, or the secretary of a recognised tenants' association, has obtained such a summary as is referred to in section 21(1) (summary of relevant costs), whether in pursuance of that section or otherwise.

(2) The tenant, or the secretary with the consent of the tenant, may within six months of obtaining the summary require the landlord in writing to afford him reasonable facilities—

(a) for inspecting the accounts, receipts and other documents supporting the summary, and

(b) for taking copies or extracts from them.

(3) A request under this section is duly served on the landlord if it is served on—

(a) an agent of the landlord named as such in the rent book or similar document, or

(b) the person who receives the rent on behalf of the landlord:

and a person on whom a request is so served shall forward it as soon as may be to the landlord.

(4) The landlord shall make such facilities available to the tenant or secretary for a period of two months beginning not later than one month after the request is made.

[(5) The landlord shall—

(a) where such facilities are for the inspection of any documents, make them so available free of charge;

(b) where such facilities are for the taking of copies or extracts, be entitled to make them so available on payment of such reasonable charge as he may determine.

(6) The requirement imposed on the landlord by subsection (5)(a) to make any facilities available to a person free of charge shall not be construed as precluding the landlord from treating as part of his costs of management any costs incurred by him in connection with making those facilities so available.][1]

[1] Ss. 22(5), (6) inserted by Landlord and Tenant Act 1987 (c.31), s. 41, Sch. 2 para. 6

s 23 Request relating to information held by superior landlord.

A6–013 (1) If a request under section 21 (request for summary of relevant costs) relates in whole or in part to relevant costs incurred by or on behalf of a supervisor landlord, and the landlord to whom the request is made is not is possession of the relevant information—

(a) he shall in turn make a written request for the relevant information to the person who is his landlord (and so on, if that person is not himself the superior landlord),

(b) the superior landlord shall comply with that request within a reasonable time, and

(c) the immediate landlord shall then comply with the tenant's or secretary's request, or that part of it which relates to the relevant costs incurred by or on behalf of the superior landlord, within the time allowed by section 21 or such further time, if any, as is reasonable in the circumstances.

(2) If a request under section 22 (request for facilities to inspect supporting accounts, &c.) relates to a summary of costs incurred by or on behalf of a superior landlord—

(a) the landlord to whom the request is made shall forthwith inform the tenant or secretary of that fact and of the name and address of the superior landlord, and

(b) section 22 shall then apply to the superior landlord as it applies to the immediate landlord.

s 24 Effect of assignment on request.

A6–014 The assignment of a tenancy does not affect the validity of a request made under section 21, 22 or 23 before the assignment; but a person is not obliged to provide a summary or make facilities available more than once for the same [dwelling][1] and for the same period.

[1] Word substituted by Landlord and Tenant Act 1987 (c.31), s. 41, Sch. 2 para. 7

s 25 Failure to comply with s 21 22, or 23 an offence.

A6–015 (1) It is a summary offence for a person to fail, without reasonable excuse, to perform a duty imposed on him by section 21, 22 or 23.
(2) A person committing such an offence is liable on conviction to a find not exceeding level 4 on the standard scale.

s 26 Exception: tenants of certain public authorities.

A6–016 (1) Sections 18 to 25 (limitation on service charges and requests for information about costs) do not apply to a service charge payable by a tenant of—

a local authority,

a National Park authority, [or][1]

a new town corporation

unless the tenancy is a long tenancy, in which case sections 18 to 24 apply but section 25 (offence of failure to comply) does not.
(2) The following are long tenancies for the purposes of subsection (1), subject to subsection (3)—

(a) a tenancy granted for a term certain exceeding 21 years, whether or not it is (or may become) terminable before the end of that term by notice given by the tenant or by re-entry or forfeiture;

(b) a tenancy for a term fixed by law under a grant with a covenant or obligation for perpetual renewal, other than a tenancy by sub-demise from one which is not a long tenancy;

(c) any tenancy granted in pursuance of Part V of the Housing Act 1985 (the right to buy), including any tenancy granted in pursuance of that

Part as it has effect by virtue of section 17 of the Housing Act 1996 (the right to acquire).

(3) A tenancy granted so as to become terminable by notice after a death is not a long tenancy for the purposes of subsection (1), unless—

(a) it is granted by a housing association which at the time of the grant is a registered social landlord,

(b) it is granted at a premium calculated by reference to a percentage of the value of the dwelling-house or the cost of providing it, and

(c) at the time it is granted it complies with the requirements of the regulations then in force under section 140(4)(b) of the Housing Act 1980 or paragraph 4(2)(b) of Schedule 4A to the Leasehold Reform Act 1967 (conditions for exclusion of shared ownership leases from Part I of Leasehold Reform Act 1967) or, in the case of a tenancy granted before any such regulations were brought into force, with the first such regulations to be in force.

[1] word inserted by Government of Wales Act (1998 c.38), Sch 15 Para 12

s 27 Exception: rent registered and not entered as variable.

A6–017 Sections 18 to 25 (limitation on service charges and requests for information about costs) do not apply to a service charge payable by the tenant of a [dwelling][1] the rent of which is registered under Part IV of the Rent Act 1977, unless the amount registered is, in pursuance of section 71(4) of that Act, entered as a variable amount.

[1] Word substituted by Landlord and Tenant Act 1987 (c.31), s. 41, Sch. 2 para. 8

s 27A Liability to pay service charges: jurisdiction

A6–018 (1) An application may be made to a leasehold valuation tribunal for a determination whether a service charge is payable and, if it is, as to–

(a) the person by whom it is payable,

(b) the person to whom it is payable,

(c) the amount which is payable,

(d) the date at or by which it is payable, and

(e) the manner in which it is payable.

(2) Subsection (1) applies whether or not any payment has been made.

(3) An application may also be made to a leasehold valuation tribunal for a determination whether, if costs were incurred for services, repairs, maintenance, improvements, insurance or management of any specified description, a service charge would be payable for the costs and, if it would, as to—

(a) the person by whom it would be payable,

(b) the person to whom it would be payable,

(c) the amount which would be payable,

(d) the date at or by which it would be payable, and

(e) the manner in which it would be payable.

(4) No application under subsection (1) or (3) may be made in respect of a matter which—

(a) has been agreed or admitted by the tenant,

(b) has been, or is to be, referred to arbitration pursuant to a post-dispute arbitration agreement to which the tenant is a party,

(c) has been the subject of determination by a court, or

(d) has been the subject of determination by an arbitral tribunal pursuant to a post-dispute arbitration agreement.

(5) But the tenant is not to be taken to have agreed or admitted any matter by reason only of having made any payment.

(6) An agreement by the tenant of a dwelling (other than a post-dispute arbitration agreement) is void in so far as it purports to provide for a determination—

(a) in a particular manner, or

(b) on particular evidence,

of any question which may be the subject of an application under subsection (1) or (3).

(7) The jurisdiction conferred on a leasehold valuation tribunal in respect of any matter by virtue of this section is in addition to any jurisdiction of a court in respect of the matter. [. . .][1]

[1] inserted subject to savings specified in SI 2004/669 Sch.2 para.6 by Commonhold and Leasehold Reform Act (2002 c. 15), Pt 2 c 5 s 155(1)

s 28 Meaning of "qualified accountant".

A6–019

(1) The reference to a "qualified account" in section 21(6) (certification of summary of information about relevant costs) is to be a person who, in accordance with the following provisions, has the necessary qualification and is not disqualified from acting.

(2) A person has the necessary qualification if he is eligible for appointment as a company auditor under section 25 of the Companies Act 1989.

(4) The following are disqualified from acting–

(b) an officer employee or partner of the landlord or, where the landlord is a company, of an associated company;

(c) a person who is partner or employee of any such officer or employee.

(d) an agent of landlord who is a managing agent for any premises to which any of the costs covered by the summary in question relate;

(e) an employee or partner of any such agent.

(5) For the purposes of subsection (4)(b) a company is associated with a landlord company if it is (within the meaning of section 736 of the Companies Act 1985) the landlord's holding company, a subsidiary of the landlord or another subsidiary of the landlord's holding company.

(5A) For the purpose of subsection (4)(d) a person is a managing agent for any premises to which any costs relate if he has been appointed to discharge any of the landlord's obligations relating to the management by him of the premises and owed to the tenants who may be required under the terms of their leases to contribute to those costs by the payment of service charges.

(6) Where the landlord is a local authority, National Park authority [or a new town corporation][1]

(a) the persons who have the necessary qualification include members of the Chartered Institute of Public Finance and Accountancy, and

(b) subsection (4)(b) (disqualification of officers and employees of landlord) does not apply.

[1] word substituted by Government of Wales Act (1998 c.38), Sch 15 Para 13

s 29 Meaning of "recognised tenants' association".

A6–020 (1) A recognised tenants' association is an association of [qualifying tenants (whether with or without other tenants)][1] which is recognised for the purposes of the provisions of this Act relating to service charges either—

(a) by notice in writing given by the landlord to the secretary of the association, or

(b) by a certificate of a member of the local rent assessment committee panel.

(2) A notice given under subsection (1)(a) may be withdrawn by the landlord by notice in writing given to the secretary of the association not less than six months before the date on which it is to be withdrawn.

(3) A certificate given under subsection (1)(b) may be cancelled by any member of the local rent assessment committee panel.

(4) In this section the "local rent assessment committee panel" means the persons appointed by the Lord Chancellor under the Rent Act 1977 to the panel of persons to act as members of a rent assessment committee for the registration area in which [the dwellings let to the qualifying tenants are situated, and for the purposes of this section a number of tenants are qualifying tenants if each of them may be required under the terms of his lease to contribute to the same costs by the payment of a service charge.][2]

[(5) The Secretary of State may be regulations specify—

(a) the procedure which is to be followed in connection with an application for, or for the cancellation of, a certificate under subsection (1)(b);

(b) the matters to which regard is to be had in giving or cancelling such a certificate;

(c) the duration of such a certificate; and

(d) any circumstances in which a certificate is not be given under subsection (1)(b).][3]

(6) Regulations under subsection (5)—

(a) may make different provisions with respect to different cases or descriptions of case, including different provision for different areas, and

(b) shall be made by statutory instrument which shall be subject to annulment in pursuance of a resolution of either House of Parliament.

[1] Words substituted by Landlord and Tenant Act 1987 (c.31), s. 41, Sch. 2 para. 10(2)
[2] Words substituted by Landlord and Tenant Act 1987 (c.31), s. 41, Sch. 2 para. 10(3)
[3] S.29(5) substituted by Landlord and Tenant Act 1987 (c.31), s. 41, Sch. 2 para. 10(4).

s 30 Meaning of "flat", "landlord" and "tenant".

In the provisions of this Act relating to service charges— **A6–021**
[. . .][1]

"landlord" includes any person who has a right to enforce payment of a service charge;

"tenant" includes

(a) a statutory tenant, and
(b) where the [dwelling][2] or part of it is sub-let, the sub-tenant.

[1] Definition of "flat" repealed by Landlord and Tenant Act 1987 (c.31), ss. 41, 61(2), Sch. 2 para. 11(a), Sch. 5
[2] Word substituted by Landlord and Tenant Act 1987 (c.31), s. 41, Sch.2 para. 11(b)

s 30A Rights of tenants with respect to insurance.

[30A. Rights of tenants with respect to insurance.
The Schedule to this Act (which confers on tenants certain rights with respect to the insurance of their dwellings) shall have effect.][1] **A6–022**

[1] S. 30A inserted by Landlord and Tenant Act 1987 (c.31), s.43(1)

s 30B Recognised tenants' associations to be consulted about managing agents.

[30B.—Recognised tenants' associations to be consulted about managing agents. **A6–023**

(1A) A recognised tenants' association may at any time serve a notice on the landlord requesting him to consult the association in accordance with this section on matters relating to the appointment or employment by him of a managing agent for any relevant premises.

(2) Where, at the time when any such notice is served by a recognised tenants' association, the landlord does not employ any managing agent for any relevant premises, the landlord shall, before appointing such a managing agent, serve on the association a notice specifying—

(a) the name of the proposed managing agent;

(b) the landlord's obligations to the tenants represented by the association which it is proposed that the managing agent should be required to discharge on his behalf; and

(c) a period of not less than one month beginning with the date of service of the notice within which the association may make observations on the proposed appointment.

(3) Where, at the time when a notice is served under subsection (1) by a recognised tenants' association, the landlord employs a managing agent for any relevant premises, the landlord shall, within the period of one month beginning with the date of service of that notice, serve on the association a notice specifying—

(a) the landlord's obligations to the tenants represented by the association which the managing agent is required to discharge on his behalf; and

(b) a reasonable period within which the association may make observations on the manner in which the managing agent has been discharging those obligations, and on the desirability of his continuing to discharge them.

(4) Subject to subsection (5), a landlord who has been served with a notice by an association under subsection (1) shall, so long as he employs a managing agent for any relevant premises—

(a) serve on that association at least once in every five years a notice specifying—

(i) any change occurring since the date of the last notice served by him on the association under this section in the obligations which the managing agent has been required to discharge on his behalf; and

(ii) a reasonable period within which the association may make observations on the manner in which the managing agent has discharged those obligations since that date, and on the desirability of his continuing to discharge them;

(b) serve on that association, whenever he proposes to appoint any new managing agent for any relevant premises, a notice specifying the matters mentioned in paragraphs (a) to (c) of subsection (2).

(5) A landlord shall not, by virtue of a notice served by an association under subsection (1), be required to serve on the association a notice under subsection (4)(a) or (b) if the association subsequently serves on the landlord a notice withdrawing its request under subsection (1) to be consulted by him.

(6) Where—

(a) a recognised tenants' association has served a notice under subsection (1) with respect to any relevant premises, and

(b) the interest of the landlord in those premises becomes vested in a new landlord,

that notice shall cease to have effect with respect to those premises (without prejudice to the service by the association on the new landlord of a fresh notice under that subsection with respect to those premises).

(7) Any notice served by a landlord under this section shall specify the name and the address in the United Kingdom of the person to whom any observations made in pursuance of the notice are to be sent; and the landlord shall have regard to any such observations that are received by that person within the period specified in the notice.

(8) In this section—

"landlord", in relation to a recognised tenants' association, means the immediate landlord of the tenants represented by the association or a person who has a right to enforce payment of service charges payable by any of those tenants;

"managing agent", in relation to any relevant premises, means an agent of the landlord appointed to discharge any of the landlord's obligations to the tenants represented by the recognised tenants' association in question which relate to the management by him of those premises; and

"tenant" includes a statutory tenant;

and for the purposes of this section any premises (whether a building or not) are relevant premises in relation to a recognised tenants' association if any of the tenants represented by the association may be required under the terms of their leases to contribute by the payment of service charges to costs relating to those premises.][1]

[1] S. 30B inserted by Landlord and Tenant Act 1987 (c.31), s. 44

SCHEDULE 1 RIGHTS OF TENANTS WITH RESPECT TO INSURANCE

Construction

Para 1

[1. In this Schedule—

A6–024

"landlord", in relation to a tenant by whom a service charge is payable which includes an amount payable directly or indirectly for insurance, includes any person who has a right to enforce payment of that service charge;

"relevant policy", in relation to a dwelling, means any policy of insurance under which the dwelling is insured (being, in the case of a flat, a policy covering the building containing it); and

"tenant" includes a statutory tenant.][1]

1 Sch. inserted by Landlord and Tenant Act 1987 (c.31), s. 43(2)

Request for summary of insurance cover

Para 2

A6–025 (1) Where a service charge is payable by the tenant of a dwelling which consists of or includes an amount payable directly or indirectly for insurance, the tenant may [by notice in writing require the landlord][1] to supply him with a written summary of the insurance for the time being effected in relation to the dwelling.

(2) If the tenant is represented by a recognised tenants' association and he consents, the [notice may be served][2] by the secretary of the association instead of by the tenant and may then be for the supply of the summary to the secretary.

(3) A [notice under this paragraph is duly][3] served on the landlord if it is served on—

(a) an agent of the landlord named as such in the rent book or similar document, or

(b) the person who receives the rent on behalf of the landlord;

and a person on [whom such a notice][4] is so served shall forward it as soon as may be to the landlord.

(4) The landlord shall, within [the period of twenty-one days beginning with the day on which he receives the notice,][5] comply with it by supplying to the tenant or the secretary of the recognised tenants' association (as the case may require) such a summary as is mentioned in sub-paragraph (1), which shall include—

(a) the insured amount or amounts under any relevant policy, and

(b) the name of the insurer under any such policy, and

(c) the risks in respect of which the dwelling or (as the case may be) the building containing it is insured under any such policy.

(5) In sub-paragraph (4)(a) "the insured amount or amounts", in relation to a relevant policy, means—

(a) in the case of a dwelling other than a flat, the amount for which the dwelling is insured under the policy; and

(b) in the case of a flat, the amount for which the building containing it is insured under the policy and, if specified in the policy, the amount for which the flat is insured under it.

(6) The landlord shall be taken to have complied with the [notice][6] if, within the period mentioned in sub-paragraph (4), he instead supplies to the tenant or the secretary (as the case may require) a copy of every relevant policy.

(7) In a case where two or more buildings are insured under any relevant policy, the summary or copy supplied under sub-paragraph (4) or (6) so far as relating to that policy need only be of such parts of the policy as relate–

(a) to the dwelling, and

(b) if the dwelling is a flat, to the building containing it. [. . .][7]

[1] modified by Commonhold and Leasehold Reform Act (2002 c. 15), Sch 10 Para 8
[2] modified by Commonhold and Leasehold Reform Act (2002 c. 15), Sch 10 Para 8
[3] modified by Commonhold and Leasehold Reform Act (2002 c. 15), Sch 10 Para 8
[4] modified by Commonhold and Leasehold Reform Act (2002 c. 15), Sch 10 Para 8
[5] modified by Commonhold and Leasehold Reform Act (2002 c. 15), Sch 10 Para 8
[6] modified by Commonhold and Leasehold Reform Act (2002 c. 15), Sch 10 Para 8
[7] modified by Commonhold and Leasehold Reform Act (2002 c. 15), Sch 10 Para 8

Request to inspect insurance policy etc.

Para 3 Inspection of insurance policy etc.

[3 Inspection of insurance policy etc. **A6–026**

(1) Where a service charge is payable by the tenant of a dwelling which consists of or includes an amount payable directly or indirectly for insurance, the tenant may by notice in writing require the landlord—

(a) to afford him reasonable facilities for inspecting any relevant policy or associated documents and for taking copies of or extracts from them, or

(b) to take copies of or extracts from any such policy or documents and either send them to him or afford him reasonable facilities for collecting them (as he specifies).

(2) If the tenant is represented by a recognised tenants' association and he consents, the notice may be served by the secretary of the association instead of by the tenant (and in that case any requirement imposed by it is to afford reasonable facilities, or to send copies or extracts, to the secretary).

(3) A notice under this paragraph is duly served on the landlord if it is served on—

(a) an agent of the landlord named as such in the rent book or similar document, or

(b) the person who receives the rent on behalf of the landlord;

and a person on whom such a notice is so served shall forward it as soon as may be to the landlord.

(4) The landlord shall comply with a requirement imposed by a notice under this paragraph within the period of twenty-one days beginning with the day on which he receives the notice.

(5) To the extent that a notice under this paragraph requires the landlord to afford facilities for inspecting documents—

(a) he shall do so free of charge, but

(b) he may treat as part of his costs of management any costs incurred by him in doing so.

(6) The landlord may make a reasonable charge for doing anything else in compliance with a requirement imposed by a notice under this paragraph.

(7) In this paragraph—

"relevant policy" includes a policy of insurance under which the dwelling was insured for the period of insurance immediately preceding that current when the notice is served (being, in the case of a flat, a policy covering the building containing it), and

"associated documents" means accounts, receipts or other documents which provide evidence of payment of any premiums due under a relevant policy in respect of the period of insurance which is current when the notice is served or the period of insurance immediately preceding that period.[1]

[1] substituted by Commonhold and Leasehold Reform Act (2002 c. 15), Sch 10 Para 9

Request relating to insurance effected by superior landlord

Para 4

A6–027 (1) If [a notice is served][1] under paragraph 2 in a case where a superior landlord has effected, in whole or in part, the insurance of the dwelling in question and the landlord [on whom the notice is served][2] is not in possession of the relevant information—

(a) he shall in turn [by notice in writing require the person who is his landlord to give him the relevant information][3] (and so on, if that person is not himself the superior landlord),

(b) the superior landlord shall comply with [the notice][4] within a reasonable time, and

(c) the immediate landlord shall then comply with the tenant's or [secretary's notice][5] in the manner provided by sub-paragraphs (4) to (7) of paragraph 2 within the time allowed by that paragraph or such further time, if any, as is reasonable in the circumstances.

(2) If, in a case where a superior landlord has effected, in whole or in part, the insurance of the dwelling in question, a [notice under paragraph 3 imposes a requirement relating][6] to any policy of insurance effected by the superior landlord—

(a) the landlord [on whom the notice is served][7] shall forthwith inform the tenant or secretary of that fact and of the name and address of the superior landlord, and

(b) that paragraph shall then apply to the superior landlord in relation to that policy as it applies to the immediate landlord. [. . .][8]

[1] modified by Commonhold and Leasehold Reform Act (2002 c. 15), Sch 10 Para 10
[2] modified by Commonhold and Leasehold Reform Act (2002 c. 15), Sch 10 Para 10
[3] modified by Commonhold and Leasehold Reform Act (2002 c. 15), Sch 10 Para 10
[4] modified by Commonhold and Leasehold Reform Act (2002 c. 15), Sch 10 Para 10
[5] modified by Commonhold and Leasehold Reform Act (2002 c. 15), Sch 10 Para 10
[6] modified by Commonhold and Leasehold Reform Act (2002 c. 15), Sch 10 Para 10
[7] modified by Commonhold and Leasehold Reform Act (2002 c. 15), Sch 10 Para 10
[8] modified by Commonhold and Leasehold Reform Act (2002 c. 15), Sch 10 Para 10

Effect of change of landlord

Para 4A

A6–028

(1) This paragraph applies where, at a time when a duty imposed on the landlord or a superior landlord by virtue of any of paragraphs 2 to 4 remains to be discharged by him, he disposes of the whole or part of his interest as landlord or superior landlord).

(2) If the landlord or superior landlord is, despite the disposal, still in a position to discharge the duty to any extent, he remains responsible for discharging it to that extent.

(3) If the other person is in a position to discharge the duty to any extent, he is responsible for discharging it to that extent.

(4) Where the other person is responsible for discharging the duty to any extent (whether or not the landlord or superior landlord is also responsible for discharging it to that or any other extent)—

(a) references to the landlord or superior landlord in paragraphs 2 to 4 are to, or include, the other person so far as is appropriate to reflect his responsibility for discharging the duty to that extent, but

(b) in connection with its discharge by that person, paragraphs 2(4) and 3(4) apply as if the reference to the day on which the landlord receives the notice were to the date of the disposal referred to in sub-paragraph (1). [. . .][1]

[1] added by Commonhold and Leasehold Reform Act (2002 c.15), Sch 10 Para 11

Effect of assignment on request

Para 5

A6–029 [5. The assignment of a tenancy does not affect any duty imposed by virtue of any of paragraphs 2 to 4A; but a person is not required to comply with more than a reasonable number of requirements imposed by any one person.][1]

[1] words substituted by Commonhold and Leasehold Reform Act (2002 c. 15), Sch 10 Para 12

Failure to comply with paragraph 2, 3 or 4 an offence

Para 6

A6–030 [6.—

(1) It is a summary offence for a person to fail, without reasonable excuse, to perform a duty imposed on him by or by virtue of any of paragraphs 2 to 4A.

(2) A person committing such an offence is liable on conviction to a fine not exceeding level 4 on the standard scale.][1]

[1] words substituted by Commonhold and Leasehold Reform Act (2002 c. 15), Sch 10 Para 13

Tenant's right to notify insurers of possible claim

Para 7

A6–031 [7.—

(1) This paragraph applies to any dwelling in respect of which the tenant pays to the landlord a service charge consisting of or including an amount payable directly or indirectly for insurance.

(2) Where—

(a) it appears to the tenant of any such dwelling that damage has been caused—

(i) to the dwelling, or

(ii) if the dwelling is a flat, to the dwelling or to any other part of the building containing it, in respect of which a claim could be made under the terms of a policy of insurance, and

(b) it is term of that policy that the person insured under the policy should give notice of any claim under it to the insurer within a specified period,

the tenant may, within that specified period, serve on the insurer a notice in writing stating that it appears to him that damage has been caused as mentioned in paragraph (a) and describing briefly the nature of the damage.

(3) Where—

(a) any such notice is served on an insurer by a tenant in relation to any such damage, and

(b) the specified period referred to in sub-paragraph (2)(b) would expire earlier than the period of six months beginning with the date on which the notice is served,

the policy in question shall have effect as regards any claim subsequently made in respect of that damage by the person insured under the policy as if for the specified period there were substituted that period of six months.

(4) Where the tenancy of a dwelling to which this paragraph applies is held by joint tenants, a single notice under this paragraph may be given by any one or more of those tenants.

(5) The Secretary of State may by regulations prescribe the form of notices under this paragraph and the particulars which such notices must contain.

(6) Any such regulations—

(a) may make different provision with respect to different cases or descriptions of case, including different provision for different areas, and

(b) shall be made by statutory instrument.][1]

[1] Sch. inserted by Landlord and Tenant Act 1987 (c. 31), s. 43(2)

Right to challenge landlord's choice of insurers

Para 8

A6–032

(1) This paragraph applies where a tenancy of a dwelling requires the tenant to insure the dwelling with an insurer nominated [or approved][1] by the landlord.

(2) The tenant or landlord may apply to a county court or leasehold valuation tribunal for a determination whether—

(a) the insurance which is available from the nominated [or approved][2] insurer for insuring the tenant's dwelling is unsatisfactory in any respect, or

(b) the premiums payable in respect of any such insurance are excessive.

(3) No such application may be made in respect of a matter which—

(a) has been agreed or admitted by the tenant,

(b) under an arbitration agreement to which the tenant is a party is to be referred to arbitration, or

(c) has been the subject of determination by a court or arbitral tribunal.

(4) On an application under this paragraph the court or tribunal may make—

(a) an order requiring the landlord to nominate [or approve][3] such other insurer as is specified in the order, or

(b) an order requiring him to nominate [or approve][4] another insurer who satisfies such requirements in relation to the insurance of the dwelling as are specified in the order.

(6) An agreement by the tenant of a dwelling (other than an arbitration agreement) is void in so fare as it purports to provide for a determination in a particular manner, or on particular evidence, of any question which may be the subject of an application under this paragraph. [. . .][5]

[1] modified by Commonhold and Leasehold Reform Act (2002 c. 15), Pt 2 c 5 s 165
[2] modified by Commonhold and Leasehold Reform Act (2002 c. 15), Pt 2 c 5 s 165
[3] modified by Commonhold and Leasehold Reform Act (2002 c. 15), Pt 2 c 5 s 165
[4] modified by Commonhold and Leasehold Reform Act (2002 c. 15), Pt 2 c 5 s 165
[5] modified by Commonhold and Leasehold Reform Act (2002 c. 15), Pt 2 c 5 s 165

Exception for tenants of certain public authorities

Para 9

A6–033 (1) Paragraphs 2 to 8 do not apply to a tenant of—

a local authority,

a National Park authority, or

a new town corporation[. . .][1]

[. . .][2] unless the tenancy is a long tenancy, in which case paragraphs 2 to 5 and 7 and 8 apply but paragraph 6 does not.

(2) Subsections (2) and (3) of section 26 shall apply for the purposes of sub-paragraph (1) as they apply for the purposes of subsection (1) of that section.

[1] words repealed by Government of Wales Act (1998 c.38), Sch 18 (IV) Para 1
[2] words repealed by Government of Wales Act (1998 c.38), Sch 18 (IV) Para 1

Table of derivations

1. The following abbreviations are used in this Table:— **A6–034**

Acts of Parliaments

1957	= The Housing Act 1957 (c.56).
1961	= The Housing Act 1961 (c.65).
1962	= The Landlord and Tenant Act 1962 (c.50).
1963 (c.33)	= The London Government Act 1963.
1968 (c.23)	= The Rent Act 1968
1969	= The Housing Act 1969 (c.33).
1972 (c.70)	= The Local Government Act 1972.
1974	= The Housing Act 1974 (c.44).
1975	= The Housing Rents and Subsidies Act 1975 (c.6).
1976 (c.80)	= The Rent (Agriculture) Act 1976.
1977 (c.42)	= The Rent Act 1977.
1980	= The Housing Act 1980 (c.51).
1980 (c.65)	= The Local Government, Planning and Land Act 1980.
1981 (c.64)	= The New Towns Act 1981.
1982 (c.48)	= The Criminal Justice Act 1982.
1985 (c.9)	= The Companies Consolidation (Consequential Provisions) Act 1985.
1985 (c.51)	= The Local Government Act 1985.
	Subordinate legislation
S.I. 1975/512	= The Isles of Scilly (Housing) Order 1975.

2. The Table does not show the effect of Transfer of Functions Orders.
3. The letter R followed by a number indicates that the provision gives effect to the Recommendation bearing that number in the Law Commissions' Report of the Consolidation of the Housing Acts (Cmnd. 9515).
4. The entry "drafting" indicates a provision of a mechanical or editorial nature affecting the arrangement of the consolidation; for instance, a provision introducing the provisions which follow or introducing a definition to avoid undue repetition of the defining words.

Provision	Derivation
1(1)	The Housing Act 1974 (c.44) s.121(1).
(2)	The Housing Act 1974 (c.44) s.121(1); The Housing Act 1980 (c.51) s.144; The Criminal Justice Act 1982 ss.37, 46(1).
(3)	The Housing Act 1974 (c.44) s.121(9).
2(1), (2)	The Housing Act 1974 (c.44) s.121(2).
(3)	The Housing Act 1974 (c.44) s.121(4).
(4)	The Housing Act 1974 (c.44) s.121(5); The Housing Act 1980 (c.51) s.144; The Criminal Justice Act 1982 ss.37, 46(1).
3(1)	The Housing Act 1974 (c.44) s.122(1), (2).
(2)	The Housing Act 1974 (c.44) s.122(4).
(3)	The Housing Act 1974 (c.44) s.122(5); The Housing Act 1980 (c.51) s.144; The Criminal Justice Act 1982 ss.37, 46(1).
(4)	The Housing Act 1974 (c.44) s. 112(8), (9)(a).
4(1)	The Landlord and Tenant act 1962 (c.50) s.1(1).
(2)	The Landlord and Tenant Act 1962 (c.50) s.1(2).
(3)	The Landlord and Tenant Act 1962 (c.50) ss.1(1), 6(1)(a).
5(1)	The Landlord and Tenant Act 1962 (c.50) s.2(1); The Rent (Agriculture) Act 1976 Sch. 8 para.9. The Rent Act 1977 Sch.23 para.31(a), (b).
(2)	The Landlord and Tenant Act 1962 (c.50) s.2(1); The Rent Act 1968 Sch. 15.
(3)	The Landlord and Tenant Act 1962 (c.50) s.6(1)(b).
6(1)	The Landlord and Tenant Act 1962 (c.50) s.3(1).
(2)	The Landlord and Tenant Act 1962 (c.50) s.3(2).
7(1), (2)	The Landlord and Tenant Act 1962 (c.50) s.4(1), (3); The Criminal Justice Act 1982 ss.37, 46(1), Sch.3.
(3)	The Landlord and Tenant Act 1962 (c.50) s.4(2), (3); The Criminal Justice Act 1982 ss.37, 46(1), Sch.3
(4)	The Landlord and Tenant Act 1962 (c.50) s.4(4).
8(1), (2)	The Housing Act 1957 (c.56) s.6(2), (3).
(3)	The Housing Act 1957 (c.56) s.6(1), (2).
(4)	The Housing Act 1957 (c.56) s.6(1); The London Government Act 1963 Sch. 8 para.2.
(5)	The Housing Act 1957 (c.56) s.6(2) proviso.
(6)	The Housing Act 1957 (c.56) s.189(1) "house" (a).
9(1), (2)	The Housing Act 1957 (c.56) s.7.
(3)	The Housing Act 1957 (c.56) ss.7, 189(1) "house" (a).
10	The Housing Act 1957 (c.56) s.4(1); The Housing Act 1969 (c.33) s.71.
11(1)	The Housing Act 1961 (c.65) s.32(1).
(2)	The Housing Act 1961 (c.65) s.32(2).

Provision	Derivation
(3)	The Housing Act 1961 (c.65) s.32(3).
(4)	The Housing Act 1961 (c.65) s.32(1), (2).
(5)	The Housing Act 1961 (c.65) s.32(1).
(6)	The Housing Act 1961 (c.65) s.32(4).
12(1)	The Housing Act 1961 (c.65) s.33(7).
(2)	The Housing Act 1961 (c.65) s.33(6).
13(1)	The Housing Act 1961 (c.65) s.33(1).
(2)	The Housing Act 1961 (c.65) s.33(2), (5).
14(1), (2)	The Housing Act 1961 (c.65) s.33(3).
(3)	The Housing Act 1961 (c.65) s.33(4).
(4)	The Rent Act 1977 ss.14, 15(3); The Housing Act 1980 (c.51) s.80(1)(a)–(c), (2), (3); The Local Government, Planning and Land Act 1980 s.155(1); The New Towns Act 1981 Sch. 12 para. 24.
(5)	The Housing Act 1980 (c.51) s.80(1)(d), (e).
15	The Housing Act 1961 (c.65) s.33(8).
16	The Housing Act 1961 (c.65) s.32(5).
17(1)	The Housing Act 1974 (c.44) s.125(1).
(2)	The Housing Act 1974 (c.44) s.125(2); R14(i).
18(1)–(3)	The Housing Act 1980 (c.51) Sch.19 para 1(1).
19(1)	The Housing Act 1980 (c.51) Sch.19 paras 2, 3.
(2)	The Housing Act 1980 (c.51) Sch.19 para 2.
(3)	The Housing Act 1980 (c.51) Sch.19 para 11.
(4)	The Housing Act 1980 (c.51) Sch.19 para 12.
20(1)	The Housing Act 1980 (c.51) Sch.19 paras 2, 4(1).
(2)	The Housing Act 1980 (c.51) Sch.19 para 4(2).
(3)	The Housing Act 1980 (c.51) Sch.19 para 5(1)–(6).
(4)	The Housing Act 1980 (c.51) Sch.19 para 5(7).
(5)	The Housing Act 1980 (c.51) Sch.19 para 6.
(6)	The Housing Act 1980 (c.51) s.151(1), (3).
21(1)	The Housing Act 1980 (c.51) Sch. 19 para.7(1), (5).
(2)	The Housing Act 1980 (c.51) Sch.19 para.7(2).
(3)	The Housing Act 1980 (c.51) Sch.19 para.9.
(4)	The Housing Act 1980 (c.51) Sch.19 para.7(1).
(5), (6)	The Housing Act 1980 (c.51) Sch.19 para.7(3).
22(1), (2)	The Housing Act 1980 (c.51) Sch.19 para.7(4).
(3)	The Housing Act 1980 (c.51) Sch.19 para.9.
(4)	The Housing Act 1980 (c.51) Sch.19 para.7(4).
23(1), (2)	The Housing Act 1980 (c.51) Sch.19 para.8(1), (2).
24	The Housing Act 1980 (c.51) Sch.19 para.10.
25(1), (2)	The Housing Act 1980 (c.51) Sch.19 para.13(1); The Criminal Justice act 1982 ss.37, 46(1).
26(1)	The Housing Act 1980 (c.51) s.50(1) "development corporation", "local authority", Sch.19 para.14(1), (2)(a).
(2), (3)	The Housing Act 1980 (c.51) Sch.3 para.1(2), (2A), (3), Sch.19 para.14(1); 1984 Sch.1 para.12, Sch.11 para.33(1).

Provision	Derivation
27	The Housing Act 1980 (c.51) Sch.19 para.15.
28(1)	drafting.
(2)	The Housing Act 1980 (c.51) Sch.16 para.3(2), Sch.19 para.17(1); The Companies Consolidation (Consequential Provisions) Act 1985 Sch.2.
(3)	The Housing Act 1980 (c.51) Sch.16 para.3(4), Sch.19 para.17(1).
(4)	The Housing Act 1980 (c.51) Sch.19 para.17(2).
(5)	The Housing Act 1980 (c.51) Sch.19 para.17(2)(b); The Companies Consolidation (Consequential Provisions) Act 1985 Sch.2.
(6)	The Housing Act 1980 (c.51) Sch.19 para.14(1), (2)(b).
29(1)	The Housing Act 1980 (c.51) Sch.19 para.20.
(2), (3)	The Housing Act 1980 (c.51) Sch.19 para.21(1).
(4)	The Housing Act 1980 (c.51) Sch.19 para.20(b).
(5)	The Housing Act 1980 (c.51) Sch.19 para.21(2).
(6)	The Housing Act 1980 (c.51) s.151(1), (3).
30	
"flat"	The Housing Act 1980 (c.51) Sch.19 para.16.
"landlord"	The Housing Act 1980 (c.51) Sch.19 para.18.
"tenant"	The Housing Act 1980 (c.51) Sch.19 para.19.
31(1)	The Housing Rents and Subsidies Act 1975 (c.6) ss.11(1), 15(1), (5).
(2)	The Housing Rents and Subsidies Act 1975 (c.6) ss.11(2), 15(5).
(3)	The Housing Rents and Subsidies Act 1975 (c.6) s.11(10), (11).
(4)	The Housing Rents and Subsidies Act 1975 (c.6) ss.11(3), 15(1).
32(1)	The Housing Act 1974 (c.44) ss.121(9), 122(8), 125(2).
(2)	The Housing Act 1961 (c.65) s.33(3)
(3)	The Housing Rents and Subsidies Act 1975 (c.6) s.11(1) "dwelling".
33(1)	The Landlord and Tenant Act 1962 (c.50) s.4(6); The Housing Act 1974 (c.44) ss.121(6), 122(6); The Housing Act 1980 (c.51) Sch.19 para.13(2).
(2)	The Housing Act 1974 (c.44) ss.121(7), 122(7); The Housing Act 1980 (c.51) Sch.19 para.13(3); R.28.
34	The Landlord and Tenant Act 1962 (c.50) s.5(2); The Rent Act 1968 Sch.15; The Local Government Act 1972 s.222(1); The Housing Act 1974 (c.44) s.121(8); The Rent Act 1977 s.149(2), Sch.23 para.32, Sch.24 para.30.
35(1), (2)	1972 s.103; The Housing Rents and Subsidies Act 1975 (c.6) s.17(11), Sch.5 para.7(1); S.I. 1972/1204; The Isles of Scilly (Housing) Order 1975; R.29.

Provision	Derivation
36	The Housing Act 1961 (c.65) s.32(5); The Housing Act 1974 (c.44) ss.121(9), 125(2); The Housing Rents and Subsidies Act 1975 (c.6) s.11(11) "new letting"; drafting.
37	The Landlord and Tenant Act 1962 (c.50) s.6(1)(a); The Housing Act 1974 (c.44) ss.121(9), 122(8), 125(2); The Rent (Agriculture) Act 1976 Sch.8 para.31; The Rent Act 1977 Sch.23 para.66; The Housing Act 1980 (c.51) Sch.19 para.18; R.14(i).
38	
"address" housing association	The Landlord and Tenant Act 1962 (c.50) s.6(2); The Housing Act 1974 (c.44) ss.121(3), 122(3), Sch.13 para.9.
"co-operative	The Rent Act 1977 s.15(3)(d); The Housing Act 1980 (c.51) s.80(1)(b); drafting
"dwelling"	The Housing Act 1974 (c.44) s.129(1) "dwelling"; The Housing Rents and Subsidies Act 1975 (c.6) s.16(1) "dwelling".
"housing association"	The Rent Act 1977 s.15(3)(a); The Housing Act 1980 (c.51) s.80(1)(b).
"local authority"	The Housing Rents and Subsidies Act 1975 (c.6) ss.11(11), 16(1) "local authority"; The Rent Act 1977 s.14(1)(a)–(c); The Housing Act 1980 (c.51) s.80(1)(c); The Local Government Act 1985 Sch.13 para.21, Sch.14 paras 56, 58(h).
"local housing authority"	The Landlord and Tenant Act 1962 (c.50) s.5(2); The Rent Act 1968 Sch.15; The Housing Act 1974 (c.44) s.121(8); The Isles of Scilly (Housing) Order 1975; The Rent Act 1977 s.149(2), Sch.23 para.32, Sch.24 para.30; The Housing Act 1980 (c.51) s.50(1) "local authority", Sch.19 para.14(1)(a).
"new town corporation"	The Rent Act 1977 s.14(d), (e); The Housing Act 1980 (c.51) ss.50(1) "development corporation, 80(1)(c), Sch.19 para.14(1)(a), (c); The New Towns Act 1981 Sch.12 para.24; drafting.
"protected tenancy"	The Landlord and Tenant Act 1962 (c.50) s.2(1); The Rent Act 1968 Sch.15; The Rent Act 1977 Sch.23 para.31(b), Sch.24 para.30.
"registered"	The Rent Act 1977 s.15(3)(a); The Housing Act 1980 (c.51) s.80(1)(b).
"restricted contract"	The Landlord and Tenant Act 1962 (c.50) s.2(1); The Rent Act 1977 Sch.23 para.31(a).
"urban development corporation"	1977 (c.42) s.14(1)(g); The Housing Act 1980 (c.51) s.80(1)(c); The Local Government Planning and Land Act 1980 s.155(1).
39	drafting.
40.	drafting.

LANDLORD AND TENANT ACT 1987 CHAPTER 31

PART 1 TENANT'S RIGHTS OF FIRST REFUSAL

Notices conferring rights of first refusal

s 5 Landlord required to serve offer notice on tenants.

A7–001 [**5.**—Landlord required to serve offer notice on tenants.

(1) Where the landlord proposes to make a relevant disposal affecting premises to which this Part applies, he shall serve a notice under this section (an "offer notice") on the qualifying tenants of the flats contained in the premises (the "constituent flats").

(2) An offer notice must comply with the requirements of whichever is applicable of the following sections—

section 5A (requirements in case of contract to be completed by conveyance, &c.),

section 5B (requirements in case of sale at auction),

section 5C (requirements in case of grant of option or right of pre-emption),

section 5D (requirements in case of conveyance not preceded by contract, &c.);

and in the case of a disposal to which section 5E applies (disposal for non-monetary consideration) shall also comply with the requirements of that section.

(3) Where a landlord proposes to effect a transaction involving the disposal of an estate or interest in more than one building (whether or not involving the same estate or interest), he shall, for the purpose of complying with this section, sever the transaction so as to deal with each building separately.

(4) If, as a result of the offer notice being served on different tenants on different dates, the period specified in the notice as the period for accepting the offer would end on different dates, the notice shall have effect in relation to all the qualifying tenants on whom it is served as if it provided for that period to end with the latest of those dates.

(5) A landlord who has not served an offer notice on all of the qualifying tenants on whom it was required to be served shall nevertheless be treated as having complied with this section—

(a) if he has served an offer notice on not less than 90% of the qualifying tenants on whom such a notice was required to be served, or

(b) where the qualifying tenants on whom it was required to be served number less than ten, if he has served such a notice on all but one of them.][1]

[1] ss.5–10 substituted and ss.5A–5E, ss.8A–8E and ss.9A–9B inserted subject to savings specified in SI 1996/2212 Sch.1 para.2 by Housing Act (1996 c.52), Sch 6(1) Para 1

PART II APPOINTMENT OF MANAGERS BY THE COURT

s 21 Tenant's right to apply to court for appointment of manager.

A7–002

(1) The tenant of a flat contained in any premises to which this Part applies may, subject to the following provisions of this Part, apply to a leasehold valuation tribunal for an order under section 24 appointing a manager to act in relation to those premises.

(2) Subject to subsection (3), this Part applies to premises consisting of the whole or part of a building if the building or part contains two or more flats.

(3) This Part does not apply to any such premises at a time when—

(a) the interest of the landlord in the premises is held by an exempt landlord or a resident landlord, or

(b) the premises are included within the functional land of any charity.

[(3A) But this Part is not prevented from applying to any premises because the interest of the landlord in the premises is held by a resident landlord if at least one-half of the flats contained in the premises are held on long leases which are not tenancies to which Part 2 of the Landlord and Tenant Act 1954 (c.56) applies.][1]

(4) An application for an order under section 24 may be made—

(a) jointly by tenants of two or more flats if they are each entitled to make such an application by virtue of this section, and

(b) in respect of two or more premises to which this Part applies;

and, in relation to any such joint application as is mentioned in paragraph (a), references in this Part to a single tenant shall be construed accordingly.

(5) Where the tenancy of a flat contained in any such premises is held by joint tenants, an application for an order under section 24 in respect of those premises may be made by any one or more of those tenants.

(6) An application to the court for it to exercise in relation to any premises any jurisdiction to appoint a receiver or manager shall not be made by a tenant (in his capacity as such) in any circumstances in which an application could be made by him for an order under section 24 appointing a manager to act in relation to those premises.

(7) References in this Part to a tenant do not include references to a tenant under a tenancy to which Part II of the Landlord and Tenant Act 1954 applies.[. . .][2]

[1] added by Commonhold and Leasehold Reform Act (2002 c.15), Pt 2 c 5 s 161
[2] added by Commonhold and Leasehold Reform Act (2002 c.15), Pt 2 c 5 s 161

s 22 Preliminary notice by tenant.

A7–003

(1) Before an application for an order under section 24 is made in respect of any premises to which this Part applies by a tenant of a flat contained in

those premises, a notice under this section must (subject to subsection (3)) be served [by the tenant on—][1]

[(i) the landlord, and

(ii) any person (other than the landlord) by whom obligations relating to the management of the premises or any part of them are owed to the tenant under his tenancy.][2]

(2) A notice under this section must—

(a) specify the tenant's name, the address of his flat and an address in England and Wales (which may be the address of his flat) at which [any person on whom the notice is served][3] may serve notices, including notices in proceedings, on him in connection with this Part;

(b) state that the tenant intends to make an application for an order under section 24 to be made by a leasehold valuation tribunal in respect of such premises to which this Part applies as are specified in the notice, but (if paragraph (d) is applicable) that he will not do so if the [requirement specified in pursuance of that paragraph is complied with][4];

(c) specify the grounds on which the court would be asked to make such an order and the matters that would be relied on by the tenant for the purpose of establishing those grounds;

(d) where those matters are capable of being remedied by [any person on whom the notice is served, require him][5], within such reasonable period as is specified in the notice, to take such steps for the purpose of remedying them as are so specified; and

(e) contain such information (if any) as the Secretary of State may by regulations prescribe.

(3) a leasehold valuation tribunal may (whether on the hearing of an application for an order under section 24 or not) by order dispense with the requirement to serve a notice under this section [on a person][6] in a case where it is satisfied that it would not be reasonably practicable to serve such a notice on the [person][7], but a leasehold valuation tribunal may, when doing so, direct that such other notices are served, or such other steps are taken, as it thinks fit.

(4) In a case where—

(a) a notice under this section has been served on the landlord, and

(b) his interest in the premises specified in pursuance of subsection (2)(b) is subject to a mortgage, the landlord shall, as soon as is reasonably practicable after receiving the notice, serve on the mortgagee a copy of the notice. [. . .][8]

[1] modified by Commonhold and Leasehold Reform Act (2002 c. 15), Pt 2 c 5 s 160 (2)

[2] modified by Commonhold and Leasehold Reform Act (2002 c. 15), Pt 2 c 5 s 160 (2)
[3] modified by Commonhold and Leasehold Reform Act (2002 c. 15), Pt 2 c 5 s 160 (2)
[4] modified by Commonhold and Leasehold Reform Act (2002 c. 15), Pt 2 c 5 s 160 (2)
[5] modified by Commonhold and Leasehold Reform Act (2002 c. 15), Pt 2 c 5 s 160 (2)
[6] modified by Commonhold and Leasehold Reform Act (2002 c. 15), Pt 2 c 5 s 160 (2)
[7] modified by Commonhold and Leasehold Reform Act (2002 c. 15), Pt 2 c 5 s 160 (2)
[8] modified by Commonhold and Leasehold Reform Act (2002 c. 15), Pt 2 c 5 s 160 (2)

s 23 Application to court for appointment of manager.

A7–004 (1) No application for an order under section 24 shall be made to a leasehold valuation tribunal unless—

(a) in a case where a notice has been served under section 22, either—

(i) the period specified in pursuance of paragraph (d) of subsection (2) of that section has expired without the person required to take steps in pursuance of that paragraph having taken them, or
(ii) that paragraph was not applicable in the circumstance of the case; or

(b) in a case where the requirement to serve such a notice has been dispensed with by an order under subsection (3) of that section, either—

(i) any notices required to be served, and any other steps required to be taken, by virtue of the order have been served or (as the case may be) taken, or
(ii) no direction was given by the court when making the order.

[. . .][1]

[1] repealed by Commonhold and Leasehold Reform Act (2002 c.15) Sch14 Para1.

s 24 Appointment of manager by the court.

A7–005 (1) A leasehold valuation tribunal may, on an application for an order under this section, by order (whether interlocutory or final) appoint a manager to carry out in relation to any premises to which this Part applies—

(a) such functions in connection with the management of the premises, or

(b) such functions of a receiver,

or both, as the court thinks fit.

(2) A leasehold valuation tribunal may only make an order under this section in the following circumstances, namely—

(a) where the court is satisfied—

(i) that any relevant person either is in breach of any obligation owed by him to the tenant under his tenancy and relating to the management of the premises in question or any part of them or (in the case of an obligation dependent on notice) would be in breach of any such obligation but for the fact that it has not been reasonably practicable for the tenant to give him the appropriate notice, and

(iii) that it is just and convenient to make the order in all the circumstances of the case; or

(ab) where the court is satisfied—

(i) that unreasonable service charges have been made, or are proposed or likely to be made, and

(ii) that it is just and convenient to make the order in all the circumstances of the case;

(aba) where the tribunal is satisfied—

(i) that unreasonable variable administration charges have been made, or are proposed or likely to be made, and

(ii) that it is just and convenient to make the order in all the circumstances of the case;

(ac) where the court is satisfied—

(i) that any relevant person has failed to comply with any relevant provision of a code of practice approved by the Secretary of State under section 87 of the Leasehold Reform, Housing and Urban Development Act 1993 (codes of management practice); and

(ii) that it is just and convenient to make the order in all the circumstances of the case;

(b) where the court is satisfied that other circumstances exist which make it just and convenient for the order to be made.

(2ZA) In this section "relevant person" means a person—

(a) on whom a notice has been served under section 22, or

(b) in the case of whom the requirement to serve a notice under that section has been dispensed with by an order under subsection (3) of that section.

(2A) For the purposes of subsection (2)(ab) a service charge shall be taken to be unreasonable—

(a) if the amount is unreasonable having regard to the items for which it is payable,

(b) if the items for which it is payable are of an unnecessarily high standard, or

(c) if the items for which it is payable are of an insufficient standard with the result that additional service charges are or may be incurred.

In that provision and this subsection "service charge" means a service charge within the meaning of section 18(1) of the Landlord and Tenant Act 1985, other than one excluded from that section by section 27 of that Act (rent of dwelling registered and not entered as variable).

(2B) In subsection (2)(aba) "variable administration charge" has the meaning given by paragraph 1 of Schedule 11 to the Commonhold and Leasehold Reform Act 2002.

(3) The premises in respect of which an order is made under this section may, if the court thinks fit, be either more or less extensive than the premises specified in the application on which the order is made.

(4) An order under this section may make provision with respect to—

(a) such matters relating to the exercise by the manager of his functions under the order, and

(b) such incidental or ancillary matters,

as the court thinks fit; and, on any subsequent application made for the purpose by the manager, the court may give him directions with respect to any such matters.

(5) Without prejudice to the generality of subsection (4), an order under this section may provide—

(a) for rights and liabilities arising under contracts to which the manager is not a party to become rights and liabilities of the manager;

(b) for the manager to be entitled to prosecute claims in respect of causes of action (whether contractual or tortious) accruing before or after the date of his appointment;

(c) for remuneration to be paid to the manger by any relevant person, or by the tenants of the premises in respect of which the order is made or by all or any of those persons;

(d) for the manager's functions to be exercisable by him (subject to subsection (9)) either during a specified period or without limit of time.

(6) Any such order may be granted subject to such conditions as the court thinks fit, and in particular its operation may be suspended on terms fixed by the court.

(7) In a case where an application for an order under this section was preceded by the service of a notice under section 22, the court may, if it thinks fit, make such an order notwithstanding—

(a) that any period specified in the notice in pursuance of subsection (2)(d) of that section was not a reasonable period, or

(b) that the notice failed in any other respect to comply with any requirement contained in subsection (2) of that section or in any regulations applying to the notice under section 54(3).

(8) The Land Charges Act 1972 and the Land Registration Act 2002 shall apply in relation to an order made under this section as they apply in relation to an order appointing a receiver or sequestrator of land.

(9) A leasehold valuation tribunal may, on the application of any person interested, vary or discharge (whether conditionally or unconditionally) an order made under this section; and if the order has been protected by an entry registered under the Land Charges Act 1972 or the Land Registration Act 2002, the court may by order direct that the entry shall be cancelled.

(9A) The [tribunal][1] shall not vary or discharge an order under subsection (9) on the application of any relevant person unless it is satisfied—

(a) that the variation or discharge of the order will not result in a recurrence of the circumstances which led to the order being made, and

(b) that it is just and convenient in all the circumstances of the case to vary or discharge the order.

(10) An order made under this section shall not be discharged by a leasehold valuation tribunal by reason only that, by virtue of section 21(3), the premises in respect of which the order was made have ceased to be premises to which this Part applies.

(11) References in this Part to the management of any premises include references to the repair, maintenance, improvement or insurance of those premises. [. . .][2]

[1] substituted by Commonhold and Leasehold Reform Act (2002 c. 15), Sch13 Para9
[2] substituted by Commonhold and Leasehold Reform Act (2002 c.15), Sch13 Para9

PART IV VARIATION OF LEASES

Applications relating to flats

s 35 Application by party to lease for variation of lease.

A7–006 (1) Any party to a long lease of a flat may make an application to [a leasehold valuation tribunal][1] for an order varying the lease in such manner as is specified in the application.

(2) The grounds on which any such application may be made are that the lease fails to make satisfactory provision with respect to one or more of the following matters, namely—

(a) the repair or maintenance of—

(i) the flat in question, or
(ii) the building containing the flat, or
(iii) any land or building which is let to the tenant under the lease or in respect of which rights are conferred on him under it;

(b) the insurance of the building containing the flat or of any such land or building as is mentioned in paragraph (a)(iii);

(c) the repair or maintenance of any installations (whether they are in the same building as the flat or not) which are reasonably necessary to ensure that occupiers of the flat enjoy a reasonable standard of accommodation;

(d) the provision or maintenance of any services which are reasonably necessary to ensure that occupiers of the flat enjoy a reasonable standard of accommodation (whether they are services connected with any such installations or not, and whether they are services provided for the benefit of those occupiers or services provided for the benefit of the occupiers of a number of flats including that flat);

(e) the recovery by one party to the lease from another party to it of expenditure incurred or to be incurred by him, or on his behalf, for the benefit of that other party or of a number of persons who include that other party;

(f) the computation of a service charge payable under the lease;

(g) such other matters as may be prescribed by regulations made by the Secretary of State.

(3) For the purposes of subsection (2)(c) and (d) the factors for determining, in relation to the occupiers of a flat, what is a reasonable standard of accommodation may include—

(a) factors relating to the safety and security of the flat and its occupiers and of any common parts of the building containing the flat; and

(b) other factors relating to the condition of any such common parts.

(3A) For the purposes of subsection (2)(e) the factors for determining, in relation to a service charge payable under a lease, whether the lease makes satisfactory provision include whether it makes provision for an amount to be payable (by way of interest or otherwise) in respect of a failure to pay the service charge by the due date.

(4) For the purposes of subsection (2)(f) a lease fails to make satisfactory provision with respect to the computation of a service charge payable under it if—

(a) it provides for any such charge to be a proportion of expenditure incurred, or to be incurred, by or on behalf of the landlord or a superior landlord; and

(b) other tenants of the landlord are also liable under their leases to pay by way of service charges proportions of any such expenditure; and

(c) the aggregate of the amounts that would, in any particular case, be payable by reference to the proportions referred to in paragraphs (a) and (b) would either exceed or be less than the whole of any such expenditure.

(5) [Procedure regulations under Schedule 12 to the Commonhold and Leasehold Reform Act 2002][2] shall make provision—

(a) for requiring notice of any application under this Part to be served by the person making the application, and by any respondent to the application, on any person who the applicant, or (as the case may be) the respondent, knows or has reason to believe is likely to be affected by any variation specified in the application, and

(b) for enabling persons served with any such notice to be joined as parties to the proceedings.

(6) For the purposes of this Part a long lease shall not be regarded as a long lease of a flat if—

(a) the demised premises consist of or include three or more flats contained in the same building; or

(b) the lease constitutes a tenancy to which Part II of the Landlord and Tenant Act 1954 applies.

(8) In this section "service charge" has the meaning given by section 18(1) of the 1985 Act. [. . .][3]

[1] modified by Commonhold and Leasehold Reform Act (2002 c. 15), Pt 2 c5 s 163 (2)
[2] modified by Commonhold and Leasehold Reform Act (2002 c. 15), Pt 2 c5 s 163 (2)
[3] modified by Commonhold and Leasehold Reform Act (2002 c. 15), Pt 2 c5 s 163 (2)

s 36 Application by respondent for variation of other leases.

A7–007 (1) Where an application ("the original application") is made under section 35 by any party to a lease, any other party to the lease may make an application to the [tribunal][1] asking it, in the event of its deciding to make an order effecting any variation of the lease in pursuance of the original application, to make an order which effects a corresponding variation of each of such one or more other leases as are specified in the application.

(2) Any lease so specified—

(a) must be a long lease of a flat under which the landlord is the same person as the landlord under the lease specified in the original application; but

(b) need not be a lease of a flat which is in the same building as the flat let under that lease, nor a lease drafted in terms identical to those of that lease.

(3) The grounds on which an application may be made under this section are—

(a) that each of the leases specified in the application fails to make satisfactory provision with respect to the matter or matters specified in the original application; and

(b) that, if any variation is effected in pursuance of the original application, it would be in the interests of the person making the application under this section, or in the interests of the other persons who are parties to the leases specified in that application, to have all of the leases in question (that is to say, the ones specified in that application together with the one specified in the original application) varied to the same effect. [. . .][2]

[1] word substituted by Commonhold and Leasehold Reform Act (2002 c. 15), Pt 2 c 5 s 163 (3).
[2] word substituted by Commonhold and Leasehold Reform Act (2002 c. 15), Pt 2 c 5 s 163 (3).

Orders varying leases

s 38 Orders varying leases.

A7–008

(1) If, on an application under section 35, the grounds on which the application was made are established to the satisfaction of the tribunal, the tribunal may (subject to subsections (6) and (7)) make an order varying the lease specified in the application in such manner as is specified in the order.

(2) If—

(a) an application under section 36 was made in connection with that application, and

(b) the grounds set out in subsection (3) of that section are established to the satisfaction of the tribunal with respect to the leases specified in the application under section 36,

the tribunal may (subject to subsections (6) and (7)) also make an order varying each of those leases in such manner as is specified in the order.

(3) If, on an application under section 37, the grounds set out in subsection (3) of that section are established to the satisfaction of the tribunal with respect to the leases specified in the application, the tribunal may (subject to subsections (6) and (7) make an order varying each of those leases in such manner as is specified in the order.

(4) The variation specified in an order under subsection (1) or (2) may be either the variation specified in the relevant application under section 35 or 36 or such other variation as the tribunal thinks fit.

(5) If the grounds referred to in subsection (2) or (3) (as the case may be) are established to the satisfaction of the tribunal with respect to some but not all of the leases specified in the application, the power to make an order under that subsection shall extend to those leases only.

(6) A tribunal shall not make an order under this section effecting any variation of a lease if it appears to the tribunal—

(a) that the variation would be likely substantially to prejudice—

(i) any respondent to the application, or

(ii) any person who is not a party to the application,

and that an award under subsection (10) would not afford him adequate compensation, or

(b) that for any other reason it would not be reasonable in the circumstances for the variation to be effected.

(7) A tribunal shall not, on an application relating to the provision to be made by a lease with respect to insurance, make an order under this section effecting any variation of the lease—

(a) which terminates any existing right of the landlord under its terms to nominate an insurer for insurance purposes; or

(b) which requires the landlord to nominate a number of insurers from which the tenant would be entitled to select an insurer for those purposes; or

(c) which, in a case where the lease requires the tenant to effect insurance with a specified insurer, requires the tenant to effect insurance otherwise than with another specified insurer.

(8) A tribunal may, instead of making an order varying a lease in such manner as is specified in the order, make an order directing the parties to the lease to vary it in such manner as is so specified, and accordingly any reference in this Part (however expressed) to an order which effects any variation of a lease or to any variation effected by an order shall include a reference to an order which directs the parties to a lease to effect a variation of it or (as the case may be) a reference to any variation effected in pursuance of such an order.

(9) A tribunal may by order direct that a memorandum of any variation of a lease effected by an order under this section shall be endorsed on such documents as are specified in the order.

(10) Where a tribunal makes an order under this section varying a lease the tribunal may, if it thinks fit, make an order providing for any party to the lease to pay, to any other party to the lease or to any other person, compensation in respect of any loss or disadvantage that the court considers he is likely to suffer as a result of the variation. [. . .][2]

[1] words repealed subject to savings specified in SI 2004/669 Sch.2 para.12 by Comonhold and Leasehold Reform Act (2002 c. 15), Sch14 Para1

[2] words repealed subject to savings specified in SI 2004/669 Sch.2 para.12 by Comonhold and Leasehold Reform Act (2002 c. 15), Sch14 Para1

s 39 Effect or orders varying leases: applications by third parties.

A7–009 (1) Any variation effected by an order under section 38 shall be binding not only on the parties to the lease for the time being but also on other persons (including any predecessors in title of those parties), whether or not they were parties to the proceedings in which the order was made or were served with a notice by virtue of section 35(5).

(2) Without prejudice to the generality of subsection (1), any variation effected by any such order shall be binding on any surety who has guaranteed the performance of any obligation varied by the order; and the surety shall accordingly be taken to have guaranteed the performance of that obligation as so varied.

(3) Where any such order has been made and a person was, by virtue of section 35(5), required to be served with a notice relating to the proceedings in which it was made, but he was not so served, he may—

(a) bring an action for damages for breach of statutory duty against the person by whom any such notice was so required to be served in respect of that person's failure to serve it;

(b) apply to [a leasehold valuation tribunal][1] for the cancellation or modification of the variation in question.

(4) [A tribunal][2] may, on an application under subsection (3)(b) with respect to any variation of a lease—

(a) by order cancel that variation or modify it in such manner as is specified in the order, or

(b) make such an order as is mentioned in section 38 (10) in favour of the person making the application,

as it thinks fit.

(5) Where a variation is cancelled or modified under paragraph (a) of subsection (4)—

(a) the cancellation or modification shall take effect as from the date of the making of the order under that paragraph or as from such later date as may be specified in the order, and

(b) the [tribunal][3] may by order direct that a memorandum of the cancellation or modification shall be endorsed on such documents as are specified in the order;

and, in a case where a variation is so modified, subsections (1) and (2) above shall, as from the date when the modification takes effect, apply to the variation as modified. [. . .][4]

1 modified by Commonhold and Leasehold Reform Act (2002 c.15), Pt 2 c 5 s 163 (6)
2 modified by Commonhold and Leasehold Reform Act (2002 c.15), Pt 2 c 5 s 163 (6)
3 modified by Commonhold and Leasehold Reform Act (2002 c.15), Pt 2 c 5 s 163 (6)
4 modified by Commonhold and Leasehold Reform Act (2002 c.15), Pt 2 c 5 s 163 (6)

PART V MANAGEMENT OF LEASEHOLD PROPERTY

Service charges

s 42 Service charge contributions to be held in trust.

A7–010 [**42.**—Service charge contributions to be held in trust.

(1) This section applies where the tenants of two or more dwellings may be required under the terms of their leases to contribute to the same costs, or the tenant of a dwelling may be required under the terms of his lease to contribute to costs to which no other tenant of a dwelling may be required to contribute, by the payment of service charges; and in this section—

"the contribution tenants" means those tenants and "the sole contributing tenant" means that tenant;

"the payee" means the landlord or other person to whom any such charges are payable by those tenants, or that tenant, under the terms of their leases, or his lease;

"relevant service charges" means any such charges;

"service charge" has the meaning given by section 18(1) of the 1985 Act, except that it does not include a service charge payable by the tenant of a dwelling the rent of which is registered under Part IV of the Rent Act 1977, unless the amount registered is, in pursuance of section 71(4) of that Act, entered as a variable amount;

"tenant" does not include a tenant of an exempt landlord; and

"trust fund" means the fund, or (as the case may be) any of the funds, mentioned in subsection (2) below.

(2) Any sums paid to the payee by the contributing tenants, or the sole contributing tenant, by way of relevant service charges, and any investments representing those sums, shall (together with any income accruing thereon) be held by the payee either as a single fund or, if he thinks fit, in two or more separate funds.

(3) The payee shall hold any trust fund—

(a) on trust to defray costs incurred in connection with the matters for which the relevant service charges were payable (whether incurred by himself or by any other person), and

(b) subject to that, on trust for the persons who are the contributing tenants for the time being, or the person who is the sole contributing tenant for the time being.

(4) Subject to subsections (6) to (8), the contributing tenants shall be treated as entitled by virtue of subsection (3)(b) to such shares in the residue of any such fund as are proportionate to their respective liabilities to pay

relevant service charges or the sole contributing tenant shall be treated as so entitled to the residue of any such fund.

(5) If the Secretary of State by order so provides, any sums standing to the credit of any trust fund may, instead of being invested in any other manner authorised by law, be invested in such manner as may be specified in the order; and any such order may contain such incidental, supplemental or transitional provisions as the Secretary of State considers appropriate in connection with the order.

(6) On the termination of the lease of any of the contributing tenants the tenant shall not be entitled to any part of any trust fund, and (except where subsection (7) applies) any part of any such fund which is attributable to relevant service charges paid under the lease shall accordingly continue to be held on the trusts referred to in subsection (3).

(7) On the termination of the lease of the last of the contributing tenants, or of the lease of the sole contributing tenant, any trust fund shall be dissolved as at the date of the termination of the lease, and any assets comprised in the fund immediately before its dissolution shall—

(a) if the payee is the landlord, be retained by him for his own use and benefit, and

(b) in any other case, be transferred to the landlord by the payee.

(8) Subsections (4), (6) and (7) shall have effect in relation to any of the contributing tenants, or the sole contributing tenant, subject to any express terms of his lease (whenever it was granted) which relate to the distribution, either before or (as the case may be) at the termination of the lease, of amounts attributable to relevant service charges paid under its terms (whether the lease was granted before or after the commencement of this section).

(9) Subject to subsection (8), the provisions of this section shall prevail over the terms of any express or implied trust created by a lease so far as inconsistent with those provisions, other than an express trust so created, in the case of a lease of any of the contributing tenants, before the commencement of this section or, in the case of the lease of the sole contributing tenant, before the commencement of paragraph 15 of Schedule 10 to the Commonhold and Leasehold Reform Act 2002.][1]

[1] modified by Commonhold and Leasehold Reform Act (2002 c.15), Sch10 Para15

s 42A Service charge contributions to be held in designated account

A7–011 (1) The payee must hold any sums standing to the credit of any trust fund in a designated account at a relevant financial institution.

(2) An account is a designed account in relation to sums standing to the credit of a trust fund if—

(a) the relevant financial institution has been notified in writing that sums standing to the credit of the trust fund are to be (or are) held in it, and

(b) no other funds are held in the account,

and the account is an account of a description specified in regulations made by the Secretary of State.

(3) Any of the contributing tenants, or the sole contributing tenant, may by notice in writing require the payee—

(a) to afford him reasonable facilities for inspecting documents evidencing that subsection (1) is complied with and for taking copies of or extracts from them, or

(b) to take copies of or extracts from any such documents and either send them to him or afford him reasonable facilities for collecting them (as he specifies).

(4) If the tenant is represented by a recognised tenants' association and he consents, the notice may be served by the secretary of the association instead of by the tenant (and in that case any requirement imposed by it is to afford reasonable facilities, or to send copies or extracts, to the secretary).

(5) A notice under this section is duly served on the payee if it is served on—

(a) an agent of the payee named as such in the rent book or similar document, or

(b) the person who receives the rent on behalf of the payee;

and a person on whom such a notice is so served must forward it as soon as may be to the payee.

(6) The payee must comply with a requirement imposed by a notice under this section within the period of twenty-one days beginning with the day on which he receives the notice.

(7) To the extent that a notice under this section requires the payee to afford facilities inspecting documents—

(a) he must do so free of charge, but

(b) he may treat as part of his costs of management any costs incurred by him in doing so.

(8) The payee may make a reasonable charge for doing anything else in compliance with a requirement imposed by a notice under this section.

(9) Any of the contributing tenants, or the sole contributing tenant, may withhold payment of a service charge if he has reasonable grounds for believing that the payee has failed to comply with the duty imposed on him by subsection (1); and any provisions of his tenancy relating to non-payment or late payment of service charges do not have effect in relation to the period for which he so withholds it.

(10) Nothing in this section applies to the payee if the circumstances are such as are specified in regulations made by the Secretary of State.

(11) In this section—

"recognised tenants' association" has the same meaning as in the 1985 Act, and

"relevant financial institution" has the meaning given by regulations made by the Secretary of State;

and expressions used both in section 42 and this section have the same meaning as in that section. [. . .][1]

[1] added by Commonhold and Leasehold Reform Act (2002 c. 15), Pt 2 c 5 s 156(1)

s 42B Failure to comply with section 42A

A7–012

(1) If a person fails, without reasonable excuse, to comply with a duty imposed on him by or by virtue of section 42A he commits an offence.
(2) A person guilty of an offence under this section is liable on summary conviction to a fine not exceeding level 4 on the standard scale.
(3) Where an offence under this section committed by a body corporate is proved—

(a) to have been committed with the consent or connivance of a director, manager, secretary or other similar officer of the body corporate, or a person purporting to act in such a capacity, or

(b) to be due to any neglect on the part of such an officer or person,

he, as well as the body corporate, is guilty of the offence and liable to be proceeded against and punished accordingly.
(4) Where the affairs of a body corporate are managed by its members, subsection (3) applies in relation to the acts and defaults of a member in connection with his functions of management as if he were a director of the body corporate.
(5) Proceeding for an offence under this section may be brought by a local housing authority (within the meaning of section 1 of the Housing Act 1985 (c. 68)). [. . .][1]

[1] added by Commonhold and Leasehold Reform Act (2002 c. 15), Pt 2 c 5 s 156(1)

PART VI INFORMATION TO BE FURNISHED TO TENANTS

s 46 Application of Par VI, etc.

A7–013

(1) This Part applies to premises which consist of or include a dwelling and are not held under a tenancy to which Part II of the Landlord and Tenant Act 1954 applies.
(2) In this Part "service charge" has the meaning given by section 18(1)of the 1985 Act. [. . .][1]

[(3) In this Part "administration charge" has the meaning given by paragraph 1 of Schedule 11 to the Commonhold and Leasehold Reform Act 2002.][2]

[1] added by Commonhold and Leasehold Reform Act (2002 c. 15), Sch. 11 (2) Para 9
[2] added by Commonhold and Leasehold Reform Act (2002 c. 15), Sch. 11 (2) Para 9

s 47 Landlord's name and address to be contained in demands for rent etc.

A7–014 (1) Where any written demand is given to a tenant of premises to which this Part applies, the demand must contain the following information, namely—

(a) the name and address of the landlord, and

(b) if that address is not in England and Wales, an address in England and Wales at which notices (including notices in proceedings) may be served on the landlord by the tenant.

(2) Where—

(a) a tenant of any such premises is given such a demand, but

(b) it does not contain any information required to be contained in it by virtue of subsection (1),

then (subject to subsection (3) any part of the amount demanded which consists of a service charge or an administration charge ("the relevant amount") shall be treated for all purposes as not being due from the tenant to the landlord at any time before that information is furnished by the landlord by notice given to the tenant.

(3) The relevant amount shall not be so treated in relation to any time when, by virtue of an order of any [or tribunal][1], there is in force an appointment of a receiver or manager whose functions include the receiving of service charges or (as the case may be) administration charges from the tenant.

(4) In this section "demand" means a demand for rent or other sums payable to the landlord under the terms of the tenancy. [. . .][2]

[1] words inserted by Commonhold and Leasehold Reform Act (2002 c. 15), Sch 13 Para 10
[2] words inserted by Commonhold and Leasehold Reform Act (2002 c. 15), Sch 13 Para 10

s 48 Notification by landlord of address for service of notices.

A7–015 (1) A landlord of premises to which this Part applies shall by notice furnish the tenant with an address in England and Wales at which notices (including notices in proceedings) may be served on him by the tenant.

(2) Where a landlord of any such premises fails to comply with subsection (1), any rent, service charge or administration charge otherwise due from

the tenant to the landlord shall (subject to subsection (3)) be treated for all purposes as not being due from the tenant to the landlord at any time before the landlord does comply with that subsection.

(3) Any such rent, service charge or administration charge shall not be so treated in relation to any time when, by virtue of an order of any court [or tribunal][1], there is in force an appointment of a received or manager whose functions include the receiving of rent, service charges or (as the case may be) administration charges from the tenant. [. . .][2]

[1] words inserted by Commonhold and Leasehold Reform Act (2002 c. 15), Sch 13 Para 11
[2] words inserted by Commonhold and Leasehold Reform Act (2002 c. 15), Sch 13 Para 11

PART VII GENERAL

s 58 Exempt landlords and resident landlords.

A7–016

(1) In this Act "exempt landlord" means a landlord who is one of the following bodies, namely—

(a) a district, county, county borough or London borough council, the Common Council of the City of London, the London Fire and Emergency Planning Authority, the Council of the Isles of Scilly, a police authority established under section 3 of the Police Act 1996, t[. . .][1] or a joint authority established by Part IV of the Local Government Act 1985;

(b) the Commission for the New Towns or a development corporation established by an order made (or having effect as if made) under the New Towns Act 1981;

(c) an urban development corporation within the meaning of Part XVI of the Local Government, Planning and Land Act 1980;

(ca) a housing action trust established under Part III of the Housing Act 1988.

(dd) the Boards Authority;

(de) a National Part authority;

(e) the Housing Corporation;

(f) a housing trust (as defined in section 6 of the Housing Act 1985) which is a charity;

(g) a registered social landlord, or a fully mutual housing association which is not a registered social landlord; or

(h) an authority established under section 10 of the Local Government Act 1985 (joint arrangements for waste disposal functions).

(1A) In subsection (1)(g)—

"fully mutual housing association" has the same meaning as in the Housing Associations Act 1985 (see section 1(1) and (2) of that Act); and

"registered social landlord" has the same meaning as in the Housing Act 1985 (see section 5(4) and (5) of that Act).

(2) For the purposes of this Act the landlord of any premises consisting of the whole or part of a building is a resident landlord of those premises at any time if—

(a) the premises are not, and do not form part of, a purpose-built block of flats; and

(b) at that time the landlord occupies a flat contained in the premises as his only or principal residence, and

(c) he has so occupied such a flat throughout a period of not less than 12 months ending with that time.

(3) In subsection (2) "purpose-built block of flats" means a building which contained as constructed, and contains, two or more flats.

[1] words repealed by Criminal Justice and Police Act (2001 c.16), Sch 7(5) (1) Para 1

s 60 General interpretation.

A7–017 (1) In this Act—

"the 1985 Act" means the Landlord and Tenant Act 1985;

"charity" means a charity within the meaning of the Charities Act 1993, and "charitable purposes", in relation to a charity, means charitable purpose whether of that charity or of that charity and other charities;

"common parts", in relation to any building or part of a building, includes the structure and exterior of that building or part and any common facilities within it;

"the court" means the High Court or a county court;

"dwelling" means a building or part of a building occupied or intended to be occupied as a separate dwelling, together with any yard, garden, outhouses and appurtenances belonging to it or usually enjoyed with it;

"exempt landlord" has the meaning given by section 58(1);

"flat" means a separate set of premises, whether or not on the same floor, which—

(a) forms part of a building, and

(b) is divided horizontally from some other part of that building, and

(c) is constructed or adapted for use for the purposes of a dwelling;

"functional land", in relation to a charity, means land occupied by the charity, or by trustees for it, and wholly or mainly used for charitable purposes;

"landlord" (except for the purposes of Part I) means the immediate landlord or, in relation to a statutory tenant, the person who, apart from the statutory tenancy, would be entitled to possession of the premises subject to the tenancy;

"lease" and related expression shall be construed in accordance with section 59(1) and (2);

"long lease" has the meaning given by section 59(3);

"mortgage" includes any charge or lien, and references to a mortgagee shall be construed accordingly;

"notices in proceedings" means notices or other documents served in, or in connection with, any legal proceedings;

[. . .][1]

"resident landlord" shall be construed in accordance with section 58(2);

"statutory tenancy" and "statutory tenant" mean a statutory tenancy or statutory tenant within the meaning of the Rent Act 1977 or the Rent (Agriculture) Act 1976;

"tenancy" includes a statutory tenancy.

[1] repealed subject to savings specified in SI 1996/2212 Sch.1 para.2 by Housing Act (1996 c.52), Sch 6 (IV) Para 10

LEASEHOLD REFORM, HOUSING AND URBAN DEVELOPMENT ACT 1993 CHAPTER 28

PART I LANDLORD AND TENANT

CHAPTER V TENANTS' RIGHT TO MANAGEMENT AUDIT

s 76 Right to audit management by landlord.

A8–001 (1) This Chapter has effect to confer on two or more qualifying tenants of dwellings held on leases from the same landlord the right, exercisable subject to and in accordance with this Chapter, to have an audit carried out on their behalf which relates to the management of the relevant premises and any appurtenant property by or an behalf of the landlord.

(2) That right shall be exercisable—

(a) where the relevant premises consist of or include two dwellings let to qualifying tenants of the same landlord, by either or both of those tenants; and

(b) where the relevant premises consist of or include three or more dwellings let to qualifying tenants of the same landlord, by not less than two-thirds of those tenants;

and in this Chapter the dwellings let to those qualifying tenants are referred to as "the constituent dwellings".

(3) In relation to an audit on behalf of two or more qualifying tenants—

(a) "the relevant premises" means so much of—

(i) the building or buildings containing the dwellings let to those tenants, and

(ii) any other building or buildings,

as constitutes premises in relation to which management functions are discharged in respect of the costs of which common service charge contributions are payable under the leases of those qualifying tenants; and

(b) "appurtenant property" means so much of any property not contained in the relevant premises as constitutes property in relation to which any such management functions are discharged.

(4) This Chapter also has effect to confer on a single qualifying tenant of a dwelling the right, exercisable subject to and in accordance with this Chapter, to have an audit carried out on his behalf which relates to the management of the relevant premises and any appurtenant property by or on behalf of the landlord.

(5) That right shall be exercisable by a single qualifying tenant of a dwelling where the relevant premises contain no other dwelling let to a qualifying tenant apart from that let to him.

(6) In relation to an audit on behalf of a single qualifying tenant—

(a) "the relevant premises" means so much of—

(i) the building containing the dwelling let to him, and
(ii) any other building or buildings,

as constitutes premises in relation to which management functions are discharged in respect of the costs of which a service charge is payable under his lease (whether as a common service charge contribution or otherwise); and

(b) "appurtenant property" means so much of any property not contained in the relevant premises as constitutes property in relation to which any such management functions are discharged.

(7) The provisions of sections 78 to 83 shall, with any necessary modifications, have effect in relation to an audit on behalf of a single qualifying tenant as they have effect in relation to an audit on behalf of two or more qualifying tenants.

(8) For the purposes of this section common service charge contributions are payable by two or more persons under their leases if they may be required under the terms of those leases to contribute to the same costs by the payment of service charges.

s 77 Qualifying tenants.

(1) Subject to the following provisions of this section, a tenant is a qualifying tenant of a dwelling for the purposes of this Chapter if— **A8–002**

(a) he is a tenant of the dwelling under a long lease other than a business lease; and

(b) any service charge is payable under the lease.

(2) For the purposes of subsection (1) a lease is a long lease if—

(a) it is a lease falling within any of paragraphs (a) to (c) of subsection (1) of section 7; or

(b) it is a shared ownership lease (within the meaning of that section), whether granted in pursuance of Part V of the Housing Act 1985 or otherwise and whatever the share of tenant under it.

(3) No dwelling shall have more than one qualifying tenant at any one time.

(4) Accordingly—

(a) where a dwelling is for the time being let under two or more leases falling within subsection (1), any tenant under any of those leases which is superior to that held by any other such tenant shall not be a qualifying tenant of the dwelling for the purposes of this Chapter; and

(b) where a dwelling is for the time being let to joint tenants under a lease falling within subsection (1), the joint tenants shall (subject to paragraph (a)) be regarded for the purposes of this Chapter as jointly constituting the qualifying tenant of the dwelling.

(5) A person can, however, be (or be among those constituting) the qualifying tenant of each of two or more dwellings at the same time, whether he is tenant of those dwellings under one lease or under two or more separate leases.

(6) Where two or more persons constitute the qualifying tenant of a dwelling in accordance with subsection (4)(b), any one or more of those persons may sign a notice under section 80 on behalf of both or all of them.

s 78 Management audits.

A8–003 (1) The audit referred to in section 76(1) is an audit carried out for the purpose of ascertaining—

(a) the extent to which the obligations of the landlord which—

(i) are owed to the qualifying tenants of the constituent dwellings, and
(ii) involve the discharge of management functions in relation to the relevant premises or any appurtenant property,

are being discharged in an efficient and effective manner; and

(b) the extent to which sums payable by those tenants by way of service charges are being applied in an efficient and effective manner;

and in this Chapter any such audit is referred to as a "management audit".

(2) In determining whether any such obligations as are mentioned in subsection (1)(a) are being discharged in an efficient and effective manner, regard shall be had to any applicable provisions of any code of practice for the time being approved by the Secretary of State under section 87.

(3) A management audit shall be carried out by a person who—

(a) is qualified for appointment by virtue of subsection (4); and
(b) is appointed—

(i) in the circumstances mentioned in section 76(2)(a), by either or both of the qualifying tenants of the constituent dwellings, or
(ii) in the circumstances mentioned in section 76(2)(b), by not less than two-thirds of the qualifying tenants of the constituent dwellings;

and in this Chapter any such person is referred to as "the auditor".

(4) A person is qualified for appointment for the purposes of subsection (3) above if—

(a) he has the necessary qualification (within the meaning of subsection (1) of section 28 of the 1985 Act (meaning of "qualified accountant")) or is a qualified surveyor;

(b) he is not disqualified from acting (within the meaning of that subsection); and

(c) he is not a tenant of any premises contained in the relevant premises.

(5) For the purposes of subsection (4)(a) above a person is a qualified surveyor if he is a fellow or professional associate of the Royal Institution of Chartered Surveyors or of the Incorporated Society of Valuers and Auctioneers or satisfies such other requirement or requirements as may be prescribed by regulations made by the Secretary of State.

(6) The auditor may appoint such persons to assist him in carrying out the audit as he thinks fit.

s 79 Rights exercisable in connection with management audits.

A8–004

(1) Where the qualifying tenants of any dwellings exercise under section 80 their right to have a management audit carried out on their behalf, the rights conferred on the auditor by subsection (2) below shall be exercisable by him in connection with the audit.

(2) The rights conferred on the auditor by this subsection are—

(a) a right to require the landlord—

(i) to supply him with such a summary as is referred to in section 21(1) of the 1985 Act (request for summary of relevant costs) in connection with any service charges payable by the qualifying tenants of the constituent dwellings, and

(ii) to afford him reasonable facilities for inspecting, or taking copies of or extracts from, the accounts, receipts and other documents supporting any such summary;

(b) a right to require the landlord or any relevant person to afford him reasonable facilities for inspecting any other documents sight of which is reasonably required by him for the purpose of carrying out the audit; and

(c) a right to require the landlord or any relevant person to afford him reasonable facilities for taking copies of or extracts from any documents falling within paragraph (b).

(3) The rights conferred on the auditor by subsection (2) shall be exercisable by him—

(a) in relation to the landlord, by means of a notice under section 80; and

(b) in relation to any relevant person, by means of a notice given to that person at (so far as is reasonably practicable) the same time as a notice under section 80 is given to the landlord;

and, where a notice is given to any relevant person in accordance with paragraph (b) above, a copy of that notice shall be given to the landlord by the auditor.

(4) The auditor shall also be entitled, on giving notice in accordance with section 80, to carry out an inspection of any common parts comprised in the relevant premises or any appurtenant property.

(5) The landlord or (as the case may be) any relevant person shall—

(a) where facilities for the inspection of any documents are required under subsection (2)(a)(ii) or (b), make those facilities available free of charge;

(b) where any documents are required to be supplied under subsection (2)(a)(i) or facilities for the taking of copies or extracts are required under subsection (2)(a)(ii) or (c), be entitled to supply those documents or (as the case may be) make those facilities available on payment of such reasonable charge as he may determine.

(6) The requirement imposed on the landlord by subsection (5)(a) to make any facilities available free of charge shall not be construed as precluding the landlord from treating as part of his costs of management any costs incurred by him in connection with making those facilities so available.

(7) In this Chapter "relevant person" means a person (other than the landlord) who—

(a) is charged with responsibility—

(i) for the discharge of any such obligations as are mentioned in section 78(1)(a), or

(ii) for the application of any such service charges as are mentioned in section 78(1)(b); or

(b) has a right to enforce payment of any such service charges.

(8) In this Chapter references to the auditor in the context of—

(a) being afforded any such facilities as are mentioned in subsection (2), or

(b) the carrying out of any inspection under subsection (4),

shall be read as including a person appointed by the auditor under section 78(6).

s 80 Exercise of right to have a management audit.

A8–005 (1) The right of any qualifying tenants to have a management audit carried out on their behalf shall be exercisable by the giving of a notice under this section.

(2) A notice given under this section—

(a) must be given to the landlord by the auditor, and

(b) must be signed by each of the tenants on whose behalf it is given.

(3) Any such notice must—

(a) state the full name of each of those tenants and the address of the dwelling of which he is a qualifying tenant;

(b) state the name and address of the auditor;

(c) specify any documents or description of documents—

(i) which the landlord is required to supply to the auditor under section 79(2)(a)(i), or
(ii) in respect of which he is required to afford the auditor facilities for inspection or for taking copies or extracts under any other provision of section 79(2); and

(d) if the auditor proposes to carry out an inspection under section 79(4), state the date on which he proposes to carry out the inspection.

(4) The date specified under subsection (3)(d) must be a date falling not less than one month nor more than two months after the date of the giving of the notice.

(5) A notice is duly given under this section to the landlord of any qualifying tenants if it is given to a person who receives on behalf of the landlord the rent payable by any such tenants; and a person to whom such a notice is so given shall forward it as soon as may be to the landlord.

s 81 Procedure following given of notice under section 80.

A8–006 (1) Where the landlord is given a notice under section 80, then within the period of one month beginning with the date of the giving of the notice, he shall—

(a) supply the auditor with any document specified under subsection (3)(c)(i) of that section, and afford him, in respect of any document falling within section 79(2)(a)(ii), any facilities specified in relation to it under subsection (3)(c)(ii) of section 80;

(b) in the case of every other document or description of documents specified in the notice under subsection (3)(c)(ii) of that section, either—

(i) afford the auditor facilities for inspection or (as the case may be) taking copies or extracts in respect of that document or those documents, or
(ii) give the auditor a notice stating that he objects to doing so for such reasons as are specified in the notice; and

(c) if a date is specified in the notice under subsection (3)(d) of that section, either approve the date or propose another date for the carrying out of an inspection under section 79(4).

(2) Any date proposed by the landlord under subsection (1)(c) must be a date falling not later than the end of the period of two months beginning with the date of the giving of the notice under section 80.

(3) Where a relevant person is given a notice under section 79 requiring him to afford the auditor facilities for inspection or taking copies or extracts in respect of any documents or description of documents specified in the notice, then within the period of one month beginning with the date of the giving of the notice, he shall, in the case of every such document or description of documents, either—

(a) afford the auditor the facilities required by him; or

(b) give the auditor a notice stating that he objects to doing so for such reasons as are specified in the notice.

(4) If by the end of the period of two months beginning with—

(a) the date of the giving of the notice under section 80, or

(b) the date of the giving of such a notice under section 79 as is mentioned in subsection (3) above,

the landlord or (as the case may be) a relevant person has failed to comply with any requirement of the notice, the court may, on the application of the auditor, make an order requiring the landlord or (as the case may be) the relevant person to comply with that requirement within such period as is specified in the order.

(5) The court shall not make an order under subsection (4) in respect of any document or documents unless it is satisfied that the document or documents falls or fall within paragraph (a) or (b) of section 79(2).

(6) If by the end of the period of two months specified in subsection (2) no inspection under section 79(4) has been carried out by the auditor, the court may, on the application of the auditor, make an order providing for such an inspection to be carried out on such date as is specified in the order.

(7) Any application for an order under subsection (4) or (6) must be made before the end of the period of four months beginning with—

(a) in the case of an application made in connection with a notice given under section 80, the date of the giving of that notice; or

(b) in the case of an application made in connection with such a notice under section 79 as is mentioned in subsection (3) above, the date of the giving of that notice.

s 82 Requirement relating to information etc. held by superior landlord.

A8–007 (1) Where the landlord is required by a notice under section 80 to supply any summary falling within section 79(2)(a), and any information necessary for complying with the notice so far as relating to any such summary is in the possession of a superior landlord—

(a) the landlord shall make a written request for the relevant information to the person who is his landlord (and so on, if that person is himself not the superior landlord);

(b) the superior landlord shall comply with that request within the period of one month beginning with the date of the making of the request; and

(c) the landlord who received the notice shall then comply with it so far as relating to any such summary within the time allowed by section 81(1) or such further time, if any, as is reasonable.

(2) Where—

(a) the landlord is required by a notice under section 80 to afford the auditor facilities for inspection or taking copies or extracts in respect of any documents or description of documents specified in the notice, and

(b) any of the documents in question is in the custody or under the control of a superior landlord,

the landlord shall on receiving the notice inform the auditor as soon as may be of that fact and of the name and address of the superior landlord, and the auditor may then give the superior landlord a notice requiring him to afford the facilities in question in respect of the document.

(3) Subsections (3) to (5) and (7) of section 81 shall, with any necessary modifications, have effect in relation to a notice given to a superior landlord under subsection (2) above as they have effect in relation to any such notice given to a relevant person as is mentioned in subsection (3) of that section.

s 83 Supplementary provisions.

(1) Where— **A8–008**

(a) a notice has been given to a landlord under section 80, and

(b) at a time when any obligations arising out of the notice remain to be discharged by him—

(i) he disposes of the whole or part of his interest as landlord of the qualifying tenants of the constituent dwellings, and
(ii) the person acquiring any such interest of the landlord is in a position to discharge any of those obligations to any extent,

that person shall be responsible for discharging those obligations to that extent, as if he had been given the notice under that section.

(2) If the landlord is, despite any such disposal, still in a position to discharge those obligations to the extent referred to in subsection (1), he shall remain responsible for so discharging them; but otherwise the person referred to in that subsection shall be responsible for so discharging them to the exclusion of the landlord.

(3) Where a person is so responsible for discharging any such obligations (whether with the landlord or otherwise)—

(a) references to the landlord in section 81 shall be read as including, or as, references to that person to such extent as is appropriate to reflect his responsibility for discharging those obligations; but

(b) in connection with the discharge of any such obligations by that person, that section shall apply as if any reference to the date of the giving of the notice under section 80 were a reference to the date of the disposal referred to in subsection (1).

(4) Where—

(a) a notice has been given to a relevant person under section 79, and

(b) at a time when any obligations arising out of the notice remain to be discharged by him, he ceases to be a relevant person, but

(c) he is, despite ceasing to be a relevant person, still in a position to discharge those obligations to any extent,

he shall nevertheless remain responsible for discharging those obligations to that extent; and section 81 shall accordingly continue to apply to him as if he were still a relevant person.

(5) Where—

(a) a notice has been given to a landlord under section 80, or

(b) a notice has been given to a relevant person under section 79,

then during the period of twelve months beginning with the date of that notice, no subsequent such notice may be given to the landlord or (as the case may be) that person on behalf of any persons who, in relation to the earlier notice, were qualifying tenants of the constituent dwellings.

s 84 Interpretation of Chapter V.

A8–009 [. . .][1] In this Chapter—

"the 1985 Act" means the Landlord and Tenant Act 1985;

"appurtenant property" shall be construed in accordance with section76(3) or (6);

"the auditor", in relation to a management audit, means such a person as is mentioned in section 78(3);

"the constituent dwellings" means the dwellings referred to in section 76(2)(a) or (b) (as the case may be);

"landlord" means immediate landlord;;

"management audit" means such an audit as is mentioned in section 78(1);

"management functions" includes functions with respect to the provision of services or the repair, maintenance [, improvement][1] or insurance of property;

"relevant person" has the meaning given by section79(7);

"the relevant premises" shall be construed in accordance with section 76(3) or (6);

"service charge" has the meaning given by section 18(1) of the 1985 Act.

[1] word inserted by Commonhold and Leasehold Reform Act (2002 c.15), Sch 9 Para 10

[1] word inserted by Commonhold and Leasehold Reform Act (2002 c.15), Sch 9 Para 10

HOUSING ACT 1996 CHAPTER 52

PART III LANDLORD AND TENANT

CHAPTER 1 TENANTS' RIGHTS

Forfeiture

s 81 Restriction on termination of tenancy for failure to pay service charge.

A9–001 (1) A landlord may not, in relation to premises let as a dwelling, exercise a right of re-entry or forfeiture for failure by a tenant to pay a service charge or administration charge unless—

(a) it is finally determined by (or on appeal from) a leasehold valuation tribunal or by a court, or by an arbitral tribunal in proceedings pursuant to a post-dispute arbitration agreement, that the amount of the service charge or administration charge is payable by him, or

(b) the tenant has admitted that it is so payable.

(2) The landlord may not exercise a right of re-entry or forfeiture by virtue of subsection (1)(a) until after the end of the period of 14 days beginning with the day after that on which the final determination is made.

(3) For the purposes of this section it is finally determined that the amount of a service charges or administration charge is payable—

(a) if a decision that it is payable is not appealed against or otherwise challenged, at the end of the time for bringing an appeal or other challenge, or

(b) if such a decision is appealed against or otherwise challenged and not set aside in consequence of the appeal or other challenge, at the time specified in subsection (3A).

(3A) The time referred to in subsection (3)(b) is the time when the appeal or other challenge is disposed of—

(a) by the determination of the appeal or other challenge and the expiry of the time for bringing a subsequent appeal (if any), or

(b) by its being abandoned or otherwise ceasing to have effect.

(4) The reference in subsection (1) to premises let as a dwelling does not include premises let on—

(a) a tenancy to which Part II of the Landlord and Tenant Act 1954 applies (business tenancies),

(b) a tenancy of an agricultural holding within the meaning of the Agricultural Holding Act 1986 in relation to which that Act applies, or

(c) a farm business tenancy within the meaning of the Agricultural Tenancies Act 1995.

(4A) References in this section to the exercise of a right of re-entry or forfeiture include the service of a notice under section 146(1) of the Law of Property Act 1925 (restriction on re-entry or forfeiture).

(5) In this section

(a) "administration charge" has the meaning given by Part 1 of Schedule 11 to the Commonhold and Leasehold Reform Act 2002,

(b) "arbitration agreement" and "arbitral tribunal" have the same meaning as in Part 1 of the Arbitration Act 1996 (c.23) and "post-dispute arbitration agreement", in relation to any matter, means an arbitration agreement made after a dispute about the matter has arisen,

(c) "dwelling" has the same meaning as in the Landlord and Tenant Act 1985 (c.70), and

(d) "service charge" means a service charge within the meaning of section 18(1) of the Landlord and Tenant Act 1985, other than one excluded from that section by section 27 of that Act (rent of dwelling registered and not entered as variable).

[(5A) Any order of a court to give effect to a determination of a leasehold valuation tribunal shall be treated as a determination by the court for the purposes of this section.][1]

(6) Nothing in this section affects the exercise of a right of re-entry or forfeiture on other grounds. [. . .][2]

[1] added by Commonhold and Leasehold Reform Act (2002 c.15), Sch 13 Para 16
[2] added by Commonhold and Leasehold Reform Act (2002 c.15), Sch 13 Para 16

Service charges

s 84 Right to appoint surveyor to advise on matters relating to service charges.

A9–002

(1) A recognised tenants' association may appoint a surveyor for the purpose of this section to advise on any matters relating to, or which may give rise to, service charges payable to a landlord by one or more members of the association.

The provisions of Schedule 4 have effect for conferring on a surveyor so appointed rights of access to documents and premises.

(2) A person shall not be so appointed unless he is a qualified surveyor.

For this purpose "qualified surveyor" has the same meaning as in section 78(4)(a) of the Leasehold Reform, Housing and Urban Development Act 1993 (persons qualified for appointment to carry out management audit).

(3) The appointment shall take effect for the purposes of this section upon notice in writing being given to the landlord by the association stating the

name and address of the surveyor, the duration of his appointment and the matters in respect of which he is appointed.

(4) An appointment shall cease to have effect for the purposes of this section if the association gives notice in writing to the landlord to that effect or if the association ceases to exist.

(5) A notice is duly given under this section to a landlord of any tenants if it is given to a person who receives on behalf of the landlord the rent payable by those tenants; and a person to whom such a notice is so given shall forward it as soon as may be to the landlord.

(6) In this section—

> "recognised tenants' association" has the same meaning as in the provisions of the Landlord and Tenant Act 1985 relating to service charges (see section 29 of that Act); and
>
> "service charge" means a service charge within the meaning of section 18(1) of that Act, other than one excluded from that section by section 27 of that Act (rent of dwelling registered and not entered as variable).

COMMONHOLD AND LEASEHOLD REFORM ACT 2002 CHAPTER 15

PART 1 COMMONHOLD

Operation of commonhold

38 Commonhold assessment

(1) A commonhold community statement must make provision— **A10–001**

(a) requiring the directors of the commonhold association to make an annual estimate of the income required to be raised from unit-holders to meet the expenses of the association,

(b) enabling the directors of the commonhold association to make estimates from time to time of income required to be raised from unit-holders in addition to the annual estimate,

(c) specifying the percentage of any estimate made under paragraph (a) or (b) which is to be allocated to each unit,

(d) requiring each unit-holder to make payments in respect of the percentage of any estimate which is allocated to his unit, and

(e) requiring the directors of the commonhold association to serve notices on unit-holders specifying payments required to be made by them and the date on which each payment is due.

(2) For the purpose of subsection (1)(c)—

(a) the percentage allocated by a commonhold community statement to the commonhold units must amount in aggregate to 100;

(b) a commonhold community statement may specify 0 per cent. in relation to a unit.

39 Reserve fund

(1) Regulations under section 32 may, in particular, require a commonhold community statement to make provision— **A10–002**

(a) requiring the directors of the commonhold association to establish and maintain one or more funds to finance the repair and maintenance of common parts;

(b) requiring the directors of the commonhold association to establish and maintain one or more funds to finance the repair and maintenance of commonhold units.

(2) Where a commonhold community statement provides for the establishment and maintenance of a fund in accordance with subsection (1) it must also make provision—

(a) requiring or enabling the directors of the commonhold association to set a levy from time to time,

(b) specifying the percentage of any levy set under paragraph (a) which is to be allocated to each unit,

(c) requiring each unit-holder to make payments in respect of the percentage of any levy set under paragraph (a) which is allocated to his unit, and

(d) requiring the directors of the commonhold association to serve notices on unit-holders specifying payments required to be made by them and the date on which each payment is due.

(3) For the purpose of subsection (2)(b)—

(a) the percentages allocated by a commonhold community statement to the commonhold units must amount in aggregate to 100;

(b) a commonhold community statement may specify 0 per cent in relation to a unit.

(4) The assets of a fund established and maintained by virtue of this section shall not be used for the purpose of enforcement of any debt except a judgment debt referable to a reserve fund activity.

(5) For the purpose of subsection (4)—

(a) "reserve fund activity" means an activity which in accordance with the commonhold community statement can or may be financed from a fund established and maintained by virtue of this section,

(b) assets are used for the purpose of enforcement of a debt if, in particular, they are taken in execution or are made the subject of a charging order under section 1 of the Charging Orders Act 1979 (c.53), and

(c) the reference to a judgment debt includes a reference to any interest payable on a judgment debt.

PART 2 LEASEHOLD REFORM

CHAPTER 1 RIGHT TO MANAGE

Introductory

s 71 The right to manage

A10–003 (1) This Chapter makes provision for the acquisition and exercise of rights in relation to the management of premises to which this Chapter applies by a company which, in accordance with this Chapter, may acquire and exercise those rights (referred to in this Chapter as a RTM company).

(2) The rights are to be acquired and exercised subject to and in accordance with this Chapter and are referred to in this Chapter as the right to manage.

Qualifying rules

s 72 Premises to which Chapter applies

(1) This Chapter applies to premises if— **A10–004**

(a) they consist of a self-contained building or part of a building, with or without appurtenant property,

(b) they contain two or more flats held by qualifying tenants, and

(c) the total number of flats held by such tenants is not less than two-thirds of the total number of flats contained in the premises.

(2) A building is a self-contained building if it is structurally detached.
(3) A part of a building is a self-contained part of the building if—

(a) it constitutes a vertical division of the building,

(b) the structure of the building is such that it could be redeveloped independently of the rest of the building, and

(c) subsection (4) applies in relation to it.

(4) This subsection applies in relation to a part of a building if the relevant service provided for occupiers of it—

(a) are provided independently of the relevant services provided for occupiers of the rest of the building, or

(b) could be so provided without involving the carrying out of works likely to result in a significant interruption in the provision of any relevant services for occupiers of the rest of the building.

(5) Relevant services are services provided by means of pipes, cables or other fixed installations.
(6) Schedule 6 (premises excepted from this Chapter) has effect.

s 73 RTM companies

(1) This section specifies what is a RTM company. **A10–005**
(2) A company is a RTM company in relation to premises if—

(a) it is a private company limited by guarantee, and

(b) its memorandum of association states that its object, or one of its objects, is the acquisition and exercise of the right to manage the premises.

(3) But a company is not a RTM company if it is a commonhold association (within the meaning of Part 1).

(4) And a company is not a RTM company in relation to premises if another company is already a RTM company in relation to the premises or to any premises containing or contained in the premises.

(5) If the freehold of any premises is [transferred][1] to a company which is a RTM company in relation to the premises, or any premises containing or contained in the premises, it ceases to be a RTM company when the [transfer][2] is executed.

[1] words substituted by Finance Act (2003 c.14), Sch 20 (20) Para 3
[2] words substituted by Finance Act (2003 c.14), Sch 20 (20) Para 3

s 74 RTM companies: membership and regulations

A10–006 (1) The persons who are entitled to be members of a company which is a RTM company in relation to premises are—

(a) qualifying tenants of flats contained in the premises, and

(b) from the date on which it acquires the right to manage (referred to in this Chapter as the "acquisition date"), landlords under leases of the whole or any part of the premises.

(2) The appropriate national authority shall make regulations about the content and form of the memorandum of association and articles of association of RTM companies.

(3) A RTM company may adopt provisions of the regulations for its memorandum or articles.

(4) The regulations may include provision which is to have effect for a RTM company whether or not it is adopted by the company.

(5) A provision of the memorandum or articles of a RTM company has no effect to the extent that it is inconsistent with the regulations.

(6) The regulations have effect in relation to a memorandum or articles—

(a) irrespective of the date of the memorandum or articles, but

(b) subject to any transitional provisions of the regulations.

(7) The following provisions of the Companies Act 1985 (c.6) do not apply to a RTM company—

(a) sections 2(7) and 3 (memorandum), and

(b) section 8 (articles).

s 75 Qualifying tenants

A10–007 (1) This section specifies whether there is a qualifying tenant of a flat for the purposes of this Chapter and, if so, who it is.

(2) Subject as follows, a person is the qualifying tenant of a flat if he is tenant of the flat under a long lease.

(3) Subsection (2) does not apply where the lease is a tenancy to which Part 2 of the Landlord and Tenant Act 1954 (c.56) (business tenancies) applies.

(4) Subsection (2) does not apply where—

(a) the lease was granted by sub-demise out of a superior lease other than a long lease,

(b) the grant was made in breach of the terms of the superior lease, and

(c) there has been no waiver of the breach by the superior landlord.

(5) No flat has more than one qualifying tenant at any one time; and subsections (6) and (7) apply accordingly.

(6) Where a flat is being let under two or more long leases, a tenant under any of those leases which is superior to that held by another is not the qualifying tenant of the flat.

(7) Where a flat is being let to joint tenants under a long lease, the joint tenants shall (subject to subsection (6)) be regarded as jointly being the qualifying tenant of the flat.

s 76 Long leases

A10–008

(1) This section and section 77 specify what is a long lease for the purposes of this Chapter.

(2) Subject to section 77, a lease is a long lease if—

(a) it is granted for a term of years certain exceeding 21 years, whether or not it is (or may become) terminable before the end of that term by notice given by or to the tenant, by re-entry or forfeiture or otherwise,

(b) it is for a term fixed by law under a grant with a covenant or obligation for perpetual renewal (but is not a lease by sub-demise from one which is not a long lease),

(c) it takes effect under section 149(6) of the Law of Property Act 1925 (c.20) (leases terminable after a death or marriage),

(d) it was granted in pursuance of the right to buy conferred by Part 5 of the Housing Act 1985 (c.68) or in pursuance of the right to acquire on rent to mortgage terms conferred by that Part of that Act,

(e) it is a shared ownership lease, whether granted in pursuance of that Part of that Act or otherwise, where the tenant's total share is 100 per cent., or

(f) it was granted in pursuance of that Part of that Act as it has effect by virtue of section 17 of the Housing Act 1996 (c. 52) (the right to acquire).

(3) "Shared ownership lease" means a lease—

(a) granted on payment of a premium calculated by reference to a percentage of the value of the demised premises or the cost of providing them, or

(b) under which the tenant (or his personal representatives) will or may be entitled to a sum calculated by reference, directly or indirectly, to the value of those premises.

(4) "Total share", in relation to the interest of a tenant under a shared ownership lease, means his initial share plus any additional share or shares in the demised premises which he has acquired.

s 77 Long leases: further provisions

A10–009 (1) A lease terminable by notice after a death or marriage is not a long lease if—

(a) the notice is capable of being given at any time after the death or marriage of the tenant,

(b) the length of the notice is not more than three months, and

(c) the terms of the lease preclude both its assignment otherwise than by virtue of section 92 of the Housing Act 1985 (assignments by way of exchange) and the sub-letting of the whole of the demised premises.

(2) Where the tenant of any property under a long lease, on the coming to an end of the lease, becomes or has become tenant of the property or part of it under any subsequent tenancy (whether by express grant or by implication of law), that tenancy is a long lease irrespective of its terms.

(3) A lease—

(a) granted for a term of years certain not exceeding 21 years, but with a covenant or obligation for renewal without payment of a premium (but not for perpetual renewal), and

(b) renewed on one or more occasions so as to bring to more than 21 years the total of the terms granted (including any interval between the end of a lease and the grant of a renewal),

is to be treated as if the term originally granted had been one exceeding 21 years.

(4) Where a long lease—

(a) is or was continued for any period under Part 1 of the Landlord and Tenant Act 1954 (c. 56) or under Schedule 10 to the Local Government and Housing Act 1989 (c. 42), or

(b) was continued for any period under the Leasehold Property (Temporary Provisions) Act 1951 (c. 38),

it remains a long lease during that period.

(5) Where in the case of a flat there are at any time two or more separate leases, with the same landlord and the same tenant, and—

(a) the property comprised in one of those leases consists of either the flat or a part of it (in either case with or without appurtenant property), and

(b) the property comprised in every other lease consists of either a part of the flat (with or without appurtenant property) or appurtenant property only,

there shall be taken to be a single long lease of the property comprised in such of those leases as are long leases.

Claim to acquire right

s 78 Notice inviting participation

A10–010

(1) Before making a claim to acquire the right to manage any premises, a RTM company must give notice to each person who at the time when the notice is given—

(a) is the qualifying tenant of a flat contained in the premises, but

(b) neither is nor has agreed to become a member of the RTM company.

(2) A notice given under this section (referred to in this Chapter as a "notice of invitation to participate") must—

(a) state that the RTM company intends to acquire the right to manage the premises,

(b) state the names of the members of the RTM company,

(c) invite the recipients of the notice to become members of the company, and

(d) contain such other particulars (if any) as may be required to be contained in notices of invitation to participate by regulations made by the appropriate national authority.

(3) A notice of invitation to participate must also comply with such requirements (if any) about the form of notices of invitation to participate as may be prescribed by regulations so made.

(4) A notice of invitation to participate must either—

(a) be accompanied by a copy of the memorandum of association and articles of association of the RTM company, or

(b) include a statement about inspection and copying of the memorandum of association and articles of association of the RTM company.

(5) A statement under subsection (4)(b) must—

(a) specify a place (in England or Wales) at which the memorandum of association and articles of association may be inspected,

(b) specify as the times at which they may be inspected periods of at least two hours on each of at least three days (including a Saturday or Sunday or both) within the seven days beginning with the day following that on which the notice is given,

(c) specify a place (in England or Wales) at which, at any time within those seven days, a copy of the memorandum of association and articles of association may be ordered, and

(d) specify a fee for the provision of an ordered copy, not exceeding the reasonable cost of providing it.

(6) Where a notice given to a person includes a statement under subsection (4)(b), the notice is to be treated as not having been given to him if he is not allowed to undertake an inspection, or is not provided with a copy, in accordance with the statement.

(7) A notice of invitation to participate is not invalidated by any inaccuracy in any of the particulars required by or by virtue of this section.

s 79 Notice of claim to acquire right

A10–011 (1) A claim to acquire the right to manage any premises is made by giving notice of the claim (referred to in this Chapter as a "claim notice"); and in this Chapter the "relevant date", in relation to any claim to acquire the right to manage, means the date on which notice of the claim is given.

(2) The claim notice may not be given unless each person required to be given a notice of invitation to participate has been given such a notice at least 14 days before.

(3) The claim notice must be given by a RTM company which complies with subsection (4) or (5).

(4) If on the relevant date there are only two qualifying tenants of flats contained in the premises, both must be members of the RTM company.

(5) In any other case, the membership of the RTM company must on the relevant date include a number of qualifying tenants of flats contained in the premises which is not less than one-half of the total number of flats so contained.

(6) The claim notice must be given to each person who on the relevant date is—

(a) landlord under a lease of the whole or any part of the premises,

(b) party to such a lease otherwise than as landlord or tenant, or

(c) a manager appointed under Part 2 of the Landlord and Tenant Act 1987 (c.31) (referred to in this Part as "the 1987 Act") to act in relation to the premises, or any premises containing or contained in the premises.

(7) Subsection (6) does not require the claim notice to be given to a person who cannot be found or whose identity cannot be ascertained; but if this subsection means that the claim notice is not required to be given to anyone at all, section 85 applies.

(8) A copy of the claim notice must be given to each person who on the relevant date is the qualifying tenant of a flat contained in the premises.

(9) Where a manager has been appointed under Part 2 of the 1987 Act to act in relation to the premises, or any premises containing or contained in the premises, a copy of the claim notice must also be given to the leasehold valuation tribunal or court by which he was appointed.

s 80 Contents of claim notice

A10–012

(1) The claim notice must comply with the following requirements.

(2) It must specify the premises and contain a statement of the grounds on which it is claimed that they are premises to which this Chapter applies.

(3) It must state the full name of each person who is both—

(a) the qualifying tenant of a flat contained in the premises, and

(b) a member of the RTM company,

and the address of his flat.

(4) And it must contain, in relation to each such person, such particulars of his lease as are sufficient to identify it, including—

(a) the date on which it was entered into,

(b) the term for which it was granted, and

(c) the date of the commencement of the term.

(5) It must state the name and registered office of the RTM company.

(6) It must specify a date, not earlier than one month after the relevant date, by which each person who was given the notice under section 79(6) may respond to it by giving a counter-notice under section 84.

(7) It must specify a date, at least three months after that specified under subsection (6), on which the RTM company intends to acquire the right to manage the premises.

(8) It must also contain such other particulars (if any) as may be required to be contained in claim notices by regulations made by the appropriate national authority.

(9) And it must comply with such requirements (if any) about the form of claim notices as may be prescribed by regulations so made.

s 81 Claim notice: supplementary

A10–013

(1) A claim notice is not invalidated by any inaccuracy in any of the particulars required by or by virtue of section 80.

(2) Where any of the members of the RTM company whose names are stated in the claim notice was not the qualifying tenant of a flat contained in the premises on the relevant date, the claim notice is not invalidated on that account, so long as a sufficient number of qualifying tenants of flats contained in the premises were members of the company on that date; and for

this purpose a "sufficient number" is a number (greater than one) which is not less than one-half of the total number of flats contained in the premises on that date.

(3) Where any premises have been specified in a claim notice, no subsequent claim notice which specifies—

(a) the premises, or

(b) any premises containing or contained in the premises,

may be given so long as the earlier claim notice continues in force.

(4) Where a claim notice is given by a RTM company it continues in force from the relevant date until the right to manage is acquired by the company unless it has previously—

(a) been withdrawn or deemed to be withdrawn by virtue of any provision of this Chapter, or

(b) ceased to have effect by reason of any other provision of this Chapter.

s 82 Right to obtain information

A10–014 (1) A company which is a RTM company in relation to any premises may give to any person a notice requiring him to provide the company with any information—

(a) which is in his possession or control, and

(b) which the company reasonably requires for ascertaining the particulars required by or by virtue of section 80 to be included in a claim notice for claiming to acquire the right to manage the premises.

(2) Where the information is recorded in a document in the person's possession or control, the RTM company may give him a notice requiring him—

(a) to permit any person authorised to act on behalf of the company at any reasonable time to inspect the document (or, if the information is recorded in the document in a form in which it is not readily intelligible, to give any such person access to it in a readily intelligible form), and

(b) to supply the company with a copy of the document containing the information in a readily intelligible form on payment of a reasonable fee.

(3) A person to whom a notice is given must comply with it within the period of 28 days beginning with the day on which it is given.

s 83 Right of access

A10–015 (1) Where a RTM company has given a claim notice in relation to any premises, each of the persons specified in subsection (2) has a right of access to any part of the premises if that is reasonable in connection with any matter arising out of the claim to acquire the right to manage.

(2) The persons referred to in subsection (1) are—

(a) any person authorised to act on behalf of the RTM company,

(b) any person who is landlord under a lease of the whole or any part of the premises and any person authorised to act on behalf of any such person,

(c) any person who is party to such a lease otherwise than as landlord or tenant and any person authorised to act on behalf of any such person, and

(d) any manager appointed under Part 2 of the 1987 Act to act in relation to the premises, or any premises containing or contained in the premises, and any person authorised to act on behalf of any such manager.

(3) The right conferred by this section is exercisable, at any reasonable time, on giving not less than ten days' notice—

(a) to the occupier of any premises to which access is sought, or

(b) if those premises are unoccupied, to the person entitled to occupy them.

s 84 Counter-notices

A10–016

(1) A person who is given a claim notice by a RTM company under section 79(6) may give a notice (referred to in this Chapter as a "counter-notice") to the company no later than the date specified in the claim notice under section 80(6).

(2) A counter-notice is a notice containing a statement either—

(a) admitting that the RTM company was on the relevant date entitled to acquire the right to manage the premises specified in the claim notice, or

(b) alleging that, by reason of a specified provision of this Chapter, the RTM company was on that date not so entitled,

and containing such other particulars (if any) as may be required to be contained in counter-notices, and complying with such requirements (if any) about the form of counter-notices, as may be prescribed by regulations made by the appropriate national authority.

(3) Where the RTM company has been given one or more counter-notices containing a statement such as is mentioned in subsection (2)(b), the company may apply to a leasehold valuation tribunal for a determination that it was on the relevant date entitled to acquire the right to manage the premises.

(4) An application under subsection (3) must be made not later than the end of the period of two months beginning with the day on which the

counter-notice (or, where more than one, the last of the counter-notices) was given.

(5) Where the RTM company has been given one or more counter-notices containing a statement such as is mentioned in subsection (2)(b), the RTM company does not acquire the right to manage the premises unless—

(a) on an application under subsection (3) it is finally determined that the company was on the relevant date entitled to acquire the right to manage the premises, or

(b) the person by whom the counter-notice was given agrees, or the persons by whom the counter-notices were given agree, in writing that the company was so entitled.

(6) If on an application under subsection (3) it is finally determined that the company was not on the relevant date entitled to acquire the right to manage the premises, the claim notice ceases to have effect.

(7) A determination on an application under subsection (3) becomes final—

(a) if not appealed against, at the end of the period for bringing an appeal, or

(b) if appealed against, at the time when the appeal (or any further appeal) is disposed of.

(8) An appeal is disposed of—

(a) if it is determined and the period for bringing any further appeal has ended, or

(b) if it is abandoned or otherwise ceases to have effect.

s 85 Landlords etc. not traceable

A10–017

(1) This section applies where a RTM company wishing to acquire the right to manage premises—

(a) complies with subsection (4) or (5) of section 79, and

(b) would not have been precluded from giving a valid notice under that section with respect to the premises,

but cannot find, or ascertain the identity of, any of the persons to whom the claim notice would be required to be given by subsection (6) of that section.

(2) The RTM company may apply to a leasehold valuation tribunal for an order that the company is to acquire the right to manage the premises.

(3) Such an order may be made only if the company has given notice of the application to each person who is the qualifying tenant of a flat contained in the premises.

(4) Before an order is made the company may be required to take such further steps by way of advertisement or otherwise as is determined proper for the purpose of tracing the persons who are—

(a) landlords under leases of the whole or any part of the premises, or

(b) parties of such leases otherwise than as landlord or tenant.

(5) If any of those persons is traced—

(a) after an application for an order is made, but

(b) before the making of an order,

no further proceedings shall be taken with a view to the making of an order.

(6) Where that happens—

(a) the rights and obligations of all persons concerned shall be determined as if the company had, at the date of the application, duly given notice under section 79 of its claim to acquire the right to manage the premises, and

(b) the leasehold valuation tribunal may give such directions as it thinks fit as to the steps to be taken for giving effect to their rights and obligations, including directions modifying or dispensing with any of the requirements imposed by or by virtue of this Chapter.

(7) An application for an order may be withdrawn at any time before an order is made and, after it is withdrawn, subsection (6)(a) does not apply.

(8) But where any step is taken for the purpose of giving effect to subsection (6)(a) in the case of any application, the application shall not afterwards be withdrawn except—

(a) with the consent of the person or persons traced, or

(b) by permission of the leasehold valuation tribunal.

(9) And permission shall be given only where it appears just that it should be given by reason of matters coming to the knowledge of the RTM company in consequence of the tracing of the person or persons traced.

s 86 Withdrawal of claim notice

A10–018

(1) A RTM company which has given a claim notice in relation to any premises may, at any time before it acquires the right to manage the premises, withdraw the claim notice by giving a notice to that effect (referred to in this Chapter as a "notice of withdrawal").

(2) A notice of withdrawal must be given to each person who is—

(a) landlord under a lease of the whole or any part of the premises,

(b) party to such a lease otherwise than as landlord or tenant,

(c) a manager appointed under Part 2 of the 1987 Act to act in relation to the premises, or any premises containing or contained in the premises, or

(d) the qualifying tenant of a flat contained in the premises.

s 87 Deemed withdrawal

A10–019 (1) If a RTM company has been given one or more counter-notices containing a statement such as is mentioned in subsection (2)(b) of section 84 but either—

(a) no application for a determination under subsection (3) of that section is made within the period specified in subsection (4) of that section, or

(b) such an application is so made but is subsequently withdrawn,

the claim notice is deemed to be withdrawn.

(2) The withdrawal shall be taken to occur—

(a) if paragraph (a) of subsection (1) applies, at the end of the period specified in that paragraph, and

(b) if paragraph (b) of that subsection applies, on the date of the withdrawal of the application.

(3) Subsection (1) does not apply if the person by whom the counter-notice was given has, or the persons by whom the counter-notices were given have, (before the time when the withdrawal would be taken to occur) agreed in writing that the RTM company was on the relevant date entitled to acquire the right to manage the premises.

(4) The claim notice is deemed to be withdrawn if—

(a) a winding-up order [. . .][1] is made, or a resolution for voluntary winding-up is passed, with respect to the RTM company, or the RTM company enters administration,

(b) a receiver or a manager of the RTM company's undertaking is duly appointed, or possession is taken, by or on behalf of the holders of any debentures secured by a floating charge, of any property of the RTM company comprised in or subject to the charge,

(c) a voluntary arrangement proposed in the case of the RTM company for the purpose of Part of 1 of the Insolvency Act 1986 (c. 45) is approved under that Part of the Act, or

(d) the RTM company's name is struck off the register under section 652 or 652A of the Companies Act 1985 (c. 6).

[1] words repealed by SI 2003/2096 (Enterprise Act 2002 (Insolvency) Order), Sch 1(1) Para 39 (a).

s 88 Costs: general

(1) A RTM company is liable for reasonable costs incurred by a person who is— **A10–020**

(a) landlord under a lease of the whole or any part of any premises,

(b) party to such a lease otherwise than as landlord or tenant, or

(c) a manager appointed under Part 2 of the 1987 Act to act in relation to the premises, or any premises containing or contained in the premises,

in consequence of a claim notice given by the company in relation to the premises.

(2) Any costs incurred by such a person in respect of professional services rendered to him by another are to be regarded as reasonable only if and to the extent that costs in respect of such services might reasonably be expected to have been incurred by him if the circumstances had been such that he was personally liable for all such costs.

(3) A RTM company is liable for any costs which such a person incurs as party to any proceedings under this Chapter before a leasehold valuation tribunal only if the tribunal dismisses an application by the company for a determination that it is entitled to acquire the right to manage the premises.

(4) Any question arising in relation to the amount of any costs payable by a RTM company shall, in default of agreement, be determined by a leasehold valuation tribunal.

s 89 Costs where claim ceases

(1) This section applies where a claim notice given by a RTM company— **A10–021**

(a) is at any time withdrawn or deemed to be withdrawn by virtue of any provision of this Chapter, or

(b) at any time ceases to have effect by reason of any other provision of this Chapter.

(2) The liability of the RTM company under section 88 for costs incurred by any person is a liability for costs incurred by him down to that time.

(3) Each person who is or has been a member of the RTM company is also liable for those costs (jointly and severally with the RTM company and each other person who is so liable).

(4) But subsection (3) does not make a person liable if—

(a) the lease by virtue of which he was a qualifying tenant has been assigned to another person, and

(b) that other person has become a member of the RTM company.

(5) The reference in subsection (4) to an assignment includes—

(a) an assent by personal representatives, and

(b) assignment by operation of law where the assignment is to a trustee in bankruptcy or to a mortgagee under section 89(2) of the Law of Property Act 1925 (c. 20) (foreclosure of leasehold mortgage).

Acquisition of right

s 90 The acquisition date

A10–022 (1) This section makes provision about the date which is the acquisition date where a RTM company acquires the right to manage any premises.

(2) Where there is no dispute about entitlement, the acquisition date is the date specified in the claim notice under section 80(7).

(3) For the purposes of this Chapter there is no dispute about entitlement if—

(a) no counter-notice is given under section 84, or

(b) the counter-notice given under that section, or (where more than one is so given) each of them, contains a statement such as is mentioned in subsection (2)(a) of that section.

(4) Where the right to manage the premises is acquired by the company by virtue of a determination under section 84(5)(a), the acquisition date is the date three months after the determination becomes final.

(5) Where the right to manage the premises is acquired by the company by virtue of subsection (5)(b) of section 84, the acquisition date is the date three months after the day on which the person (or the last person) by whom a counter-notice containing a statement such as is mentioned in subsection (2)(b) of that section was given agrees in writing that the company was on the relevant date entitled to acquire the right to manage the premises.

(6) Where an order is made under section 85, the acquisition date is (subject to any appeal) the date specified in the order.

s 91 Notices relating to management contracts

A10–023 (1) Section 92 applies where—

(a) the right to manage premises is to be acquired by a RTM company (otherwise than by virtue of an order under section 85), and

(b) there are one or more existing management contracts relating to the premises.

(2) A management contract is a contract between—

(a) an existing manager of the premises (referred to in this Chapter as the "manager party"), and

(b) another person (so referred to as the "contractor party"), under which the contractor party agrees to provide services, or do any other thing, in connection with any matter relating to a function which will be a function of the RTM company once it acquires the right to manage.

(3) And in this Chapter "existing management contract" means a management contract which—

(a) is subsisting immediately before the determination date, or

(b) is entered into during the period beginning with the determination date and ending with the acquisition date.

(4) An existing manager of the premises is any person who is—

(a) landlord under a lease relating to the whole or any part of the premises,

(b) party to such a lease otherwise than as landlord or tenant, or

(c) a manager appointed under Part 2 of the 1987 Act to act in relation to the premises, or any premises containing or contained in the premises.

(5) In this Chapter "determination date" means—

(a) where there is no dispute about entitlement, the date specified in the claim notice under section 80(6),

(b) where the right to manage the premises is acquired by the company by virtue of a determination under section 84(5)(a), the date when the determination becomes final, and

(c) where the right to manage the premises is acquired by the company by virtue of subsection (5)(b) of section 84, the day on which the person (or the last person) by whom a counter-notice containing a statement such as is mentioned in subsection (2)(b) of that section was given agrees in writing that the company was on the relevant date entitled to acquire the right to manage the premises.

s 92 Duties to give notice of contracts

A10–024

(1) The person who is the manager party in relation to an existing management contract must give a notice in relation to the contract—

(a) to the person who is the contractor party in relation to the contract (a "contractor notice"), and

(b) to the RTM company (a "contract notice").

(2) A contractor notice and a contract notice must be given—

(a) in the case of a contract subsisting immediately before the determination date, on that date or as soon after that date as is reasonably practicable, and

(b) in the case of a contract entered into during the period beginning with the determination date and ending with the acquisition date, on the date on which it is entered into or as soon after that date as is reasonably practicable.

(3) A contractor notice must—

(a) give details sufficient to identify the contract in relation to which it is given,

(b) state that the right to manage the premises is to be acquired by a RTM company,

(c) state the name and registered office of the RTM company,

(d) specify the acquisition date, and

(e) contain such other particulars (if any) as may be required to be contained in contractor notices by regulations made by the appropriate national authority,

and must also comply with such requirements (if any) about the form of contractor notices as may be prescribed by regulations so made.

(4) Where a person who receives a contractor notice (including one who receives a copy by virtue of this subsection) is party to an existing management sub-contract with another person (the "sub-contractor party"), the person who received the notice must—

(a) send a copy of the contractor notice to the sub-contractor party, and

(b) give to the RTM company a contract notice in relation to the existing management sub-contract.

(5) An existing management sub-contract is a contract under which the sub-contractor party agrees to provide services, or do any other thing, in connection with any matter relating to a function which will be a function of the RTM company once it acquires the right to manage and which—

(a) is subsisting immediately before the determination date, or

(b) is entered into during the period beginning with the determination date and ending with the acquisition date.

(6) Subsection (4) must be complied with—

(a) in the case of a contract entered into before the contractor notice is received, on the date on which it is received or as soon after that date as is reasonably practicable, and

(b) in the case of a contract entered into after the contractor notice is received, on the date on which it is entered into or as soon after that date as is reasonably practicable.

(7) A contract notice must—

(a) give particulars of the contract in relation to which it is given and of the person who is the contractor party, or sub-contractor party, in relation to that contract, and

(b) contain such other particulars (if any) as may be required to be contained in contract notices by regulations made by the appropriate national authority,

and must also comply with such requirements (if any) about the form of contract notices as may be prescribed by such regulations so made.

s 93 Duty to provide information

A10–025 (1) Where the right to manage premises is to be acquired by a RTM company, the company may give notice to a person who is—

(a) landlord under a lease of the whole or any part of the premises,

(b) party to such a lease otherwise than as landlord or tenant, or

(c) a manager appointed under Part 2 of the 1987 Act to act in relation to the premises, or any premises containing or contained in the premises,

requiring him to provide the company with any information which is in his possession or control and which the company reasonably requires in connection with the exercise of the right to manage.

(2) Where the information is recorded in a document in his possession or control the notice may require him—

(a) to permit any person authorised to act on behalf of the company at any reasonable time to inspect the document (or, if the information is recorded in the document in a form in which it is not readily intelligible, to give any such person access to it in a readily intelligible form), and

(b) to supply the company with a copy of the document containing the information in a readily intelligible form.

(3) A notice may not require a person to do anything under this section before the acquisition date.

(4) But, subject to that, a person who is required by a notice to do anything under this section must do it within the period of 28 days beginning with the day on which the notice is given.

s 94 Duty to pay accrued uncommitted service charges

A10–026 (1) Where the right to manage premises is to be acquired by a RTM company, a person who is—

(a) landlord under a lease of the whole or any part of the premises,

(b) party to such a lease otherwise than as landlord or tenant, or

(c) a manager appointed under Part 2 of the 1987 Act to act in relation to the premises, or any premises containing or contained in the premises,

must make to the company a payment equal to the amount of any accrued uncommitted service charges held by him on the acquisition date.

(2) The amount of any accrued uncommitted service charges is the aggregate of—

(a) any sums which have been paid to the person by way of service charges in respect of the premises, and

(b) any investments which represent such sums (and any income which has accrued on them),

less so much (if any) of that amount as is required to meet the costs incurred before the acquisition date in connection with the matters for which the service charges were payable.

(3) He or the RTM company may make an application to a leasehold valuation tribunal to determine the amount of any payment which falls to be made under this section.

(4) This duty imposed by this section must be complied with on the acquisition date or as soon after that date as is reasonably practicable.

Exercising right

s 95 Introductory

A10–027 Sections 96 to 103 apply where the right to manage premises has been acquired by a RTM company (and has not ceased to be exercisable by it).

s 96 Management functions under leases

A10–028 (1) This section and section 97 apply in relation to management functions relating to the whole or any part of the premises.

(2) Management functions which a person who is landlord under a lease of the whole or any part of the premises has under the lease are instead functions of the RTM company.

(3) And where a person is party to a lease of the whole or any part of the premises otherwise than as landlord or tenant, management functions of his under the lease are also instead functions of the RTM company.

(4) Accordingly, any provisions of the lease making provision about the relationship of—

(a) a person who is landlord under the lease, and

(b) a person who is party to the lease otherwise than as landlord or tenant,

in relation to such functions do not have effect.

(5) "Management functions" are functions with respect to services, repairs, maintenance, improvements, insurance and management.

(6) But this section does not apply in relation to—

(a) functions with respect to a matter concerning only a part of the premises consisting of a flat or other unit not held under a lease by a qualifying tenant, or

(b) functions relating to re-entry or forfeiture.

(7) An order amending subsection (5) or (6) may be made by the appropriate national authority.

s 97 Management functions: supplementary

A10–029

(1) Any obligation owned by the RTM company by virtue of section 96 to a tenant under a lease of the whole or any part of the premises is also owed to each person who is landlord under the lease.

(2) A person who is—

(a) landlord under a lease of the whole or any part of the premises,

(b) party to such a lease otherwise than as landlord or tenant, or

(c) a manager appointed under Part 2 of the 1987 Act to act in relation to the premises, or any premises containing or contained in the premises,

is not entitled to do anything which the RTM company is required or empowered to do under the lease by virtue of section 96, except in accordance with an agreement made by him and the RTM company.

(3) But subsection (2) does not prevent any person from insuring the whole or any part of the premises at his own expense.

(4) So far as any function of a tenant under a lease of the whole or any part of the premises—

(a) relates to the exercise of any function under the lease which is a function of the RTM company by virtue of section 96, and

(b) is exercisable in relation to a person who is landlord under the lease or party to the lease otherwise than as landlord or tenant,

it is instead exercisable in relation to the RTM company.

(5) But subsection (4) does not require or permit the payment to the RTM company of so much of any service charges payable by a tenant under a lease of the whole or any part of the premises as is required to meet costs incurred before the right to manage was acquired by the RTM company in connection with matters for which the service charges are payable.

s 98 Functions relating to approvals

A10–030

(1) This section and section 99 apply in relation to the grant of approvals under long leases of the whole or any part of the premises; but nothing in this

section or section 99 applies in relation to an approval concerning only a part of the premises consisting of a flat or other unit not held under a lease by a qualifying tenant.

(2) Where a person who is—

(a) landlord under a long lease of the whole or any part of the premises, or

(b) party to such a lease otherwise than as landlord or tenant,

has functions in relation to the grant of approvals to a tenant under the lease, the functions are instead functions of the RTM company.

(3) Accordingly, any provisions of the lease making provision about the relationship of—

(a) a person who is landlord under the lease, and

(b) a person who is party to the lease otherwise than as landlord or tenant,

in relation to such functions do not have effect.

(4) The RTM company must not grant an approval by virtue of subsection (2) without having given—

(a) in the case of an approval relating to assignment, underletting, charging, parting with possession, the making of structural alterations or improvements or alterations of use, 30 days' notice, or

(b) in any other case, 14 days' notice,

to the person who is, or each of the persons who are, landlord under the lease.

(5) Regulations increasing the period of notice to be given under subsection (4)(b) in the case of any description of approval may be made by the appropriate national authority.

(6) So far as any function of a tenant under a long lease of the whole or any part of the premises—

(a) relates to the exercise of any function which is a function of the RTM company by virtue of this section, and

(b) is exercisable in relation to a person who is landlord under the lease or party to the lease otherwise than as landlord or tenant,

it is instead exercisable in relation to the RTM company.

(7) In this Chapter "approval" includes consent or licence and "approving" is to be construed accordingly; and an approval required to be obtained by virtue of a restriction entered on the register of title kept by the Chief Land Registrar is, so far as relating to a long lease of the whole or any part of any premises, to be treated for the purposes of this Chapter as an approval under the lease.

s 99 Approvals: supplementary

A10–031

(1) If a person to whom notice is given under section 98(4) objects to the grant of the approval before the time when the RTM company would first be entitled to grant it, the RTM company may grant it only—

(a) in accordance with the written agreement of the person who objected, or

(b) in accordance with a determination of (or on an appeal from) a leasehold valuation tribunal.

(2) An objection to the grant of the approval may not be made by a person unless he could withhold the approval if the function of granting it were exercisable by him (and not by the RTM company).

(3) And a person may not make an objection operating only if a condition or requirement is not satisfied unless he could grant the approval subject to the condition or requirement being satisfied if the function of granting it were so exercisable.

(4) An objection to the grant of the approval is made by giving notice of the objection (and of any condition or requirement which must be satisfied if it is not to operate) to—

(a) the RTM company, and

(b) the tenant,

and, if the approval is to a tenant approving an act of a sub-tenant, to the sub-tenant.

(5) An application to a leasehold valuation tribunal for a determination under subsection (1)(b) may be made by—

(a) the RTM company,

(b) the tenant,

(c) if the approval is to a tenant approving an act of a sub-tenant, the sub-tenant, or

(d) any person who is landlord under the lease.

s 100 Enforcement of tenant covenants

A10–032

(1) This section applies in relation to the enforcement of untransferred tenant covenants of a lease of the whole or any part of the premises.

(2) Untransferred tenant covenants are enforceable by the RTM company, as well as by any other person by whom they are enforceable apart from this section, in the same manner as they are enforceable by any other such person.

(3) But the RTM company may not exercise any function of re-entry or forfeiture.

(4) In this Chapter "tenant covenant", in relation to a lease, means a covenant falling to be complied with by a tenant under the lease; and a tenant

covenant is untransferred if, apart from this section, it would not be enforceable by the RTM company.

(5) Any power under a lease of a person who is—

(a) landlord under the lease, or

(b) party to the lease otherwise than as landlord or tenant,

to enter any part of the premises to determine whether a tenant is complying with any untransferred tenant covenant is exercisable by the RTM company (as well as by the landlord or party).

s 101 Tenant covenants: monitoring and reporting

A10–033 (1) This section applies in relation to failures to comply with tenant covenants of leases of the whole or any part of the premises.

(2) The RTM company must—

(a) keep under review whether tenant covenants of leases of the whole or any part of the premises are being complied with, and

(b) report to any person who is landlord under such a lease any failure to comply with any tenant covenant of the lease.

(3) The report must be made before the end of the period of three months beginning with the day on which the failure to comply comes to the attention of the RTM company.

(4) But the RTM company need not report to a landlord a failure to comply with a tenant covenant if—

(a) the failure has been remedied,

(b) reasonable compensation has been paid in respect of the failure, or

(c) the landlord has notified the RTM company that it need not report to him failures of the description of the failure concerned.

s 102 Statutory functions

A10–034 (1) Schedule 7 (provision for the operation of certain enactments with modifications) has effect.

(2) Other enactments relating to leases (including enactments contained in this Act or any Act passed after this Act) have effect with any such modifications as are prescribed by regulations made by the appropriate national authority.

s 103 Landlord contributions to service charges

A10–035 (1) This section applies where—

(a) the premises contain at least one flat or other unit not subject to a lease held by a qualifying tenant (an "excluded unit"),

(b) the service charges payable under leases of flats contained in the premises which are so subject fall to be calculated as a proportion of the relevant costs, and

(c) the proportions of the relevant costs so payable, when aggregated, amount to less than the whole of the relevant costs.

(2) Where the premises contain only one excluded unit, the person who is the appropriate person in relation to the excluded unit must pay to the RTM company the difference between—

(a) the relevant costs, and

(b) the aggregate amount payable in respect of the relevant costs under leases of flats contained in the premises which are held by qualifying tenants.

(3) Where the premises contain more than one excluded unit, each person who is the appropriate person in relation to an excluded unit must pay to the RTM company the appropriate proportion of that difference.

(4) And the appropriate proportion in the case of each such person is the proportion of the internal floor area of all of the excluded units which is internal floor area of the excluded unit in relation to which he is the appropriate person.

(5) The appropriate person in relation to an excluded unit—

(a) if it is subject to a lease, is the landlord under the lease,

(b) if it is subject to more than one lease, is the immediate landlord under whichever of the leases is inferior to all the others, and

(c) if it is not subject to any lease, is the freeholder.

Supplementary

s 104

[. . .][1] **A10–036**

[1] repealed by Commonhold and Leasehold Reform Act (2000 c.15), Sch 14 Para1

s 105 Cessation of management

A10–037 (1) This section makes provision about the circumstances in which, after a RTM company has acquired the right to manage any premises, that right ceases to be exercisable by it.

(2) Provision may be made by an agreement made between—

(a) the RTM company, and

(b) each person who is landlord under a lease of the whole or any part of the premises, for the right to manage the premises to cease to be exercisable by the RTM company.

(3) The right to manage the premises ceases to be exercisable by the RTM company if—

(a) a winding-up order [. . .][1] is made, or a resolution for voluntary winding-up is passed, with respect to the RTM company, or the RTM company enters administration,

(b) a receiver or a manager of the RTM company's undertaking is duly appointed, or possession is taken, by or on behalf of the holders of any debentures secured by a floating charge, of any property of the RTM company comprised in or subject to the charge,

(c) a voluntary arrangement proposed in the case of the RTM company for the purposes of Part 1 of the Insolvency Act 1986 (c. 45) is approved under that Part of that Act, or

(d) the RTM company's name is struck off the register under section 652 or 652A of the Companies Act 1985 (c. 6).

(4) The right to manage the premises ceases to be exercisable by the RTM company if a manager appointed under Part 2 of the 1987 Act to act in relation to the premises, or any premises containing or contained in the premises, begins so to act or an order under that Part of that Act that the right to manage the premises is to cease to be exercisable by the RTM company takes effect.

(5) The right to manage the premises ceases to be exercisable by the RTM company if it ceases to be a RTM company in relation to the premises.

[1] words repealed by SI 2003/2096 (Enterprise Act 2002 (Insolvency) Order), Sch 1 (1) Para 40 (a)

s 106 Agreements excluding or modifying right

A10–038 Any agreement relating to a lease (whether contained in the instrument creating the lease or not and whether made before the creation of the lease or not) is void in so far as it—

(a) purports to exclude or modify the right of any person to be, or do any thing as, a member of a RTM company,

(b) provides for the termination or surrender of the lease if the tenant becomes, or does any thing as, a member of a RTM company or if a RTM company does any thing, or

(c) provides for the imposition of any penalty or disability if the tenant becomes, or does any thing as, a member of a RTM company or if a RTM company does any thing.

s 107 Enforcement of obligations

A10–039

(1) A county court may, on the application of any person interested, make an order requiring a person who has failed to comply with a requirement imposed on him by, under or by virtue of any provision of this Chapter to make good the default within such time as is specified in the order.
(2) An application shall not be made under subsection (1) unless—

(a) a notice has been previously given to the person in question requiring him to make good the default, and

(b) more than 14 days have elapsed since the date of the giving of that notice without his having done so.

s 108 Application to Crown

A10–040

(1) This Chapter applies in relation to premises in which there is a Crown interest.
(2) There is a Crown interest in premises if there is in the premises an interest or estate—

(a) which is comprised in the Crown Estate,

(b) which belongs to Her Majesty in right of the Duchy of Lancaster,

(c) which belongs to the Duchy of Cornwall, or

(d) which belongs to a government department or is held on behalf of Her Majesty for the purposes of a government department.

(3) Any sum payable under this Chapter to a RTM company by the Chancellor of the Duchy of Lancaster may be raised and paid under section 25 of the Duchy of Lancaster Act 1817 (c. 97) as an expense incurred in improvement of land belonging to Her Majesty in right of the Duchy.
(4) Any sum payable under this Chapter to a RTM company by the Duke of Cornwall (or any other possessor for the time being of the Duchy of Cornwall) may be raised and paid under section 8 of the Duchy of Cornwall Management Act 1863 (c. 49) as an expense incurred in permanently improving the possessions of the Duchy.

s 109 Powers of trustees in relation to right

A10–041

(1) Where trustees are the qualifying tenant of a flat contained in any premises, their powers under the instrument regulating the trusts include power to be a member of a RTM company for the purpose of the acquisition and exercise of the right to manage the premises.
(2) But subsection (1) does not apply where the instrument regulating the trusts contains an explicit direction to the contrary.
(3) The power conferred by subsection (1) is exercisable with the same consent or on the same direction (if any) as may be required for the exercise of the trustees' powers (or ordinary powers) of investment.

(4) The purposes—

(a) authorised for the application of capital money by section 73 of the Settled Land Act 1925 (c. 18), and

(b) authorised by section 71 of that Act as purposes for which moneys may be raised by mortgage,

include the payment of any expenses incurred by a tenant for life or statutory owner as a member of a RTM company.

s 110 Power to prescribe procedure

A10–042 (1) Where a claim to acquire the right to manage any premises is made by the giving of a claim notice, except as otherwise provided by this Chapter—

(a) the procedure for giving effect to the claim notice, and

(b) the rights and obligations of all parties in any matter arising in giving effect to the claim notice,

shall be such as may be prescribed by regulations made by the appropriate national authority.

(2) Regulations under this section may, in particular, make provision for a person to be discharged from performing any obligations arising out of a claim notice by reason of the default or delay of some other person.

s 111 Notices

A10–043 (1) Any notice under this Chapter—

(a) must be in writing, and

(b) may be in sent by post.

(2) A company which is a RTM company in relation to premises may give a notice under this Chapter to a person who is landlord under a lease of the whole or any part of the premises at the address specified in subsection (3) (but subject to subsection (4)).

(3) That address is—

(a) the address last furnished to a member of the RTM company as the landlord's address for service in accordance with section 48 of the 1987 Act (notification of address for service of notice on landlord), or

(b) if no such address has been so furnished, the address last furnished to such a member as the landlord's address in accordance with section 47 of the 1987 Act (landlord's name and address to be contained in demands for rent).

(4) But the RTM company may not give a notice under this Chapter to a person at the address specified in subsection (3) if it has been notified by him

of a different address in England and Wales at which he wishes to be given any such notice.

(5) A company which is a RTM company in relation to premises may give a notice under this Chapter to a person who is the qualifying tenant of a flat contained in the premises at the flat unless it has been notified by the qualifying tenant of a different address in England and Wales at which he wishes to be given any such notice.

Interpretation

s 112 Definitions

(1) In this Chapter— **A10–044**

"appurtenant property", in relation to a building or part of a building or a flat, means any garage, outhouse, garden, yard or appurtenances belonging to, or usually enjoyed with, the building or part or flat,

"copy", in relation to a document in which information is recorded, means anything onto which the information has been copied by whatever means and whether directly or indirectly,

"document" means anything in which information is recorded,

"dwelling" means a building or part of a building occupied or intended to be occupied as a separate dwelling,

"flat" means a separate set of premises (whether or not on the same floor)—

(a) which forms part of a building,
(b) which is constructed or adapted for use for the purposes of a dwelling, and
(c) either the whole or a material part of which lies above or below some other part for the building,

"relevant costs" has the meaning given by section 18 of the 1985 Act,

"service charge" has the meaning given by that section, and

"unit" means—

(a) a flat,
(b) any other separate set of premises which is constructed or adapted for use for the purposes of a dwelling, or
(c) a separate set of premises let, or intended for letting, on a tenancy to which Part 2 of the Landlord and Tenant Act 1954 (c. 56) (business tenancies) applies.

(2) In this Chapter "lease" and "tenancy" have the same meaning and both expressions include (where the context permits)—

(a) a sub-lease or sub-tenancy, and

(b) an agreement for a lease or tenancy (or for a sub-lease or sub-tenancy),

but do not include a tenancy at will or at sufferance.

(3) The expressions "landlord" and "tenant", and references to letting, to the grant of a lease or to covenants or the terms of a lease, shall be construed accordingly.

(4) In this Chapter any reference (however expressed) to the lease held by the qualifying tenant of a flat is a reference to a lease held by him under which the demised premises consist of or include the flat (whether with or without one or more other flats).

(5) Where two or more persons jointly constitute either the landlord or the tenant or qualifying tenant in relation to a lease of a flat, any reference in this Chapter to the landlord or to the tenant or qualifying tenant is (unless the context otherwise requires) a reference to both or all of the persons who jointly constitute the landlord or the tenant or qualifying tenant, as the case may require.

(6) In the case of a lease which derives (in accordance with section 77(5)) from two or more separate leases, any reference in this Chapter to the date of the commencement of the term for which the lease was granted shall, if the terms of the separate leases commenced at different dates, have effect as references to the date of the commencement of the term of the lease with the earliest date of commencement.

s 113 Index of defined expressions

A10–045 In this Chapter the expressions listed below are defined by the provisions specified.

Expression	*Interpretation provision*
Approval (and approving)	Section 98(7)
Appurtenant property	Section 112(1)
Acquisition date	Sections 74(1)(b) and 90
Claim notice	Section 79(1)
Contractor party	Section 91(2)(b)
Copy	Section 112(1)
Counter-notice	Section 84(1)
Date of the commencement of the term of a lease	Section 112(6)
Determination date	Section 91(5)
Document	Section 112(1)
Dwelling	Section 112(1)
Existing management contract	Section 91(3)
Flat	Section 112(1)
Landlord	Section 112(3) and (5)
Lease	Section 112(2) to (4)

Letting	Section 112(3)
Long lease	Sections 76 and 77
Manager party	Section 91(2)(a)
No dispute about entitlement	Section 90(3)
Notice of invitation to participate	Section 78
Notice of withdrawal	Section 86(1)
Premises to which this Chapter applies	Section 72 (and Schedule 6)
Qualifying tenant	Section 75 and 112(4) and (5)
Relevant costs	Section 112(1)
Relevant date	Section 79(1)
Right to manage	Section 71(2)
RTM company	Section 71(1) and 73
Service charge	Section 112(1)
Tenancy	Section 112(2)
Tenant	Section 112(3) and (5)
Tenant covenant	Section 100(4)
Unit	Section 112(1)

CHAPTER 5 OTHER PROVISIONS ABOUT LEASES

Service Charges, Administration Charges etc.

s 151 Consultation about service charges

For section 20 of the 1985 Act (limitation of service charges: estimates and consultation) substitute— **A10–046**

"20 Limitation of service charges: consultation requirements

(1) Where this section applies to any qualifying works or qualifying long term agreement, the relevant contributions of tenants are limited in accordance with subsection (6) or (7) (or both) unless the consultation requirements have been either—

(a) complied with in relation to the works or agreement, or
(b) dispensed with in relation to the works or agreement by (or on appeal from) a leasehold valuation tribunal.

(2) In this section 'relevant contribution', in relation to a tenant and any works or agreement, is the amount which he may be required under the terms of his lease to contribute (by the payment of service charges) to relevant costs incurred on carrying out the works or under the agreement.

(3) This section applies to qualifying works if relevant costs incurred on carrying out the works exceed an appropriate amount.

(4) The Secretary of State may by regulations provide that this section applies to a qualifying long term agreement—

(a) if relevant costs incurred under the agreement exceed an appropriate amount, or

(b) if relevant costs incurred under agreement during a period prescribed by the regulations exceed an appropriate amount.

(5) An appropriate amount is an amount set by regulations made by the Secretary of State; and the regulations may make provision for either or both of the following to be an appropriate amount—

(a) an amount prescribed by, or determined in accordance with, the regulations, and
(b) an amount which results in the relevant contribution of any one or more tenants being an amount prescribed by, or determined in accordance with, the regulations.

(6) Where an appropriate amount is set by virtue of paragraph (a) of subsection (5), the amount of the relevant costs incurred on carrying out the works or under the agreement which may be taken into account in determining the relevant contributions of tenants is limited to the appropriate amount.

(7) Where an appropriate amount is set by virtue of paragraph (b) of that subsection, the amount of the relevant contribution of the tenant, or each of the tenants, whose relevant contribution would otherwise exceed the amount prescribed by, or determined in accordance with, the regulations is limited to the amount so prescribed or determined.

20ZA Consultation requirements: supplementary

(1) Where an application is made to a leasehold valuation tribunal for a determination to dispense with all or any of the consultation requirements in relation to any qualifying works or qualifying long term agreement, the tribunal may make the determination if satisfied that it is reasonable to dispense with the requirements.

(2) In section 20 and this section—

'qualifying works' means works on a building or any other premises, and
'qualifying long term agreement' means (subject to subsection (3)) an agreement entered into, by or on behalf of the landlord or a superior landlord, for a term of more than twelve months.

(3) The Secretary of State may by regulations provide that an agreement is not a qualifying long term agreement—

(a) if it is an agreement of a description prescribed by the regulations, or
(b) in any circumstances so prescribed.

(4) In section 20 and this section 'the consultation requirements' means requirements prescribed by regulations made by the Secretary of State.

(5) Regulations under subsection (4) may in particular include provision requiring the landlord—

(a) to provide details of proposed works or agreements to tenants or the recognised tenants' association representing them,
(b) to obtain estimates for proposed works or agreements,

(c) to invite tenants or the recognised tenants' association to propose the names of persons from whom the landlord should try to obtain other estimates,
(d) to have regard to observations made by tenants or the recognised tenants' association in relation to proposed works or agreements and estimates, and
(e) to give reasons in prescribed circumstances for carrying out works or entering into agreements.

(6) Regulations under section 20 or this section—

(a) may make provision generally or only in relation to specific cases, and
(b) may make different provision for different purposes.

(7) Regulations under section 20 or this section shall be made by statutory instrument which shall be subject to annulment in pursuance of a resolution of either House of Parliament."

s 152 Statements of account

For section 21 of the 1985 Act (request for summary of relevant costs) substitute— **A10–047**

"21 Regular statements of account

(1) The landlord must supply to each tenant by whom service charges are payable, in relation to each accounting period, a written statement of account dealing with—

(a) service charges of the tenant and the tenants of dwellings associated with his dwelling,
(b) relevant costs relating to those service charges,
(c) the aggregate amount standing to the credit of the tenant and the tenants of those dwellings—

(i) at the beginning of the accounting period, and
(ii) at the end of the accounting period, and

(d) related matters.

(2) The statement of account in relation to an accounting period must be supplied to each such tenant not later than six months after the end of the accounting period.

(3) Where the landlord supplies a statement of account to a tenant he must also supply to him—

(a) a certificate of a qualified accountant that, in the accountant's opinion, the statement of account deals fairly with the matters with which it is required to deal and is sufficiently supported by accounts, receipts and other documents which have been produced to him, and
(b) a summary of the rights and obligations of tenants of dwellings in relation to service charges.

(4) The Secretary of State may make regulations prescribing requirements as to the form and content of—

(a) statements of account,
(b) accountants' certificates, and
(c) summaries of rights and obligations,

required to be supplied under this section.

(5) The Secretary of State may make regulations prescribing exceptions from the requirement to supply an accountant's certificate.

(6) If the landlord has been notified by a tenant of an address in England and Wales at which he wishes to have supplied to him documents required to be so supplied under this section, the landlord must supply them to him at that address.

(7) And the landlord is to be taken to have been so notified if notification has been given to—

(a) an agent of the landlord named as such in the rent book or similar document, or
(b) the person who receives the rent on behalf of the landlord;

and where notification is given to such an agent or person he must forward it as soon as may be to the landlord.

(8) For the purposes of this section a dwelling is associated with another dwelling if the obligations of the tenants of the dwellings under the terms of their leases as regards contributing to relevant costs relate to the same costs.

(9) In this section 'accounting period' means such period—

(a) beginning with the relevant date, and
(b) ending with such date, not later than twelve months after the relevant date,

as the landlord determines.

(10) In the case of the first accounting period in relation to any dwellings, the relevant date is the later of—

(a) the date on which service charges are first payable under a lease of any of them, and
(b) the date on which section 152 of the Commonhold and Leasehold Reform Act 2002 comes into force,

and, in the case of subsequent accounting periods, it is the date immediately following the end of the previous accounting period.

(11) Regulations under subsection (4) may make different provision for different purposes.

(12) Regulations under this section shall be made by statutory instrument which shall be subject to annulment in pursuance of a resolution of either House of Parliament.

21A Withholding of service charges

(1) A tenant may withhold payment of a service charge if—

(a) the landlord has not supplied a document to him by the time by which he is required to supply it under section 21, or

(b) the form or content of a document which the landlord has supplied to him under that section (at any time) does not conform exactly or substantially with the requirements prescribed by regulations under subsection (4) of that section.

(2) The maximum amount which the tenant may withhold is an amount equal to the aggregate of—

(a) the service charges paid by him in the accounting period to which the document concerned would or does relate, and
(b) so much of the aggregate amount required to be dealt with in the statement of account for that accounting period by section 21(1)(c)(i) as stood to his credit.

(3) An amount may not be withheld under this section—

(a) in a case within paragraph (a) of subsection (1), after the document concerned has been supplied to the tenant by the landlord, or
(b) in a case within paragraph (b) of that subsection, after a document conforming exactly or substantially with the requirements prescribed by regulations under section 21(4) has been supplied to the tenant by the landlord by way of replacement of the one previously supplied.

(4) If, on an application made by the landlord to a leasehold valuation tribunal, the tribunal determines that the landlord has a reasonable excuse for a failure giving rise to the right of a tenant to withhold an amount under this section, the tenant may not withhold the amount after the determination is made.

(5) Where a tenant withholds a service charge under this section, any provisions of the tenancy relating to non-payment or late payment of service charges do not have effect in relation to the period for which he so withholds it."

s 154 Inspection etc. of documents

For section 22 of the 1985 Act (request to inspect documents supporting summary of relevant costs) substitute— **A10–048**

"22 Inspection etc. of documents

(1) A tenant may by notice in writing require the landlord—

(a) to afford him reasonable facilities for inspecting accounts, receipts or other documents relevant to the matters which must be dealt with in a statement of account required to be supplied to him under section 21 and for taking copies of or extracts from them, or
(b) to take copies of or extracts from any such accounts, receipts or other documents and either send them to him or afford him reasonable facilities for collecting them (as he specifies).

(2) If the tenant is represented by a recognised tenants' association and he consents, the notice may be served by the secretary of the association instead of by the tenant (and in that case any requirement imposed by it is to afford reasonable facilities, or to send copies or extracts, to the secretary).

(3) A notice under this section may not be served after the end of the period of six months beginning with the date by which the tenant is required to be supplied with the statement of account under section 21.

(4) But if—

(a) the statement of account is not supplied to the tenant on or before that date, or
(b) the statement of account so supplied does not conform exactly or substantially with the requirements prescribed by regulations under section 21(4),

the six month period mentioned in subsection (3) does not begin until any later date on which the statement of account (conforming exactly or substantially with those requirements) is supplied to him.

(5) A notice under this section is duly served on the landlord if it is served on—

(a) an agent of the landlord named as such in the rent book or similar document, or
(b) the person who receives the rent on behalf of the landlord;

and a person on whom such a notice is so served must forward it as soon as may be to the landlord.

(6) The landlord must comply with a requirement imposed by a notice under this section within the period of twenty-one days beginning with the day on which he receives the notice.

(7) To the extent that a notice under this section requires the landlord to afford facilities for inspecting documents—

(a) he must do so free of charge, but
(b) he may treat as part of his costs of management any costs incurred by him in doing so.

(8) The landlord may make a reasonable charge for doing anything else in compliance with a requirement imposed by a notice under this section."

s 158 Administration charges

A10–049 Schedule 11 (which makes provision about administration charges payable by tenants of dwellings) has effect.

s 159 Charges under estate management schemes

A10–050 (1) This section applies where a scheme under—

(a) section 19 of the 1967 Act (estate management schemes in connection with enfranchisement under that Act),

(b) Chapter 4 of Part 1 of the 1993 Act (estate management schemes in connection with enfranchisement under the 1967 Act or Chapter 1 of Part 1 of the 1993 Act), or

(c) section 94(6) of the 1993 Act (corresponding schemes in relation to areas occupied under leases from Crown),

includes provision imposing on persons occupying or interested in property an obligation to make payments ("estate charges").

(2) A variable estate charge is payable only to the extent that the amount of the charge is reasonable; and "variable estate charge" means an estate charge which is neither—

(a) specified in the scheme, nor

(b) calculated in accordance with a formula specified in the scheme.

(3) Any person on whom an obligation to pay an estate charge is imposed by the scheme may apply to a leasehold valuation tribunal for an order varying the scheme in such manner as is specified in the application on the grounds that—

(a) any estate charge specified in the scheme is unreasonable, or

(b) any formula specified in the scheme in accordance with which any estate charge is calculated is unreasonable.

(4) If the grounds on which the application was made are established to the satisfaction of the tribunal, it may make an order varying the scheme in such manner as is specified in the order.

(5) The variation specified in the order may be—

(a) the variation specified in the application, or

(b) such other variation as the tribunal thinks fit.

(6) An application may be made to a leasehold valuation tribunal for a determination whether an estate charge is payable by a person and, if it is, as to—

(a) the person by whom it is payable,

(b) the person to whom it is payable,

(c) the amount which is payable,

(d) the date at or by which it is payable, and

(e) the manner in which it is payable.

(7) Subsection (6) applies whether or not any payment has been made.

(8) The jurisdiction conferred on a leasehold valuation tribunal in respect of any matter by virtue of subsection (6) is in addition to any jurisdiction of a court in respect of the matter.

(9) No application under subsection (6) may be made in respect of a matter which—

(a) has been agreed or admitted by the person concerned,

(b) has been, or is to be, referred to arbitration pursuant to a post-dispute arbitration agreement to which that person is a party,

(c) has been the subject of determination by a court, or

(d) has been the subject of determination by an arbitral tribunal pursuant to a post-dispute arbitration agreement.

(10) But the person is not to be taken to have agreed or admitted any matter by reason only of having made any payment.

(11) An agreement (other than a post-dispute arbitration agreement) is void in so far as it purports to provide for a determination—

(a) in a particular manner, or

(b) on particular evidence,

of any question which may be the subject matter of an application under subsection (6).

(12) In this section—

"post-dispute arbitration agreement", in relation to any matter, means an arbitration agreement made after a dispute about the matter has arisen, and

"arbitration agreement" and "arbitral tribunal" have the same meanings as in Part 1 of the Arbitration Act 1996 (c. 23).

Insurance

s 164 Insurance otherwise than with landlord's insurer

A10–051 (1) This section applies where a long lease of a house requires the tenant to insure the house with an insurer nominated or approved by the landlord ("the landlord's insurer").

(2) The tenant is not required to effect the insurance with the landlord's insurer if—

(a) the house is insured under a policy of insurance issued by an authorised insurer,

(b) the policy covers the interests of both the landlord and the tenant,

(c) the policy covers all the risks which the lease requires be covered by insurance provided by the landlord's insurer,

(d) the amount of the cover is not less than that which the lease requires to be provided by such insurance, and

(e) the tenant satisfies subsection (3).

(3) To satisfy this subsection the tenant—

(a) must have given a notice of cover to the landlord before the end of the period of fourteen days beginning with the relevant date, and

(b) if (after that date) he has been requested to do so by a new landlord, must have given a notice of cover to him within the period of fourteen days beginning with the day on which the request was given.

(4) For the purposes of subsection (3)—

(a) if the policy has not been renewed the relevant date is the day on which it took effect and if it has been renewed it is the day from which it was last renewed, and

(b) a person is a new landlord on any day if he acquired the interest of the previous landlord under the lease on a disposal made by him during the period of one month ending with that day.

(5) A notice of cover is a notice specifying—

(a) the name of the insurer,

(b) the risks covered by the policy,

(c) the amount and period of the cover, and

(d) such further information as may be prescribed.

(6) A notice of cover—

(a) must be in the prescribed form, and

(b) may be sent by post.

(7) If a notice of cover is sent by post, it may be addressed to the landlord at the address specified in subsection (8).

(8) That address is—

(a) the address last furnished to the tenant as the landlord's address for service in accordance with section 48 of the 1987 Act (notification of address for service of notices on landlord), or

(b) if no such address has been so furnished, the address last furnished to the tenant as the landlord's address in accordance with section 47 of the 1987 Act (landlord's name and address to be contained in demands for rent).

(9) But the tenant may not give a notice of cover to the landlord at the address specified in subsection (8) if he has been notified by the landlord of a different address in England and Wales at which he wishes to be given any such notice.

(10) In this section—

"authorised insurer", in relation to a policy of insurance, means a person who may carry on in the United Kingdom the business of effecting or carrying out contracts of insurance of the sort provided under the policy without contravening the prohibition imposed by section 19 of the Financial Services and Markets Act 2000 (c. 8),

"house" has the same meaning as for the purposes of Part 1 of the 1967 Act,

"landlord" and "tenant" have the same meanings as in Chapter 1 of this Part,

"long lease" has the meaning given by sections 76 and 77 of this Act, and

"prescribed" means prescribed by regulations made by the appropriate national authority.

Ground rent

s 166 Requirement to notify long leaseholders that rent is due

A10–052 (1) A tenant under a long lease of a dwelling is not liable to make a payment of rent under the lease unless the landlord has given him a notice relating to the payment; and the date on which he is liable to make the payment is that specified in the notice.

(2) The notice must specify—

(a) the amount of the payment,

(b) the date on which the tenant is liable to make it, and

(c) if different from that date, the date on which he would have been liable to make it in accordance with the lease,

and shall contain any such further information as may be prescribed.

(3) The date on which the tenant is liable to make the payment must not be—

(a) either less than 30 days or more than 60 days after the day on which the notice is given, or

(b) before that on which he would have been liable to make it in accordance with the lease.

(4) If the date on which the tenant is liable to make the payment is after that on which he would have been liable to make it in accordance with the lease, any provisions of the lease relating to non-payment or late payment of rent have effect accordingly.

(5) The notice—

(a) must be in the prescribed form, and

(b) may be sent by post.

(6) If the notice is sent by post, it must be addressed to a tenant at the dwelling unless he has notified the landlord in writing of a different address in England and Wales at which he wishes to be given notices under this section (in which case it must be addressed to him there).

(7) In this section "rent" does not include—

(a) a service charge (within the meaning of section 18(1) of the 1985 Act), or

(b) an administration charge (within the meaning of Part 1 of Schedule 11 to this Act).

(8) In this section "long lease of a dwelling" does not include—

(a) a tenancy to which Part 2 of the Landlord and Tenant Act 1954 (c. 56) (business tenancies) applies,

(b) a tenancy of an agricultural holding within the meaning of the Agricultural Holdings Act 1986 (c. 5) in relation to which that Act applies, or

(c) a farm business tenancy within the meaning of the Agricultural Tenancies Act 1995 (c. 8).

(9) In this section—

"dwelling" has the same meaning as in the 1985 Act,

"landlord" and "tenant" have the same meanings as in Chapter 1 of this Part,

"long lease" has the meaning given by sections 76 and 77 of this Act, and

"prescribed" means prescribed by regulations made by the appropriate national authority.

Forfeiture of leases of dwellings

s 167 Failure to pay small amount for short period

A10–053

(1) A landlord under a long lease of a dwelling may not exercise a right of re-entry or forfeiture for failure by a tenant to pay an amount consisting of rent, service charges or administration charges (or a combination of them) ("the unpaid amount") unless the unpaid amount—

(a) exceeds the prescribed sum, or

(b) consists of or includes an amount which has been payable for more than a prescribed period.

(2) The sum prescribed under subsection (1)(a) must not exceed £500.

(3) If the unpaid amount includes a default charge, it is to be treated for the purposes of subsection (1)(a) as reduced by the amount of the charge; and for this purpose "default charge" means an administration charge payable in respect of the tenant's failure to pay any part of the unpaid amount.

(4) In this section "long lease of a dwelling" does not include—

(a) a tenancy to which Part 2 of the Landlord and Tenant Act 1954 (c. 56) (business tenancies) applies,

(b) a tenancy of an agricultural holding within the meaning of the Agricultural Holdings Act 1986 (c. 5) in relation to which that Act applies, or

(c) a farm business tenancy within the meaning of the Agricultural Tenancies Act 1995 (c. 8).

(5) In this section —

"administration charge" has the same meaning as in Part 1 of Schedule 11,

"dwelling" has the same meaning as in the 1985 Act,

"landlord" and "tenant" have the same meaning as in Chapter 1 of this Part,

"long lease" has the meaning given by sections 76 and 77 of this Act, except that a shared ownership lease is a long lease whatever the tenant's total share,

"prescribed" means prescribed by regulations made by the appropriate national authority, and

"service charge" has the meaning given by section 18(1) of the 1985 Act.

s 168 No forfeiture notice before determination of breach

A10–054 (1) A landlord under a long lease of a dwelling may not serve a notice under section 146(1) of the Law of Property Act 1925 (c. 20) (restriction of forfeiture) in respect of a breach by a tenant of a covenant or condition in the lease unless subsection (2) is satisfied.

(2) This subsection is satisfied if—

(a) it has been finally determined on an application under subsection (4) that the breach has occurred,

(b) the tenant has admitted the breach, or

(c) a court in any proceedings, or an arbitral tribunal in proceedings pursuant to a post-dispute arbitration agreement, has finally determined that the breach has occurred.

(3) But a notice may not be served by virtue of subsection (2)(a) or (c) until after the end of the period of 14 days beginning with the day after that on which the final determination is made.

(4) A landlord under a long lease of a dwelling may make an application to a leasehold valuation tribunal for a determination that a breach of a covenant or condition in the lease has occurred.

(5) But a landlord may not make an application under subsection (4) in respect of a matter which—

(a) has been, or is to be, referred to arbitration pursuant to a post-dispute arbitration agreement to which the tenant is a party,

(b) has been the subject of determination by a court, or

(c) has been the subject of determination by an arbitral tribunal pursuant to a post-dispute arbitration agreement.

s 169 Section 168: supplementary

A10–055

(1) An agreement by a tenant under a long lease of a dwelling (other than a post-dispute arbitration agreement) is void in so far as it purports to provide for a determination—

(a) in a particular manner, or

(b) on particular evidence,

of any question which may be the subject of an application under section 168(4).

(2) For the purpose of section 168 it is finally determined that a breach of a convenant or condition in a lease has occurred—

(a) if a decision that it has occurred is not appealed against or otherwise challenged, at the end of the period for bringing an appeal or other challenge, or

(b) if such a decision is appealed against or otherwise challenged and not set aside in consequence of the appeal or other challenge, at the time specified in subsection (3).

(3) The time referred to in subsection (2)(b) is the time when the appeal or other challenge is disposed of—

(a) by the determination of the appeal or other challenge and the expiry of the time for bringing a subsequent appeal (if any), or

(b) by its being abandoned or otherwise ceasing to have effect.

(4) In section 168 and this section "long lease of a dwelling" does not include—

(a) a tenancy to which Part 2 of the Landlord and Tenant Act 1954 (c. 56) (business tenancies) applies,

(b) a tenancy of an agricultural holding within the meaning of the Agricultural Holdings Act 1986 (c. 5) in relation to which that Act applies, or

(c) a farm business tenancy within the meaning of the Agricultural Tenancies Act 1995 (c. 8).

(5) In section 168 and this section—

"arbitration agreement" and "arbitral tribunal" have the same meaning as in Part 1 of the Arbitration Act 1996 (c. 23) and "post-dispute arbitration agreement", in relation to any breach (or alleged breach), means an arbitration agreement made after the breach has occurred (or is alleged to have occurred),

"dwelling" has the same meaning as in the 1985 Act,

"landlord" and "tenant" have the same meaning as in Chapter 1 of this Part, and

"long lease" has the meaning given by sections 76 and 77 of this Act, except that a shared ownership lease is a long lease whatever the tenant's total share.

(6) Section 146(7) of the Law of Property Act 1925 (c. 20) applies for the purposes of section 168 and this section.

(7) Nothing in section 168 affects the service of a notice under section 146(1) of the Law of Property Act 1925 in respect of a failure to pay—

(a) a service charge (within the meaning of section 18(1) of the 1985 Act), or

(b) an administration charge (within the meaning of Part 1 of Schedule 11 to this Act).

s 170 Forfeiture for failure to pay service charge etc

A10–056 (1) Section 81 of the Housing Act 1996 (c. 52) (restriction on forfeiture for failure to pay service charge) is amended as follows.

(2) In subsection (1), for the words from "to pay" to the end substitute

"by a tenant to pay a service charge or administration charge unless—

(a) it is finally determined by (or on appeal from) a leasehold valuation tribunal or by a court, or by an arbitral tribunal in proceedings pursuant to a post-dispute arbitration agreement, that the amount of the service charge or administration charge is payable by him, or

(b) the tenant has admitted that it is so payable."

(3) For subsection (2) substitute—

"(2) The landlord may not exercise a right of re-entry or forfeiture by virtue of subsection (1)(a) until after the end of the period of 14 days beginning with the day after that on which the final determination is made."

(4) For subsection (3) substitute—

"(3) For the purposes of this section it is finally determined that the amount of a service charge or administration charge is payable—

(a) if a decision that it is payable is not appealed against or otherwise challenged, at the end of the time for bringing an appeal or other challenge, or
(b) if such a decision is appealed against or otherwise challenged and not set aside in consequence of the appeal or other challenge, at the time specified in subsection (3A).

(3A) The time referred to in subsection (3)(b) is the time when the appeal or other challenge is disposed of—

(a) by the determination of the appeal or other challenge and the expiry of the time for bringing a subsequent appeal (if any), or
(b) by its being abandoned or otherwise ceasing to have effect."

(5) After subsection (4) insert—

"(4A) References in this section to the exercise of a right of re-entry or forfeiture include the service of a notice under section 146(1) of the Law of Property Act 1925 (restriction on re-entry or forfeiture)."

(6) In subsection (5), after "this section" insert—

(a) "administration charge" has the meaning given by Part 1 of Schedule 11 to the Commonhold and Leasehold Reform Act 2002,
(b) "arbitration agreement" and "arbitral tribunal" have the same meaning as in Part 1 of the Arbitration Act 1996 (c. 23) and "post-dispute arbitration agreement", in relation to any matter, means an arbitration agreement made after a dispute about the matter has arisen,
(c) "dwelling" has the same meaning as in the Landlord and Tenant Act 1985 (c. 70), and
(d) ".

s 171 Power to prescribe additional or different requirements

A10–057 (1) The appropriate national authority may by regulations prescribe requirements which must be met before a right of re-entry or forfeiture may be exercised in relation to a breach of a covenant or condition in a long lease of an unmortgaged dwelling.

(2) The regulations may specify that the requirements are to be in addition to, or instead of, requirements imposed otherwise than by the regulations.

(3) In this section "long lease of a dwelling" does not include—

(a) a tenancy to which Part 2 of the Landlord and Tenant Act 1954 (c. 56) (business tenancies) applies,

(b) a tenancy of an agricultural holding within the meaning of the Agricultural Holdings Act 1986 (c. 5) in relation to which that Act applies, or

(c) a farm business tenancy within the meaning of the Agricultural Tenancies Act 1995 (c. 8).

(4) For the purposes of this section a dwelling is unmortgaged if it is not subject to a mortgage, charge or lien.

(5) In this section—

"dwelling" has the same meaning as in the 1985 Act, and

"long lease" has the meaning given by sections 76 and 77 of this Act, except that a shared ownership lease is a long lease whatever the tenant's total share.

SCHEDULE 6 PREMISES EXCLUDED FROM RIGHT TO MANAGE

Para 1 Buildings with substantial non-residential parts

A10–058 (1) This Chapter does not apply to premises falling within section 72(1) if the internal floor area—

(a) of any non-residential part, or

(b) (where there is more than one such part) of those parts (taken together),

exceeds 25 per cent of the internal floor area of the premises (taken as a whole).

(2) A part of premises is a non-residential part if it is neither—

(a) occupied, or intended to be occupied, for residential purposes, nor

(b) comprised in any common parts of the premises.

(3) Where in the case of any such premises any part of the premises (such as, for example, a garage, parking space or storage area) is used, or intended for use, in conjunction with a particular dwelling contained in the premises (and accordingly is not comprised in any common parts of the premises), it shall be taken to be occupied, or intended to be occupied, for residential purposes.

(4) For the purpose of determining the internal floor area of a building or of any part of a building, the floor or floors of the building or part shall be taken to extend (without interruption) throughout the whole of the interior of the building or part, except that the area of any common parts of the building or part shall be disregarded.

Para 2 Buildings with self-contained parts in different ownership

Where different persons own the freehold of different parts of premises falling within section 72(1), this Chapter does not apply to the premises if any of those parts is a self-contained part of a building. **A10–059**

Para 3 Premises with resident landlord and no more than four units

(1) This Chapter does not apply to premises falling within section 72(1) if the premises— **A10–060**

(a) have a resident landlord, and

(b) do not contain more than four units.

(2) Premises have a resident landlord if—

(a) the premises are not, and do not form part of, a purpose-built block of flats (that is, a building which, as constructed, contained two or more flats),

(b) a relevant freeholder, or an adult member of a relevant freeholder's family, occupies a qualifying flat as his only or principal home, and

(c) sub-paragraph (4) or (5) is satisfied.

(3) A person is a relevant freeholder, in relation to any premises, if he owns the freehold of the whole or any part of the premises.

(4) This sub-paragraph is satisfied if—

(a) the relevant freeholder, or

(b) the adult member of his family,

has throughout the last twelve months occupied the flat as his only or principal home.

(5) This sub-paragraph is satisfied if—

(a) immediately before the date when the relevant freeholder acquired his interest in the premises, the premises were premises with a resident landlord, and

(b) he, or an adult member of his family, entered into occupation of the flat during the period of 28 days beginning with that date and has occupied the flat as his only or principal home ever since.

(6) "Qualifying flat", in relation to any premises and a relevant freeholder or an adult member of his family, means a flat or other unit used as a dwelling—

(a) which is contained in the premises, and

(b) the freehold of the whole of which is owned by the relevant freeholder.

(7) Where the interest of a relevant freeholder in any premises is held on trust, the references in sub-paragraphs (2), (4) and (5)(b) to a relevant freeholder are to a person having an interest under the trust (whether or not also a trustee).

(8) A person is an adult member of another's family if he is—

(a) the other's spouse,

(b) a son, daughter, son-in-law or daughter-in-law of the other, or of the other's spouse, who has attained the age of 18, or

(c) the father or mother of the other or of the other's spouse;

and "son" and "daughter" include stepson and stepdaughter ("son-in-law" and "daughter-in-law" being construed accordingly).

Para 4 Premises owned by local housing authority

A10–061 (1) This Chapter does not apply to premises falling within section 72(1) if a local housing authority is the immediate landlord of any of the qualifying tenants of flats contained in the premises.

(2) "Local housing authority" has the meaning given by section 1 of the Housing Act 1985 (c. 68).

Para 5 Premises in relation to which rights previously exercised

A10–062 (1) This Chapter does not apply to premises falling within section 72(1) at any time if—

(a) the right to manage the premises is at that time exercisable by a RTM company, or

(b) that right has been so exercisable but has ceased to be so exercisable less than four years before that time.

(2) Sub-paragraph (1)(b) does not apply where the right to manage the premises ceased to be exercisable by virtue of section 73(5).

(3) A leasehold valuation tribunal may, on an application made by a RTM company, determine that sub-paragraph (1)(b) is not to apply in any case if it considers that it would be unreasonable for it to apply in the circumstances of the case.

SCHEDULE 7 RIGHT TO MANAGE: STATUTORY PROVISIONS

Para 1 Covenants not to assign etc.

A10–063 (1) Section 19 of the Landlord and Tenant Act 1927 (c. 36) (covenants not to assign without approval etc.) has effect with the modifications provided by this paragraph.

(2) Subsection (1) applies as if—

(a) the reference to the landlord, and

(b) the final reference to the lessor,

were to the RTM company.

(3) Subsection (2) applies as if the reference to the payment of a reasonable sum in respect of any damage to or diminution in the value of the premises or neighbouring premises belonging to the landlord were omitted.

(4) Subsection (3) applies as if—

(a) the first and final references to the landlord were to the RTM company, and

(b) the reference to the right of the landlord to require payment of a reasonable sum in respect of any damage to or diminution in the value of the premises or neighbouring premises belonging to him were omitted.

Para 2 Defective premises

A10–064 (1) Section 4 of the Defective Premises Act 1972 (c. 35) (landlord's duty of care by virtue of obligation or right to repair demised premises) has effect with the modifications provided by this paragraph.

(2) References to the landlord (apart from the first reference in subsections (1) and (4)) are to the RTM company.

(3) The reference to the material time is to the acquisition date.

Para 3 Repairing obligations

A10–065 (1) The obligations imposed on a lessor by virtue of section 11 (repairing obligations in short leases) of the Landlord and Tenant Act 1985 (c. 70) (referred to in this Part as "the 1985 Act") are, so far as relating to any lease of any flat or other unit contained in the premises, instead obligations of the RTM company.

(2) The RTM company owes to any person who is in occupation of a flat or other unit contained in the premises otherwise than under a lease the same obligations as would be imposed on it by virtue of section 11 if that person were a lessee under a lease of the flat or other unit.

(3) But sub-paragraphs (1) and (2) do not apply to an obligation to the extent that it relates to a matter concerning only the flat or other unit concerned.

(4) The obligations imposed on the RTM company by virtue of sub-paragraph (1) in relation to any lease are owed to the lessor (as well as to the lessee).

(5) Subsections (3A) to (5) of section 11 have effect with the modifications that are appropriate in consequence of sub-paragraphs (1) to (3).

(6) The references in subsection (6) of section 11 to the lessor include the RTM company; and a person who is in occupation of a flat or other unit contained in the premises otherwise than under a lease has, in relation to the flat or other unit, the same obligation as that imposed on a lessee by virtue of that subsection.

(7) The reference to the lessor in section 12(1)(a) of the 1985 Act (restriction on contracting out of section 11) includes the RTM company.

Para 4 Service charges

A10–066 (1) Sections 18 to 30 of the 1985 Act (service charges) have effect with the modifications provided by this paragraph.

(2) References to the landlord are to the RTM company.

(3) References to a tenant of a dwelling include a person who is landlord under a lease of the whole or any part of the premises (so that sums paid by him in pursuance of section 103 of this Act are service charges).

(4) Section 22(5) applies as if paragraph (a) were omitted and the person referred to in paragraph (b) were a person who receives service charges on behalf of the RTM company.

(5) Section 26 does not apply.

Para 5 Right to request information on insurance

A10–067 (1) Section 30A of, and the Schedule to, the 1985 Act (rights of tenants with respect to insurance) have effect with the modifications provided by this paragraph.

(2) References to the landlord are to the RTM company.

(3) References to a tenant include a person who is landlord under a lease of the whole or any part of the premises and has to make payments under section 103 of this Act.

(4) Paragraphs 2(3) and 3(3) of the Schedule apply as if paragraph (a) were omitted and the person referred to in paragraph (b) were a person who receives service charges on behalf of the RTM company.

Para 6 Managing agents

A10–068 Section 30B of the 1985 Act (recognised tenants' associations to be consulted about landlord's managing agents) has effect as if references to the landlord were to the RTM company (and as if subsection (6) were omitted).

Para 7 Right of first refusal

A10–069 Where section 5 of the 1987 Act (right of first refusal: requirement that landlord serve offer notice on tenant) requires the landlord to serve an offer notice on the qualifying tenants of the flats contained in the premises, he must serve a copy of the offer notice on the RTM company.

Para 8 Appointment of manager

A10–070 (1) Part 2 of the 1987 Act (appointment of manager by leasehold valuation tribunal) has effect with the modifications provided by this paragraph.

(2) References to the landlord are to the RTM company.

(3) References to a tenant of a flat contained in the premises include a person who is landlord under a lease of the whole or any part of the premises.

(4) Section 21(3) (exception for premises where landlord is exempt or resident or where premises are functional land of a charity) does not apply.

(5) The references in paragraph (a)(i) of subsection (2) of section 24 to any obligation owed by the RTM company to the tenant under his tenancy include any obligations of the RTM company under this Act.

(6) And the circumstances in which a leasehold valuation tribunal may make an order under paragraph (b) of that subsection include any in which the RTM company no longer wishes the right to manage the premises to be exercisable by it.

(7) The power in section 24 to make an order appointing a manager to carry out functions includes a power (in the circumstances specified in subsection (2) of that section) to make an order that the right to manage the premises is to cease to be exercisable by the RTM company.

(8) And such an order may include provision with respect to incidental and ancillary matters (including, in particular, provision about contracts to which the RTM company is a party and the prosecution of claims in respect of causes of action, whether tortuous or contractual, accruing before or after the right to manage ceases to be exercisable).

Para 9 Right to acquire landlord's interest

A10–071 Part 3 of the 1987 Act (compulsory acquisition by tenants of landlord's interest) does not apply.

Para 10 Variation of leases

A10–072 Sections 35, 36, 38 and 39 of the 1987 Act (variation of long leases relating to flats) have effect as if references to a party to a long lease (apart from those in section 38(8)) included the RTM company.

Para 11 Service charges to be held in trust

A10–073 (1) Sections 42 to 42B of the 1987 Act (service charge contributions to be held in trust and in designated account) have effect with the modifications provided by this paragraph.

(2) References to the payee are to the RTM company.

(3) The definition of "tenant" in section 42(1) does not apply.

(4) References to a tenant of a dwelling include a person who is landlord under a lease of the whole or any part of the premises.

(5) The reference in section 42(2) to sums paid to the payee by the contributing tenants by way of relevant service charges includes payments made to the RTM company under section 94 or 103 of this Act.

(6) Section 42A(5) applies as if paragraph (a) were omitted and the person referred to in paragraph (b) were a person who receives service charges on behalf of the RTM company.

Para 12 Information to be furnished to tenants

A10–074 (1) Sections 46 to 48 of the 1987 Act (information to be furnished to tenants) have effect with the modifications provided by this paragraph.

(2) References to the landlord include the RTM company.

(3) References to a tenant include a person who is landlord under a lease of the whole or any part of the premises; and in relation to such a person the references in section 47(4) to sums payable to the landlord under the terms of the tenancy are to sums paid by him under section 103 of this Act.

Para 13 Statutory duties relating to certain covenants

A10–075 (1) The Landlord and Tenant Act 1988 (c. 26) (statutory duties in connection with covenants against assigning etc.) has effect with the modifications provided by this paragraph.

(2) The reference in section 1(2)(b) to the covenant is to the covenant as it has effect subject to section 98 of this Act.

(3) References in section 3(2), (4) and (5) to the landlord are to the RTM company.

Para 14 Tenants' right to management audit

A10–076 (1) Chapter 5 of Part 1 (tenants' right to management audit by landlord) of the Leasehold Reform, Housing and Urban Development Act 1993 (c. 28) (referred to in this Part as "the 1993 Act") has effect with the modifications provided by this paragraph.

(2) References to the landlord (other than the references in section 76(1) and (2) to "the same landlord") are to the RTM company.

(3) References to a tenant include a person who is landlord under a lease of the whole or any part of the premises and has to make payments under section 103 of this Act.

(4) Section 80(5) applies as if the reference to a person who receives rent were to a person who receives service charges.

Para 15 Right to appoint surveyor

A10–077 (1) Section 84 of the Housing Act 1996 (c. 52) and Schedule 4 to that Act (apart from paragraph 7) (right of recognised tenants' association to appoint surveyor to advise on matters relating to service charges) have effect as if references to the landlord were to the RTM company.

(2) Section 84(5) and paragraph 4(5) of Schedule 4 apply as if the references to a person who receives rent were to a person who receives service charges.

Para 16 Administration charges

A10–078 Schedule 11 to this Act has effect as if references to the landlord (or a part to a lease) included the RTM company.

SCHEDULE 11 ADMINISTRATION CHARGES

SCHEDULE PART 1 REASONABLENESS OF ADMINISTRATION CHARGES

Meaning of "administration charge"

Para 1

(1) In this Part of this Schedule "administration charge" means an amount payable by a tenant of a dwelling as part of or in addition to the rent which is payable, directly or indirectly— **A10–079**

(a) for or in connection with the grant of approvals under his lease, or applications for such approvals,

(b) for or in connection with the provision of information or documents by or on behalf of the landlord or a person who is party to his lease otherwise than as landlord or tenant,

(c) in respect of a failure by the tenant to make a payment by the due date to the landlord or a person who is party to his lease otherwise than as landlord or tenant, or

(d) in connection with a breach (or alleged breach) of a covenant or condition in his lease.

(2) But an amount payable by the tenant of a dwelling the rent of which is registered under Part 4 of the Rent Act 1977 (c. 42) is not an administration charge, unless the amount registered is entered as a variable amount in pursuance of section 71(4) of that Act.

(3) In this Part of this Schedule "variable administration charge" means an administration charge payable by a tenant which is neither—

(a) specified in his lease, nor

(b) calculated in accordance with a formula specified in his lease.

(4) An order amending sub-paragraph (1) may be made by the appropriate national authority.

Reasonableness of administration charges

Para 2

A variable administration charge is payable only to the extent that the amount of the charge is reasonable. **A10–080**

Para 3

(1) Any party to a lease of a dwelling may apply to a leasehold valuation tribunal for an order varying the lease in such manner as is specified in the application on the grounds that— **A10–081**

(a) any administration charge specified in the lease is unreasonable, or

(b) any formula specified in the lease in accordance with which any administration charge is calculated is unreasonable.

(2) If the grounds on which the application was made are established to the satisfaction of the tribunal, it may make an order varying the lease in such manner as is specified in the order.

(3) The variation specified in the order may be—

(a) the variation specified in the application, or

(b) such other variation as the tribunal thinks fit.

(4) The tribunal may, instead of making an order varying the lease in such manner as is specified in the order, make an order directing the parties to the lease to vary it in such manner as is so specified.

(5) The tribunal may by order direct that a memorandum of any variation of a lease effected by virtue of this paragraph be endorsed on such documents as are specified in the order.

(6) Any such variation of a lease shall be binding not only on the parties to the lease for the time being but also on other persons (including any predecessors in title), whether or not they were parties to the proceedings in which the order was made.

Notice in connection with demands for administration charges

Para 4

A10–082 (1) A demand for the payment of an administration charge must be accompanied by a summary of the rights and obligations of tenants of dwellings in relation to administration charges.

(2) The appropriate national authority may make regulations prescribing requirements as to the form and content of such summaries of rights and obligations.

(3) A tenant may withhold payment of an administration charge which has been demanded from him if sub-paragraph (1) is not complied with in relation to the demand.

(4) Where a tenant withholds an administration charge under this paragraph, any provisions of the lease relating to non-payment or late payment of administration charges do not have effect in relation to the period for which he so withholds it.

Liability to pay administration charges

Para 5

A10–083 (1) An application may be made to a leasehold valuation tribunal for a determination whether an administration charge is payable and, if it is, as to—

(a) the person by whom it is payable,

(b) the person to whom it is payable,

(c) the amount which is payable,

(d) the date at or by which it is payable, and

(e) the manner in which it is payable.

(2) Sub-paragraph (1) applies whether or not any payment has been made.

(3) The jurisdiction conferred on a leasehold valuation tribunal in respect of any matter by virtue of sub-paragraph (1) is in addition to any jurisdiction of a court in respect of the matter.

(4) No application under sub-paragraph (1) may be made in respect of a matter which—

(a) has been agreed or admitted by the tenant,

(b) has been, or is to be, referred to arbitration pursuant to a post-dispute arbitration agreement to which the tenant is a party,

(c) has been the subject of determination by a court, or

(d) has been the subject of determination by an arbitral tribunal pursuant to a post-dispute arbitration agreement.

(5) But the tenant is not to be taken to have agreed or admitted any matter by reason only of having made any payment.

(6) An agreement by the tenant of a dwelling (other than a post-dispute arbitration agreement) is void in so far as it purports to provide for a determination—

(a) in a particular manner, or

(b) on particular evidence,

of any question which may be the subject of an application under sub-paragraph (1).

Interpretation

Para 6

(1) This paragraph applies for the purposes of this Part of this Schedule. **A10–084**

(2) "Tenant" includes a statutory tenant.

(3) "Dwelling" and "statutory tenant" (and "landlord" in relation to a statutory tenant) have the same meanings as in the 1985 Act.

(4) "Post-dispute arbitration agreement", in relation to any matter, means an arbitration agreement made after a dispute about the matter has arisen.

(5) "Arbitration agreement" and "arbitral tribunal" have the same meanings as in Part 1 of the Arbitration Act 1996 (c. 23).

SCHEDULE PART 2 AMENDMENTS OF LANDLORD AND TENANT ACT 1987

Para 7

A10–085 The 1987 Act has effect subject to the following amendments.

Para 8

A10–086 (1) Section 24 (appointment of manager by leasehold valuation tribunal) is amended as follows.

(2) In subsection (2), after paragraph (ab) insert—

"(aba) where the tribunal is satisfied—

(i) that unreasonable variable administration charges have been made, or are proposed or likely to be made, and
(ii) that it is just and convenient to make the order in all the circumstances of the case;".

(3) After subsection (2A) insert—

"(2B) In subsection (2)(aba) "variable administration charge" has the meaning given by paragraph 1 of Schedule 11 to the Commonhold and Leasehold Reform Act 2002."

Para 9

A10–088 In section 46 (interpretation of provisions concerning information to be furnished to tenants), insert at the end—

"(3) In this Part "administration charge" has the meaning given by paragraph 1 of Schedule 11 to the Commonhold and Leasehold Reform Act 2002."

Para 10

A10–089 (1) Section 47 (landlord's name and address to be contained in demands for rent etc.) is amended as follows.

(2) In subsection (2), after "service charge" insert "or an administration charge".

(3) In subsection (3), after "service charges" insert "or (as the case may be) administration charges".

Para 11

A10–090 (1) Section 48 (notification by landlord of address for service of notices) is amended as follows.

(2) In subsection (2), for "or service charge" substitute ",service charge or administration charge".

(3) In subsection (3)—

(a) for "or service charge" substitute, "service charge or administration charge", and

(b) for "or (as the case may be) service charges" substitute ",service charges or (as the case may be) administration charges".

The Service Charge Contributions (Authorised Investments) Order 1988

1988 No. 1284

A11–001 The Secretary of State, in exercise of the powers conferred on him by section 42(5) of the Landlord and Tenant Act 1987[1] and of all other powers enabling him in that behalf, hereby makes the following Order:

1. This Order may be cited as the Service Charge Contributions (Authorised Investments) Order 1987 and shall come into force on 1st April 1989.

2. Any sums standing to the credit of any trust fund to which section 42 of the Landlord and Tenant Act 1987 applies may be—

(a) deposited at interest with the Bank of England; or

(b) deposited in the United Kingdom at interest with a person carrying on in the United Kingdom a deposit-taking business within the meaning of the Banking Act 1987[2]; or

(c) deposited at interest with, or invested in shares in, a building society within the meaning of the Building Societies Act 1986[3].

[1] 1987 c. 31.
[2] 1987 c. 22.
[3] 1986 c. 53.

The Service Charge (Estimates and Consultation) Order 1988

1988 No. 1285

A12–001

The Secretary of State for the Environment, as respects England, and the Secretary of State for Wales, as respects Wales, in exercise of the powers conferred on them by section 20(3) and (10) of the Landlord and Tenant Act 1985[1] and all other powers enabling them in that behalf, hereby make the following Order:

1. This Order may be cited as the Service Charge (Estimates and Consultation) Order 1988 and shall come into force on 1st September 1988.

2. Except in a case where relevant costs have been incurred before this Order comes into force—

(a) the amount prescribed for the purposes of section 20(3)(a) of the Landlord and Tenant Act 1985 is £50, and

(b) the amount prescribed for the purposes of section 20(3)(b) of that Act is £1,000.

[1] 1985 c. 70; section 20 was substituted by paragraph 3 of Schedule 2 to the Landlord and Tenant Act 1987 (c. 31).

The Unfair Terms in Consumer Contracts Regulations 1999

1999 No. 2083

A13–001 Whereas the Secretary of State is a Minister designated[1] for the purposes of section 2(2) of the European Communities Act 1972[2] in relation to measures relating to consumer protection:

Now, the Secretary of State, in exercise of the powers conferred upon him by section 2(2) of that Act, hereby makes the following Regulations:—

Citation and commencement

A13–002 **1.** These Regulations may be cited as the Unfair Terms in Consumer Contracts Regulations 1999 and shall come into force on 1st October 1999.

Revocation

A13–003 **2.** The Unfair Terms in Consumer Contracts Regulations 1994[3] are hereby revoked.

Interpretation

A13–004 **3.**—(1) In these Regulations—

"the Community" means the European Community;

"consumer" means any natural person who, in contracts covered by these Regulations, is acting for purposes which are outside his trade, business or profession;

"court" in relation to England and Wales and Northern Ireland means a county court or the High Court, and in relation to Scotland, the Sheriff or the Court of Session;

"Director" means the Director General of Fair Trading;

"EEA Agreement" means the Agreement on the European Economic Area signed at Oporto on 2nd May 1992 as adjusted by the protocol signed at Brussels on 17th March 1993[4];

"Member State" means a State which is a contracting party to the EEA Agreement;

"notified" means notified in writing;

"qualifying body" means a person specified in Schedule 1;

"seller or supplier" means any natural or legal person who, in contracts covered by these Regulations, is acting for purposes relating to his trade, business or profession, whether publicly owned or privately owned;

"unfair terms" means the contractual terms referred to in regulation 5.

(2) In the application of these Regulations to Scotland for references to an "injunction" or an "interim injunction" there shall be substituted references to an "interdict" or "interim interdict" respectively.

Terms to which these Regulations apply

A13–005

4.—(1) These Regulations apply in relation to unfair terms in contracts concluded between a seller or a supplier and a consumer.

(2) These Regulations do not apply to contractual terms which reflect—

(a) mandatory statutory or regulatory provisions (including such provisions under the law of any Member State or in Community legislation having effect in the United Kingdom without further enactment);

(b) the provisions or principles of international conventions to which the Member States or the Community are party.

Unfair Terms

A13–006

5.—(1) A contractual term which has not been individually negotiated shall be regarded as unfair if, contrary to the requirement of good faith, it cause a significant imbalance in the parties' rights and obligations arising under the contract, to the detriment of the consumer.

(2) A term shall always be regarded as not having been individually negotiated where it has been drafted in advance and the consumer has therefore not been able to influence the substance of the term.

(3) Notwithstanding that a specific term or certain aspects of it in a contract has been individually negotiated, these Regulations shall apply to the rest of a contract if an overall assessment of it indicates that it is a pre-formulated standard contract.

(4) It shall be for any seller or supplier who claims that a term was individually negotiated to show that it was.

(5) Schedule 2 to these Regulations contains an indicative and non-exhaustive list of the terms which may be regarded as unfair.

Assessment of unfair terms

A13–007

6.—(1) Without prejudice to regulation 12, the unfairness of a contractual term shall be assessed, taking into account the nature of the goods or services for which the contract was concluded and by referring, at the time of conclusion of the contract, to all the circumstances attending the conclusion of the contract and to all the other terms of the contract or of another contract on which it is dependent.

(2) In so far as it is in plain intelligible language, the assessment of fairness of a term shall not relate—

(a) to the definition of the main subject matter of the contract, or

(b) to the adequacy of the price or remuneration, as against the goods or services supplied in exchange.

Written contracts

A13–008 **7.**—(1) A seller or supplier shall ensure that any written term of a contract is expressed in plain, intelligible language.

(2) If there is doubt about the meaning of a written term, the interpretation which is most favorable to the consumer shall prevail but this rule shall not apply in proceedings brought under regulation 12.

Effect of unfair term

A13–009 **8.**—(1) An unfair term in a contract concluded with a consumer by a seller or supplier shall not be binding on the consumer.

(2) The contract shall continue to bind the parties if it is capable of continuing in existence without the unfair term.

Choice of law clauses

A13–010 **9.** These Regulations shall apply notwithstanding any contract term which applies or purports to apply the law of a non-Member State, if the contract has a close connection with the territory of the Member States.

Complaints – consideration by Director

A13–011 **10.**—(1) It shall be the duty of the Director to consider any complaint made to him that any contract term drawn up for general use is unfair, unless—

(a) the complaint appears to the Director to be frivolous or vexatious; or

(b) a qualifying body has notified the Director that it agrees to consider the complaint.

(2) The Director shall give reasons for his decision to apply or not to apply, as the case may be, for an injunction under regulation 12 in relation to any complaint which these Regulations require him to consider.

(3) In deciding whether or not to apply for an injunction in respect of a term which the Director considers to be unfair, he may, if he considers it appropriate to do so, have regard to any undertakings given to him by or on behalf of any person as to the continued use of such a term in contracts concluded with consumers.

Complaints – consideration by qualifying bodies

A13–012 **11.**—(1) If a qualifying body specified in Part One of Schedule 1 notifies the Director that it agrees to consider a complaint that any contract term drawn up for general use is unfair, it shall be under a duty to consider that complaint.

(2) Regulation 10(2) and (3) shall apply to a qualifying body which is under a duty to consider a complaint as they apply to the Director.

Injunction to prevent continued use of unfair terms

12.—(1) The Director or, subject to paragraph (2), any qualifying body may apply for an injunction (including an interim injunction) against any person appearing to the Director or that body to be using, or recommending use of, an unfair term drawn up for general use in contracts concluded with consumers. **A13–013**

(2) A qualifying body may apply for an injunction only where—

(a) it has notified the Director of its intention to apply at least fourteen days before the date on which the application is made, beginning with the date on which the notification was given; or

(b) the Director consents to the application being made within a shorter period.

(3) The court on an application under this regulation may grant an injunction on such terms as it thinks fit.

(4) An injunction may relate not only to use of a particular contract term drawn up for general use but to any similar term, or a term having like effect, used or recommended for use by any person.

Powers of the Director and qualifying bodies to obtain documents and information

13.—(1) The Director may exercise the power conferred by this regulation for the purpose of— **A13–014**

(a) facilitating his consideration of a complaint that a contract term drawn up for general use is unfair; or

(b) ascertaining whether a person has complied with an undertaking or court order as to the continued use, or recommendation for use, of a term in contracts concluded with consumers.

(2) A qualifying body specified in Part One of Schedule 1 may exercise the power conferred by this regulation for the purpose of—

(a) facilitating its consideration of a complaint that a contract term drawn up for general use is unfair; or

(b) ascertaining whether a person has complied with—

(i) an undertaking given to it or to the court following an application by that body, or

(ii) a court order made on an application by that body,

as to the continued use, or recommendation for use, of a term in contracts concluded with consumers.

(3) The Director may require any person to supply to him, and a qualifying body specified in Part One of Schedule 1 may require any person to supply to it—

(a) a copy of any document which that person has used or recommended for use, at the time the notice referred to in paragraph (4) below is given, as a pre-formulated standard contract in dealings with consumers;

(b) information about the use, or recommendation for use, by that person of that document or any other such document in dealings with consumers.

(4) The power conferred by this regulation is to be exercised by a notice in writing which may—

(a) specify the way in which and the time within which it is to be complied with; and

(b) be varied or revoked by a subsequent notice.

(5) Nothing in this regulation compels a person to supply any document or information which he would be entitled to refuse to produce or give in civil proceedings before the court.

(6) If a person makes default in complying with a notice under this regulation, the court may, on the application of the Director or of the qualifying body, make such order as the court thinks fit for requiring the default to be made good, and any such order may provide that all the costs or expenses of and incidental to the application shall be borne by the person in default or by any officers of a company or other association who are responsible for its default.

Notification of undertakings and orders to Director

A13–015 **14.** A qualifying body shall notify the Director—

(a) of any undertaking given to it by or on behalf of any person as to the continued use of a term which that body considers to be unfair in contracts concluded with consumers;

(b) of the outcome of any application made by it under regulation 12, and of the terms of any undertaking given to, or order made by, the court;

(c) of the outcome of any application made by it to enforce a previous order of the court.

Publication, information and advice

A13–016 **15.**—(1) The Director shall arrange for the publication in such form and manner as he considers appropriate, of—

(a) details of any undertaking or order notified to him under regulation 14;

(b) details of any undertaking given to him by or on behalf of any person as to the continued use of a term which the Director considers to be unfair in contracts concluded with consumers;

(c) details of any application made by him under regulation 12, and of the terms of any undertaking given to, or order made by, the court;

(d) details of any application made by the Director to enforce a previous order of the court.

(2) The Director shall inform any person on request whether a particular term to which these Regulations apply has been—

(a) the subject of an undertaking given to the Director or notified to him by a qualifying body; or

(b) the subject of an order of the court made upon application by him or notified to him by a qualifying body;

and shall give that person details of the undertaking or a copy of the order, as the case may be, together with a copy of any amendments which the person giving the undertaking has agreed to make to the term in question.

(3) The Director may arrange for the dissemination in such form and manner as he considers appropriate of such information and advice concerning the operation of these Regulations as may appear to him to be expedient to give to the public and to all persons likely to be affected by these Regulations.

SCHEDULE 1

Regulation 3

QUALIFYING BODIES

PART ONE

A13–017

1. The Data Protection Registrar.
2. The Director General of Electricity Supply.
3. The Director General of Gas Supply.
4. The Director General of Electricity Supply for Northern Ireland.
5. The Director General of Gas for Northern Ireland.
6. The Director General of Telecommunications.
7. The Director General of Water Services.
8. The Rail Regulator.
9. Every weights and measures authority in Great Britain.
10. The Department of Economic Development in Northern Ireland.

PART TWO

11. Consumers' Association.

SCHEDULE 2

Regulation 5(5)

INDICATIVE AND NON-EXHAUSTIVE LIST OF TERMS WHICH MAY BE REGARDED AS UNFAIR

A13–018 **1.** Terms which have the object or effect of—

(a) excluding or limiting the legal liability of a seller or supplier in the event of the death of a consumer or personal injury to the latter resulting from an act or omission of that seller or supplier;

(b) inappropriately excluding or limiting the legal rights of the consumer vis-à-vis the seller or supplier or another party in the event of total or partial non-performance or inadequate performance by the seller or supplier of any of the contractual obligations, including the option of offsetting a debt owed to the seller or supplier against any claim which the consumer may have against him;

(c) making an agreement binding on the consumer whereas provision of services by the seller or supplier is subject to a condition whose realisation depends on his own will alone;

(d) permitting the seller or supplier to retain sums paid by the consumer where the latter decides not to conclude or perform the contract, without providing for the consumer to receive compensation of an equivalent amount from the seller or supplier where the latter is the party canceling the contract;

(e) requiring any consumer who fails to fulfil his obligation to pay a disproportionately high sum in compensation;

(f) authorising the seller or supplier to dissolve the contract on a discretionary basis where the same facility is not granted to the consumer, or permitting the seller or supplier to retain the sums paid for services not yet supplied by him where it is the seller or supplier himself who dissolves the contract;

(g) enabling the seller or supplier to terminate a contract of indeterminate duration without reasonable notice except where there are serious grounds for doing so;

(h) automatically extending a contract of fixed duration where the consumer does not indicate otherwise, when the deadline fixed for the consumer to express his desire not to extend the contract is unreasonably early;

(i) irrevocably binding the consumer to terms with which he had no real opportunity of becoming acquainted before the conclusion of the contract;

(j) enabling the seller or supplier to alter the terms of the contract unilaterally without a valid reason which is specified in the contract;

(k) enabling the seller or supplier to alter unilaterally without a valid reason any characteristics of the product or service to be provided;

(l) providing for the price of goods to be determined at the time of delivery or allowing a seller of goods or supplier of services to increase their price without in both cases giving the consumer the corresponding right to cancel the contract if the final price is too high in relation to the price agreed when the contract was concluded;

(m) giving the seller or supplier the right to determine whether the goods or services supplied are in conformity with the contract, or giving him the exclusive right to interpret any term of the contract;

(n) limiting the seller's or supplier's obligation to respect commitments undertaken by his agents or making his commitments subject to compliance with a particular formality;

(o) obliging the consumer to fulfill all his obligations where the seller or supplied does not perform his;

(p) giving the seller or supplier the possibility of transferring his rights and obligations under the contract, where this may serve to reduce the guarantees for the consumer, without the latter's agreement;

(q) excluding or hindering the consumer's right to take legal action or exercise any other legal remedy, particularly by requiring the consumer to take disputes exclusively to arbitration not covered by legal provisions, unduly restricting the evidence available to him or imposing on him a burden of proof which, according to the applicable law, should lie with another party to the contract.

2. Scope of paragraph 1(g), (j) and (1) **A13–019**

(a) Paragraph 1(g) is without hindrance to terms by which a supplier of financial services reserves the right to terminate unilaterally a contract of indeterminate duration without notice where there is a valid reason, provided that the supplier is required to inform the other contracting party or parties thereof immediately.

(b) Paragraph 1(j) is without hindrance to terms under which a supplier of financial services reserves the right to alter the rate of interest payable by the consumer or due to the latter, or the amount of other charges for financial services without notice where there is a valid reason, provided that the supplier is required to inform the other contracting party or parties thereof at the earliest opportunity and that the latter are free to dissolve the contract immediately.

Paragraph 1(j) is also without hindrance to terms under which a seller or supplier reserves the right to alter unilaterally the conditions of a contract of indetermine duration, provided that he is required to inform the consumer with reasonable notice and that the consumer is free to dissolve the contract.

(c) Paragraphs 1(g), (j) and (1) do not apply to:
- — transactions in transferable securities, financial instruments and other products or services where the price is linked to fluctuations in a stock exchange quotation or index or a financial market rate that the seller or supplier does not control;
- — contracts for the purchase or sale of foreign currency, traveller's cheques or international money orders denominated in foreign currency;

(d) Paragraph 1(1) is without hindrance to price indexation clauses, where lawful, provided that the method by which prices vary is explicitly described.

[1] S.I 1993/2661.
[2] 1972 c. 68
[3] S.I. 1994/3159.
[4] Protocol 47 and certain Annexes to the EEA Agreement were amended by Decision No. 7/94 of the EEA Joint Committee which came into force on 1st July 1994, (O.J. No. L160, 28.6.94, p.1). Council Directive 9/13/EEC was added to Annex XIX to the Agreement by Annex 17 to the said Decision No. 7/94

The Service Charges (Consultation Requirements) (England) Regulations 2003

2003 No. 1987

The First Secretary of State, in exercise of the powers conferred by section 2(4) and (5) and 20ZA(3) to (6) of the Landlord and Tenant Act 1985[1], hereby makes the following Regulations: **A14–001**

Citation, commencement and application

1.—(1) These Regulations may be cited as the Service Charges (Consultation Requirements) (England) Regulations 2003 and shall come into force on 31st October 2003. **A14–002**

(2) These Regulations apply in relation to England only.

(3) These Regulations apply where a landlord—

(a) intends to enter into a qualifying long term agreement to which section 20 of the Landlord and Tenant Act 1985 applies[2] on or after the date on which these Regulations come into force; or

(b) intends to carry out qualifying works to which that section[3] applies on or after that date.

Interpretation

2.—(1) In these Regualtions— **A14–003**

"the 1985 Act" means the Landlord and Tenant Act 1985;

"close relative", in relation to a person, means a spouse or cohabitee, a parent, parent-in-law, son, son-in-law, daughter, daughter-in-law, brother, brother-in-law, sister, sister-in-law, step-parent, step-son or step daughter of that person;

"cohabitee", in relation to a person, means—

(a) a person of the opposite sex who is living with that person as husband or wife; or
(b) a person of the same sex living with that person in a relationship which has the characteristics of the relationship between husband and wife;

"nominated person" means a person whose name is proposed in response to an invitation made as mentioned in paragraph 1(3) of Schedule 1 or paragraph 1(3) of Part 2 of Schedule 4; and "nomination" means any such proposal;

"public notice" means notice published in the Official Journal of the European Union pursuant to the Public Works Contracts Regulations

1991[4], the Public Services Contracts Regulations 1993[5] or the Public Supply Contracts Regulations 1995[6];

"relevant period", in relation to a notice, means the period of 30 days beginning with the date of the notice;

"RTB tenancy" means the tenancy of an RTB tenant;

"RTB tenant", in relation to a landlord, means a person who has become a tenant of the landlord by virtue of section 138 of the Housing Act 1985 (duty of landlord to convey freehold or grant lease), section 171A of that Act (cases in which right to buy is preserved), or section 16 of the Housing Act 1996 (right of tenant to acquire dwelling)[7] under a lease whose terms include a requirement that the tenant shall bear a reasonable part of such costs incurred by the landlord as are mentioned in paragraphs 16A to 16D of Schedule 6 to that Act (service charges and other contributions payable by the tenant)[8];

"section 20" means section 20 (limitation of service charges: consultation requirements) of the 1985 Act;

"section 20ZA" means section 20ZA (consultation requirements: supplementary) of that Act;

"the relevant matters", in relation to a proposed agreement, means the goods or services to be provided or the works to be carried out (as the case may be) under the agreement.

(2) For the purposes of any estimate required by any provision of these Regulations to be made by the landlord—

(a) value added tax shall be included where applicable; and
(b) where the estimate relates to a proposed agreement, it shall be assumed that the agreement will terminate only by effluxion of time.

Agreements that are not qualifying long term agreements

A14–004 **3.**—(1) An agreement is not a qualifying long term agreement[9]—

(a) if it is a contract of employment; or
(b) if it is a management agreement made by a local housing authority[10] and—
    (i) a tenant management organisation; or
    (ii) a body established under section 2 of the Local Government Act 2000[11];
(c) if the parties to the agreement are—
    (i) a holding company and one or more of its subsidiaries; or
    (ii) two or more subsidiaries of the same holding company;

(d) if—

(i) when the agreement is entered into, there are no tenants of the building or other premises to which the agreement relates; and
(ii) the agreement is for a term not exceeding five years.

(2) An agreement entered into, by or on behalf of the landlord or a superior landlord—

(a) before the coming into force of these Regulations; and

(b) for a term of more than twelve months,

is not a qualifying long term agreement, notwithstanding that more than twelve months of the term remain unexpired on the coming into force of these Regulations.

(3) An agreement for a term of more than twelve months entered into, by or on behalf of the landlord or a superior landlord, which provides for the carrying out of qualifying works for which public notice has been given before the date on which these Regulations come into force, is not a qualifying long term agreement.

(4) In paragraph (1)—

"holding company" and "subsidiaries" have the same meaning as in the Companies Act 1985[12];

"management agreement" has the meaning given by section 27(2) of the Housing Act 1985[13]; and

"tenant management organisation" has the meaning given by section 27AB(8) of the Housing Act 1985[14].

Application of section 20 to qualifying long term agreements

A14–005

4.—(1) Section 20 shall apply to a qualifying long term agreement if relevant costs[15] incurred under the agreement in any accounting period exceed an amount which results in the relevant contribution of any tenant, in respect of that period, being more than £100.

(2) In paragraph (1), "accounting period" means the period—

(a) beginning with the relevant date, and

(b) ending with the date that falls twelve months after the relevant date.

(3) In the case of the first accounting period, the relevant date is—

(a) if the relevant accounts are made up for periods of twelve months, the date on which the period that includes the date on which these Regulations come into force ends, or

(b) if the accounts are not so made up, the date on which these Regulations come into force.

(4) In the case of subsequent accounting periods, the relevant date is the date immediately following the end of the previous accounting period.

The consultation requirements: qualifying long term agreements

A14–006 **5.**—(1) Subject to paragraphs (2) and (3), in relation to qualifying long term agreements to which section 20 applies, the consultation requirements for the purposes of that section and section 20ZA are the requirements specified in Schedule 1.

(2) Where public notice is required to be given of the relevant matters to which a qualifying long term agreement relates, the consultation requirements for the purposes of sections 20 and 20ZA, as regards the agreement, are the requirements specified in Schedule 2.

(3) In relation to a RTB tenant and a particular qualifying long term agreement, nothing in paragraph (1) or (2) requires a landlord to comply with any of the consultation requirements applicable to that agreement that arise before the thirty-first day of the RTB tenancy.

Application of section 20 to qualifying works

A14–007 **6.** For the purposes of subsection (3) of section 20 the appropriate amount is an amount which results in the relevant contribution of any tenant being more than £250.

The consultation requirements: qualifying works

A14–008 **7.**—(1) Subject to paragraph (5), where qualifying works are the subject (whether alone or with other matters) of a qualifying long term agreement to which section 20 applies, the consultation requirements for the purposes of that section and section 20ZA, as regards those works, are the requirements specified in Schedule 3.

(2) Subject to paragraph (5), in a case to which paragraph (3) applies the consultation requirements for the purposes of sections 20 and 20ZA, as regards qualifying works referred to in that paragraph, are those specified in Schedule 3.

(3) This paragraph applies where—

(a) under an agreement entered into, by or on behalf of the landlord or a superior landlord, before the coming into force of these Regulations, qualifying works are carried out at any time on or after the date that falls two months after the date on which these Regulations come into force; or

(b) under an agreement for a term of more than twelve months entered into, by or on behalf of the landlord or a superior landlord, qualifying works for which public notice has been given before the date on which these Regulations come into force are carried out at any time on or after the date.

(4) Except in a case to which paragraph (3) applies, and subject to paragraph (5), where qualifying works are not the subject of a qualifying long term agreement to which section 20 applies, the consultation requirements for the purposes of that section and section 20ZA, as regards those works—

(a) in a case where public notice of those works is required to be given, are those specified in Part 1 of Schedule 4;

(b) in any other case, are those specified in Part 2 of that Schedule.

(5) In relation to a RTB tenant and particular qualifying works, nothing in paragraph (1), (2) or (4) requires a landlord to comply with any of the consultation requirements applicable to that agreement that arise before the thirty-first day of the RTB tenancy.

SCHEDULE 1

Regulation 5(1)

CONSULTATION REQUIREMENTS FOR QUALIFYING LONG TERM AGREEMENTS OTHER THAN THOSE FOR WHICH PUBLIC NOTICE IS REQUIRED

Notice of intention

A14–009

1.—(1) The landlord shall give notice in writing of his intention to enter into the agreement—

(a) to each tenant; and

(b) where a recognised tenants' association[16] represents some or all of the tenants, to the association.

(2) The notice shall—

(a) describe, in general terms, the relevant matters or specify the place and hours at which a description of the relevant matters may be inspected;

(b) state the landlord's reasons for considering it necessary to enter into the agreement;

(c) where the relevant matters consist of or include qualifying works, state the landlord's reasons for considering it necessary to carry out those works;

(d) invite the making, in writing, of observations in relation to the proposed agreement; and

(e) specify—

(i) the address to which such observations may be sent;
(ii) that they must be delivered within the relevant period; and
(iii) the date on which the relevant period ends.

(3) The notice shall also invite each tenant and the association (if any) to propose, within the relevant period, the name of a person from whom the landlord should try to obtain an estimate in respect of the relevant matters.

Inspection of description of relevant matters

A14–010 **2.**—(1) Where a notice under paragraph 1 specifies a place and hours for inspection—

(a) the place and hours so specified must be reasonable; and

(b) a description of the relevant matters must be available for inspection, free of charge, at that place and during those hours.

(2) If facilities to enable copies to be taken are not made available at the times at which the description may be inspected, the landlord shall provide to any tenant, on request and free of charge, a copy of the description.

Duty to have regard to observations in relation to proposed agreement

A14–011 **3.** Where, within the relevant period, observations are made in relation to the proposed agreement by any tenant or recognised tenants' association, the landlord shall have regard to those observations.

Estimates

A14–012 **4.**—(1) Where, within the relevant period, a single nomination is made by a recognised tenants' association (whether or not a nomination is made by any tenant), the landlord shall try to obtain an estimate from the nominated person.

(2) Where, within the relevant period, a single nomination is made by only one of the tenants (whether or not a nomination is made by a recognised tenants' association), the landlord shall try to obtain an estimate from the nominated person.

(3) Where, within the relevant period, a single nomination is made by more than one tenant (whether or not a nomination is made by a recognised tenants' association), the landlord shall try to obtain an estimate—

(a) from the person who received the most nominations; or

(b) if there is no such person, but two (or more) persons received the same number of nominations, being a number in excess of the nominations received by any other person, from one of those two (or more) persons; or

(c) in any other case, from any nominated person.

(4) Where, within the relevant period, more than one nomination is made by any tenant and more than one nomination is made by a recognised tenants' association, the landlord shall try to obtain an estimate—

(a) from at least one person nominated by a tenant; and

(b) from at least one person nominated by the association, other than a person from whom an estimate is sought as mentioned in paragraph (a).

Preparation of landlord's proposals

5.—(1) The landlord shall prepare, in accordance with the following provisions of this paragraph, at least two proposals in respect of the relevant matters. **A14–013**

(2) At least one of the proposals must propose that goods or services are provided, or works are carried out (as the case may be), by a person wholly unconnected with the landlord.

(3) Where an estimate has been obtained from a nominated person, the landlord must prepare a proposal based on that estimate.

(4) Each proposal shall contain a statement of the relevant matters.

(5) Each proposal shall contain a statement, as regards each party to the proposed agreement other than the landlord—

(a) of the party's name and address; and

(b) of any connection (apart from the proposed agreement) between the party and the landlord.

(6) For the purposes of sub-paragraphs (2) and (5)(b), it shall be assumed that there is a connection between a party (as the case may be) and the landlord—

(a) where the landlord is a company, if the party is, or is to be, a director or manager of the company or is a close relative of any such director or manager;

(b) where the landlord is a company, and the party is a partner in a partnership, if any partner in that partnership is, or is to be, a director or manager of the company or is a close relative of any such director or manager;

(c) where both the landlord and the party are companies, if any director or manager of one company is, or is to be, a director or manager of the other company;

(d) where the party is a company, if the landlord is a director or manager of the company or is a close relative of any such director or manager; or

(e) where the party is a company and the landlord is a partner in a partnership, if any partner in that partnership is a director or manager of the company or is a close relative of any such director or manager.

(7) Where, as regards each tenant's unit of occupation and the relevant matters, it is reasonably practicable for the landlord to estimate the relevant

contribution attributable to the relevant matters to which the proposed agreement relates, each proposal shall contain a statement of that estimated contribution.

(8) Where—

(a) it is not reasonably practicable for the landlord to make the estimate mentioned in sub-paragraph (7); and

(b) it is reasonably practicable for the landlord to estimate, as regards the building or other premises to which the proposed agreement relates, the total amount of his expenditure under the proposed agreement,

each proposal shall contain a statement of that estimated expenditure.

(9) Where—

(a) it is not reasonably practicable for the landlord to make the estimate mentioned in sub-paragraph (7) or (8)(b); and

(b) it is reasonably practicable for the landlord to ascertain the current unit cost or hourly or daily rate applicable to the relevant matters,

each proposal shall contain a statement of that cost or rate.

(10) Where the relevant matters comprise or include the proposed appointment by the landlord of an agent to discharge any of the landlord's obligations to the tenants which relate to the management by him of premises to which the agreement relates, each proposal shall contain a statement—

(a) that the person whose appointment is proposed—

(i) is or, as the case may be, is not, a member of a professional body or trade association; and

(ii) subscribes or, as the case may be, does not subscribe, to any code of practice or voluntary accreditation scheme relevant to the functions of managing agents; and

(b) if the person is a member of a professional body trade association, of the name of the body or association.

(11) Each proposal shall contain a statement as to the provisions (if any) for variation of any amount specified in, or to be determined under, the proposed agreement.

(12) Each proposal shall contain a statement of the intended duration of the proposed agreement.

(13) Where the landlord has received observations to which (in accordance with paragraph 3) he is required to have regard, each proposal shall contain a statement summarising the observations and setting out the landlord's response to them

Notification of landlord's proposals

A14–014

6.—(1) The landlord shall give notice in writing of proposals prepared under paragraph 5—

(a) to each tenant; and

(b) where a recognised tenants' association represents some or all of the tenants, to the association.

(2) The notice shall—

(a) be accompanied by a copy of each proposal or specify the place and hours at which the proposals may be inspected;

(b) invite the making, in writing, of observations in relation to the proposals; and

(c) specify—

(i) the address to which such observations may be sent;
(ii) that they must be delivered within the relevant period; and
(iii) the date on which the relevant period ends.

(3) Paragraph 2 shall apply to proposals made available for inspection under this paragraph as it applies to a description of the relevant matters made available for inspection under that paragraph.

Duty to have regard to observations in relation to proposals

7. Where, within the relevant period, observations are made in relation to the landlord's proposals by any tenant or recognised tenants' association, the landlord shall have regard to those observations. **A14–015**

Duty on entering into agreement

8.—(1) Subject to sub-paragraph (2), where the landlord enters into an agreement relating to relevant matters, he shall, within 21 days of entering into the agreement, by notice in writing to each tenant and the recognised tenants' association (if any)— **A14–016**

(a) state his reasons for making that agreement or specify the place and hours at which a statement of those reasons may be inspected; and

(b) where he has received observations to which (in accordance with paragraph 7) he is required to have regard, summarise the observations and respond to them or specify the place and hours at which that summary and response may be inspected.

(2) The requirements of sub-paragraph (1) do not apply where the person with whom the agreement is made is a nominated person or submitted the lowest estimate.

(3) Paragraph 2 shall apply to a statement, summary and response made available for inspection under this paragraph as it applies to a description of the relevant matters made available for inspection under that paragraph.

SCHEDULE 2

Regulation 5(2)

CONSULTATION REQUIREMENTS FOR QUALIFYING LONG TERM AGREEMENTS FOR WHICH PUBLIC NOTICE IS REQUIRED

Notice of intention

A14–017 **1.**—(1) The landlord shall give notice in writing of his intention to enter into the agreement—

(a) to each tenant; and

(b) where a recognised tenants' association represents some or all of the tenants, to the association.

(2) The notice shall—

(a) describe, in general terms, the relevant matters or specify the place and hours at which a description of the relevant matters may be inspected;

(b) state the landlord's reasons for considering it necessary to enter into the agreement;

(c) where the relevant matters consist of or include qualifying works, state the landlord's reasons for considering it necessary to carry out those works;

(d) state that the reason why the landlord is not inviting recipients of the notice to nominate persons from whom he should try to obtain an estimate for the relevant matters is that public notice of the relevant matters is to be given;

(e) invite the making, in writing, of observations in relation to the relevant matters; and

(f) specify—

(i) the address to which such observations may be sent;
(ii) that they must be delivered within the relevant period; and
(iii) the date on which the relevant period ends.

Inspection of description of relevant matters

A14–018 **2.**—(1) Where a notice under paragraph 1 specifies a place and hours for inspection—

(a) the place and hours so specified must be reasonable; and

(b) a description of the relevant matters must be available for inspection, free of charge, at that place and during those hours.

(2) If facilities to enable copies to be taken are not made available at the times at which the description may be inspected, the landlord shall provide to any tenant, on request and free of charge, a copy of the description.

Duty to have regard to observations in relation to relevant matters

A14–019 **3.** Where, within the relevant period, observations are made, in relation to the relevant matters by any tenant or recognised tenants' association, the landlord shall have regard to those observations.

Preparation of landlord's proposal

A14–020 **4.**—(1) The landlord shall prepare, in accordance with the following provisions of this paragraph, a proposal in respect of the proposed agreement.

(2) The proposal shall contain a statement—

(a) of the name and address of every party to the proposed agreement (other than the landlord); and

(b) of any connection (apart from the proposed agreement) between the landlord and any other party.

(3) For the purpose of sub-paragraph (2)(b), it shall be assumed that there is a connection between the landlord and a party—

(a) where the landlord is a company, if the party is, or is to be, a director or manager of the company or is a close relative of any such director or manager;

(b) where the landlord is a company, and the party is a partner in a partnership, if any partner in that partnership is, or is to be, a director or manager of the company or is a close relative of any such director or manager;

(c) where both the landlord and the party are companies, if any director or manager of one company is, or is to be, a director or manager of the other company;

(d) where the party is a company, if the landlord is a director or manager of the company or is a close relative of any such director or manager; or

(e) where the party is a company and the landlord is a partner in a partnership, if any partner in that partnership is a director or manager of the company or is a close relative of any such director or manager.

(4) Where, as regards each tenant's unit of occupation, it is reasonably practicable for the landlord to estimate the relevant contribution to be incurred by the tenant attributable to the relevant matters to which the proposed agreement relates, the proposal shall contain a statement of that contribution.

(5) Where—

(a) it is not reasonably practicable for the landlord to make the estimate mentioned in sub-paragraph (4); and

(b) it is reasonably practicable for the landlord to estimate, as regards the building or other premises to which the proposed agreement relates, the total amount of his expenditure under the proposed agreement,

the proposal shall contain a statement of the amount of that estimate expenditure.

(6) Where—

(a) it is not reasonably practicable for the landlord to make the estimate mentioned in sub-paragraph (4) or (5)(b); and

(b) it is reasonably practicable for the landlord to ascertain the current unit cost or hourly or daily rate applicable to the relevant matters to which the proposed agreement relates,

the proposal shall contain a statement of that cost or rate.

(7) Where it is not reasonably practicable for the landlord to make the estimate mentioned in sub-paragraph (6)(b), the proposal shall contain a statement of the reasons why eh cannot comply and the date by which he expects to be able provide an estimate, cost or rate.

(8) Where the relevant matters comprise or include the proposed appointment by the landlord of an agent to discharge any of the landlord's obligations to the tenants which relate to the management by him of premises to which the agreement relates, each proposal shall contain a statement—

(a) that the person whose appointment is proposed—

(i) is or, as the case may be, is not, a member of a professional body or trade association; and

(ii) subscribes or, as the case may be, does not subscribes, to any code of practice or voluntary accreditation scheme relevant to the functions of managing agents; and

(b) if the person is a member of a professional body trade association, of the name of the body or association.

(9) Each proposal shall contain a statement of the intended duration of the proposed agreement.

(10) Where the landlord has received observations to which (in accordance with paragraph 3) he is required to have regard, the proposal shall contain a statement summarising the observations and setting out the landlord's response to them.

Notification of landlord's proposal

A14–021 **5.**—(1) The landlord shall give notice in writing of the proposal prepared under paragraph 4—

(a) to each tenant; and

(b) where a recognised tenants' association represents some or all of the tenants, to the association.

(2) The notice shall—

(a) be accompanied by a copy of the proposal or specify the place and hours at which the proposal may be inspected;

(b) invite the making, in writing, of observations in relation to the proposal; and

(c) specify—

(i) the address to which such observations may be sent;
(ii) that they must be delivered within the relevant period; and
(iii) the date on which the relevant period ends.

(3) Paragraph 2 shall apply to a proposal made available for inspection under this paragraph as it applies to a description made available for inspection under that paragraph.

Duty to have regard to observations in relation to proposal

6. Where, within the relevant period, observations are made in relation to the landlord's proposal by any tenant or recognised tenants' association, the landlord shall have regard to those observations. **A14–022**

Landlord's response to observations

7. Where the landlord receives observations to which (in accordance with paragraph 6) he is required to have regard, he shall, within 21 days of their receipt, by notice in writing to the person by whom the observations were made, state his response to the observations. **A14–023**

Supplementary information

8. Where a proposal prepared under paragraph 4 contains such a statement as is mentioned in sub-paragraph (7) of that paragraph, the landlord shall, within 21 days of receiving sufficient information to enable him to estimate the amount, cost or rate referred to in sub-paragraph (4), (5) or (6) of that paragraph, give notice in writing of the estimated amount, cost or rate (as the case may be)— **A14–024**

(a) to each tenant; and

(b) where a recognised tenants' association represents some or all of the tenants, to the association.

SCHEDULE 3

Regulation 7(1) and (2)

CONSULTATION REQUIREMENTS FOR QUALIFYING WORKS UNDER QUALIFYING LONG TERM AGREEMENTS AND AGREEMENTS TO WHICH REGULATION 7(3) APPLIES

Notice of intention

A14–025

1.—(1) The landlord shall give notice in writing of his intention to carry out qualifying works—

(a) to each tenant; and

(b) where a recognised tenants' association represents some or all of the tenants, to the association.

(2) The notice shall—

(a) describe, in general terms, the works proposed to be carried out or specify the place and hours at which a description of the proposed works may be inspected;

(b) state the landlord's reasons for considering it necessary to carry out the proposed works;

(c) contain a statement of the total amount of the expenditure estimated by the landlord as likely to be incurred by him on and in connection with the proposed works;

(d) invite the making, in writing, of observations in relation to the proposed works or the landlord's estimated expenditure;

(e) specify—

(i) the address to which such observations may be sent;
(ii) that they must be delivered within the relevant period; and
(iii) the date on which the relevant period ends.

Inspection of description of proposed works

A14–026

2.—(1) Where a notice under paragraph 1 specifies a place and hours for inspection—

(a) the place and hours so specified must be reasonable; and

(b) a description of the proposed works must be available for inspection, free of charge, at that place and during those hours.

(2) If facilities to enable copies to be taken are not made available at the times at which the description may be inspected, the landlord shall provide to any tenant, on request and free of charge, a copy of the description.

Duty to have regard to observations in relation to proposed works and estimated expenditure

3. Where, within the relevant period, observations are made in relation to the proposed works or the landlord's estimated expenditure by and tenant or the recognised tenants' association, the landlord shall have regard to those observations. **A14–027**

Landlord's response to observations

4. Where the landlord receives observations to which (in accordance with paragraph 3) he is required to have regard, he shall, within 21 days of their receipt, by notice in writing to the person by whom the observations were made, state his response to the observations. **A14–028**

SCHEDULE 4

Regulation 7(4)

CONSULTATION REQUIREMENTS FOR QUALIFYING WORKS OTHER THAN WORKS UNDER QUALIFYING LONG TERM OR AGREEMENTS TO WHICH REGULATION 7(3) APPLIES

PART 1

CONSULTATION REQUIREMENTS FOR QUALIFYING WORKS FOR WHICH PUBLIC NOTICE IS REQUIRED

Notice of intention

1.—(1) The landlord shall give notice in writing of his intention to carry out qualifying works— **A14–029**

(a) to each tenant; and

(b) where a recognised tenants' association represents some or all of the tenants, to the association.

(2) The notice shall—

(a) describe, in general terms, the works proposed to be carried out or specify the place and hours at which a description of the proposed works may be inspected;

(b) state the landlord's reasons for considering it necessary to carry out the proposed works;

(c) state that the reason why the landlord is not inviting recipients of the notice to nominate persons from whom he should try to obtain an estimate for carrying out the works is that public notice of the works is to be given;

(d) invite the making, in writing, of observations in relation to the proposed works; and

(e) specify—

(i) the address to which such observations may be sent;
(ii) that they must be delivered within the relevant period; and
(iii) the date on which the relevant period ends.

Inspection of description of proposed works

A14–030 **2.**—(1) Where a notice under paragraph 1 specifies a place and hours for inspection—

(a) the place and hours so specified must be reasonable; and

(b) a description of the proposed works must be available for inspection, free of charge, at that place and during those hours.

(2) If facilities to enable copies to be taken are not made available at the times at which the description may be inspected, the landlord shall provide to any tenant, on request and free of charge, a copy of the description.

Duty to have regard to observations in relation to proposed works

A14–031 **3.** Where, within the relevant period, observations are made in relation to the proposed works by any tenant or the recognised tenants' association, the landlord shall have regard to those observations.

Preparation of landlord's contract statement

A14–032 **4.**—(1) The landlord shall prepare, in accordance with the following provisions of this paragraph, a statement in respect of the proposed contract under which the proposed works are to be carried out.

(2) The statement shall set out—

(a) the name and address of the person with whom the landlord proposes to contract; and

(b) particulars of any connection between them (apart from the proposed contract).

(3) For the purpose of sub-paragraph (2)(b) it shall be assumed that there is a connection between a person and the landlord—

(a) where the landlord is a company, if the person, or is to be, a director or manager of the company or is a close relative of any such director or manager;

(b) where the landlord is a company, and the person is a partner in a partnership, if any partner in that partnership is, or is to be, a director or manager of the company or is a close relative of any such director or manager;

(c) where both the landlord and the person are companies, if any director or manager of one company is, or is to be, a director or manager of the other company;

(d) where the person is a company, if the landlord is a director or manager of the company or is a close relative of any such director or manager; or

(e) where the person is a company and the landlord is a partner in a partnership, if any partner in that partnership is a director or manager of the company or is a close relative of any such director or manager.

(4) Where, as regards each tenant's unit of occupation, it is reasonably practicable for the landlord to estimate the amount of the relevant contribution to be incurred by the tenant attributable to the works to which the proposed contract relates, that estimated amount shall be specified in the statement.

(5) Where—

(a) it is not reasonably practicable for the landlord to make the estimate mentioned in sub-paragraph (4); and

(b) it is reasonably practicable for the landlord to estimate, as regards the building or other premises to which the proposed contract relates, the total amount of his expenditure under the proposed contract, that estimated amount shall be specified in the statement.

(6) Where—

(a) it is not reasonably practicable for the landlord to make the estimate mentioned in sub-paragraph (4) or (5)(b); and

(b) it is reasonably practicable for the landlord to ascertain the current unit cost or hourly or daily rate applicable to the works to which the proposed contract relates,

that cost or rate shall be specified in the statement.

(7) Where it is not reasonably practicable for the landlord to make the estimate mentioned in sub-paragraph (6)(b), the reasons why he cannot comply and the date by which he expects to be able to provide an estimated amount, cost or rate shall be specified in the statement.

(8) Where the landlord has received observations to which (in accordance with paragraph 3) he is required to have regard, the statement shall summarise the observations and set out his response to them.

Notification of proposed contract

A14–033 **5.**—(1) The landlord shall give notice in writing of his intention to enter into the proposed contract—

(a) to each tenant; and

(b) where a recognised tenants' association represents some or all of the tenants, to the association.

(2) The notice shall—

(a) comprise, or be accompanied by, the statement prepared in accordance with paragraph 4 ("the paragraph 4 statement") or specify the place and hours at which that statement may be inspected;

(b) invite the making, in writing, of observations in relation to any matter mentioned in the paragraph 4 statement;

(c) specify—

(i) the address to which such observations may be sent;
(ii) that they must be delivered within the relevant period; and
(iii) the date on which the relevant period ends.

(3) Where the paragraph 4 statement is made available for inspection, paragraph 2 shall apply in relation to that statement as it applies in relation to a description of proposed works made available for inspection under that paragraph.

Landlord's response to observations

A14–034 **6.** Where, within the relevant period, the landlord receives observations in response to the invitation in the notice under paragraph 5, he shall, within 21 days of their receipt, by notice in writing to the person by whom the observations were made, state his response to the observations.

Supplementary information

A14–035 **7.** Where a statement prepared under paragraph 4 sets out the landlord's reasons for being unable to comply with sub-paragraph (6) of that paragraph, the landlord shall, within 21 days of receiving sufficient information to enable him to estimate the amount, cost or rate referrered to in sub-paragraph (4), (5) or (6) of that paragraph, give notice in writing of the estimated amount, cost or rate (as the case may be)—

(a) to each tenant; and

(b) where a recognised tenants' association represents some or all of the tenants, to the association.

PART 2

CONSULTATION REQUIREMENTS FOR QUALIFYING WORKS FOR WHICH PUBLIC NOTICE IS NOT REQUIRED

Notice of intention

1.[a]—(1) The landlord shall give notice in writing of his intention to carry out qualifying works— **A14–036**

(a) to each tenant; and

(b) where a recognised tenants' association represents some or all of the tenants, to the association.

(2) The notice shall—

(a) describe, in general terms, the works proposed to be carried out or specify the place and hours at which a description of the proposed works may be inspected;

(b) state the landlord's reasons for considering it necessary to carry out the proposed works;

(c) invite the making, in writing, of observations in relation to the proposed works; and

(d) specify—

(i) the address to which such observations may be sent;
(ii) that they must be delivered within the relevant period; and
(iii) the date on which the relevant period ends.

(3) The notice shall also invite each tenant and the association (if any) to propose, within the relevant period, the names of a person from whom the landlord should try to obtain an estimate for the carrying out of the proposed works.

Inspection of description of proposed works

2.—(1) Where a notice under paragraph 1 specifies a place and hours for inspection— **A14–037**

(a) the place and hours so specified must be reasonable; and

(b) a description of the proposed works must be available for inspection, free of charge, at that place and during those hours.

(2) If facilities to enable copies to be taken are not made available at the times at which the description may be inspected, the landlord shall provide to any tenant, on request and free of charge, a copy of the description.

Duty to have regard to observations in relation to proposed works

A14–038 **3.** Where, within the relevant period, observations are made, in relation to the proposed works by any tenant or recognised tenants' association, the landlord shall have regard to those observations.

Estimates and response to observations

A14–039 **4.**—(1) Where, within the relevant period, a nomination is made by a recognised tenants' association (whether or not a nomination is made by any tenant), the landlord shall try to obtain an estimate from the nominated person.

(2) Where, within the relevant period, a nomination is made by only one of the tenants (whether or not a nomination is made by a recognised tenants' association), the landlord shall try to obtain an estimate from the nominated person.

(3) Where, within the relevant period, a single nomination is made by more than one tenant (whether or not a nomination is made by a recognised tenants' association), the landlord shall try to obtain an estimate—

(a) from the person who received the most nominations; or

(b) if there is no such person, but two (or more) persons received the same number of nominations, being a number in excess of the nominations received by any other person, from one of those two (or more) persons; or

(c) in any other case, from any nominated person.

(4) Where, within the relevant period, more than one nomination is made by any tenant and more than one nomination is made by a recognised tenants' association, the landlord shall try to obtain an estimate—

(a) from at least one person nominated by a tenant; and

(b) from at least one person nominated by the association, other than a person from whom an estimate is sought as mentioned in paragraph (a).

(5) The landlord shall, in accordance with this sub-paragraph and sub-paragraphs (6) to (9)—

(a) obtain estimates for the carrying out of the proposed works;

(b) supply, free of charge, a statement ("the paragraph (b) statement") setting out—

(i) as regards at least two of the estimates, the amount specified in the estimate as the estimated cost of the proposed works; and

(ii) where the landlord has received observations to which (in accordance with paragraph 3) he is required to have regard, a summary of the observations and his response to them; and

(c) make all of the estimates available for inspection.

(6) At least one of the estimates must be that of a person wholly unconnected with the landlord.

(7) For the purpose of paragraph (6), it shall be assumed that there is a connection between a person and the landlord—

(a) where the landlord is a company, if the person is, or is to be, a director or manager of the company or is a close relative of any such director or manger;

(b) where the landlord is a company, and the person is a partner in a partnership, if any partner in that partnership is, or is to be, a director or manager of the company or is a close relative of any such director or manager;

(c) where both the landlord and the person are companies, if any director or manager of one company is, or is to be, a director or manager of the other company;

(d) where the person is a company if the landlord is a director or manager of the company or is a close relative of any such director or manager; or

(e) where the person is a company and the landlord is a partner in a partnership, if any partner in that partnership is a director or manager of the company or is a close relative of any such director or manager.

(8) Where the landlord has obtained an estimate from a nominated person, that estimate must be one of those to which the paragraph (b) statement relates.

(9) The paragraph (b) statement shall be supplied to, and the estimates made available for inspection by—

(a) each tenant; and

(b) the secretary of the recognised tenants' association (if any).

(10) The landlord shall, by notice in writing to each tenant and the association (if any)—

(a) specify the place and hours at which the estimates may be inspected;

(b) invite the making, in writing, of observations in relation to those estimates;

(c) specify—

(i) the address to which such observations may be sent;
(ii) that they must be delivered within the relevant period; and
(iii) the date on which the relevant period ends.

(11) Paragraph 2 shall apply to estimates made available for inspection under this paragraph as it applies to a description of proposed works made available for inspection under that paragraph.

Duty to have regard to observations in relation to estimates

A14–040 **5.** Where, within the relevant period, observations are made in relation to the estimates by a recognised tenants' association or, as the case may be, any tenant, the landlord shall have regard to those observations.

Duty on entering into contract

A14–041 **6.**—(1) Subject to sub-paragraph (2), where the landlord enters into a contract for the carrying out of qualifying works, he shall, within 21 days of entering into the contract, by notice in writing to each tenant and the recognised tenants' association (if any)—

(a) state his reasons for awarding the contract or specify the place and hours at which a statement of those reasons may be inspected; and

(b) there he received observations to which (in accordance with paragraph 5) he was required to have regard, summarise the observations and set out his response to them.

(2) The requirements of sub-paragraph (1) do not apply where the person with whom the contract is made is a nominated person or submitted the lowest estimate.

(3) Paragraph 2 shall apply to a statement made available for inspection under this paragraph as it applies to a description of proposed works made available for inspection under that paragraph.

[1] 1985 c.70. Section 20 was substituted, and section 20ZA inserted, by section 151 of the Commonhold and Leasehold Reform Act 2002 (c. 15). *See also* paragraph 4 of Schedule 7 to that Act for medications relevant to sections 20 and 20ZA associated with the right to manage under Chapter 1 of Part 2 of that Act. The functions of the Secretary of State under sections 20 and 20ZA are, so far as exercisable in relation to Wales, transferred to the National Assembly for Wales by the National Assembly for Wales (Transfer of Functions) Order 1999 (S.I. 1999/672), article 2; *see* the entry in Schedule 1 for the Landlord and Tenant Act 1985. *see also* section 177 of the Commonhold and Leasehold Reform Act 2002.
[2] *See* section 20ZA(2) and regulations 3 and 4 of these Regulations.
[3] *See* section 20(3) and regulation 6 of these Regulations. For the application of section 20, as originally enacted, in transitional cases, see article 3 of the Commonhold and Leasehold Reform Act 2002 (Commencement No.2 and Savings) England) Order 2003 (S.I. 2003/1986 (c. 82).
[4] S.I. 1991/2680, to which there are amendments not relevant to these Regulations.
[5] S.I. 1993/3228, to which there are amendments not relevant to these Regulations.

[6] S.I. 1995/201, to which there are amendments not relevant to these Regulations.
[7] Section 138 of the Housing Act 1985 (c. 68) is applied in relation to section 171A by section 171C. Section 171A and 171C were inserted by the Housing and Planning Act 1996 (c. 52), section 8. *See also* the Housing (Extension of Right to Buy) Order 1993 (S.I. 1993/2240) and the Housing (preservation of Right to Buy) Regulations 1993 (S.I. 1993/2241). Section 138 is applied in relation to section 16 of the Housing Act 1996 (c. 52) by section 17 of that Act. *See also* the Housing (Right to Acquire) Regulations 1997 (S.I. 1997/619).
[8] *See also* section 139 and Parts 1 and 3 of Schedule 6 to the Housing Act 1985. Paragraphs 16A to 16D in Part 3 of Schedule 6 were inserted by the Housing and Planning Act 1986 (c. 63), section 4(4).
[9] *See* the definition in section 20ZA(2) of the Landlord and Tenant Act 1985, inserted by section 151 of the Commonhlod and Leasehold Reform Act 2002.
[10] *See* section 38 of the Landlord and Tenant Act 1985 and section 1 of the Housing Act 1985.
[11] 2000 c.22.
[12] 1985 c. 6. Definition of "holding company" and "subsidiary" are in section 736. That section and section 736A were substituted for the original section 736 by the Companies Act 1989 (c. 40), section 144(1).
[13] 1985 c. 68. Section 27(2) was substituted by S.I. 2003/940.
[14] Section 27AB was inserted by the Leasehold Reform, Housing and Urban Development Act 1993 (c. 28), section 132. *See also* regulation 1(4) of the Housing (Right to Manage) Regulations 1994 (S.I. 1994/627).
[15] *See* section 18(2) of the Landlord and Tenant Act 1985.
[16] *See* section 29(1) of the Landlord and Tenant Act 1985, which was amended by the Landlord and Tenant Act 1987 (c. 31), Schedule 2, paragraph 10.
[a] Amended by Correction Slip. The paragraph numbering in Schedule 4, Part 2, on page 14 should start at paragraph 1 (instead of paragraph 8) and run consecutively to finish at paragraph 6 (instead of paragraph 13) on page 16.

The Right to Manage (Prescribed Particulars and Forms) (England) Regulations 2003

2003 No. 1988

A15–001 The First Secretary of State[1], in exercise of the powers conferred by sections 78(2)(d) and (3), 80(8) and (9), 84(2), 92(3)(e) and (7)(b) and 178(1) (b) and (c) of the Commonhold and Leasehold Reform Act 2002[2], hereby makes the following Regulations:

Citation, commencement and application

A15–002 **1.**—(1) These Regulations may be cited as the Right to Manage (Prescribed Particulars and Forms) (England) Regulations 2003 and shall come into force on 30th September 2003.

(2) These Regulations apply in relation to premises in England only.

Interpretation

A15–003 **2.** In these Regulations—

"the 2002 Act" means the Commonhold and Leasehold Reform Act 2002;

"landlord", in relation to RTM premises, means a person who is landlord under a lease of the whole or any part of the premises[3];

"RTM premises" means premises as regards which a RTM company intends to acquire the right to manage[4];

"third party", in relation to RTM premises, means a person who is party to a lease of the whole or any part of the premises otherwise than as landlord or tenant[5].

Additional content of notice of invitation to participate

A15–004 **3.**—(1) A notice of invitation to participate[6] shall contain (in addition to the statements and invitation referred to in paragraphs (a) to (c) of subsection (2) of section 78 (notice inviting participation) of the 2002 Act), the particular mentioned in paragraph (2).

(2) The particulars referred to in paragraph (1) are—

(a) the RTM company's registered number[7], the address of its registered office and the names of its directors and secretary;

(b) the names of the landlord and any third party;

(c) a statement that, subject to the exclusions mentioned in sub-paragraph(e), if the right to manage is acquired by the RTM company, will be responsible for—

(i) the discharge of the landlord's duties under the lease; and
(ii) the exercise of his powers under the lease,

with respect to services, repairs, maintenance, improvements, insurance and management;

(d) a statement that, subject to the exclusion mentioned in sub-paragraph (e)(ii), if the right to manage is acquired by the RTM company, the company may enforce untransferred tenant covenants[8];

(e) a statement that, if the right to manage is acquired by the RTM company, the company will not be responsible for the discharge of the landlord's duties or the exercise of his powers under the lease—

(i) with respect to a matter concerning only a part of the premises consisting of a flat or other unit not subject to a lease held by a qualifying tenant[9]; or
(ii) relating to re-entry or forfeiture;

(f) a statement that, if the right to manage is acquired by the RTM company, the company will have functions under the statutory provisions referred to in Schedule 7 to the 2002 Act;

(g) a statement that the RTM company intends or, as the case may be, does not intend, to appoint a managing agent within the meaning of section 30B(8) of the Landlord and Tenant Act 1985[10]; and—

(i) if it does so intend, a statement—

(aa) of the name and address of the proposed managing agent (if known); and
(bb) if it be the case, that the person is the landlord's managing agent; or

(ii) if it does not so intend, the qualifications or experience (if any) of the existing members of the RTM company in relation to the management of residential property;

(h) a statement that, where the company gives a claim notice[11], a person who is or has been a member of the company may be liable for costs incurred by the landlord and others in consequence of the notice;

(i) a statement that, if the recipient of the notice (of invitation to participate) does not fully understand its purpose or implications, he is advised to seek professional help; and

(j) the information, provided in the notes to the form set out in Schedule 1 to these Regulations.

Additional content of claim notice

A15–005

4. A claim notice[12] shall contain (in addition to the particulars required by subsections (2) to (7) of section 80 (contents of claim notice) of the 2002 Act)—

(a) a statement that a person who—

(i) does not dispute the RTM's company's entitlement to acquire the right to manage[13]; and
(ii) is the manager party under a management contract[14] subsisting immediately before the date specified in the claim notice under section 80(6) of the 2002 Act,

must, in accordance with section 92 (duties to give notice of contracts) of the 2002 Act, give a notice in relation to the contract to the person who is the contractor party[15] in relation to the contract and to the RTM company;

(b) a statement that, from the acquisition date[16], landlords under leases of the whole or any part of the premises to which the claim notice relates are entitled to be members of the RTM company;

(c) a statement that the notice is not invalidated by any inaccuracy in any of the particulars required by section 80(2) to (7) of the 2002 Act or this regulation, but that a person who is of the opinion that any of the particulars contained in the claim notice are inaccurate may—
(i) identify the particulars in question to the RTM company by which the notice was given; and
(ii) indicate the respects in which they are considered to be inaccurate;

(d) a statement that a person who receives the notice but does not fully understand its purpose, is advised to seek professional help; and

(e) the information provided in the notes to the form set out in Schedule 2 to these Regulations.

Additional content of counter-notice

A15–006 **5.** A counter-notice shall contain (in addition to the statement referred to in paragraph (a) or (b) of subsection (2) of section 84 (counter-notices) of the 2002 Act)—

(a) a statement that, where the RTM company has been given one or more counter-notices containing such a statement as is mentioned in paragraph (b) of subsection (2) of section 84 of the 2002 Act, the company may apply to a leasehold valuation tribunal for a determination that, on the date on which notice of the claim was given, the company was entitled to acquire the right to manage the premises specified in the claim notice;

(b) a statement that, where the RTM company has been given one or more counter-notices containing such a statement as is mentioned in paragraph (b) of subsection (2) of section 84 of the 2002 Act, the company does not acquire the right to manage the premises specified in the claim notice unless—
(i) on an application to a leasehold valuation tribunal, it is finally determined[17] that the company was entitled to acquire the right to manage the premises; or

(ii) the person by whom the counter-notice was given agrees, or the persons by whom the counter-notices were given agree, in writing that the company was so entitled; and

(c) the information provided in the notes to the form set out in Schedule 3 to these Regulations.

Additional content of contractor notice

6. A contractor notice[18] shall contain (in addition to the particulars referred to in paragraphs (a) to (d) of subsection (3) of section 92 (duties to give notice of contracts) of the 2002 Act) the statement that, should the person to whom the notice is given wish to provide to the RTM company services which, as the contractor party, it has provided to the manager party[19] under the contract of which details are given in the notice, it is advised to contact the RTM company at the address given in the notice. **A15–007**

Additional content of contract notice

7. A contract notice[20] shall contain (in addition to the particulars referred to in paragraph (a) of subsection (7) of section 92 of the 2002 Act)— **A15–008**

(a) the address of the person who is the contractor party, or sub-contractor party[21], under the contract of which particulars are given in the notice; and

(b) a statement that, should the RTM company wish to avail itself of the services which the contractor party, or sub-contractor party, has provided to the manager party under that contract, it is advised to contact the contractor party, or sub-contractor party, at the address given in the notice.

Form of notices

8.—(1) Notices of invitation to participate shall be in the form set out in Schedule 1 to these Regulations. **A15–009**

(2) Claim notices shall be in the form set out in Schedule 2 to these Regulations.

(3) Counter-notices shall be in the form set out in Schedule 3 to these Regulations.

SCHEDULE 1

regulations 3(2)(j) and 8(1)

FORM OF NOTICE OF INVITATION TO PARTICIPATE

COMMONHOLD AND LEASEHOLD REFORM ACT 2002

Notice of invitation to participate in right to manage

A15–010 To *[name and address]* **(See Note 1 below)**

1. [*name of RTM* company] ("the company"), a private company limited by guarantee, of [*address of registered office*], and of which the registered number is [*number under Companies Act 1985*], is authorised by its memorandum of association to acquired and exercise the right to manage [*name of premises to which notice relates*] ("the premises"). The company intends to acquire the right to manage the premises.

2. *The company's memorandum of association, together with its articles of association, accompanies this notice.

*The company's memorandum of association, together with its articles of association, may be inspected at [*address for inspection*] between [*specify times*]. **(See Note 2 below)** At any time within the period of seven days beginning with the day after this notice is given, a copy of the memorandum of association and articles of association may be ordered from [*specify address*] on payment of [*specify fee*]. **(See Note 3 below)**

**Delete one of these statements, as the circumstances require.*

3. The names of—

(a) the members of the company;

(b) the company's director; and

(c) the company's secretary,

are set out in the Schedule below.

4. The names of the landlord and of the person (if any) who is party to a lease of the whole or any part of the premises otherwise than as landlord or tenant are [*specify*].

5. Subject to the exclusions mentioned in paragraph 7, if the right to manage is acquired by the company, the company will responsible for—

(a) the discharge of the landlord's duties under the lease; and

(b) the exercise of his powers under the lease,

with respect to services, repairs, maintenance, improvements, insurance and management.

6. Subject to the exclusion mentioned in paragraph 7(b), if the right to manage is acquired by the company, the company may enforce untransferred tenant covenants. **(See Note 4 below)**

7. If the right to manage is acquired by the company, the company will not be responsible for the discharge of the landlord's duties or the exercise of his powers under the lease—

(a) with respect to a matter concerning only a part of the premises consisting of a flat or other unit not subject to a lease held by a qualifying tenant; or

(b) relating to re-entry or forfeiture.

8. If the right to manage is acquired by the company, the company will have functions under the statutory provisions referred to in Schedule 7 to the Commonhold and Leasehold Reform Act 2002. **(See Note 5 below)**

9. *The company intends to appoint a managing agent within the meaning of section 30B(8) of the Landlord and Tenant Act 1985. [If known, give the name and address of the proposed managing agent here. If that person is the current managing agent, that fact must also be stated here.]
*The company does not intend to appoint a managing agent within the meaning of section 30B(8) of the Landlord and Tenant Act 1985. [*If any existing member of the company has qualifications or experience in relation to the management of residential property, give details in the Schedule below.*]
**Delete one of these statements, as the circumstances require.*

10. If the company gives notice of its claim to acquire the right to manage the premises (a "claim notice"), a person who is or has been a member of the company may be liable for costs incurred by the landlord and others in consequence of the claim notice. **(See Note 6 below)**

11. You are invited to become a member of the company. **(See Note 7 below)**

12. If you do not fully understand the purpose or implications of this notice you are advised to seek professional help.

SCHEDULE

A15–011 The name of the members of the company are: [*state names of company members*]

The names of the company's directors are: [*state directors' names*]

The name of the company's secretary is: [*state company secretary's name*]

[*If applicable; see the second alternative in paragraph 9 above*]
The following member[s] of the company [has][have] qualifications or experience in relation to the management of residential property: [*give details*]

Signed by authority of the company,

[*Signature of authorised member or officer*]

[*Insert date*]

Notes

1. The notice inviting participation must be sent to each person who is at the time the notice is given a qualifying tenant of a flat in the premises but who is not already, and has not agreed to become, a member of the company. A qualifying tenant is defined in section 75 of the Commonhold and Leasehold Reform Act 2002 ("the 2002 Act").

2. The specified times must be periods of at least 2 hours on each of at least 3 days (including a Saturday or Sunday or both) within the 7 days beginning with the day following that on which the notice is given.

3. The ordering facility must be available throughout the 7 day period referred to in Note 2. The fee must not exceed the reasonable cost of providing the ordered copy.

4. An untransferred tenant covenant is a covenant in a tenant's lease that he must comply with, but which can be enforced by the company only by virtue of section 100 of the 2002 Act.

5. The functions relate to matters such as repairing obligations, administration and service charges, and information to be furnished to tenants. Details may be obtained from the RTM company.

6. If the claim notice is at any time withdrawn, deemed to be withdrawn or otherwise ceases to have effect, each person who is or has been a member of the company is liable (except in the circumstances mentioned at the end of this note) for reasonable costs incurred by—

(a) the landlord,

(b) any person who is party to a lease of the whole or any part of the premises otherwise than as landlord or tenant, or

(c) a manager appointed under Part 2 of the Landlord and Tenant Act 1987 to act in relation to the premises to which this notice relates, or any premises containing or contained in the premises to which this notice relates,

in consequence of the claim notice.

A current or former member of the company is liable both jointly with the company and every other person who is or has been a member of the company, and individually. However, a former member is not liable if he has assigned the lease by virtue of which he was a qualifying tenant to another person and that other person has become a member of the company.

7. All qualifying tenants of flats contained in the premises are entitled to be members. Landlords under leases of the whole or any part of the premises are also entitled to be members, but only once the right to manage has been acquired by the company. An application for membership may be made in accordance with the company's articles of association which, if they do not accompany this notice, may be inspected as mentioned in paragraph 2 of the notice.

8. If the right to manage is acquired by the company, the company must report to any person who is landlord under a lease of the whole or any part of premises any failure to comply with any tenant covenant of the lease unless, within the period of three months beginning with the day on which the failure to comply comes to the attention of the company—

(a) the failure has been remedied,

(b) reasonable compensation has been paid in respect of the failure, or

(c) the landlord has notified the company that it need not report to him failures of the description of the failure concerned.

9. If the right to manage is acquired by the company, management functions of a person who is party to a lease of the whole or any part of the premises otherwise than as landlord or tenant will become functions of the company. The company will be responsible for the discharge of that person's duties under the lease and the exercise of his powers under the lease, with respect to services, repairs, maintenance, improvements, insurance and management. However, the company will not be responsible for matters concerning only a part of the premises consisting of a flat or other unit not subject to a lease held by a qualifying tenant, or relation to re-entry forfeiture.

10. If the right to manage is acquired by the company, the company will be responsible for the exercise of the powers relating to the grant of approvals to a tenant under the lease, but will not be responsible for the exercise of those powers in relation to an approval concerning only a part of the premises consisting of a flat or other unit not subject to a lease held by a qualifying tenant.

SCHEDULE 2

regulations 4(e) and 8(2)

FORM OF CLAIM NOTICE

COMMONHOLD AND LEASEHOLD REFORM ACT 2002

Claim Notice

A15–012

To *[name and address]* **(See Note 1 below)**

1. [*Name of RTM company*] ("the company"), of [*address of registered office*], and of which the registered number is [*number under Companies Act 1985*], in accordance with Chapter 1 of Part 2 of the Commonhold and Leasehold Reform Act 2002 ("the 2002 Act") claims to acquire the right to manage [*name of premises to which notice relates*] ("the premises").

2. The company claims that the premises are ones to which Chapter 1 of the 2002 Act applies on the grounds that [*state grounds*]. **(See Note 2 below)**

3. The full names of each person who is both—

(a) the qualifying tenant of a flat contained in the premises, and

(b) a member of the company,

and the address of his flat are set out in Part 1 of the Schedule below.

4. There are set out, in Part 2 of the Schedule, in relation to each person named in Part 1 of the Schedule—

(a) the date on which his lease was entered into,

(b) the term for which it was granted,

(c) the date of commencement of the term,

(d) *such other particulars of his lease as are necessary to identify it.

* *(d) may be ignored if no other particulars need to be given.*

5. If you are—

(a) landlord under a lease of the whole or any part of the premises,

(b) party to such a lease otherwise than as landlord or tenant, or

(c) a manager appointed under Part 2 of the Landlord and Tenant Act 1987 to act in relation to the premises, or any premises containing or contained in the premises,

you may respond to this claim notice by giving a counter-notice under section 84 of the 2002 Act. A counter-notice must be in the form set out in Schedule 3 to the Right to Manage (Prescribed Particulars and Forms) (England) Regulations 2003. It must be given to the company, at the address in paragraph 1, not later than [*specify date not earlier than one month after the date on which the claim notice is given*]. If you do not fully understand the purpose or implications of this notice you are advised to seek professional help.

6. The company intends to acquire the right to manage the premises on [specify date, being at least three months after that specified in paragraph 5].

7. If you are a person to whom paragraph 5 applies and—

(a) you do not dispute the company's entitlement to acquire the right to manage; and

(b) you are the manager party under a management contract subsisting immediately before the date specified in this notice,

you must, in accordance with section 92 (duties to give notice of contracts) of the 2002 Act, give a notice in relation to the contract to the person who is the contractor party in relation to the contract and to the company. **(See Note 3 below)**.

8. From the date on which the company acquires the right to manage the premises, landlords under leases of the whole or any part of the premises are entitled to be members of the company **(See Note 4 below)**.

9. This notice is not invalidated by any inaccuracy in any of the particulars required by section 80(2) to (7) of the 2002 Act or regulation 4 of the Right to Manage (Prescribed Particulars and Forms) (England) Regulations 2003. If you are of the opinion that any of the particulars contained in the claim notice are inaccurate you may notify the company of the particulars in question, indicating the respects in which you think that they are inaccurate.

SCHEDULE

PART 1

FULL NAMES AND ADDRESSES OF PERSONS WHO ARE BOTH QUALIFYING TENANTS AND MEMBERS OF THE COMPANY

A15–013

[*set out here the particulars required by paragraph 3 above*]

PART 2

PARTICULARS OF LEASES OF PERSONS NAMED IN PART 1

[*set out here the particulars required by paragraph 4 above*]

Signed by authority of the company,

[*Signature of authorised member or officer*]

[*Insert date*]

Notes

1. A claim notice (a notice in the form set out in Schedule 2 to the Right to Manage (Prescribed Particulars and Forms) (England) Regulations 2003 of a claim to exercise the right to manage specified premises) must be given to each person who, on the date on which the notice is given, is—

(a) landlord under a lease of the whole or any part of the premises to which the notice relates,

(b) party to such a lease otherwise than as landlord or tenant, or

(c) a manager appointed under Part 2 of the Landlord and Tenant Act 1987 to act in relation to the premises, or any premises containing or contained in the premises.

But notice need not be given to such a person if he cannot be found, or if his identify cannot be ascertained. If that means that there is no one to whom the notice must be given, the company may apply to a leasehold valuation tribunal for an order that the company is to acquire the right to manage the premises. In that case, the procedures specified in section 85 of the 2002 Act (landlords etc. not traceable) will apply.

2. The relevant provisions are contained in section 72 of the 2002 Act (premises to which Chapter 1 applies). The company is advised to consider, in particular, Schedule 6 to the 2002 Act (premises excepted from Chapter 1).

3. The terms "management contract", "manager party" and "contractor party" are defined in section 91(2) of the 2002 Act (notices relating to management contracts).

4. Landlords under leases of the whole or any part of the premises are entitled to be members of the company, but only once the right to manage has been acquired by the company. An application for membership may be made in accordance with the company's articles of association, which may be inspected at the company's registered office, free of charge, at any reasonable time.

SCHEDULE 3

regulations 5(c) and 8(3)

FORM OF COUNTER-NOTICE

COMMONHOLD AND LEASEHOLD REFORM ACT 2002

Counter-notice

A15–014 To *[name and address]* **(See Note 1 below)**

1. * 1 admit that, on [*insert date on which claim notice was given*], [*insert name of company by which claim notice was given*] ("the company") was entitled to acquire the right to manage the premises specified in the claim notice.

* I allege that, by reason of [specify provision of Chapter 1 of Part 2 of the Commonhold and Leasehold Reform Act 2002 relied on], on [insert date on which claim notice was given], [insert name of company by which claim notice was given] ("the company") was not entitled to acquire the right to manage the premises specified in the claim notice.

* *Delete one of these statements, as the circumstances require.*

2. If the company has been given one or more counter-notices containing such a statement as is mentioned in paragraph (b) of subsection (2) of section 84 of the Commonhold and Leasehold Reform Act 2002, the company may apply to a leasehold valuation tribunal for a determination that, on the date on which notice of the claim was given, the company was entitled to acquire the right to manage the premises specified in the claim notice (**See Note 2 below**).

3. If the company has been given one or more counter-notices containing such a statement as is mentioned in paragraph (b) of subsection (2) of section 84 of the Commonhold and Leasehold Reform Act 2002, the company does not acquire the right to manage those premises unless—

(a) on an application to a leasehold valuation tribunal, it is finally determined that the company was entitled to acquire the right to manage the premises; or

(b) the persons by whom the counter-notice was given agrees, or the persons by whom the counter-notices were given agree, in writing that the company was so entitled. **(See Note 3 below)**

Signed:

[*Signature of person on whom claim notice served, or of agent of such person. Where an agent signs, insert also* "Duly authorised agent of [*insert name of person on whom claim notice served*]"

Address:
[*Give the address to which future communications relating to the subject-matter of the notice should be sent*]

Date:

[*Insert date*]

OR

Signed by authority of the company on whose behalf this notice is given

[*Signature of authorised member or officer and statement of position in company*]
Address:

[*Give the address to which future communications relating to the subject-matter of the notice should be sent*]

Date:

[*Insert date*]

Notes

1. The counter-notice is to be given to the company that gave the claim notice (a notice in the form set out in Schedule 2 to the Right to Manage (Prescribed Particulars and Forms) (England) Regulations 2003 of a claim to exercise the right to manage specified premises). The company's name and address are given in that notice.

2. An application to a leasehold valuation tribunal must be made within the period of two months beginning with the day on which the counter-notice (or, where more than one, the last of the counter-notices) was given.

3. For the time at which an application is finally determined, see section 84(7) and (8) of the Commonhold and Leasehold Reform Act 2002.

[1] By virtue section 179(1) of the Commonhold and Leasehold Reform Act 2002 (c.15), the Secretary of State is "the appropriate national authority" as respects England. The powers conferred by sections 78(2)(d) and (3), 80(8) and (9), 84(2) and 92(3)(e) and (7)(b) of that Act are exercisable, as respects Wales, by the National Assembly for Wales.
[2] 2002 c.15.
[3] As to "landlord" *see* section 112(2), (3) and (5) of the Commonhold and Leasehold Reform Act 2002.
[4] As to "RTM company", *see* sections 71(1) and 73 of the Commonhold and Leasehold Reform Act 2002. As to "the right to manage" *see* section 71(2) of that Act.
[5] As to "tenant" *see* section 112(2), (3) and (5) of the Commonhold and Leasehold Reform Act 2002.
[6] *See* section 78(2) of the Commonhold and Leasehold Reform Act 2002.
[7] *See* section 705(1) of the Companies Act 1985 (c.6). Section 705 was substituted by the Companies Act 1989 (c.40), Schedule 19, paragraph 14.

[8] As to "untransferred tenant covenants" *see* section 100(4) of the Commonhold and Leasehold Reform Act 2002.
[9] As to premises to which Chapter 1 of Part 2 of the Commonhold and Leasehold Reform Act 2002 applies, *see* section 72 (and Schedule 6). As to "flat" and "unit" *see* section 112(1). As to "lease" *see* section 112(2). As to "qualifying tenant", *see* sections 75 and 112(4) and (5).
[10] 1985 c.70. Section 30B was inserted by the Landlord and Tenant Act 1987 (c.31), section 44.
[11] As to "claim notice" *see* section 79(1) of the Commonhold and Leasehold Reform Act 2002.
[12] *See* section 79(1) of the Commonhold and Leasehold Reform Act 2002.
[13] As to the circumstances in which there is no dispute about entitlement, *see* section 90(3) of the Commonhold and Leasehold Reform Act 2002.
[14] As to "manager party" *see* section 91(2) and (4) of the Commonhold and Leasehold Reform Act 2002. As to "management contract" *see* section 91(2) of that Act.
[15] As to "contractor party" *see* section 91(2)(b) of the Commonhold and Leasehold Reform Act 2002.
[16] *See* sections 74(1)(b) and 90 of the Commonhold and Leasehold Reform Act 2002.
[17] *See* section 84(7) and (8) of the Commonhold and Leasehold Reform Act 2002.
[18] *See* section 92(1)(a) of the Commonhold and Leasehold Reform Act 2002.
[19] As to "manager party" *see* section 91(2)(a) of the Commonhold and Leasehold Reform Act 2002.
[20] *See* section 92(1)(b) of the Commonhold and Leasehold Reform Act 2002.
[21] As to sub-contractor party *see* section 92(4) of the Commonhold and Leasehold Reform Act 2002.

Leasehold Valuation Tribunals (Procedure) (England) Regulations 2003

As amended by the Leasehold Valuation Tribunals (Procedure) (England) (Amendment) Regulations 2004

Citation, commencement, and application

1.—(1) These Regulations may be cited as the Leasehold Valuation Tribunals (Procedure) (England) Regulations 2003 **A16–001**

(2) These Regulations shall come into force—

(a) for all purposes other than paragraph 2(a) of Schedule 1, on 30th September 2003; and

(b) for the purposes of paragraph 2(a) of Schedule 1, on 31st October 2003.

(3) These Regulations apply in relation to any application made, or proceedings transferred from a court, to a leasehold valuation tribunal in respect of premises in England on or after—

[(a) in the case of an application—

(i) of the description specified in paragraph 2(a) of Schedule 1, 31st October 2003;
(ii) of the description specified in paragraph 8 of that Schedule, 28th February 2005; and]

(b) in any other case, 30th September 2003.

Interpretation

2. In these Regulations— **A16–002**

"the 1985 Act" means the Landlord and Tenant Act 1985;

"the 1987 Act" means the Landlord and Tenant Act 1987;

"the 1993 Act" means the Leasehold Reform, Housing and Urban Development Act 1993;

"the 2002 Act" means the Commonhold and Leasehold Reform Act 2002;

"applicant" means—

(a) the person making an application to a tribunal, or
(b) the person who is the claimant or applicant in proceedings before a court which are transferred by order of the court to a tribunal;

"application" means, other than for the purposes of regulations 1, 20 and 25—

(a) an application to a tribunal of a description specified in Schedule 1, or
(b) a transferred application;

"recognised tenants' association" has the same meaning as in section 29 of the 1985 Act;

"representative application" has the meaning given in regulation 8;

"respondent" means—

(a) the person against whom an applicant seeks an order or determination from a tribunal; or
(b) the person who is the defendant or respondent in proceedings before a court which are transferred by order of the court to a tribunal;

"transferred application" means so much of proceedings before a court as relate to a question falling within the jurisdiction of a tribunal as have been transferred to the tribunal for determination by order of the court; and

"tribunal" means a leasehold valuation tribunal.

Particulars of applications

A16–003 **3.**—(1) The particulars to be included with an application are—

(a) the name and address of the applicant;

(b) the name and address of the respondent;

(c) the name and address of any landlord or tenant of the premises to which the application relates;

(d) the address of the premises to which the application relates; and

(e) a statement that the applicant believes that the facts stated in the application are true.

(2) Where an application is of a description specified in paragraph 1 of Schedule 1 (enfranchisement and extended leases) the particulars and documents listed in paragraph 1 of Schedule 2 shall be included with the application.
(3) Where an application is of a description specified in [any of subparagraphs (b) to (f) of paragraph 2] of Schedule 1 (service charges, administration charges and estate charges) the particulars and documents listed in paragraph 2 of Schedule 2 shall be included with the application.
(4) Where an application is of a description specified in paragraph 3 of Schedule 1 (estate management schemes) the particulars and documents listed in paragraph 3 of Schedule 2 shall be included with the application.

(5) Where an application is of a description specified in paragraph 4 of Schedule 1 (right to manage) the particulars and documents listed in paragraph 4 of Schedule 2 shall be included with the application.

(6) Where an application is of a description specified in paragraph 5 of Schedule 1 (appointment of manager) the particulars and documents listed in paragraph 5 of Schedule 2 shall be included with the application.

(7) Where an application is of a description specified in paragraph 6 of Schedule 1 (variation of leases) the particulars and documents listed in paragraph 6 of Schedule 2 shall be included with the application.

[(7A) Where an application is of the description specified in paragraph 8 of Schedule 1 (determination as to breach of covenant or condition) the particulars and documents listed in paragraph 7 of Schedule 2 shall be included with the application]

(8) Any of the requirements in the preceding paragraphs may be dispensed with or relaxed if the tribunal is satisfied that—

(a) the particulars and documents included with an application are sufficient to enable the application to be determined; and

(b) no prejudice will, or is likely to, be caused to any party to the application.

Notice of application under Part 4 of the 1987 Act

A16–004 **4.**—(1) The applicant shall give notice of an application under Part 4 of the 1987 Act (variation of leases) to the respondent and to any person who the applicant knows, or has reason to believe, is likely to be affected by any variation specified in the application.

(2) On receipt of the notice under paragraph (1) the respondent shall give notice of the application to any person not already notified under that paragraph, who the respondent knows, or has reason to believe, is likely to be affected by any variation specified in the application.

Notice of application by tribunal

A16–005 **5.**—(1) On receipt of an application, other than an application made under Part 4 of the 1987 Act, the tribunal shall send a copy of the application and each of the documents accompanying it to each person named in it as a respondent.

(2) On receipt of an application of a description specified in paragraph 2 of Schedule 1 (service charges, administration charges and estate charges), the tribunal shall give notice of the application to—

(a) the secretary of any recognised tenants' association mentioned in the particulars included in the application; and

(b) any person, whose name and address the tribunal has, who the tribunal considers is likely to be significantly affected by the application.

(3) On receipt of an application the tribunal may give notice to any other person it considers appropriate.

(4) Any notice given under paragraph (2) or (3) shall include a statement that any person may make a request to the tribunal under regulation 6 to be joined as a party to the proceedings with details as to how such a request can be made.

(5) Any notice given under paragraph (2) or (3) may be given by local advertisement.

(6) In this regulation, "local advertisement" means publication of the notice in two newspapers (at least one of which should be a freely distributed newspaper) circulating in the locality in which the premises to which the application relates is situated.

Request to be treated as an applicant or respondent

A16–006 **6.**—(1) Any person may make a request to the tribunal to be joined as a party to the proceedings.

(2) Any request under paragraph (1)—

(a) may be made without notice; and

(b) shall specify whether the person making the request wishes to be treated as—

(i) an applicant; or
(ii) a respondent

to the application.

(3) The tribunal may grant or refuse a request under paragraph (1).

(4) As soon as possible after reaching its decision on a request under paragraph (1), the tribunal shall—

(a) notify the person making the request of the decision and the reasons for it; and

(b) send a copy of the notification to the applicant and the respondent.

(5) Any person whose request under paragraph (1) is granted shall be treated as an applicant or respondent, as the case may be, for the purposes of regulations 8 to 18, 20 and 24.

(6) In the regulations mentioned in paragraph (5) any reference to—

(a) an applicant, or

(b) a respondent,

shall be construed as including a person treated as such under this regulation and any reference to a party shall be construed as including any such person.

Non-payment of fees

A16–007 **7.**—(1) In any case where a fee which is payable under regulation 4 or 5 of the Leasehold Valuation Tribunals (Fees) (England) Regulations 2003 is not paid in accordance with those Regulations, the tribunal shall not proceed further with the application to which the fee relates until the fee is paid.

(2) Where a fee remains unpaid for a period of one month from the date on which it becomes due, the application shall be treated as withdrawn unless the tribunal is satisfied that there are reasonable grounds not to do so.

Representative applications and other provisions for securing consistency

8.—(1) Where it appears to a tribunal that numerous applications— **A16–008**

(a) have been made in respect of the same or substantially the same matters; or

(b) include some matters which are the same or substantially the same,

the tribunal may propose to determine only one of those applications ("the representative application") as representative of all of the applications on those matters which are the same or substantially the same ("the common matters"), and shall give notice of the proposal to the parties to all such applications.

(2) A notice under paragraph (1) shall—

(a) specify the common matters;

(b) specify the application which the tribunal proposes to determine as the representative application;

(c) explain that the tribunal's decision on the common matters in the representative application will apply to the common matters in any application made by a person to whom notice has been given under that paragraph;

(d) invite objections to the tribunal's proposal to determine the representative application; and

(e) specify the address to which objections may be sent and the date (being not less than 21 days after the date that the notice was sent) by which the objections must be received by the tribunal.

(3) Where no objection is received on or before the date specified in the notice—

(a) the tribunal shall determine the representative application in accordance with these Regulations;

(b) the tribunal need not determine the matters mentioned in paragraph (1)(a) in any other application made by a person to whom a notice under paragraph (1) has been given; and

(c) the decision of the tribunal in respect of the representative application shall be recorded as the decision of the tribunal in respect of the common matters in any such other application.

(4) Where an objection is received on or before the date specified in the notice—

(a) sub-paragraphs (a) to (c) of paragraph (3) shall apply only to those applications in respect of which no objection was made, and

(b) the application in respect of which an objection was made may be determined together with the representative application.

Subsequent applications where notice of the representative application given

A16–009 **9.**—(1) If, after a representative application has been determined, a subsequent application is made which includes any of the common matters on which the tribunal has made a decision in its determination of the representative application, and the applicant is a person to whom a notice under regulation 8(1) was given, the tribunal shall give notice to the parties to the subsequent application of—

(a) the matters which, in the opinion of the tribunal, are the common matters in the subsequent application and the representative application;

(b) the decision recorded in respect of the common matters in the representative application;

(c) the date on which notice under regulation 8(1) was given to the applicant;

(d) the tribunal's proposal to record the tribunal's decision on the common matters in the subsequent application in identical terms to the decision in the representative application;

(e) the address to which objections to the tribunal's proposal may be sent and the date (being not less than 21 days after the date that the notice was sent) by which such objections must be received by the tribunal; and

(f) a statement that any objection must include the grounds on which it is made and, in particular, whether it is alleged that the notice under regulation 8(1) was not received by the person making the objection.

(2) Where no objection is received on or before the date specified in the notice—

(a) the tribunal need not determine the matters mentioned in paragraph 1(a); and

(b) the decision of the tribunal in respect of the common matters in the representative application shall be recorded as the decision of the tribunal in respect of the common matters in the subsequent application.

(3) Where an objection is received to the tribunal's proposal on or before the date specified in the notice—

(a) the tribunal shall consider the objection when determining the subsequent application; and

(b) if the tribunal dismisses the objection, it may record the decision mentioned in paragraph (1)(b) as the decision of the tribunal in the subsequent application.

Subsequent applications where notice of representative application not given

A16–010

10.—(1) If, after a representative application has been determined, a subsequent application is made which includes any of the common matters on which the tribunal has made a decision in its determination of the representative application, and the applicant is not a person to whom a notice under regulation 8(1) was given, the tribunal shall give notice to the parties to the subsequent application of—

(a) the matters which, in the opinion of the tribunal, are the common matters in the subsequent application and the representative application;

(b) the decision recorded in respect of those common matters in the representative application;

(c) the tribunal's proposal to record its decision on the common matters in the subsequent application in identical terms to the decision in the representative application; and

(d) the address to which objections to the tribunal's proposal may be sent and the date (being not less than 21 days after the date that the notice was sent) by which such objections must be received by the tribunal.

(2) Where no objection is received on or before the date specified in the notice—

(a) the tribunal need not determine the matters mentioned in paragraph (1)(a); and

(b) the decision of the tribunal in respect of the common matters in the representative application shall be recorded as the decision of the tribunal in respect of the common matters in the subsequent application.

(3) Where an objection is received to the tribunal's proposal on or before the date specified in the notice the tribunal shall determine the application in accordance with the following provisions of these Regulations.

Dismissal of frivolous etc. applications

A16–011

11.—(1) Subject to paragraph (2), where—

(a) it appears to a tribunal that an application is frivolous or vexatious or otherwise an abuse of process of the tribunal; or

(b) the respondent to an application makes a request to the tribunal to dismiss an applications as frivolous or vexatious or otherwise an abuse of the process of the tribunal,

the tribunal may dismiss the applications, in whole or in part.

(2) Before dismissing an application under paragraph (1) the tribunal shall give notice to the applicant in accordance with paragraph (3).

(3) Any notice under paragraph (2) shall state—

(a) that the tribunal is minded to dismiss the application;

(b) the grounds on which it is minded to dismiss the application;

(c) the date (being not less than 21 days after the date that the notice was sent) before which the applicant may request to appear before and be heard by the tribunal on the question whether the application should be dismissed.

(4) An application may not be dismissed unless—

(a) the applicant makes no request to the tribunal before the date mentioned in paragraph (3)(c); or

(b) where the applicant makes such a request, the tribunal has heard the applicant and the respondent, or such of them as attend the hearing, on the question of the dismissal of the application.

Pre-trial review

A16–012 **12.**—(1) The tribunal may, whether on its own initiative or at the request of a party, hold a pre-trial review in respect of an application.

(2) The tribunal shall give the parties not less than 14 days notice (or such shorter notice as the parties agree to) of the date, time and place of the pre-trial review.

(3) At the pre-trial review the tribunal shall—

(a) give any direction that appears to the tribunal necessary or desirable for securing the just, expeditious and economical disposal of proceedings;

(b) endeavour to secure that the parties make all such admissions and agreements as ought reasonably to be made by them in relation to the proceedings; and

(c) record in any order made at the pre-trial review any such admission or agreement or any refusal to make such admission or agreement.

(4) The functions of the tribunal in relation to, or at, a pre-trial review may be exercised by any single member of the panel provided for in Schedule 10 to the Rent Act 1977 who is qualified to exercise them.

Determination without a hearing

13.—(1) A tribunal may determine an application without an oral hearing, in accordance with the following provisions of this regulation, if— **A16–013**

[(a) it has given to both the applicant and the respondent not less than 28 days' notice in writing of its intention to proceed without an oral hearing; and (b) neither the applicant nor the respondent has made a request to the tribunal to be heard,

but this paragraph is without prejudice to paragraph (3)]

(2) The tribunal shall—

(a) notify the parties that the application is to be determined without an oral hearing;

(b) invite written representations on the application;

(c) set time limits for sending any written representations to the tribunal; and

(d) set out how the tribunal intends to determine the matter without an oral hearing.

(3) At any time before the application is determined—

(a) the applicant or the respondent may make a request to the tribunal to be heard; or

(b) the tribunal may give notice to the parties that it intends to determine the application at a hearing in accordance with regulation 14.

(4) Where a request is made or a notice given under paragraph (3) the application shall be determined in accordance with regulation 14.

(5) The functions of the tribunal in relation to an application to be determined without an oral hearing may be exercised by a single member of the panel provided for in Schedule 10 to the Rent Act 1977, if he was appointed to that panel by the Lord Chancellor.

Hearings

14.—(1) Subject to regulations 8(3), 9(2) and 10(2), a hearing shall be on the date and at the time and place appointed by the tribunal. **A16–014**

(2) The tribunal shall give notice to the parties of the appointed date, time and place of the hearing.

(3) Subject to paragraph (4), notice under paragraph (2) shall be given not less than 21 days (or such shorter period as the parties may agree) before the appointed date.

(4) In exceptional circumstances the tribunal may, without the agreement of the parties, give less than 21 days notice of the appointed date, time and place of the hearing; but any such notice must be given as soon as possible

before the appointed date and the notice must specify what the exceptional circumstances are.

(5) The tribunal may arrange that an application shall be heard together with one or more other applications.

(6) A hearing shall be in public unless, in the particular circumstances of the case, the tribunal decide that a hearing or part of a hearing shall be held in private.

(7) At the hearing—

(a) the tribunal shall determine the procedure (subject to these Regulations) and the order in which the persons appearing before it are to be heard;

(b) a person appearing before the tribunal may do so either in person or by a representative authorised by him, whether or not that representative is a barrister or a solicitor; and

(c) a person appearing before the tribunal may give evidence on his own behalf, call witnesses, and cross-examine any witnesses called by any other person appearing.

(8) If a party does not appear at a hearing, the tribunal may proceed with the hearing if it is satisfied that notice has been given to that party in accordance with these Regulations.

Postponement and adjournment

A16–015 **15.**—(1) Subject to paragraph (2) the tribunal may postpone or adjourn a hearing or pre-trial review either on its own initiative or at the request of a party.

(2) Where a postponement or adjournment has been requested the tribunal shall not postpone or adjourn the hearing except where it considers it is reasonable to do so having regard to—

(a) the grounds for the request;

(b) the time at which the request is made; and

(c) the convenience of the other parties.

(3) The tribunal shall give reasonable notice of any postponed or adjourned hearing to the parties.

Documents

A16–016 **16.**—(1) Before the date of the hearing, the tribunal shall take all reasonable steps to ensure that each of the parties is given—

(a) a copy of any document relevant to the proceedings (or sufficient extracts from or particulars of the document) which has been received from any other party (other than a document already in his possession or one of which he has previously been supplied with a copy); and

(b) a copy of any document which embodies the results of any relevant enquiries made by or for the tribunal for the purposes of the proceedings.

(2) At a hearing, if a party has not previously received a relevant document or a copy of, or sufficient extracts from a particulars of, a relevant document, then unless—

(a) that person consents to the continuation of the hearing; or

(b) the tribunal considers that that person has a sufficient opportunity to deal with the matters to which the document relates without an adjournment of the hearing,

the tribunal shall adjourn the hearing for a period which it considers will give that person a sufficient opportunity to deal with those matters.

Inspections

17.—(1) A tribunal may inspect— **A16–017**

(a) the house, premises or area which is the subject of the application; or

(b) any comparable house, premises or area to which its attention is directed.

(2) Subject to paragraph (3), the tribunal shall give the parties an opportunity to attend an inspection.

(3) The making of, and attendance at, an inspection is subject to any necessary consent being obtained.

[(4) Where an inspection is to be made, the tribunal shall give notice to the parties.

(5) A notice under paragraph (4) shall—

(a) state the date, time and place of the inspection; and

(b) be given not less than 14 days before that date.

(6) . . .

(7) . . .]

(8) Where an inspection is made after the close of a hearing, the tribunal may reopen the hearing on account of any matter arising from the inspection.

(9) The tribunal shall give reasonable notice of the date, time and place of the reopened hearing to the parties.

(10) Any of the requirements for notice in the preceding paragraphs may be dispensed with or relaxed—

(a) with the consent of the parties; or

(b) if the tribunal is satisfied that the parties have received sufficient notice.

Decisions

A16–018 **18.**—(1) This regulations applies to a decision on the determination of an application by—

(a) a tribunal; or

(b) a single member, as mentioned in regulation 13(5).

(2) If a hearing was held, the decision may be given orally at the end of the hearing.

(3) A decision shall, in every case, be recorded in a document as soon as possible after the decision has been made.

(4) A decision given or recorded in accordance with paragraph (2) or (3) need not record the reasons for the decision.

(5) Where the document mentioned in paragraph (3) does not record the reasons for the decision, they shall be recorded in a separate document as soon as possible after the decision has been recorded.

(6) A document recording a decision, or the reasons for a decision, shall be signed and dated by an appropriate person.

(7) An appropriate person may, by means of a certificate signed and dated by him, correct any clerical mistakes in a document or any errors arising in it from an accidental slip or omission.

(8) In this regulation, "appropriate person" means—

(a) where an application was determined by a single member as mentioned in regulation 13(5)—

(i) the single member; or
(ii) in the event of his absence or incapacity, another member of the tribunal who was appointed by the Lord Chancellor;

(b) in any other case—

(i) the chairman of the tribunal; or
(ii) in the event of his absence or in capacity, another member of the tribunal.

(9) A copy of any document recording a decision, or the reasons for a decision, and a copy of any correction certified under paragraph (7) shall be sent to each party.

Enforcement

A16–019 **19.** Any decision of the tribunal may, with the permission of the county court, be enforced in the same way as orders of such a court.

Permission to appeal

A16–020 **20.** Where a party makes an application to a tribunal for permission to appeal to the Lands Tribunal—

(a) the application shall be made to the tribunal within the period of 21 days starting with the date on which the document which records the reasons for the decision under regulation 18 was sent to that party; and

(b) a copy of the application shall be served by the tribunal on every other party.

Attendance by member of Council on Tribunals

21. A member of the Council on Tribunals, who is acting in that capacity, may— **A16–021**

(a) attended any hearings held, whether in public or private, in accordance with these Regulations;

(b) attend any inspection for which any necessary consent has been obtained;

(c) be present during, but not take part in, a tribunal's deliberations in respect of an application.

Information required by tribunal

22. Where a tribunal serves a notice requiring information to be given under paragraph 4 of Schedule 12 to the 2002 Act, the notice shall contain a statement to the effect that any person who fails without reasonable excuse to comply with the notice commits an offence and is liable on summary conviction to a fine not exceeding level 3 on the standard scale. **A16–022**

Notices

23.—(1) Where any notice or other document is required under these Regulations to be given or sent to a person by the tribunal, it shall be sufficient compliance with the requirement if— **A16–023**

(a) it is delivered or sent by pre-paid post to that person at his usual or last known address;

(b) it is sent to that person by fax or other means of electronic communication which produces a text of the document;

(c) where that person has appointed an agent or representative to act on his behalf—

  (i) it is delivered or sent by pre-paid post to the agent or representative at the address of the agent or representative supplied to the tribunal; or
  (ii) it is sent to the agent or representative by fax or other means of electronic communication which produces a text of the document.

(2) A notice or other document may be sent as mentioned in paragraphs (1)(b) or (c)(ii) only if that person or his agent has given his consent.

(3) A notice or other document sent as mentioned in paragraphs (1) (b) or (c)(ii) shall be regarded as sent when the text of it is received in legible form.

(4) This paragraph applies where—

(a) an intended recipient—

(i) cannot be found after all diligent enquiries have been made;
(ii) has died and has no personal representative; or
(iii) is out of the United Kingdom; or

(b) for any other reason a notice or other document cannot readily be given or sent in accordance with these Regulations.

(5) Where paragraph (4) applies, the tribunal may—

(a) dispense with the giving or sending of the notice or other document; or

(b) may give directions for substituted service in such other form (whether by advertisement in a newspaper or otherwise) or manner as the tribunal think fit.

Allowing further time

A16–024 **24.**—(1) In a particular case, the tribunal may extend any period prescribed by these Regulations, or prescribed by a notice given under these Regulations, within which anything is required or authorised to be done.

(2) A party may make a request to the tribunal to extend any such period but must do so before that period expires.

Revocation and saving

A16–025 **25.**—(1) Subject to paragraph (2) the Rent Assessment Committee (England and Wales) (Leasehold Valuation Tribunal) Regulations 1993 ("the 1993 Regulations") are hereby revoked in relation to England.

(2) The revocation in paragraph (1) shall not have effect in relation to any application made, or proceedings transferred from a court, to a tribunal before 30 September 2003.

SCHEDULE 1

Descriptions of Applications

Enfranchisement and extended leases

A16–026 **1.** Applications under—

(a) section 21 of the Leasehold Reform Act 1967;

(b) section 13 of the 1987 Act;

(c) section 31 of that Act;

(d) section 24 of that 1993 Act;

(e) section 25 of that Act;

(f) section 27 of that Act;

(g) section 48 of that Act;

(h) section 51 of that Act;

(i) section 88 of that Act;

(j) section 91 of that Act;

(k) section 94 of that Act; and

(l) paragraph 2 of Schedule 14 to that Act.

Service Charges, administration charges and estate charges

2. Applications under— **A16–027**

(a) section 20ZA of the 1985 Act[11];

(b) section 27A of that Act[12];

(c) paragraph 8 of the Schedule to that Act[13];

(d) section 159 of the 2002 Act;

(e) paragraph 3 of Schedule 11 to that Act; and

(f) paragraph 5 of Schedule 11 to that Act.

Estate management schemes

3. Applications under Chapter 4 of Part 1 to the 1993 Act. **A16–028**

Right to manage

4. Applications under— **A16–029**

(a) section 84 of the 2002 Act;

(b) section 85 of that Act;

(c) section 88 of that Act;

(d) section 94 of that Act;

(e) section 99 of that Act; and

(f) paragraph 5 of Schedule 6 to that Act.

Appointment of a manager

5. Applications under— **A16–030**

(a) section 22 of the Landlord and Tenant Act 1987; and

(b) section 24 of that Act.

Variation of leases

A16–031 **6.** Applications under Part 4 of the 1987 Act.

Cost of proceedings

A16–032 **7.** Applications under section 20C of the 1985 Act.

[Determination as to breach of covenant or condition

A16–033 **8.** Applications under section 168(4) of the 2002 Act.]

SCHEDULE 2

Particulars of Applications

Enfranchisement and extended leases

A16–034 **1.**—(1) A copy of any notice served in relation to the enfranchisement.

(2) The name and address of the freeholder and any intermediate landlord.

(3) The name and address of any person having a mortgage or other charge over an interest in the premises the subject of the application held by the freeholder or other landlord.

(4) Where an application is made under section 21(2) of the Leasehold Reform Act 1967, the name and address of the sub-tenant, and a copy of any agreement for the sub-tenancy.

(5) Where an application is made under section 13 of the 1987 Act[15], the date on which the landlord acquired the property and the terms of acquisition including the sums paid.

[(6) Except where an application is made under section 24, 25 or 27 of the 1993 Act, a copy of the lease.

Service charges, administration charges and estate charges

A16–035 **2.**—(1) Where an application is made under section 27A of the 1985 Act, the name and address of the secretary of any recognised tenants' association.

(2) Where an application is made under paragraph 3 of Schedule 11 to the 2002 Act, a draft of the proposed variation.

[(3) A copy of the lease or, where appropriate, a copy of the estate management scheme.]

Estate management charges

A16–036 **3.**—(1) A copy of any estate management agreement or the proposed estate management scheme.

(2) A statement that the applicant is either—

(a) a natural person;

(b) a representative body within the meaning of section 71(3) of the 1993 Act; or

(c) a relevant authority within the meaning of section 73(5) of that Act.

(3) Where an application is made under section 70 of the 1993 Act, a copy of the notice given by the applicant under section 70(4) of that Act.

(4) Where—

(a) approval is sought for a scheme;

(b) approval is sought to modify the area of an existing scheme; or

(c) approval is sought to vary an existing scheme,

a description of the area of—

(i) the proposed scheme;
(ii) the proposed modification; or
(iii) the proposed variation,

including identification of the area by a map or plan.

(5) Where an application is made under section 70 of the 1993 Act, a copy of any consent given by the Secretary of State under section 72(1) of that Act.

Right to manage

A16–037

4.—(1) The name and address for service of the RTM company (within the meaning of Chapter 1 of Part 2 of the 2002 Act).

(2) The name and address of the freeholder, any intermediate landlord and any manager.

(3) A copy of the memorandum and articles of association of the RTM company.

(4) Where an application is made under section 84(3) of the 2002 Act, a copy of the claim notice and a copy of the counter notice received.

(5) Where an application is made under section 85(2) of the 2002 Act—

(a) a statement that the requirements of sections 78 and 79 of the 2002 Act are fulfilled;

(b) a copy of the notice given under section 85(3) of the 2002 Act together with a statement that such notice has been served on all qualifying tenants;

(c) a statement describing the circumstances in which the landlord cannot be identified or traced.

(6) Where an application is made under section 94(3) of the 2002 Act an estimate of the amount of the accrued uncommitted service charges.

(7) Where an application is made under section 99(1) of the 2002 Act, a description of the approval sought and a copy of the relevant lease.

(8) Where an application is made under paragraph 5 of Schedule 6 to the 2002 Act, the date and circumstances in which the right to exercise the right to manage has ceased within the past four years.

Appointment of manager

A16–038 **5.**—(1) Other than where an application is made under section 22(3) of the 1987 Act, a copy of the notice served under section 22 of that Act.

(2) Where an application is made under section 24(9) of that Act, a copy of the management order.

Variation of leases

A16–039 **6.**—(1) The names and addresses of any person served with a notice in accordance with regulation 4 of these Regulations.

(2) A draft of the variation sought.

[(3) A copy of the lease.]

[Determination of breach of covenant or condition

A16–040 **7.**—(1) A statement giving particulars of the alleged breach of covenant or condition.

(2) A copy of the lease concerned.]

Words in square brackets amended by the Leasehold Valuation Tribunals (Procedure) (England) (Amendment) Regulations 2004.

The RTM Companies (Memorandum and Articles of Association) (England) Regulations 2003

2003 No. 2120

A17–001 The First Secretary of State, in exercise of the powers conferred by sections 7 (2), (4) and (6) and 178(1) of the Commonhold and Leasehold Reform Act 2002[1], hereby makes the following Regulations:

Citation, commencement and application

A17–002 **1.**—(1) These Regulations may be cited as the RTM Companies (Memorandum and Articles of Association) (England) Regulations 2003 and shall come into force on 30th September 2003.

(2) These Regulations apply to RTM companies[2] in relation to premises [3] in England.

Form and content of memorandum and articles of association of RTM companies

A17–003 **2.**—(1) The memorandum of association of a RTM company shall take the form, and include the provisions, set out in Part 1 of the Schedule to these Regulations.

(2) The articles of association of a RTM company shall take the form, and include the provisions, set out in Part 2 of that Schedule.

(3) The provisions referred to in paragraphs (1) and (2) shall have effect for a RTM company whether or not they are adopted by the company.

(4) Where—

(a) a RTM company has adopted a memorandum of association and articles of association before the coming into force of these Regulations and

(b) the memorandum and the articles, or either of them, do not comply, as to content, with the requirements of paragraphs (1) and (2),

the memorandum and articles shall be treated, on and after the coming into force of these Regulations, as including such of the provisions set out in the Schedule as are required to secure compliance with those requirements (whether in addition to or, as the circumstances require, in substitution for their original content).

SCHEDULE

Regulation 2

MEMORANDUM AND ARTICLES OF ASSOCIATION OF RTM COMPANIES

PART 1

MEMORANDUM OF ASSOCIATION

THE COMPANIES ACTS 1985 AND 1989

COMPANY LIMITED BY GUARANTEE AND NOT HAVING A SHARE CAPITAL

MEMORANDUM OF ASSOCIATION OF [*NAME*] RTM COMPANY LIMITED

A17–004 **1.** The name of the company is "[*name*] RTM Company Limited".

A17–005 **2.** The registered office of the Company will be situated in [*England and Wales*] [*Wales*].

A17–006 **3.** The objects for which the Company is established are to acquire and exercise in accordance with the Commonhold and Leasehold Reform Act 2002 ("the 2002 Act") the right to manage the premises known as [*name and address*] ("the Premises"). These objects shall not be restrictively construed but the widest interpretation shall be given to them.

A17–007 **4.** In furtherance of the objects, but not otherwise, the Company shall have power to do all such things as may be authorised or required to be done by a RTM company by and under the 2002 Act, and in particular (but without derogation from the generality of the foregoing)—

(a) to prepare, make, pursue or withdraw a claim to acquire the right to manage the Premises;

(b) to exercise management functions under leases of the whole or any part of the Premises in accordance with sections 96 and 97 of the 2002 Act;

(c) to exercise functions in relation to the grant of approvals under long leases of the whole or any part of the Premises in accordance with sections 98 and 99 of the 2002 Act;

(d) in accordance with sections 100 and 101 of the 2002 Act, to monitor, keep under review, report to the landlord, and procure or enforce the performance by any person of the terms of any covenant, undertaking, duty or obligation in any way connected with or affecting the Premises or any of its occupants;

(e) to negotiate for and make applications for the variation of leases pursuant to Part 4 of the Landlord and Tenant Act 1987 ("the 1987 Act");

(f) to do such other things and to perform such other functions in relation to the Premises or any leases of the whole or any part of the Premises as may be agreed from time to time with the landlord or landlords or any other parties to the leases, as the case may be;

(g) to provide and maintain service and amenities of every description in relation to the Premises; to maintain, repair, renew, redecorate, repaint and clean the Premises; and to cultivate, maintain, landscape and plant any land, gardens and grounds comprised in the Premises;

(h) to enter into contracts with buildings, decorators, cleaners, tenants, contractors, gardeners, or any other person; to consult and retain any professional advisers and to employ any staff and managing or other agents; and to pay, reward or remunerate in any way any person supplying goods or services to the Company;

(i) to make any appropriate or consequential agreements or arrangements for the right to manage the Premises to cease to be exercisable by the Company;

(j) to issue and receive any notice, counter-notice, consent or other communication and to enter into any correspondence concerning or in any way affecting the Premises, the management of the Premises, the occupants of the Premises, the Company, any of its activities, or any of its members;

(k) to commence, pursue, defend or participate in any application to, or other proceeding before, any court or tribunal of any description;

(l) to insure the Premises or any other property of the Company or in which it has an interest against damage or destruction and such other risks as may be considered necessary, appropriate or desirable and to insure the Company and its directors, officers or auditors against public liability and any other risks which it may consider prudent or desirable to insure against;

(m) to collect in or receive monies from any person on account of service charges, administration charges and other charges in relation to the Premises and, where required by law to do so, to hold, invest and deal with the monies in accordance with the provisions of the 1987 Act and any regulations or orders made under that Act from time to time;

(n) to establish, undertake and execute any trusts which may lawfully be, or which are required by law to be, established, undertaken or executed by the Company;

(o) to establish and maintain capital reserves, management funds and any form of sinking fund in order to pay, or contribute towards, all fees, costs and other expenses incurred in the implementation of the Company's objects;

(p) to invest any money of the Company in the United Kingdom by depositing it at interest with any financial institution with which a trust fund of service charge contributions might be held in accordance with the 1987 Act; or to invest it in such other manner (including the purchase of securities and other investments) as the Company in general meeting may authorise from time to time; and to hold, sell or otherwise dispose of any such investments;

(q) subject to any limitations or conditions imposed by the Company in general meeting from time to time, to lend and advance money or give credit on any terms, with or without security to any person; to enter into guarantees, contracts of indemnity and suretyship of all kinds; to receive money on deposit or loan upon any terms; and to secure or guarantee in any manner and upon any terms the payment of any sum of money or the performance of any obligation by any person;

(r) subject to any limitations or conditions imposed by the Company in general meeting from time to time, to borrow and raise money in any manner and to secure the repayment of any money borrowed, raised or owing by mortgage, charge, standard security, lien or other security upon the whole or part of the Company's property or assets (whether present or future) and also by a similar mortgage, charge, standard security, lien or security to secure and guarantee the performance by the Company of any obligation or liability it may undertake or which may become binding on it;

(s) to operate bank accounts and to draw, make, accept, endorse, discount, negotiate, execute and issue cheques, bills of exchange, promissory notes, debentures and other negotiable or transferable instruments;

(t) to pay all or any expenses incurred in connection with the promotion, formation and incorporation of the Company, or to contract with any person to pay such expenses;

(u) with the consent of the Company in general meeting, to give or award pensions, annuities, gratuities, and superannuation or other allowances or benefits or charitable aid and generally to provide advantages, facilities and services for any persons who are or have been directors of, or who are or have been employed by, or who are serving or have served the Company and to the spouses, surviving spouses, children and other relatives and dependants of such persons; to make payments towards insurance; and to set up, establish, support and maintain superannuation and other funds or schemes (whether contributory or non-contributory) for the benefit of any such persons and of their spouses, surviving spouses, children and other relatives and dependants;

(v) to monitor and determine for the purpose of voting, or for any other purpose, the physical dimensions of the Premises and any part or parts of the Premises and to take or obtain any appropriate measurements;

(w) to enter into any agreements or arrangements with any government or authority (central, municipal, local, or otherwise) that may seem conducive to the attainment of the Company's objects, and to obtain from any such government or authority any charters, decrees, rights, privileges or concessions which the Company may think desirable, and to carry out, exercise, and comply with any such charters, decrees, rights, privileges, and concessions;

(x) to do all things specified for the time being in the articles of association of the Company;

(y) to do or procure or arrange for the doing of all or any of the things or matters mentioned above in any part of the world and either as principals, agents, contractors or otherwise, and by or through agents, brokers, sub-contractors or otherwise and either alone or in conjunction with others; and

(z) to do all such other lawful things as may be incidental or conducive to the pursuit or attainment of the Company's objects.

A17–008 **5.** The income of the Company, from wherever derived, shall be applied solely in promoting the Company's objects, and, save on a winding up of the Company, no distribution shall be made to its members in cash or otherwise.

A17–009 **6.** The liability of the members is limited.

A17–010 **7.** Every member of the Company undertakes to contribute such amount as may be required, not exceeding £1, to the assets of the Company in the event of the Company being wound up while he is a member, or within one year after he ceases to be a member, for payment of the debts and liabilities of the Company contracted before he ceases to be a member, and of the costs, charges, and expenses of winding up the Company, and for the adjustment of the rights of the contributories among themselves.

A17–011 **8.** If, on the winding up of the Company, there remains any surplus after the satisfaction of all its debts and liabilities, the surplus shall be paid to or distributed among the members of the Company.

A17–012 **9.** In this Memorandum, references to an Act include any statutory modification or re-enactment of the Act for the time being in force.

We, the subscribers to this memorandum of association, wish to be formed into a company pursuant to this memorandum.

Names and address of subscribers:

Dated

Witness to the above signatures

PART 2

ARTICLES OF ASSOCIATION

THE COMPANIES ACTS 1985 AND 1989

[COMPANY LIMITED BY GUARANTEE AND NOT HAVING A SHARE CAPITAL]

ARTICLES OF ASSOCIATION OF [*NAME*] **RTM COMPANY LIMITED**

Interpretation

A17–013 **1.** In these articles—

"the Companies Act" means the Companies Act 1985[4];

"the 2002 Act" means the Commonhold and Leasehold Reform Act 2002;

"address", in relation to electronic communications, includes any number or address used for the purposes of such communications;

"clear days", in relation to a period of notice, means that period excluding the day when the notice is given or deemed to be given and the day for which it is given or on which it is to take effect;

"communication" and "electronic communication" have the same meaning as in the Electronic Communications Act 2000[5];

"the Company" means [*name*] RTM Company Limited;

"immediate landlord", in relation to a unit in the Premises, means the person who—

(a) if the unit is subject to a lease, is the landlord under the lease; or
(b) if the unit is subject to two or more leases, is the landlord under whichever of the leases is inferior to the others;

"the Premises" means [*name and address*];

"residential unit" means a flat or any other separate set of premises which is constructed or adapted for use for the purposes of a dwelling;

"registered office" means the registered office of the Company;

"secretary" means the secretary of the Company or any other person appointed to perform the duties of the secretary of the Company, including a joint, assistant or deputy secretary.

A17–014 **2.** Unless the context otherwise requires, words or expressions contained in these articles bear the same meaning as in the Companies Act.

A17–015 **3.** In these articles, references to an Act shall include any statutory modification or re-enactment of the Act for the time being in force.

Members

4. Subject to the following articles, the subscribers to the Memorandum of Association of the Company, and such other persons as are admitted to membership in accordance with these articles shall be members of the Company. Membership of the Company shall not be transferable. **A17–016**

5. No person shall be admitted to membership of the Company unless that person, whether alone or jointly with others, is— **A17–017**

(a) a qualifying tenant of a flat contained in the Premises as specified in section 75 of the 2002 Act; or

(b) from the date upon which the Company acquires the right to manage the Premises pursuant to the 2002 Act, a landlord under a lease of the whole or any part of the Premises.

6. A person who, together with another or others, is to be regarded as jointly being the qualifying tenant of a flat, or as jointly constituting the landlord under a lease of the whole or any part of the Premises, shall, once admitted, be regarded as jointly being a member of the Company in respect of that flat or lease (as the case may be). **A17–018**

7. Every person who is entitled to be, and who wishes to become a member of the Company, shall deliver to the Company an application for membership executed by him in the following form (or in a form as near to the following form as circumstances allow or in any other form which is usual or which the directors may approve)— **A17–019**

To the Board of [*name of Company*]

I, [*name*]

of [*address*]

am a qualifying tenant of [address of flat] and wish to become a member of [name of Company] subject to the provisions of the Memorandum and Articles of Association of the Company and to any Rules made under those Articles. I agree to pay to the Company an amount of up to £1 if the Company is wound up while I am a member or for up to 12 months after I have ceased to be a member.

Signed

Dated

8. Applications for membership by persons who are to be regarded as jointly being the qualifying tenant of a flat, or who jointly constitute the landlord under a lease of the whole or any part of the Premises, shall state the names and addresses of all others who are jointly interested with them, and the order in which they wish to appear on the register of members in respect of such flat or lease (as the case may be). **A17–020**

A17–021 **9.** The directors shall, upon being satisfied as to a person's application and entitlement to membership, register such person as a member of the Company.

A17–022 **10.** Upon the Company becoming an RTM company in relation to the Premises, any of the subscribers to the Memorandum of Association who do not also satisfy the requirements for membership set out in article 5 above shall cease to be members of the Company with immediate effect. Any member who at any time ceases to satisfy those requirements shall also cease to be a member of the Company with immediate effect.

A17–023 **11.** If a member (or joint member) dies or becomes bankrupt, his personal representatives or trustee in bankruptcy will be entitled to be registered as a member (or joint member as the case may be) upon notice in writing to the Company.

A17–024 **12.** A member may withdraw from the Company and thereby cease to be a member by giving at least seven clear days' notice in writing to the Company. Any such notice shall not be effective if given in the period beginning with the date on which the Company gives notice of its claim to acquire the right to manage the Premises and ending with the date which is either—

(a) the acquisition date in accordance with section 90 of the 2002 Act; or

(b) the date of withdrawal or deemed withdrawal of that notice in accordance with sections 86 or 87 of that Act.

A17–025 **13.** If, for any reason—

(a) a person who is not a member of the Company becomes a qualifying tenant or landlord jointly with persons who are members of the Company, but fails to apply for members hip within 28 days, or

(b) a member who is a qualifying tenant or landlord jointly with such persons dies or becomes bankrupt and his personal representatives or trustee in bankruptcy do not apply for membership within 56 days pursuant to article 11, or

(c) a member who is a qualifying tenant or landlord jointly with such persons resigns from membership pursuant to article 12,

those persons shall, unless they are otherwise entitled to be members of the Company by reason of their interest in some other flat or lease, also cease to be members of the Company with immediate effect. All such persons shall, however, be entitled to re-apply for membership in accordance with articles 7 to 9.

General meetings

A17–026 **14.** All general meetings, other than annual general meetings, shall be called extraordinary general meetings.

A17–027 **15.** The directors may call general meetings and, on the requisition of members pursuant to the provisions of the Companies Act, shall forthwith (and in any event within twenty-one days) proceed to convene an extraordinary general meeting for a date not more than twenty-eight days after the date of the notice convening the meeting. If there are not within the United Kingdom sufficient directors to call a general meeting, any director or any member of the Company may call a general meeting.

16. All general meetings shall be held at the Premises or at such other suitable place as is near to the Premises and reasonably accessible to all members. **A17–028**

Notice of general meetings

17. An annual general meeting and an extraordinary general meeting called for the passing of a special resolution or a resolution appointing a person as a director shall be called by at least twenty-one clear days' notice. All other extraordinary general meetings shall be called by at least fourteen clear days' notice but a general meeting may be called by shorter notice if it is so agreed, **A17–029**

(a) in the case of an annual general meeting, by all the members entitled to attend and vote; and

(b) in the case of any other meeting, by a majority in number of the members having a right to attend and vote, being a majority together holding not less than ninety-five per cent of the total voting rights at the meeting of all the members.

18. The notice shall specify the time and place of the meeting and, in the case of an annual general meeting, shall specify the meeting as such. **A17–030**

19. The notice shall also include or be accompanied by a statement and explanation of the general nature of the business to be transacted at the meeting. **A17–031**

20. Subject to the provisions of these articles, the notice shall be given to all the members and to the directors and auditors. **A17–032**

21. The accidental omission to give notice of a meeting to, or the non-receipt of notice of a meeting by, any person entitled to receive notice shall not invalidate the proceedings at that meeting. **A17–033**

Proceedings at general meetings

22. No business shall be transacted at any general meeting unless it was included in the notice convening the meeting in accordance with article 19. **A17–034**

23. No business shall be transacted at any general meeting unless a quorum is present. The quorum for the meeting shall be 20 per cent of the members of the Company entitled to vote upon the business to be transacted, or two members of the Company so entitled (whichever is the greater) present in person or by proxy. **A17–035**

24. If such a quorum is not present within half an hour from the time appointed for the meeting, or if during a meeting such a quorum ceases to be present, the meeting shall stand adjourned to the same day in the next week at the same time and place or to such time and place as the directors may determine. **A17–036**

A17–037 **25.** The chairman, if any, of the board of directors or in his absence some other director nominated by the directors shall preside as chairman of the meeting, but if neither the chairman nor such other director (if any) is present within fifteen minutes after the time appointed for holding the meeting and willing to act, the directors present shall elect one of their number to be chairman and, if there is only one director present and willing to act, he shall be chairman.

A17–038 **26.** If no director is willing to act as chairman, or if no director is present within fifteen minutes after the time appointed for holding the meeting, the members present and entitled to vote shall choose one of their number to be chairman.

A17–039 **27.** A director shall, notwithstanding that he is not a member, be entitled to attend, speak and propose (but, subject to article 33, not vote upon) a resolution at any general meeting of the Company.

A17–040 **28.** The chairman may, with the consent of a meeting at which a quorum is present (and shall if so directed by the meeting), adjourn the meeting from time to time and from place to place, but no business shall be transacted at an adjourned meeting other than business which might properly have been transacted at the meeting if the adjournment had not taken place. When a meeting is adjourned for fourteen days or more, at least seven clear days' notice shall be given specifying the time and place of the adjourned meeting and the general nature of the business to be transacted. Otherwise it shall not be necessary to give any such notice.

A17–041 **29.** A resolution put to the vote of a meeting shall be decided on a show of hands unless before, or on the declaration of the result of, the show of hands a poll is duly demanded. Subject to the provisions of the Companies Act, a poll may be demanded—

(a) by the chairman; or

(b) by at least two members having the right to vote at the meeting; or

(c) by a member or members representing not less than one-tenth of the total voting rights of all the members having the right to vote at the meeting;

and a demand by a person as proxy for a member shall be the same as demand by the member.

A17–042 **30.** Unless a poll is duly demanded, a declaration by the chairman that a resolution has been carried or carried unanimously, or by a particular majority, or lost, or not carried by a particular majority and an entry to that effect in the minutes of the meeting shall be convulsive evidence of the fact without proof of the number or proportion of the votes recorded in favour of or against the resolution.

A17–043 **31.** The demand for a poll may, before the poll is taken, be withdrawn but only with the consent of the chairman and a demand so withdrawn shall not be taken to have invalidated the result of a show of hands declared before the demand was made.

A17–044 **32.** A poll shall be taken as the chairman directs and he may appoint scrutineers (who need not be members) and fix a time and place for declaring the result of the poll. The result of the poll shall be deemed to be the resolution of the meeting at which the poll was demanded.

33. In the case of an equality of votes, whether on a show of hands or on a poll, the chairman shall be entitled to a casting vote in addition to any other vote he may have. **A17–045**

34. A poll demanded on the election of a chairman or on a question of adjournment shall be taken forthwith. A poll demanded on any other question shall be taken either forthwith or at such time and place as the chairman directs, not being more than thirty days after the poll is demanded. The demand for a poll shall not prevent the continuance of a meeting for the transaction of any business other than the question on which the poll was demanded. If a poll is demanded before the declaration of the result of a show of hands and the demand is duly withdrawn, the meeting shall continue as if the demand had not been made. **A17–046**

35. No notice need be given of a poll not taken forthwith if the time and place at which it is to be taken are announced at the meeting at which it is demanded. In any other case at least seven clear days' notice shall be given specifying the time and place at which the poll is to be taken. **A17–047**

36. A resolution in writing executed by or on behalf of each member who would have been entitled to vote upon it if it had been proposed at a general meeting at which he was present shall be as effectual as if it had been passed at a general meeting duly convened and held and may consist of several instruments in the like form each executed by or on behalf of one or more members. **A17–048**

Votes of members

37. On a show of hands every member who (being an individual) is present in person or (being a corporation) is present by a duly authorised representative, not being himself a member entitled to vote, shall have one vote and on a poll, each member shall have the number of votes determined in accordance with articles 38 to 40. **A17–049**

38. If there are no landlords under leases of the whole or any part of the Premises who are members of the Company, then one vote shall be available to be cast in respect of each flat in the Premises. The vote shall be cast by the member who is the qualifying tenant of the flat. **A17–050**

39. At any time at which there are any landlords under leases of the whole or any part of the Premises who are members of the Company, the votes available to be cast shall be determined as follows— **A17–051**

(a) there shall first be allocated to each residential unit in the Premises the same number of votes as equals the total number of members of the Company who are landlords under leases of the whole or any part of the Premises. Landlords under a lease who are regarded as jointly being a member of the Company shall be counted as one member for this purpose;

(b) if at any time the Premises includes any non-residential part, a total number of votes shall be allocated to that part as shall equal the total number of votes allocated to the residential units multiplied by a factor of A/B, where A is the total internal floor area of the non-residential parts and B is the total internal area of all the residential parts. Internal floor area shall be determined in accordance with paragraph 1(4) of Schedule 6 to the 2002 Act. Calculations of the internal floor area shall be measured in square metres, fractions of floor area of less than half a square metre shall be ignored and fractions of floor area in excess of half a square metre shall be counted as a whole square metre;

(c) the votes allocated to each residential unit shall be entitled to be cast by the member who is the qualifying tenant of that unit, or if there is no member who is a qualifying tenant of the unit, by the member who is the immediate landlord;

(d) the votes allocated to any non-residential part included in the Premises shall be entitled to be cast by the immediate landlord of that part, or where there is no lease of a non-residential part, by the freeholder. Where there is more than one such person, the total number of votes allocated to the non-residential part shall be divided between them in proportion to the internal floor area of their respective parts. Any resulting entitlement to a fraction of a vote shall be ignored;

(e) If a residential unit is not subject to any lease, no votes shall be entitled to be cast in respect of it;

(f) any person who is a landlord under a lease or leases of the whole or any part of the Premises and who is a member of the Company but is not otherwise entitled to any votes, shall be entitled to one vote.

A17–052 **40.** In the case of any persons who are to be regarded as jointly being members of the Company, any such person may exercise the voting rights to which such members are jointly entitled, but where more than one such person tenders a vote, whether in person or by proxy, the vote of the senior shall be accepted to the exclusion of the votes of the others, and seniority shall be determined by the order in which the names of such persons appear in the register of members in respect of the flat or lease (as the case may be) in which they are interested.

A17–053 **41.** The Company shall maintain a register showing the respective entitlements of each of its members to vote on a poll at any meeting of the Company.

A17–054 **42.** Any objection to the qualification of any voter or to the computation of the number of votes to which he is entitled that is raised in due time at a meeting or adjourned meeting shall be referred to the chairman of the meeting, whose decision shall, for all purposes relating to that meeting or adjourned meeting, be final and conclusive. Subject to that, any dispute between any member and the Company or any other member, that arises out of the member's contract of membership and concerns the measurement of floor areas, shall be referred for determination by an independent chartered surveyor selected by agreement between the parties or, in default, by the President of the Royal Institution of Chartered Surveyors. Such independent chartered surveyor shall, in determining the measurements of the floor areas in question, act as an expert and not as an arbitrator and his decision shall be final and conclusive. The Company shall be responsible to such surveyor for payment of his fees and expenses, but he shall have the power, in his absolute discretion, to direct that some or all of such fees and expenses shall be reimbursed by the member(s) in question to the Company, in which event such monies shall be paid by the member(s) to the Company forthwith.

43. A member in respect of whom an order has been made by any court having jurisdiction (whether in the United Kingdom or elsewhere) in matters concerning mental disorder may vote, whether on a show of hands or on a poll, by his receiver, curator bonis or other person, authorised in that behalf appointed by that court, and any such receiver, curator bonis or other person may, on a poll, vote by proxy. Evidence to the satisfaction of the directors of the authority of the person claiming to exercise the right to vote shall be deposited at the registered office, or at such other place as is specified in accordance with these articles for the deposit of instruments of proxy, not less than 48 hours before the time appointed for holding the meeting or adjourned meeting at which the right to vote is to be exercised and in default the right to vote shall not be exercisable. **A17–055**

44. On a poll votes may be given either personally or by proxy. A member may appoint more than one proxy to attend on the same occasion. **A17–056**

45. An instrument appointing a proxy shall be writing, executed by or on behalf of the appointor and shall be in the following form (or in a form as near to the following form as circumstances allow or in any other form which is usual or which the directors may approve)— **A17–057**

[Name of Company]

[Name of member(s)], of [address], being a member/members of the above-named company, hereby appoint [name] of [address], or failing him, [name] of [address], as my/our proxy to vote in my/our name[s] and on my/our behalf at the annual/extraordinary general meeting of the company to be held on [date], and at any adjournment of the meeting.

Signed on [date]

46. Where it is desired to afford members an opportunity of instructing the proxy how he shall act, the instrument appointing a proxy shall be in the following form (on in a form as near to the following form as circumstances allow or in any other form which is usual or which the directors may approve)— **A17–058**

[Name of Company]

[Name of member(s)], of [address], being a member/members of the above-named company, hereby appoint [name] of [address], or failing him, [name] of [address], as my/our proxy to vote in my/our name[s] and on my/our behalf at the annual/extraordinary general meeting of the company to be held on [date], and at any adjournment of the meeting.

This form is to be used in respect of the resolutions mentioned below as follows:

Resolution No. 1 [for] [against]

Resolution No. 2 [for] [against]

[Strike out whichever is not desired]

Unless otherwise instructed, the proxy may vote as he thinks fit or abstain from voting.

Signed on [date]

A17–059 **47.** The instrument appointing a proxy and any authority under which it is executed or a copy of such authority certified notarially or in some other way approved by the directors may—

(a) in the case of an instrument in writing, be deposited at the registered office or at such other place within the United Kingdom as is specified in the notice convening the meeting or in any instrument of proxy sent out by the Company in relation to the meeting not less than 48 hours before the time for holding the meeting or adjourned meeting at which the person named in the instrument proposes to vote; or

(b) in the case of an appointment contained in an electronic communication, where an address has been specified for the purpose of receiving electronic communications—

(i) in the notice convening the meeting, or
(ii) in any instrument of proxy sent out by the Company in relation to the meeting, or
(iii) in any invitation contained in an electronic communication to appoint a proxy issued by the Company in relation to the meeting,

be received at such address not less than 48 hours before the time for holding the meeting or adjourned meeting at which the person named in the appointment proposes to vote;

(c) in the case of a poll taken more than 48 hours after it is demanded, be deposited or received as mentioned in paragraph (a) or (b) after the poll has been demanded and not less than 24 hours before the time appointed for the taking of the poll; or

(d) where the poll is taken forthwith but is taken not more than 48 hours after it was demanded, be delivered at the meeting at which the poll was demanded to the chairman or to the secretary or to any director;

and an instrument of proxy which is not deposited, delivered or received in a manner permitted by this article shall be invalid.

48. A vote give or poll demanded by proxy or by the duly authorised representative of a corporation shall be valid notwithstanding the previous termination of the authority of the person voting or demanding a poll unless notice of the termination was received by the Company at the registered office or at such other place at which the instrument of proxy was duly deposited or, where the appointment of the proxy was contained in an electronic communication, at the address at which such appointment was duly received before the commencement of the meeting or adjourned meeting at which the vote is given or the poll demanded or (in the case of a poll taken otherwise than on the same day as the meeting or adjourned meeting) the time appointed for taking the poll. **A17–060**

Qualification of directors

49. A director need not be a member of the Company. **A17–061**

Number of directors

50. Unless otherwise determined by ordinary resolution, the number of directors (other than alternate directors) shall not be subject to any maximum but shall be not less than two. **A17–062**

Appointment and removal of directors

51. At the first annual general meeting, all of the directors shall retire from office, and at every subsequent annual general meeting one-third of the directors who are subject to retirement by rotation or, if their number is not three or a multiple of three, the number nearest to one-third shall retire from office; but if there is only one director who is subject to retirement by rotation, he shall retire. **A17–063**

52. Subject to the provisions of the Companies Act, the directors to retire by rotation shall be those who have been longest in office since their last appointment or reappointment, but as between persons who became or who were last reappointed directors on the same day those to retire shall (unless they otherwise agree among themselves) be determined by lot. **A17–064**

53. If the Company, at the meeting at which a director retires by rotation, does not fill the vacancy, the retiring director shall, if willing to act, be deemed to have been reappointed unless at the meeting it is resolved not fill the vacancy or unless a resolution for the appointment of the director is put to the meeting and lost. **A17–065**

54. A person other than a director retiring by rotation shall not be appointed or reappointed as a director at any general meeting unless— **A17–066**

(a) he is recommended by the directors; or

(b) not less than fourteen nor more than thirty-five clear days before the date appointed for the meeting, notice executed by a member qualified to vote at the meeting has been given to the Company of the intention to propose that person for appointment or reappointment stating the particulars which would, if he were so appointed or reappointed, be required to be included in the Company's register of directors together with notice executed by that person of his willingness to be appointed or reappointed.

A17–067 **55.** Not less than seven nor more than twenty-eight clear days before the date appointed for holding a general meeting, notice shall be given to all who are entitled to receive notice of the meeting of any person who is recommended by the directors for appointment or reappointment as a director at the meeting or in respect of whom notice has been duly given to the Company of the intention to propose him at the meeting for appointment or reappointment as a director. The notice shall give the particulars of that person which would, if he were so appointed or reappointed, be required to be included in the Company's register of directors.

A17–068 **56.** Subject to articles 51 to 55, the Company may by ordinary resolution appoint a person who is willing to act to be a director either to fill a vacancy, or as an additional director and may also determine the rotation in which any additional directors are to retire.

A17–069 **57.** The directors may appoint a person who is willing to act to be a director, either to fill a vacancy or as an additional director, provided that the appointment does not cause the number of directors to exceed any number fixed by or in accordance with the articles as the maximum number of directors. A director so appointed shall hold office only until the next following annual general meeting. If not reappointed at such annual general meeting, he shall vacate office at the conclusion thereof.

A17–070 **58.** Subject to those articles, a director who retires at an annual general meeting may, if willing to act, be reappointed. If he is not reappointed, he shall retain office until the meeting appoints someone in his place, or if it does not do so, until the end of the meeting.

Alternate directors

A17–071 **59.** Any director (other than an alternate director) may appoint any other director, or any other person approved by resolution of the directors and willing to act, to be an alternate director and may remove from office an alternate director so appointed by him.

A17–072 **60.** An alternate director shall be entitled to receive notice of all meetings of directors and of all meetings of committees of directors of which his appointor is a member, to attend and vote at any such meeting at which the director appointing him is not personally present and generally to perform all the functions of his appointor as a director in his absence but shall not be entitled to receive any remuneration from the Company for his service as an alternate director. It shall not be necessary to give notice of such a meeting to an alternate director who is absent from the United Kingdom unless he has given to the Company an address to which notices may be sent using electronic communications.

A17–073 **61.** An alternate director shall cease to be an alternate director if his appointor ceases to be a director. If a director retires but is reappointed or deemed to have been reappointed at the meeting at which he retires, any appointment of an alternate director made by him which was in force immediately prior to his retirement shall continue after his reappointment.

62. Any appointment or removal of an alternate director shall be by notice to the Company signed by the director making or revoking the appointment or in any other manner approved by the directors. **A17–074**

63. Except where otherwise provided in these articles, an alternate director shall be deemed for all purposes to be a director and shall alone be responsible for his own acts and defaults and he shall not be deemed to be the agent of the director appointing him. **A17–075**

Disqualification and removal of directors

64. The office of a director shall be vacated if— **A17–076**

(a) he ceases to be a director by virtue of any provision of the Companies Act or he becomes prohibited by law from being a director; or

(b) he becomes bankrupt and shall continue to be disqualified from acting as a director whilst he remains undischarged from his bankruptcy, or makes any arrangement or composition with his creditors generally; or

(c) he is, or may be, suffering from mental disorder and either—

(i) he is admitted to hospital in pursuance of an application for admission for treatment under the Mental Health Act 1983 or, in Scotland, an application for admission under the Mental Health (Scotland) Act 1960, or

(ii) an order is made by a court having jurisdiction (whether in the United Kingdom or elsewhere) in matters concerning mental disorder for his detention or for the appointment of a receiver, curator bonis or other person to exercise powers with respect to his property or affairs; or

(d) having been a member of the Company, he ceases to be a member of the Company; or

(e) he resigns his office by notice to the Company; or

(f) he shall for more than six consecutive months have been absent without permission of the directors from meetings of directors held during that period and the directors resolve that his office be vacated.

Powers of directors

65. Subject to the provisions of the Companies Act, the memorandum and these articles and to any directions given by special resolution, the business of the Company shall be managed by the directors who may exercise all the powers of the Company. No alteration of the memorandum or articles and no such direction shall invalidate any prior act of the directors which would have been valid if that alteration had not been made or that direction had not **A17–077**

been given. The powers given by this article shall not be limited by any special power given to the directors by these articles and a meeting of directors at which a quorum is present may exercise all powers exercisable by the directors.

A17–078 **66.** The directors may, by power of attorney or otherwise, appoint any person to be the agent of the Company for such purposes and on such conditions as they determine, including authority for the agent to delegate all or any of his powers.

Delegation of directors' powers

A17–079 **67.** The directors may delegate any of their powers to any committee consisting of one or more directors, members of the Company and others as they shall think fit. The majority of the members of any such committee from time to time shall be members of the Company. The directors may also delegate to any managing director, or any director holding any other executive office, such of their powers as they consider desirable to be exercised by him. Any such delegation may be made subject to any conditions the directors may impose, and either collaterally with or to the exclusion of their own powers and may be revoked or altered. Subject to any such conditions, the proceedings of a committee with two or more members shall be governed by the articles regulating the proceedings of directors so far as they are capable of applying.

Remuneration of directors

A17–080 **68.** Except with the consent of the Company in general meeting, the directors shall not be entitled to any remuneration. Any resolution giving such consent shall specify the amount of remuneration to be paid to the directors, and unless the resolution provides otherwise, the remuneration shall be deemed to accrue from day to day.

Directors' expenses

A17–081 **69.** The directors may be paid all expenses properly incurred by them in connection with their attendance at meetings of directors or committees of directors or general meetings of the Company or otherwise in connection with the discharge of their duties.

Directors' appointments and interests

A17–082 **70.** Subject to the provisions of the Companies Act, and provided that the terms of any such appointment, agreement or arrangement have been approved in advance by the Company, the directors may appoint one or more of their number to the office of managing director or to any other executive office under the Company and may enter into an agreement or arrangement with any director for his employment by the Company or for the provision by him of any services outside the scope of the ordinary duties of a director. Any appointment of a director to an executive office shall terminate if he ceases to be a director but without prejudice to any claim to damages for breach of the contract of service between the director and the Company.

71. Subject to the provisions of the Companies Act, and provided that he has disclosed to the directors the nature and extent of any material interest of his, a director notwithstanding his office— **A17–083**

(a) may be a party to, or otherwise interested in, any transaction or arrangement with the Company or in which the Company is otherwise interested; and

(b) may be a director or other officer of, or employed by, or a party to any transaction or arrangement with, or otherwise interested in, any body corporate promoted by the Company or in which the Company is otherwise interested; and

(c) shall not, by reason of his office, be accountable to the Company for any benefit which he derives from any such office or employment or from any such transaction or arrangement or from any interest in any such body corporate and no such transaction or arrangement shall be liable to be avoided on the ground of any such interest or benefit.

72. For the purposes of article 71— **A17–084**

(a) a general notice given to the directors that a director is to be regarded as having an interest of the nature and extent specified in the notice in any transaction or arrangement in which a specified person or class of persons is interested shall be deemed to be a disclosure that the director has an interest in any such transaction of the nature and extent so specified; and

(b) an interest of which a director has no knowledge and of which it is unreasonable to except him to have knowledge shall not be treated as an interest of his.

Directors' gratuities and pensions

73. The directors may provide benefits, whether by the payment of gratuities or pensions or by insurance or otherwise, for any director who has held but no longer holds any executive office or employment with the Company or with any body corporate which is or has been a subsidiary of the Company, and for any member of his family (including a spouse and a former spouse) or any person who is or was dependent on him, and may (as well before as after he ceases to hold such office or employment) contribute to any fund and pay premiums for the purchase or provision of any such benefit. **A17–085**

Proceedings of directors

74. Subject to the provisions of these articles, the directors may regulate their proceedings as they think fit. A director may, and the secretary at the request of a director shall, call a meeting of the directors. It shall not be necessary to give notice of a meeting to a director who is absent from the United Kingdom unless he has given to the Company an address to which notices **A17–086**

may be sent using electronic communications. Questions arising at a meeting shall be decided by a majority of votes. In the case of an equality of votes, the chairman shall have a second or casting vote. A director who is also an alternate director shall be entitled in the absence of his appointor to a separate vote on behalf of his appointor in addition to his own vote.

A17–087 **75.** The quorum for the transaction of the business of the directors may be fixed by the directors and, unless so fixed at any other greater number, shall be the greater of 50 per cent of the number of appointed directors for the time being, or two. A person who holds office only as an alternate director shall, if his appointor is not present, be counted in the quorum. A person who holds office both as a director and as an alternate director shall only be counted once in the quorum.

A17–088 **76.** The continuing directors or a sole continuing director may act notwithstanding any vacancies in their number, but, if the number of directors is less than the number fixed as the quorum, the continuing director may act only for the purpose of filling vacancies or of calling a general meeting.

A17–089 **77.** The directors may appoint one of their number to be the chairman of the board of directors and may at any time remove him from that office. Unless he is unwilling to do so, the director so appointed shall preside at every meeting of directors at which he is present. But if there is no director holding that office, or if the director holding it is unwilling to preside or is not present within fifteen minutes after the time appointed for the meeting, the directors present may appoint one of their number to be chairman of the meeting.

A17–090 **78.** All acts done by a meeting of directors, or of a committee of directors, or by a person acting as a director shall, notwithstanding that it be afterwards discovered that there was a defect in the appointment of any director or that any of them were disqualified from holding office, or had vacated office, or were not entitled to vote, be as valid as if every such person had been duly appointed and was qualified and had continued to be a director and had been entitled to vote.

A17–091 **79.** A resolution in writing signed by all the directors entitled to receive notice of a meeting of directors or of a committee of directors shall be as valid and effectual as if it had been passed at a meeting of directors or (as the case may be) a committee of directors duly convened and held and may consist of several documents in the like form each signed by one or more directors; but a resolution signed by an alternate director need not also be signed by his appointor and, if it is signed by a director who had appointed an alternate director, it need not be signed by the alternate director in that capacity.

A17–092 **80.** A director who is not a member of the Company shall not vote at a meeting of directors or of a committee of directors on any resolution concerning a matter in which he has, directly or indirectly, an interest or duty which is material and which conflicts or may conflict with the interests of the Company. For the purposes of this article, an interest of a person who is, for any purpose of the Companies Act, connected with a director shall be treated as an interest of the director and, in relation to an alternate director, an interest of his appointor shall be treated as an interest of the alternate director without prejudice to any interest which the alternate director has otherwise. A director shall not be counted in the quorum present at a meeting in relation to a resolution on which he is not entitled to vote.

81.A director who is a member of the Company may vote at any meeting of directors or of any committee of directors of which he is a member notwithstanding that it in any way concerns or relates to a matter in which he has any interest whatsoever, directly or indirectly, and if he votes on such a resolution, his vote shall be counted; and, in relation to any such resolution, he shall (whether or not he votes on it) be taken into account in calculating the quorum present at the meeting. **A17–093**

82. If a question arises at a meeting of directors or of a committee of directors as to the right of a director to vote, the question may, before the conclusion of the meeting, be referred to the chairman of the meeting and his ruling in relation to any director other than himself shall be final and conclusive. **A17–094**

Secretary

83. Subject to the provisions of the Companies Act, the secretary shall be appointed by the directors for such terms, at such remuneration and upon such conditions as they may think fit; and any secretary so appointed may be removed by them. The secretary may resign his office at any time by giving notice in writing to the Company. **A17–095**

Minutes

84. The directors shall cause minutes to be made in books kept for the purpose— **A17–096**

(a) of all appointments of officers made by the directors; and

(b) of all proceedings at meetings of the Company, of members and of the directors, and of committees of directors, including the names of the directors present at each such meeting.

No distribution of profits

85. Except in the case of a winding up, the Company shall not make any distribution to its members of its profits or assets, whether in cash or otherwise. **A17–097**

Winding up

86. If the Company is wound up, the liquidator may, with the sanction of an extraordinary resolution of the Company and any other sanction required by the Companies Act, divide among the members the whole or any part of the assets of the Company and may, for that purpose, value any assets and determine how the division shall be carried out as between the members or different classes of members. The liquidator may, with the like sanction, vest the whole or any part of the assets in trustees upon such trusts for the benefit of the members as he, with the like sanction, determines but no member shall be compelled to accept any asset upon which there is a liability. **A17–098**

Inspection and copying of books and records

A17–099 **87.** In addition to, and without derogation from, any right conferred by statute, any member shall have the right, on reasonable notice, at such time and place as shall be convenient to the Company, to inspect, and to be provided with a copy of, any book, minute, document or accounting record of the Company, upon payment of any reasonable charge for copying. Such rights shall be subject to any resolution of the Company in general meeting, and, in the case of any book, minute, document or accounting record which the directors reasonably consider contains confidential material, the disclosure of which would be contrary to the interests of the Company, to the exclusion or excision of such confidential material (the fact of such exclusion or excision being disclosed to the member), and to any other reasonable conditions that the directors may impose.

Notices

A17–100 **88.** Any notice to be given to or by any person pursuant to these articles shall be in writing or shall be given using electronic communications to an address for the time being notified for that purpose to the person giving the notice. A notice calling a meeting of the directors need not be in writing or given using electronic communications if there is insufficient time to give such notice having regard to the urgency of the business to be conducted at the meeting.

A17–101 **89.** The Company may give any notice to a member either personally or by sending it by first class post in a prepaid envelope addressed to the member at his registered address or by leaving it at that address or by giving it using electronic communications in accordance with any of the methods described in subsections (4A)–(4D) of section 369 of the Companies Act. A member whose registered address is not within the United Kingdom and who gives to the Company an address within the United Kingdom at which notices may be given to him, or an address to which notices may be sent by electronic communications, shall be entitled to have notices given to him at that address, but otherwise no such member shall be entitled to receive any notice from the Company.

A17–102 **90.** A member present, either in person or by proxy, at any meeting of the Company shall be deemed to have received notice of the meeting and, where requisite, of the purposes for which it was called.

A17–103 **91.** Proof that an envelope containing a notice was properly addressed, prepaid and posted by first class post shall be conclusive evidence that the notice was given. Proof that a notice contained in an electronic communication was sent in accordance with guidance issued by the Institute of Chartered Secretaries and Administration shall be conclusive evidence that the notice was given.

A17–104 **92.** A notice shall by first class post shall be deemed to be given at the expiration of 48 hours after the envelope containing it was posted. A notice contained in an electronic communication sent in accordance with section 369(4A) of the Companies Act shall be deemed to be given at the expiration of 48 hours after the time it was sent. A notice contained in an electronic communication given in accordance with section 369(4B) of the Companies Act shall be deemed to be given when treated as having been so given in accordance with that subsection.

Indemnity

93. Subject to the provisions of the Companies Act, and in particular section 310 of that Act— **A17–105**

(a) without prejudice to any indemnity to which a director may otherwise be entitled, every director or other office or auditor of the Company shall be indemnified out of the assets of the Company against any losses or liabilities which he may sustain or incur in or about, or otherwise in relation to, the execution of the duties of his office, including any liability incurred by him in defending any proceedings, whether civil or criminal, in which judgment is given in his favour or in which he is acquitted or in connection with any application in which relief is granted to him by the court from liability for negligence, default, breach of duty or breach of trust in relation to the affairs of the Company; and

(b) no director or other officer shall be liable for any loss, damage or other misfortune which may happen to or be incurred by the Company in, or in relation to, the execution of the duties of his office.

94. The directors shall have power to purchase and maintain for any director, officer or auditor of the Company, insurance against any such liability as is referred to in section 310(1) of the Companies Act. **A17–106**

Rules or bye-laws

95. The directors may from time to time make such rules or bye-laws as they may deem necessary or expedient or convenient for the proper conduct and management of the Company. Any such rules or bye-laws shall not be inconsistent with the Memorandum and these articles and may, in particular (but without prejudice to the generality of the directors' powers), regulate— **A17–107**

(a) the conduct of the members of the Company in relation to one another and to the Company and the Company's servants;

(b) the procedure at general meetings and meetings of the directors and committees of the directors of the Company in so far as such procedure is not regulated by these articles.

96. The Company in general meeting shall have power to alter, repeal or add to any such rules or bye-laws and the directors shall adopt such means as they deem sufficient to bring to the notice of the members of the Company any such rules or bye-laws, which so long as they shall be in force, shall be binding on all members of the Company. **A17–108**

Name and Addresses of Members:
[list names and addresses of members]

[1] 2002 c. 15. For the definition of "the appropriate national authority" *see* section 179(1).
[2] For the definition "RTM company" *see* sections 7(1) and 73 of the Commonhold and Leasehold Reform Act 2002.
[3] For the premises relevant to RTM companies, *see* section 72 of, and Schedule 6 to, the Commonhold and Leasehold Reform Act 2002.
[4] 1985 c. 6.
[5] 2000 c. 7. *See* section 15 of that Act.

The Service Charges (Consultation Requirements) (Amendment) (England) Regulations 2004

2004 No. 2665

The First Secretary of State, in exercise of the powers conferred by sections 2 (4) and (5) and 20ZA(3) to (6) of the Landlord and Tenant Act 1985[1], hereby makes the following Regulations: **A18–001**

Citation, commencement and application

1.—(1) These Regulations may be cited as the Service Charges (Consultation Requirements) (Amendment) (England) Regulations 2004 and shall come into force on 8th November 2004. **A18–002**

(2) These Regulations apply in relation to England only.

Amendment of Regulations

2.—Regulation 4 (application of section 20 to qualifying long term agreements) of the Service Charges (Consultation Requirements) (England) Regulations 2003[2] is amended— **A18–003**

(a) in paragraph (3), by the substitution, for "In", of "Subject to paragraph (3A), in"; and

(b) by the insertion, after paragraph (3) of the following paragraph—

"(3A) Where—

(a) a landlord intends to enter into a qualifying long term agreement on or after *date* November 2004; and

(b) he has not at any time between 31st October 2003 and *date* November 2004 made up accounts relating to service charges referable to a qualifying long term agreement and payable in respect of the dwellings to which the intended agreement is to relate,

the relevant date is the date on which begins the first period for which service charges referable to that intended agreement are payable under the terms of the leases of those dwellings.".

[1] 1985 c. 70. Section 20 was substituted, and section 20ZA inserted, by section 151 of the Commonhold and Leasehold Reform Act 2002 (c. 15). *See also* paragraph 4 of Schedule 7 to that Act for modifications relevant to sections 20 and 20ZA associated with the right to manage under Chapter 1 of Part 2 of that Act. The functions of the Secretary of State under sections 20 and 20ZA are, so far as exercisable in relation to Wales, transferred to the National Assembly for Wales by the National Assembly for Wales (Transfer of Functions) Order 1999 (S.I. 1999/672), article 2; *see* the entry in Schedule 1 for the Landlord and Tenant Act 1985. *See also* section 177 of the Commonhold and Leasehold Reform Act 2002.

[2] S.I. 2003/1987.

The Rights of Re-entry and Forfeiture (Prescribed Sum and Period) (England) Regulations 2004

2004 No. 3086

A19–001 The First Secretary of State, in exercise of the powers conferred by section 16 (1) of the Commonhold and Leasehold Reform Act 2002[1], hereby makes the following Regulations, of which a draft has been laid before, and approved by resolution of, each House of Parliament:

Citation, commencement and application

A19–002 **1.**—(1) These Regulations may be cited as the Rights of Re-entry and Forfeiture (Prescribed Sum and Period) (England) Regulations 2004 and shall come into force on the day after that on which they are made.

(2) These Regulations apply in relation to dwellings in England that are occupied under a long lease[2].

Prescribed sum and period

A19–003 **2.**—(1) The sum prescribed for the purposes of subsection (1)(a) of section 167 (failure to pay small amount for short period) of the Commonhold and Leasehold Reform Act 2002 is £350.

(2) The period prescribed for the purposes of subsection (1)(b) of that section is three years.

[1] 2002 c. 15. *See* the definition of "prescribed" in section 167(5) and the definition of "appropriate national authority" in section 179(1).
[2] As to "dwelling" and "long lease", *see* section 167(5) of the Commonhold and Leasehold Reform Act 2002.

Appendix B

Miscellaneous Notices

SECTION 20 STATEMENT OF ESTIMATES IN RELATION TO PROPOSED WORKS

To all the Leaseholders of [*insert name of premises*] and the [*insert recognised tenants' association*[1]] **B1–001**

RE [*insert name of premises*]

1. This notice is given pursuant to the notice of intention to carry out works issued on *[insert date of notice of intention]*. The consultation period in respect of the notice of intention ended on *[insert relevant date]*.
2. It is your Landlord's obligation to supply, free of charge, a statement setting out the following information: as regards at least two of the estimates, the amount specified in the estimate as the estimated cost of the proposed works and, where observations have been made by any tenant, a summary of those observations and your Landlord's response to them. Your Landlord is obliged to make all the estimates available for inspection. It is also necessary that at least one of the estimates must be that of a person wholly unconnected with the Landlord. We confirm that each of the companies which provided estimates are wholly unconnected with the Landlord.
3. We have now obtained estimates in respect of the works to be carried out. We have selected *[insert number, at least two]* estimates from which to make the final choice of contractor.
4. The amount specified in the selected estimates as the estimated cost of the proposed works is as follows: *[insert amount of each selected estimate against the name of each contractor concerned]*.
5. All of the estimates obtained may be inspected at *[insert place and hours for inspection]* [or if requested we shall send you a copy].

6. We did not receive within the consultation period any written observations in relation to the notice of proposals given on *[insert date of notice of proposals]*

   OR

7. The written observations in relation to the proposals received during the consultation period may be summarised as follows: *[insert summary of observations]*. Our response to the observations is: *[state response]*

   OR

8. A summary of the written response received during the consultation period, together with our response to them, may be inspected at: *[specify place and hours for inspection]*[or if requested we shall send you a copy].

Signed:

[Duly authorised agent of [*insert name of Landlord or Manager*]]

Address:

[*insert address to which future correspondence relating to the subject matter of the notice should be sent*]

Dated:

[1] Delete if appropriate

SECTION 20 NOTICE OF REASONS FOR AWARDING A CONTRACT TO CARRY OUT WORKS/MAKING A LONG TERM AGREEMENT[1]

B2–001

To all the Leaseholders of [*insert name of premises*] and the [*insert recognised tenants' association*[2]]

RE [*insert name of premises*]

1. This notice is given pursuant to the statement of estimates / notice of proposals served on [insert date]. The consultation period in respect of the notice of proposals ended on [insert relevant date].
2. We have now entered into a contract for the carrying out of the works first described in the notice of intention dated [insert date of notice of intention] with [name of chosen contractor].
3. Our reasons for doing so are: [state reasons]

   OR

4. A statement of our reasons for doing so may be inspected at [insert address and time for inspection] [or if requested, we will send you a copy[3]].
5. We did not receive within the consultation period any written observations in relation to the statement of estimates / notice of proposals given on [insert date]

   OR

6. The written observations in relation to the estimates / proposals received during the consultation period may be summarised as follows: [insert a summary of observations].
7. Our response to the observations is: [insert response].

   OR

8. A summary of the written observations received during the consultation period, together with our response to them, may be inspected at [insert address and time for inspection] or if requested we will send you a copy.

Signed:

[Duly authorised agent of [*insert name of Landlord or Manager*]]

Address:

[*insert address to which future correspondence relating to the subject matter of the notice should be sent*]

Dated:

[1] Delete as appropriate throughout pleading
[2] Delete if appropriate
[3] Not necessary, although may be appropriate in certain circumstances

SECTION 20 NOTICE OF PROPOSALS TO ENTER INTO A LONG-TERM AGREEMENT

B3–001

To all the Leaseholders of [*insert name of premises*] and the [*insert recognised tenants' association*[1]]

RE [*insert name of premises*]

1. This notice is given pursuant to the notice of intention to enter into a long term agreement issued on *[insert date of notice of intention]*. The consultation period in respect of the notice of intention ended on *[insert relevant date]*.
2. We have now obtained proposals in respect of the works to be provided under the agreement based on the estimates received and a copy of each proposal is attached to this notice / can be inspected at [*insert place and hours of inspection*].
3. We invite you to make written observations in relation to the proposals by sending them to [*insert address*]. Written observations must be made within the consultation period of 30 days from the date of this notice, and the consultation period will end on [*insert date*].

Signed:

[Duly authorised agent of [*insert name of Landlord or Manager*]]

Address:

[*insert address to which future correspondence relating to the subject matter of the notice should be sent*]

Dated:

[1] Delete if appropriate

SECTION 20 NOTICE OF INTENTION TO CARRY OUT WORK/ENTER INTO A LONG TERM AGREEMENT[1]

B4–001 To all leaseholders of *[insert name of the premises]* and the *[insert name of recognised tenants' association[2]]*.

RE [*insert name of premises*]

It is the intention of *[insert name of landlord or manager]* to enter into an agreement to carry out works / or a long term agreement in respect of which we are required to consult leaseholders.

1. The works to be carried out under the agreement are specified as follows: *[insert a specification of works]*

   OR

2. A description of the works to be carried out under the agreement may be inspected at *[insert address and time for inspection]*. [Or if you require a copy of the specification, please inform [*insert name of landlord or manager*] of this and they will provide you with a copy free of charge[3]].
3. The reason your Landlord considers it necessary to carry out these works/enter into this agreement is *[insert statement of reasons]*.
4. We invite you to make written observations in relation to the proposed works by sending them to *[insert address of landlord or manager]*. Observations must be made within the consultation period of 30 days from the date of this notice. The consultation period will end on [*insert date 30 days from the date of the notice]*.
5. We also invite you to propose, within 30 days from the date of this notice, the name of a person from whom we should try to obtain an estimate for the carrying out of the proposed works / matters detailed above.

Signed:

[*Signature of person giving the notice.*]
[duly authorised agent of *[insert name of Landlord or manager]*]

Address:

[*Give the address to which future communications relating to the subject matter of the notice should be sent.*]

Date:

[1] Delete as appropriate throughout notice
[2] Delete is not applicable
[3] Not necessary, although may be appropriate in certain circumstances

SECTION 20 NOTICE ACCOMPANYING STATEMENT OF ESTIMATES IN RELATION TO PROPOSED WORKS

B5–001

To all the Leaseholders of [*insert name of premises*] and the [*insert recognised tenants' association*[1]]

RE [*insert name of premises*]

1. This notice is to accompany the statement of estimates in relation to proposed works which is attached, issued on *(insert date of statement of estimates)*.
2. All of the estimates obtained may be inspected at *[insert place and hours for inspection]* [or if requested we will send you a copy[2]].
3. We invite you to make written observations in relation to any of the estimates by sending them to *[address of landlord or manager]*. Observations must be made within the consultation period of 30 days from the date of this notice. The consultation period will end on *[insert date 30 days from the date of the notice]*.

Signed:

[Duly authorised agent of [*insert name of Landlord or Manager*]]

Address:

[*insert address to which future correspondence relating to the subject matter of the notice should be sent*]

Dated:

[1] Delete if appropriate
[2] Not necessary, although may be appropriate in certain circumstances

NOTICE PURSUANT TO SECTION 146 OF THE LAW OF PROPERTY ACT 1925

B6–001 **TO:** Sunshine Drinks Ltd.

Or the Lessee of Unit 8, Pina Colada Way, Sandbeach ("the Premises") comprised in the Lease dated 23rd July 1989 and made between Grim & Darke Ltd. of the one part as "Lessor" and Gaye Abandon of the other part as "Lessee".

AND TO ALL OTHERS WHOM IT MAY CONCERN

We Pestilence & Plague, solicitors and agents for Killjoy & Doom, hereby give you notice as follows:-

(1) By the said Lease, the said Gaye Abandon covenants in relation to the Premises as follows:-

Not to use the said premises for the manufacture of any goods

(2) The abovementioned covenants have been broken and you have:-

Used the said premises as a factory for the manufacture of alcoholic beverages and general party paraphenalia

(3) We require you to remedy the aforesaid breach in so far as the same is capable of remedy. You are also required to make reasonable compensation in money due to the lessor for the breach of covenant.

(4) Now take notice that on your failure to comply with this Notice within a reasonable time it is the intention of the said Killjoy & Doom to re-enter upon the Premises by action or otherwise and forfeit the said Lease and to claim damages for the aforesaid breaches of covenant.

Further by clause 5(3) of the said lease the said Gaye Abandon covenanted to pay the costs of and incurred by the landlord in the preparation of any notice under s.146 of the Law of Property Act 1925. Costs of £1175 have been incurred in the preparation of this notice and you are hereby required to make payment of that sum to the lessor within 14 days of the date of this notice.

DATE and SIGN

NOTICE PURSUANT TO SECTION 146 OF THE LAW OF PROPERTY ACT 1925

TO: Mr Adam Son **B7–001**

Or the Lessee of Flat 136 Helm Mansions London ("the Premises") comprised in the Lease dated 22nd April 1977 and made between Tate Limited of the one part as "Lessor" and Adam Son of the other part as "Lessee".

AND TO ALL OTHERS WHOM IT MAY CONCERN

We Davey & Sons solicitors and agents for Tate Limited, hereby give you notice as follows:-

(1) By the said Lease, the said Mr Adam Son covenants in relation to the Premises as follows:-

Under clause 3(2) to pay to the Lessor without any deduction or set off whatsoever a proportionate part (being 4.2%) of the costs, expenses and outgoings incurred by the Lessor in each service charge year (being the year ending 24th June) in respect of the repair maintenance and insurance of the Building and the provision of services therein and the other heads of expenditure as the same are provided for and set out in the 3rd Schedule hereto ("the Service Charge"), such sum to be certified by the lessor's surveyor as having been expended in accordance with the terms of the lease as soon as practicable after the 24th June in each year and such sum to be payable within 14 days of being demanded.

(2) The abovementioned covenant has been broken and you have:-

Failed to pay the Service Charge in accordance with clause 3(2) of the Lease:

(i) In respect of the year end 24th June 2004 the sum incurred by the lessor in the preceding year was certified on the 9th July 2004 by the lessor's surveyor, Mr Matthew Hannah, in the sum of £79,462.
(ii) The proportion of that cost owed by you is £3,337.40.
(iii) The sum of £3,337.40 was demanded of you in a letter dated 15th July 2004.
(iv) As at the 27th August 2004 the said sum remains unpaid.

(3) We require you to remedy the aforesaid breach in so far as the same is capable of remedy. You are also required to make reasonable compensation in money due to the lessor for the breach of covenant.

(4) Now take notice that on your failure to comply with this Notice within a reasonable time it is the intention of the said Tate Limited to re-enter upon the Premises by action or otherwise and forfeit the said Lease and to claim damages for the aforesaid breaches of covenant.

(5) Take notice that Section 81 of the Housing Act 1996 applies to this Notice. This means that the lessor may not, in relation to premises let as a dwelling, exercise the right of re-entry or forfeiture for failure by a lessee to pay a service charge or administration charge unless:

 (i) The lessee has admitted that it is payable; or
 (ii) It is finally determined by (or on appeal from) a leasehold valuation tribunal or by a court, or by an arbitral tribunal in proceedings pursuant to a post-dispute arbitration agreement, that the amount of the service charge or administration charge is payable by him.

(6) Where the amount is the subject of a final determination, the day on which the decision of the leasehold valuation tribunal, court or arbitral tribunal is given shall be taken to be the day on which the service charge or administration charge is taken to be determined, and the landlord may not exercise any such right of re-entry or forfeiture until after the end of the period of 14 days beginning with the day such decision is given.

For these purposes it is finally determined that the amount of a service charge or administration charge is payable:-

 (i) If a decision that it is payable is not appealed against or otherwise challenged, at the end of the time for bringing an appeal or other challenge; or
 (ii) If such a decision is appealed against or otherwise challenged and not set aside in consequence of the appeal or other challenge, at the time the appeal or other challenge is disposed of:—

  (a) By the determination of the appeal or other challenge and the expiry of the time for bringing a subsequent appeal (if any), or
  (b) By its being abandoned or otherwise ceasing to have effect.

(7) The reference to premises let as a dwelling does not include premises let on:—

 (i) a tenancy to which Part II of the Landlord and Tenant Act 1954 applies (business tenancy)
 (ii) a tenancy of an agricultural holding within the meaning of the Agricultural Holdings Act 1986 in relation to which that Act applies, or
 (iii) a farm business tenancy within the meaning of the Agricultural Tenancies Act 1995.

(8) "Service Charge" in section 81 means a service charge within the meaning of section 18(1) of the Landlord and Tenant Act 1985, other than one excluded form [*sic*] that section by section 27 of that Act (rent of dwelling registered and not entered as variable).

(9) "Administration Charge" has the meaning given by Part I of Schedule 11 to the Commonhold and Leasehold Reform Act 2002; "arbitration agreement" and "arbitral tribunal" have the same meaning as Part I of the Arbitration Act 1996; "post-dispute arbitration agreement", in relation to any matter, means an arbitration agreement made after a dispute about the matter has arisen; and "dwelling" has the same meaning as in the Landlord and Tenant Act 1985.

(10) On the 27th October 2004 proceedings were issued against you in the Romsey County Court (claim number 4RO725) claiming judgment for the unpaid Service Charge referred to above in the sum of £3,337.40. You defended those proceedings and the matter proceeded to trial. On the 24th August 2005 HHJ Herbert Moses QC having heard the trial (at which you were present) gave judgment to the lessor for the unpaid Service Charge in the full amount claimed. You have not appealed that decision and the time for you so doing has now passed.

(11) By clause 3.7 of the Lease you covenant to pay on an indemnity basis all costs charges fees disbursements and expenses (including the fees of Solicitors and Counsel) incurred by the lessor of and incidental to any Notice served under Section 146 of the Law of Property Act 1925 and all proceedings commenced thereunder notwithstanding that forfeiture for such breach shall be avoided otherwise than by relief granted by the court.

(12) By reason of the matters referred to above in this Notice, Tate Limited have incurred not less that £275 costs in respect of the preparation and service of this Notice and you are required to repay the said sum to them.

Dated this 17th September 2005

Signed

NOTICE PURSUANT TO SECTION 27 OF THE LANDLORD AND TENANT ACT 1987

B8–001 To: *Mr. Robert Clive* of 22 Large House, London and of PO Box 1234, Cresta 1234, South Africa ("the Landlord").

We, Busy Solicitors of 90–92 High Street, Small Village, London as Solicitors and Agents for the Tenants of the property known as 100 Long Road, London ("the Tenants") namely:

Flat A Mr. Hills
Flat B Mr and Mrs White
Flat C Mr. N. Brown
GIVE YOU NOTICE as follows:

1. The Tenants intend to pursue an application to the Lastditch County Court for an order *under section 28 of* the Landlord & Tenant Act 1997 ("the Act") in respect of the whole of the premises situated at and known as 100 Long Road, London ("the Property").
2. If the Landlord within 28 days of the date of this Notice remedies the following breaches as set out below the Tenants will not pursue their application for an acquisition order.

The alleged breaches are as follows:-

(i) To perform its covenant at paragraphs 4(l) to (7) of the Tenants' leases as *follows:-*

(a) To maintain and keep in good order repair condition and where necessary painted the external wall surfaces bearing walls foundations and roofs
(b) to keep all water gas and other pipes sewers drains tubes meters wires and cables in good and substantial repair.
(c) At all times to keep the Parts of the Estate and building . . . in common clean tidy and properly lighted and where applicable carpeted.
(d) To defray such other costs as may be necessary to maintain the Estate as a good class residential Estate . . .
(e) To pay and discharge any rates . . .
(f) Without prejudice to the foregoing to do or cause to be done **all** such works installations acts matters and things . . . for the proper maintenance safety and administration of the Estate and the building
(g) To employ a firm of managing agents . . . to manage and maintain the Estate and the building . . .

(ii) To perform his covenant at clause 5(2) of the leases to keep the building insured in the joint names of the Landlord and the Tenants and their mortgagees against loss or damage etc.

3. The Tenants will ask the Court to make an order on the grounds that the Landlord is in breach of the above stated obligations. Matters that the Tenants will rely on for the purposes of establishing those grounds are that the Landlord has not complied with the obligations or taken any steps to comply with the obligations since at least 1995 and further that it is believed that the Landlord resides in South Africa and accordingly the circumstances by virtue of which the Landlord is in breach of the aforesaid obligations are likely to continue.

Dated:

NOTICE UNDER SECTION 48 OF THE LANDLORD AND TENANT ACT 1987

B9–001 To: [insert name of Tenant and address]

Being the Tenant of premises known as [insert address of premises].

We [name and address of Landlord's agent or solicitors], on behalf of your Landlord [insert name of Landlord], give you notice pursuant to section 48(1) of the Landlord and Tenant Act 1987 that the address of your Landlord for service of notices (including notices of proceedings) is:

[insert Landlord's address for service]

Signed:

Dated:

Further pursuant to section 47 of the Landlord and Tenant Act 1986, the following information must be included in any demand for rent or other sums payable to the landlord under the terms of the tenancy:

(a) Name and address of the landlord; and

(b) if that address is not in England and Wales, an address in England and Wales at which notices (including notices in proceedings) may be served on the landlord by the tenant.

Appendix C

Leasehold Valuation Tribunal Precedents

PRECEDENT: APPLICATION FOR A DETERMINATION OF LIABILITY TO PAY SERVICE CHARGES (LEASEHOLD VALUATION TRIBUNAL)

C1–001

Application Form
S27A Landlord and Tenant Act 1985
Application for a determination of liability to pay service charges

This is the correct form to use if you want the Leasehold Valuation Tribunal to determine the liability to pay any service charge. This includes the question of whether or not the service charge is reasonable.

Please do not send any documents with this application form except a copy of the lease. If and when further evidence is needed you will be asked to send it in separately. If you have any questions about how to fill in this form or the procedures the Tribunal will use, please call us on 0845 600 3178. **Please send this completed application form together with the application fee and a copy of the lease to the appropriate panel (see page 6 for panel addresses).**

1. DETAILS OF APPLICANT(S) (if there are multiple Applicants please continue on a separate sheet)

Name *Constance Brown*

Address (including postcode) *14 Tanfield Mansions London N5 3DR*

Address for correspondence (*if different*) *As above*

Telephone: *Day:* *020 8123 4567* *Evening:* *020 8123 4567*
Mobile: *07885 123456*

Email address: *constancebrown@isp.com*

Capacity (e.g. landlord/tenant/managing agent) *tenant*

Representative details *Breef & Co solicitors, 100 Equity St, London N5 3XD*

Where details of a representative have been given, all correspondence and communications will be with them until the tribunal is notified that they are no longer acting.

2. ADDRESS (including postcode) OF PROPERTY (if not already given)

As above

3. BRIEF DESCRIPTION OF PROPERTY (*e.g., 2-bedroom flat in Victorian block*)

3 storey mansion block c.1890 comprising 35 flats over shops

4. DETAILS OF RESPONDENT(S)(if there are multiple Respondents please continue on a separate sheet)

Name *The Brookhouse Property Trust Limited*

Address (including postcode) *Property House, Land Street, London N5 3PT*

Address for correspondence (*if different*) *As above*

Telephone: *Day*: *020 8987 6543* *Evening:* ____________________
Mobile: ____________________

Email address (if known): *mail@brookfieldproperty.co.uk*

Capacity (*e.g. landlord/tenant/managing agent*) *Landlord*

5. DETAILS OF LANDLORD (if not already given)

Name *As above*

Address (including postcode)____________________

____

____

Telephone: *Day:* ____________________ *Evening:* ____________________
Mobile: ____________________

Email address (if known): ____________________

6. DETAILS OF ANY RECOGNISED TENANTS' ASSOCIATION (if known)

Name of Secretary *None*

Address (including postcode)____________________

____

____

Telephone: *Day:* ____________________ *Evening:* ____________________
Mobile: ____________________

Email address (if known): ____________________

7. SERVICE CHARGES TO BE CONSIDERED BY THE TRIBUNAL

a. **Service charges for past years**

Please list years for which a determination is sought

1. *1 April 2004 to 31 March 2005* 2. ____________________

3. ____________________ 4. ____________________

5. ____________________ 6. ____________________

For each service charge year, fill in one of the sheets of paper entitled **Service Charges in Question.**

b. **Service charges for current or future years**

Please list years for which a determination is sought

1. ______________________ 2. ______________________

3. ______________________ 4. ______________________

5. ______________________ 6. ______________________

For each service charge year, fill in one of the sheets of paper entitled **Service Charges in Question.**

8. OTHER APPLICATIONS

Do you know of any other cases involving either: (a) the same or similar issues about the service charge as in this application; or (b) the same landlord or tenant or property as in this application? If so please give details.

The tenants of flats 1 and 3 have brought related applications under application Number LON/LIS/00AA/2005/1234

9. LIMITATION OF COSTS

If you are a tenant, do you wish to make a s.20C application (see Guidance Notes) YES ☒ NO ☐

If so, why? *(1) The landlord has behaved improperly or unreasonably in that it has failed to reply to letters from me dated 25 March 2005, 24 June 2005 and 29 September 2005. (2) I have paid £1,100 in respect of the undisputed service charges (3) the landlord has refused an offer to mediate made in my letter of 10 October 2005.*

Guidance notes
Some leases allow a landlord to recover costs incurred in connection with the proceedings before the LVT as part of the service charge. Section 20C of the Landlord and Tenant Act 1985 gives the tribunal power, on application by a tenant, to make an order preventing a landlord from taking this step. If you are a tenant you should indicate here whether you want the tribunal to consider making such an order.

10. CAN WE DEAL WITH YOUR APPLICATION WITHOUT A HEARING?

If the Tribunal thinks it is appropriate, and all the parties agree, it is possible for your application to be dealt with entirely on the basis of written representations and documents and without the need for parties to attend and make oral representations. This means you would not be liable for a hearing fee of £150 but it would also mean that you would not be able to explain your case in person. Please let us know if you would be happy for your application to be dealt with in this way.

I would be happy for the case to be dealt with on paper if the Tribunal thinks it is appropriate YES ☐ NO ☒

NB: Even if you have asked for a determination on paper the Tribunal may decide that a hearing is necessary. Please go on to answer questions 11 to 13 on the assumption that a hearing will be heard.

11. TRACK PREFERENCES

We need to decide whether to deal with the case on the Fast Track or the Standard Track.

(see Guidance Notes for an explanation of what a track is). Please let us know which track you think appropriate for this case.

Fast Track ☐ Standard Track ☒

Is there any special reason for urgency in this case? YES ☐ NO ☒

If there is, please explain how urgent it is and why: ____________________

____

____

The Tribunal will normally deal with a case in one of three ways: on paper, on the "fast track", and on the "standard track." The fast track is designed for cases that need a hearing but are very simple and will not generate a great deal of paperwork or argument. A fast track case will usually be heard within 10 weeks of your application. You should indicate here if you think the case is very simple and can easily be dealt with. The standard track is designed for more complicated cases where there may be numerous issues to be decided or where, for example, a lot of documentation is involved. A standard track case may involve the parties being invited to a Pre-Trial Review which is a meeting at which the steps that need to be taken to bring the case to a final hearing can be discussed.

12. AVAILABILITY

If there are dates or days we must avoid during the next three months (either for your convenience or the convenience of any expert you may wish to call) please list them here.

Dates on which you will NOT be available ____________________

____

____

13. VENUE REQUIREMENTS

Please provide details of any special requirements you or anyone who will be coming with you may have (e.g., the use of a wheelchair and/or the presence of a translator) ____________________

____

____

In London cases are usually heard in Alfred Place, which is fully wheelchair accessible. Elsewhere hearings are held in local venues which are no all so accessible and the Clerks will find it useful to know if you or anyone you want to come to the hearing with you has any special requirements of this kind.

14. CHECK LIST

Please check that you have completed this form fully. The tribunal will not process your application until this has been done and it has both a copy of the lease and the application fee:

A copy of the lease(s) is/are enclosed ☒

A crossed cheque or postal order for the application fee (if applicable) is enclosed ☒

Amount of fee enclosed *£350* Please put your name and address on the back of any cheque you send.

DO NOT send cash under any circumstances. Cash payment will not be accepted and any application accompanied by cash will be returned to the applicant.

Please ONLY send this application form, a copy of the lease and the application fee and nothing else.

Guidance notes:

The amount of the application fee will depend on the total amount of service charge that is in dispute. To find out how much you will need to pay you should consult the following table: ***Fees should be paid by a crossed cheque made payable to or a postal order drawn in favour of the Office of the Deputy Prime Minister.***

Waiver and Fees

You will not be liable to pay a fee if you or your partner is in receipt of:

- *Income Support*
- *Housing Benefit*
- *Income Based Job Seeker's Allowance*

Amount of Service Charge in dispute	***Application Fee***
Not more than £500	£50
More than £500 but less than £1,000	£70
More than £1,000 but less than £5,000	£100
More than £5,000 but less than £15,000	£200
More than £15,000	£350

- *A working tax credit, and either:*
  - *you or your partner receive a tax credit with a disability or severe disability element; or*
  - *you or your partner is also in receipt of a child tax credit*
- *a guarantee credit under the State Pensions Credit Act 2002*
- *certificate issued under the Funding Code which has not been revoked or discharged and which is in respect of the proceedings before the tribunal the whole or part of which have been transferred from the county court for determination by a tribunal*

- *A Working Tax Credit where the Gross Annual Income used to calculate the Tax Credit is £14,213 or less*

If you wish to claim a waiver of fees you must complete another form available from the Panel office. The waiver form will not be copied to other parties in the proceedings.

If you are making several applications at the same time, even if you are using different application forms or the applications relate to different parts of the Tribunal's jurisdiction, you do not have to pay a separate fee for each application. The overall fee will be the biggest of the fees payable for each application on its own.

If you are in any doubt about the amount of fee or have any other questions about how to fill in this form please telephone the RPTS help line on 0845 600 3178.

15. STATEMENT OF TRUTH

I believe that the facts stated in this application are true.

Signed: ____*Constance Brown*__________________ Dated: *1 October 2005*

PANEL ADDRESSES

Northern Rent Assessment Panel

20th Floor, Sunley Tower, Piccadilly Plaza, Manchester M1 4BE

Telephone: 0845 1002614

Facsimile: 0161 2367 3656

Midland Rent Assessment Panel

2nd Floor, East Wing, Ladywood House

45-46 Stephenson Street

Birmingham B2 4DH

Telephone: 0845 1002615

Facsimile: 0121 643 7605

Eastern Rent Assessment Panel

Great Eastern House, Tenison Road, Cambridge CB1 2TR

Telephone: 0845 1002616

Facsimile: 01223 505116

London Rent Assessment Panel

2nd Floor, 10 Alfred Place, London WC1E 7LR

Telephone: 020 7446 7700

Facsimile: 020 7637 1250

Southern Rent Assessment Panel

1st Floor, 1 Market Avenue, Chichester PO19 1JU

Telephone: 0845 1002617

Facsimile: 01243 779389

SERVICE CHARGES IN QUESTION

PLEASE USE THE SPACE BELOW TO PROVIDE INFORMATION REGARDING EACH OF THE YEARS MENTIONED IN PART 7 OF THE MAIN APPLICATION FORM.

You will be given an opportunity later to give further details of your case and to supply the Tribunal with any documents that support it. At this stage you should give a clear outline of your case so that the Tribunal understands what your application is about.

The year in question *1 April 2004 to 31 March 2005*

A list of the items of service charge that are in issue (or relevant) and their value

1. Cost of major works to roof and front elevation: £123,456

2. Insurance: £17,890

3. Legal costs: £3,210

Description of the question(s) you wish the tribunal to decide
A determination under section 27A of the Landlord and Tenant Act 1985 of the amount of service charges payable by me in the service charge year 2004/5. I wish to argue:

1. In respect the major works, the landlord failed to follow the consultation requirements of section 20 of the Landlord and Tenant Act 1985 and the Service Charges (Consultation Requirements) (England) Regulations 2003 in that it did not serve a statement under paragraph 4(5)(b) of Part 2 of Schedule 4 of the regulations.

2. The cost of insurance was not reasonably incurred within the meaning of section 19 of the Landlord and Tenant Act 1985 because the premium was excessive. A reasonable insurance premium for this block of flats ought properly to be £3,500. The landlord failed to obtain any other quotations for insurance.

3. There is no provision in the lease that allows the landlord to recover legal costs.

Any further comments you may wish to make: *I accept liability to pay the remainder of the service charges set out in the landlord's demand dated 25 April 2005 (amounting to £750). I further accept liability to pay £250 for the qualifying works under section 20(1) of the Landlord and Tenant Act 1985 and £100 as my contribution to insurance. I therefore seek a determination that I am liable to pay service charges of £1,100 for service charges in 2004/5.*

RESIDENTIAL PROPERTY TRIBUNAL SERVICE DIRECTIONS BY THE LEASEHOLD VALUATION TRIBUNAL

C2–001 **COMMONHOLD AND LEASEHOLD REFORM ACT 2002**

LANDLORD AND TENANT ACT 1985/1987 **Ref:**
HOUSING ACT 1996

Premises:

Applicant: **(Landlord/Tenant/Managing Agent)**

Represented by:

Respondent: **(Landlord/Tenant/Managing Agent)**

Represented by:

Preliminary

1. A Pre-Trial Review was held on ______________. The applicant attended and was represented by _____________ /did not attend and was not represented. The respondent attended and was represented by _____________/did not attend and was not represented.

2. The application/s dated _____________ is/are for:

(a) A determination of reasonableness and/or liability to pay service charges under Section 27A of the Landlord and Tenant Act 1985.
(b) Dispensation of all or any of the consultation requirements contained in Section 20 of the Landlord and Tenant Act 1985.
(c) Limitation of the landlord's costs in the proceedings under Section 20C of the Landlord and Tenant Act 1985.
(d) The appointment of a manager or for the variation or discharge of an order appointing a manager under Section 24 of the Landlord and Tenant Act 1987.
(e) For the variation of a lease or leases under Part IV of the Landlord and Tenant Act 1987.

3. The application/s was/were transferred to the Tribunal by an Order of the ___________ County Court dated ________________.

4. The issue/s in dispute is/are—

(a)

(b)

(c)

(d)

5. A copy/copies of the relevant lease/s is/are in the case file.
6. The following was/were admitted/agreed by the parties at the Pre-Trial Review:

(a)

(b)

(c)

(d)

7. The applicant seeks to have the application/s dealt with at a hearing/on paper. Having regarded to the complexity of the issues to be determined, the Tribunal considered it appropriate to deal with the application/s by way of a hearing on the fast track/standard track/by paper and the parties have agreed to this in writing.
8. The Tribunal thinks it is appropriate, and the parties have agreed, for the application/s to be dealt with entirely on the basis of written representations and documents; without the need for the parties to attend and make oral representations at a hearing. However, at any time before the application/s is/are determined, the parties may make a request to the Tribunal to be heard or the Tribunal may give notice to the parties that it intends to determine the application/s at a hearing.[1]
9. Accordingly the Tribunal makes the directions set out below.

Directions
(1) The application/s is/are to be dealt with on the fast track/standard track/without a hearing and on the basis of a consideration of documents and written representations only.
(2) On or before ____________ 200_, the applicant shall prepare a Bundle of documents relevant to the application/s and send four copies to the Tribunal and one copy to the respondent. The Bundle shall include:

(a) A statement setting out the full grounds for the application/s including:

(i) Identify the service charge provisions in the lease.
(ii) Evidence of service charge accounts and payments, including the percentage of the service charge costs payable by each lessee.
(iii) What is regarded as reasonable alternative figures for the costs in dispute.
(iv) Any legal submissions in support of the application.

(b) Copies of all documents the applicant wishes the Tribunal to consider at the determination of the application/s including:

(i) The application/s to the Tribunal and all documents lodged with the application/s.
(ii) A copy of any written quotation received or alternative figures in (a)(iii) above.

(iii) Copies of any relevant correspondence between the applicant and the respondent.

The Bundle will be regarded as the applicant's case.

(3) On or before __________ 200_, the respondent shall prepare a Bundle of documents relevant to the application/s and send four copies to the Tribunal and one copy to the applicant. The Bundle shall include:

(a) A statement in response to (2) above setting out fully the grounds for opposing the application/s.

(b) Copies of all documents the respondent wishes the Tribunal to consider at the determination of the application/s not already included in the applicant's Bundle.

The Bundle will be regarded as the respondent's case.

(4) The applicant/s will prepare a brief Response to (3) above identifying those issues now agreed and those still in dispute with reasons. The Response should be in a file, indexed and numbered page by page. It must include a copy of the application/s, all relevant information and supporting documentary evidence which are to be considered by the Tribunal. It should also include the Report or Proof of Evidence of any Expert Witness. Four copies must be sent to the Tribunal and one copy to the respondent/s by ________________ 200_. This Response will be regarded as the applicant/s case.

(5) The parties shall seek to limit the use of expert witnesses to one witness for each party. A statement setting out the substance of the evidence of any witness whom either party wishes to call, whether as an expert or witness of fact, shall be served on the other party by __________ 200_.

(6) The person whom the applicant/s desire to be appointed the manager shall be called to give evidence at the hearing on matters relevant to being a manager, such as qualifications, experience and terms of employment. A written statement in this respect must be included in the Response in (4) above.

(7) The parties shall agree a single Bundle of documents relevant to the outstanding issues in the applications. It must be filed, indexed and numbered page by page, and the applicant/s shall no later than _____________ 200_ send one copy to the respondent and 4 copies to the Tribunal. The Bundle shall contain the application/s lease and other documents filed in support of the application/s; supplemental statement in support of the applicant's case together with the statements of case in answer and reply; any documents on which either party wishes to rely, and any witness statements lodged in accordance with these directions.

(8) The parties should note that at the hearing the Tribunal will consider whether the respondent should reimburse the applicant with the whole or part of the fees paid in these proceedings[2]. The parties if they wish should make representations on this in their bundles/at or before the hearing.

(9) The hearing of the application/s will be on _________ 200_ at 9.45am/1:30pm continuing on ________ 200_ if necessary at 10 Alfred Place,

London WC1E 7LR. The Tribunal will inspect the subject premises at 10:30am on the same day. The Tribunal will make arrangements with the parties at the hearing if they wish to inspect the premises. The hearing is expected to last no more than _______ day/s.

(10) Letters/documents should not be sent to the Tribunal unless they have been copied to the other party and this is noted on each letter/document.

Non-compliance with the Tribunal's Directions may result in prejudice to a party's case. In particular, failure to provide evidence as directed may result in the Tribunal deciding to debar the defaulter from relying on such evidence at the full hearing. In the case of the Applicant non-compliance could result in dismissal of the application/s in accordance with regulation 11 of the Leasehold Valuation Tribunal (Procedure) (England) Regulations 2003.

Chairman: ______________________________

Date: ________________________________

[1] Leasehold Valuation Tribunals (Procedure) (England) Regulations 2003 SI 2003 No. 2099. reg 13.

[2] Leasehold Valuation Tribunals (Fees) (England) Regulations 2003 SI 2003 No. 2098 reg 9.

PRECEDENT: APPLICANT'S STATEMENT OF CASE (LEASEHOLD VALUATION TRIBUNAL)

C3–001

Case No. LON/00AE/LAC/2005/9999

IN THE LEASEHOLD VALUATION TRIBUNAL

IN THE MATTER of Flat 14, Tanfield Mansions, London N5 3DR

AND IN THE MATTER of The Landlord and Tenant Act 1985

BETWEEN: MS CONSTANCE BROWN (Applicant) and
THE BROOKHOUSE PROPERTY TRUST LIMITED (Respondent)

APPLICANT'S STATEMENT OF CASE

1. This statement is prepared pursuant to paragraph (2)(a) of the Tribunal's directions dated 31 October 2005. Also pursuant to those directions, a bundle of relevant documents is attached and references are to tab numbers within that bundle.
2. The Applicant is the leaseholder owner of Flat 14, Tanfield Mansions, London N5 3DR ("the Property") pursuant to a lease dated 25 June 1985 and granted for a term of 125 years from 1 July 1985 ("the Lease"). A copy of the Lease appears at tab 1. The Respondent is the freehold owner of Tanfield Mansions ("the Building") in which there are 35 flats.
3. The leaseholders of flats 1 and 3, Tanfield Mansions have brought related applications under applications number LON/LIS/00AA/2005/1234.
4. The Applicant seeks a determination under section 27A of the Landlord and Tenant Act 1985 ("the Act") as to the amount of service charges payable for the financial year 1 April 2004 to 31 March 2005. A copy of the service charge demand for this period dated 25 April 2005 and the landlord's service charge accounts for 2004/5 appear at tab 2.
5. The items of service charge which are in issue are as follows;
   1) Cost of major works to the roof and front elevation ("the Major Works"): £123,456
   2) Insurance: £17,890
   3) Legal Costs: £3,210
6. The Applicant accepts her liability to pay the remainder of the service charges set out in the said demand and in the sum of £750. Further and in respect of the above items the Applicant accepts that she is liable to pay £250 in respect of the major works and £100 in respect of insurance. Consequently, the Applicant seeks a determination that she is liable to pay service charges of £1,100 for the period 2004/5.

The Lease

7. Clause 5(d) of the Lease provides for the recovery of "Service Charges". Clause 5(e) provides that the annual amount of the "Service Charge" payable by the Applicant is 1/35 of the aggregate of the expenses referred to in the sixth schedule to the Lease incurred by the landlord in any one year. The sixth schedule of the Lease sets out what expenses can be recovered as "Service Charges". The expenses are those incurred by the landlord in complying with its repairing obligations in clauses 6(b) to (e) and in insuring the Building.

The Major Works

8. The Major Works were carried out in February 2005 and involved works to the roof and front elevation of the Building. The Applicant does not dispute the liability to pay service charges in respect of such works, which the Applicant accepts fall within the landlords obligations contained in clauses 6(b) and (c) of the Lease i.e. to keep in repair the structure and exterior of the flat and the building and to make good any defects affecting the structure and to keep in good repair and condition the communal areas.

Section 20 Consultation

9. The Respondent served a notice of intention to carry out the Major Works dated 1 November 2004 pursuant to section 20 of the Act and paragraph 1 of Schedule 4 to the Service Charges (Consultation Requirements) (England) Regulations 2003 ("the Regulations"). A copy of the said notice appears at tab 3.

10. On or around 15 November 2004 the Applicant telephoned the Respondent's managing agent and proposed Mr. John Wayne as a person from whom the Respondent should try and obtain an estimate for the carrying out of the proposed works.

11. By letter dated 16 December 2005, the Respondent's managing agents wrote to the Applicant and informed her that all the estimates, which had been obtained were available for inspection at their offices. A copy of the said letter appears at tab 4.

12. Due to work commitments, the Applicant did not inspect the estimates, which had been obtained and does not know the identity of the person or persons who carried out the major works.

13. In the premises, the Respondent failed to comply with the consultation requirements of section 20 of the Act and the Regulations in that it did not serve a statement under paragraph 4(5)(b) of Part 2 of Schedule 4 of the Regulations. Consequently, it is averred that the Applicant's contribution towards the Major Works should be limited to £250 pursuant to section 20(1) of the Act.

Insurance

14. A copy of the certificate of insurance for the Building appears at tab 5. This shows that the annual premium paid by the Respondent in respect of insurance for the Building is £17,890. No quotations for insurance have been provided by the Respondent and it is believed that only one quotation was obtained.
15. At tab 6 appear four quotes which the Applicant has obtained from reputable insurers, which range from £3,500 to £7,000.
16. In the premises, it is averred that the insurance premium of £17,890 is excessive and, as such, was not reasonably incurred.

Legal Costs

17. The Respondent has included within the service charge account the sum of £3,210 in respect of legal costs. Legal costs are not included in the sixth schedule to the Lease and therefore are not recoverable as service charges.

Section 20C Application

18. In the event that the tribunal decides that there is provision in the Lease to recover legal costs, the Applicant asks that the tribunal to make an order preventing the Respondent from seeking to recover the costs of this application as part of the service charges for the following reasons;
    1) The Respondent has behaved improperly and/or unreasonably in that it has failed to reply to letters from the Applicant dated 25 March 2005, 24 June 2005 and 29 September 2005, copies of which appear at tab 7;
    2) The Applicant has paid £1,100 in respect of the undisputed service charges; and
    3) The Respondent has refused an offer to mediate contained in the Applicant's letter of 10 October 2005, a copy of which appears at tab 8.

Elaine Barristor

STATEMENT OF TRUTH

The Applicant believes that the facts stated in this statement of case are true.

Signed: **Kevin Moore**
Name: KEVIN MOORE
Position: Solicitor, Breef & Co solicitors
Date: 7 November 2005

PRECEDENT: RESPONDENT'S STATEMENT OF CASE (LEASEHOLD VALUATION TRIBUNAL)

Case No. LON/00AE/LAC/2005/9999 **C4–001**

IN THE LEASEHOLD VALUATION TRIBUNAL

IN THE MATTER of Flat 14, Tanfield Mansions, London N5 3DR

AND IN THE MATTER of The Landlord and Tenant Act 1985

BETWEEN: MS CONSTANCE BROWN (Applicant) and
THE BROOKHOUSE PROPERTY TRUST LIMITED (Respondent)

RESPONDENT'S STATEMENT OF CASE

1. Paragraph 1 of the Applicant's Statement of Case is noted. This Reply is prepared pursuant to paragraph 3(b) of the directions and a bundle of documents is attached hereto.
2. Paragraphs 2 and 3 are admitted.
3. Paragraph 4 is noted. The respondent relies on the demand attached at Tab 2 in the Applicant's bundle of documents.
4. Paragraphs 5 and 6 are noted.

The Lease

5. As to paragraph 7, it is admitted that:

    i) the Applicant is obliged to pay 1/35th of the aggregate of the expenses referred to in the sixth schedule;
    ii) the sixth schedule sets out what expenses can be recovered as service charges;
    iii) that schedule includes expenses incurred by the landlord in complying with its repairing covenants under clauses 6(b) to (e) and in insuring the building.

    but it is averred that paragraph 8 of the sixth schedule also makes reference to "professional fees properly incurred in connection with the management of the building".

Major works

6. As to paragraph 8, the Major Works commenced in February 2005 but carried on until June of that year. It is admitted that they consisted of works to the roof and front elevation of the building. The Applicant's acceptance of her liability to pay service charges is noted.
7. Paragraph 9 is admitted.

8. Paragraph 10 is admitted. However the Applicant was the only person to nominate Mr Wayne. By contrast three tenants nominated a Mr Errol Flynn, and so, in accordance with sub-paragraph 4(3)(a) of Part 2 of Schedule 4 to the Regulations ("Part 2"), the Respondent sought and obtained an estimate from Mr Flynn.

9. Paragraph 11 is admitted. The said letter was written in accordance with the obligation contained in sub-paragraph 4(5)(c) of Part 2.

10. If which is not admitted paragraph 12 is correct, the Applicant's failure is through no fault of the Respondent. The person who undertook the work was Mr Flynn.

11. It is admitted that the Respondent did not supply a statement under Rule 4(5)(b) of Part 2 ("a paragraph b statement"). The Respondent invites the Tribunal to dispense with the requirement to supply a statement under section 20ZA of the Act on the following grounds:

    i) The Respondent in fact received no observations under paragraph 3 of Part 2;
    ii) a paragraph b statement would thus have served the sole purpose of setting out the amount specified in 2 of the estimates;
    iii) the estimates were in any event on display in the Respondent's office, which was adjacent to the building and was open until 8pm every night except Sunday;
    iv) the Respondent did in fact use the services of the builder who received most nominations from the tenants;
    v) in the premises, it is reasonable to dispense with the requirement of a paragraph b statement.

12. A form of application to dispense with the consultation requirements under section 20ZA of the Act accompanies this statement of case.

Insurance

13. Paragraph 14 is admitted. The Respondent uses the services of Dodge and Weave Underwriters who supply a block policy in relation to all the Respondent's properties. The block policy has been obtained in the ordinary course of business and the underwriters are respectable and in the circumstances even if (which is not admitted) the quotes obtained by the Applicant are genuine and provide for like cover, the charge for insurance is reasonably incurred.

14. Save as aforesaid, paragraphs 15 and 16 are denied.

Legal Costs

15. As to paragraph 17, legal costs fall within the scope of "professional fees properly incurred in the management of the building" within the meaning of paragraph 8 of the sixth schedule, and accordingly are recoverable as service charges. Paragraph 17 is therefore denied.

16. The Respondent resists the Applicant's request for an order under s.20C. As to the reasons given:

    i) receipt of the letters of 25th March 2005 and 24th June 2005 is denied. The Respondent did reply to the letter of 29th September 2005 by making a telephone call to the Applicant;
    ii) the payment of undisputed service charges is not a reason to dispense with an entitlement to legal costs;
    iii) there was no refusal to mediate. The Respondent acknowledged the request and was considering it but events were superseded by this Application.

ARTHUR BRAIN

STATEMENT OF TRUTH
The Respondent believes that the facts stated in this statement of case are true.

Signed: **Paul Green**
Name: Paul Green
Position: Solicitor, Lore & Co solicitors
Date: 22 November 2005

PRECEDENT: NOTICE OF APPEAL TO LANDS TRIBUNAL FROM A DECISION OF THE LEASEHOLD VALUATION TRIBUNAL

C5–001 **LANDS TRIBUNAL** **LR / /**

NOTICE OF APPLICATION FOR PERMISSION TO APPEAL / NOTICE OF APPEAL AGAINST A DECISION OF A LEASEHOLD VALUATION TRIBUNAL

First open out the whole sheet, then read the notes opposite the form

1. Type of Case
← *[see Note 1 opposite]*
This appeal relates to a decision of Leasehold Valuation Tribunal concerning: (☑ *tick one*)

A. ☐ Leasehold enfranchisement **B.** ☑ Other matters

2. Name of Applicant/Appellant...*Ms Constance Brown*...........................
← *[see Note 2 opposite]*
Address:...............*Flat 14, Tanfield Mansions, London N5 3DR*...................

....

....

Telephone No. ....*0207 123 4567*........ Fax No. ....

3. **Name of Applicant/Appellant's solicitors or other representative .** Mr. Kevin Moore.
← *[see Note 3 opposite]*
Address:...............*Breef & Co solicitors, 100 Equity Street, London N5 3XD*

....

....

Telephone No. .....*0207 121 3141*..Fax No. *0207 891 0111*..Status..*Solicitor*..

4. Name(s) and address(es) of potential Respondent(s) and their representative(s)
← *[see Note 4 opposite]*
Name:..................*The Brookhouse Property Trust Limited*...........................
Address:...............*Property House, Land Street, London N5 3PT* ....
.............................*c/o. Lore & Co Solicitors, 66 Fieldsend Court,*..................
.............................*London WC1R 1BJ*...
Telephone No. .... *0207 111 1111*.........Fax No. ....*0207 222 2222*.................

5. Description & Address of the property ...*Flat within a mansion block*
← *[see Note 5 opposite]*
Address:...............*Flat 14, Tanfield Mansions, London N5 3DR*...................

....

....

6. Leasehold Valuation Tribunal Details
🡐 *[see Note 6 opposite]*

6A. Name of Leasehold Valuation Tribunal.........*London*.........................

6B. LVT Appeal Number..................... *LON/00AE/LAC/2005/9999*.........

6C. Date when main LVT Decision was sent to Applicant/Appellant........
20 December 2005..

7. Date when LVT Decision granting or refusing permission to appeal was sent to Applicant/Appellant *[see Note A opposite]* 🡒

Date....3 January 2006......☐ Permission granted........☑ Permission refused

8. Grounds of appeal *[see Note B opposite]* 🡒
The Leasehold Valuation Tribunal erred in law in construing paragraph 8 of the sixth ...... schedule to the lease in that legal costs are not.. "professional fees properly incurred in the management of the building" ....

....

....

9. Reasons for application for permission to appeal
[see Note C opposite] 🡒

(☑ tick one or more boxes)
(a) ☑ The decision shows that the LVT wrongly interpreted or wrongly applied the relevant law
(b) ☐ The decision shows that the LVT wrongly applied or misinterpreted or disregarded a relevant principle of valuation or other professional practice
(c) ☐ The LVT took account of irrelevant considerations, or failed to take account of relevant consideration or evidence, or there was a substantial procedural defect
(d) ☐ The point or points at issue is or are of potentially wide implications
(e) ☐ Reasons other than (a) to (d) above

10. Extension of time *[see Note D opposite]* 🡒

Have more than 28 days elapsed since the date at 7 above ☐ yes ☑ No

If so, you will need to ask for permission to proceed out of time. Apply by ticking this box: ☐
and giving the reasons for lateness here:

....

....

....

11. Type of Procedure Arrangements (if permission to appeal is granted)
[see Note E] ➔
(☑ *tick one or box on each line)*

11A Do you intend to call an expert witness at the hearing of the appeal? Yes ☐ No ☑

11B Do you intend to apply for permission to call more than one expert witness at the hearing of the appeal? Yes ☐ No ☑

11C Which type of procedure do you wish to be used in this appeal?
Standard procedure ☑ Special procedure ☐ Simplified procedure ☐ Written representation procedure ☐

12. Fees *[see Note F opposite]* ➔
Have you enclosed:.................the appeal fee of £50? Yes ☑ No ☐
................the application for permission fee of £40? Yes ☑ No ☐
................the extension of time application fee of a further £40? Yes ☐ No ☑

13. Declaration, Signature and Date *[see Note G opposite]* ➔
I accept responsibility for the conduct of the case and the payment of fees due

Signed .....*Kevin Moore* ....Name in Capitals.........*MR. KEVIN MOORE*.....
Date.........*20/1/06*.............Status............................ *Appellant's Solicitor*.....

For official use only

SPECIMEN ORDER APPOINTING A MANAGER

LEASEHOLD VALUATION TRIBUNAL **C6–001**

MANAGEMENT ORDER DATED [ ]

Re: [property]

Case Number [ ]

BETWEEN:

[ ] Applicant
[ ] Respondent

1. In this order:

   A. "The property" includes all those parts of the property known as [ ] save for those parts known as [ ].
   B. "The landlord" means [ ] or in the event of the vesting of the reversion of the residential under-leases of the property in another, the landlord's successors in title.
   C. "The manager" means [ ].

   It is hereby ordered as follows:

2. In accordance with s.24(1) of the Landlord and Tenant Act 1987 the manager shall be appointed as receiver and manager of the property.
3. The order shall continue for a period of [ ] years from the date of this order.
4. That the manager shall manage the property in accordance with:
   (a) The Directions and Schedule of Functions and Services attached to this order.
   (b) The respective obligations of the landlord and the leases and/or under-lessees by which the flats at the property are demised by the landlord and in particular with regard to repair, decoration, provision of services to and insurance of the property.
   (c) The duties of manager set out in the Service Charge Residential Management Code ("The Code") or such other replacement Code published by the Royal Institution of Chartered Surveyors and approved by the Secretary of State pursuant to section 87 of the Leasehold Reform Housing and Urban Development Act 1993.
5. No order shall be made under s.20C of the Landlord and Tenant Act 1987 that the applicants' costs before the Tribunal shall not be added to the service charges.

....

[Chairman]

[Date]

DIRECTIONS

1. That from the date of appointment and throughout the appointment the manager shall ensure that he has appropriate professional indemnity cover in the sum of at least £1,000,000 and shall provide copies of the current cover note upon a request being made by any lessee or under-lessee of the property, the landlord or the Tribunal.
2. That not later than four weeks after the date of this order the parties to this application shall provide all necessary information to and arrange with the manager an orderly transfer of responsibilities. No later than this date, the applicants and the landlords shall transfer to the manager all the accounts, books, records and funds (including without limitation, service charge reserve fund).
3. The rights and liabilities of the landlord arising under any contracts of insurance, and/or any contract for the provision of any services to the property shall upon the date four weeks from the date of this order become rights and liabilities of the manager.
4. That the manager shall account forthwith to the landlord for the payment of ground rent received by him and shall apply the remaining amounts received by him (other than those representing his fees) in the performance of the landlord's covenants contained in the said leases.
5. That he shall be entitled to remuneration (which for the avoidance of doubt shall be recoverable as part of the service charges of the underleases and/or leases of the property) in accordance with the Schedule of Functions and Services attached.
6. That at the expiry of [ ] months from the date of this order, the manager shall prepare a brief written report for the Tribunal on the progress of the management of the property up to that date and shall submit the same to the Tribunal by no later than [date].
7. That the manager shall be entitled to apply to the Tribunal for further directions in accordance with section 24(4) of the Landlord and Tenant Act 1987, with particular regard (but not limited to) the following events:
   (a) any failure by any party to comply with paragraph 2 of these directions and/or;
   (b) (if so advised) upon the service of the report in paragraph 6 of these directions, and/or;
   (c) in the event that there are insufficient sums held by him to pay the manager's remuneration.

SCHEDULE OF FUNCTIONS AND SERVICES

A. SERVICE CHARGE

1.1 Prepare an annual service charge budget, administer the service charge and prepare and distribute appropriate service charge accounts to the under-lessees as per the percentage share of under the terms of their under-lease.

1.2 Demand and collect rents, service charges, insurance premiums and any other payments due from the under-lessees. Instruct solicitors to recover unpaid rents and service charges and any other monies due to the landlord upon the landlord's instructions.

1.3 Place, supervise and administer contacts and check demands for payment for goods, services and equipment supplied for the benefit of the property within the service charge budget.

B. ACCOUNTS

2.1 Prepare and submit to the landlord an annual statement of account detailing all monies received and expended on its behalf. The accounts to be certified by an external auditor if required by the manager.

2.2 Produce for inspection, receipts or other evidence of expenditure.

2.3 All monies collected on the landlord's behalf will be accounted for in accordance with the Accounts Regulations as issued by the Royal Institution for Chartered Surveyors, subject to the manager receiving interest on the monies whilst they are in his client account. Any reserve fund monies to be held in a separate client account with interest accruing to the landlord.

C. MAINTENANCE

3.1 Deal with routine repair and maintenance issues and instruct contractors to attend and rectify problems. Deal with all building maintenance relating to the services and structure of the building.

3.2 The consideration of works to be carried out to the property in the interest of good estate management and making the appropriate recommendations to the landlord and the under-lessees.

3.3 The setting up of a planned maintenance programme to allow for the periodic re-decorations of the exterior and interior common parts are and other.

D. FEES

4.1 Fees for the above mentioned management services would be a basic fee of £175 per annum per unit for the flats within the property. Those services to include the services set out in paragraph 2.5 of the Service Charge Residential Management Code published by the RICS.

4.2 Major works carried out to the property (where it is necessary to prepare a specification of works, obtain competitive tenders, serve relevant notices on lessees informing them of the works and supervising the works) will be subject to a charge of 10% of the cost (subject to a minimum fee of £250.00). This in respect of the professional fees of an architect, surveyor, or other appropriate person in the administration of a contract for such works.

4.3 If required to act in the capacity of Company Secretary an additional fee of £250 per annum will be charged.

4.4 An additional charge for dealing with solicitors enquires on transfer will be made on a time related basis payable by the outgoing lessee.

4.5 VAT to be payable on all the fees quoted above, where appropriate, at the rate prevailing on the date of invoicing.

4.6 The preparation of insurance valuations and the undertaking of other tasks which fall outside those duties described at 4.1 above, are to be charged for on a fee basis to be agreed.

E. COMPLAINTS PROCEDURE

5.1 The manager shall operate a complaints procedure in accordance with the requirements of the Royal Institution of Chartered Surveyors. Details of the procedure are available from the institution on request.

Appendix D

County Court Precedents

Particulars of Claim (Basic Debt Claim)

D1–001

NEW BUILDING LIMITED (claimant) and
BAD INVESTMENTS LIMITED (defendant)

PARTICULARS OF CLAIM

1. The Claimant is the freehold owners of a residential block of flats at 3 Long Acre, London NW2 ('the Building').
2. By a lease dated 16th January 2002 ('the Lease') the Claimant let Flat 6 within the Building ('the Flat') to the Defendant for a term of 999 years commencing 16th January 2002 at an annual rent of £100 payable in advance on 25th March in each year. A copy of the Lease is attached at Schedule 1.
3. The Lease provides for payment by the lessee of a Service Charge as defined in the 4th Schedule thereto.
4. Under the Lease the Defendant covenanted and agreed as follows

    4.1. To pay the respective yearly and other rents [clause 2(1)];
    4.2. To pay to the Landlord by way of Service Charge such yearly sum as shall represent a fair and reasonable proportion of the annual service costs (being the proportion of the floor area that the flat bears to the floor area of all flats in the Building) estimated by the Landlord to be incurred for the following twelve months together with the same proportion of the Reserve Fund[clause 4(iv)]
    4.3. On the 24th day of June next following the preparation by the Landlord of an Annual Service Account there shall be paid by the Tenant to the Landlord or refunded by the Landlord to the Tenant as the case may be the difference (if any) between the total of all Service Charge payments (except those attributable to the Reserve Fund) paid by the Tenant and the amount of the Tenant's proper proportion. [clause 4(v)]
    4.4. To pay interest on any rent in arrear or other sum due under the lease whether the same has been demanded or not at the rate of 3 per centum per annum above the Base Lending Rate

of Barclays Bank Plc on a day to day basis from the date that the such sum fell due until the date of actual payment whether before or after judgment and such interest shall for all purposes be treated as rent in arrear. [clause 2(12)]

5. Further by clause 2.7 of the Lease the Defendant covenanted and agreed to pay on an indemnity basis all costs charges fees disbursements and expenses (including the fees of Solicitors and Counsel) incurred by the landlord for the purpose of or incidental to any breach of any of the stipulations and covenants on the part of the tenant including the cost of proceedings and in respect of the recovery of arrears of rent (including service charge recoverable as rent).
6. The Claimant will refer to the lease at any trial hereof as to its full terms their meaning and effect.
7. In breach of the covenants referred to above the Defendant has failed to pay Service Charge as follows:

Year Ending 31st March 2002	£740.46
Year Ending 31st March 2003	£6,845.07
Year Ending 31st March 2004	£851.97
Total:	**£8,537.50**

8. Copies of the Annual Service Accounts and written demands for payment are attached hereto at Schedule 2.
9. The Claimant claims and is entitled to interest on the above sums under clause 2(12) of the lease at the rate of 3 per centum per annum above the Base Lending Rate of Barclays Bank Plc on a day to day basis from the date that the such sums fell due until payment. Particulars of interest claimed are set out in the schedule of interest annexed hereto.
10. In the alternative the Claimant claims interest pursuant to section 69 of the County Courts Act 1984 at the rate of 8% per annum or alternatively at such rate and for such period as the Court deems fit.

AND THE CLAIMANT CLAIMS

1. The sum of £8,537.50;
2. In the alternative damages for breach of covenant (not exceeding £15,000);
3. Interest pursuant to clause 2(ix) of the lease or alternatively section 69 of the County Courts Act 1984.
4. Costs to be assessed on an indemnity basis in accordance with clause 2(7) of the lease.

A BARRISTER

STATEMENT OF TRUTH

The Claimant believes that the facts stated in this Particulars of Claim are true.

Defence and Part 20 Claim (Basic Debt Claim)

NEW BUILDING LIMITED (Claimant/Part 20 Defendant ("Claimant")) and BAD INVESTMENTS LIMITED (Defendant/Part 20 Claimant ("Defendant")) **D2–001**

DEFENCE AND COUNTERCLAIM

DEFENCE

1. Paragraphs 1to 5 of the Particulars of Claim are admitted.
2. As to paragraph 6 of the Particulars of Claim the Defendant will do likewise.
3. The Defendant denies that the Claimant is entitled to the sums claimed by reason of the matters set out below.

Year end March 2002

4. On 19th December 2001 the Leasehold Valuation Tribunal determined in proceedings numbered LON/2000/839 between the Defendant (and others) (as Applicant) and the Claimant (as Respondent) that service charges claimed for the year ending March 2001 had been unreasonably incurred in accordance with s.19 of the Landlord and Tenant Act 1985. The Defendant's proportion of such costs was £750.
5. The Defendant had paid in full the service charges demanded for the year ending March 2001 and in correspondence thereafter requested the Claimant to credit the Defendant's service charge account with the £750 overpaid. The Claimant wrongfully refused and failed so to do.
6. The Defendant contends that it is not obliged to pay £720 claimed for the year ending March 2002 because:

   (i) On a true interpretation of the lease the obligation upon the landlord at clause 4(5) of the lease to refund sums paid by the tenant in excess of its "proper proportion" include sums paid in respect of service charges unreasonably incurred;

   (ii) The sum of £750 paid by the Defendant for the year ending March 2001 was paid under a mistake of fact and/or law the Defendant at the time believing that the same was due whereby the Defendant is entitled to repayment of the same and to set-off such sum against the sum claimed for the year ending March 2002 and hereby seeks to set-off such sum.

Year ending March 2003

7. By clause 3.4 of the lease the Claimant covenanted and agreed that prior to carrying out "major works" (being defined as works for which the cost will exceed £5000) it would provide a detailed breakdown of

the works involved and obtain and provide to the lessee 2 estimates and seek the lessee's approval to the same (such approval not to be unreasonably withheld).

8. In the circumstances the obligation to provide a breakdown and obtain 2 estimates and seek approval was a condition precedent to the Defendant's liability to pay service charge in respect of major works.

9. In breach of its obligations referred to in paragraph 3 above the Claimant failed to provide a breakdown and/or 2 estimates and seek the Defendant's approval prior to carrying out the works the subject of the sum claimed for the year ending 31st March 2003 namely £6,845.07.

10. By reason thereof the Defendant is not liable to pay £6,845.07 in respect of year ending 31st March 2003 as alleged or at all.

11. Further or in the alternative the Claimant failed to comply with the provisions of section 20 of the Landlord and Tenant Act 1985 whereby the Defendant's liability for service charges for the works the subject of the demand for year ending 31st March 2003 is limited to £250 in any event.

Year ending March 2004

12. On 24th June 2003 the Defendant sent a cheque made out to the Claimant in the sum of £851.97 (and numbered 8899001122) to the Claimant's managing agents.

13. The cheque has been returned erroneously on the basis that to accept the same would waive the right to forfeit for non-payment of earlier service charges.

14. In the circumstances the sum of £851.97 has been paid and/or tendered and in accordance with CPR 37.3 the Defendant at the time of filing this defence has paid £851.97 into Court.

Interest

15. By reason of the matters above no sums are due to the Claimant whereby the claim for interest is denied.

Costs

16. Whilst it is admitted that the lease contains an indemnity costs clause it is denied that the Claimant is entitled to its costs on an indemnity basis. These proceedings were issued without any warning letter by the Claimant. The Defendant has written numerous letters to the Claimant seeking to resolve the matter and suggesting that if it cannot be agreed an application should be made to the Leasehold Valuation Tribunal to determine what sums if any are due. In such circumstances the Defendant will rely on the above matters in support of an application that the Claimant pay its costs on an indemnity basis.

Set off

17. As set out above the Defendant seeks to set-off against the Claimants claim herein such sums as it is awarded on its counterclaim in extinction or diminution thereof.

COUNTER CLAIM

18. Paragraphs 1 to 17 above are repeated.
19. As set out in paragraphs 4 to 6 of the Defendant the Defendant has paid to the Claimant £750 under a mistake of fact and/or law whereby the Claimant has been unjustly enriched at the expense of the Defendant.
20. By reason of the matters above the Defendant claims and is entitled to payment of £750.
21. Further the Claimant claims interest on the sum of £750 pursuant to section 69 of the County Courts Act 1984 at such rate and for such period as the Court deems fit.

AND THE DEFENDANT COUNTERCLAIMS

1. The sum of £750;
2. In the alternative damages;
3. Interest pursuant to section 69 of the County Courts Act 1984.
4. Costs to be assessed on an indemnity basis or as determined by the Court.

A BARRISTER

STATEMENT OF TRUTH
The Defendant believes that the facts stated in this Defence and Counterclaim are true.

Particulars of Claim (Business Tenancy)

D3–001

A BUSINESS LIMITED (Claimant) and
A TRADER LIMITED (Defendant)

PARTICULARS OF CLAIM

1. The Claimant is the leasehold owner entitled to possession of warehouse premises situate at and know as 101 Fire Street London SE1. ("the premises").
2. The premises are business premises and do not include or comprise a dwelling-house and in the circumstances this claim does not relate to residential property.
3. By an underlease dated 15th May 2000 ("the lease") made between the Claimant's predecessors in title The Busy Property Trust Plc (as landlord) and the Defendant (as tenant) the premises were demised to the Defendant for a term of 21 years expiring on 14th May 2021 on the following rents namely:
   - (i) Firstly an initial annual rent of £20,000 payable in advance by equal quarterly payments on the usual quarter days;
   - (ii) Secondly by way of further rent on demand such sum as the landlord may expend on insuring the premises;
   - (iii) Thirdly by way of further rent 50% of such sum as the landlord may expend in each service charge year (being the year ending 24th June) on repairing and maintaining the building containing the premises, such sum to certified by the landlord's surveyor as having been expended in accordance with the terms of the lease as soon as practicable after 24th June in each year and such sum to be payable in full without any deduction within 14 days of being demanded;
   - (iv) Fourthly and by way of further rent on demand all costs charges and expenses that the landlord may from time to time incur in connection with any breach of covenant on the part of the tenant.
4. The reversion expectant upon determination of the lease has at all material times been and remains vested in the Claimant.
5. The lease contains amongst others the following covenants on the part of the tenant:
   - (i) By clause 3.1 to pay the rents reserved in the manner provided for;
   - (ii) By clause 3.7 to pay on an indemnity basis all costs charges fees disbursements and expenses (including the fees of Solicitors and Counsel) incurred by the landlord for the purpose of or incidental to any breach of any of the stipulations and covenants on the part of the tenant including the cost of proceedings.

6. Clause 5.1 of the lease contains a proviso for re-entry entitling the Claimant to forfeit the lease and re-enter the premises in the event (amongst others) that the rent reserved or any part thereof is in arrear for 21 days after the same has become due whether legally demanded or not such forfeiture being without prejudice to any right of action in respect of any antecedent breach of covenant.
7. Clauses 5.1.1 and 1.1(m) of the lease provide that the Defendant shall pay interest on any rent in arrear or other sum due under the lease whether the same has been demanded or not at the rate of 3 per centum per annum above the Base Lending Rate of Barclays Bank Plc on a day to day basis from the date that the such sum fell due until the date of actual payment whether before or after judgment and such interest shall for all purposes be treated as rent in arrear.
8. In breach of the covenant referred to at paragraph 5(i) aforesaid the Defendant is in arrears of rent and service charges (due as rent).

PARTICULARS

Rent due on 24th June 2004	£5,000.00
Service charge as rent demanded 25th August 2004	£6,750.00
Rent due 29th September 2004	£5,000.00
Insurance demanded 15th October 2004	£3,457.54
Rent due 25th December 2004	£5,000.00
Rent due 25th March 2005	£5,000.00
Rent due 24th June 2005	£5,000.00

9. By reason thereof the lease has become liable to be forfeited to the Claimant and by these proceedings is forfeit whereby the Claimant claims and is entitled to possession of the premises.
10. Further the Claimant claims and is entitled to interest on the arrears of rent set out at paragraph 8 above by reason of the covenants pleaded at paragraph 7 above and as provided for therein. Details of such interest are set out in the schedule annexed hereto.
11. In the alternative the Claimant seeks interest on the said sums pursuant to section 69 of the County Courts Act 1984 at such rate and for such period as the Court deems fit.
12. The Claimant is not aware of any person entitled to relief against forfeiture as underlessee or mortgagee.
13. The open market letting value of the premises is £54.79 per day and the Claimant claims and is entitled to damages at such rate in respect of the Defendant's continued occupation of the premises from the date hereof until possession is given up or alternative at such rate and for such period as the Court deems fit.

14. The Claimant seeks its costs of and in connection with this claim on an indemnity basis in accordance with the clause referred to in paragraph 5(ii) aforesaid.

15. The daily rate at which the rent set out in paragraph 3(i) is to be calculated is £54.79 per day. The other rents are of varying amounts and a daily rate cannot be stated.

16. In the event that the Defendant seeks or is granted relief from forfeiture the Claimant contends that in order to obtain such relief the Defendant must pay all of the following sums:

    (i) All rents in arrear (including insurance premium and service charge) up to the date that the issue of the obtaining of relief from forfeiture is determined and all rents falling due thereafter until all terms of relief are complied with; and
    (ii) All interest accrued as provided for in paragraph 7 above (which forms part of the "rent" payable under the terms of the lease); and
    (iii) The costs of and in connection with these proceedings (which in any event forms part of the "rent" payable under the terms of the lease) to be assessed on an indemnity basis. (If a figure for costs is required prior to the hearing of this case the Claimant's solicitor will provide the same if a written request is made).

17. Save for the Defendant herein the Claimant is not aware of any other person who is in possession of the premises.

18. The value of the Claim exceeds £15,000.00.

AND THE CLAIMANT CLAIMS:

1. Possession of the premises;
2. £35,207.54 arrears of rent;
3. Interest as set out for in paragraphs 10 or alternative 11 above;
4. If appropriate damages in respect of the Defendant's continued occupation of the premises as set out in paragraph 13 above;
5. Costs on an indemnity basis.

A BARRISTER

STATEMENT OF TRUTH

The Claimant believes that the facts stated in these Particulars of Claim are true.

Defence and Part 20 Claim (Business Tenancy)

A BUSINESS LIMITED (Claimant/Part 20 Defendant) and A TRADER LIMITED (Defendant/Part 20 Claimant) **D4–001**

DEFENCE AND PART 20 CLAIM

DEFENCE

1. Paragraphs 1 and 2 are admitted. The Defendant is in the business of importing and distributing computer and other electronic equipment and uses the warehouse (as the Claimant knows) for the purpose of storage of such equipment before onward transportation to retail outlets around the UK.
2. Paragraph 3 is admitted but it is averred, in so far as the Claimant alleges otherwise, that the use of the words "without any deduction" in relation to the payment of service charges is ineffective to preclude the Defendant's right to raise an equitable set-off as set out herein. Further, it is an implied term of the lease that the Claimant would only be entitled to recover service charges in so far as the same were reasonably incurred.
3. Paragraphs 4, 5, 6 and 7 are admitted.
4. The lease contained the following additional clauses:
   - 4.1. by clause 4.3, an obligation on the part of the Claimant to keep in good repair the structure and exterior of the premises, including *inter alia* the roof thereof;
   - 4.2. by clause 4.7, an obligation on the part of the Claimant to permit the Defendant quiet enjoyment of the demised premises.
5. In breach of the aforesaid obligations, the Claimant has permitted the roof of the premises to fall into disrepair, with the result that rain-water has entered the warehouse and has caused irreparable damage to certain items of the Defendant's equipment stored therein as more particularly set out below:

PARTICULARS OF LOSS AND DAMAGE

5.1.	12 x Toshiba XP90 computers at a value of £2499 each, amounting to	£29,988.00
5.2.	6 x Sony Panasonic "Voyeur" Video Cameras at £899 each, amounting to	£5,394.00
5.3.	27 x Nintendo X-box Game Consoles at £129.99 each, amounting to	£3,509.73
	TOTAL	**£38,891.73**

6. As to paragraph 8:
   - 6.1. it is admitted that the payments of rent referred to have not been made;

6.2. it is further admitted that the payment of service charge demanded on 25th August 2004 has not been made, but averred that the said service charge was not reasonably incurred in that it purported to relate to repairs carried out to the roof and as set out herein those repairs were not properly effected. Further, even if they had been properly effected the sums claimed were not reasonable;

6.3. it is further admitted that the payment of insurance demanded on 15th October 2004 has not been made, but no admissions are made as to whether the Claimant has expended the sum claimed or any sum on the insurance of the premises and the Claimant is put to proof thereof;

6.4. in any event, the Defendant is entitled to set off and hereby does set off in diminution or extinction of any liability which is admitted herein or established at trial the sums set out in paragraph 5 above.

7. Further, the condition of the premises and in particular the roof thereof was discussed at a meeting between Mr Smith on the part of the Claimant and Mr Jones on the part of the Defendant in the course of a meeting which took place at the premises on or about 15th June 2004.

8. In the course of that meeting Mr Smith assured Mr Jones that repairs would be carried out to the roof as a matter of urgency and stated that the Claimant would not seek to recover any rent or service charges from the Defendant until such repairs were complete.

9. In the premises there arose a collateral contract whereby in consideration of the Defendant's implied promise not to enforce by injunction or otherwise the terms of the lease, the Claimant agreed to a suspension of the obligation to pay rent or service charge pending the execution of proper repairs to the roof.

10. Further or alternatively, the Defendant has relied on the assurances given by Mr Smith and has acted to its detriment by a) not taking any steps to enforce the Claimant's obligations and b) arranging its affairs so as to meet the demands of other creditors over and above those of the Claimant; and in the premises the Claimant is estopped from enforcing the provisions of the lease in so far as they are inconsistent with the promise made at the meeting referred to.

11. In the premises, paragraph 9 is denied. Further or alternatively, if contrary to the Defendant's defence herein the Claimant is entitled to forfeit the lease, the Defendant hereby claims relief from forfeiture unconditionally, alternatively on such terms as the Court thinks fit.

12. The Claimant's entitlement to the relief claimed in paragraphs 10, 11, 13, 14, 15 and 16 is denied.

13. Paragraph 12 is noted. There is no underlessee or mortgagee of the premises.

14. Paragraph 17 is noted. The Defendant is the only person in occupation of the premises.

PART 20 CLAIM

15. Paragraphs 1 to 14 hereof are repeated.
16. The Defendant claims interest on all sums found to be due to it pursuant to s.69 of the *County Courts Act* 1984, at such rate and for such period as the Court thinks fit.

AND THE Defendant claims

1. Damages;
2. Interest pursuant to statute as aforesaid;
3. Insofar as may be appropriate, relief from forfeiture unconditionally or alternatively on such terms as the Court thinks fit.

ANN OTHER-BARRISTER

STATEMENT OF TRUTH

The Defendant believes that the facts stated in this Defence and Part 20 Claim are true.

Particulars of Claim (Forfeiture)

D5–001 FORM N119: PARTICULARS OF CLAIM FOR POSSESSION (RENTED RESIDENTIAL PREMISES)

CLAIM NUMBER 5CL00075

NEW BUILDINGS LIMITED (Claimant) and (1) BAD INVESTMENTS LIMITED, (2) MR. JOHN SMITH (Defendants)

1. The Claimant has a right to possession of a residential flat at:

   Flat 6, 3 Long Acre, London NW2 ('the Property').

2. To the best of the Claimant's knowledge the following persons are in possession of the property:

   The First Defendant is in possession of the property. The property is occupied by the Second Defendant who is a director of the first Defendant. The Claimant is not aware of any other person in occupation/possession of the property.

About the Tenancy

3.
   (a) The premises are let to the First Defendant~~(s)~~ under a~~(n)~~ long lease (~~tenancy~~) which began on 16th January 2002 whereby the property was let for a term of 999 years commencing 16th January 2002.
   (b) The current rent is £100 per year and is payable in advance on 25th March in each year.
   (c) Any unpaid rent or charge for use and occupation should be calculated at £0.27 per day. (The Claimant will seek damages for continued use and occupation at a market rate as set out below).

The Basis of the Claim for Possession

4. The reason the Claimant is asking for possession is:

   (a) Because the First Defendant has not paid rent and service charges due under the terms of the lease. (*Details are set out below*)(~~*Details are shown on the attached rent statement*~~)

   Unpaid service charges amounting to £8,537.50

   PARTICULARS OF ARREARS OF SERVICE CHARGES

Year Ending 31st March 2002	£740.46
Year Ending 31st March 2003	£6,845.07
Year Ending 31st March 2004	£851.97
Total:	**£8,537.50**

PARTICULARS OF UNPAID RENT

1) On 17 August 2005 in proceedings in this Court in claim numbered CTYCT007892 the Claimant following trial (at which the First Defendant did not attend and was not represented) obtained judgment against the First Defendant for unpaid service charges in the sum of £8,537.50. The Claimant also obtained judgment for interest in the sum of £1000.00 and costs of £2000.00. Interest and costs under the terms of the lease are recoverable as rent in arrears. The First Defendant has not paid the costs and interest of £3000.00.

~~(b) Because the Defendant has failed to comply with other terms of the tenancy. *Details are set out below:*~~

(c) Because: (including any (other) statutory grounds)

Forfeiture

1) Clause 5 of the lease contains a proviso for re-entry entitling the Claimant to forfeit the lease when any sum due thereunder remains unpaid for 21 days. As set out above on 17 August 2005 the Claimant entered judgment against the First Defendant for unpaid service charges in the sum of £8,537.50 and interest thereon and costs amounting to £3000.00. The First Defendant has not appealed or applied to set aside the judgment at the date hereof. A copy of the claim form, particulars of claim and judgment are attached at Schedule 1.
2) The judgment amounts to a final determination by a court for the purposes of section 81 of the Housing Act 1996 as amended by section 170 of the Commonhold and Leasehold Reform Act 2002.
3) By service of these proceedings the lease is forfeit and the Claimant claims and is entitled to possession of the property.

Claim against Second Defendant

4) The Claimant does not know on what basis the Second Defendant occupies the property but assumes it is as licensee of the First Defendant. If the Second Defendant occupies under a licence the same is not binding upon the Claimant and/or does not create any interest entitling the Second Defendant to remain in occupation of the property.
5) In any event the lease at clause 2(13) contains an absolute prohibition on assigning, sub-letting or parting with possession of all or part of the property.
6) If which the Claimant is unable to admit the Second Defendant occupies as sub-tenant (which the Second

Defendant is required to prove if it be alleged) such tenancy is "unlawful" whereby the Second Defendant is not entitled as against the Claimant to the protection of the Housing Act 1988.

7) By reason of the matters above upon forfeiture of the lease the Claimant is entitled to possession of the property as against the Second Defendant as well as the First Defendant.

5. The following steps have already been taken to recover any arrears:

See paragraph 4(c) above

Further the Claimant has served a notice in accordance with s. 146 of the Law of Property Act 1925 as set out below.

Section 146 Notice

6. The appropriate ~~(notice to quit)~~ (notice of breach of lease)~~(notice seeking possession) (notice seeking a demotion order) (*other* ....)~~ was served on the Defendant on 29th September 2005 such notice being served pursuant to section 146 of the Law of Property Act 1925 and in accordance with section 82 of the Housing Act 1996.

About the Defendant

7. The following information is known about the Defendant's circumstances: The Defendant is a limited company.

About the Claimant

8. The Claimant is asking the court to take the following financial or other information into account when making its decision whether or not to grant an order for possession: The arrears are substantial and no payment of any kind has been made for over 2 years.

Forfeiture

9.

~~(a) There is no underlessee or mortgagee entitled to claim relief against forfeiture.~~

~~or~~

(b) Swallows & Co Bank PLC of 1 Smith Street, London, EC1R 5PP is entitled to claim relief against forfeiture as underlessee or mortgagee.

The Claimant does not know whether there is any underlessee. If which is not admitted the Second Defendant occupies as underlessee technically he is entitled to apply for relief from forfeiture but any such application will be opposed as the lease prohibits underletting in any event.

Claim for use and occupation

9A By reason of the matters above the Claimant claims and is entitled as against both Defendants to damages for continued use and occupation of the property. The open market letting value of the property is £`100 per day (£36,400 per annum) and the Claimant claims and is entitled to damages at such rate from the date of service of these proceedings until possession is given up or in the alternative at such rate and for such period as the Court deems fit.

Claim for Interest

9B By clause 2(12) of the lease the First Defendant covenanted and agreed to pay interest on any rent in arrear or other sum due under the lease whether the same has been demanded or not at the rate of 3 per centum per annum above the Base Lending Rate of Barclays Bank Plc on a day to day basis from the date that the such sum fell due until the date of actual payment whether before or after judgment and such interest shall for all purposes be treated as rent in arrear. By reason thereof the Claimant claims and is entitled interest on the sums outstanding as set out in the schedule annexed hereto.

In the alternative the Claimant claims interest pursuant to section 69 of the County Courts Act 1984 at such rate and for such period as the Court deems fit.

Costs

9C by clause 2.7 of the Lease the Defendant covenanted and agreed to pay on an indemnity basis all costs charges fees disbursements and expenses (including the fees of Solicitors and Counsel) incurred by the landlord for the purpose of or incidental to any breach of any of the stipulations and covenants on the part of the tenant including the cost of proceedings and in respect of the recovery of arrears of rent (including all sums recoverable as rent). By reason thereof the Claimant will seek an order that the First and/or Second Defendant pay the costs of these proceedings on an indemnity basis.

Further and in any event the Claimant will contend that it is appropriate for costs to be assessed on an indemnity basis as no payment has been made for over 2 years and the Claimant has already had to issue proceedings to recover the arrears.

Costs of s.146 notice

9D By clause 2(8) of the lease the First Defendant covenanted and agreed to pay the costs of and incidental to the preparation and service of a notice under s.146 of the Law of Property Act 1925 such sum to be recoverable as rent in arrear. The costs of the notice referred to at paragraph 6 above were £750 and the Claimant claims and is entitled to judgment for the same as against the First Defendant.

Relief from forfeiture

9E In the event that an application is made for relief from forfeiture and in any event on the making of an order for possession under s.138 of the County Courts Act 1984 the Claimant will contend that the sum required in order to obtain relief from forfeiture will be:

i) £8,537.50 arrears of service charge as set out in paragraph 3 above; and
ii) £3000.00 costs and interest in proceedings numbered CTYCT007892; and
iii) Interest as set out in paragraph 9B above (which includes continuing interest; and
iv) The costs of the section 146 notice as set out in paragraph 9D above; and
v) The costs of these proceedings; and
vi) Such further sums in respect of service charges or otherwise as would have fallen due under the terms of the lease but for the issue and service of these proceedings.

What the court is being asked to do:

10. **The Claimant asks the court to order that the Defendants:**

(a) give the Claimant possession of the premises (the lease being forfeit);
(b) pay the unpaid rent and any charge/damages for use and occupation up to the date an order is made as set out in paragraph 9A above;
(c) pay rent and any damages/charge for use and occupation from the date of the order until the claimant recovers possession of the property as set out in paragraph 9A above;
(d) pay the claimant's costs of making this claim on an indemnity basis or as the Court deems fit by reason of the matters set out in paragraph 9C above;

and that the First Defendant

(e) pay interest as set out in paragraph 9B above on unpaid rent (including sums recoverable as rent) and use and occupation charges due hereafter.
(f) Pay £750 in respect of the costs of the section 146 notice as set out in paragraph 9D above.

A. BARRISTER

STATEMENT OF TRUTH
The Claimant believes that the facts stated in this Particulars of Claim are true.

Defence and Part 20 Claim (Forfeiture)

NEW BUILDING LIMITED (Claimant/Part 20 Defendant ("Claimant")) and (1) BAD INVESTMENTS LIMITED (First Defendant/Part 20 Claimant ("First Defendant"), (2) MR. JOHN SMITH (Second Defendant) **D6–001**

DEFENCE AND COUNTERCLAIM OF THE FIRST DEFENDANT AND ADMISSION ON THE PART OF THE SECOND DEFENDANT

DEFENCE

1. Save that it is denied that the Claimant is entitled to possession of the property and/or is entitled to forfeit the lease paragraphs 1 to 4 of the Particulars of Claim are admitted.

Defective s. 146 notice

2. As to paragraphs 5 and 6 of the Particulars of Claim whilst it is admitted that the Claimant served a notice purportedly in accordance with section 146 of the Law of Property Act 1925 and section 82 of the Housing Act 1996 it is denied that the notice was a valid notice.

3. The First Defendant contends that the Claimant has failed to serve a notice in accordance with section 146 of the Law of Property Act 1925 with the information required by section 82 of the Housing Act 1996 in that the particulars given in the said notice under section 82 of the 1996 were in very small print significantly less conspicuous than the remainder of the notice.

Waiver

4. Further and insofar as the Claimant contends that it is entitled to forfeit the lease by reason of non-payment of costs and insurance recoverable as rent or by reason of the arrears of service charge it is denied that the Claimant is entitled to forfeit the lease in any event as the Claimant has waived any right to forfeit.

5. By a written demand dated 15th September 2005 (such demand being unqualified and not headed "without prejudice") the Claimant demanded the First Defendant's proportion of the insurance payable in advance in accordance with clause 2(2) of the lease whereby the Claimant recognised the continued existence of the lease.

6. By reason thereof the Claimant has waived any right to forfeit and is not entitled to possession of the property.

7. Paragraphs 7 to 9 of the Particulars of Claim are noted. The Second Defendant is not in a position to plead to the same save that it admits that Swallow & Co Bank plc are entitled to seek relief from forfeiture if which is denied the lease is forfeit.

Money Claims

8. By reason of the matters above the Claimant's entitlement to damages for continued occupation as set out in paragraph 9A of the Particulars of Claim is denied as is its entitlement to the costs of the notice purportedly served in accordance with s. 146 of the 1925 Act as claimed in paragraph 9D of the Particulars of Claim.

9. The Claimant's entitlement to interest as set out in paragraph 9B of the Particulars of Claim is admitted.

10. Whilst it is admitted that the lease contains an "indemnity costs" clause as alleged in paragraph 9C of the Particulars of Claim it is denied that the Claimant is entitled to its costs of the Claim on an indemnity basis or at all. The matters above are repeated. Further by an open letter dated 20th September 2005 the First Defendant offered to pay all of the arrears in 42 days and offered to secure payment by way of a charge over its leasehold interest. Such open offer if accepted would have brought about payment sooner than the issue of proceedings and prevented the need for issue of proceedings.

The Second Defendant

11. For the avoidance of doubt the Second Defendant admits and avers that he occupies as licensee of the First Defendant only and therefore has no defence in the event that the Claimant establishes its right to forfeit. Further the Second Defendant does not intend to take part in these proceedings and will be bound by any decision made against the First Defendant.

COUNTER CLAIM BY THE FIRST DEFENDANT

12. Paragraphs 1 to 11 above are repeated.

13. If which is denied the Claimant is entitled to forfeit the lease the First Defendant claims and is entitled to relief from forfeiture on such terms as the Court deems appropriate.

AND THE FIRST DEFENDANT COUNTERCLAIMS:

1. Relief from Forfeiture.

STATEMENT OF TRUTH

The Defendants believe that the facts stated in this Defence and Counterclaim are true.

A BARRISTER

STATEMENT OF TRUTH

The Defendant believes that the facts stated in this Defence and Counterclaim are true.

N27—Forfeiture Order

In the CENTRAL LONDON COUNTY COURT

D7–001

Order for possession on forfeiture
(for rent arrears)

Claim No.5CL00075

LONGLEASE LIMITED Claimant

SHANE WARNOUT Defendant(s)

On 1st November 2005, Deputy District Bowden

sitting at 13–14 Park Crescent, London W1B 1HT

SEAL

heard Counsel for the Claimant and Counsel for the Defendant

and the court orders that

1. The defendant give the claimant possession of Flat 13, Lucky Mansions, Rough Street, London W1 5PC on or before 1st December 2005.
2. The defendant pay the claimant £21,000, for unpaid rent + interest ~~and £ per day from 20~~ and £100 per day from 30th November 2005 until possession is given to the claimant or payment is made under paragraph 5 below.
3. The defendant pay the claimant's costs of £1,500

   [~~The defendant pay the claimant's costs, within 14 days after they are assessed [and in the meantime pay the claimant £ on account of those costs~~]
4. The defendant pay the total of the sums mentioned above to the claimant [on or before 1st December 2005.] [~~by instalments of £ per , the first instalment to be paid to the claimant on or before 20.~~]
5. If the defendant pays the claimant the sums mentioned above on or before 1st December 2005 this order **shall have no effect and the lease will continue.**

To the defendant

The court has **ordered you to leave** the property by the date stated in paragraph 1 above. However that order **will not take effect if you pay** the arrears of rent, any use and occupation charge, and costs by the date stated above. Payment should be made to the claimant, not to the court. If you need more information about making payment, you should contact the claimant.

If you do not make the payment or leave the property, the claimant can ask the court, without a further hearing, to authorise a bailiff or Sheriff to evict you. In that case, you can apply to the court to stay the eviction; a judge will decide if there are grounds for doing so.

SHANE WARNOUT Flat 13 Lucky Mansions Rough Street London W1 5PC Ref

(If detailed assessment of costs is ordered)
The claimant will send you a copy of the bill of costs with a notice telling you what to do if you object to the amount. If you do object, the claimant will ask the court to fix a hearing to assess the amount.

(If there is an order to pay money, made in a county court)
If you do not pay the money owed when it is due and the claimant takes steps to enforce payment, the order will be registered in the Register of County Court Judgments. This may make it difficult for you to get credit. Further information about registration is available in a leaflet which you can get from any county court office.

Application Under LTA 1987

D8–001

IN THE MATTER OF PART III OF THE LANDLORD AND TENANT ACT 1987 AND IN THE MATTER OF 84 PLEASANT PARK ROAD, GREEN VILLAGE, LONDON

(1) COLIN RED, (2) SIMON YELLOW, (3) TIMOTHY BLUE, (4) JOHN GREEN, (5) 84 PLEASANT PARK ROAD MANAGEMENT LIMITED (Claimants) and (1) RICHARD WHITE, (2) LINDA WHITE (Defendants)

PARTICULARS OF CLAIM

We

Apply to the Court for the following order:

THE RELIEF SOUGHT

1. That service of the Claim Form be dispensed with.
2. That pursuant to Section 27(3) of the Landlord and Tenant Act 1927 ("the Act") the Court dispense with the requirement to serve a notice under section 27 of the Act.
3. That the person nominated by the Claimants being **84 Pleasant Park Road Management Limited** be entitled to acquire the Defendants' freehold interest in the premises at 84 Pleasant Park Road Green Village London and being the whole of the land and buildings thereon comprised in HM Land Registry Title Number K123 456 ("the premises") on such terms as may be determined by the Court pursuant to Section 33 of the Act.
4. That upon the Claimants paying into Court:
   (i) such amount as represents the value of the Defendants' interest in the premises as valued and certified by a surveyor selected by the President of the Lands Tribunal in accordance with and pursuant to section 33(2)(a) of the Act; and
   (ii) such further amount determined by the Court as being due to the Defendants from the Claimants being all the tenants in the premises in accordance with and pursuant to section 33(2)(b) of the Act;

   the Defendants' freehold interest in the premises shall vest in 84 Pleasant Park Road Management Limited absolutely.
5. The Defendants do pay the Claimants' costs of this Application to be summarily assessed by the Court together with the reasonable costs of and occasioned by the appointment of a surveyor pursuant to sub-section 33(2)(a) of the Act.
6. That the above costs to be set-off against and/or paid out from the sums paid into Court by the Claimants in respect of the sums payable

for acquisition of the Defendants' freehold interest pursuant to and in accordance with section 33 of the Act.

7. That the Court grant such further or other relief as it thinks appropriate.
8. (A complete draft of the order, which the Claimants are seeking, is annexed hereto.)

THE GROUNDS OF THE APPLICATION
The Defendants

1. The Defendants are the registered Proprietors of the freehold reversionary interest ("the freehold") in the premises at 84 Pleasant Park Road Green Village London and being the whole of the land comprising HM Land Registry Title Number K123 456 ("the premises").

The Premises

2. At the date hereof the premises consist of a building containing 4 residential flats held by the Claimants respectively as tenants of the Defendants under leases which are long leases and such flats are occupied for residential purposes whereby the premises are premises to which section 25 of the Landlord and Tenant Act 1987 ("the Act") and Part III thereof applies. The premises include 4 garages, which are demised to the Claimants respectively under their leases.

The Claimants

3. At the hereof the Claimants are "qualifying tenants" within the meaning of section 26(1) of the Act and they constitute the requisite majority of such tenants as they are all the tenants of the premises. The Claimants hold long leases of their flats (120 years from 25th December 1981) and each flat is occupied for residential purposes.

The Nominated Person

4. The person nominated by the Claimants in whom the Defendants' interest in the premises should vest pursuant to section 33 of the Act is 84 Pleasant Park Road Management Limited of [1]

Other Interested Parties

5. There are no intermediate landlords and the freehold is not subject to any mortgage/charge. All lessees of the premises are a party to this claim and the Claimants are not aware of any person other than the Claimants and Defendants herein who are likely to be affected by this application.

Attempts to locate the Defendants

6. The Defendants cannot be found. They have not been heard of since mid 1988. The Claimants have taken reasonable steps to locate the Defendants including placing advertisements in the national press and instructing an enquiry agent and notwithstanding the same the Defendants cannot be found. Further details of the steps taken are contained in the witness statement of Brian Brown, which is served herewith.

Notice under Section 27 of the Act

7. It was and is not reasonably practicable to serve a preliminary notice pursuant to Section 27 of the Act on the Defendants as they cannot be found and the Claimants have not served such notice. Further it is not reasonably practicable for the Claimants to serve any further notice or take any further steps to locate the Defendants.

The Defendants Breaches of Covenant

10. The lease to each flat in the premises is in substantially the same form. By clause 4 and the sixth schedule to the leases the landlord covenants to repair, maintain insure and manage the premises. (At the hearing of this application the same shall be referred to as to their terms and full effect).
11. The Defendants have been and are in breach of their covenants under the Claimants' leases. For at least 10 years the Defendants have failed to repair, maintain, insure or manage the premises or have any dealings with them whatsoever. The lessees have had to insure repair maintain and manage the premises themselves.
12. The circumstances by which the Defendants are in breach of their covenants in the leases with the Claimants in this regard or will be in breach in the future are likely to continue.

Rent and Service Charge arrears

13. The leases make provision for payment of service charges by the lessees. As far as the Claimants are aware there are no arrears of service charge owing by their predecessors in title to the Defendants and the Claimants herein are not in arrears of service charge none having been incurred or demanded by the Defendants.
14. The leases provide that ground rent is payable at the rate of £50 per annum payable by equal installments on 24th June and 25th December in each year. The Claimants are not aware whether there are arrears of ground rent owing by their predecessors in title. The Claimants have not paid ground rent. It is averred that the recovery of ground rent falling due more than 6 years prior to the date hereof is statute barred by operation of section 5 of the Limitation Act 1980. Therefore the aggregate of the recoverable amounts remaining due

from the Claimants (being all the tenants of the premises) to the Defendants under the terms of their leases is £

THE APPROPRIATE RELIEF

15. In the circumstances it is contended that it is appropriate that the Court grant the relief set out above in the form of the draft order annexed hereto or in such form and on such terms as the Court deems appropriate.

16. The Claimants seek an order that the Defendants pay the costs of and occasioned by this application to include the costs of a surveyor. It is contended that it is appropriate that such costs should be offset and/or paid out from the sums paid into Court by the Claimants pursuant to this application.

Procedure

17. These proceedings are issued under and are subject to CPR Part 8.

STATEMENT OF TRUTH etc.

[1] Insert company reg. office

Appendix E

Useful Website Addresses

E1–001

www.lease-advice.org
Leasehold Advisory Service, funded by the Government to provide free advice. Contains useful information on Residential Long Leasehold Property and Commonhold, including LVT Decisions, LEASE Reports, LEASE Publications and precedents.

www.rpts.gov.uk
Residential Property Tribunal Service.
Contains information on LVT and Rent Assessment Committees, including guidance, procedures, forms and relevant contact details.

www.landstribunal.gov.uk
Lands Tribunal Website.
Includes information on the functions and powers of the Lands Tribunal, an explanation of the rules and procedures and a searchable database of decisions.

www.hmcourts-service.gov.uk
Court Service Website.
Contains details of Courts, Procedure, Guidance and Forms.

www.opsi.gov.uk
Office of Public Sector Information.
Contains online access to UK legislation. Replaced HMSO website.

Index